SUPERMAN RED and BLUE

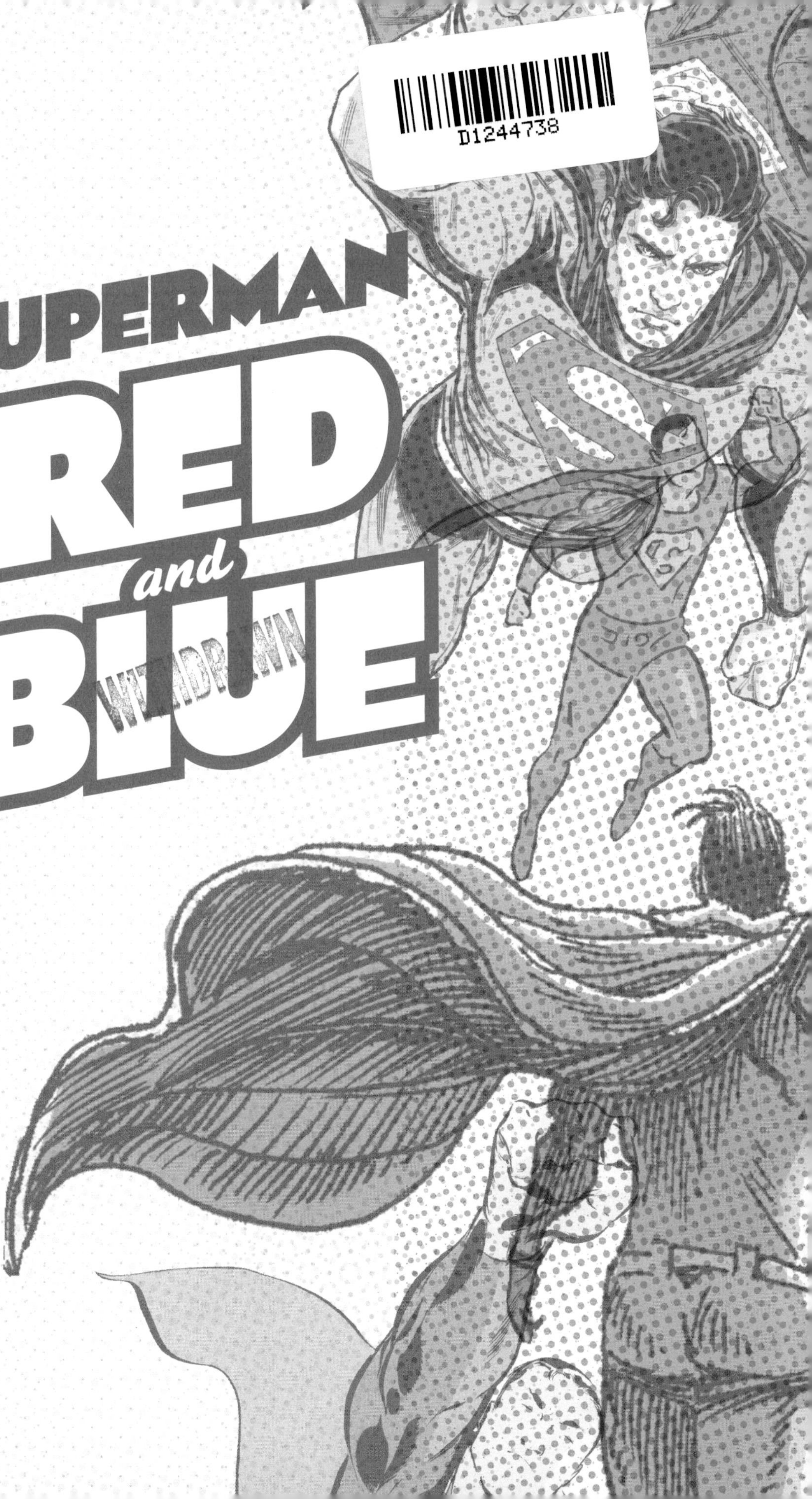

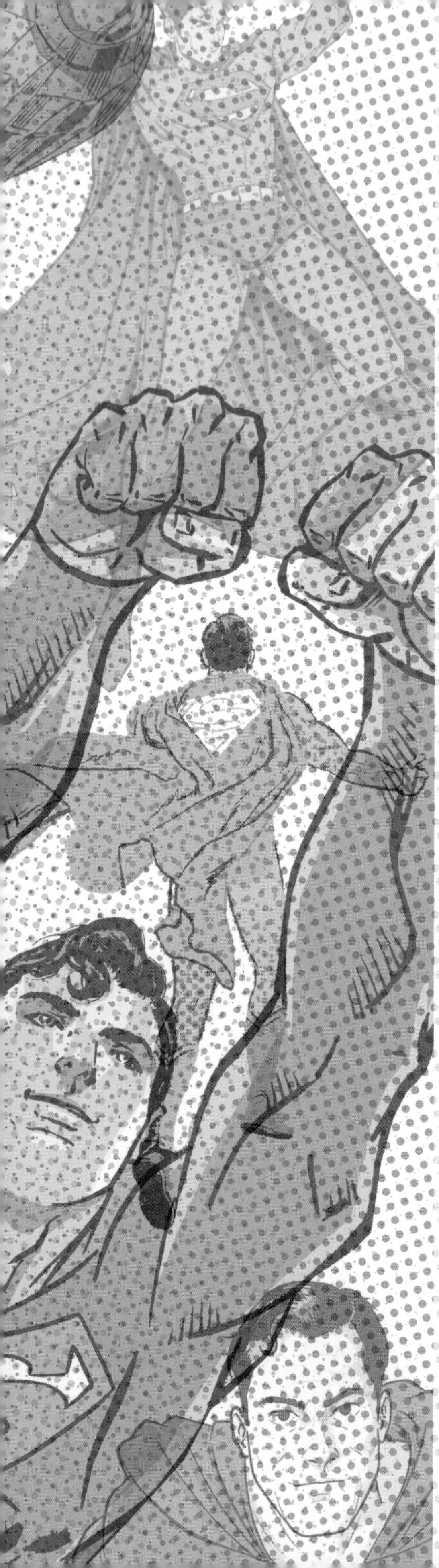

writers

John Ridley, Brandon Easton,
Wes Craig, Dan Watters,
Marguerite Bennett, Steven T. Seagle,
Chuck Brown, Dan Panosian,
Stephanie Phillips, Jason Howard,
Jesse J. Holland, Michel Fiffe,
Brandon Thomas, Nick Spencer,
James Stokoe, Mark Waid, Francis Manapul,
Robert Venditti, Michael W. Conrad,
Rich Douek, Judd Winick, G. Willow Wilson,
Joshua Williamson, Mark Buckingham,
Daniel Warren Johnson, Sophie Campbell,
Matt Wagner, Tom King,
Darcie Little Badger, Rex Ogle

artists

Clayton Henry, Steve Lieber, Wes Craig,
Dani, Jill Thompson, Duncan Rouleau,
Denys Cowan, John Stanisci, Dan Panosian,
Marley Zarcone, Jason Howard,
Laura Braga, Michel Fiffe, Berat Pekmezci,
Christian Ward, James Stokoe, Audrey Mok,
Francis Manapul, Alitha Martinez,
Cully Hamner, Joe Quinones,
Ibrahim Moustafa, Valentine De Landro,
Chris Sprouse, Karl Story, Mark Buckingham,
Daniel Warren Johnson, Sophie Campbell,
Matt Wagner, Paolo Rivera,
Steve Pugh, Mike Norton

colorists

Jordie Bellaire, Ron Chan, Wes Craig,
Dani, Jill Thompson, Duncan Rouleau,
Chris Sotomayor, Dan Panosian,
Marley Zarcone, Jason Howard, Hi-Fi,
Michel Fiffe, Berat Pekmezci,
Christian Ward, James Stokoe,
Francis Manapul, Emilio Lopez,
Cully Hamner, Joe Quinones,
Ibrahim Moustafa, Valentine De Landro,
Lee Loughridge, Daniel Warren Johnson,
Sophie Campbell, Brennan Wagner,
Paolo Rivera, Steve Pugh, Mike Norton

SUPERMAN
RED *and* BLUE

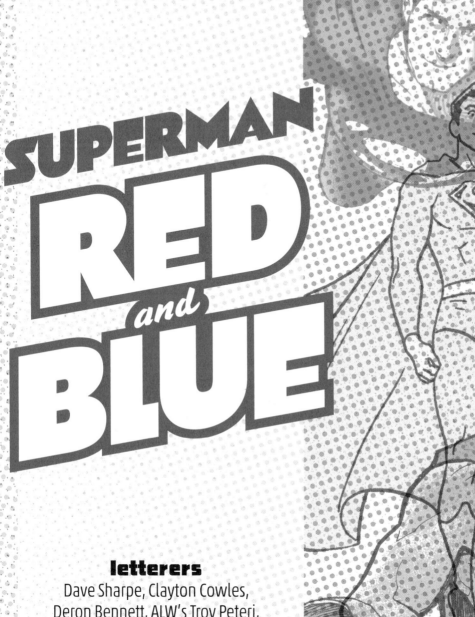

letterers
Dave Sharpe, Clayton Cowles,
Deron Bennett, ALW's Troy Peteri,
Pat Brosseau, Dan Panosian, Rob Leigh,
Tom Napolitano, Michel Fiffe, James
Stokoe, Wes Abbott, Josh Reed,
Daniel Warren Johnson,
Dave Lanphear, Steve Wands

collection cover artists
Gary Frank and Brad Anderson

SUPERMAN created by
JERRY SIEGEL and JOE SHUSTER.
By special arrangement with
the JERRY SIEGEL FAMILY.

Brittany Holzherr Editor - Original Series & Collected Edition
Jamie S. Rich, Diego Lopez Editors - Original Series
Bixie Mathieu Assistant Editor - Original Series
Steve Cook Design Director - Books
Amie Brockway-Metcalf Publication Design
Christy Sawyer Publication Production

Marie Javins Editor-in-Chief, DC Comics

Daniel Cherry III Senior VP - General Manager
Jim Lee Publisher & Chief Creative Officer
Joen Choe VP - Global Brand & Creative Services
Don Falletti VP - Manufacturing Operations & Workflow Management
Lawrence Ganem VP - Talent Services
Alison Gill Senior VP - Manufacturing & Operations
Nick J. Napolitano VP - Manufacturing Administration & Design
Nancy Spears VP - Revenue

SUPERMAN RED & BLUE

DC Comics, 2900 West Alameda Ave., Burbank, CA 91505
Printed by Transcontinental Interglobe,
Beauceville, QC, Canada. 11/19/21.
First Printing.
ISBN: 978-1-77951-280-2

PEFC Certified
This product is
from sustainably
managed forests and
controlled sources
PEFC/01-31-106   www.pefc.org

Library of Congress Cataloging-in-Publication Data is available.

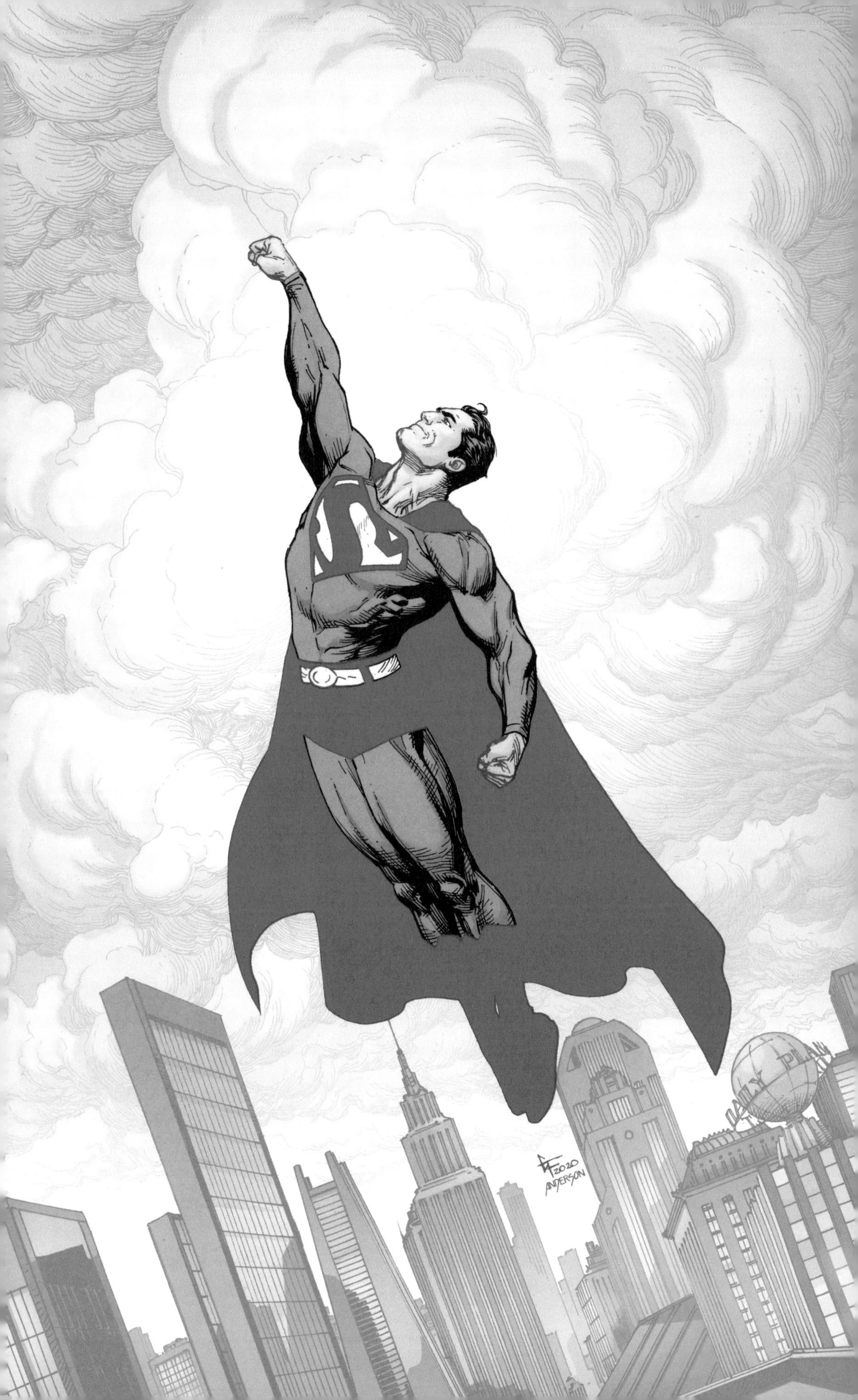
2020
ANDERSON

Cover by Gary Frank and Brad Anderson

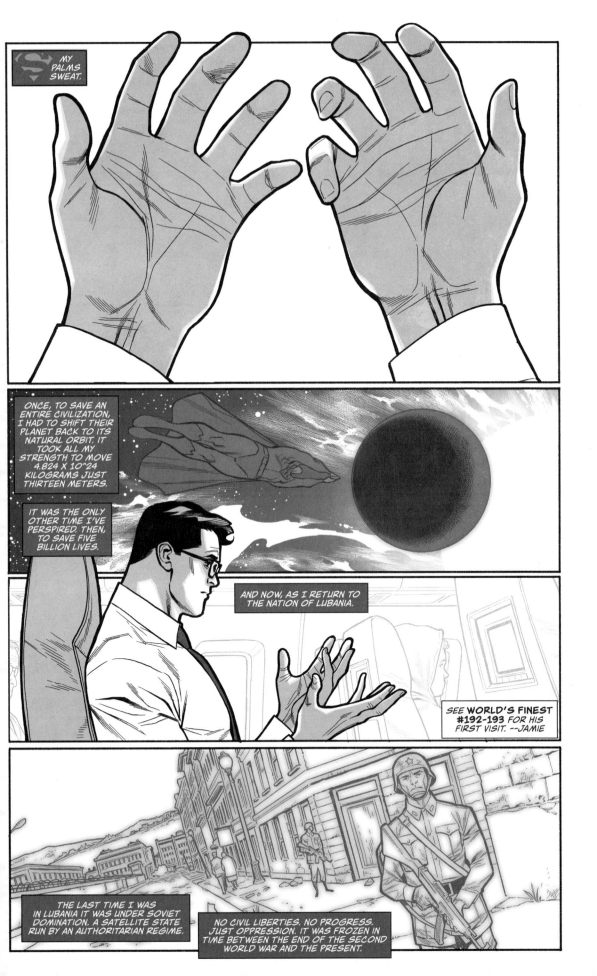

MY PALMS SWEAT.

ONCE, TO SAVE AN ENTIRE CIVILIZATION, I HAD TO SHIFT THEIR PLANET BACK TO ITS NATURAL ORBIT. IT TOOK ALL MY STRENGTH TO MOVE 4.824 X 10^24 KILOGRAMS JUST THIRTEEN METERS.

IT WAS THE ONLY OTHER TIME I'VE PERSPIRED. THEN, TO SAVE FIVE BILLION LIVES.

AND NOW, AS I RETURN TO THE NATION OF LUBANIA.

SEE **WORLD'S FINEST** #192-193 FOR HIS FIRST VISIT. --JAMIE

THE LAST TIME I WAS IN LUBANIA IT WAS UNDER SOVIET DOMINATION. A SATELLITE STATE RUN BY AN AUTHORITARIAN REGIME.

NO CIVIL LIBERTIES. NO PROGRESS. JUST OPPRESSION. IT WAS FROZEN IN TIME BETWEEN THE END OF THE SECOND WORLD WAR AND THE PRESENT.

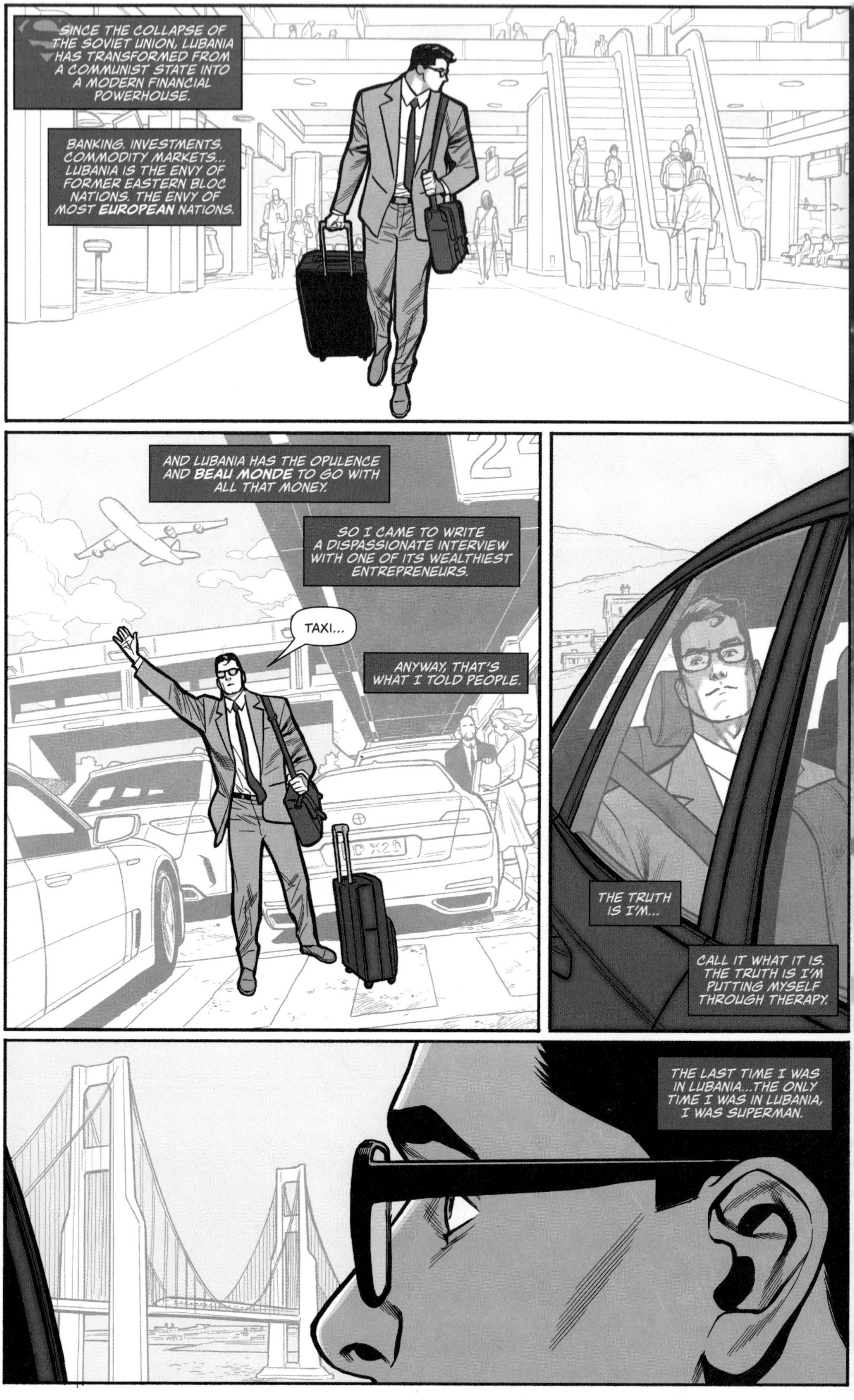
SINCE THE COLLAPSE OF THE SOVIET UNION, LUBANIA HAS TRANSFORMED FROM A COMMUNIST STATE INTO A MODERN FINANCIAL POWERHOUSE.
BANKING. INVESTMENTS. COMMODITY MARKETS... LUBANIA IS THE ENVY OF FORMER EASTERN BLOC NATIONS. THE ENVY OF MOST **EUROPEAN** NATIONS.
AND LUBANIA HAS THE OPULENCE AND **BEAU MONDE** TO GO WITH ALL THAT MONEY.
SO I CAME TO WRITE A DISPASSIONATE INTERVIEW WITH ONE OF ITS WEALTHIEST ENTREPRENEURS.
TAXI...
ANYWAY, THAT'S WHAT I TOLD PEOPLE.
THE TRUTH IS I'M...
CALL IT WHAT IT IS. THE TRUTH IS I'M PUTTING MYSELF THROUGH THERAPY.
THE LAST TIME I WAS IN LUBANIA...THE ONLY TIME I WAS IN LUBANIA, I WAS SUPERMAN.

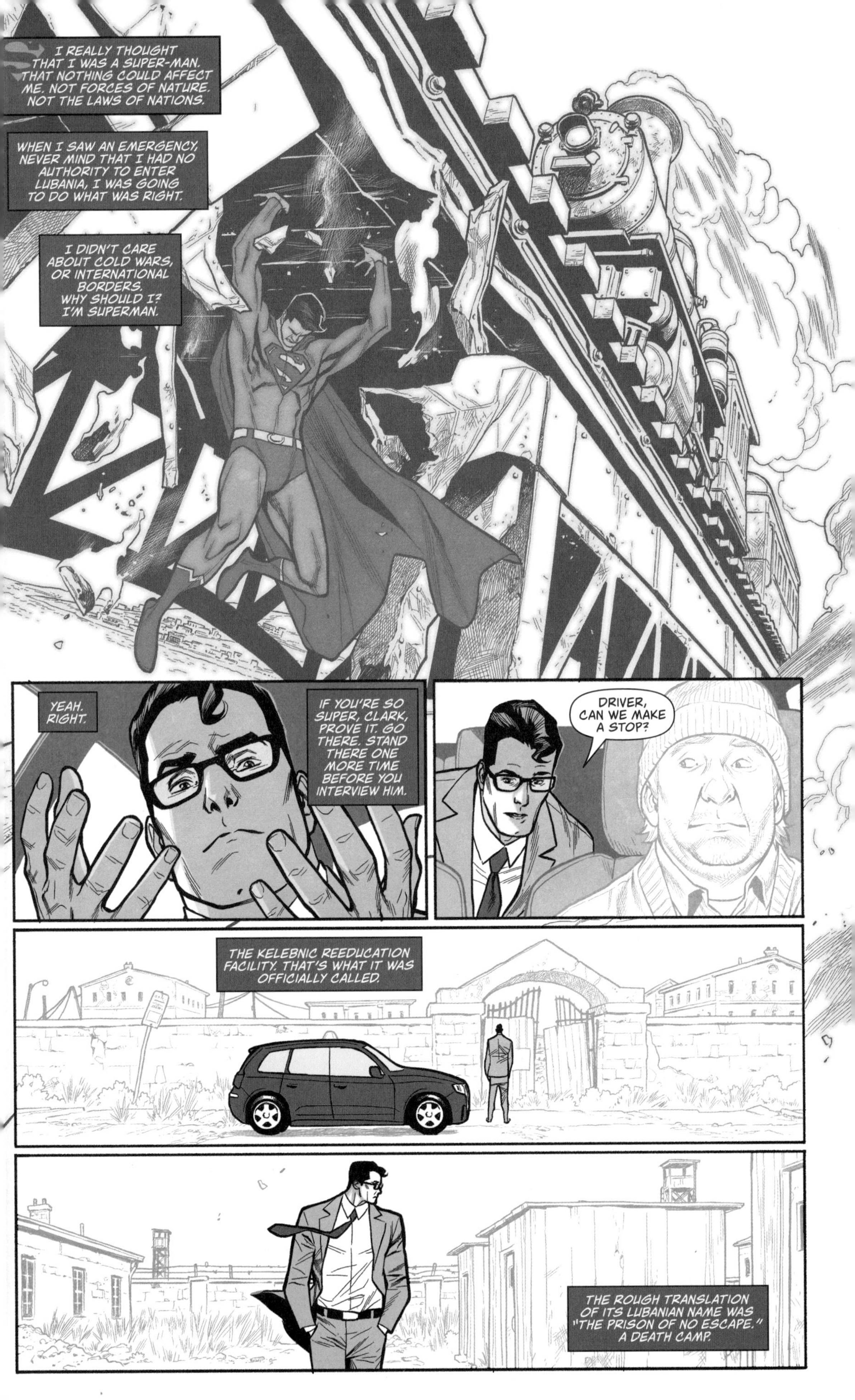
I REALLY THOUGHT THAT I WAS A SUPER-MAN. THAT NOTHING COULD AFFECT ME. NOT FORCES OF NATURE. NOT THE LAWS OF NATIONS.
WHEN I SAW AN EMERGENCY, NEVER MIND THAT I HAD NO AUTHORITY TO ENTER LUBANIA, I WAS GOING TO DO WHAT WAS RIGHT.
I DIDN'T CARE ABOUT COLD WARS, OR INTERNATIONAL BORDERS. WHY SHOULD I? I'M SUPERMAN.
YEAH. RIGHT.
IF YOU'RE SO SUPER, CLARK, PROVE IT. GO THERE. STAND THERE ONE MORE TIME BEFORE YOU INTERVIEW HIM.
DRIVER, CAN WE MAKE A STOP?
THE KELEBNIC REEDUCATION FACILITY. THAT'S WHAT IT WAS OFFICIALLY CALLED.
THE ROUGH TRANSLATION OF ITS LUBANIAN NAME WAS "THE PRISON OF NO ESCAPE." A DEATH CAMP.

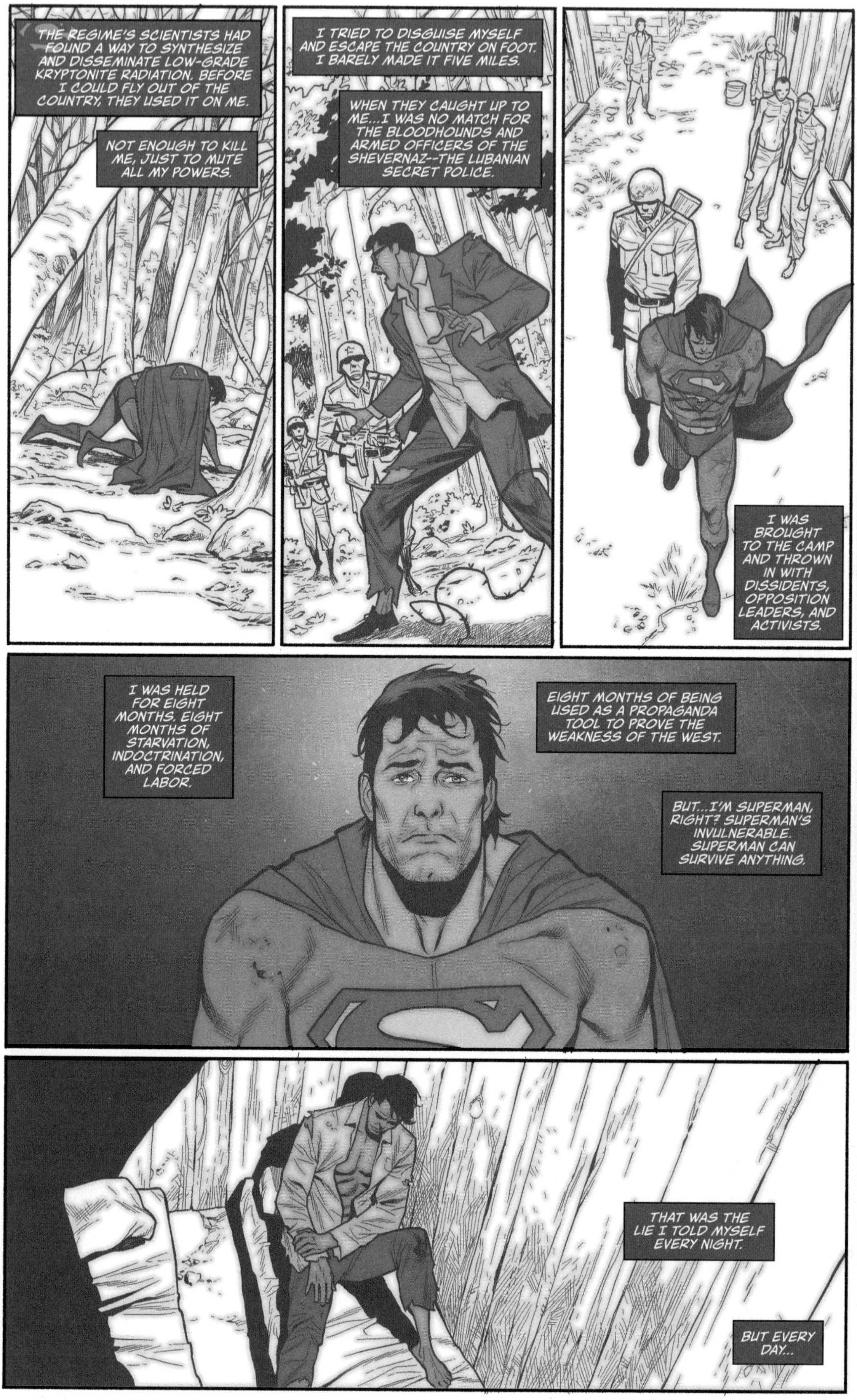

THE REGIME'S SCIENTISTS HAD FOUND A WAY TO SYNTHESIZE AND DISSEMINATE LOW-GRADE KRYPTONITE RADIATION. BEFORE I COULD FLY OUT OF THE COUNTRY, THEY USED IT ON ME.
NOT ENOUGH TO KILL ME, JUST TO MUTE ALL MY POWERS.
I TRIED TO DISGUISE MYSELF AND ESCAPE THE COUNTRY ON FOOT. I BARELY MADE IT FIVE MILES.
WHEN THEY CAUGHT UP TO ME...I WAS NO MATCH FOR THE BLOODHOUNDS AND ARMED OFFICERS OF THE SHEVERNAZ--THE LUBANIAN SECRET POLICE.
I WAS BROUGHT TO THE CAMP AND THROWN IN WITH DISSIDENTS, OPPOSITION LEADERS, AND ACTIVISTS.
I WAS HELD FOR EIGHT MONTHS. EIGHT MONTHS OF STARVATION, INDOCTRINATION, AND FORCED LABOR.
EIGHT MONTHS OF BEING USED AS A PROPAGANDA TOOL TO PROVE THE WEAKNESS OF THE WEST.
BUT...I'M SUPERMAN, RIGHT? SUPERMAN'S INVULNERABLE. SUPERMAN CAN SURVIVE ANYTHING.
THAT WAS THE LIE I TOLD MYSELF EVERY NIGHT.
BUT EVERY DAY...

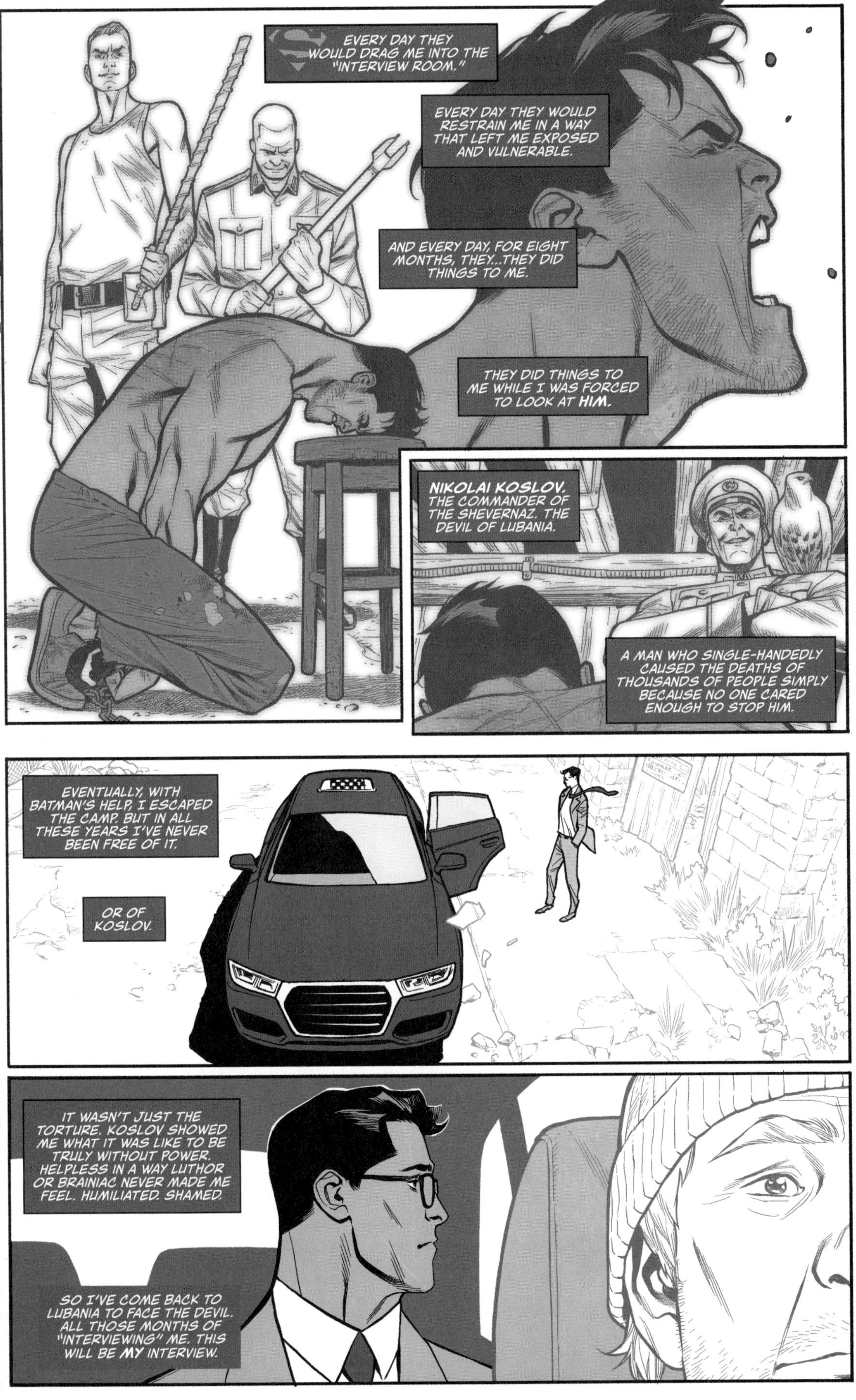
EVERY DAY THEY WOULD DRAG ME INTO THE "INTERVIEW ROOM."
EVERY DAY THEY WOULD RESTRAIN ME IN A WAY THAT LEFT ME EXPOSED AND VULNERABLE.
AND EVERY DAY, FOR EIGHT MONTHS, THEY...THEY DID THINGS TO ME.
THEY DID THINGS TO ME WHILE I WAS FORCED TO LOOK AT **HIM.**
NIKOLAI KOSLOV. THE COMMANDER OF THE SHEVERNAZ. THE DEVIL OF LUBANIA.
A MAN WHO SINGLE-HANDEDLY CAUSED THE DEATHS OF THOUSANDS OF PEOPLE SIMPLY BECAUSE NO ONE CARED ENOUGH TO STOP HIM.
EVENTUALLY, WITH BATMAN'S HELP, I ESCAPED THE CAMP. BUT IN ALL THESE YEARS I'VE NEVER BEEN FREE OF IT.
OR OF KOSLOV.
IT WASN'T JUST THE TORTURE. KOSLOV SHOWED ME WHAT IT WAS LIKE TO BE TRULY WITHOUT POWER. HELPLESS IN A WAY LUTHOR OR BRAINIAC NEVER MADE ME FEEL. HUMILIATED. SHAMED.
SO I'VE COME BACK TO LUBANIA TO FACE THE DEVIL. ALL THOSE MONTHS OF "INTERVIEWING" ME. THIS WILL BE **MY** INTERVIEW.

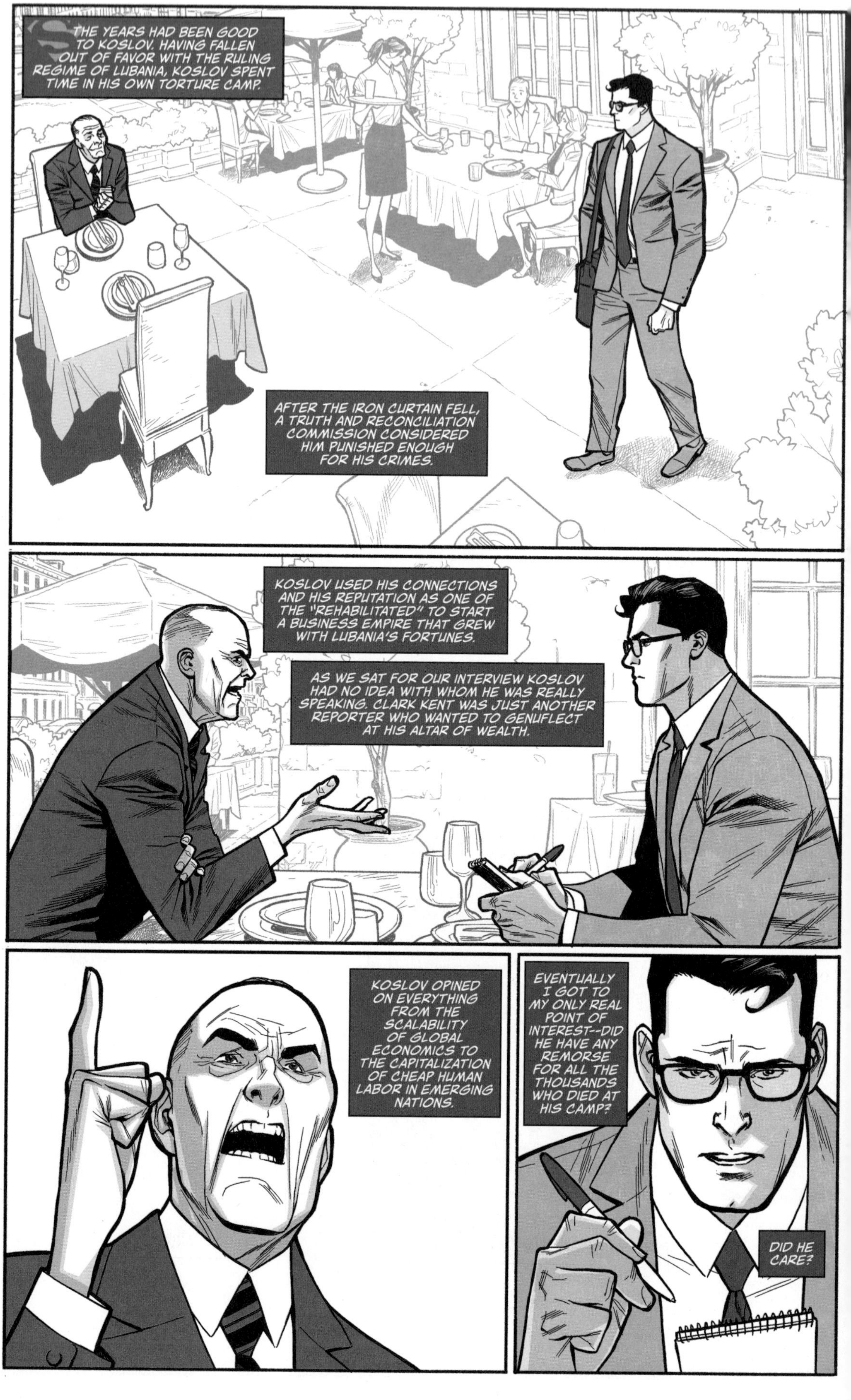
THE YEARS HAD BEEN GOOD TO KOSLOV. HAVING FALLEN OUT OF FAVOR WITH THE RULING REGIME OF LUBANIA, KOSLOV SPENT TIME IN HIS OWN TORTURE CAMP.
AFTER THE IRON CURTAIN FELL, A TRUTH AND RECONCILIATION COMMISSION CONSIDERED HIM PUNISHED ENOUGH FOR HIS CRIMES.
KOSLOV USED HIS CONNECTIONS AND HIS REPUTATION AS ONE OF THE "REHABILITATED" TO START A BUSINESS EMPIRE THAT GREW WITH LUBANIA'S FORTUNES.
AS WE SAT FOR OUR INTERVIEW KOSLOV HAD NO IDEA WITH WHOM HE WAS REALLY SPEAKING. CLARK KENT WAS JUST ANOTHER REPORTER WHO WANTED TO GENUFLECT AT HIS ALTAR OF WEALTH.
KOSLOV OPINED ON EVERYTHING FROM THE SCALABILITY OF GLOBAL ECONOMICS TO THE CAPITALIZATION OF CHEAP HUMAN LABOR IN EMERGING NATIONS.
EVENTUALLY I GOT TO MY ONLY REAL POINT OF INTEREST--DID HE HAVE ANY REMORSE FOR ALL THE THOUSANDS WHO DIED AT HIS CAMP?
DID HE CARE?

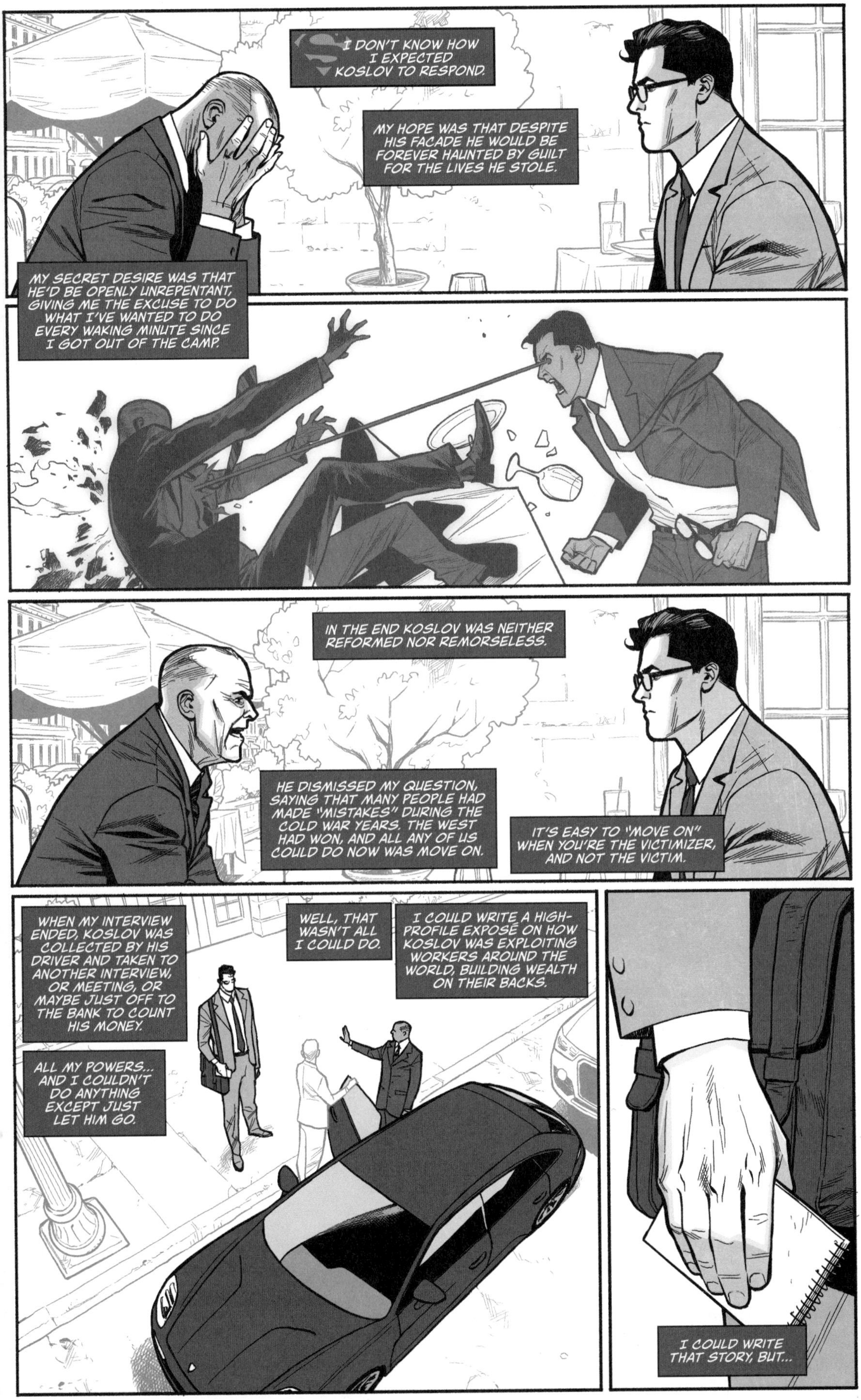
I DON'T KNOW HOW I EXPECTED KOSLOV TO RESPOND.
MY HOPE WAS THAT DESPITE HIS FACADE HE WOULD BE FOREVER HAUNTED BY GUILT FOR THE LIVES HE STOLE.
MY SECRET DESIRE WAS THAT HE'D BE OPENLY UNREPENTANT, GIVING ME THE EXCUSE TO DO WHAT I'VE WANTED TO DO EVERY WAKING MINUTE SINCE I GOT OUT OF THE CAMP.
IN THE END KOSLOV WAS NEITHER REFORMED NOR REMORSELESS.
HE DISMISSED MY QUESTION, SAYING THAT MANY PEOPLE HAD MADE "MISTAKES" DURING THE COLD WAR YEARS. THE WEST HAD WON, AND ALL ANY OF US COULD DO NOW WAS MOVE ON.
IT'S EASY TO "MOVE ON" WHEN YOU'RE THE VICTIMIZER, AND NOT THE VICTIM.
WHEN MY INTERVIEW ENDED, KOSLOV WAS COLLECTED BY HIS DRIVER AND TAKEN TO ANOTHER INTERVIEW, OR MEETING, OR MAYBE JUST OFF TO THE BANK TO COUNT HIS MONEY.
ALL MY POWERS... AND I COULDN'T DO ANYTHING EXCEPT JUST LET HIM GO.
WELL, THAT WASN'T ALL I COULD DO.
I COULD WRITE A HIGH-PROFILE EXPOSÉ ON HOW KOSLOV WAS EXPLOITING WORKERS AROUND THE WORLD, BUILDING WEALTH ON THEIR BACKS.
I COULD WRITE THAT STORY, BUT...

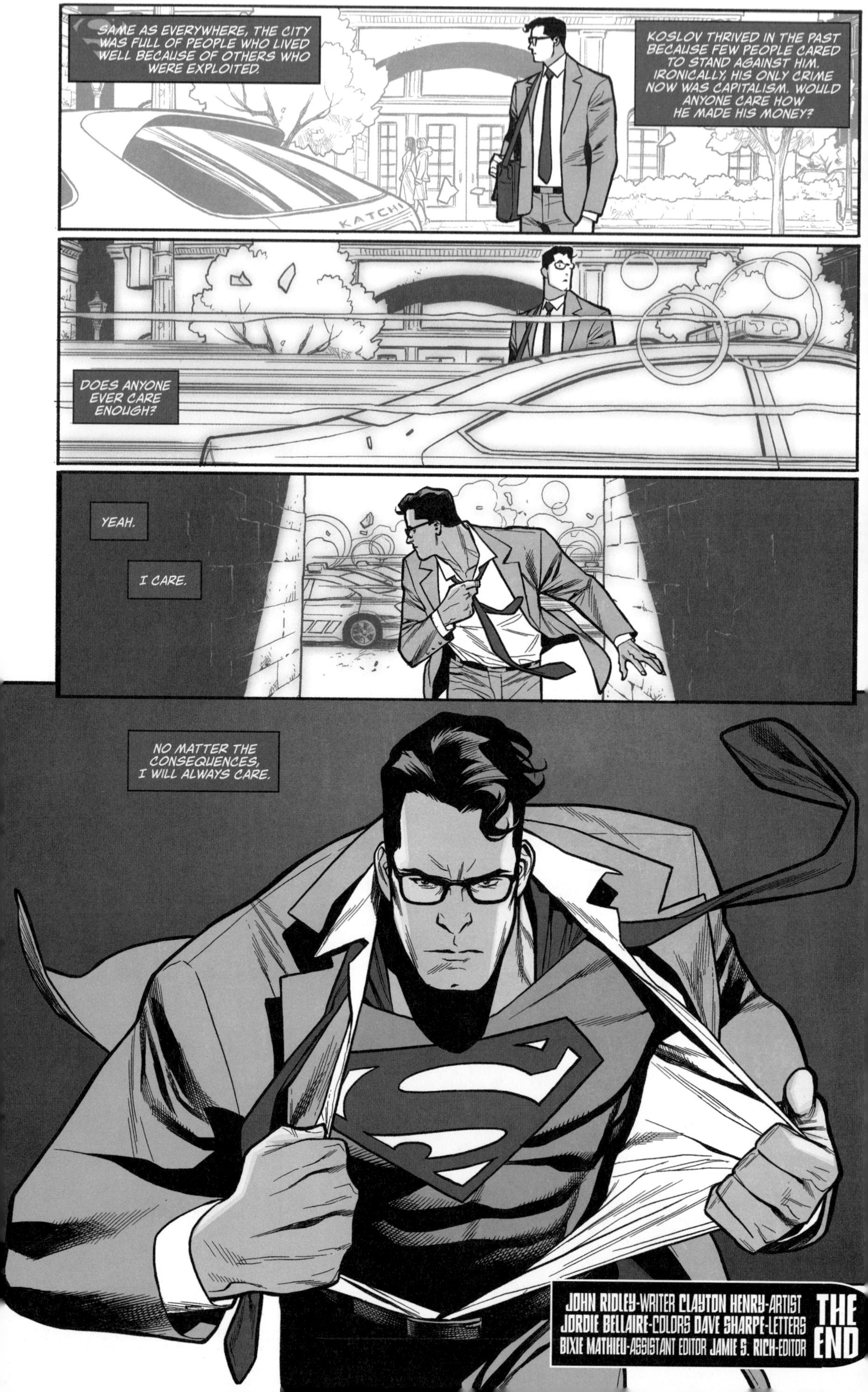
SAME AS EVERYWHERE, THE CITY WAS FULL OF PEOPLE WHO LIVED WELL BECAUSE OF OTHERS WHO WERE EXPLOITED.
KOSLOV THRIVED IN THE PAST BECAUSE FEW PEOPLE CARED TO STAND AGAINST HIM. IRONICALLY, HIS ONLY CRIME NOW WAS CAPITALISM. WOULD ANYONE CARE HOW HE MADE HIS MONEY?
KATCHI
DOES ANYONE EVER CARE ENOUGH?
YEAH.
I CARE.
NO MATTER THE CONSEQUENCES, I WILL ALWAYS CARE.
JOHN RIDLEY-WRITER CLAYTON HENRY-ARTIST
JORDIE BELLAIRE-COLORS DAVE SHARPE-LETTERS
BIXIE MATHIEU-ASSISTANT EDITOR JAMIE S. RICH-EDITOR
THE END

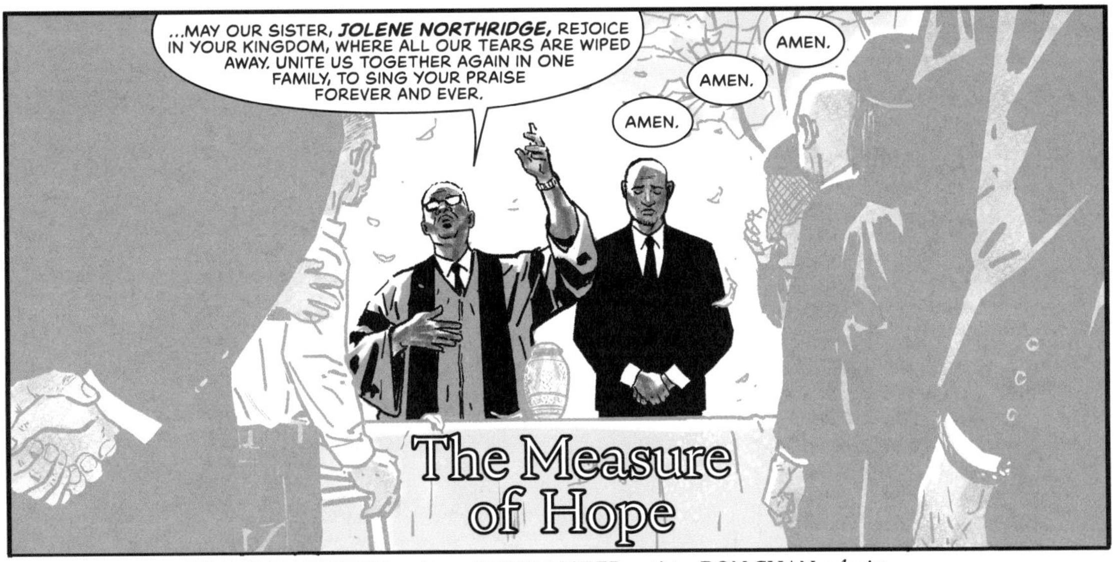
...MAY OUR SISTER, JOLENE NORTHRIDGE, REJOICE IN YOUR KINGDOM, WHERE ALL OUR TEARS ARE WIPED AWAY. UNITE US TOGETHER AGAIN IN ONE FAMILY, TO SING YOUR PRAISE FOREVER AND EVER.
AMEN.
AMEN.
AMEN.
The Measure of Hope

BRANDON EASTON *writer* • STEVE LIEBER *artist* • RON CHAN *colorist*
CLAYTON COWLES *letterer* • DIEGO LOPEZ *assoc. editor* • JAMIE S. RICH *editor*

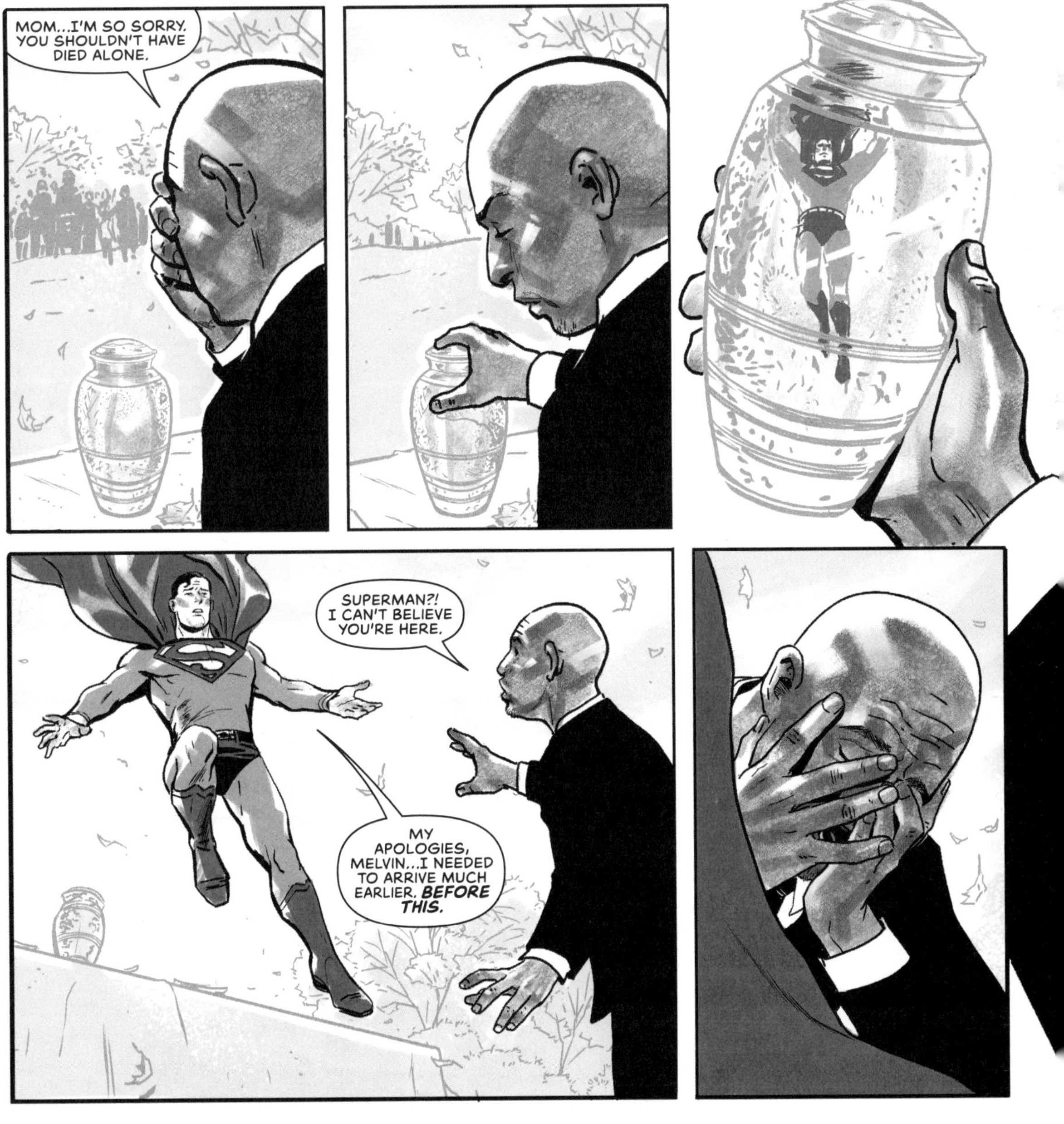
MOM...I'M SO SORRY. YOU SHOULDN'T HAVE DIED ALONE.
SUPERMAN?! I CAN'T BELIEVE YOU'RE HERE.
MY APOLOGIES, MELVIN...I NEEDED TO ARRIVE MUCH EARLIER. BEFORE THIS.

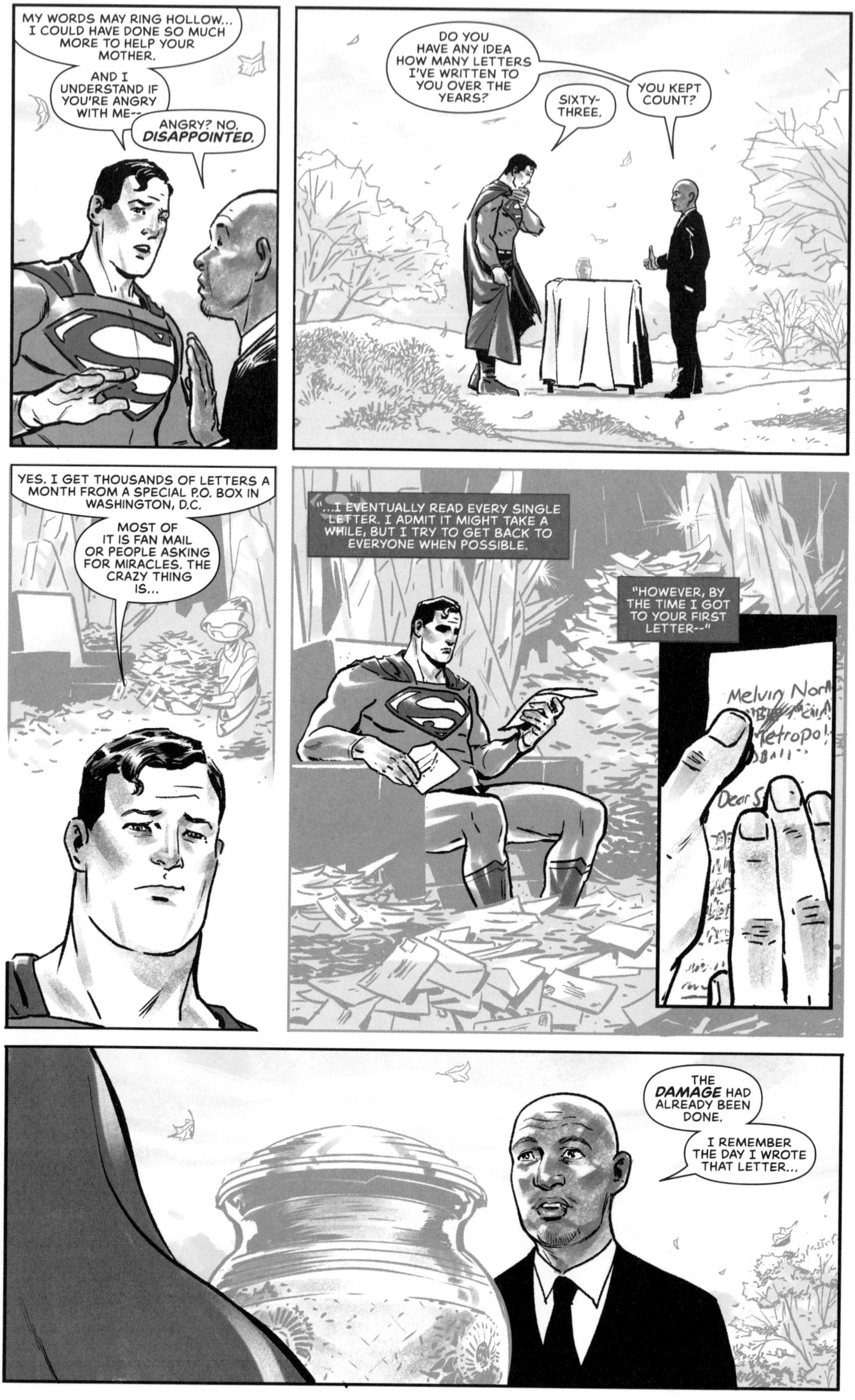
MY WORDS MAY RING HOLLOW... I COULD HAVE DONE SO MUCH MORE TO HELP YOUR MOTHER.
AND I UNDERSTAND IF YOU'RE ANGRY WITH ME--
ANGRY? NO. DISAPPOINTED.
DO YOU HAVE ANY IDEA HOW MANY LETTERS I'VE WRITTEN TO YOU OVER THE YEARS?
SIXTY-THREE.
YOU KEPT COUNT?
YES. I GET THOUSANDS OF LETTERS A MONTH FROM A SPECIAL P.O. BOX IN WASHINGTON, D.C.
MOST OF IT IS FAN MAIL OR PEOPLE ASKING FOR MIRACLES. THE CRAZY THING IS...
"...I EVENTUALLY READ EVERY SINGLE LETTER. I ADMIT IT MIGHT TAKE A WHILE, BUT I TRY TO GET BACK TO EVERYONE WHEN POSSIBLE.
"HOWEVER, BY THE TIME I GOT TO YOUR FIRST LETTER--"
THE DAMAGE HAD ALREADY BEEN DONE.
I REMEMBER THE DAY I WROTE THAT LETTER...

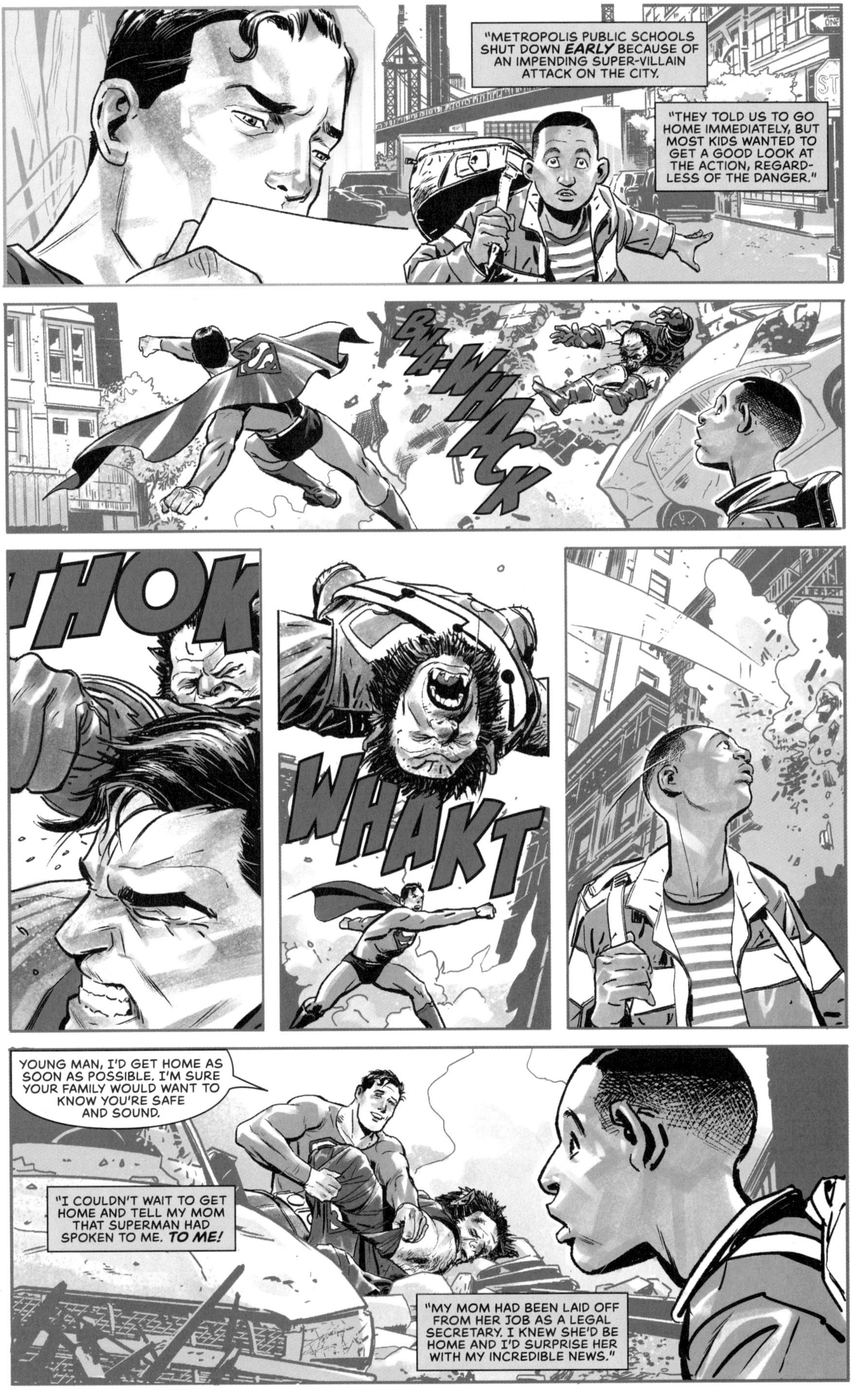

"METROPOLIS PUBLIC SCHOOLS SHUT DOWN EARLY BECAUSE OF AN IMPENDING SUPER-VILLAIN ATTACK ON THE CITY.
"THEY TOLD US TO GO HOME IMMEDIATELY, BUT MOST KIDS WANTED TO GET A GOOD LOOK AT THE ACTION, REGARDLESS OF THE DANGER."
BWA-WHACK
THOK
WHAKT
YOUNG MAN, I'D GET HOME AS SOON AS POSSIBLE. I'M SURE YOUR FAMILY WOULD WANT TO KNOW YOU'RE SAFE AND SOUND.
"I COULDN'T WAIT TO GET HOME AND TELL MY MOM THAT SUPERMAN HAD SPOKEN TO ME. TO ME!
"MY MOM HAD BEEN LAID OFF FROM HER JOB AS A LEGAL SECRETARY. I KNEW SHE'D BE HOME AND I'D SURPRISE HER WITH MY INCREDIBLE NEWS."

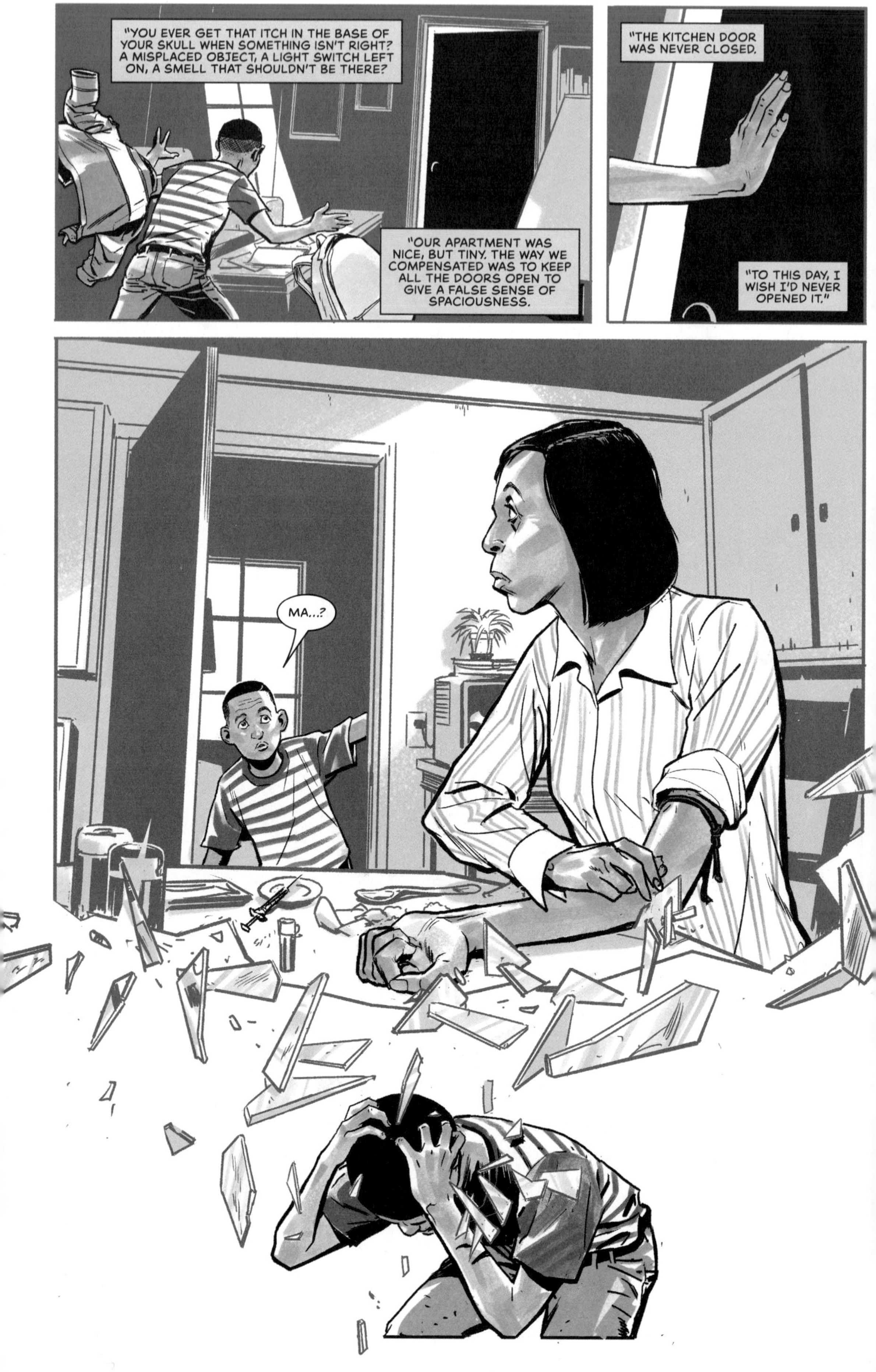
"YOU EVER GET THAT ITCH IN THE BASE OF YOUR SKULL WHEN SOMETHING ISN'T RIGHT? A MISPLACED OBJECT, A LIGHT SWITCH LEFT ON, A SMELL THAT SHOULDN'T BE THERE?
"OUR APARTMENT WAS NICE, BUT TINY. THE WAY WE COMPENSATED WAS TO KEEP ALL THE DOORS OPEN TO GIVE A FALSE SENSE OF SPACIOUSNESS.
"THE KITCHEN DOOR WAS NEVER CLOSED.
"TO THIS DAY, I WISH I'D NEVER OPENED IT."
MA...?

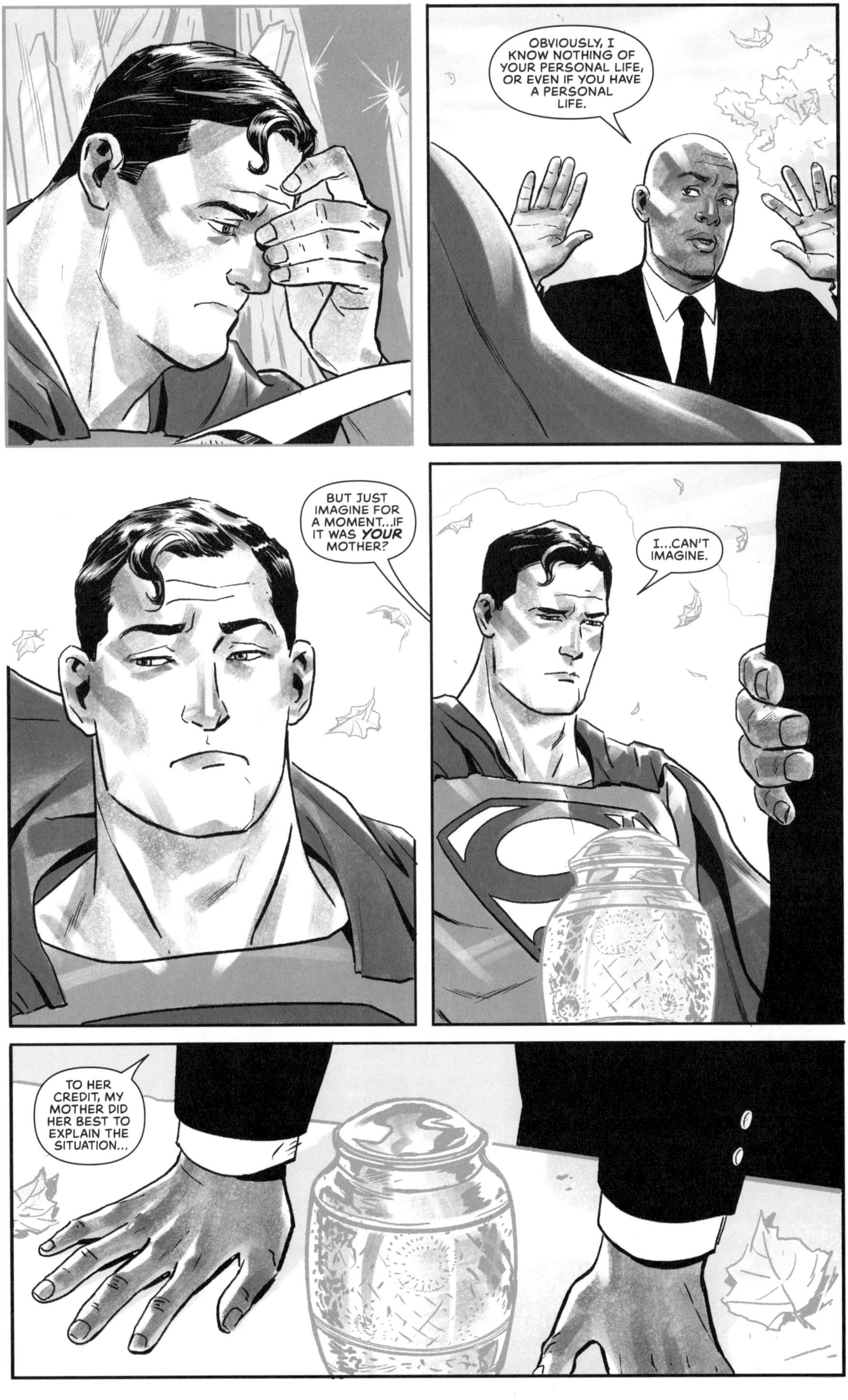
OBVIOUSLY, I KNOW NOTHING OF YOUR PERSONAL LIFE, OR EVEN IF YOU HAVE A PERSONAL LIFE.
BUT JUST IMAGINE FOR A MOMENT...IF IT WAS YOUR MOTHER?
I...CAN'T IMAGINE.
TO HER CREDIT, MY MOTHER DID HER BEST TO EXPLAIN THE SITUATION...

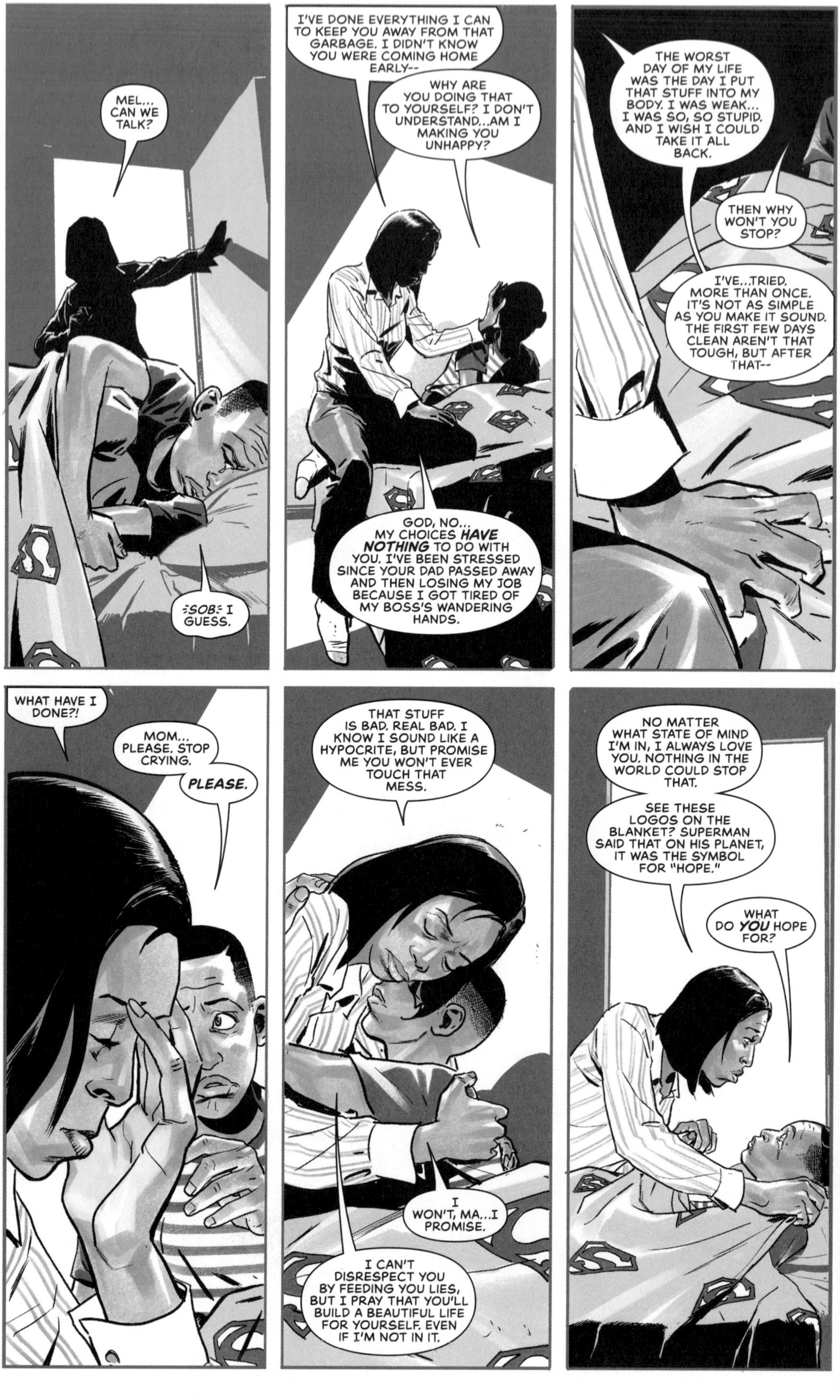

MEL... CAN WE TALK?
=SOB= I GUESS.
I'VE DONE EVERYTHING I CAN TO KEEP YOU AWAY FROM THAT GARBAGE. I DIDN'T KNOW YOU WERE COMING HOME EARLY--
WHY ARE YOU DOING THAT TO YOURSELF? I DON'T UNDERSTAND...AM I MAKING YOU UNHAPPY?
GOD, NO... MY CHOICES **HAVE NOTHING** TO DO WITH YOU. I'VE BEEN STRESSED SINCE YOUR DAD PASSED AWAY AND THEN LOSING MY JOB BECAUSE I GOT TIRED OF MY BOSS'S WANDERING HANDS.
THE WORST DAY OF MY LIFE WAS THE DAY I PUT THAT STUFF INTO MY BODY. I WAS WEAK... I WAS SO, SO STUPID. AND I WISH I COULD TAKE IT ALL BACK.
THEN WHY WON'T YOU STOP?
I'VE...TRIED. MORE THAN ONCE. IT'S NOT AS SIMPLE AS YOU MAKE IT SOUND. THE FIRST FEW DAYS CLEAN AREN'T THAT TOUGH, BUT AFTER THAT--
WHAT HAVE I DONE?!
MOM... PLEASE. STOP CRYING.
PLEASE.
THAT STUFF IS BAD. REAL BAD. I KNOW I SOUND LIKE A HYPOCRITE, BUT PROMISE ME YOU WON'T EVER TOUCH THAT MESS.
I WON'T, MA...I PROMISE.
I CAN'T DISRESPECT YOU BY FEEDING YOU LIES, BUT I PRAY THAT YOU'LL BUILD A BEAUTIFUL LIFE FOR YOURSELF, EVEN IF I'M NOT IN IT.
NO MATTER WHAT STATE OF MIND I'M IN, I ALWAYS LOVE YOU. NOTHING IN THE WORLD COULD STOP THAT.
SEE THESE LOGOS ON THE BLANKET? SUPERMAN SAID THAT ON HIS PLANET, IT WAS THE SYMBOL FOR "HOPE."
WHAT DO **YOU** HOPE FOR?

A BETTER TOMORROW. THAT'S THE ONLY WAY TO **MEASURE HOPE,** BY YOUR CAPACITY TO BELIEVE THAT THINGS CAN IMPROVE.

OTHERWISE, THERE'S NO POINT IN GETTING UP IN THE MORNING.

"YOU HAVE GREAT TASTE IN HEROES, SON. ALWAYS KEEP AN EYE ON HIM."

THEY FOUND HER BODY LAST WEEK. SHE'D GOTTEN A BAD BATCH OF HEROIN, BUT SOMEHOW MANAGED TO MAKE IT INTO A CHURCH FOR HER FINAL MOMENTS OF LIFE.

THE PARAMEDICS SAID THE ONLY THINGS SHE HAD IN HER PURSE WERE HER I.D. AND A **PHOTOGRAPH.** IT'S THE PICTURE ON HER FUNERAL PROGRAM.

I...I NEED TO DO MORE. NOTHING I SAY CAN BRING YOUR MOTHER BACK.

THERE'S NO SUPERPOWER IN THE WORLD THAT CAN CHANGE THE FLOW OF PERSONAL RESPONSIBILITY.

I LOVED MY MOTHER MORE THAN FLOWERS LOVE THE SUN. BUT SHE MADE A LOT OF BAD CHOICES.

PART OF ME WONDERS IF THOSE CHOICES WOULD EXIST IF YOU AND YOUR COLLEAGUES DESTROYED THE FLOW OF NARCOTICS INTO DEPRESSED AND UNDERSERVED COMMUNITIES.

NONE OF YOU ARE OUR GODS OR EMPERORS AND I'M NOT QUALIFIED TO OFFER ABSOLUTION OR JUDGMENT.

BUT WHAT STOPS YOU FROM BEING COMPLETELY USELESS ON THE STREET LEVEL ARE THE FEELINGS OF HOPE YOU INSPIRE IN THE MOST **BROKEN** OF SOULS.

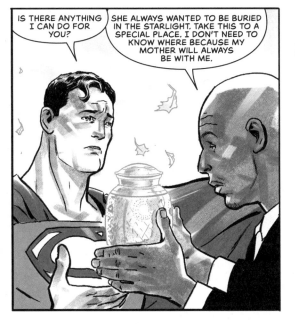

IS THERE ANYTHING I CAN DO FOR YOU?

SHE ALWAYS WANTED TO BE BURIED IN THE STARLIGHT. TAKE THIS TO A SPECIAL PLACE. I DON'T NEED TO KNOW WHERE BECAUSE MY MOTHER WILL ALWAYS BE WITH ME.

I'VE BUILT AN EXCELLENT LIFE FOR MYSELF. I'VE GOT A CAREER, A GREAT HOME, A FIANCÉE, AND WONDERFUL FRIENDS. ALL BECAUSE MY MOTHER GAVE ME THE GIFT OF HOPE...

...BY TEACHING ME TO FOLLOW YOUR **EXAMPLE.**

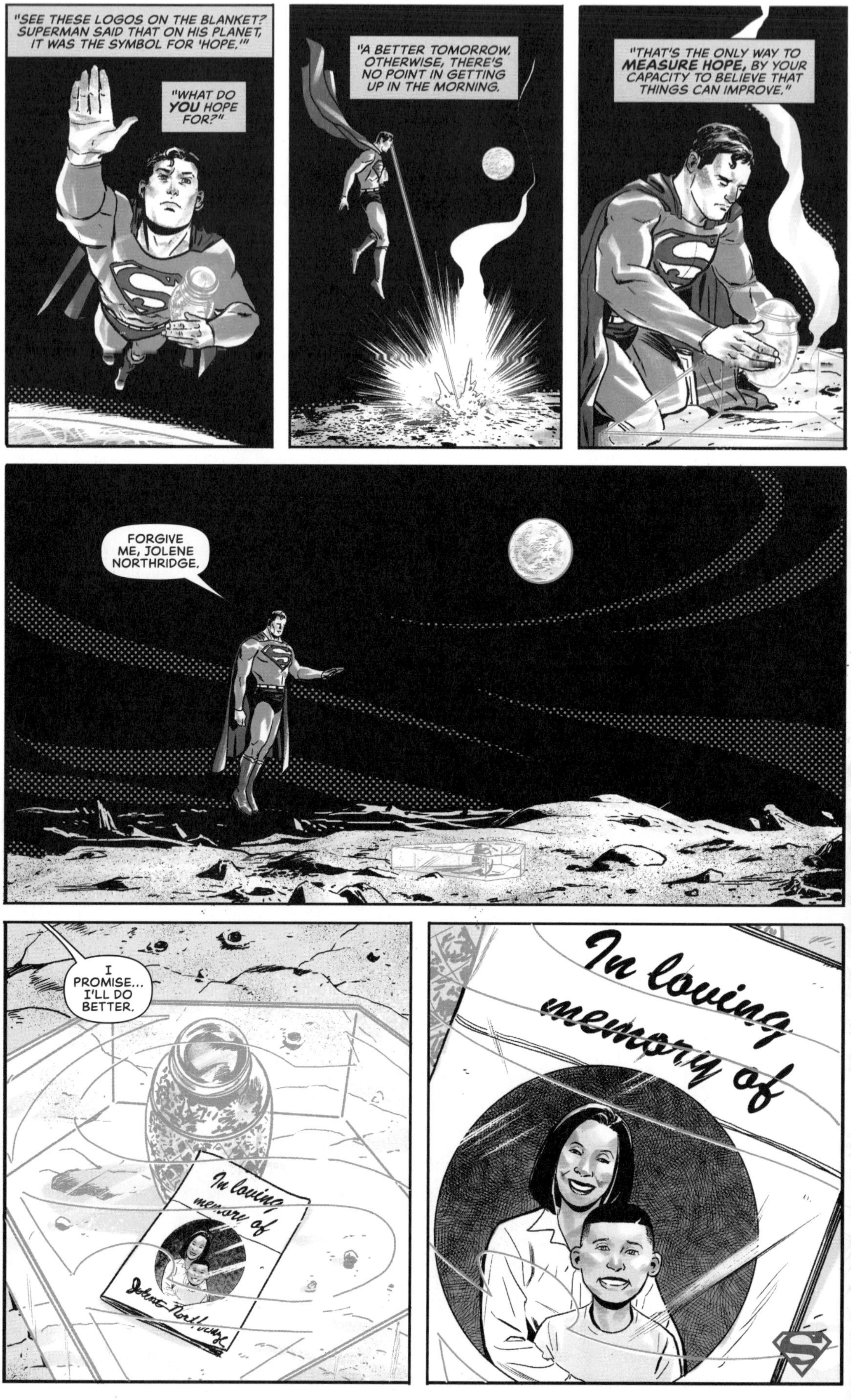
"SEE THESE LOGOS ON THE BLANKET? SUPERMAN SAID THAT ON HIS PLANET, IT WAS THE SYMBOL FOR 'HOPE.'"
"WHAT DO YOU HOPE FOR?"
"A BETTER TOMORROW. OTHERWISE, THERE'S NO POINT IN GETTING UP IN THE MORNING.
"THAT'S THE ONLY WAY TO MEASURE HOPE, BY YOUR CAPACITY TO BELIEVE THAT THINGS CAN IMPROVE."
FORGIVE ME, JOLENE NORTHRIDGE.
I PROMISE... I'LL DO BETTER.
In loving memory of
In loving memory of

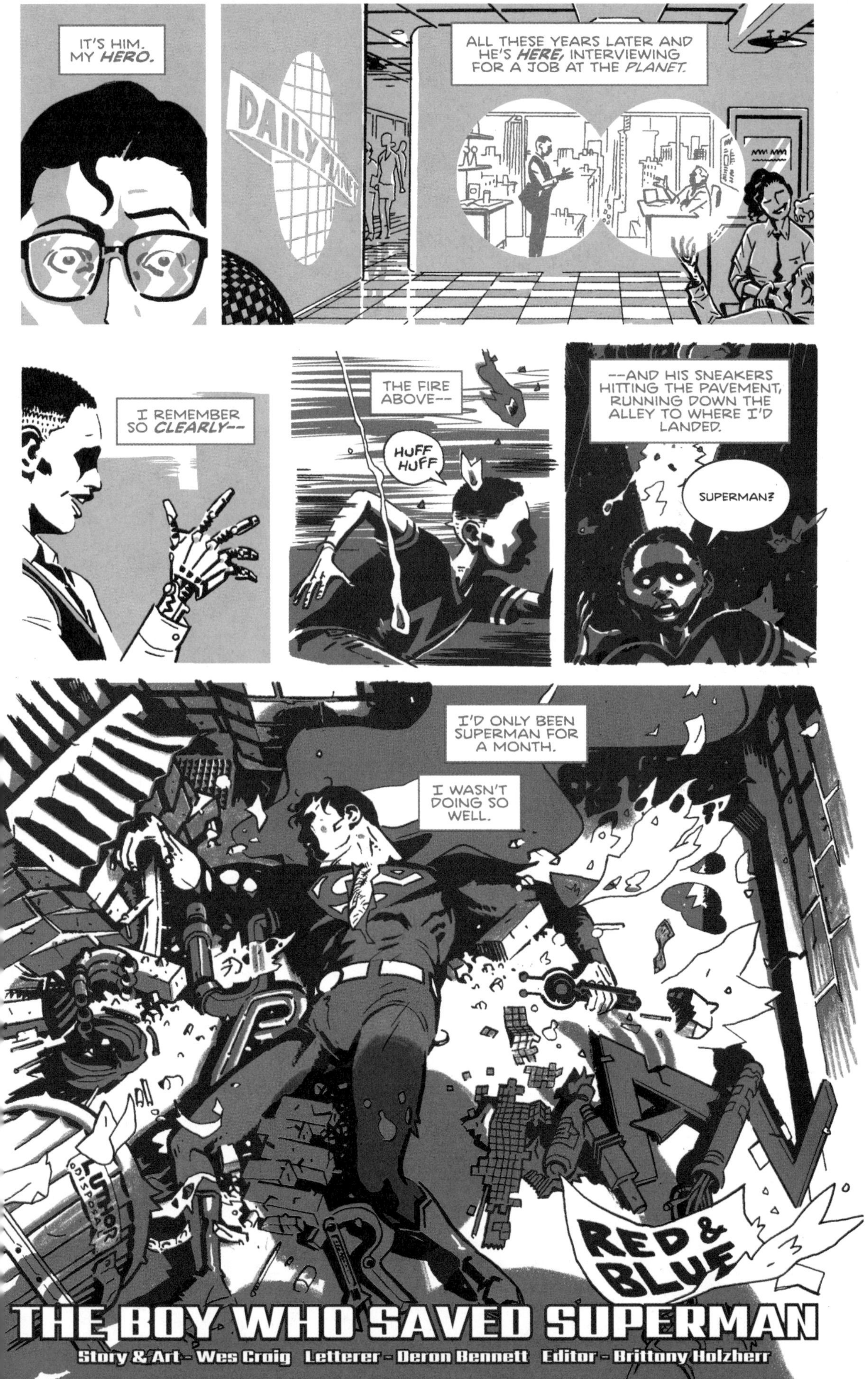
IT'S HIM. MY HERO.
ALL THESE YEARS LATER AND HE'S HERE, INTERVIEWING FOR A JOB AT THE PLANET.
DAILY PLANET
I REMEMBER SO CLEARLY--
THE FIRE ABOVE--
HUFF HUFF
--AND HIS SNEAKERS HITTING THE PAVEMENT, RUNNING DOWN THE ALLEY TO WHERE I'D LANDED.
SUPERMAN?
I'D ONLY BEEN SUPERMAN FOR A MONTH.
I WASN'T DOING SO WELL.
LUTHOR
RED & BLUE
THE BOY WHO SAVED SUPERMAN
Story & Art - Wes Craig Letterer - Deron Bennett Editor - Brittany Holzherr

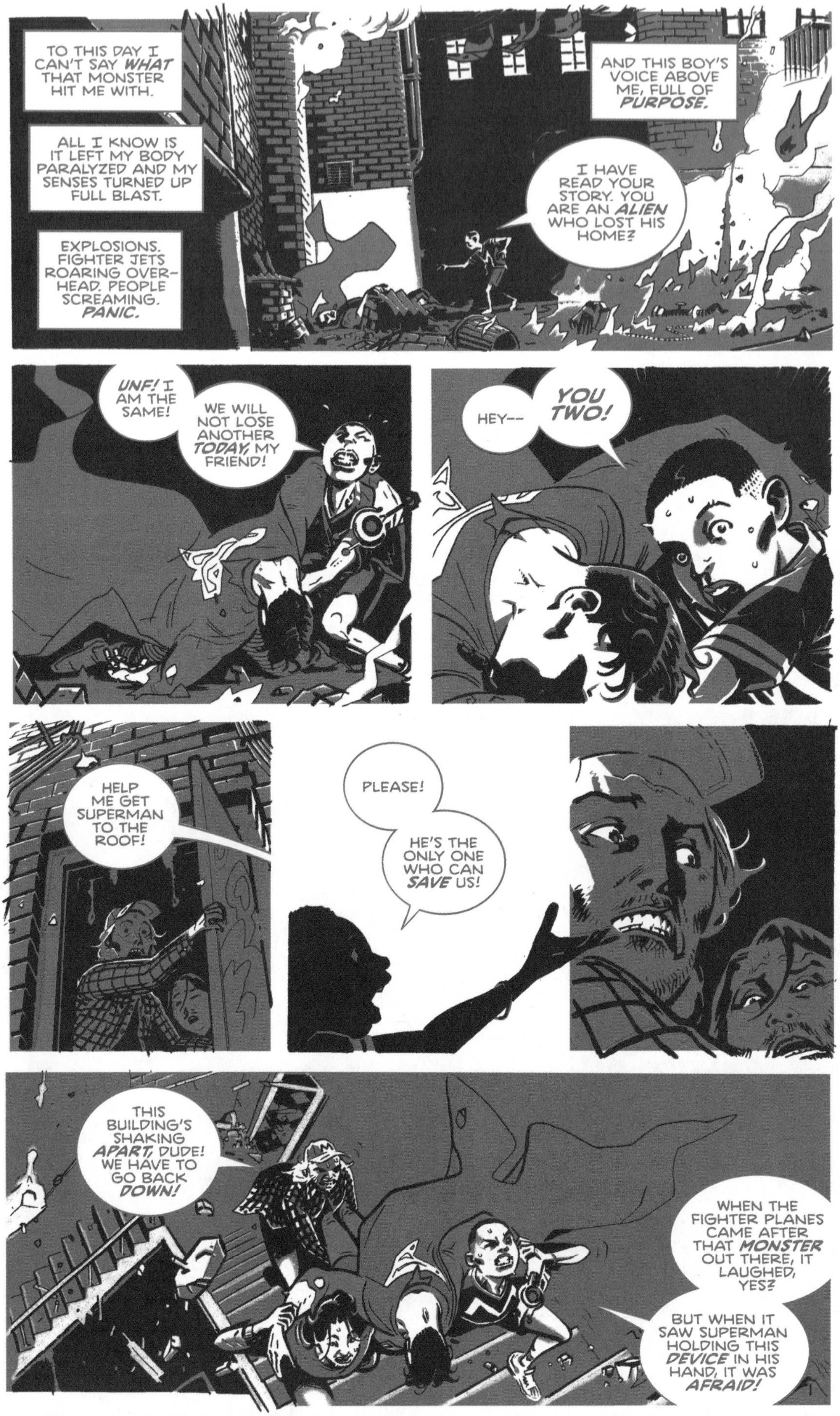

TO THIS DAY I CAN'T SAY WHAT THAT MONSTER HIT ME WITH.
ALL I KNOW IS IT LEFT MY BODY PARALYZED AND MY SENSES TURNED UP FULL BLAST.
EXPLOSIONS. FIGHTER JETS ROARING OVER-HEAD. PEOPLE SCREAMING. PANIC.
AND THIS BOY'S VOICE ABOVE ME, FULL OF PURPOSE.
I HAVE READ YOUR STORY. YOU ARE AN ALIEN WHO LOST HIS HOME?
UNF! I AM THE SAME!
WE WILL NOT LOSE ANOTHER TODAY, MY FRIEND!
HEY--
YOU TWO!
HELP ME GET SUPERMAN TO THE ROOF!
PLEASE!
HE'S THE ONLY ONE WHO CAN SAVE US!
THIS BUILDING'S SHAKING APART, DUDE! WE HAVE TO GO BACK DOWN!
WHEN THE FIGHTER PLANES CAME AFTER THAT MONSTER OUT THERE, IT LAUGHED, YES?
BUT WHEN IT SAW SUPERMAN HOLDING THIS DEVICE IN HIS HAND, IT WAS AFRAID!

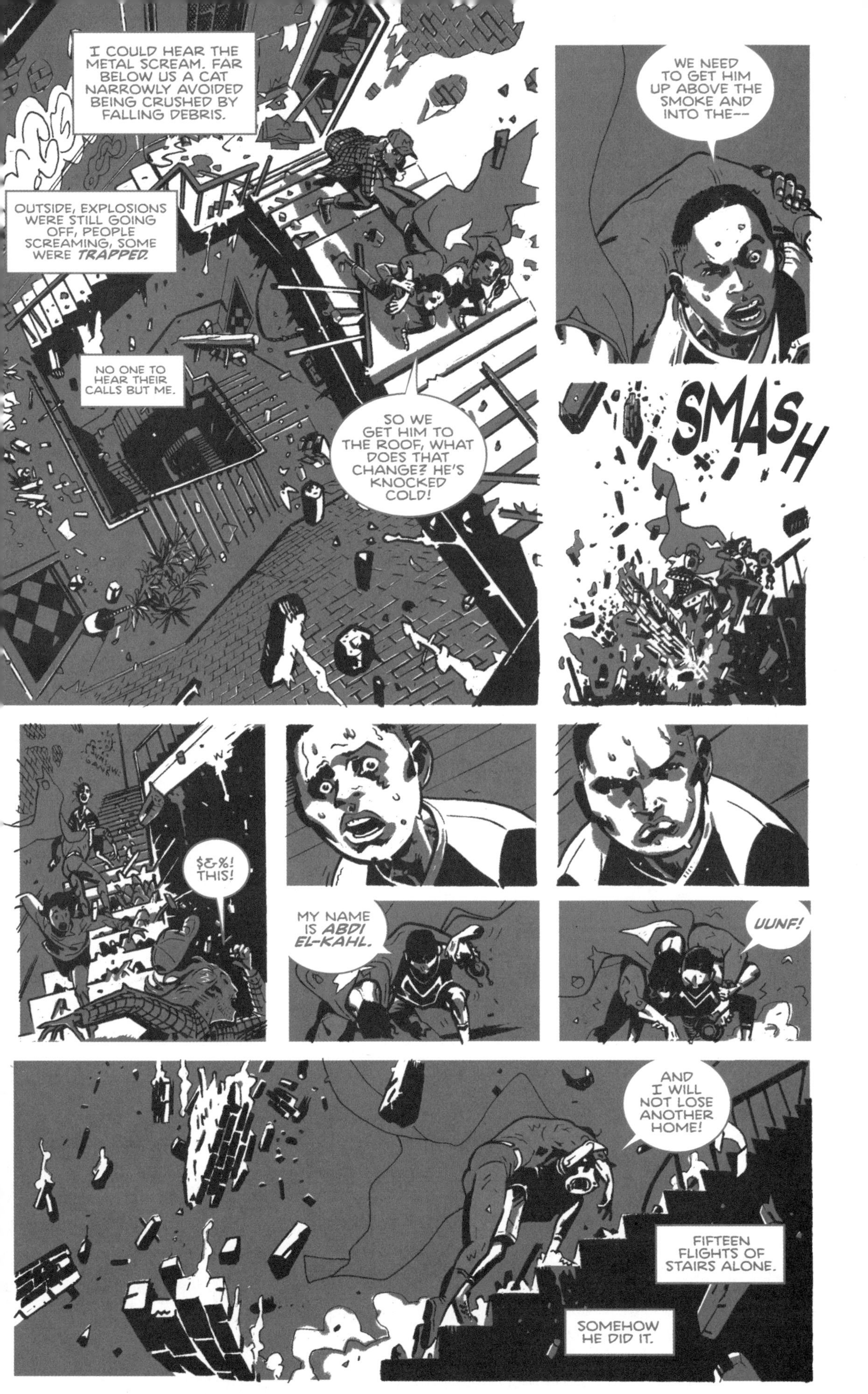
I COULD HEAR THE METAL SCREAM. FAR BELOW US A CAT NARROWLY AVOIDED BEING CRUSHED BY FALLING DEBRIS.
OUTSIDE, EXPLOSIONS WERE STILL GOING OFF, PEOPLE SCREAMING, SOME WERE *TRAPPED.*
NO ONE TO HEAR THEIR CALLS BUT ME.
SO WE GET HIM TO THE ROOF, WHAT DOES THAT CHANGE? HE'S KNOCKED COLD!
WE NEED TO GET HIM UP ABOVE THE SMOKE AND INTO THE--
SMASH
$&%! THIS!
MY NAME IS *ABDI EL-KAHL.*
UUNF!
AND I WILL NOT LOSE ANOTHER HOME!
FIFTEEN FLIGHTS OF STAIRS ALONE.
SOMEHOW HE DID IT.

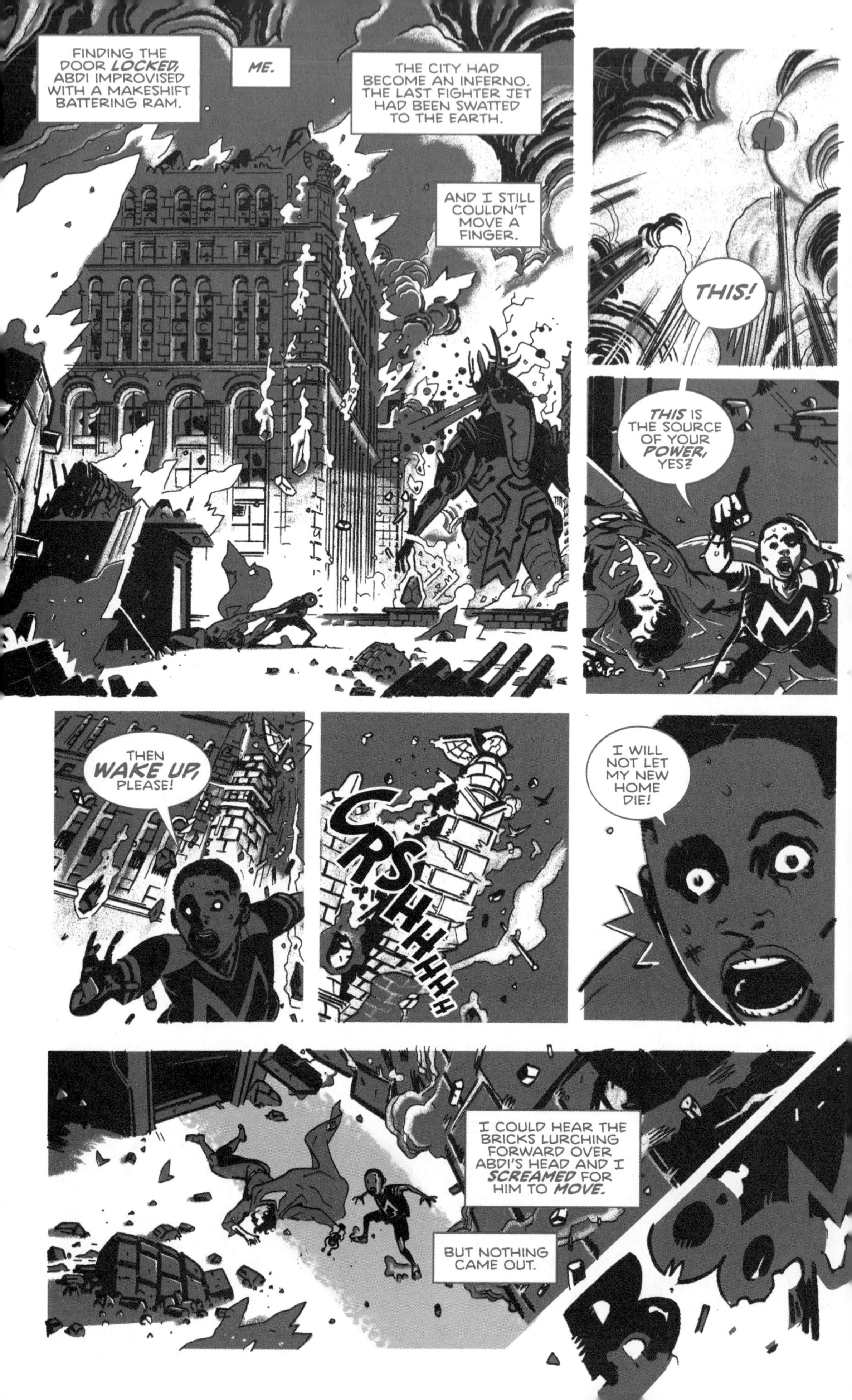
FINDING THE DOOR LOCKED, ABDI IMPROVISED WITH A MAKESHIFT BATTERING RAM.
ME.
THE CITY HAD BECOME AN INFERNO. THE LAST FIGHTER JET HAD BEEN SWATTED TO THE EARTH.
AND I STILL COULDN'T MOVE A FINGER.
THIS!
THIS IS THE SOURCE OF YOUR POWER, YES?
THEN WAKE UP, PLEASE!
CRSHHHHH
I WILL NOT LET MY NEW HOME DIE!
I COULD HEAR THE BRICKS LURCHING FORWARD OVER ABDI'S HEAD AND I SCREAMED FOR HIM TO MOVE.
BUT NOTHING CAME OUT.
BOOM

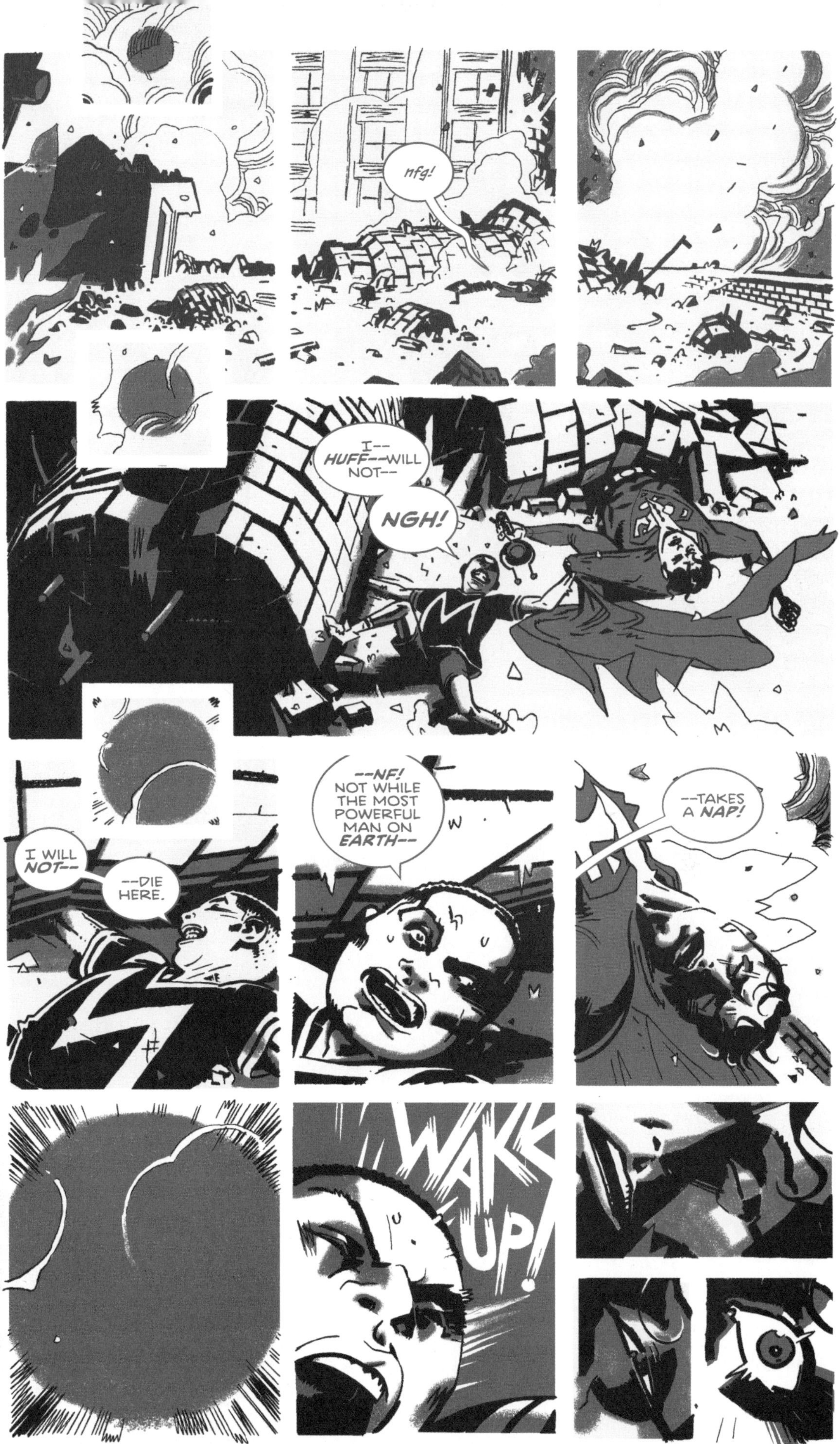
nfg!
I-- HUFF--WILL NOT--
NGH!
I WILL NOT--
--DIE HERE.
--NF! NOT WHILE THE MOST POWERFUL MAN ON EARTH--
--TAKES A NAP!
WAKE UP!

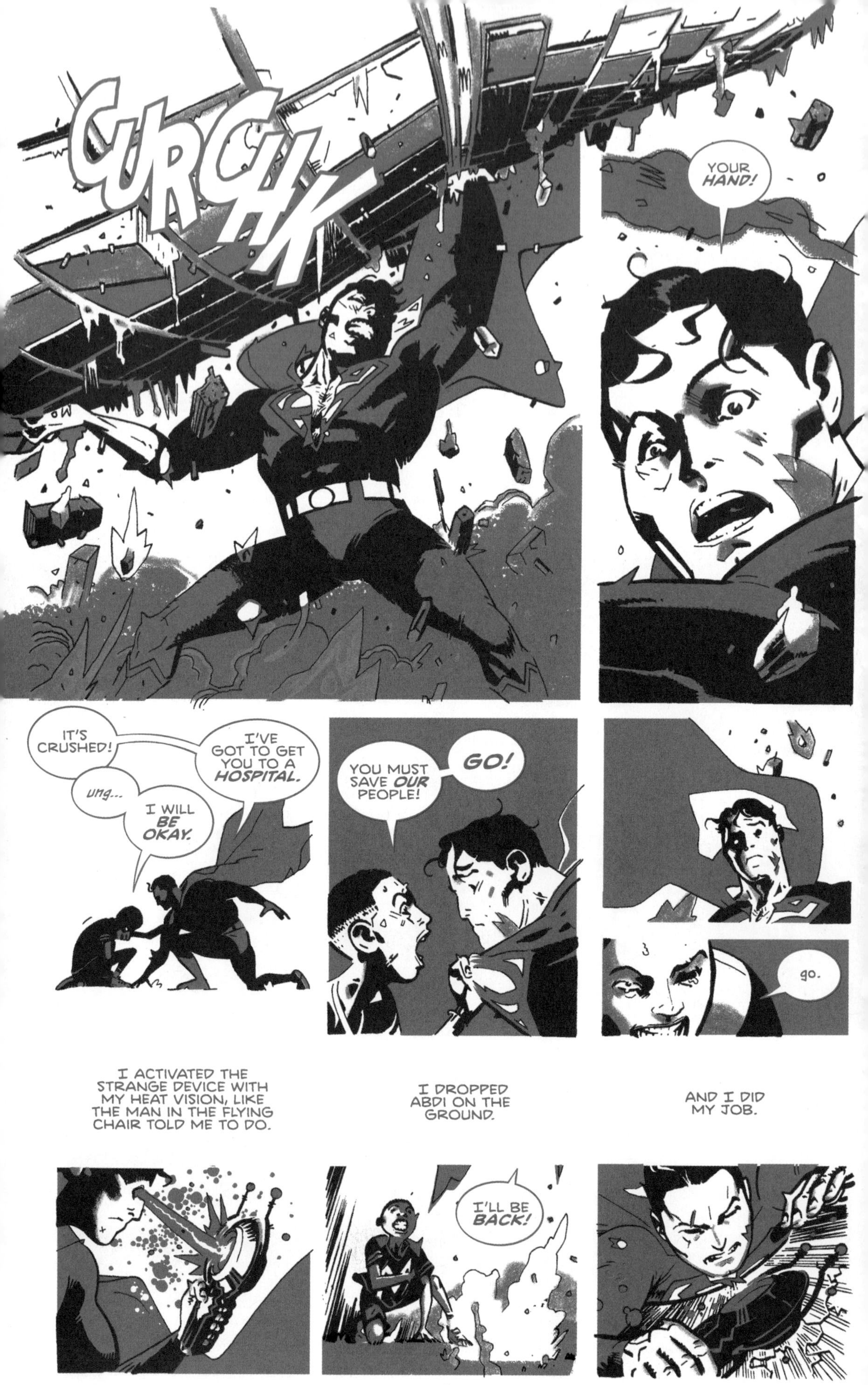
GURCHK
YOUR HAND!
IT'S CRUSHED!
I'VE GOT TO GET YOU TO A HOSPITAL.
ung...
I WILL BE OKAY.
YOU MUST SAVE OUR PEOPLE!
GO!
go.
I ACTIVATED THE STRANGE DEVICE WITH MY HEAT VISION, LIKE THE MAN IN THE FLYING CHAIR TOLD ME TO DO.
I DROPPED ABDI ON THE GROUND.
I'LL BE BACK!
AND I DID MY JOB.

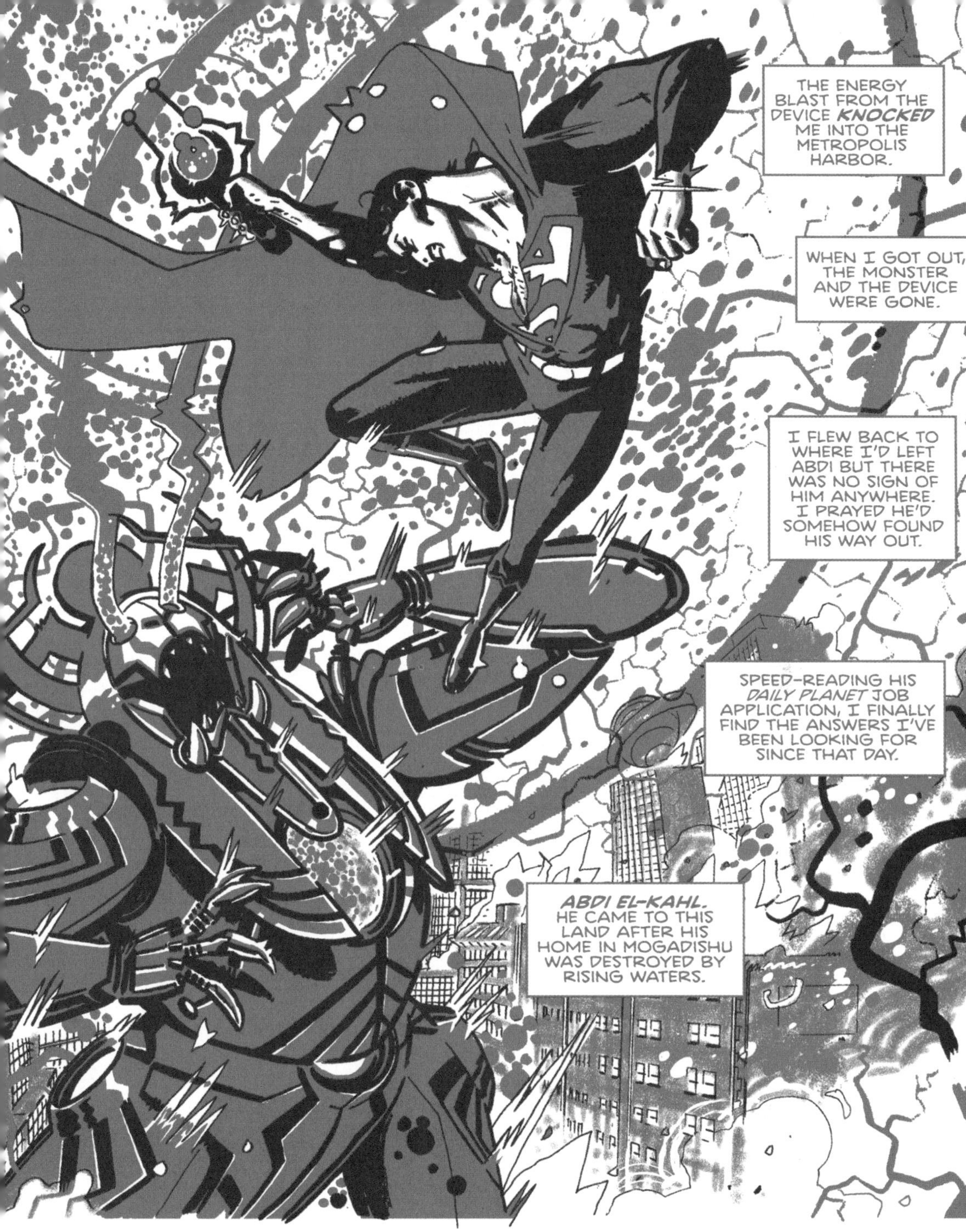
THE ENERGY BLAST FROM THE DEVICE *KNOCKED* ME INTO THE METROPOLIS HARBOR.
WHEN I GOT OUT, THE MONSTER AND THE DEVICE WERE GONE.
I FLEW BACK TO WHERE I'D LEFT ABDI BUT THERE WAS NO SIGN OF HIM ANYWHERE. I PRAYED HE'D SOMEHOW FOUND HIS WAY OUT.
SPEED-READING HIS *DAILY PLANET* JOB APPLICATION, I FINALLY FIND THE ANSWERS I'VE BEEN LOOKING FOR SINCE THAT DAY.
ABDI EL-KAHL. HE CAME TO THIS LAND AFTER HIS HOME IN MOGADISHU WAS DESTROYED BY RISING WATERS.

HE GRADUATED TOP OF HIS CLASS IN PHOTOGRAPHY AT METROPOLIS UNIVERSITY.

THEN HE RETURNED TO HIS OLD HOME TO RECORD THE DAMAGE AS A PHOTOJOURNALIST IN THE PEACE CORPS.

HE EARNED A MASTER'S IN POLITICAL PHILOSOPHY.

RAN A MARATHON.

...SAVED SUPERMAN'S *LIFE.*

HE LEFT THAT OFF HIS APPLICATION, THOUGH. DIDN'T WANT TO SEEM BOASTFUL, I GUESS.

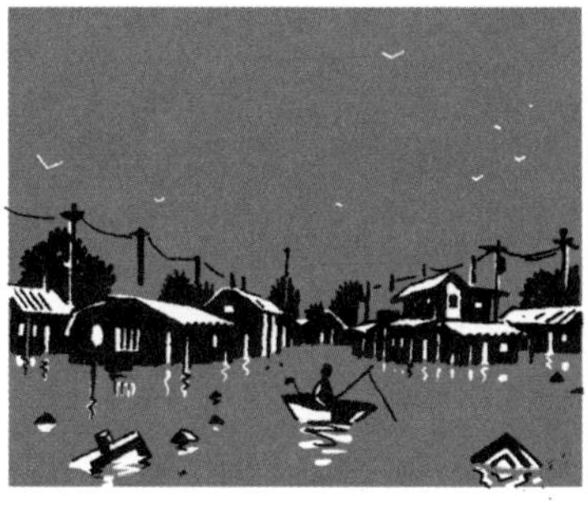

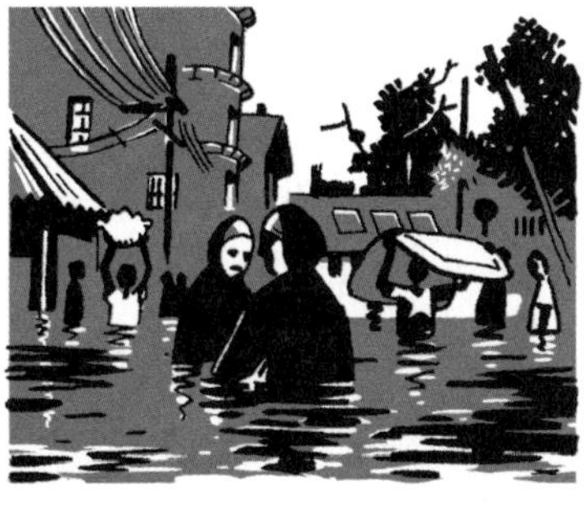

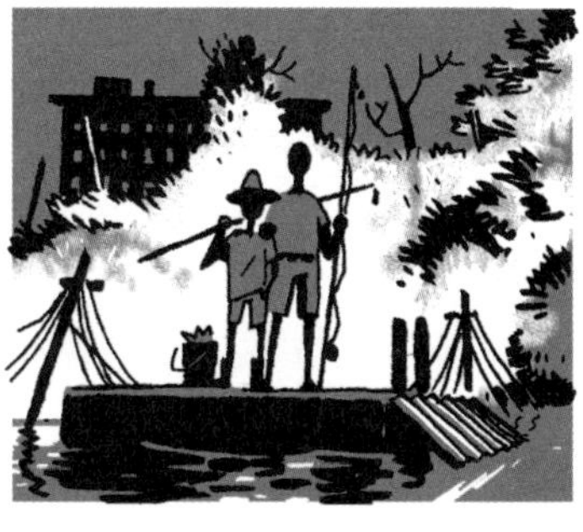

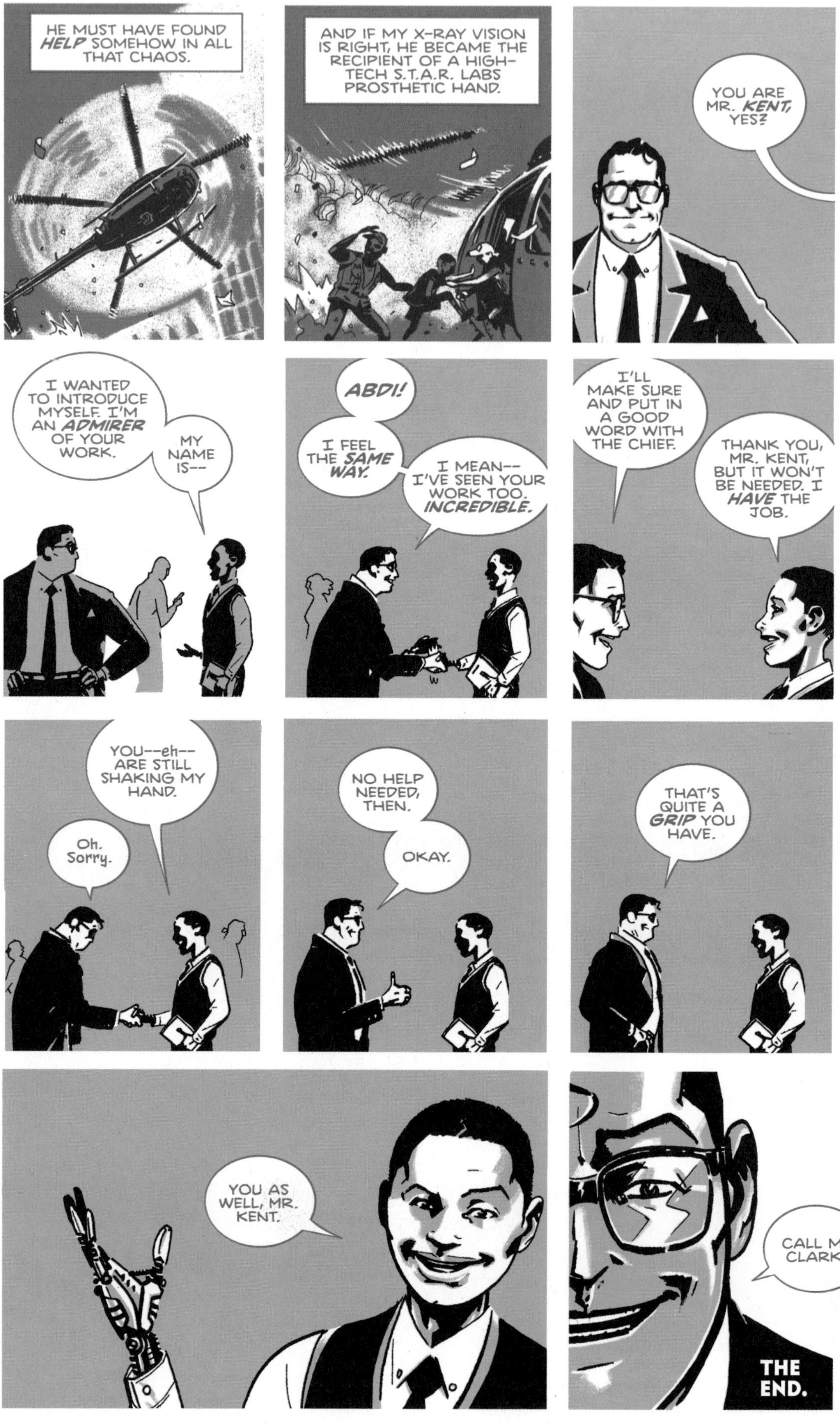
HE MUST HAVE FOUND HELP SOMEHOW IN ALL THAT CHAOS.
AND IF MY X-RAY VISION IS RIGHT, HE BECAME THE RECIPIENT OF A HIGH-TECH S.T.A.R. LABS PROSTHETIC HAND.
YOU ARE MR. KENT, YES?
I WANTED TO INTRODUCE MYSELF. I'M AN ADMIRER OF YOUR WORK.
MY NAME IS--
ABDI!
I FEEL THE SAME WAY.
I MEAN-- I'VE SEEN YOUR WORK TOO. INCREDIBLE.
I'LL MAKE SURE AND PUT IN A GOOD WORD WITH THE CHIEF.
THANK YOU, MR. KENT, BUT IT WON'T BE NEEDED. I HAVE THE JOB.
YOU--eh-- ARE STILL SHAKING MY HAND.
Oh. Sorry.
NO HELP NEEDED, THEN.
OKAY.
THAT'S QUITE A GRIP YOU HAVE.
YOU AS WELL, MR. KENT.
CALL ME CLARK.
THE END.

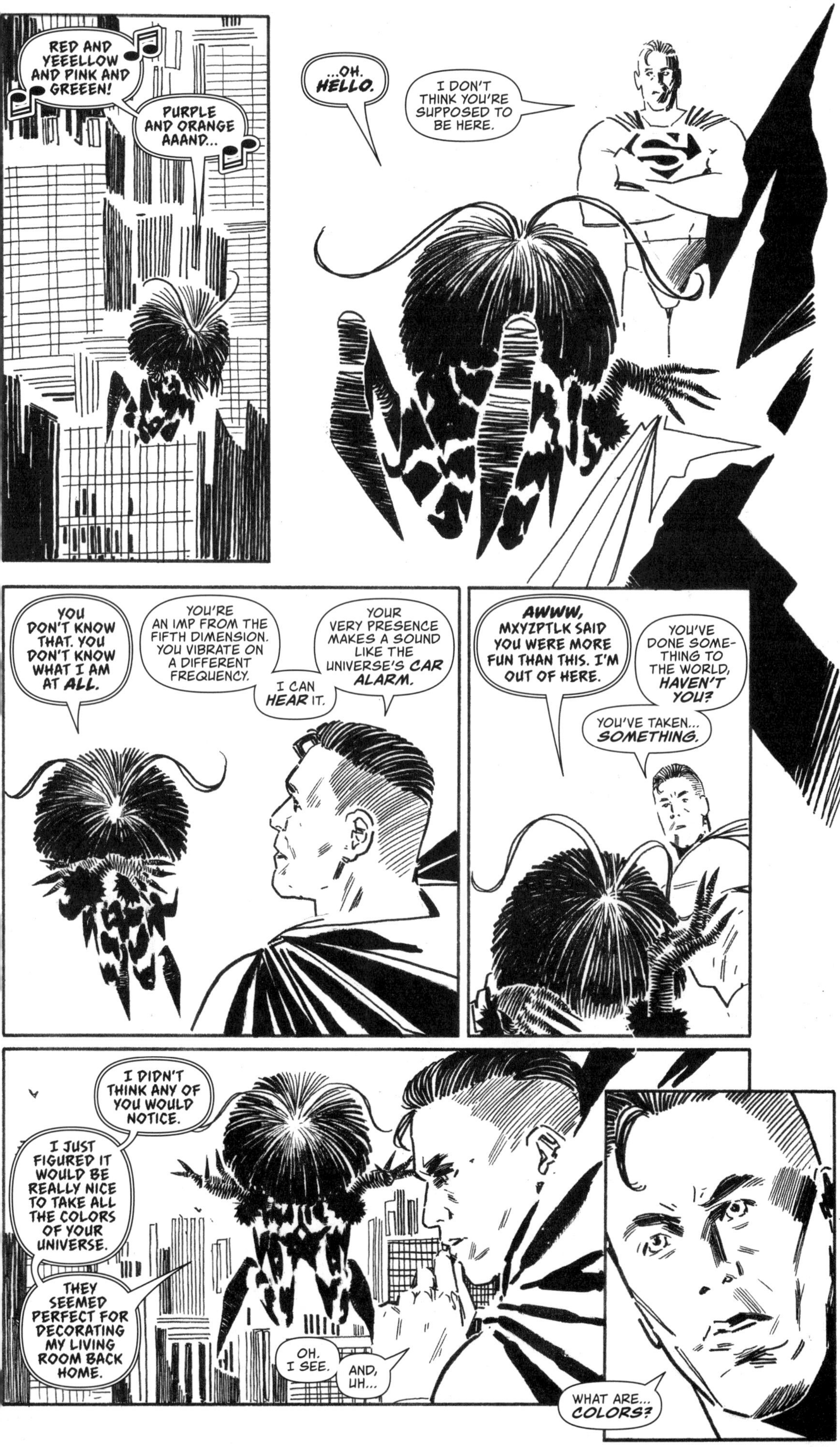
RED AND YEEELLOW AND PINK AND GREEEN!
PURPLE AND ORANGE AAAND...
...OH. HELLO.
I DON'T THINK YOU'RE SUPPOSED TO BE HERE.
YOU DON'T KNOW THAT. YOU DON'T KNOW WHAT I AM AT ALL.
YOU'RE AN IMP FROM THE FIFTH DIMENSION. YOU VIBRATE ON A DIFFERENT FREQUENCY.
I CAN HEAR IT.
YOUR VERY PRESENCE MAKES A SOUND LIKE THE UNIVERSE'S CAR ALARM.
AWWW, MXYZPTLK SAID YOU WERE MORE FUN THAN THIS. I'M OUT OF HERE.
YOU'VE DONE SOMETHING TO THE WORLD, HAVEN'T YOU?
YOU'VE TAKEN... SOMETHING.
I DIDN'T THINK ANY OF YOU WOULD NOTICE.
I JUST FIGURED IT WOULD BE REALLY NICE TO TAKE ALL THE COLORS OF YOUR UNIVERSE.
THEY SEEMED PERFECT FOR DECORATING MY LIVING ROOM BACK HOME.
OH. I SEE.
AND, UH...
WHAT ARE... COLORS?

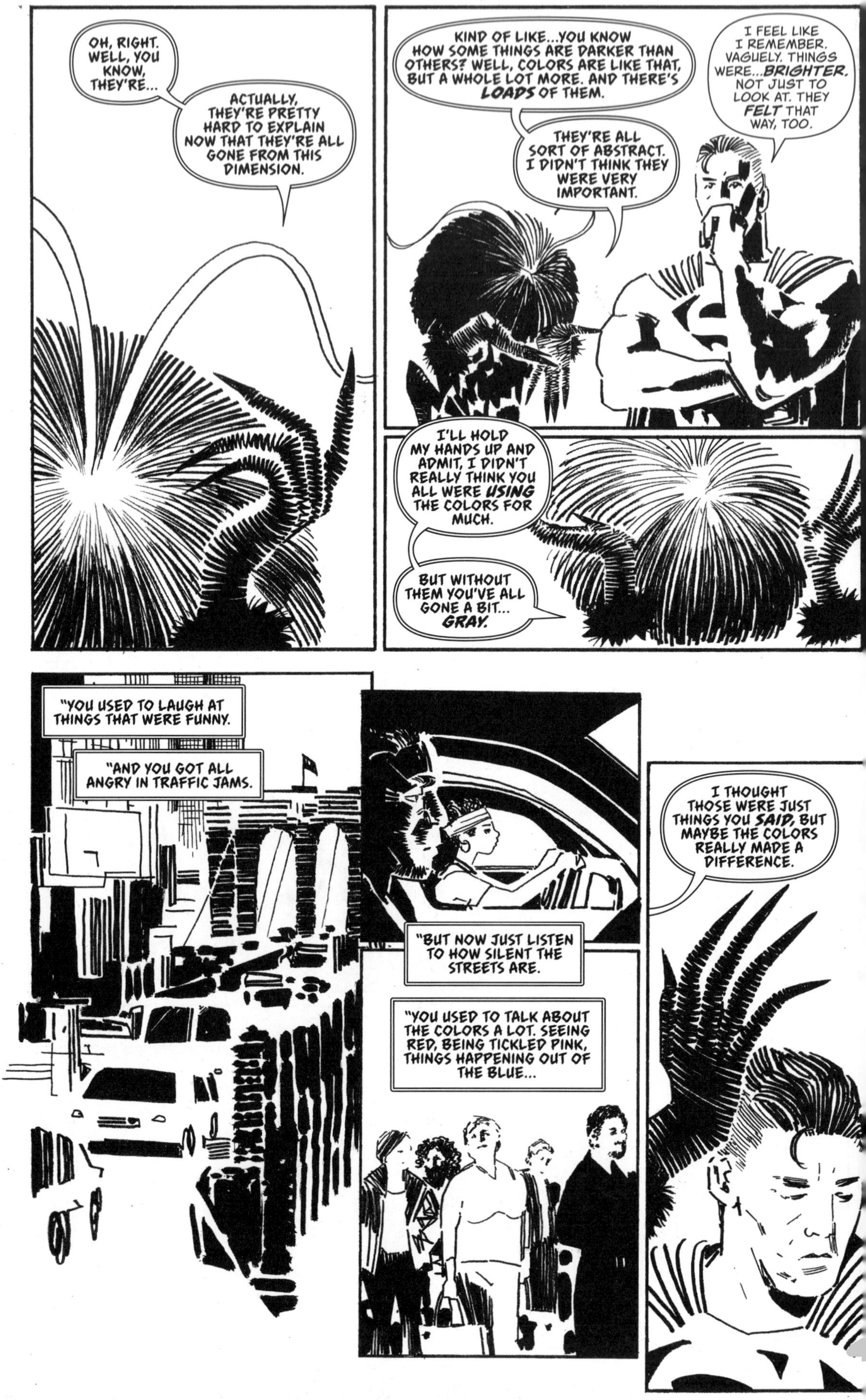
OH, RIGHT. WELL, YOU KNOW, THEY'RE...
ACTUALLY, THEY'RE PRETTY HARD TO EXPLAIN NOW THAT THEY'RE ALL GONE FROM THIS DIMENSION.
KIND OF LIKE...YOU KNOW HOW SOME THINGS ARE DARKER THAN OTHERS? WELL, COLORS ARE LIKE THAT, BUT A WHOLE LOT MORE. AND THERE'S LOADS OF THEM.
THEY'RE ALL SORT OF ABSTRACT. I DIDN'T THINK THEY WERE VERY IMPORTANT.
I FEEL LIKE I REMEMBER. VAGUELY. THINGS WERE...BRIGHTER. NOT JUST TO LOOK AT. THEY FELT THAT WAY, TOO.
I'LL HOLD MY HANDS UP AND ADMIT, I DIDN'T REALLY THINK YOU ALL WERE USING THE COLORS FOR MUCH.
BUT WITHOUT THEM YOU'VE ALL GONE A BIT... GRAY.
"YOU USED TO LAUGH AT THINGS THAT WERE FUNNY.
"AND YOU GOT ALL ANGRY IN TRAFFIC JAMS.
"BUT NOW JUST LISTEN TO HOW SILENT THE STREETS ARE.
"YOU USED TO TALK ABOUT THE COLORS A LOT. SEEING RED, BEING TICKLED PINK, THINGS HAPPENING OUT OF THE BLUE...
I THOUGHT THOSE WERE JUST THINGS YOU SAID, BUT MAYBE THE COLORS REALLY MADE A DIFFERENCE.

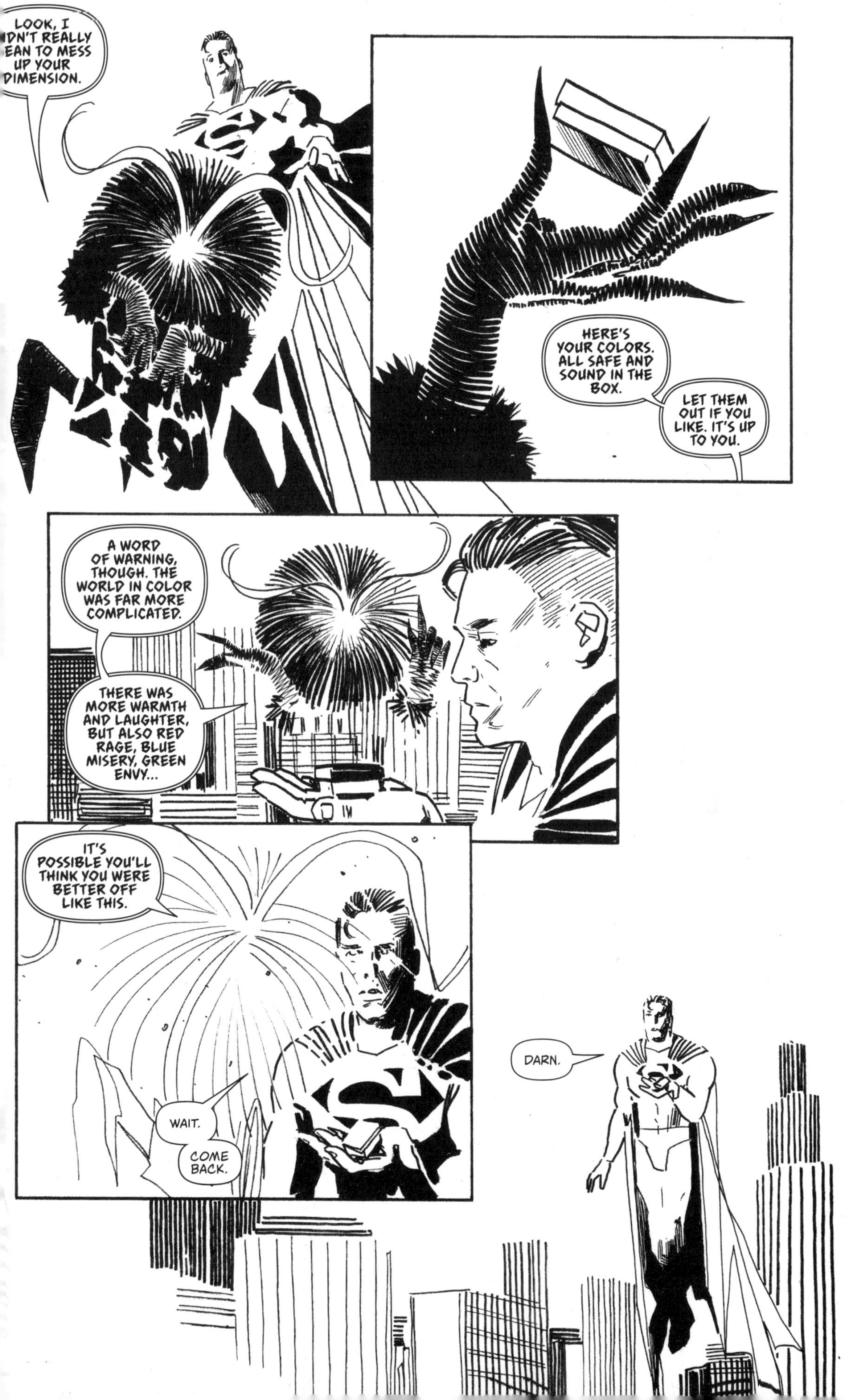
LOOK, I DN'T REALLY EAN TO MESS UP YOUR DIMENSION.
HERE'S YOUR COLORS. ALL SAFE AND SOUND IN THE BOX.
LET THEM OUT IF YOU LIKE. IT'S UP TO YOU.
A WORD OF WARNING, THOUGH. THE WORLD IN COLOR WAS FAR MORE COMPLICATED.
THERE WAS MORE WARMTH AND LAUGHTER, BUT ALSO RED RAGE, BLUE MISERY, GREEN ENVY...
IT'S POSSIBLE YOU'LL THINK YOU WERE BETTER OFF LIKE THIS.
WAIT.
COME BACK.
DARN.

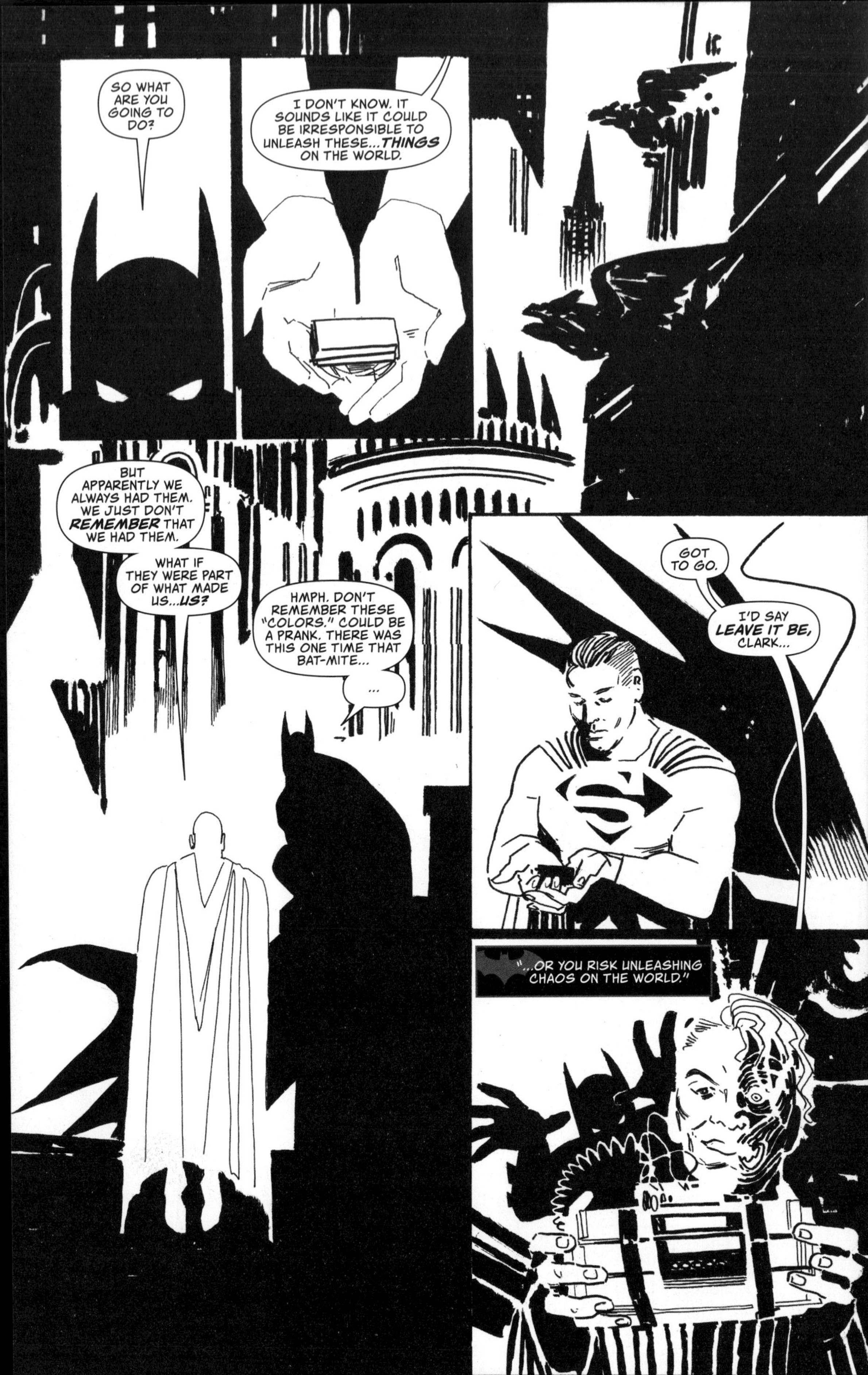
SO WHAT ARE YOU GOING TO DO?
I DON'T KNOW. IT SOUNDS LIKE IT COULD BE IRRESPONSIBLE TO UNLEASH THESE...THINGS ON THE WORLD.
BUT APPARENTLY WE ALWAYS HAD THEM. WE JUST DON'T REMEMBER THAT WE HAD THEM.
WHAT IF THEY WERE PART OF WHAT MADE US...US?
HMPH. DON'T REMEMBER THESE "COLORS." COULD BE A PRANK. THERE WAS THIS ONE TIME THAT BAT-MITE...
...
GOT TO GO.
I'D SAY LEAVE IT BE, CLARK...
"...OR YOU RISK UNLEASHING CHAOS ON THE WORLD."

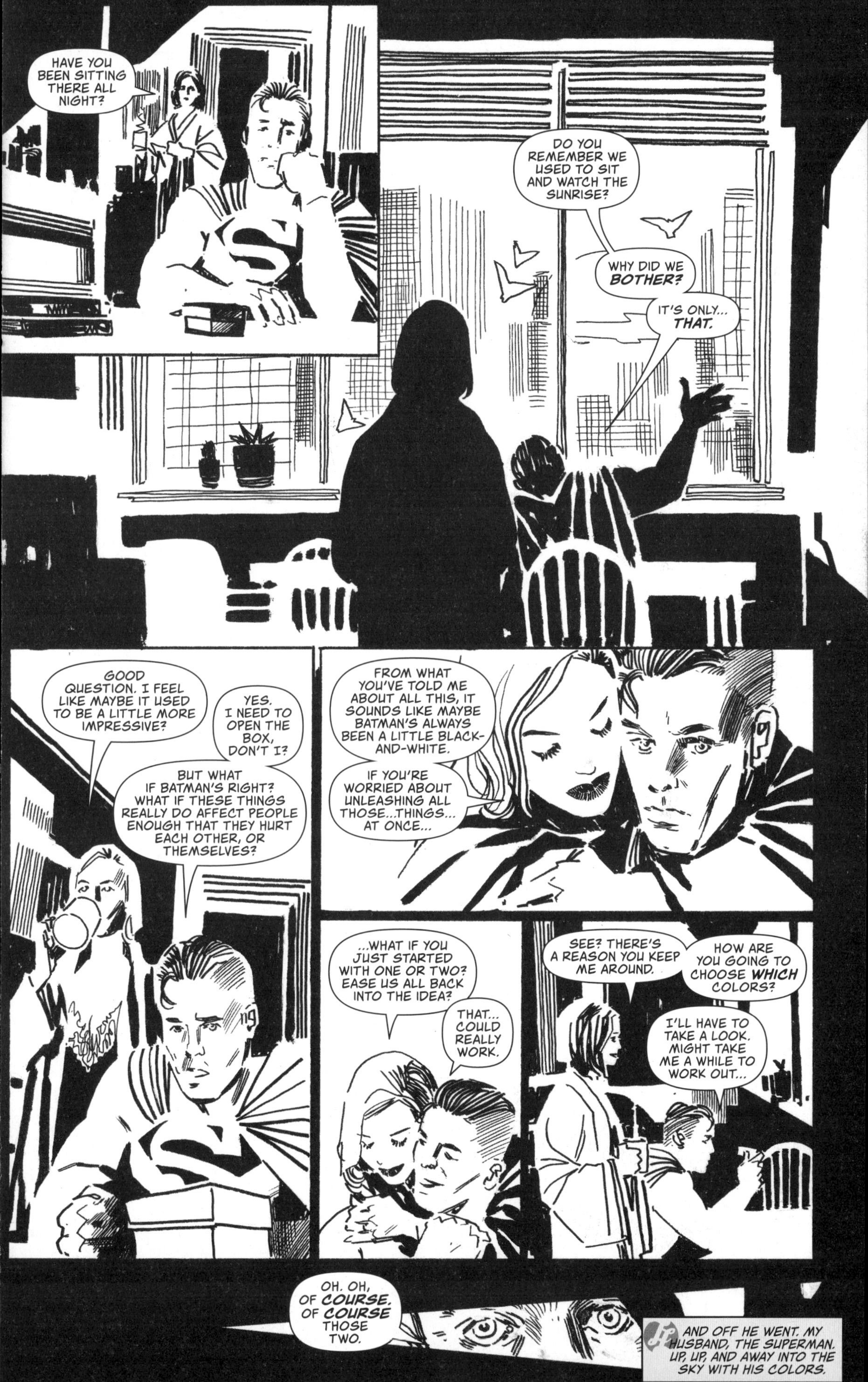
HAVE YOU BEEN SITTING THERE ALL NIGHT?
DO YOU REMEMBER WE USED TO SIT AND WATCH THE SUNRISE?
WHY DID WE BOTHER?
IT'S ONLY... THAT.
GOOD QUESTION. I FEEL LIKE MAYBE IT USED TO BE A LITTLE MORE IMPRESSIVE?
YES. I NEED TO OPEN THE BOX, DON'T I?
BUT WHAT IF BATMAN'S RIGHT? WHAT IF THESE THINGS REALLY DO AFFECT PEOPLE ENOUGH THAT THEY HURT EACH OTHER, OR THEMSELVES?
FROM WHAT YOU'VE TOLD ME ABOUT ALL THIS, IT SOUNDS LIKE MAYBE BATMAN'S ALWAYS BEEN A LITTLE BLACK-AND-WHITE.
IF YOU'RE WORRIED ABOUT UNLEASHING ALL THOSE...THINGS... AT ONCE...
...WHAT IF YOU JUST STARTED WITH ONE OR TWO? EASE US ALL BACK INTO THE IDEA?
THAT... COULD REALLY WORK.
SEE? THERE'S A REASON YOU KEEP ME AROUND.
HOW ARE YOU GOING TO CHOOSE WHICH COLORS?
I'LL HAVE TO TAKE A LOOK. MIGHT TAKE ME A WHILE TO WORK OUT...
OH. OH, OF COURSE. OF COURSE THOSE TWO.
AND OFF HE WENT. MY HUSBAND, THE SUPERMAN. UP, UP, AND AWAY INTO THE SKY WITH HIS COLORS.

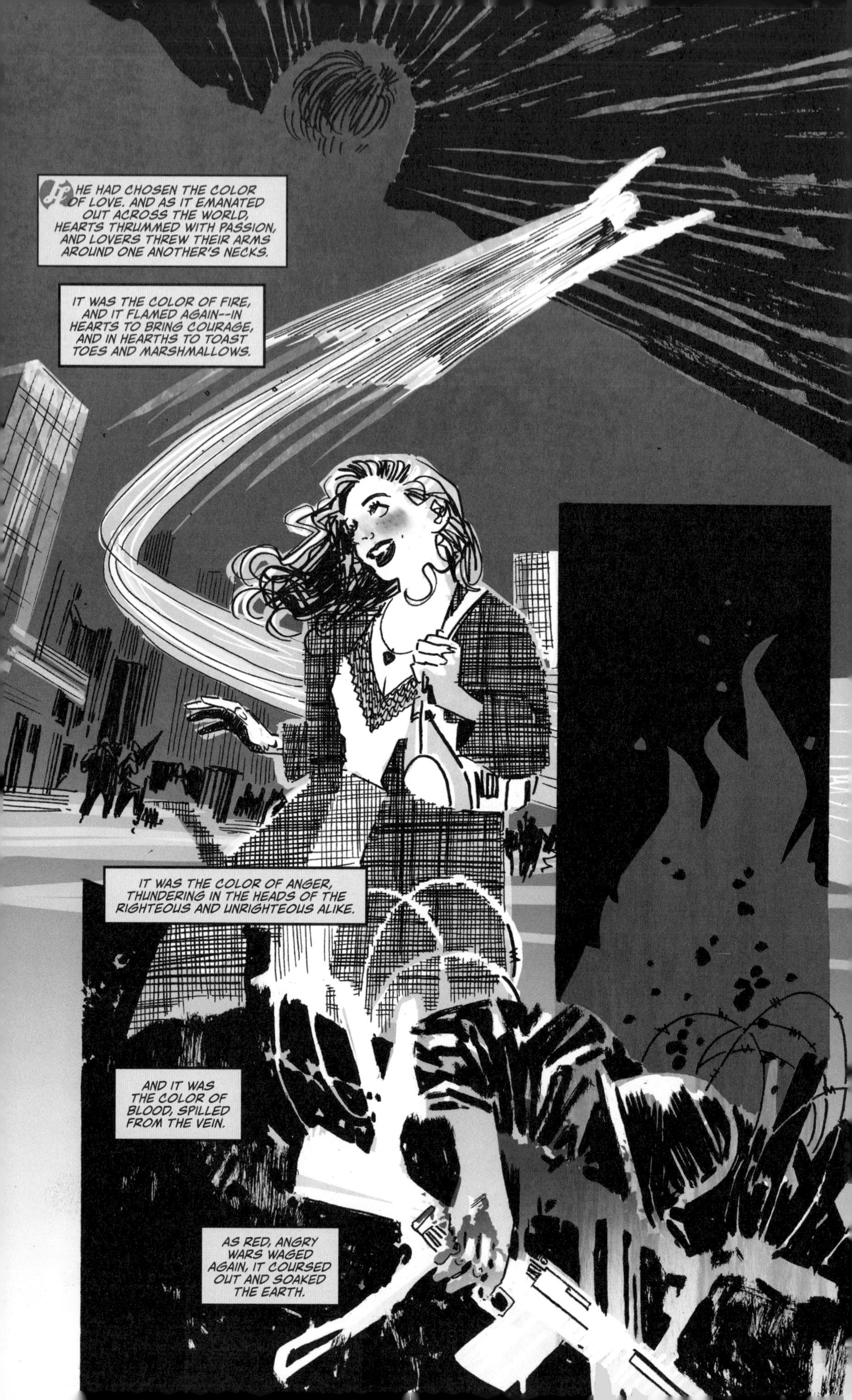
HE HAD CHOSEN THE COLOR OF LOVE. AND AS IT EMANATED OUT ACROSS THE WORLD, HEARTS THRUMMED WITH PASSION, AND LOVERS THREW THEIR ARMS AROUND ONE ANOTHER'S NECKS.
IT WAS THE COLOR OF FIRE, AND IT FLAMED AGAIN--IN HEARTS TO BRING COURAGE, AND IN HEARTHS TO TOAST TOES AND MARSHMALLOWS.
IT WAS THE COLOR OF ANGER, THUNDERING IN THE HEADS OF THE RIGHTEOUS AND UNRIGHTEOUS ALIKE.
AND IT WAS THE COLOR OF BLOOD, SPILLED FROM THE VEIN.
AS RED, ANGRY WARS WAGED AGAIN, IT COURSED OUT AND SOAKED THE EARTH.

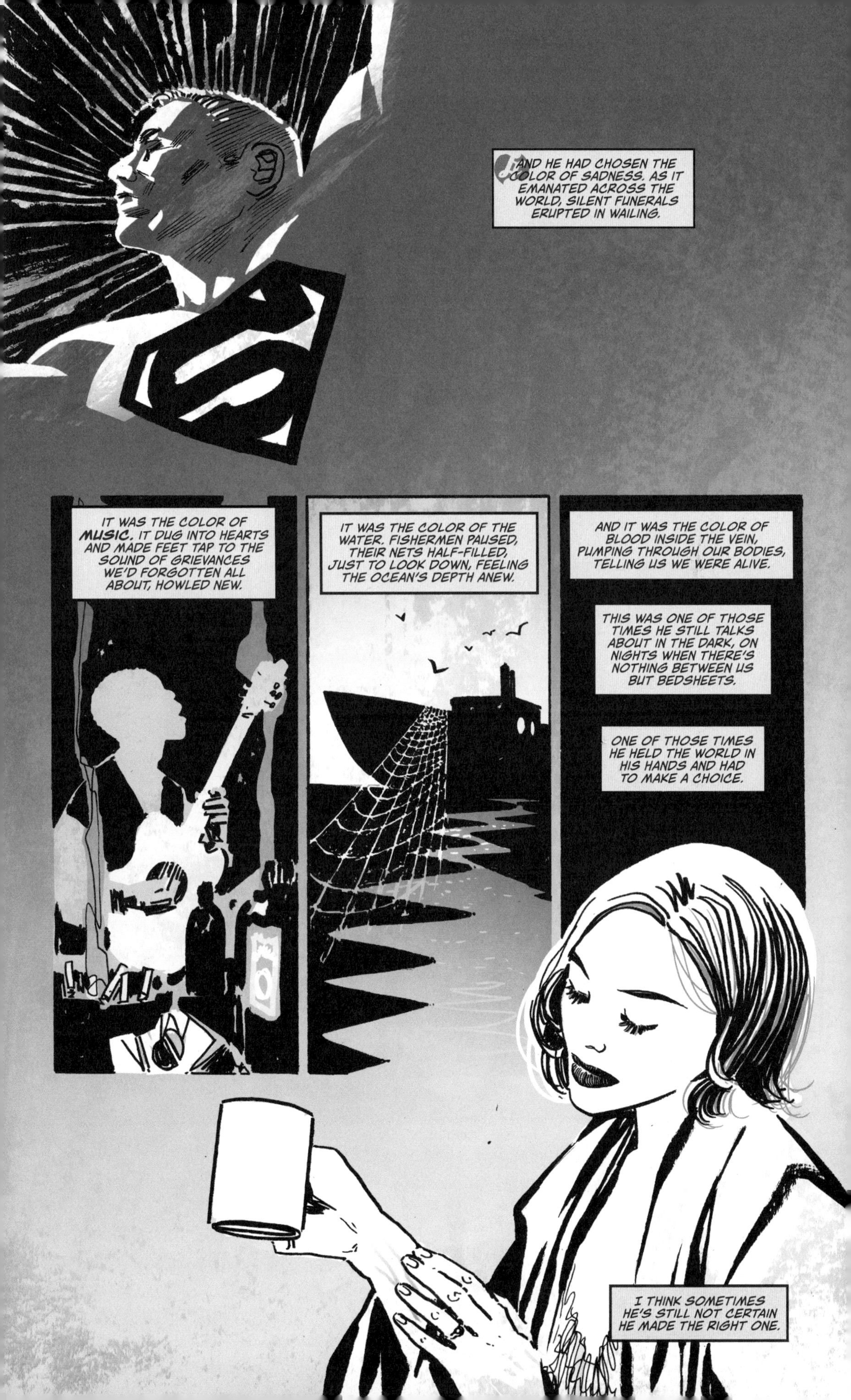
AND HE HAD CHOSEN THE COLOR OF SADNESS. AS IT EMANATED ACROSS THE WORLD, SILENT FUNERALS ERUPTED IN WAILING.
IT WAS THE COLOR OF MUSIC. IT DUG INTO HEARTS AND MADE FEET TAP TO THE SOUND OF GRIEVANCES WE'D FORGOTTEN ALL ABOUT, HOWLED NEW.
IT WAS THE COLOR OF THE WATER. FISHERMEN PAUSED, THEIR NETS HALF-FILLED, JUST TO LOOK DOWN, FEELING THE OCEAN'S DEPTH ANEW.
AND IT WAS THE COLOR OF BLOOD INSIDE THE VEIN, PUMPING THROUGH OUR BODIES, TELLING US WE WERE ALIVE.
THIS WAS ONE OF THOSE TIMES HE STILL TALKS ABOUT IN THE DARK, ON NIGHTS WHEN THERE'S NOTHING BETWEEN US BUT BEDSHEETS.
ONE OF THOSE TIMES HE HELD THE WORLD IN HIS HANDS AND HAD TO MAKE A CHOICE.
I THINK SOMETIMES HE'S STILL NOT CERTAIN HE MADE THE RIGHT ONE.

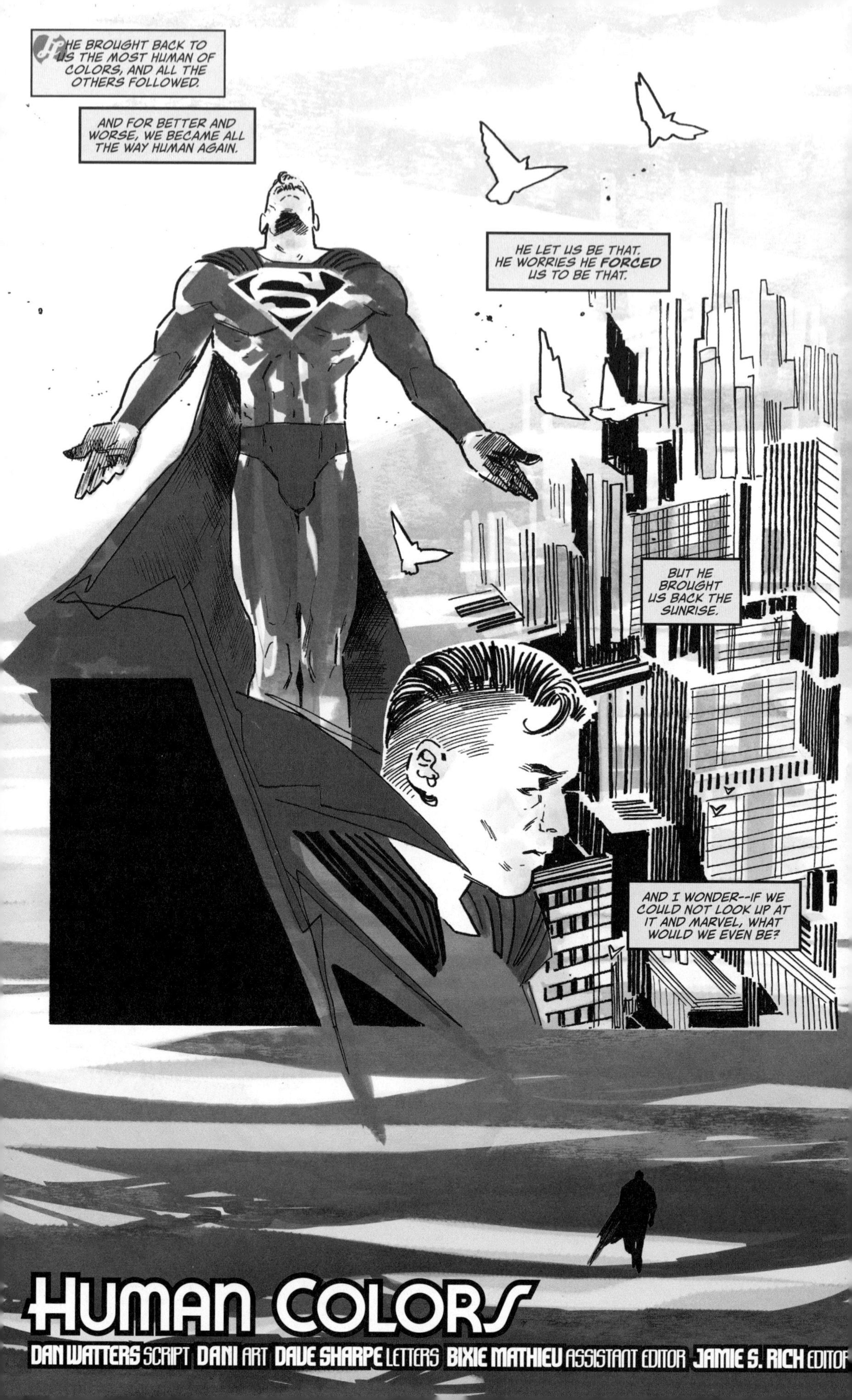
HE BROUGHT BACK TO US THE MOST HUMAN OF COLORS, AND ALL THE OTHERS FOLLOWED.
AND FOR BETTER AND WORSE, WE BECAME ALL THE WAY HUMAN AGAIN.
HE LET US BE THAT. HE WORRIES HE FORCED US TO BE THAT.
BUT HE BROUGHT US BACK THE SUNRISE.
AND I WONDER--IF WE COULD NOT LOOK UP AT IT AND MARVEL, WHAT WOULD WE EVEN BE?
HUMAN COLORS
DAN WATTERS SCRIPT DANI ART DAVE SHARPE LETTERS BIXIE MATHIEU ASSISTANT EDITOR JAMIE S. RICH EDITOR

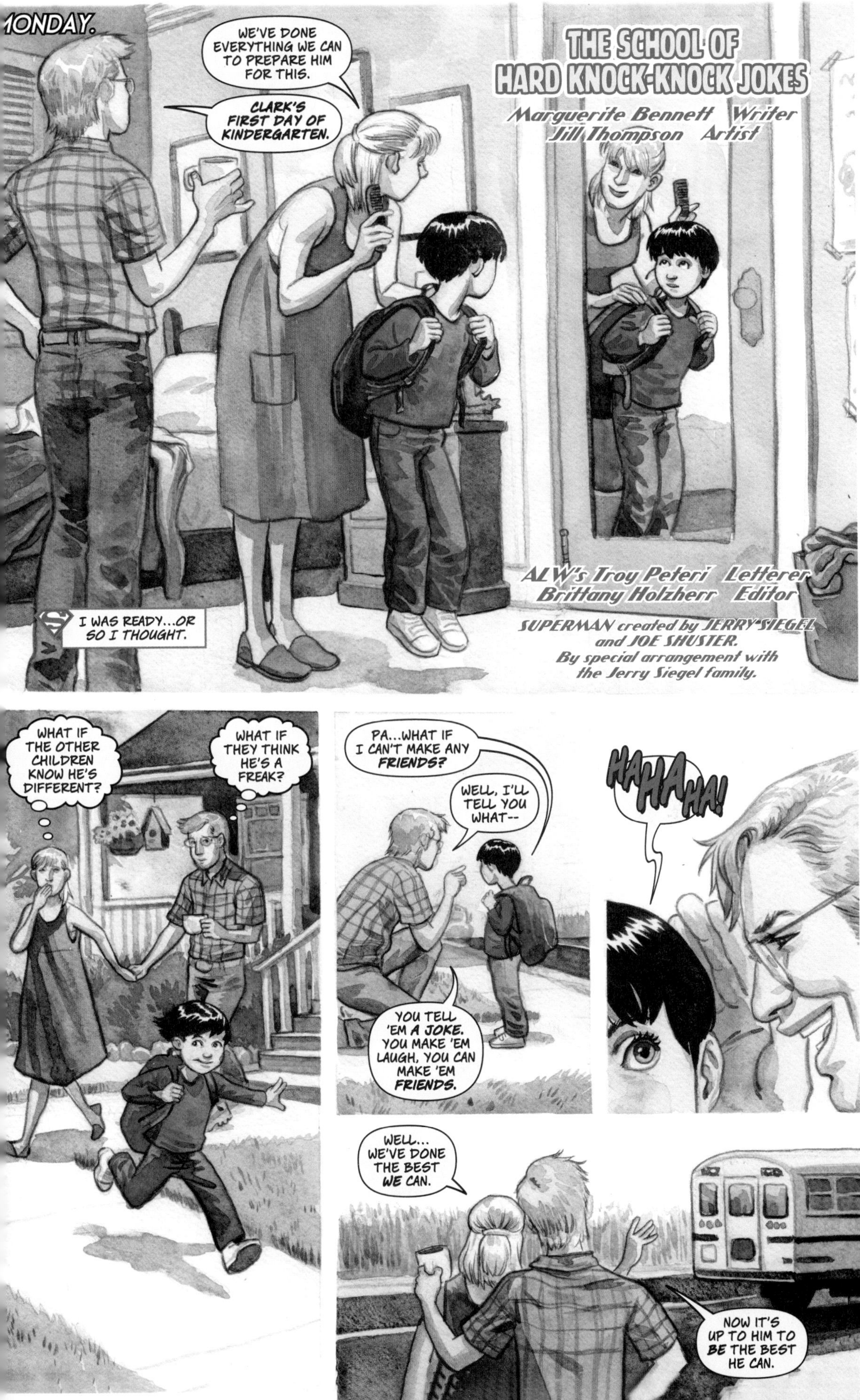
MONDAY.
WE'VE DONE EVERYTHING WE CAN TO PREPARE HIM FOR THIS.
CLARK'S FIRST DAY OF KINDERGARTEN.
THE SCHOOL OF HARD KNOCK-KNOCK JOKES
Marguerite Bennett Writer
Jill Thompson Artist
ALW's Troy Peteri Letterer
Brittany Holzherr Editor
SUPERMAN created by JERRY SIEGEL and JOE SHUSTER.
By special arrangement with the Jerry Siegel family.
I WAS READY...OR SO I THOUGHT.
WHAT IF THE OTHER CHILDREN KNOW HE'S DIFFERENT?
WHAT IF THEY THINK HE'S A FREAK?
PA...WHAT IF I CAN'T MAKE ANY FRIENDS?
WELL, I'LL TELL YOU WHAT--
YOU TELL 'EM A JOKE. YOU MAKE 'EM LAUGH, YOU CAN MAKE 'EM FRIENDS.
HAHAHAHA!
WELL... WE'VE DONE THE BEST WE CAN.
NOW IT'S UP TO HIM TO BE THE BEST HE CAN.

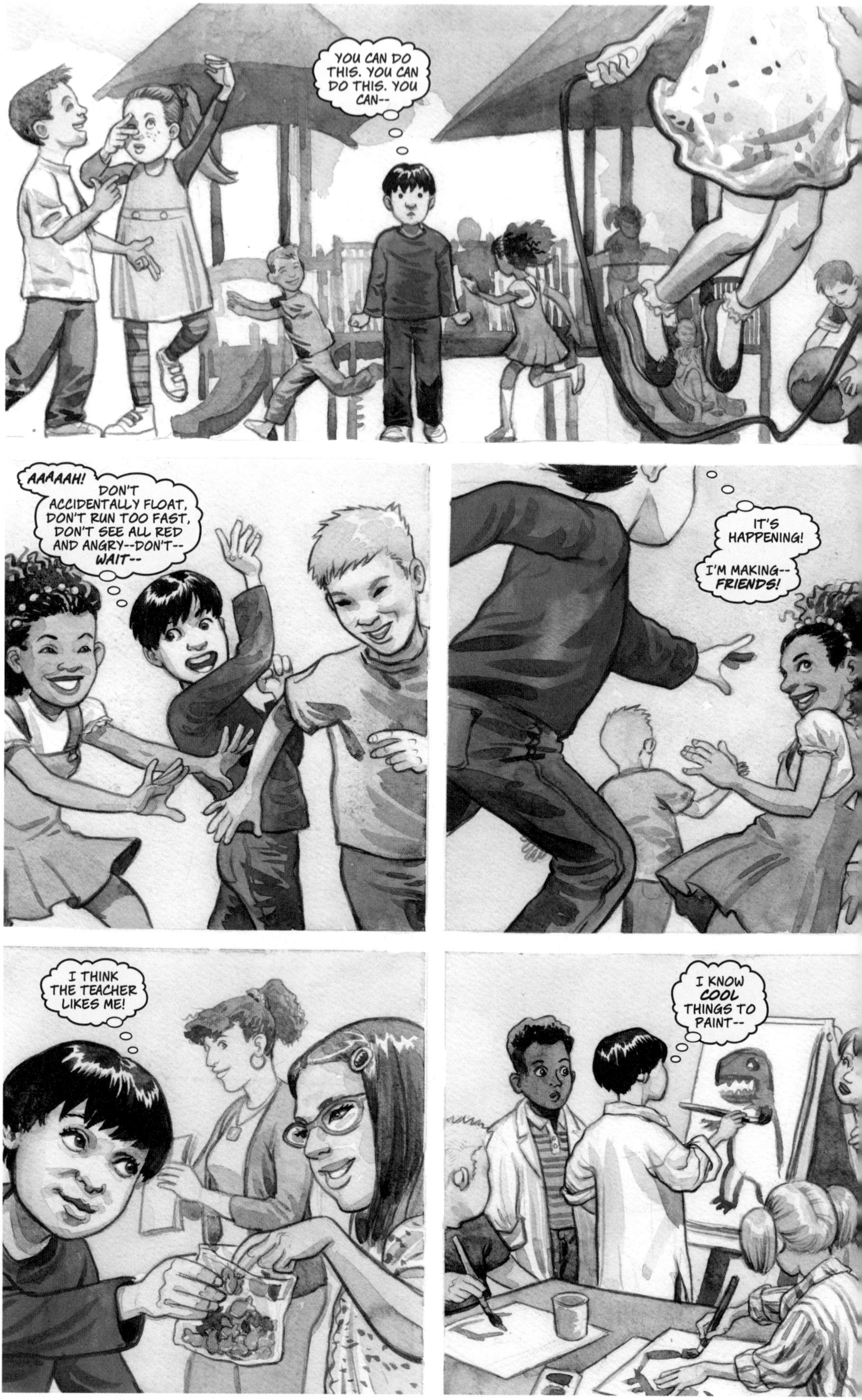
YOU CAN DO THIS. YOU CAN DO THIS. YOU CAN--
AAAAAH!
DON'T ACCIDENTALLY FLOAT, DON'T RUN TOO FAST, DON'T SEE ALL RED AND ANGRY--DON'T-- WAIT--
IT'S HAPPENING!
I'M MAKING-- FRIENDS!
I THINK THE TEACHER LIKES ME!
I KNOW COOL THINGS TO PAINT--

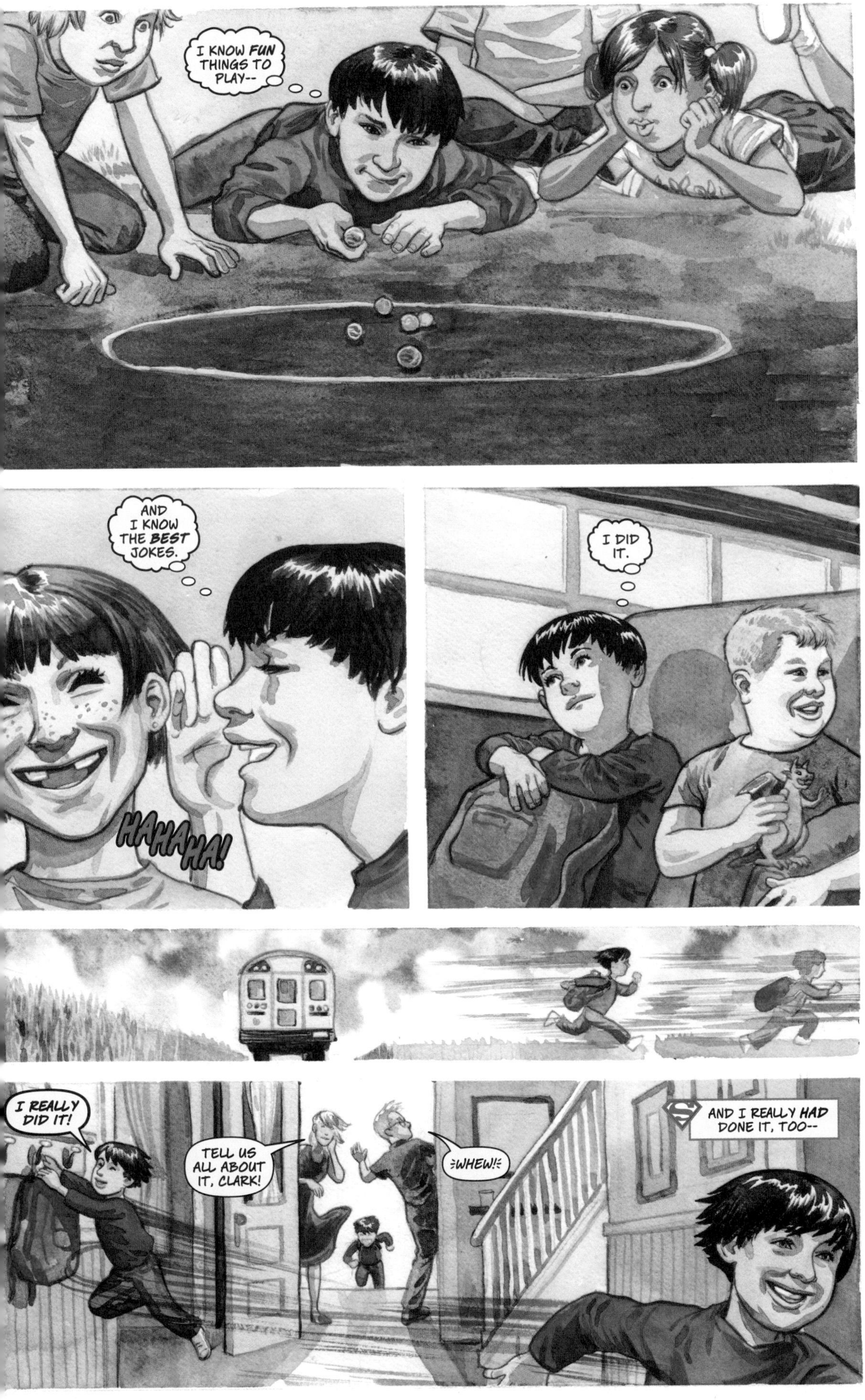
I KNOW FUN THINGS TO PLAY--
AND I KNOW THE BEST JOKES.
HAHAHA!
I DID IT.
I REALLY DID IT!
TELL US ALL ABOUT IT, CLARK!
WHEW!
AND I REALLY HAD DONE IT, TOO--

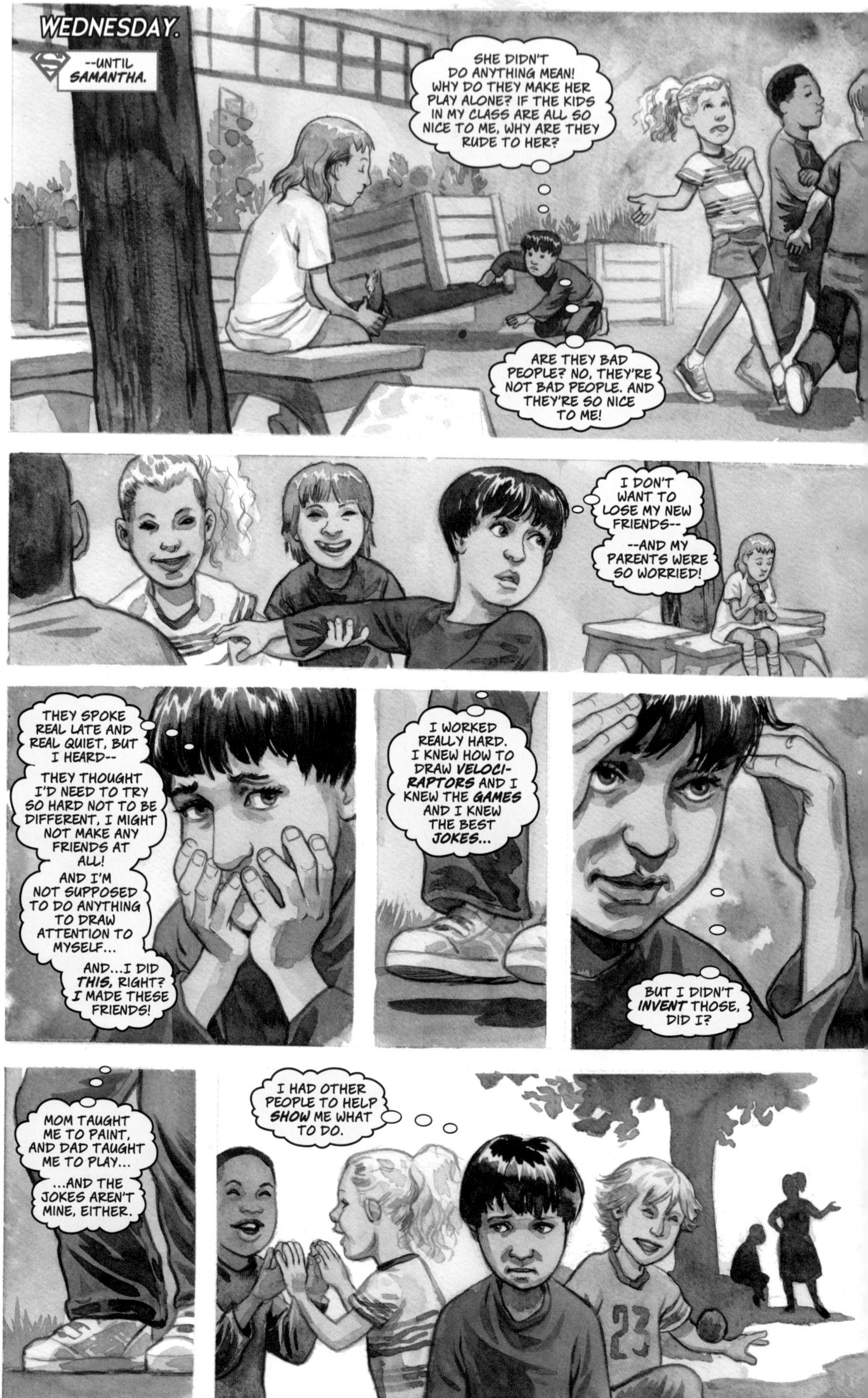
WEDNESDAY.
--UNTIL SAMANTHA.
SHE DIDN'T DO ANYTHING MEAN! WHY DO THEY MAKE HER PLAY ALONE? IF THE KIDS IN MY CLASS ARE ALL SO NICE TO ME, WHY ARE THEY RUDE TO HER?
ARE THEY BAD PEOPLE? NO, THEY'RE NOT BAD PEOPLE. AND THEY'RE SO NICE TO ME!
I DON'T WANT TO LOSE MY NEW FRIENDS--
--AND MY PARENTS WERE SO WORRIED!
THEY SPOKE REAL LATE AND REAL QUIET, BUT I HEARD--
THEY THOUGHT I'D NEED TO TRY SO HARD NOT TO BE DIFFERENT, I MIGHT NOT MAKE ANY FRIENDS AT ALL!
AND I'M NOT SUPPOSED TO DO ANYTHING TO DRAW ATTENTION TO MYSELF...
AND...I DID THIS, RIGHT? I MADE THESE FRIENDS!
I WORKED REALLY HARD. I KNEW HOW TO DRAW VELOCI-RAPTORS AND I KNEW THE GAMES AND I KNEW THE BEST JOKES...
BUT I DIDN'T INVENT THOSE, DID I?
MOM TAUGHT ME TO PAINT, AND DAD TAUGHT ME TO PLAY...
...AND THE JOKES AREN'T MINE, EITHER.
I HAD OTHER PEOPLE TO HELP SHOW ME WHAT TO DO.
23

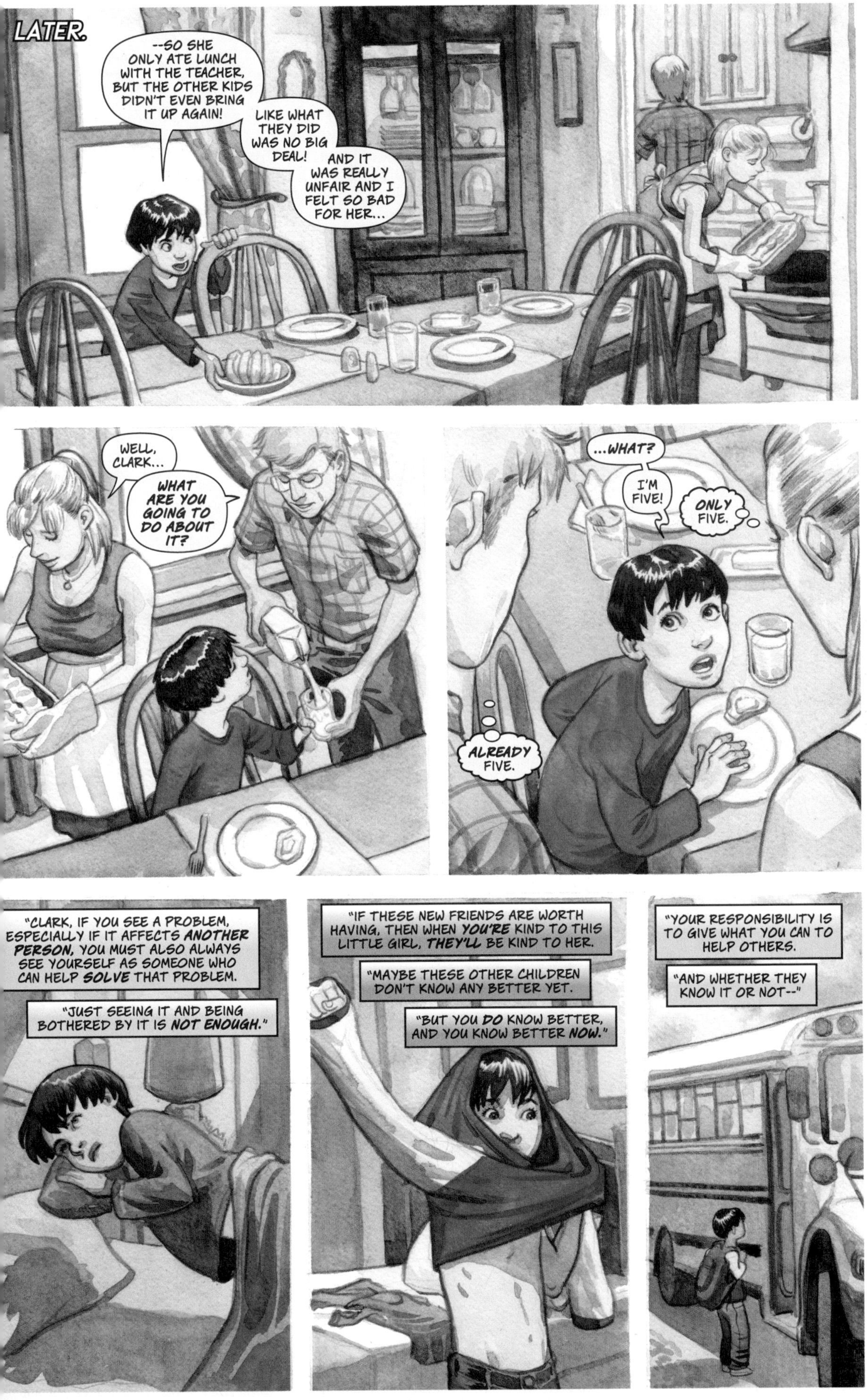
LATER.
--SO SHE ONLY ATE LUNCH WITH THE TEACHER, BUT THE OTHER KIDS DIDN'T EVEN BRING IT UP AGAIN!
LIKE WHAT THEY DID WAS NO BIG DEAL!
AND IT WAS REALLY UNFAIR AND I FELT SO BAD FOR HER...
WELL, CLARK...
WHAT ARE YOU GOING TO DO ABOUT IT?
...WHAT?
I'M FIVE!
ONLY FIVE.
ALREADY FIVE.
"CLARK, IF YOU SEE A PROBLEM, ESPECIALLY IF IT AFFECTS ANOTHER PERSON, YOU MUST ALSO ALWAYS SEE YOURSELF AS SOMEONE WHO CAN HELP SOLVE THAT PROBLEM.
"JUST SEEING IT AND BEING BOTHERED BY IT IS NOT ENOUGH."
"IF THESE NEW FRIENDS ARE WORTH HAVING, THEN WHEN YOU'RE KIND TO THIS LITTLE GIRL, THEY'LL BE KIND TO HER.
"MAYBE THESE OTHER CHILDREN DON'T KNOW ANY BETTER YET.
"BUT YOU DO KNOW BETTER, AND YOU KNOW BETTER NOW."
"YOUR RESPONSIBILITY IS TO GIVE WHAT YOU CAN TO HELP OTHERS.
"AND WHETHER THEY KNOW IT OR NOT--"

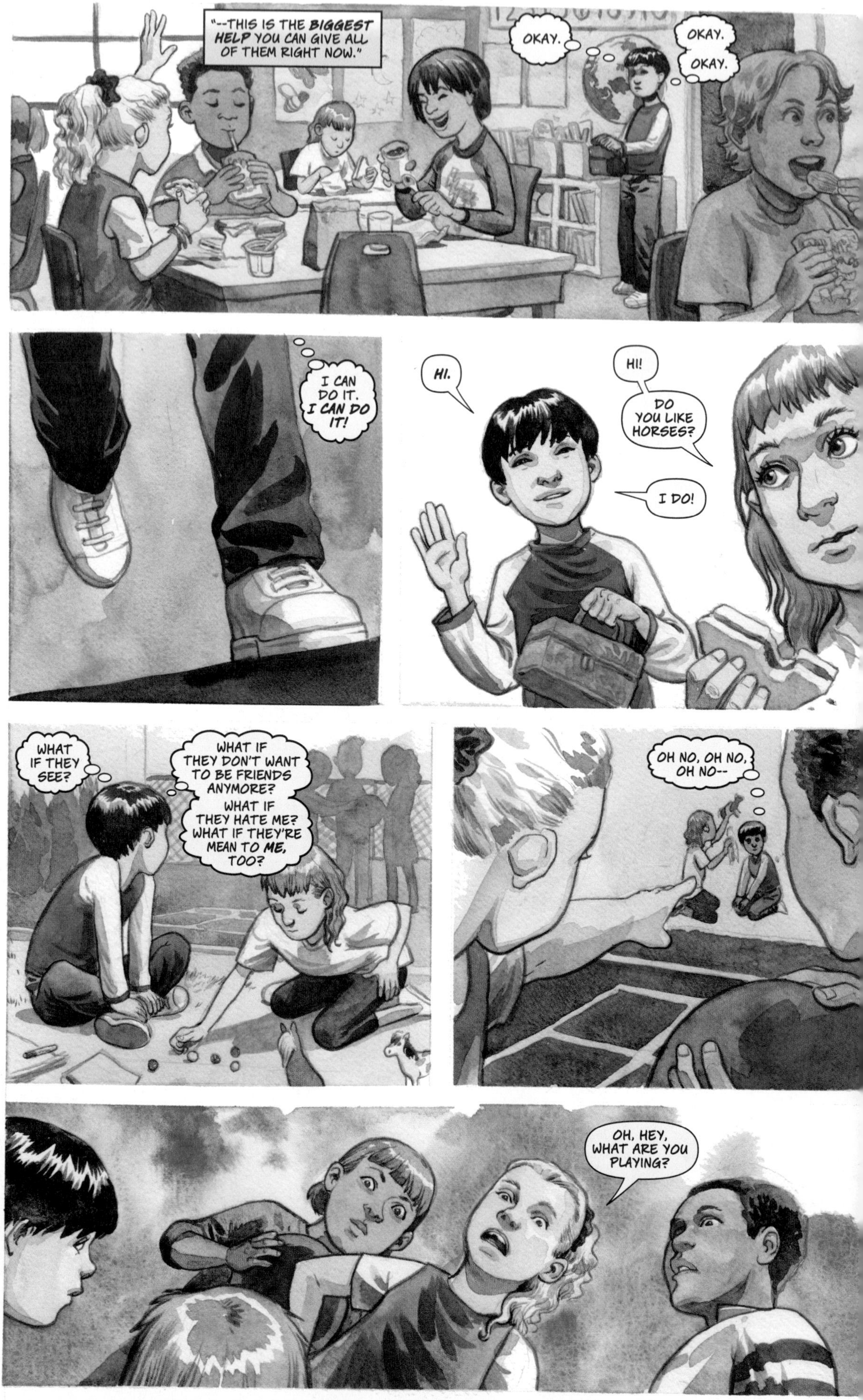
"--THIS IS THE **BIGGEST HELP** YOU CAN GIVE ALL OF THEM RIGHT NOW."
OKAY.
OKAY.
OKAY.
I CAN DO IT. ***I CAN DO IT!***
HI.
HI!
DO YOU LIKE HORSES?
I DO!
WHAT IF THEY SEE?
WHAT IF THEY DON'T WANT TO BE FRIENDS ANYMORE?
WHAT IF THEY HATE ME? WHAT IF THEY'RE MEAN TO **ME,** TOO?
OH NO, OH NO, OH NO--
OH, HEY, WHAT ARE YOU PLAYING?

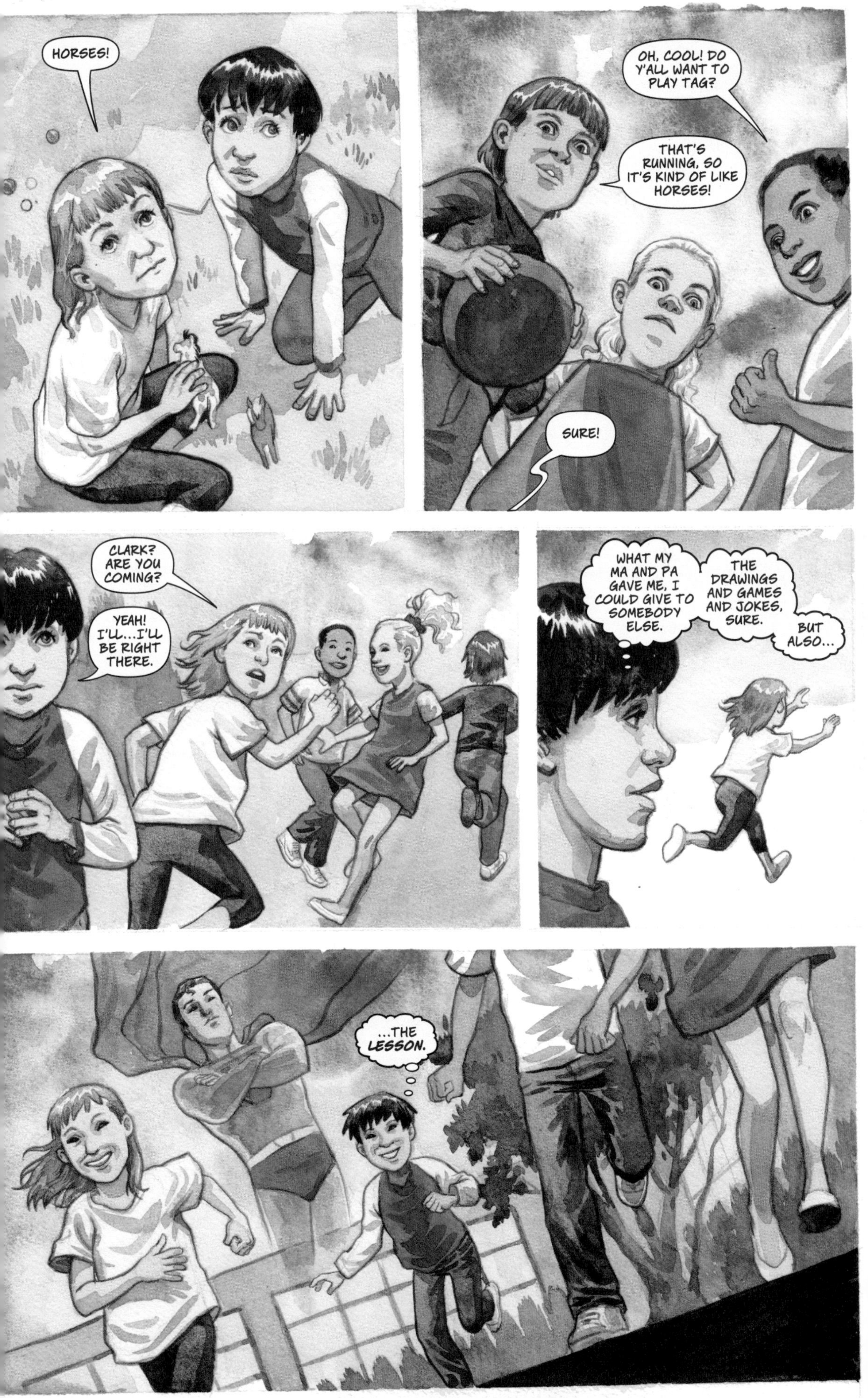
HORSES!
OH, COOL! DO Y'ALL WANT TO PLAY TAG?
THAT'S RUNNING, SO IT'S KIND OF LIKE HORSES!
SURE!
CLARK? ARE YOU COMING?
YEAH! I'LL...I'LL BE RIGHT THERE.
WHAT MY MA AND PA GAVE ME, I COULD GIVE TO SOMEBODY ELSE.
THE DRAWINGS AND GAMES AND JOKES, SURE.
BUT ALSO...
...THE LESSON.

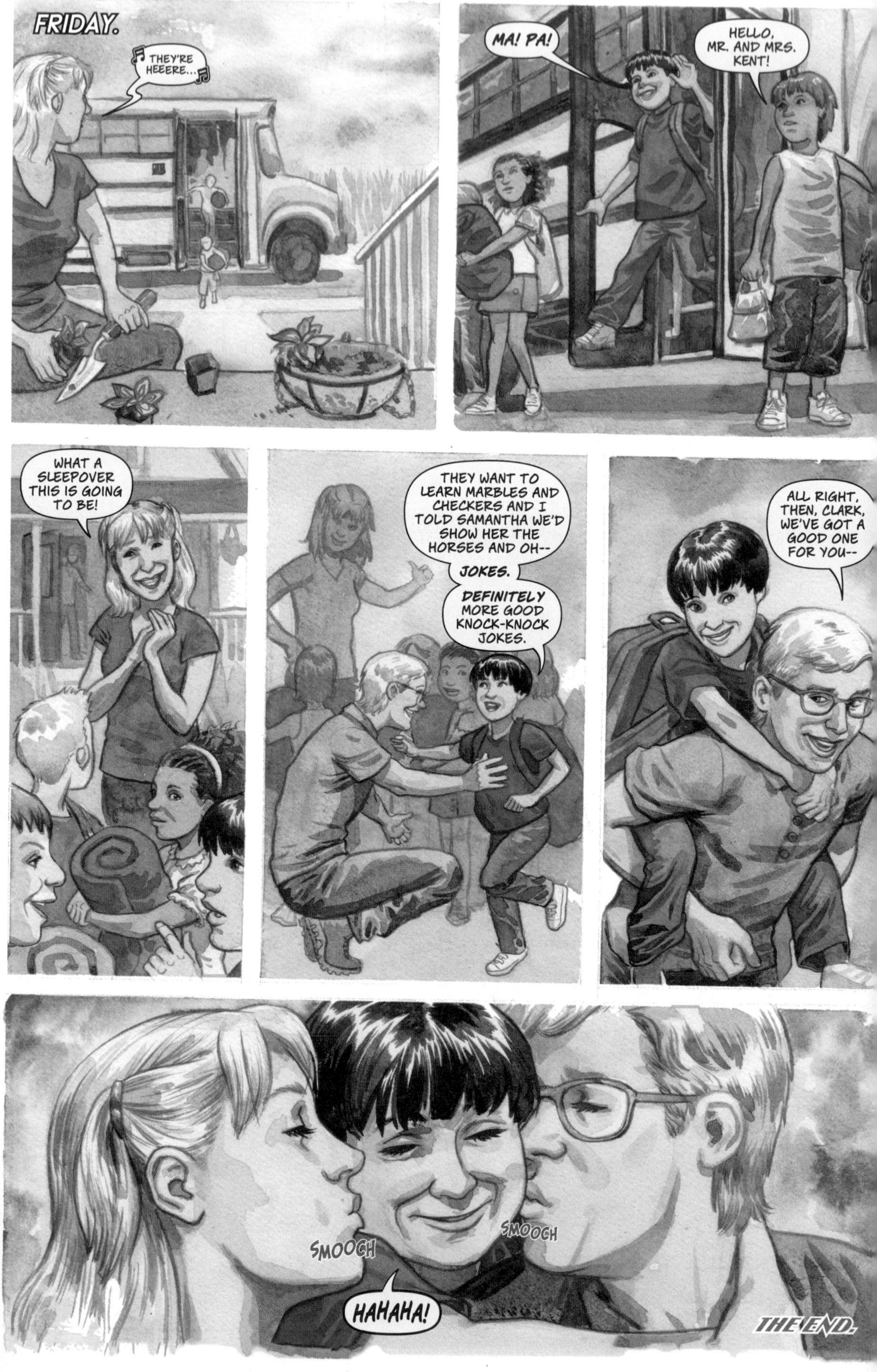
FRIDAY.
THEY'RE HEEERE...
MA! PA!
HELLO, MR. AND MRS. KENT!
WHAT A SLEEPOVER THIS IS GOING TO BE!
THEY WANT TO LEARN MARBLES AND CHECKERS AND I TOLD SAMANTHA WE'D SHOW HER THE HORSES AND OH--
JOKES.
DEFINITELY MORE GOOD KNOCK-KNOCK JOKES.
ALL RIGHT, THEN, CLARK, WE'VE GOT A GOOD ONE FOR YOU--
SMOOCH
SMOOCH
HAHAHA!
THE END.

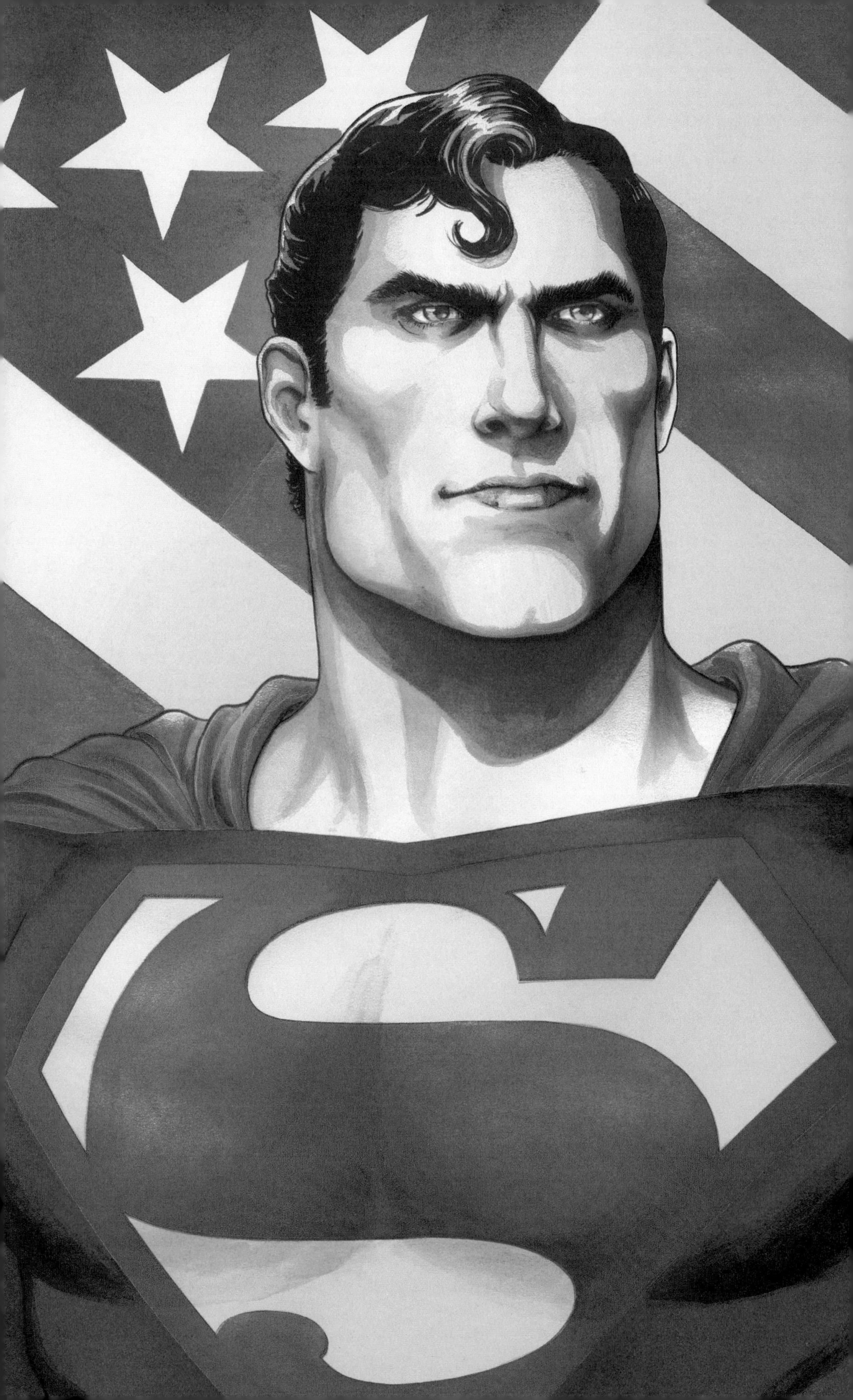

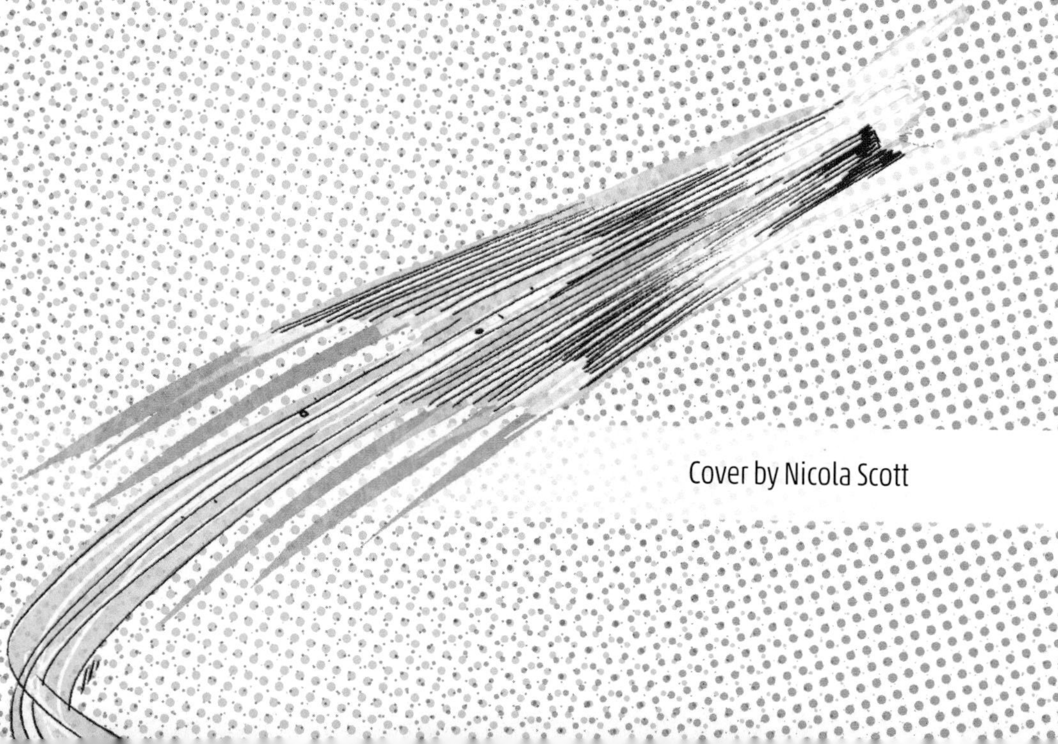

Cover by Nicola Scott

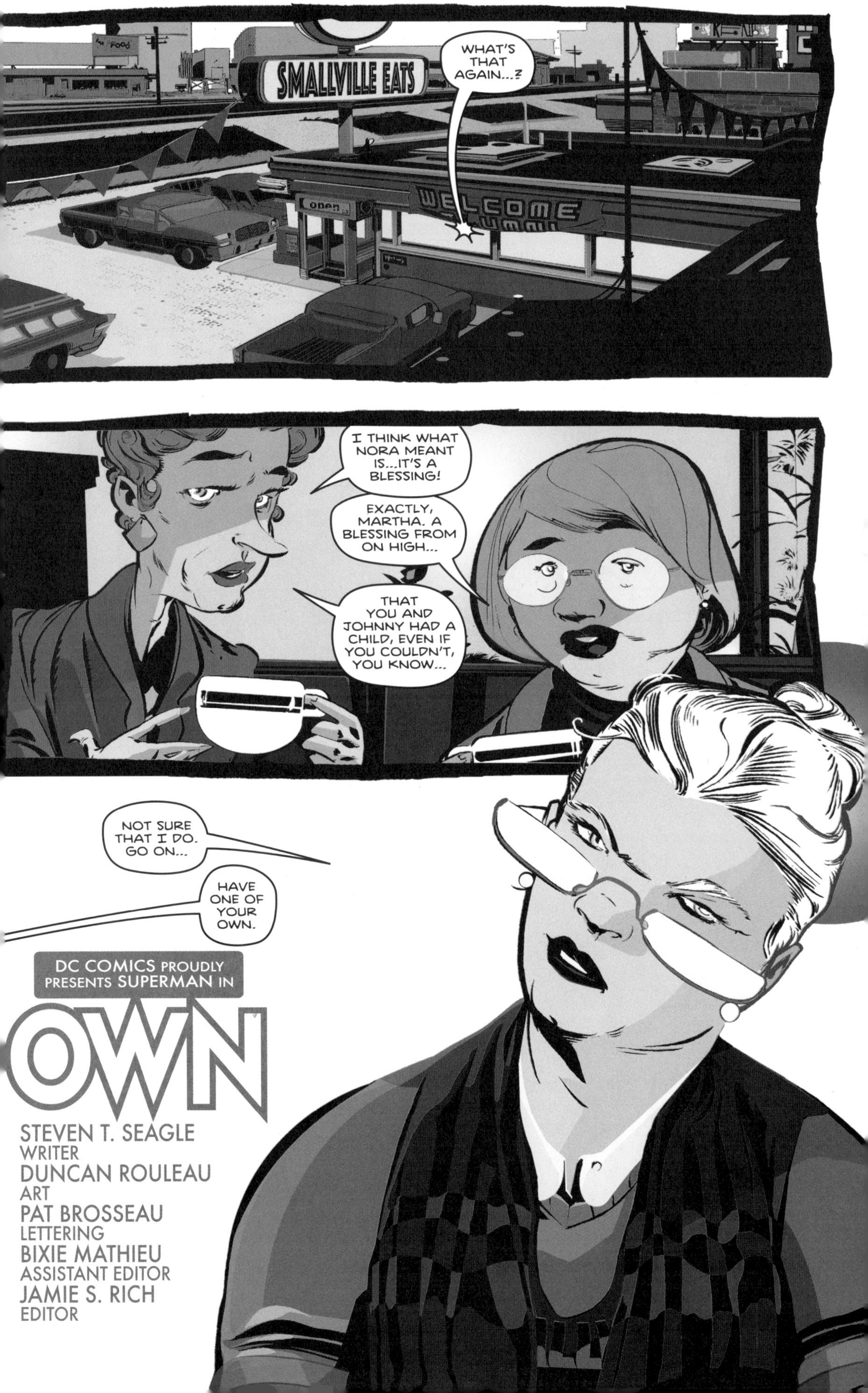
SMALLVILLE EATS
open
WELCOME
WHAT'S THAT AGAIN...?
I THINK WHAT NORA MEANT IS...IT'S A BLESSING!
EXACTLY, MARTHA. A BLESSING FROM ON HIGH...
THAT YOU AND JOHNNY HAD A CHILD, EVEN IF YOU COULDN'T, YOU KNOW...
NOT SURE THAT I DO. GO ON...
HAVE ONE OF YOUR OWN.
DC COMICS PROUDLY PRESENTS SUPERMAN IN
OWN
STEVEN T. SEAGLE
WRITER
DUNCAN ROULEAU
ART
PAT BROSSEAU
LETTERING
BIXIE MATHIEU
ASSISTANT EDITOR
JAMIE S. RICH
EDITOR

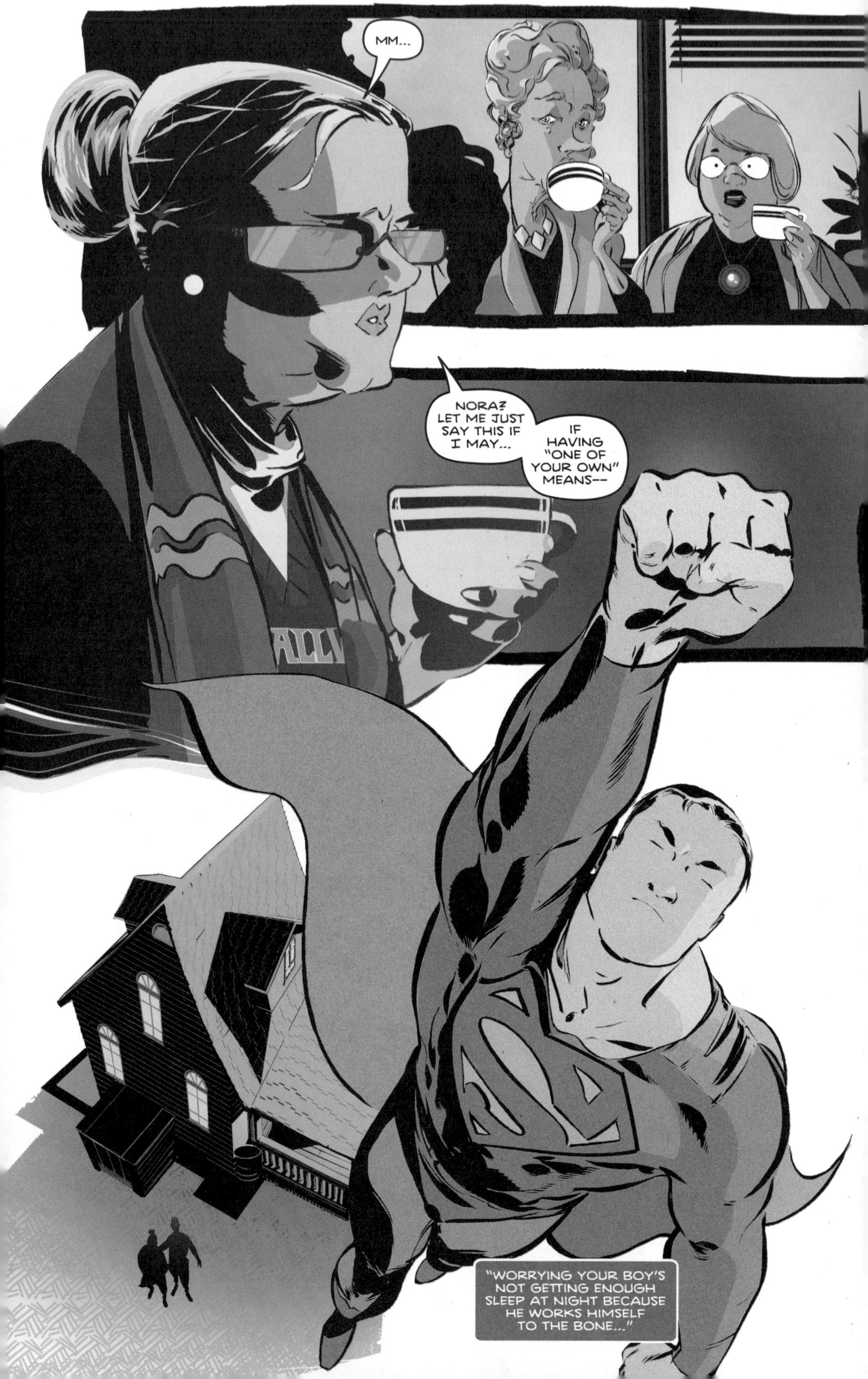
MM...
NORA? LET ME JUST SAY THIS IF I MAY...
IF HAVING "ONE OF YOUR OWN" MEANS--
"WORRYING YOUR BOY'S NOT GETTING ENOUGH SLEEP AT NIGHT BECAUSE HE WORKS HIMSELF TO THE BONE..."

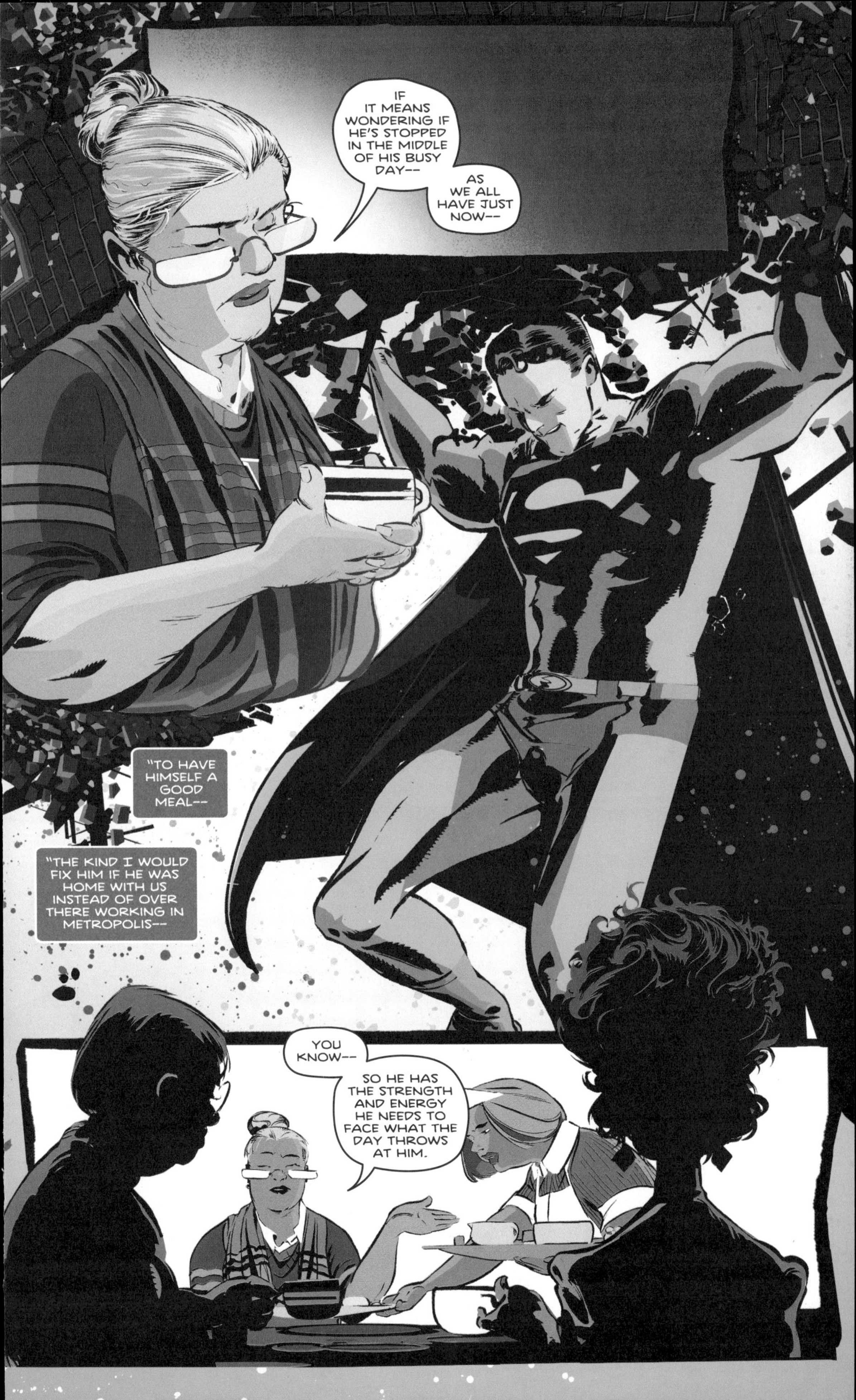

IF IT MEANS WONDERING IF HE'S STOPPED IN THE MIDDLE OF HIS BUSY DAY--
AS WE ALL HAVE JUST NOW--
"TO HAVE HIMSELF A GOOD MEAL--
"THE KIND I WOULD FIX HIM IF HE WAS HOME WITH US INSTEAD OF OVER THERE WORKING IN METROPOLIS--
YOU KNOW--
SO HE HAS THE STRENGTH AND ENERGY HE NEEDS TO FACE WHAT THE DAY THROWS AT HIM.

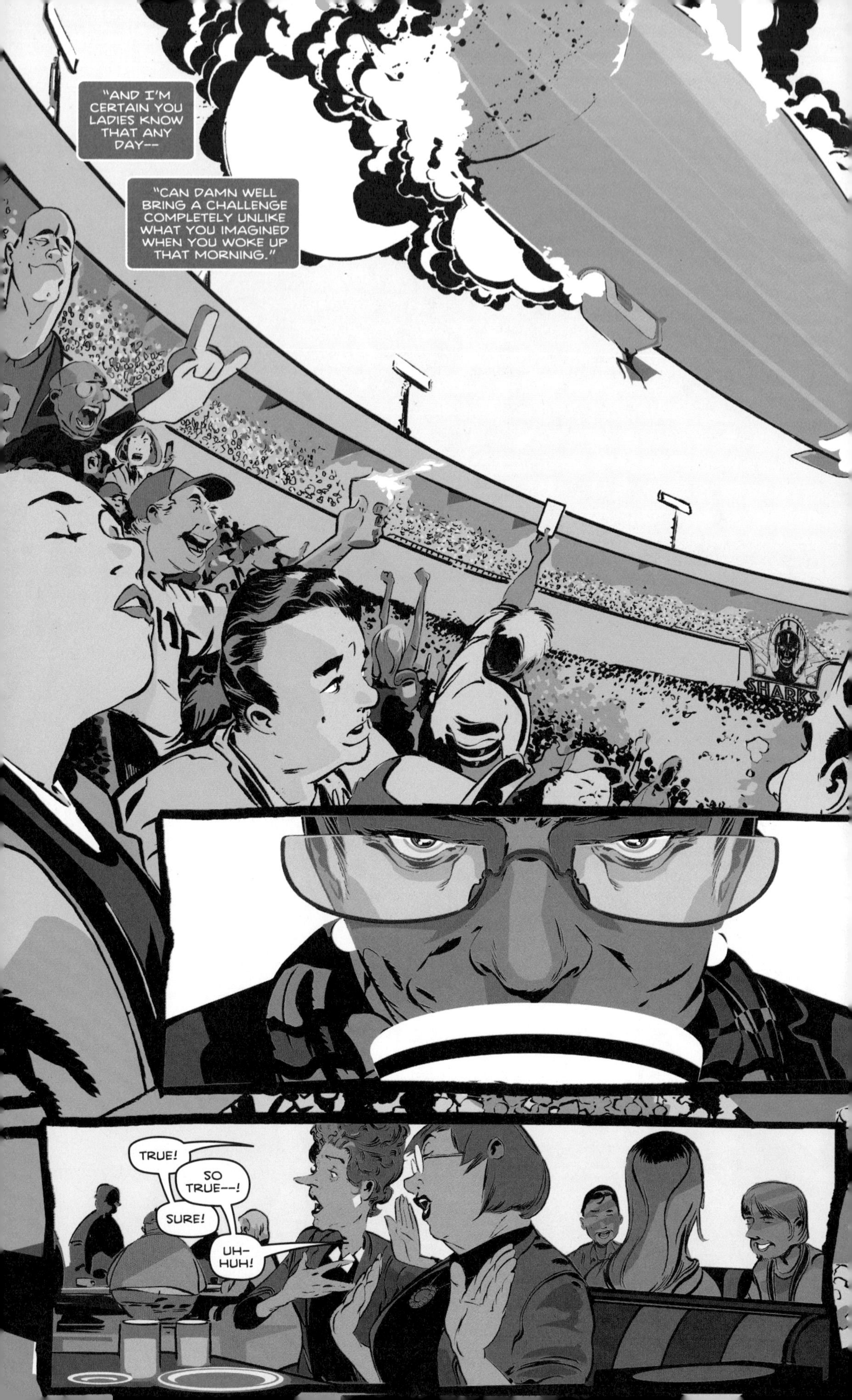
"AND I'M CERTAIN YOU LADIES KNOW THAT ANY DAY--
"CAN DAMN WELL BRING A CHALLENGE COMPLETELY UNLIKE WHAT YOU IMAGINED WHEN YOU WOKE UP THAT MORNING."
SHARKS
TRUE!
SO TRUE--!
SURE!
UH-HUH!

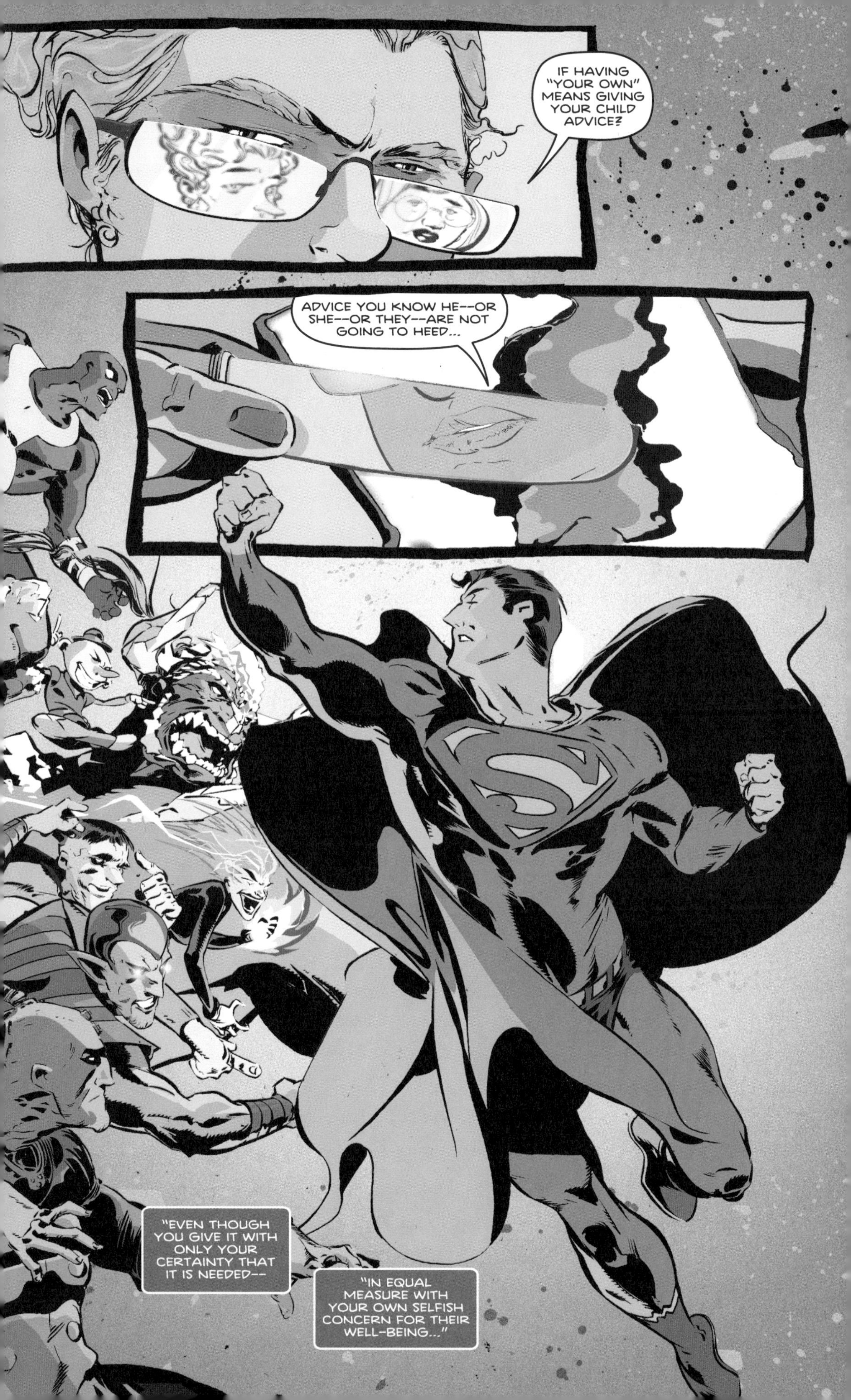
IF HAVING "YOUR OWN" MEANS GIVING YOUR CHILD ADVICE?
ADVICE YOU KNOW HE--OR SHE--OR THEY--ARE NOT GOING TO HEED...
"EVEN THOUGH YOU GIVE IT WITH ONLY YOUR CERTAINTY THAT IT IS NEEDED--
"IN EQUAL MEASURE WITH YOUR OWN SELFISH CONCERN FOR THEIR WELL-BEING..."

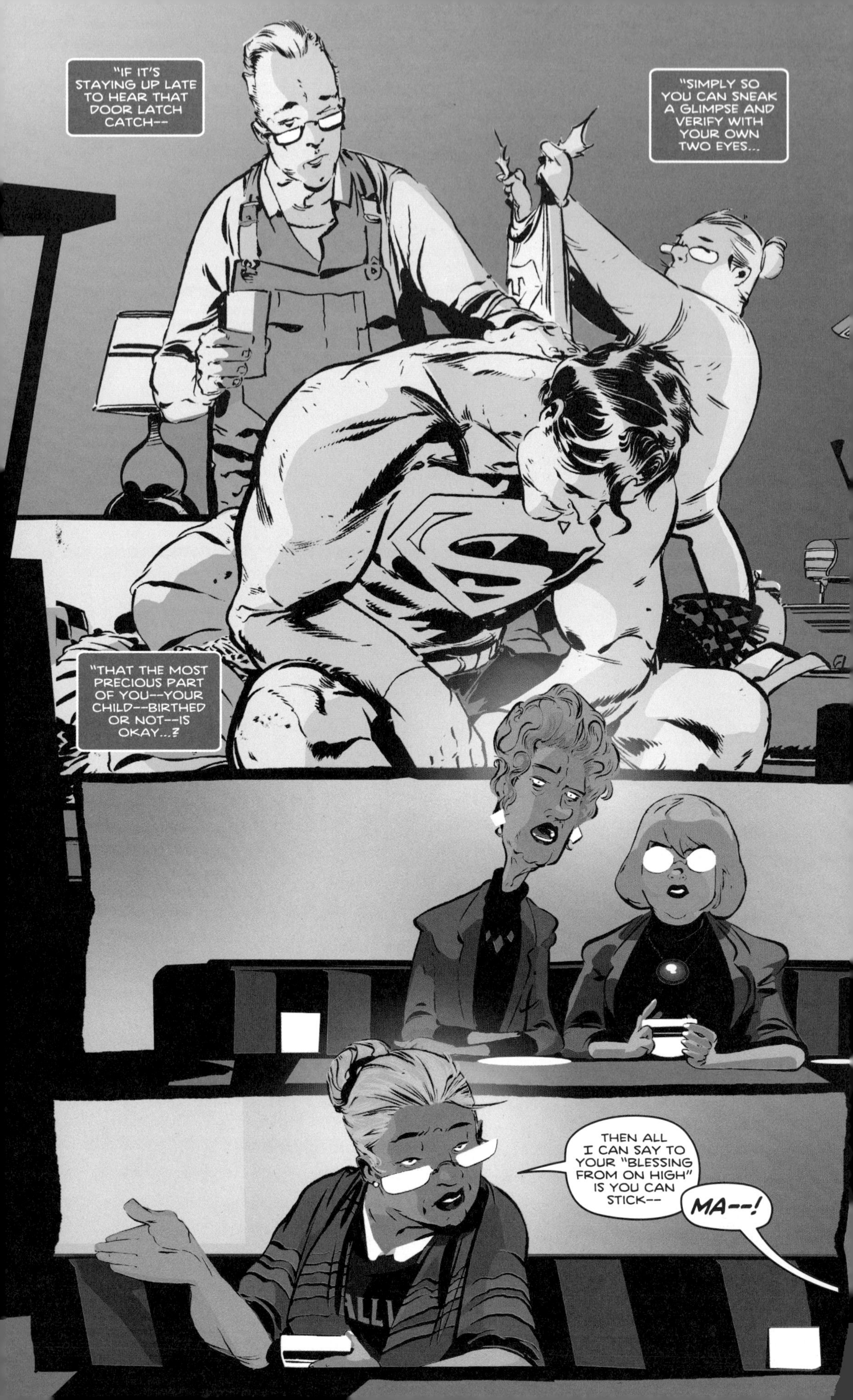
"IF IT'S STAYING UP LATE TO HEAR THAT DOOR LATCH CATCH--
"SIMPLY SO YOU CAN SNEAK A GLIMPSE AND VERIFY WITH YOUR OWN TWO EYES...
"THAT THE MOST PRECIOUS PART OF YOU--YOUR CHILD--BIRTHED OR NOT--IS OKAY...?
THEN ALL I CAN SAY TO YOUR "BLESSING FROM ON HIGH" IS YOU CAN STICK--
MA--!

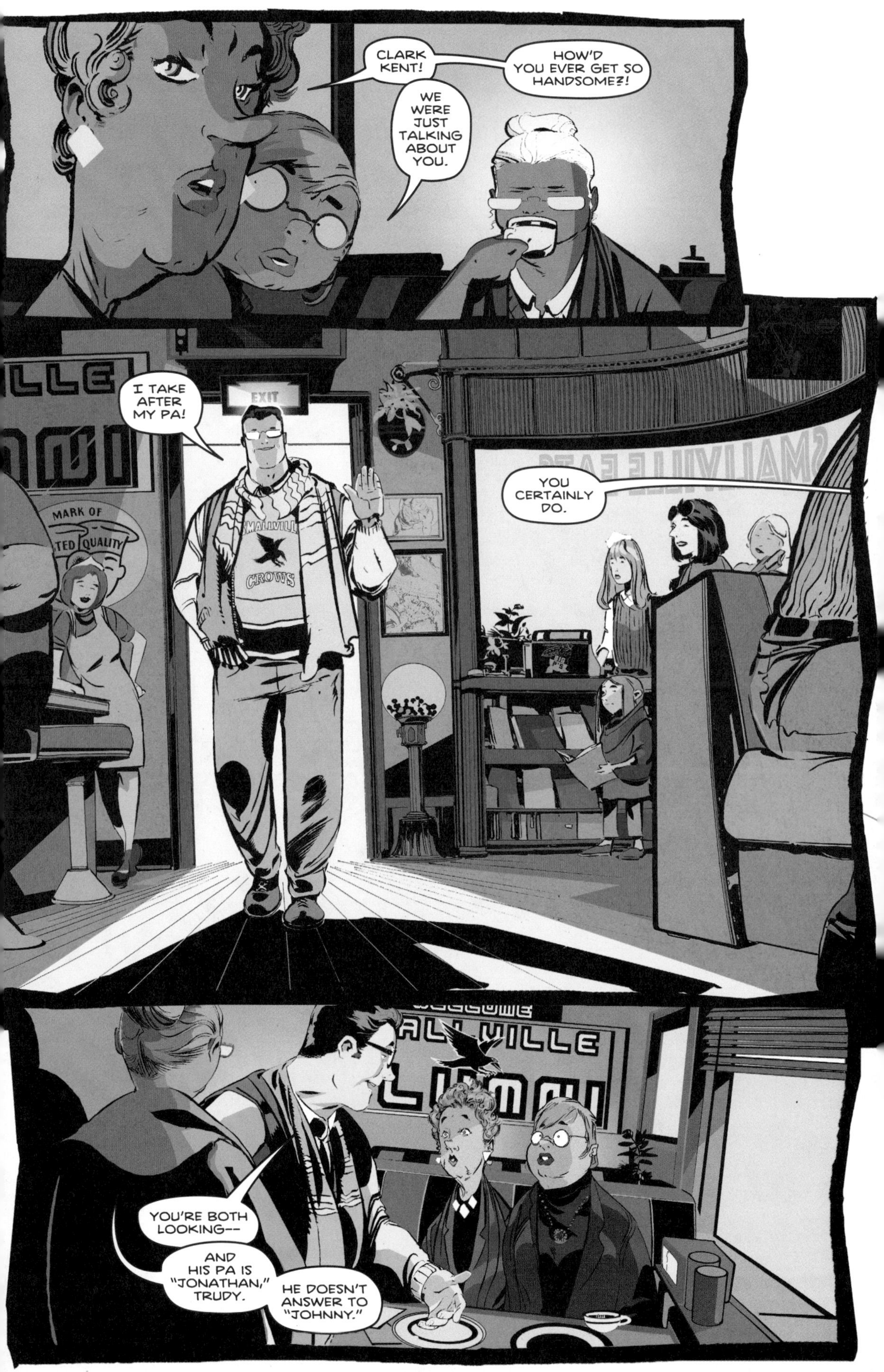
CLARK KENT!
HOW'D YOU EVER GET SO HANDSOME?!
WE WERE JUST TALKING ABOUT YOU.
I TAKE AFTER MY PA!
EXIT
SMALLVILLE CROWS
MARK OF
TED QUALITY
YOU CERTAINLY DO.
SMALLVILLE
YOU'RE BOTH LOOKING--
AND HIS PA IS "JONATHAN," TRUDY.
HE DOESN'T ANSWER TO "JOHNNY."

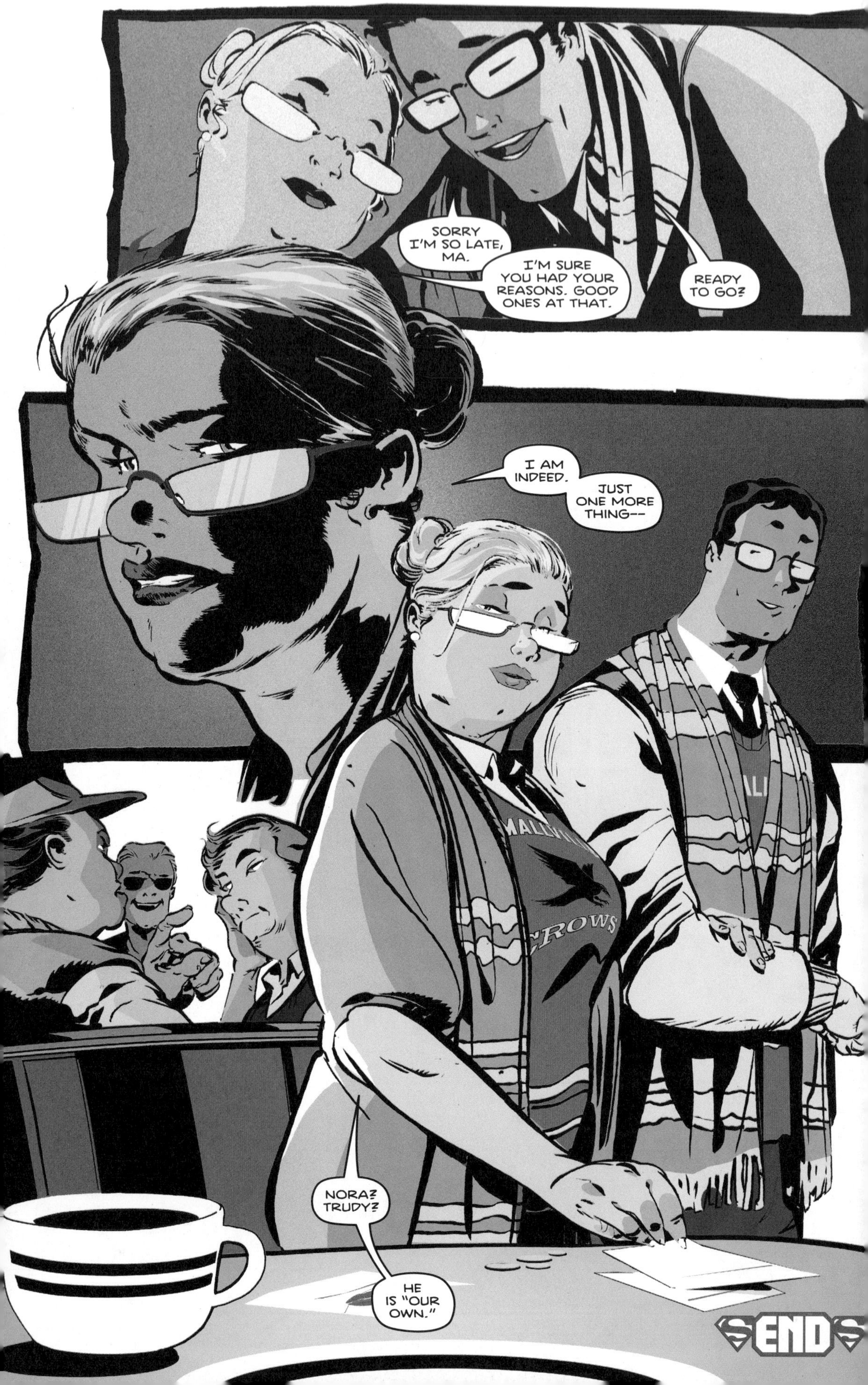

SORRY I'M SO LATE, MA.
I'M SURE YOU HAD YOUR REASONS. GOOD ONES AT THAT.
READY TO GO?
I AM INDEED.
JUST ONE MORE THING--
SMALLVILLE
CROWS
NORA? TRUDY?
HE IS "OUR OWN."
END

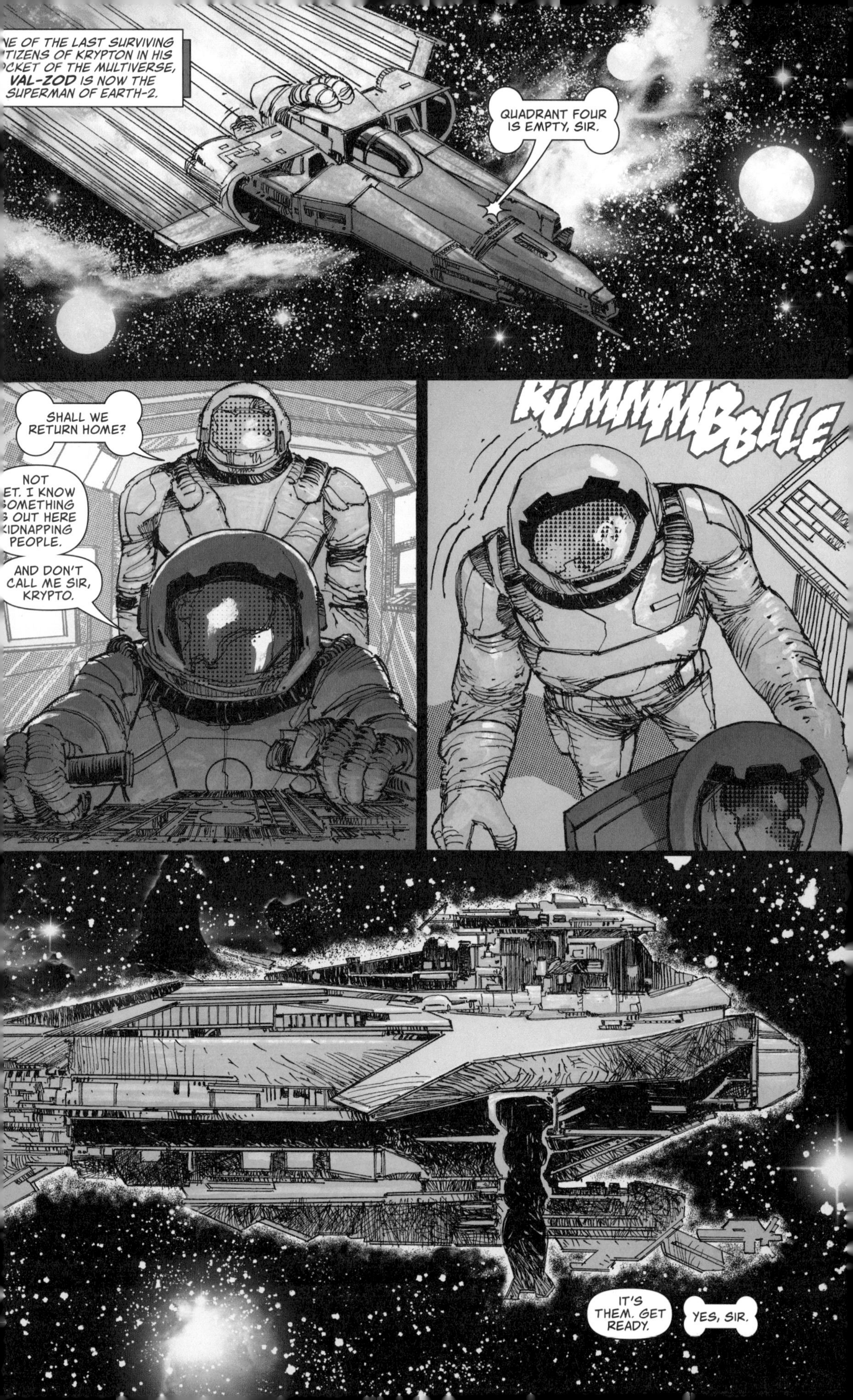
NE OF THE LAST SURVIVING TIZENS OF KRYPTON IN HIS OCKET OF THE MULTIVERSE, VAL-ZOD IS NOW THE SUPERMAN OF EARTH-2.
QUADRANT FOUR IS EMPTY, SIR.
SHALL WE RETURN HOME?
NOT ET. I KNOW SOMETHING S OUT HERE KIDNAPPING PEOPLE.
AND DON'T CALL ME SIR, KRYPTO.
RUMMMBBLLE
IT'S THEM. GET READY.
YES, SIR.

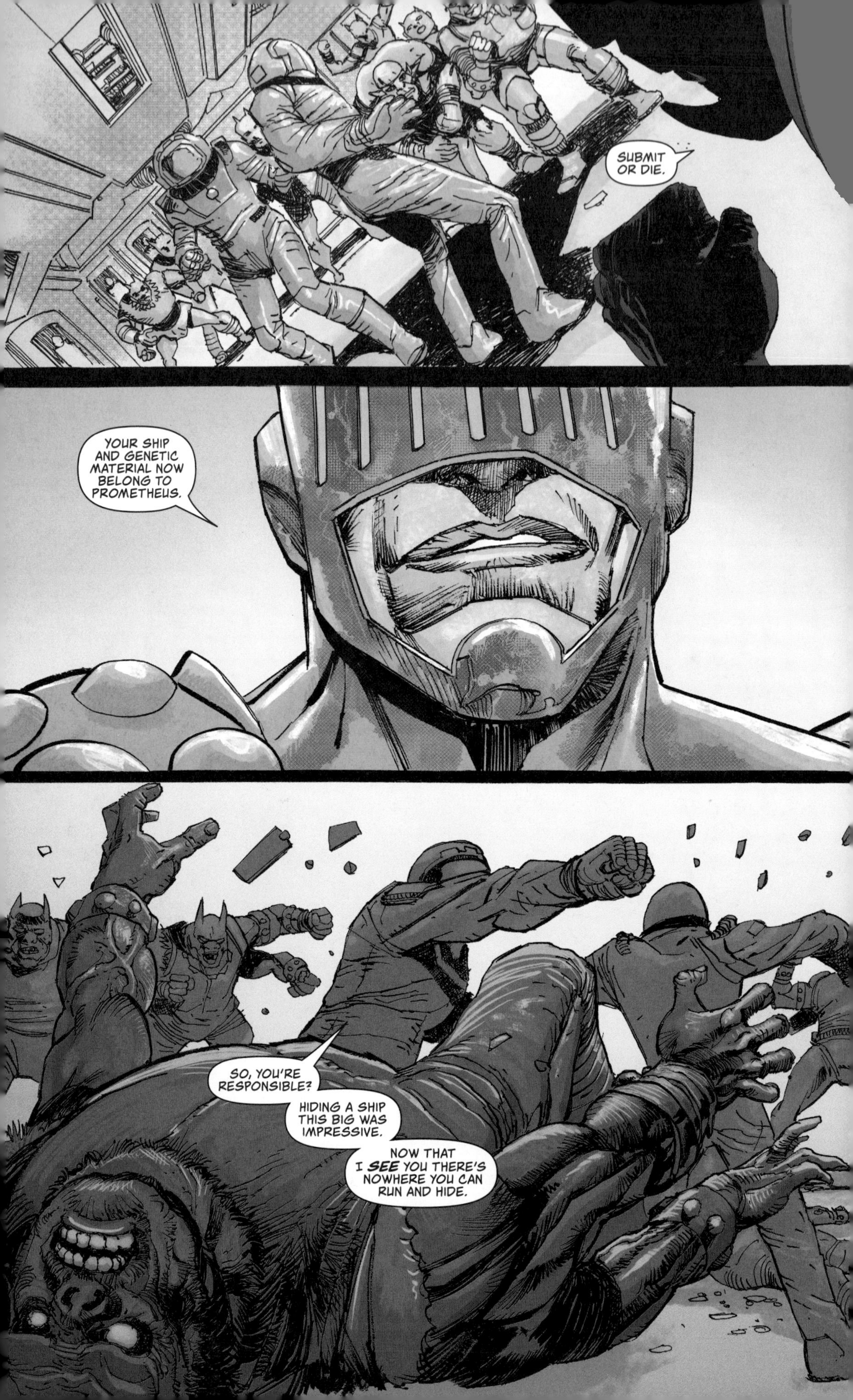
SUBMIT OR DIE.
YOUR SHIP AND GENETIC MATERIAL NOW BELONG TO PROMETHEUS.
SO, YOU'RE RESPONSIBLE?
HIDING A SHIP THIS BIG WAS IMPRESSIVE.
NOW THAT I **SEE** YOU THERE'S NOWHERE YOU CAN RUN AND HIDE.

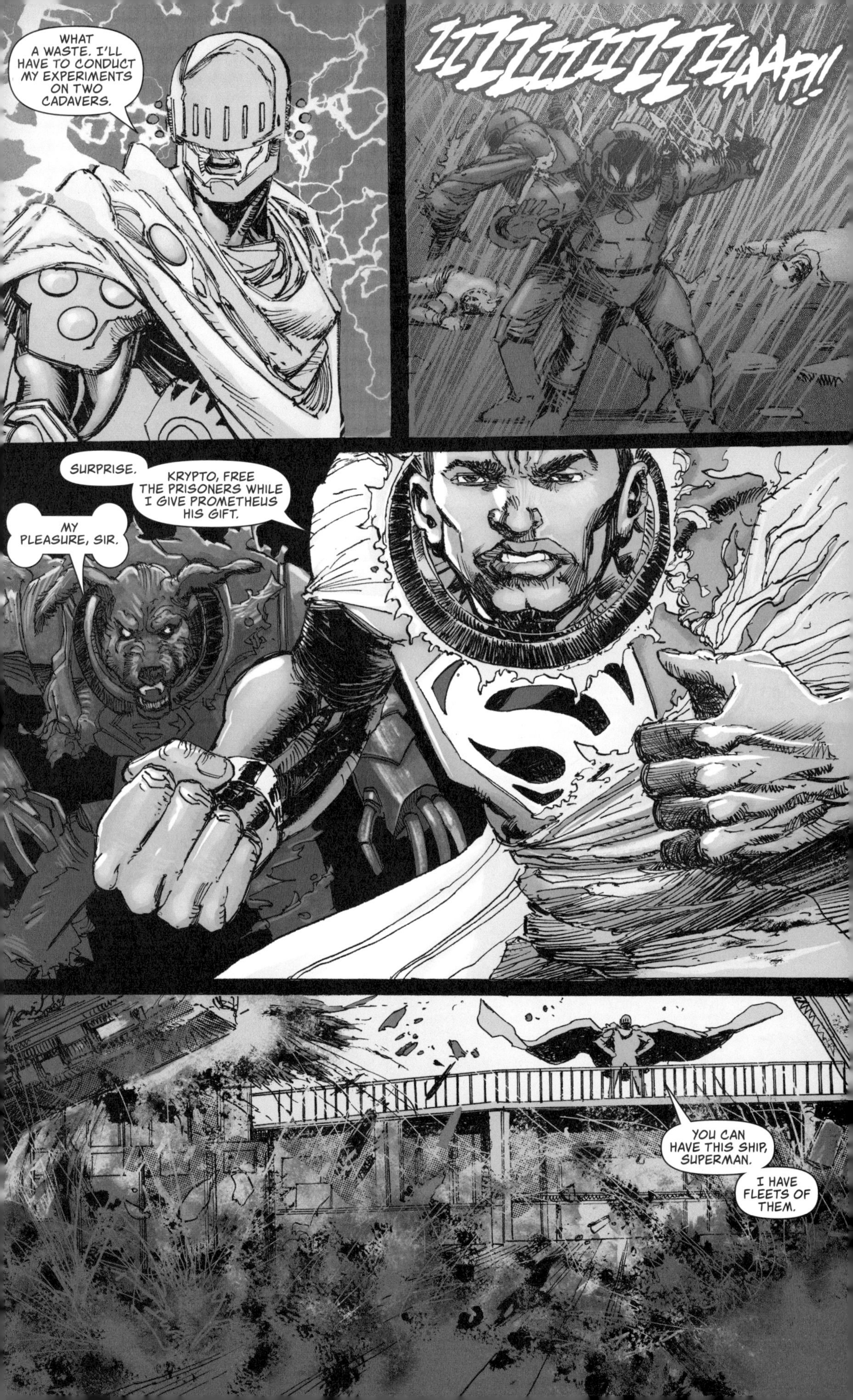
WHAT A WASTE. I'LL HAVE TO CONDUCT MY EXPERIMENTS ON TWO CADAVERS.
ZZZZZZZZZZZAAP!!
SURPRISE.
KRYPTO, FREE THE PRISONERS WHILE I GIVE PROMETHEUS HIS GIFT.
MY PLEASURE, SIR.
YOU CAN HAVE THIS SHIP, SUPERMAN.
I HAVE FLEETS OF THEM.

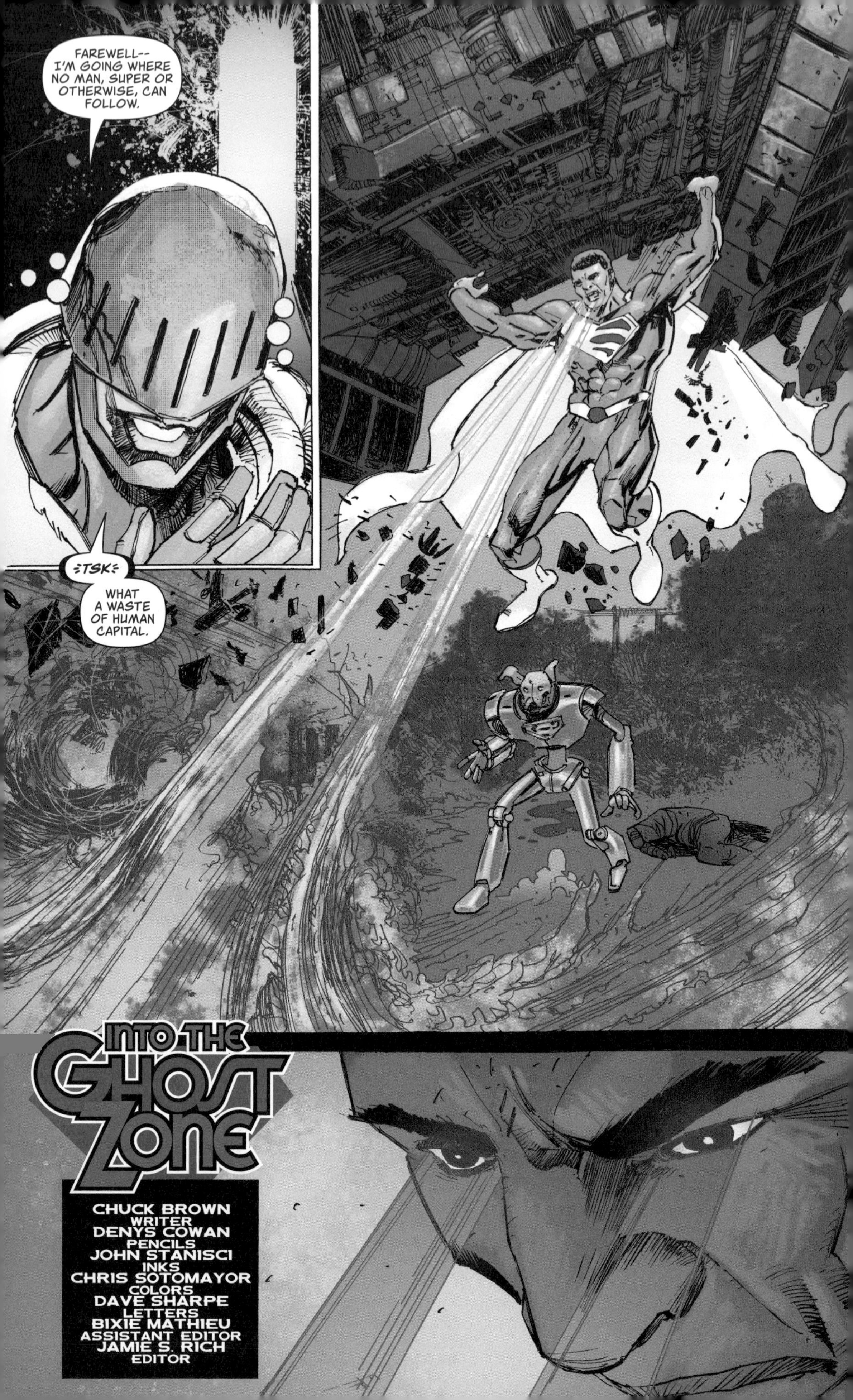
FAREWELL-- I'M GOING WHERE NO MAN, SUPER OR OTHERWISE, CAN FOLLOW.
TSK
WHAT A WASTE OF HUMAN CAPITAL.
INTO THE GHOST ZONE
CHUCK BROWN WRITER
DENYS COWAN PENCILS
JOHN STANISCI INKS
CHRIS SOTOMAYOR COLORS
DAVE SHARPE LETTERS
BIXIE MATHIEU ASSISTANT EDITOR
JAMIE S. RICH EDITOR

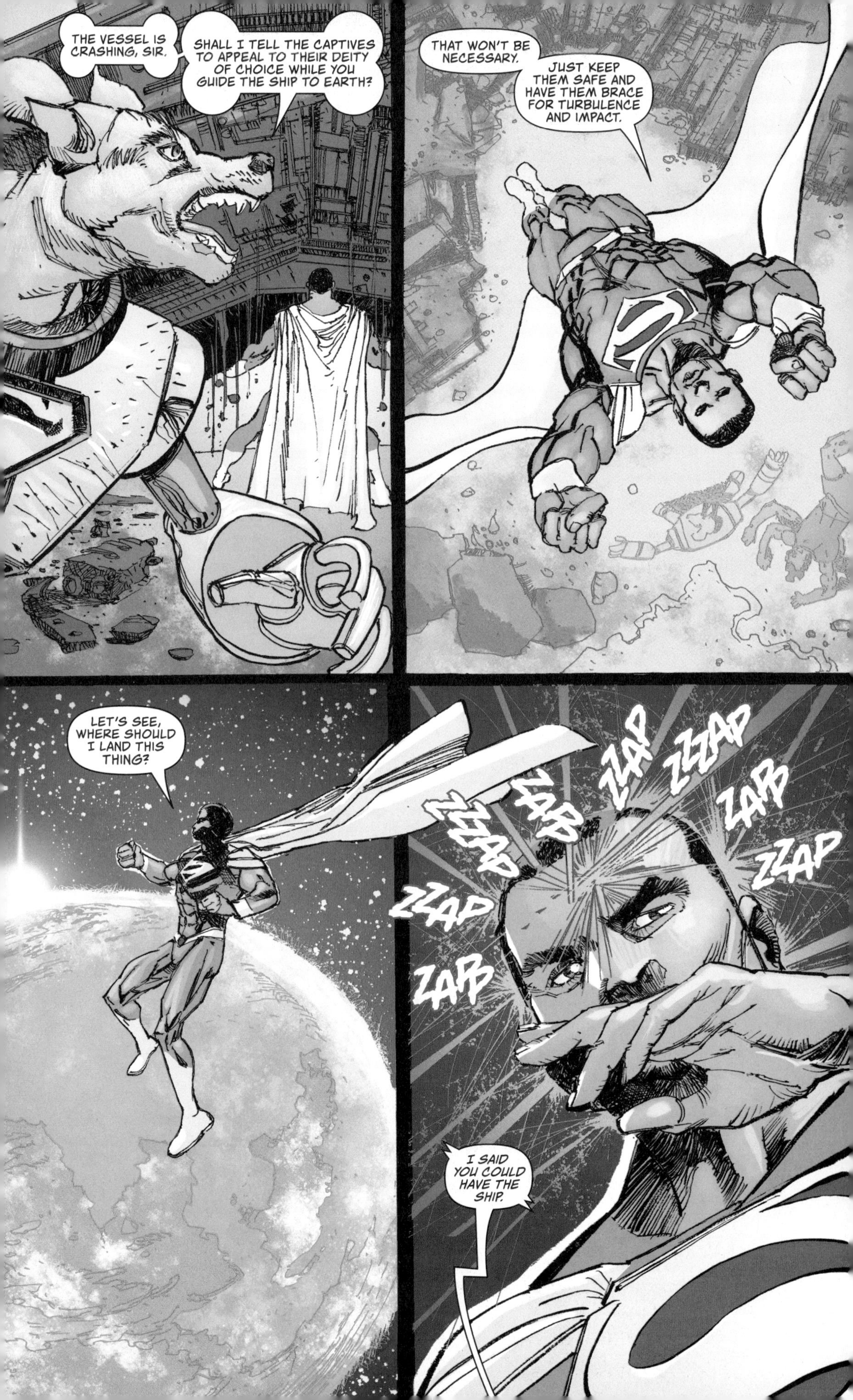
THE VESSEL IS CRASHING, SIR.
SHALL I TELL THE CAPTIVES TO APPEAL TO THEIR DEITY OF CHOICE WHILE YOU GUIDE THE SHIP TO EARTH?
THAT WON'T BE NECESSARY.
JUST KEEP THEM SAFE AND HAVE THEM BRACE FOR TURBULENCE AND IMPACT.
LET'S SEE, WHERE SHOULD I LAND THIS THING?
ZZZAP
ZAP
ZZAP
ZZZAP
ZAP
ZZAP
ZZZAP
ZAP
I SAID YOU COULD HAVE THE SHIP.

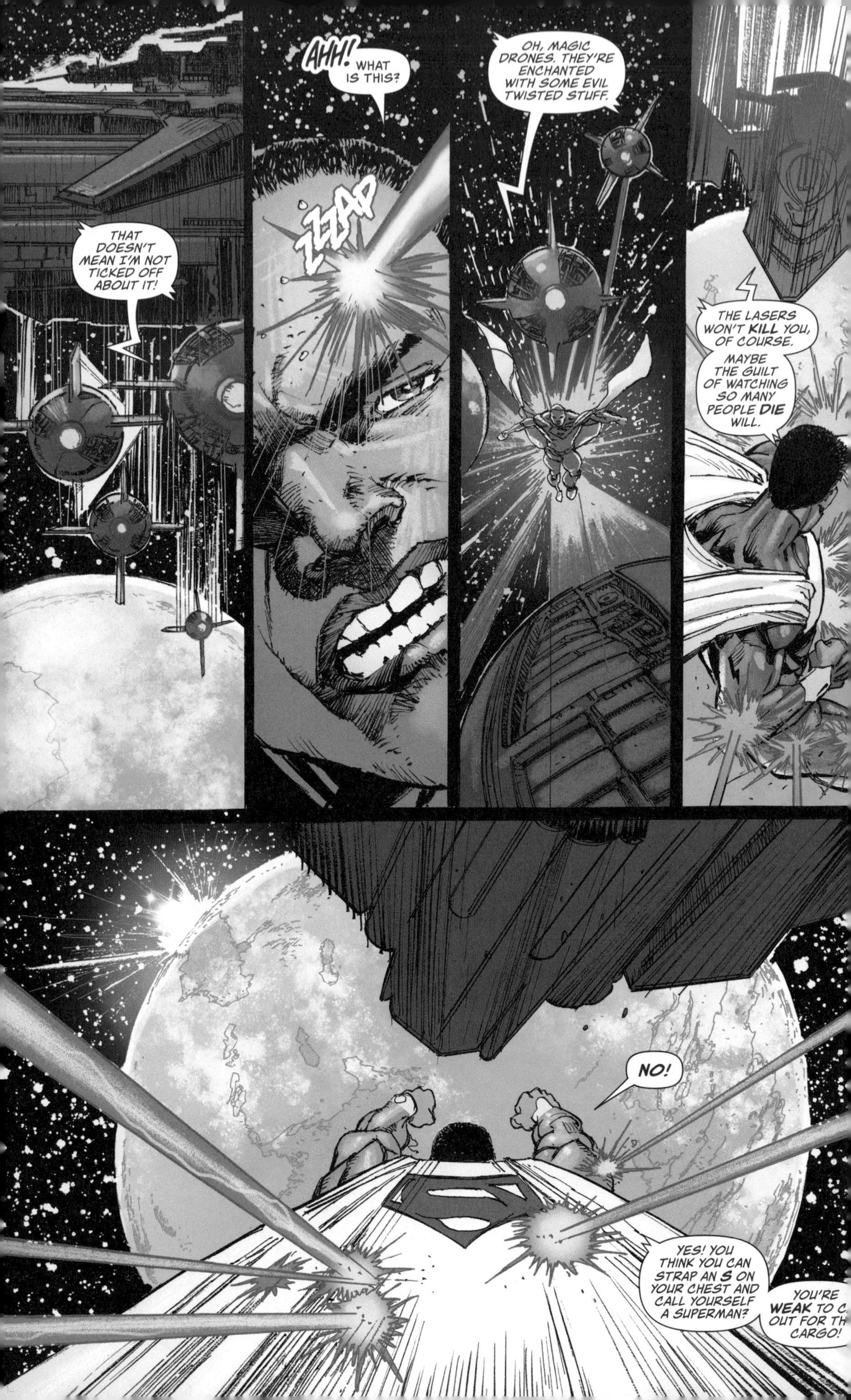
THAT DOESN'T MEAN I'M NOT TICKED OFF ABOUT IT!
AHH! WHAT IS THIS?
ZZZAP
OH, MAGIC DRONES. THEY'RE ENCHANTED WITH SOME EVIL TWISTED STUFF.
THE LASERS WON'T KILL YOU, OF COURSE.
MAYBE THE GUILT OF WATCHING SO MANY PEOPLE DIE WILL.
NO!
YES! YOU THINK YOU CAN STRAP AN S ON YOUR CHEST AND CALL YOURSELF A SUPERMAN?
YOU'RE WEAK TO C OUT FOR TH CARGO!

I WON'T LET GO!

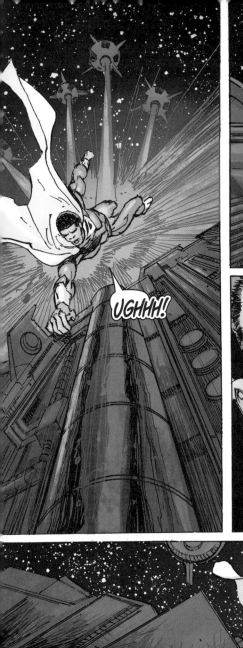

UGHHH!

I HAVE THE UTMOST CONFIDENCE THAT YOU WOULD NOT LET GO, SIR.

KRYPTO?

YES, SIR.

I'VE TAKEN CONTROL OF THE DRONE TO HELP MAKE YOUR SAVE MORE--

COMFORTABLE.

GOOD DOGGIE.

MY PLEASURE, SIR.

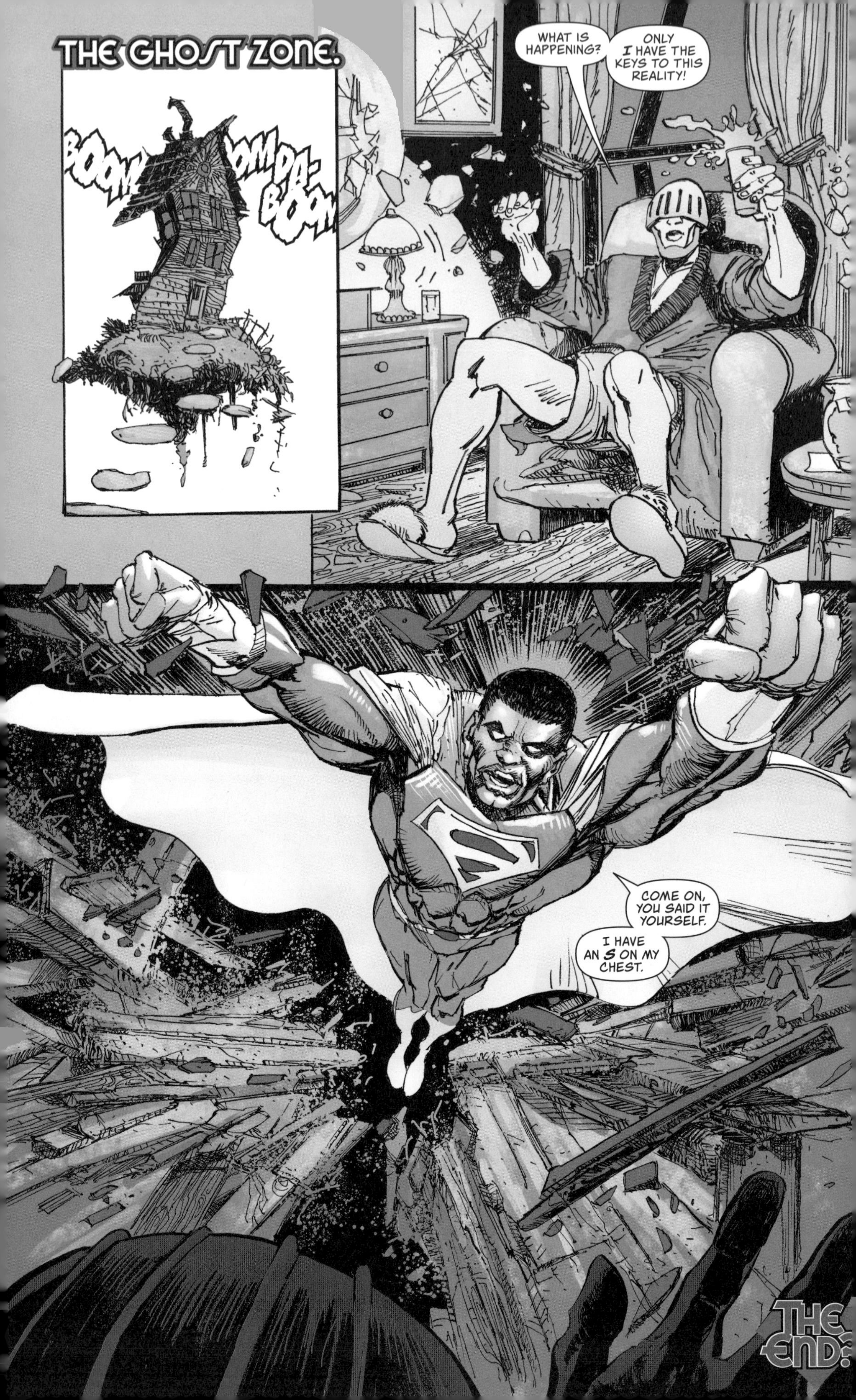
THE GHOST ZONE.
BOOM
BOOMDA-BOOM
WHAT IS HAPPENING?
ONLY I HAVE THE KEYS TO THIS REALITY!
COME ON, YOU SAID IT YOURSELF.
I HAVE AN S ON MY CHEST.
THE END?

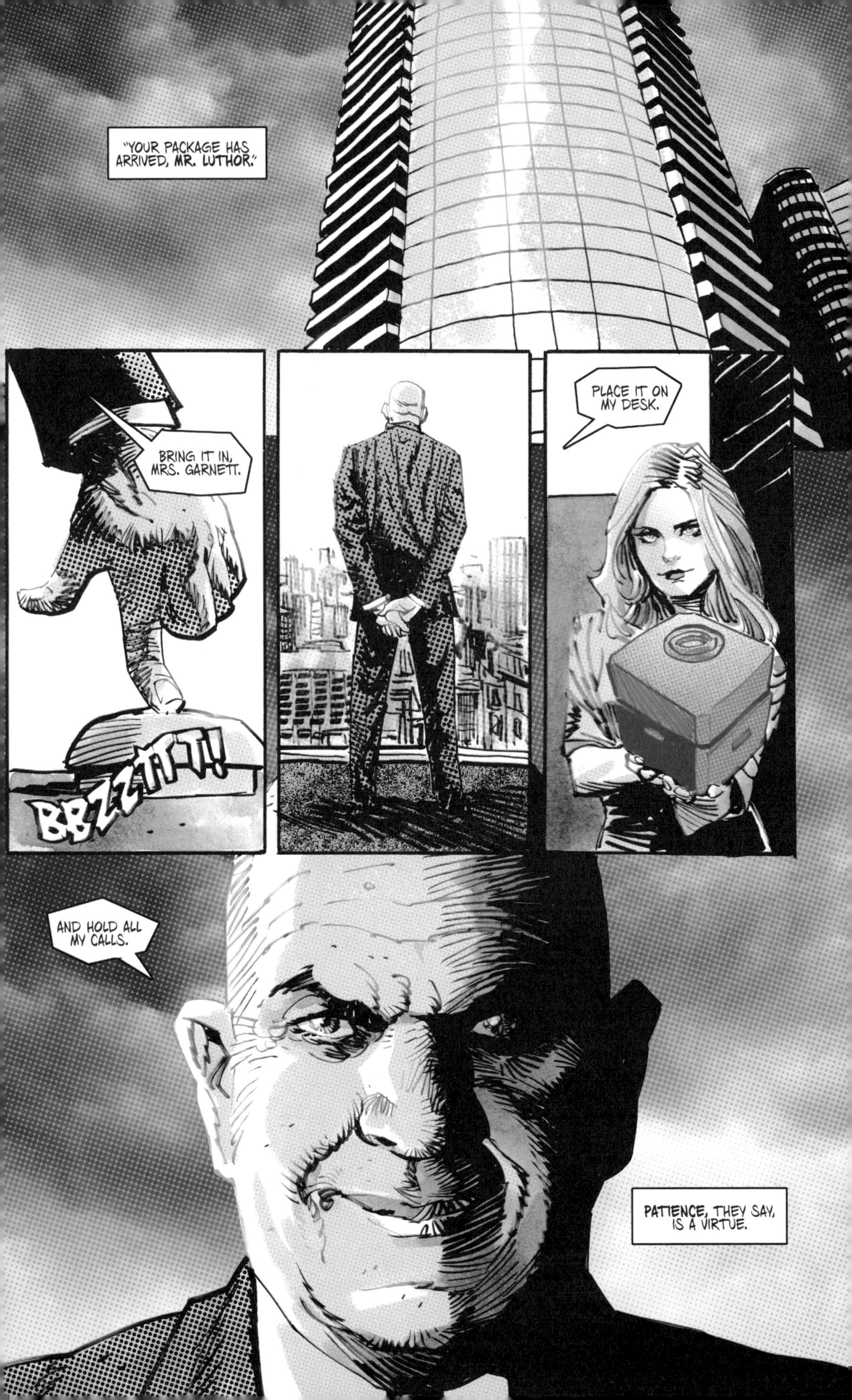
"YOUR PACKAGE HAS ARRIVED, MR. LUTHOR."
BRING IT IN, MRS. GARNETT.
BBZZZTTTT!
PLACE IT ON MY DESK.
AND HOLD ALL MY CALLS.
PATIENCE, THEY SAY, IS A VIRTUE.

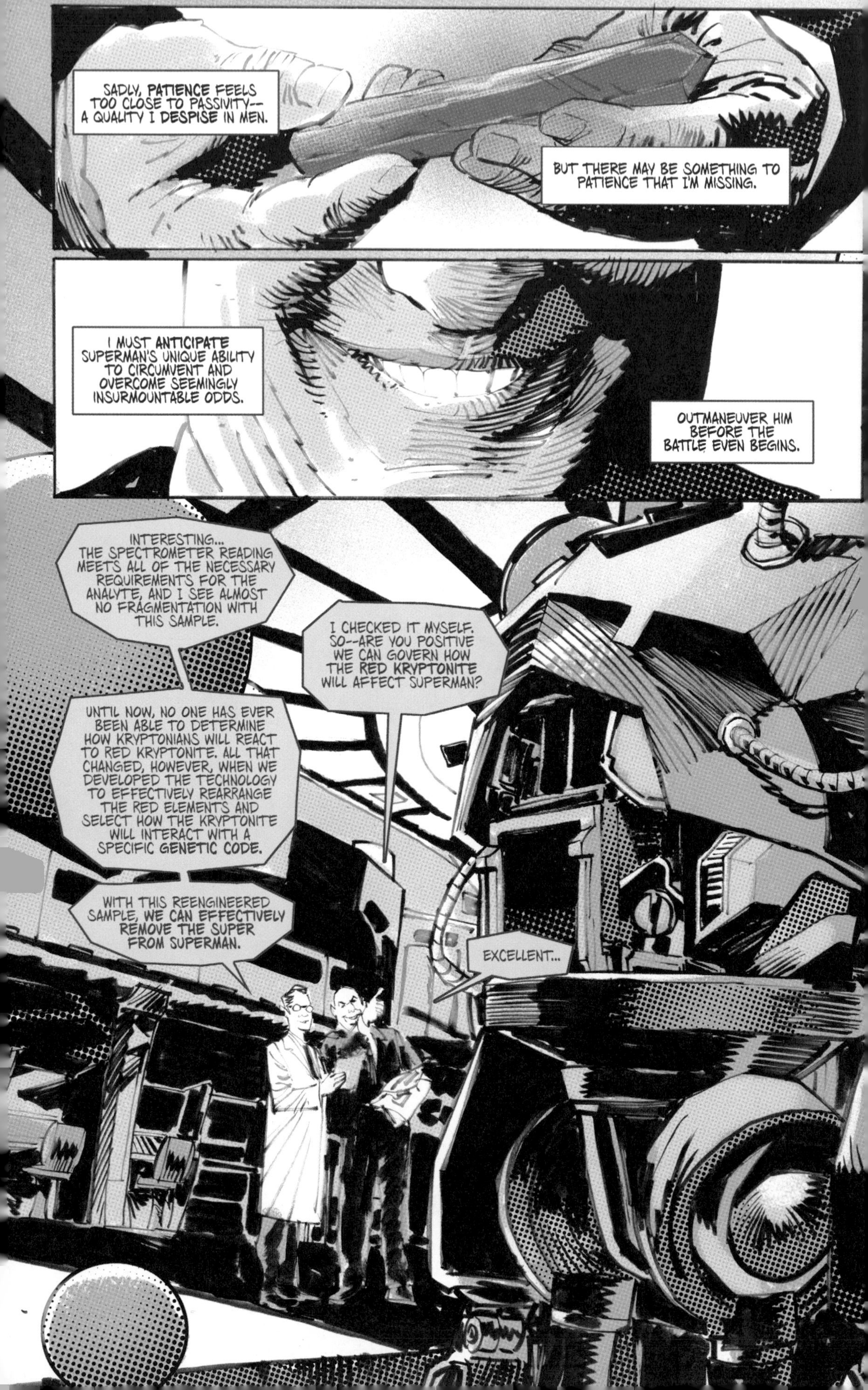
SADLY, PATIENCE FEELS TOO CLOSE TO PASSIVITY-- A QUALITY I DESPISE IN MEN.
BUT THERE MAY BE SOMETHING TO PATIENCE THAT I'M MISSING.
I MUST ANTICIPATE SUPERMAN'S UNIQUE ABILITY TO CIRCUMVENT AND OVERCOME SEEMINGLY INSURMOUNTABLE ODDS.
OUTMANEUVER HIM BEFORE THE BATTLE EVEN BEGINS.
INTERESTING... THE SPECTROMETER READING MEETS ALL OF THE NECESSARY REQUIREMENTS FOR THE ANALYTE, AND I SEE ALMOST NO FRAGMENTATION WITH THIS SAMPLE.
I CHECKED IT MYSELF. SO--ARE YOU POSITIVE WE CAN GOVERN HOW THE RED KRYPTONITE WILL AFFECT SUPERMAN?
UNTIL NOW, NO ONE HAS EVER BEEN ABLE TO DETERMINE HOW KRYPTONIANS WILL REACT TO RED KRYPTONITE. ALL THAT CHANGED, HOWEVER, WHEN WE DEVELOPED THE TECHNOLOGY TO EFFECTIVELY REARRANGE THE RED ELEMENTS AND SELECT HOW THE KRYPTONITE WILL INTERACT WITH A SPECIFIC GENETIC CODE.
WITH THIS REENGINEERED SAMPLE, WE CAN EFFECTIVELY REMOVE THE SUPER FROM SUPERMAN.
EXCELLENT...

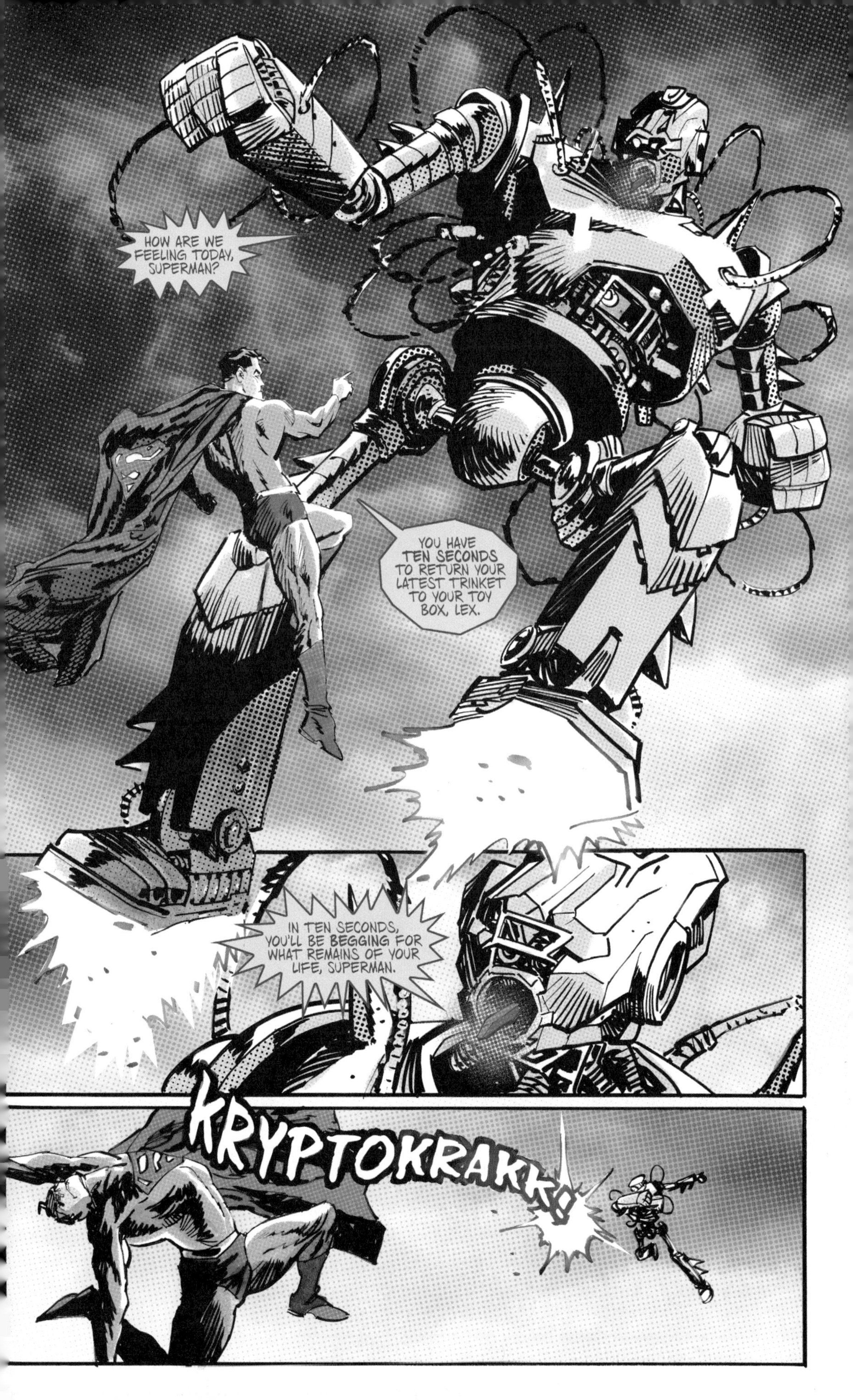
HOW ARE WE FEELING TODAY, SUPERMAN?
YOU HAVE TEN SECONDS TO RETURN YOUR LATEST TRINKET TO YOUR TOY BOX, LEX.
IN TEN SECONDS, YOU'LL BE BEGGING FOR WHAT REMAINS OF YOUR LIFE, SUPERMAN.
KRYPTOKRAKK!

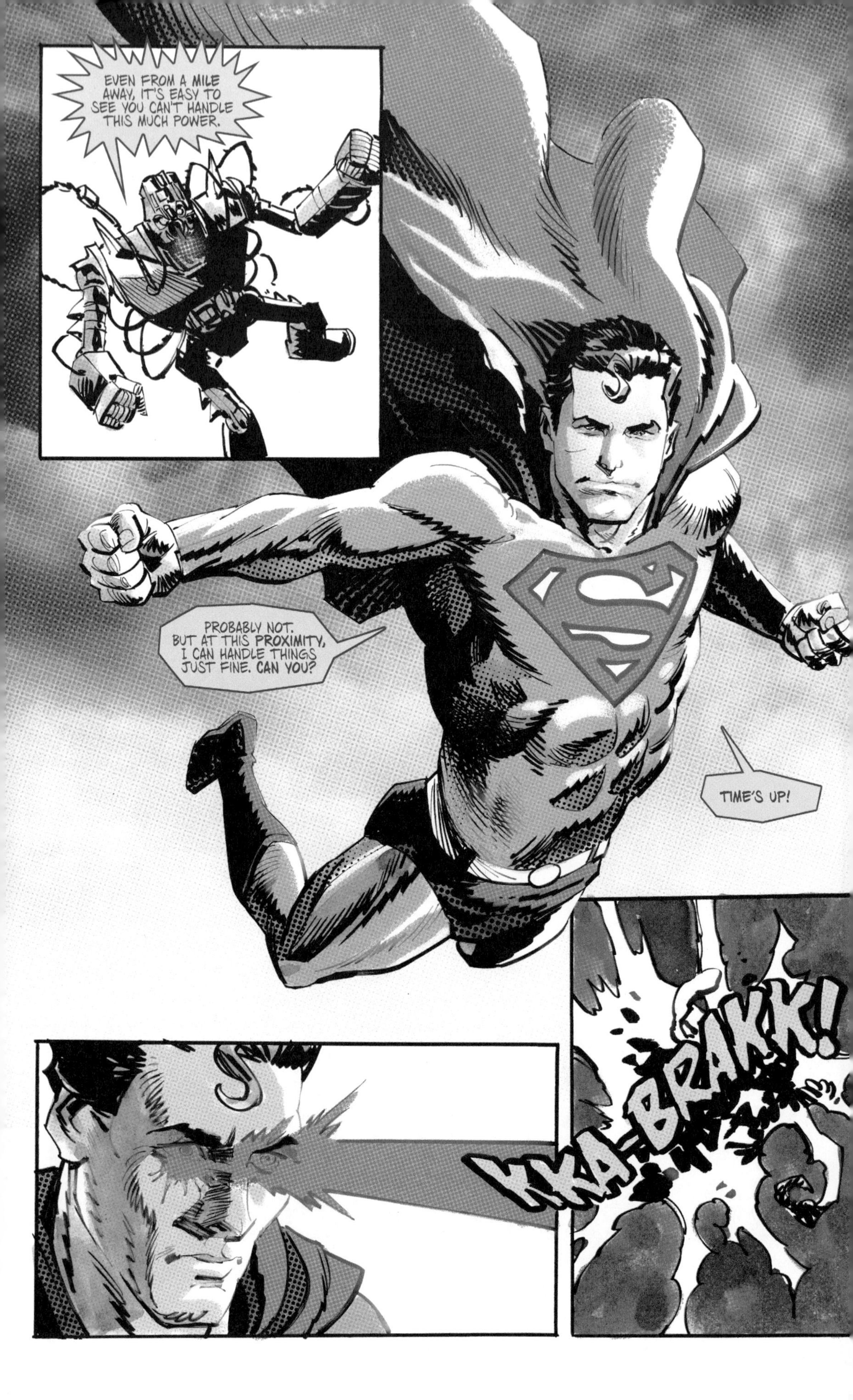
EVEN FROM A MILE AWAY, IT'S EASY TO SEE YOU CAN'T HANDLE THIS MUCH POWER.
PROBABLY NOT. BUT AT THIS PROXIMITY, I CAN HANDLE THINGS JUST FINE. CAN YOU?
TIME'S UP!
KKA-BRAKK!

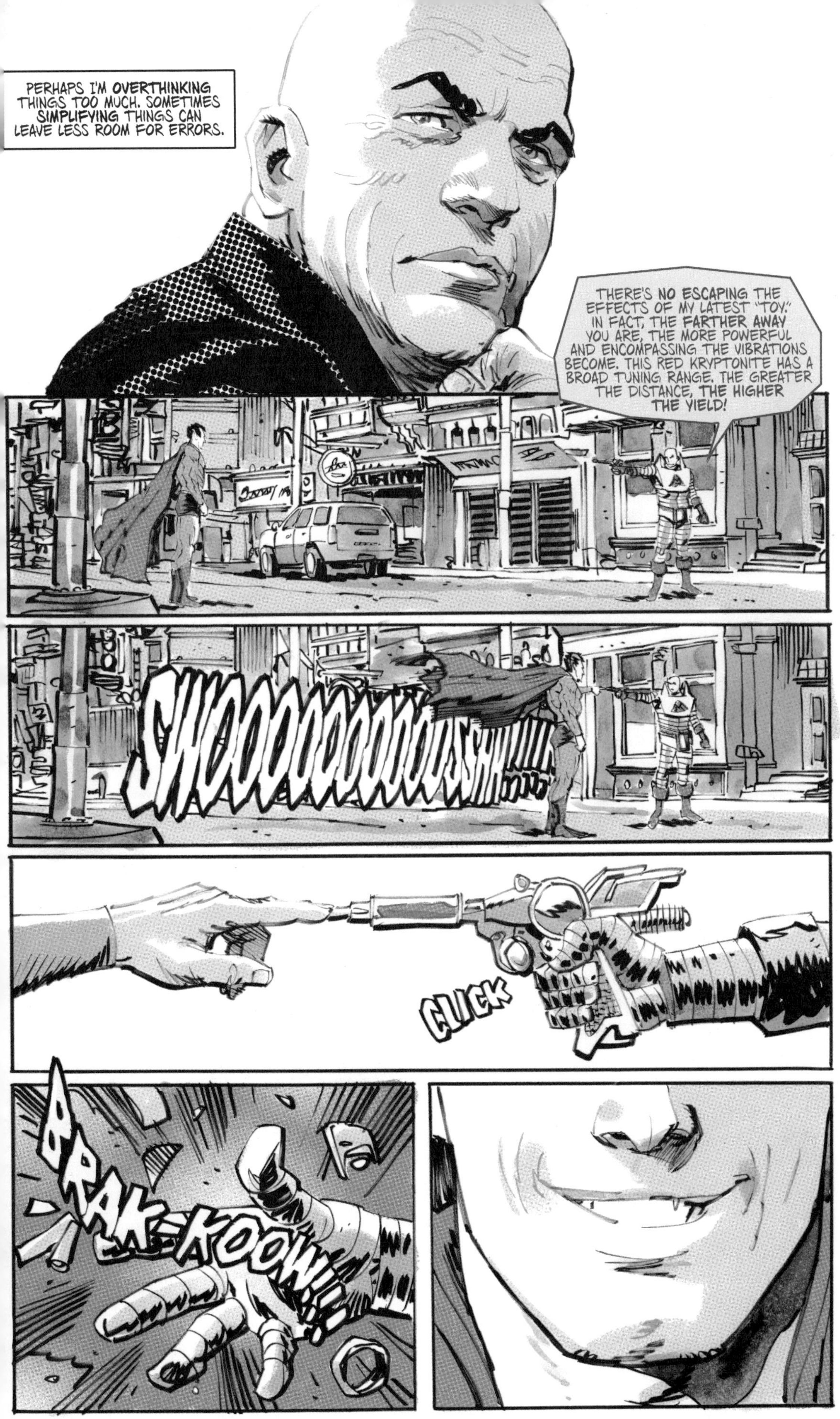
PERHAPS I'M OVERTHINKING THINGS TOO MUCH. SOMETIMES SIMPLIFYING THINGS CAN LEAVE LESS ROOM FOR ERRORS.
THERE'S NO ESCAPING THE EFFECTS OF MY LATEST "TOY." IN FACT, THE FARTHER AWAY YOU ARE, THE MORE POWERFUL AND ENCOMPASSING THE VIBRATIONS BECOME. THIS RED KRYPTONITE HAS A BROAD TUNING RANGE. THE GREATER THE DISTANCE, THE HIGHER THE YIELD!
SHOOOOOOOOOOSHH!!!
CLICK
BRAK-KOOM!!

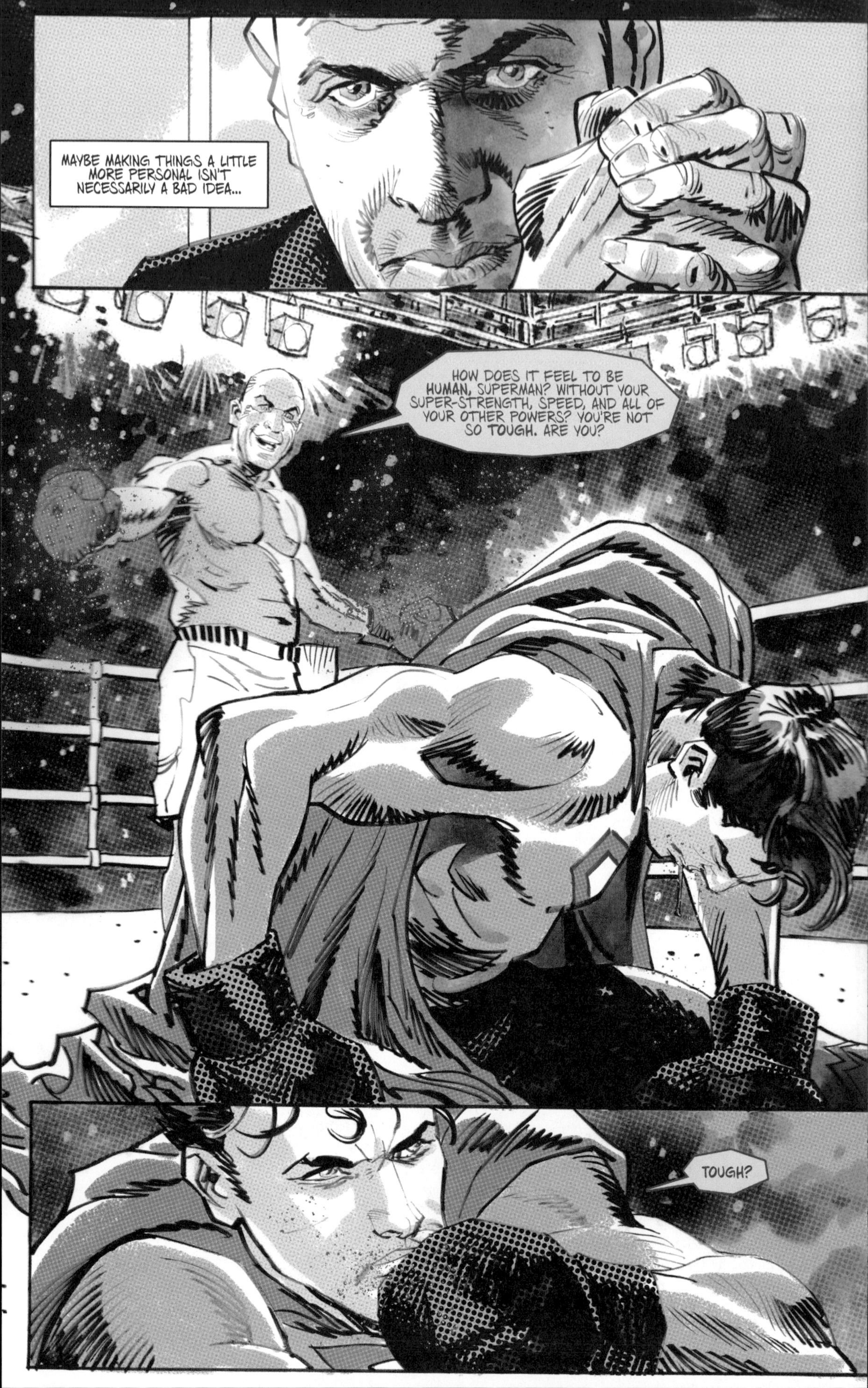
MAYBE MAKING THINGS A LITTLE MORE PERSONAL ISN'T NECESSARILY A BAD IDEA...
HOW DOES IT FEEL TO BE HUMAN, SUPERMAN? WITHOUT YOUR SUPER-STRENGTH, SPEED, AND ALL OF YOUR OTHER POWERS? YOU'RE NOT SO TOUGH. ARE YOU?
TOUGH?

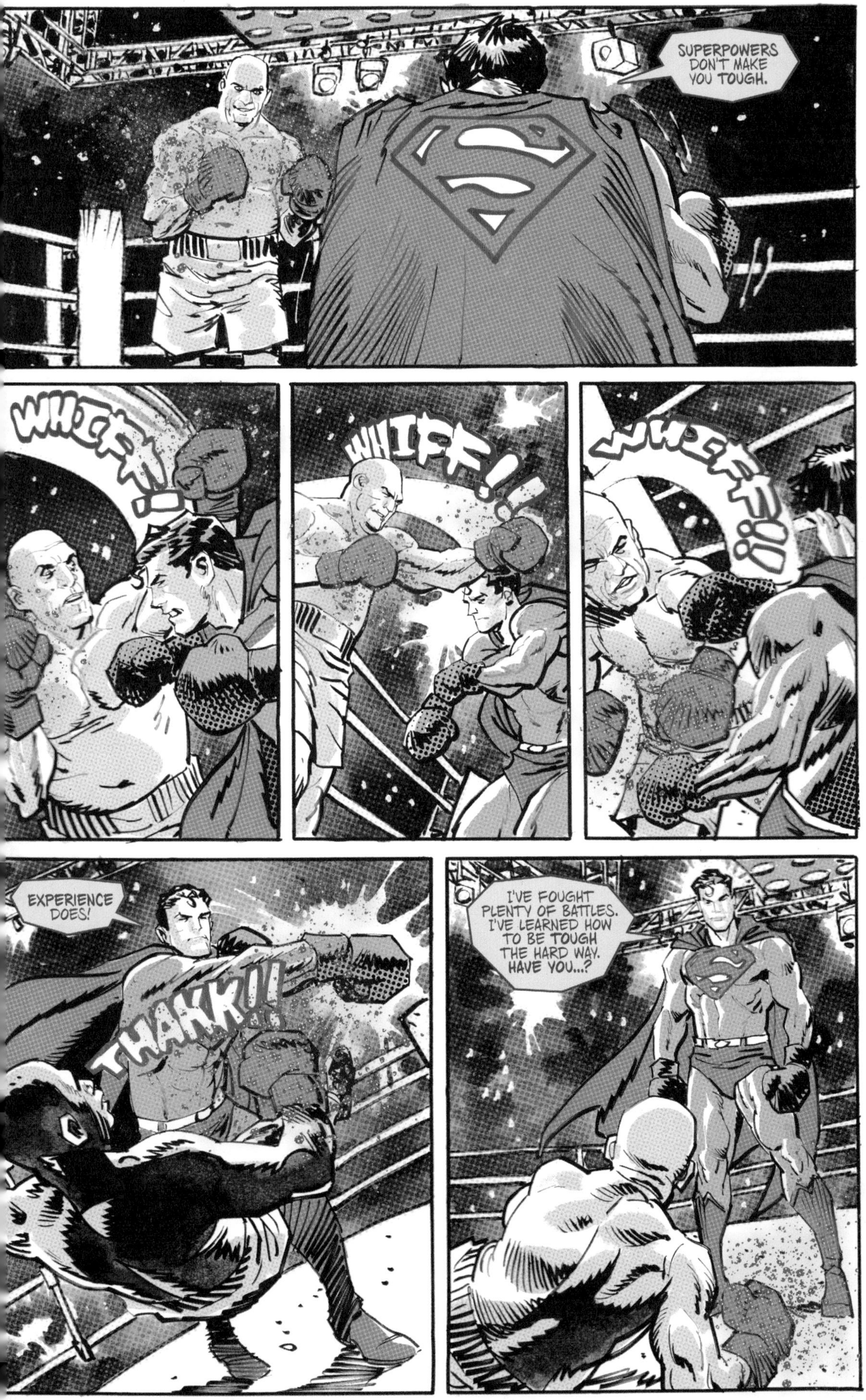
SUPERPOWERS DON'T MAKE YOU TOUGH.
WHIFF!!
WHIFF!!
WHIFF!!
EXPERIENCE DOES!
THAKK!!
I'VE FOUGHT PLENTY OF BATTLES. I'VE LEARNED HOW TO BE TOUGH THE HARD WAY. HAVE YOU...?

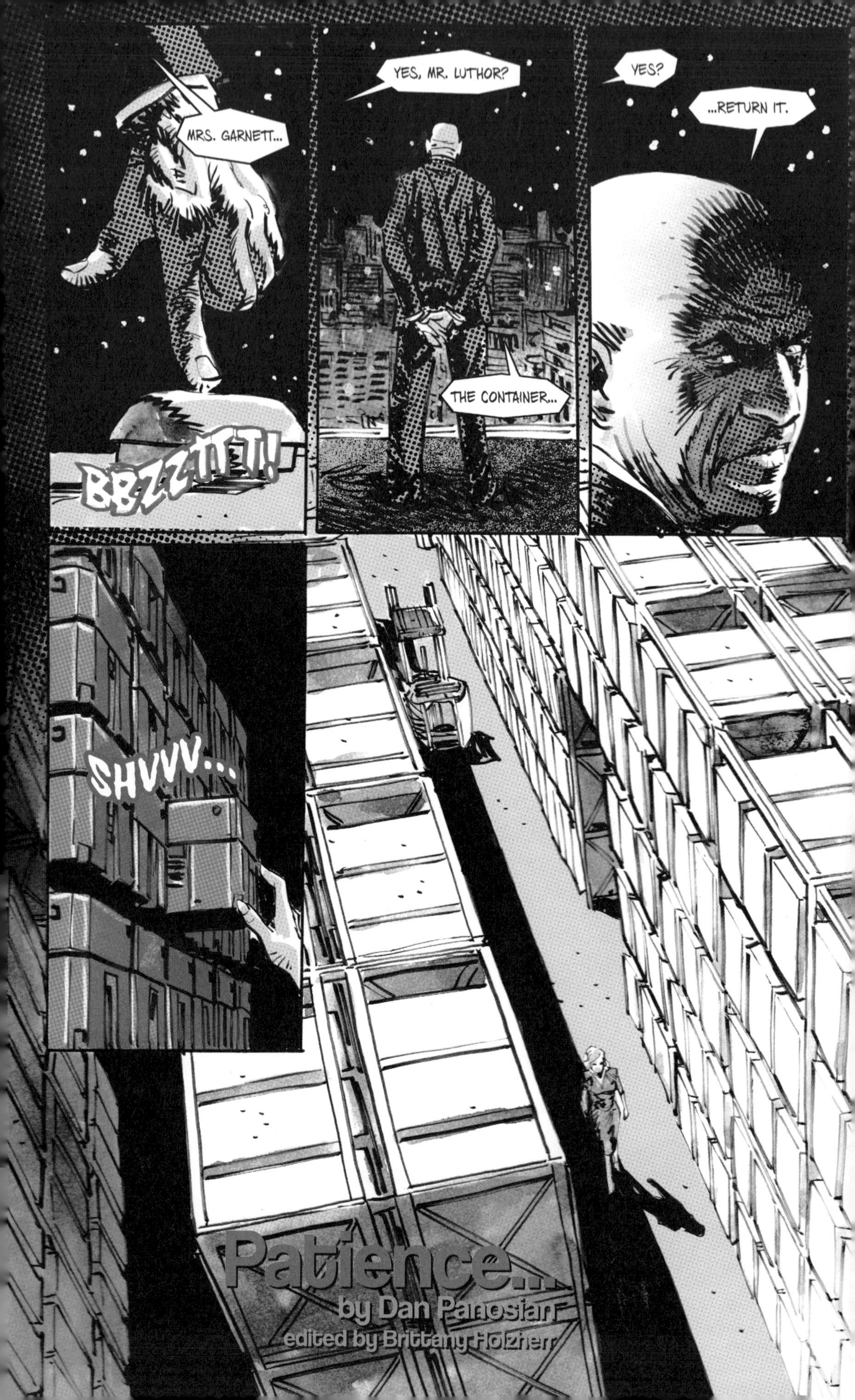
MRS. GARNETT...
BBZZTTTT!
YES, MR. LUTHOR?
THE CONTAINER...
YES?
...RETURN IT.
SHVVV...
Patience...
by Dan Panosian
edited by Brittany Holzherr

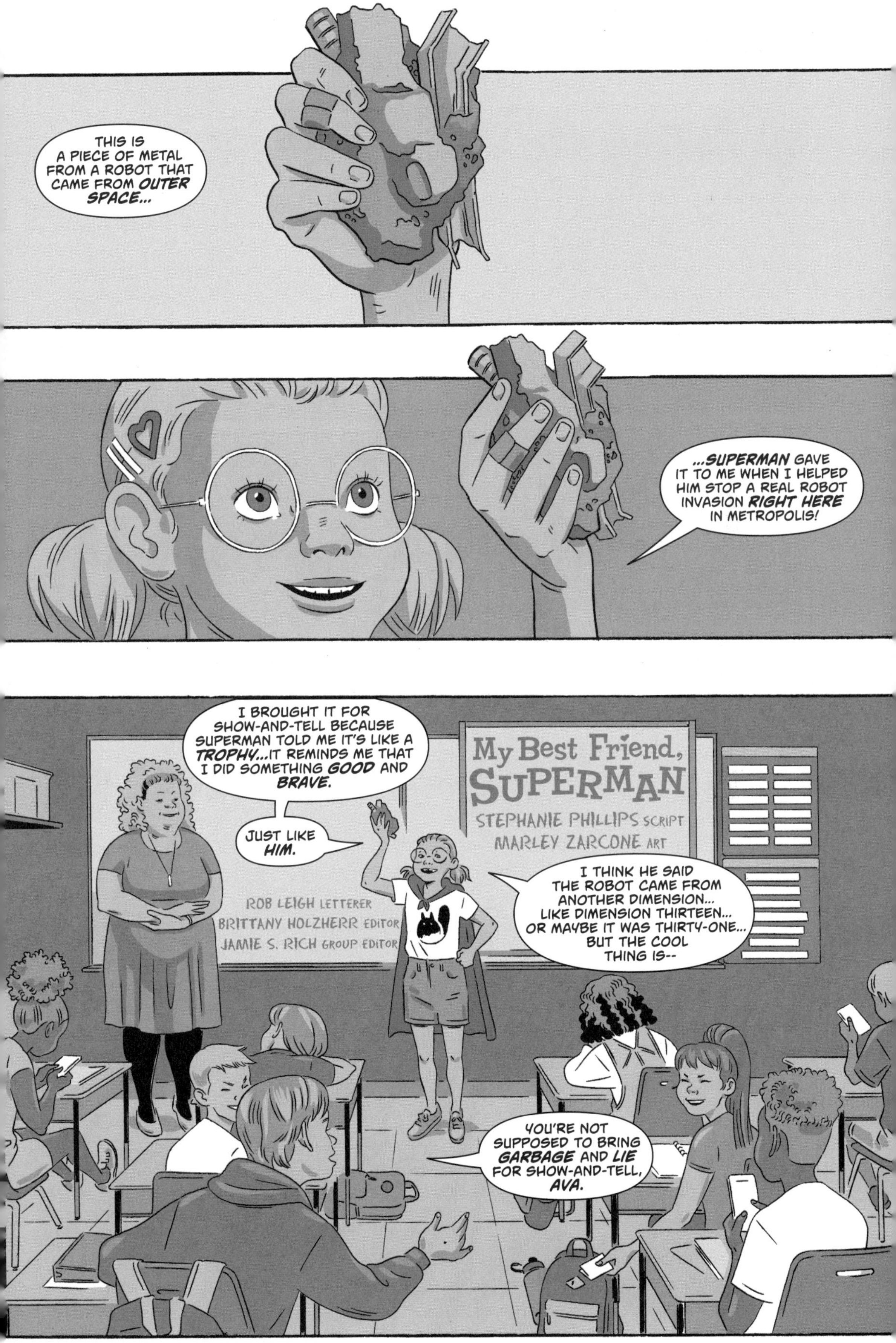
THIS IS A PIECE OF METAL FROM A ROBOT THAT CAME FROM OUTER SPACE...
...SUPERMAN GAVE IT TO ME WHEN I HELPED HIM STOP A REAL ROBOT INVASION RIGHT HERE IN METROPOLIS!
I BROUGHT IT FOR SHOW-AND-TELL BECAUSE SUPERMAN TOLD ME IT'S LIKE A TROPHY...IT REMINDS ME THAT I DID SOMETHING GOOD AND BRAVE.
JUST LIKE HIM.
My Best Friend, SUPERMAN
STEPHANIE PHILLIPS SCRIPT
MARLEY ZARCONE ART
ROB LEIGH LETTERER
BRITTANY HOLZHERR EDITOR
JAMIE S. RICH GROUP EDITOR
I THINK HE SAID THE ROBOT CAME FROM ANOTHER DIMENSION... LIKE DIMENSION THIRTEEN... OR MAYBE IT WAS THIRTY-ONE... BUT THE COOL THING IS--
YOU'RE NOT SUPPOSED TO BRING GARBAGE AND LIE FOR SHOW-AND-TELL, AVA.

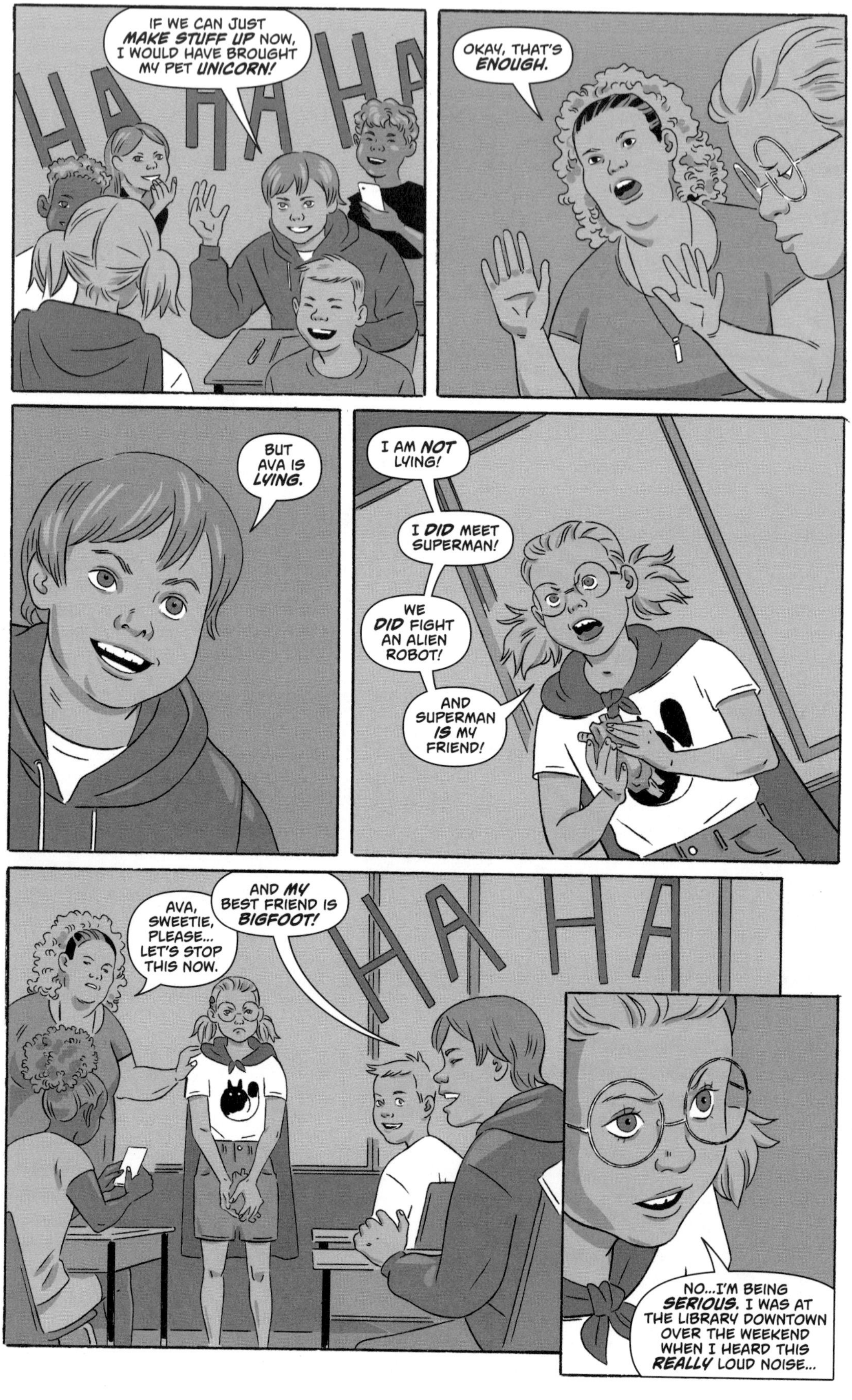

IF WE CAN JUST MAKE STUFF UP NOW, I WOULD HAVE BROUGHT MY PET UNICORN!
HA HA HA
OKAY, THAT'S ENOUGH.
BUT AVA IS LYING.
I AM NOT LYING!
I DID MEET SUPERMAN!
WE DID FIGHT AN ALIEN ROBOT!
AND SUPERMAN IS MY FRIEND!
AVA, SWEETIE, PLEASE... LET'S STOP THIS NOW.
AND MY BEST FRIEND IS BIGFOOT!
HA HA
NO...I'M BEING SERIOUS. I WAS AT THE LIBRARY DOWNTOWN OVER THE WEEKEND WHEN I HEARD THIS REALLY LOUD NOISE...

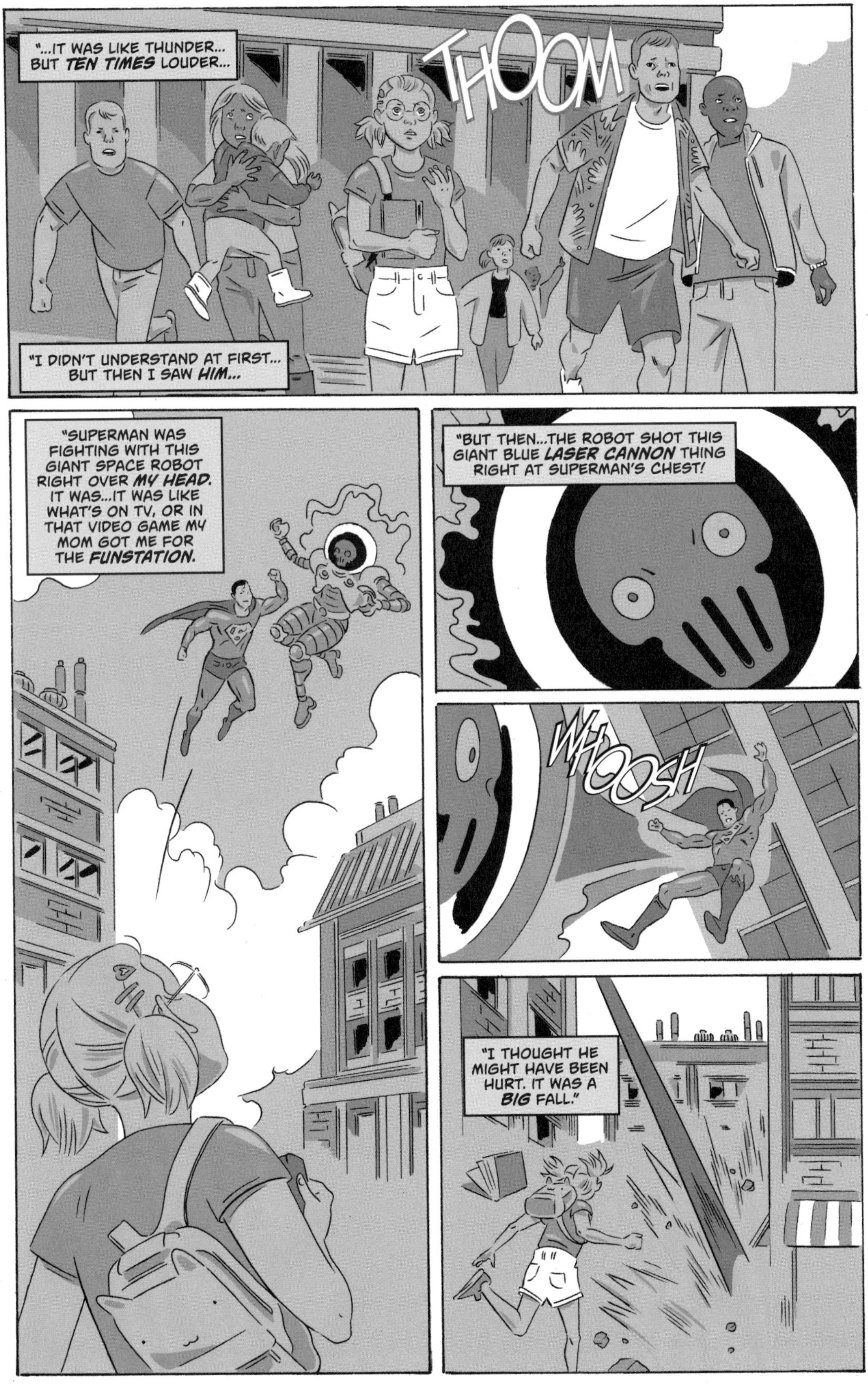
"...IT WAS LIKE THUNDER... BUT TEN TIMES LOUDER...
THOOM
"I DIDN'T UNDERSTAND AT FIRST... BUT THEN I SAW HIM...
"SUPERMAN WAS FIGHTING WITH THIS GIANT SPACE ROBOT RIGHT OVER MY HEAD. IT WAS...IT WAS LIKE WHAT'S ON TV, OR IN THAT VIDEO GAME MY MOM GOT ME FOR THE FUNSTATION.
"BUT THEN...THE ROBOT SHOT THIS GIANT BLUE LASER CANNON THING RIGHT AT SUPERMAN'S CHEST!
WHOOSH
"I THOUGHT HE MIGHT HAVE BEEN HURT. IT WAS A BIG FALL."

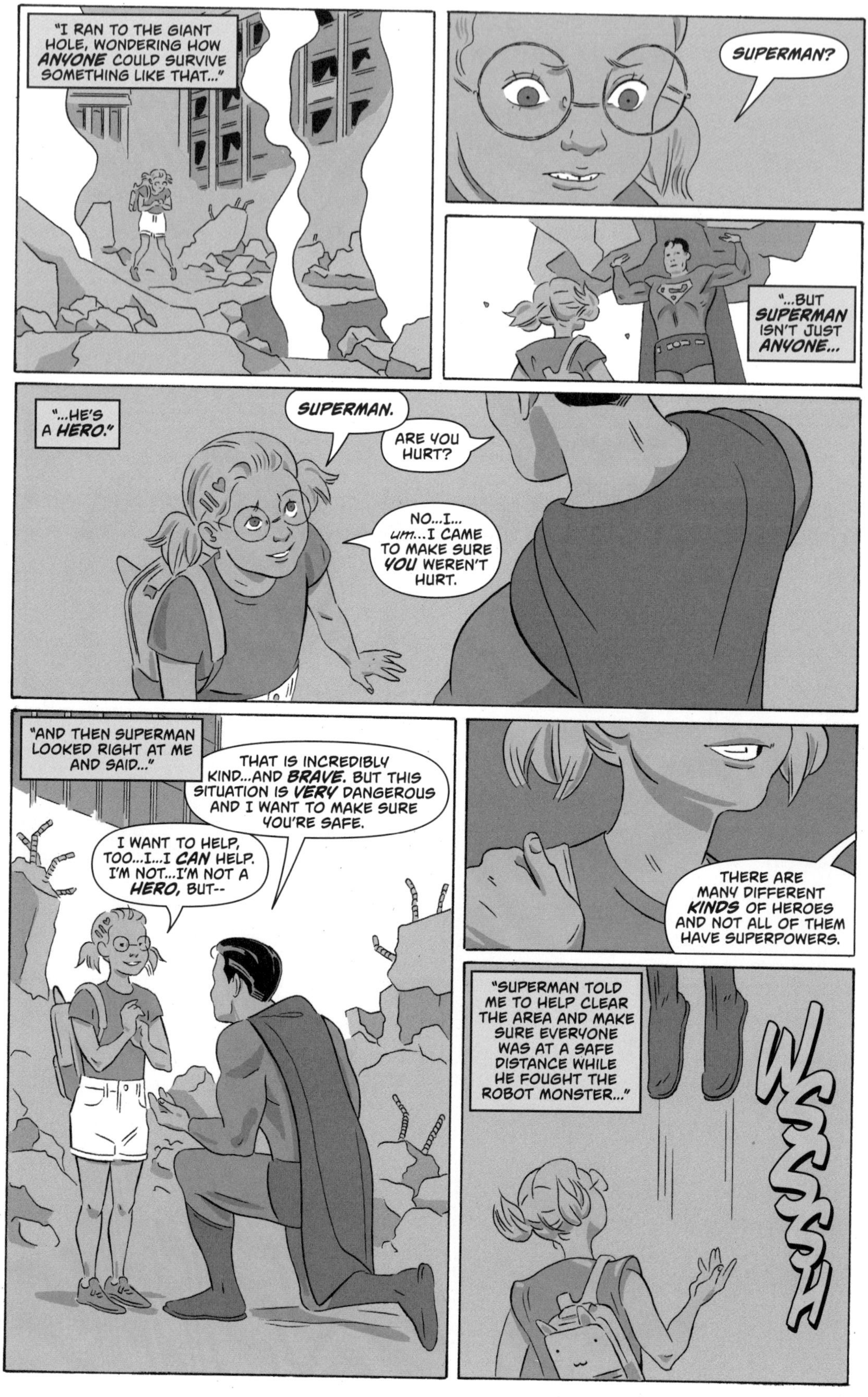
"I RAN TO THE GIANT HOLE, WONDERING HOW ANYONE COULD SURVIVE SOMETHING LIKE THAT..."
SUPERMAN?
"...BUT SUPERMAN ISN'T JUST ANYONE...
"...HE'S A HERO."
SUPERMAN.
ARE YOU HURT?
NO...I... um...I CAME TO MAKE SURE YOU WEREN'T HURT.
"AND THEN SUPERMAN LOOKED RIGHT AT ME AND SAID..."
THAT IS INCREDIBLY KIND...AND BRAVE. BUT THIS SITUATION IS VERY DANGEROUS AND I WANT TO MAKE SURE YOU'RE SAFE.
I WANT TO HELP, TOO...I...I CAN HELP. I'M NOT...I'M NOT A HERO, BUT--
THERE ARE MANY DIFFERENT KINDS OF HEROES AND NOT ALL OF THEM HAVE SUPERPOWERS.
"SUPERMAN TOLD ME TO HELP CLEAR THE AREA AND MAKE SURE EVERYONE WAS AT A SAFE DISTANCE WHILE HE FOUGHT THE ROBOT MONSTER..."
WSSSH

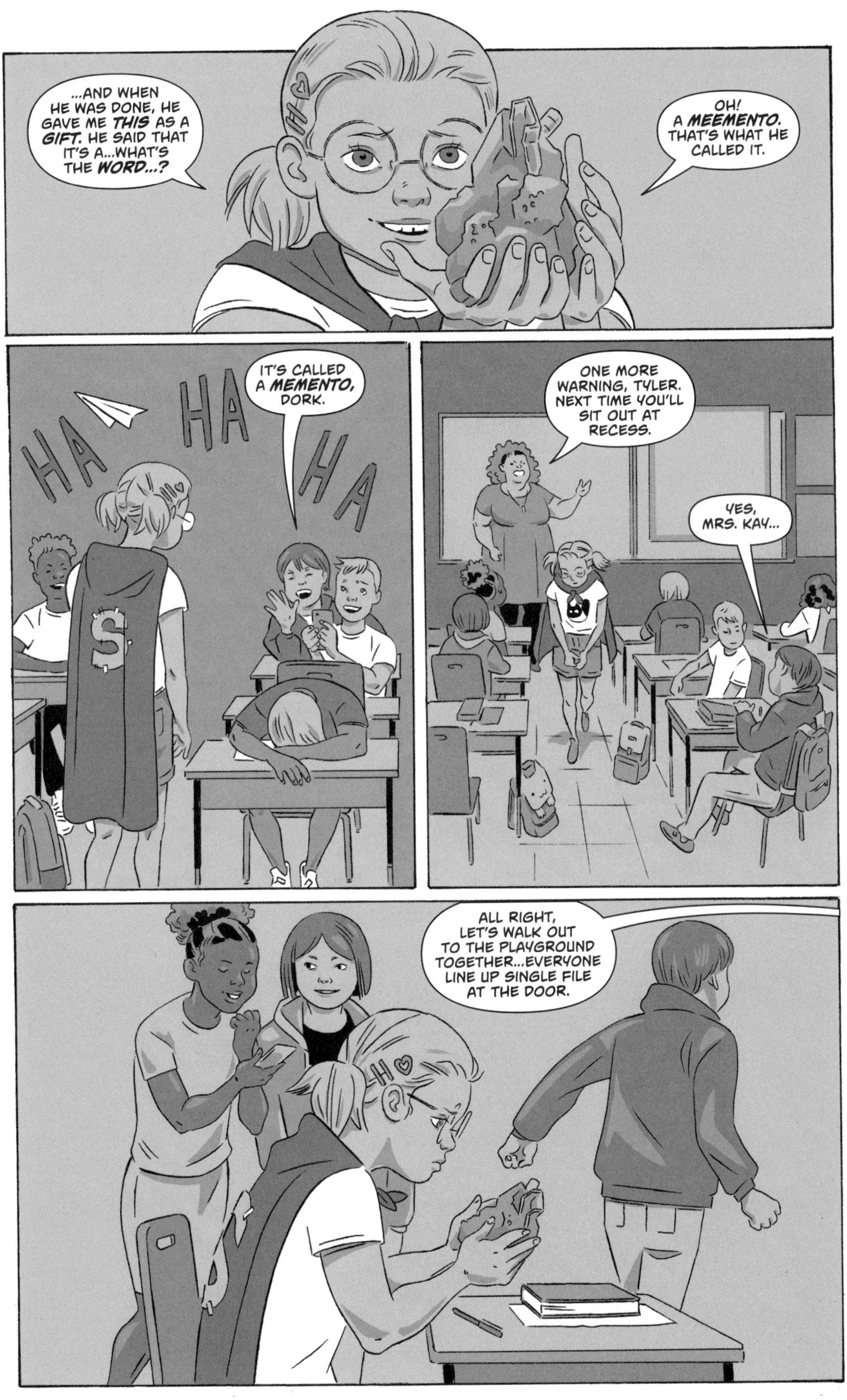
...AND WHEN HE WAS DONE, HE GAVE ME THIS AS A GIFT. HE SAID THAT IT'S A...WHAT'S THE WORD...?
OH! A MEEMENTO. THAT'S WHAT HE CALLED IT.
HA HA HA
IT'S CALLED A MEMENTO, DORK.
ONE MORE WARNING, TYLER. NEXT TIME YOU'LL SIT OUT AT RECESS.
YES, MRS. KAY...
ALL RIGHT, LET'S WALK OUT TO THE PLAYGROUND TOGETHER...EVERYONE LINE UP SINGLE FILE AT THE DOOR.

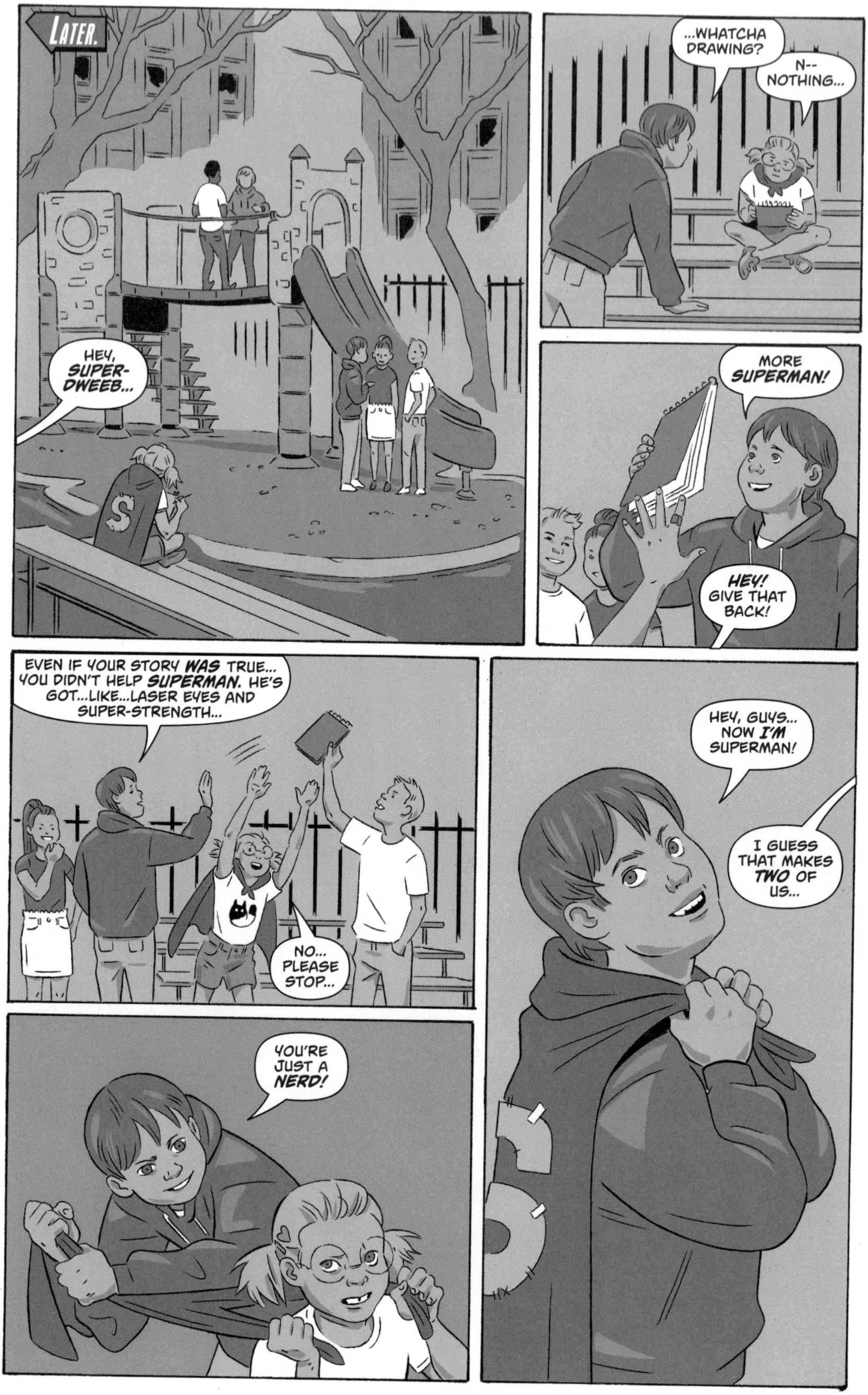
LATER.
HEY, SUPER-DWEEB...
...WHATCHA DRAWING?
N-- NOTHING...
MORE SUPERMAN!
HEY! GIVE THAT BACK!
EVEN IF YOUR STORY WAS TRUE... YOU DIDN'T HELP SUPERMAN. HE'S GOT...LIKE...LASER EYES AND SUPER-STRENGTH...
NO... PLEASE STOP...
YOU'RE JUST A NERD!
HEY, GUYS... NOW I'M SUPERMAN!
I GUESS THAT MAKES TWO OF US...

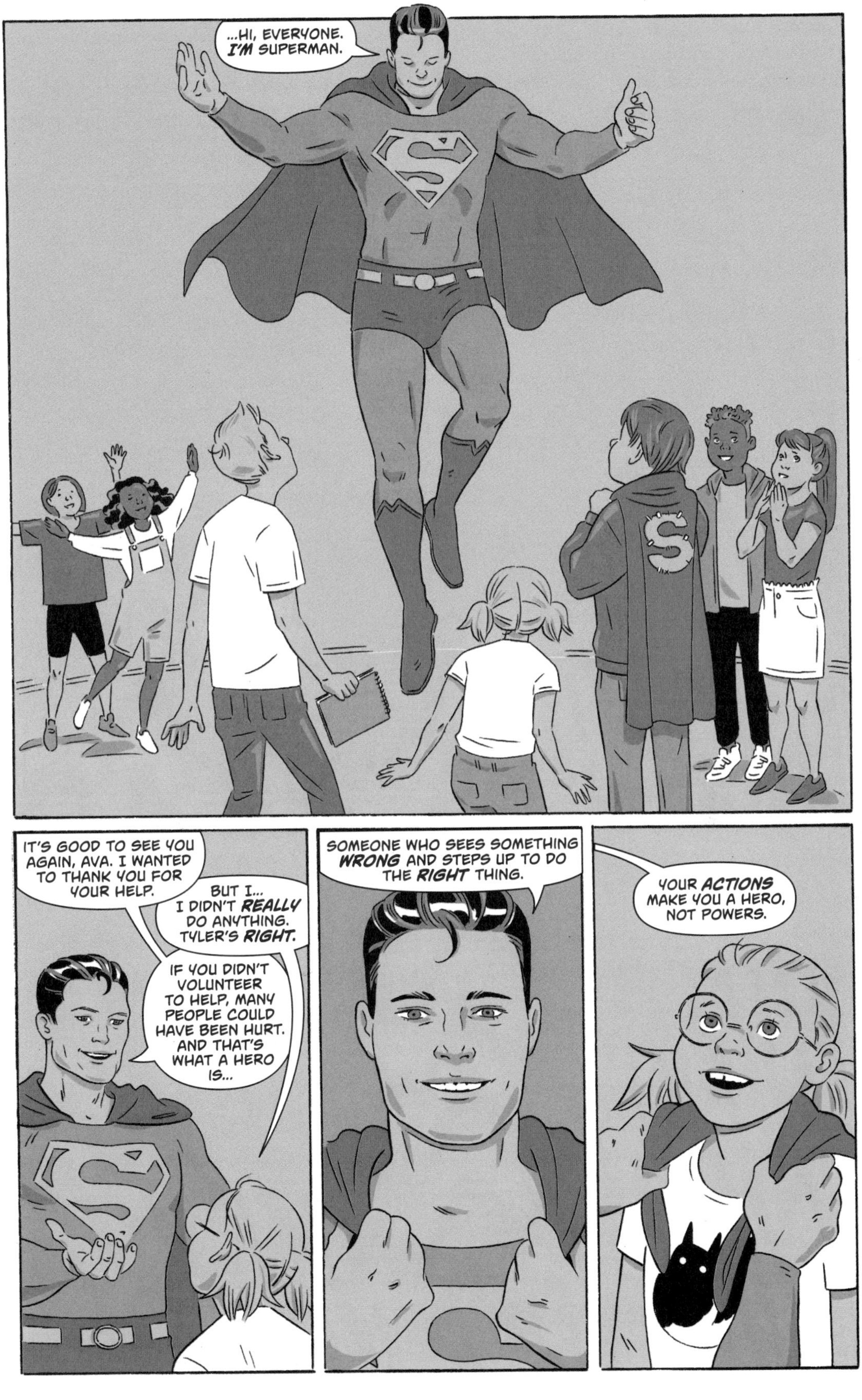
...HI, EVERYONE. I'M SUPERMAN.
IT'S GOOD TO SEE YOU AGAIN, AVA. I WANTED TO THANK YOU FOR YOUR HELP.
BUT I... I DIDN'T REALLY DO ANYTHING. TYLER'S RIGHT.
IF YOU DIDN'T VOLUNTEER TO HELP, MANY PEOPLE COULD HAVE BEEN HURT. AND THAT'S WHAT A HERO IS...
SOMEONE WHO SEES SOMETHING WRONG AND STEPS UP TO DO THE RIGHT THING.
YOUR ACTIONS MAKE YOU A HERO, NOT POWERS.

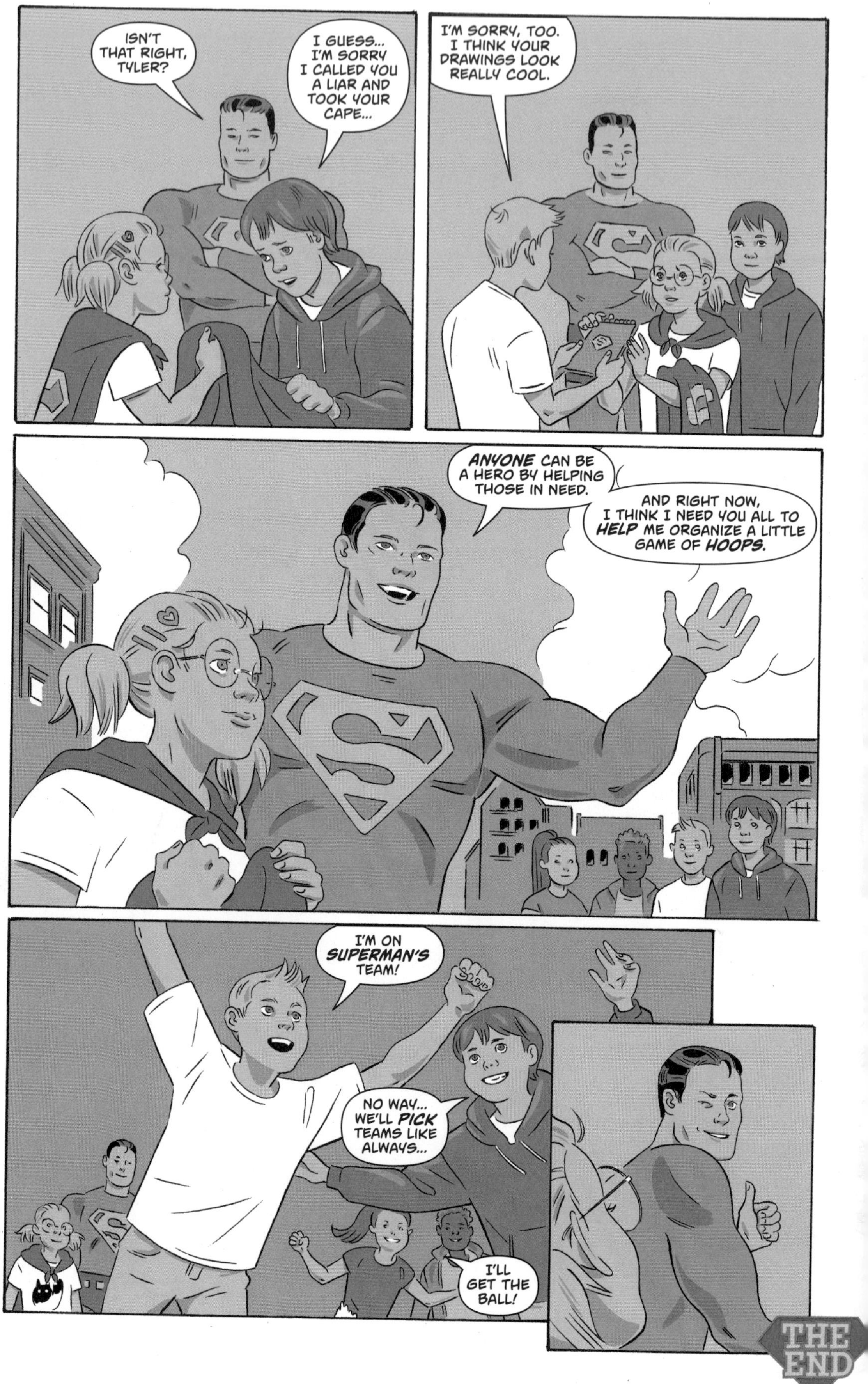
ISN'T THAT RIGHT, TYLER?
I GUESS... I'M SORRY I CALLED YOU A LIAR AND TOOK YOUR CAPE...
I'M SORRY, TOO. I THINK YOUR DRAWINGS LOOK REALLY COOL.
ANYONE CAN BE A HERO BY HELPING THOSE IN NEED.
AND RIGHT NOW, I THINK I NEED YOU ALL TO HELP ME ORGANIZE A LITTLE GAME OF HOOPS.
I'M ON SUPERMAN'S TEAM!
NO WAY... WE'LL PICK TEAMS LIKE ALWAYS...
I'LL GET THE BALL!
THE END

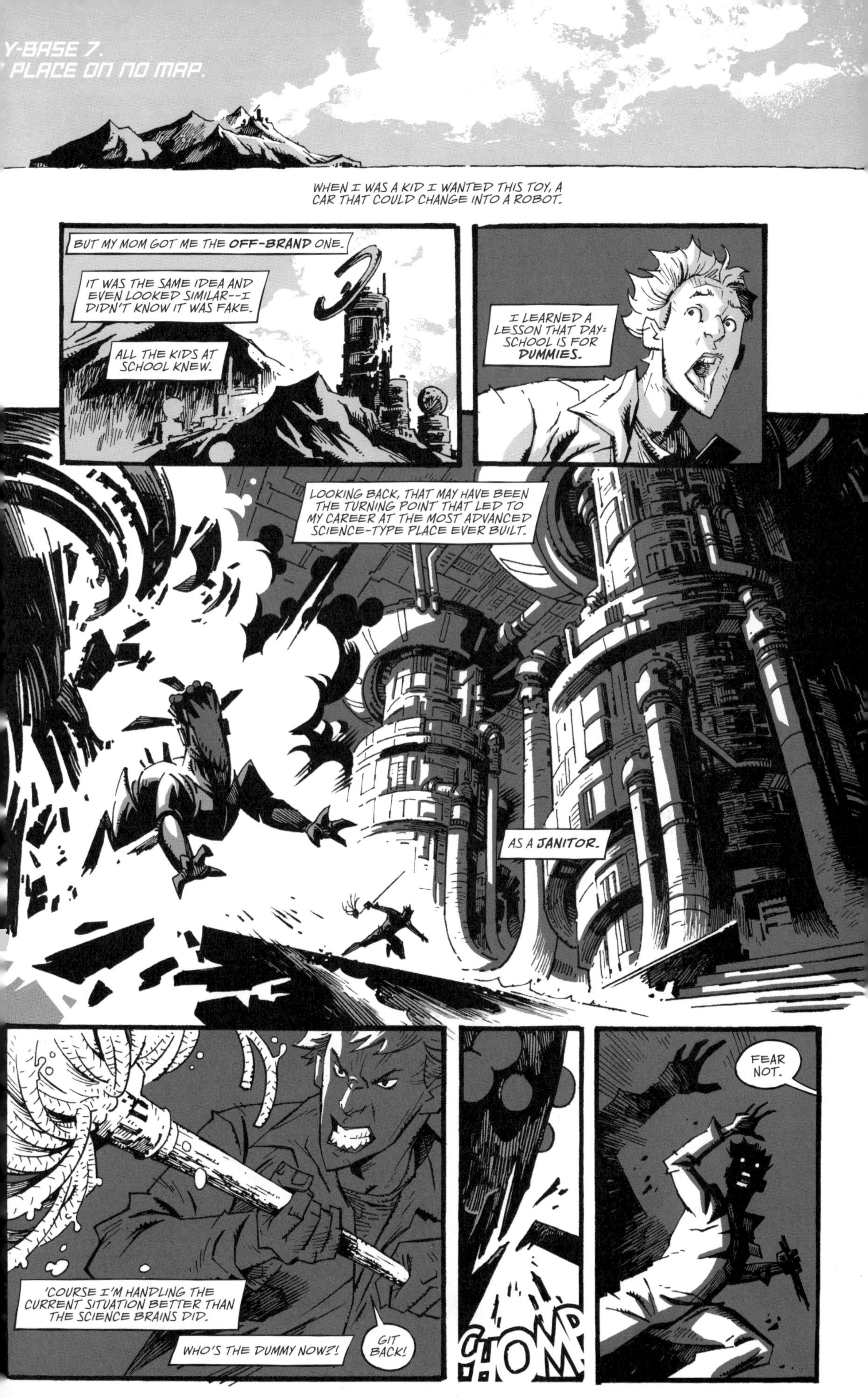
Y-BASE 7.
PLACE ON NO MAP.
WHEN I WAS A KID I WANTED THIS TOY, A CAR THAT COULD CHANGE INTO A ROBOT.
BUT MY MOM GOT ME THE OFF-BRAND ONE.
IT WAS THE SAME IDEA AND EVEN LOOKED SIMILAR--I DIDN'T KNOW IT WAS FAKE.
ALL THE KIDS AT SCHOOL KNEW.
I LEARNED A LESSON THAT DAY: SCHOOL IS FOR DUMMIES.
LOOKING BACK, THAT MAY HAVE BEEN THE TURNING POINT THAT LED TO MY CAREER AT THE MOST ADVANCED SCIENCE-TYPE PLACE EVER BUILT.
AS A JANITOR.
'COURSE I'M HANDLING THE CURRENT SITUATION BETTER THAN THE SCIENCE BRAINS DID.
WHO'S THE DUMMY NOW?!
GIT BACK!
CHOMP
FEAR NOT.

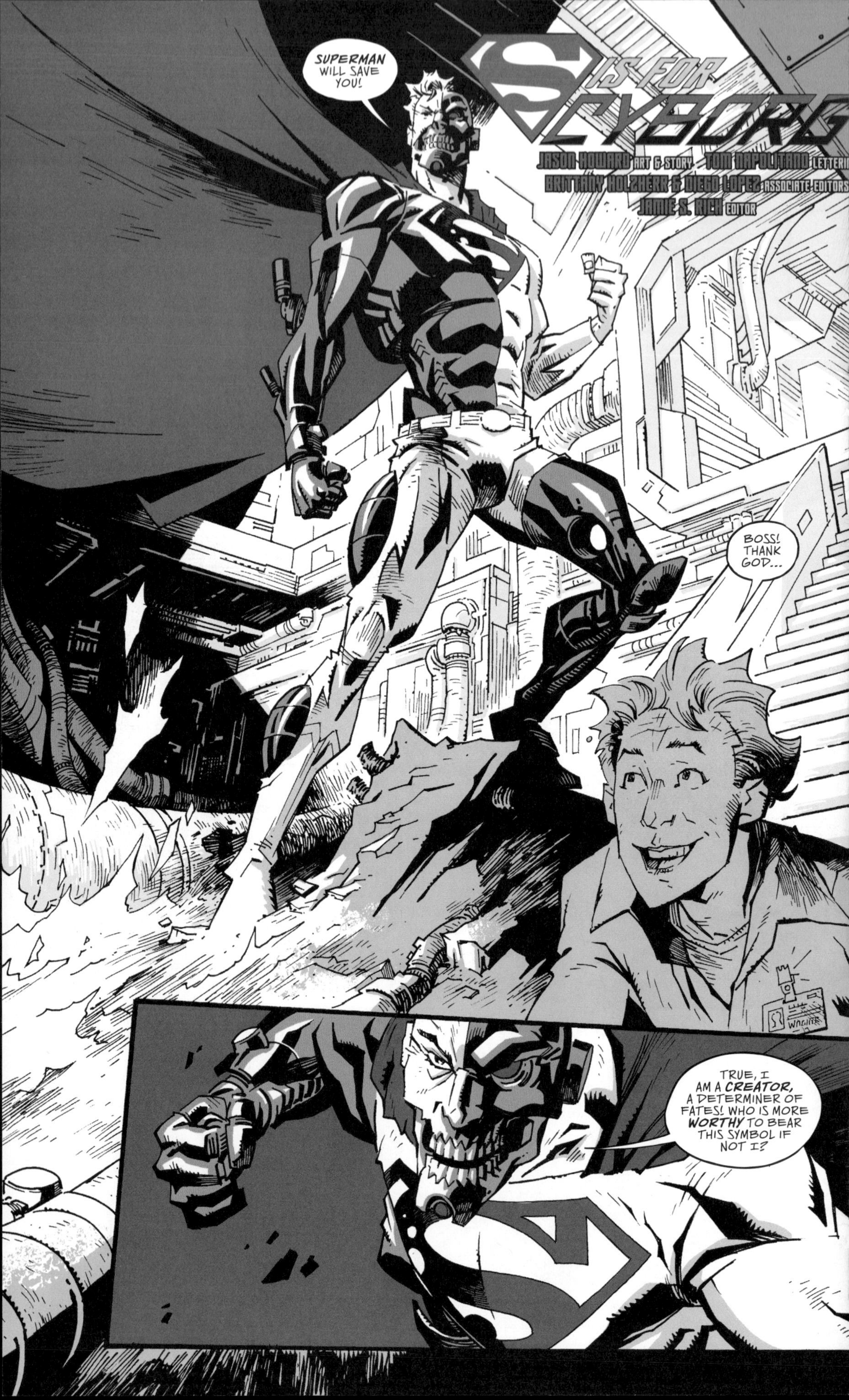
S IS FOR CYBORG
JASON HOWARD ART & STORY TOM NAPOLITANO LETTERIN
BRITTANY HOLZHERR & DIEGO LOPEZ ASSOCIATE EDITORS
JAMIE S. RICH EDITOR
SUPERMAN WILL SAVE YOU!
BOSS! THANK GOD...
TRUE, I AM A CREATOR, A DETERMINER OF FATES! WHO IS MORE WORTHY TO BEAR THIS SYMBOL IF NOT I?

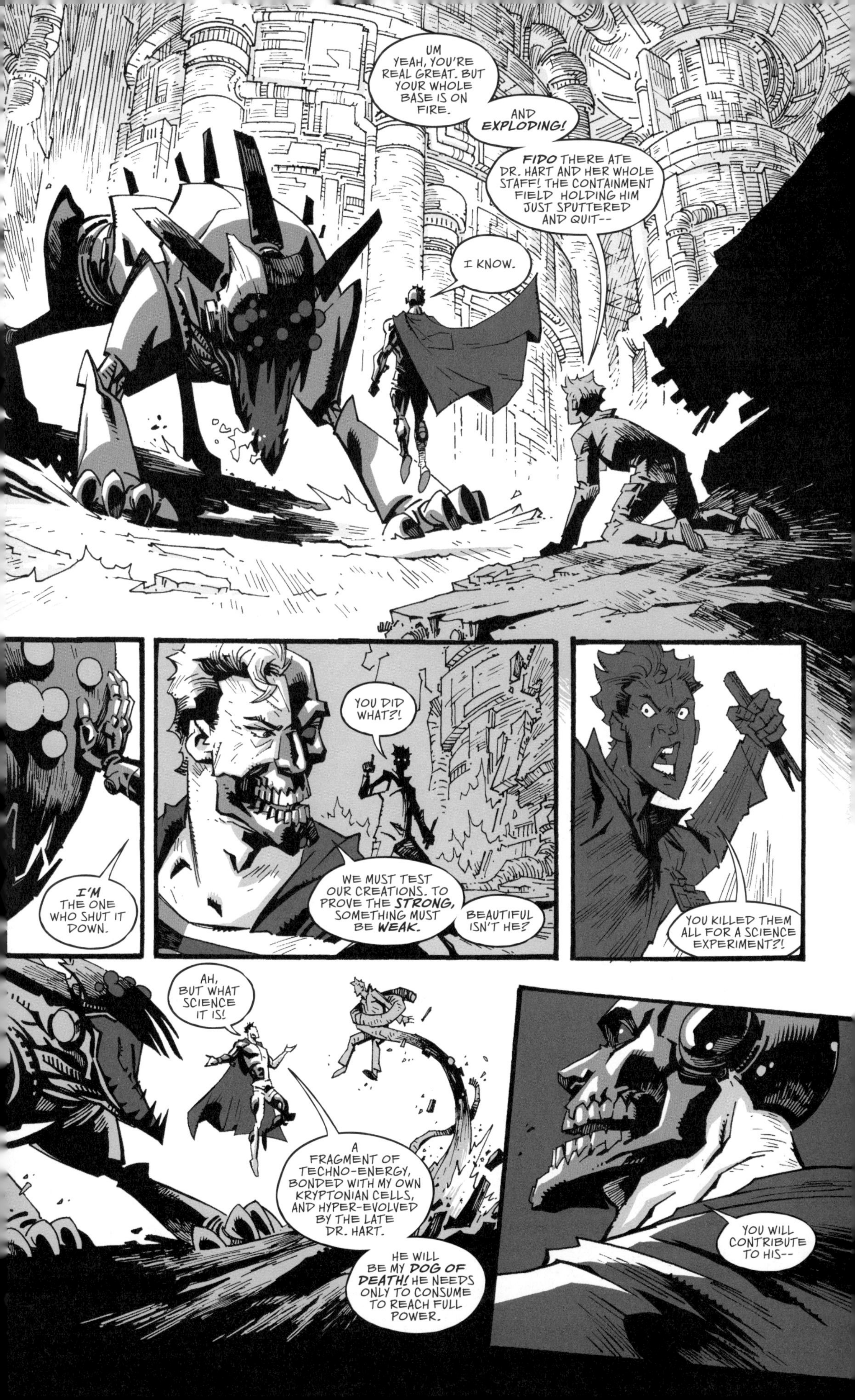
UM YEAH, YOU'RE REAL GREAT. BUT YOUR WHOLE BASE IS ON FIRE.
AND EXPLODING!
FIDO THERE ATE DR. HART AND HER WHOLE STAFF! THE CONTAINMENT FIELD HOLDING HIM JUST SPUTTERED AND QUIT--
I KNOW.
I'M THE ONE WHO SHUT IT DOWN.
YOU DID WHAT?!
WE MUST TEST OUR CREATIONS. TO PROVE THE STRONG, SOMETHING MUST BE WEAK.
BEAUTIFUL ISN'T HE?
YOU KILLED THEM ALL FOR A SCIENCE EXPERIMENT?!
AH, BUT WHAT SCIENCE IT IS!
A FRAGMENT OF TECHNO-ENERGY, BONDED WITH MY OWN KRYPTONIAN CELLS, AND HYPER-EVOLVED BY THE LATE DR. HART.
HE WILL BE MY DOG OF DEATH! HE NEEDS ONLY TO CONSUME TO REACH FULL POWER.
YOU WILL CONTRIBUTE TO HIS--

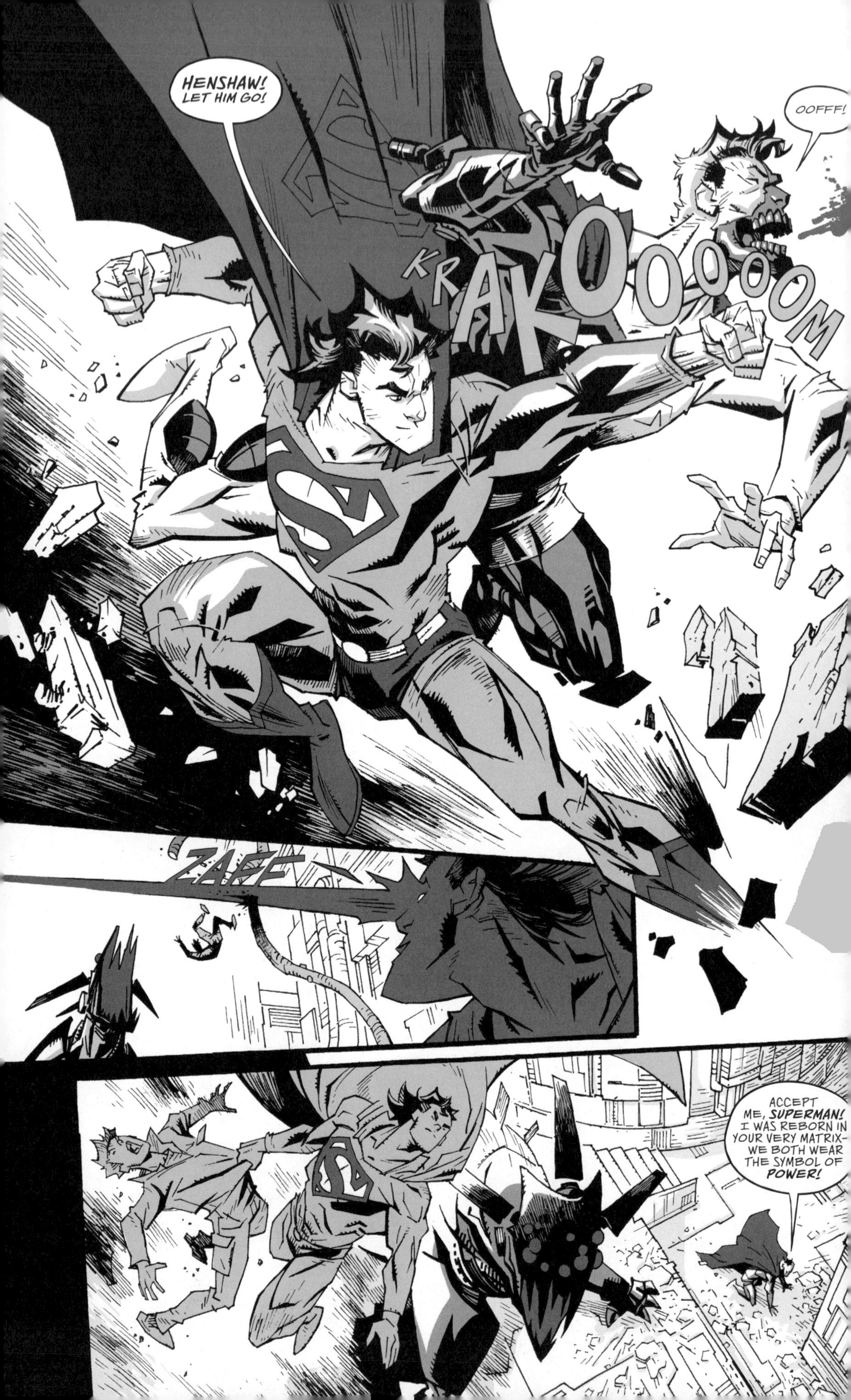
HENSHAW! LET HIM GO!
OOFFF!
KRAKOOOOOOM
ZAFF
ACCEPT ME, SUPERMAN! I WAS REBORN IN YOUR VERY MATRIX-WE BOTH WEAR THE SYMBOL OF POWER!

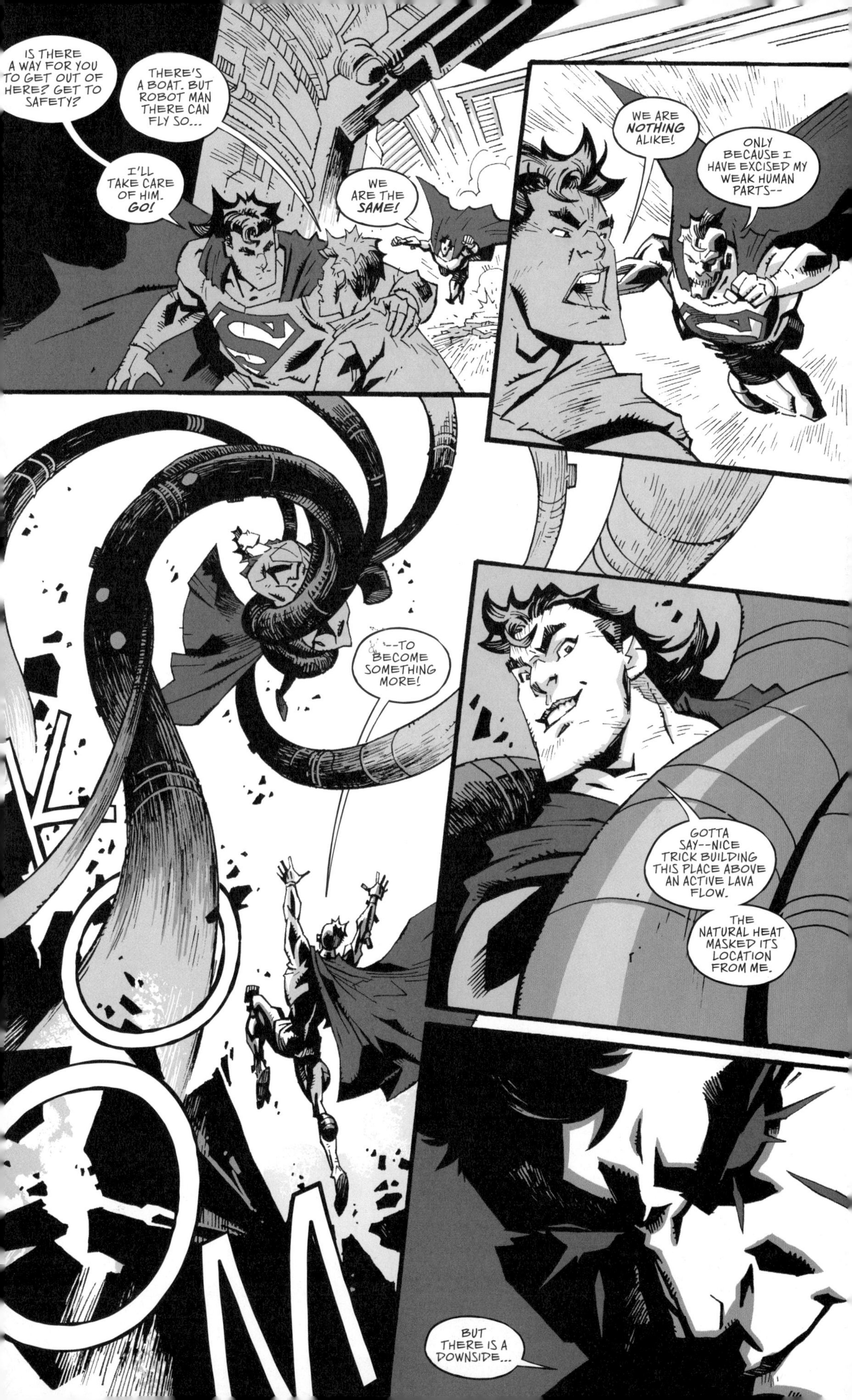
IS THERE A WAY FOR YOU TO GET OUT OF HERE? GET TO SAFETY?
THERE'S A BOAT. BUT ROBOT MAN THERE CAN FLY SO...
I'LL TAKE CARE OF HIM. GO!
WE ARE THE SAME!
WE ARE NOTHING ALIKE!
ONLY BECAUSE I HAVE EXCISED MY WEAK HUMAN PARTS--
--TO BECOME SOMETHING MORE!
GOTTA SAY--NICE TRICK BUILDING THIS PLACE ABOVE AN ACTIVE LAVA FLOW.
THE NATURAL HEAT MASKED ITS LOCATION FROM ME.
BUT THERE IS A DOWNSIDE...

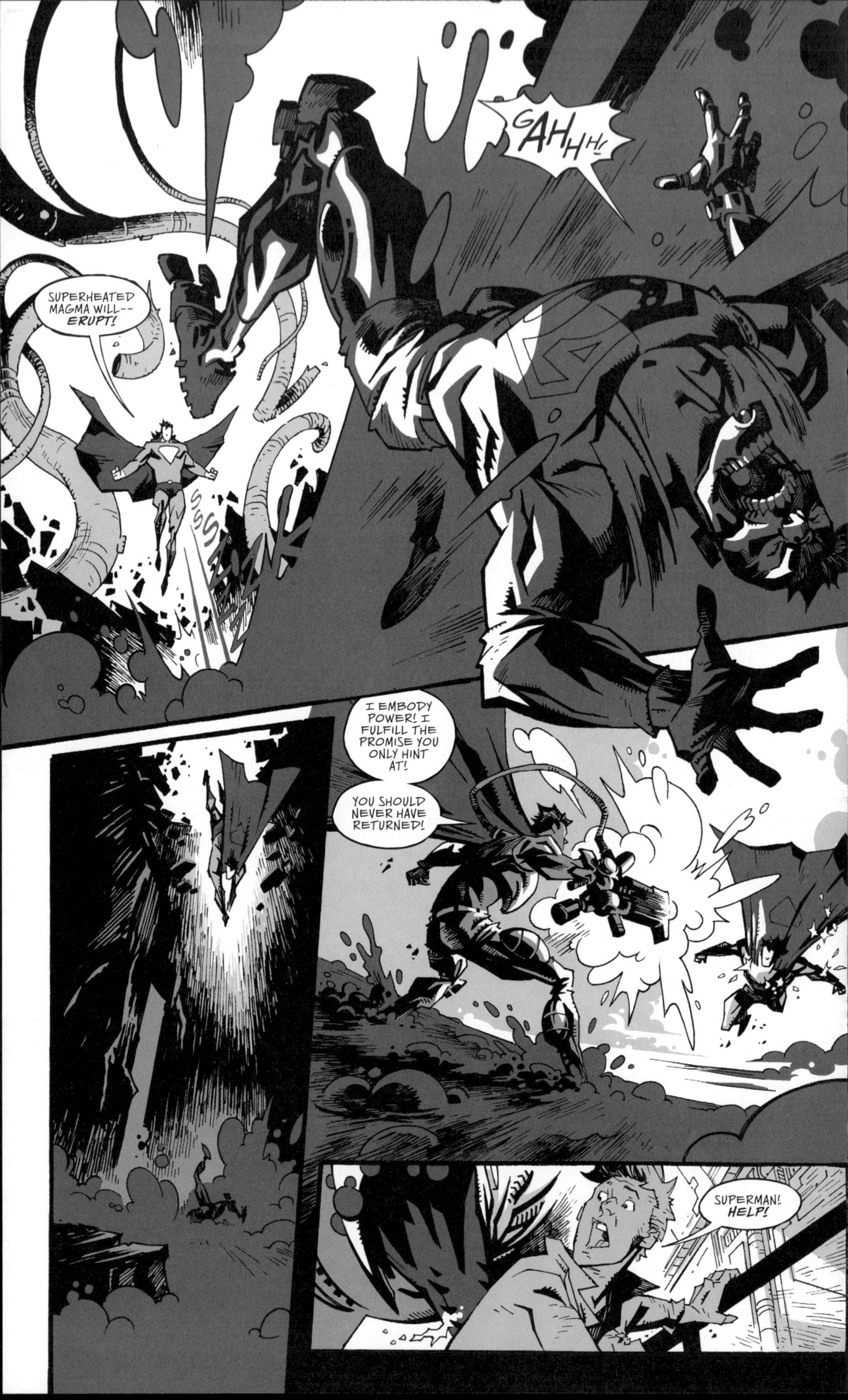
GAHHH!
SUPERHEATED MAGMA WILL-- ERUPT!
SSSHANK
I EMBODY POWER! I FULFILL THE PROMISE YOU ONLY HINT AT!
YOU SHOULD NEVER HAVE RETURNED!
SUPERMAN! HELP!

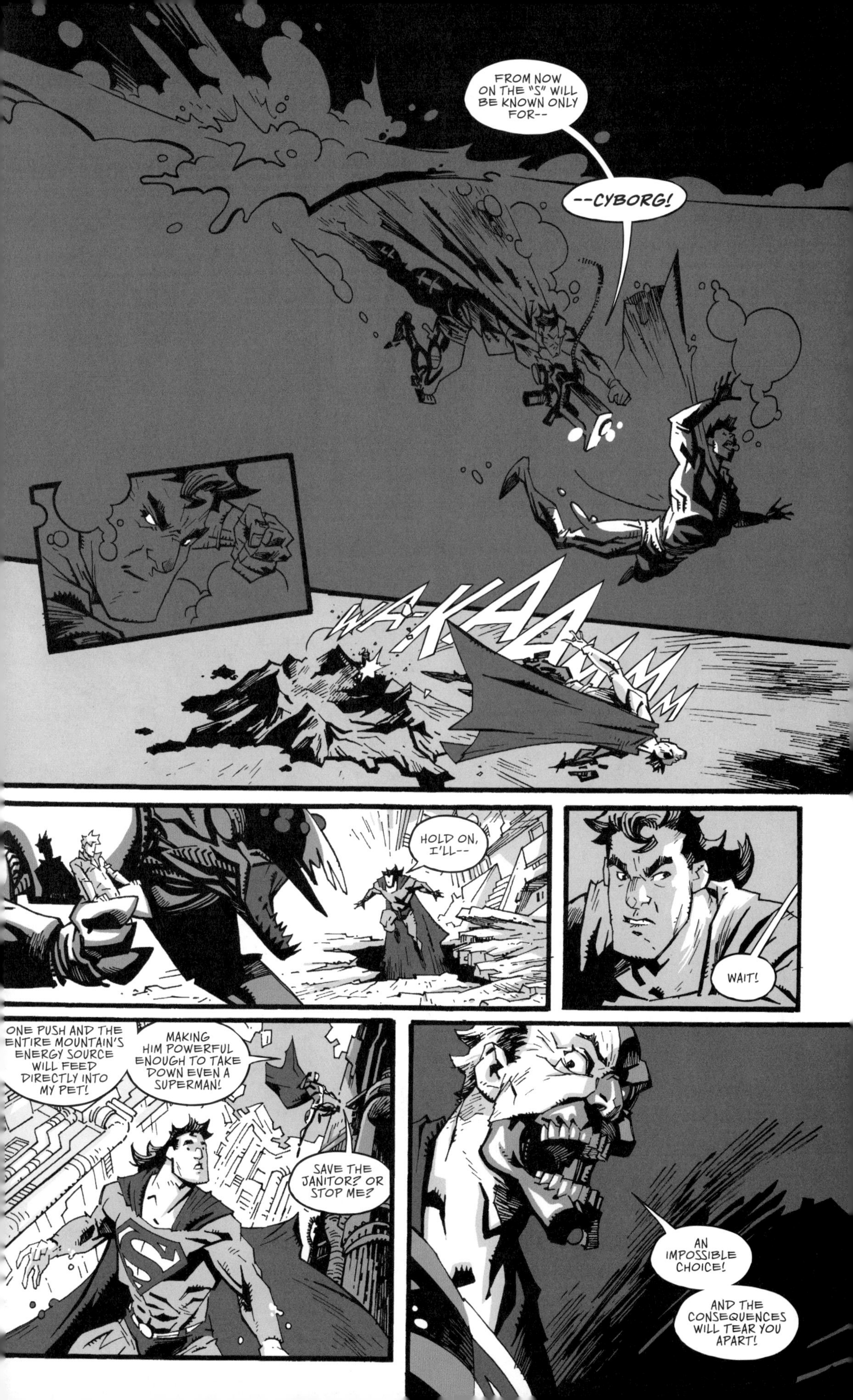
FROM NOW ON THE "S" WILL BE KNOWN ONLY FOR--
--CYBORG!
WA-KAAMMMM
HOLD ON, I'LL--
WAIT!
ONE PUSH AND THE ENTIRE MOUNTAIN'S ENERGY SOURCE WILL FEED DIRECTLY INTO MY PET!
MAKING HIM POWERFUL ENOUGH TO TAKE DOWN EVEN A SUPERMAN!
SAVE THE JANITOR? OR STOP ME?
AN IMPOSSIBLE CHOICE!
AND THE CONSEQUENCES WILL TEAR YOU APART!

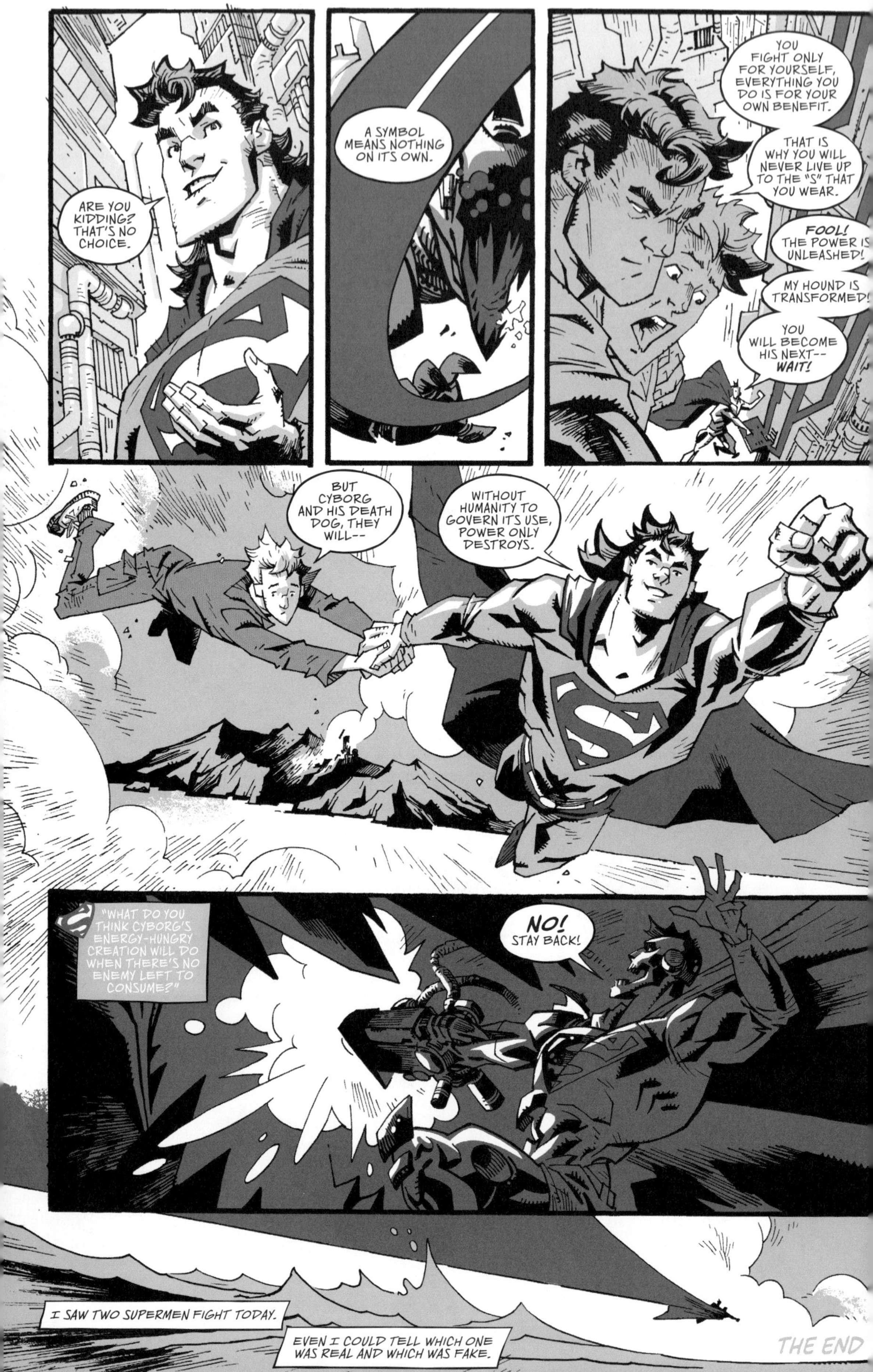
ARE YOU KIDDING? THAT'S NO CHOICE.
A SYMBOL MEANS NOTHING ON ITS OWN.
YOU FIGHT ONLY FOR YOURSELF, EVERYTHING YOU DO IS FOR YOUR OWN BENEFIT.
THAT IS WHY YOU WILL NEVER LIVE UP TO THE "S" THAT YOU WEAR.
FOOL! THE POWER IS UNLEASHED!
MY HOUND IS TRANSFORMED!
YOU WILL BECOME HIS NEXT-- WAIT!
BUT CYBORG AND HIS DEATH DOG, THEY WILL--
WITHOUT HUMANITY TO GOVERN ITS USE, POWER ONLY DESTROYS.
"WHAT DO YOU THINK CYBORG'S ENERGY-HUNGRY CREATION WILL DO WHEN THERE'S NO ENEMY LEFT TO CONSUME?"
NO! STAY BACK!
I SAW TWO SUPERMEN FIGHT TODAY.
EVEN I COULD TELL WHICH ONE WAS REAL AND WHICH WAS FAKE.
THE END

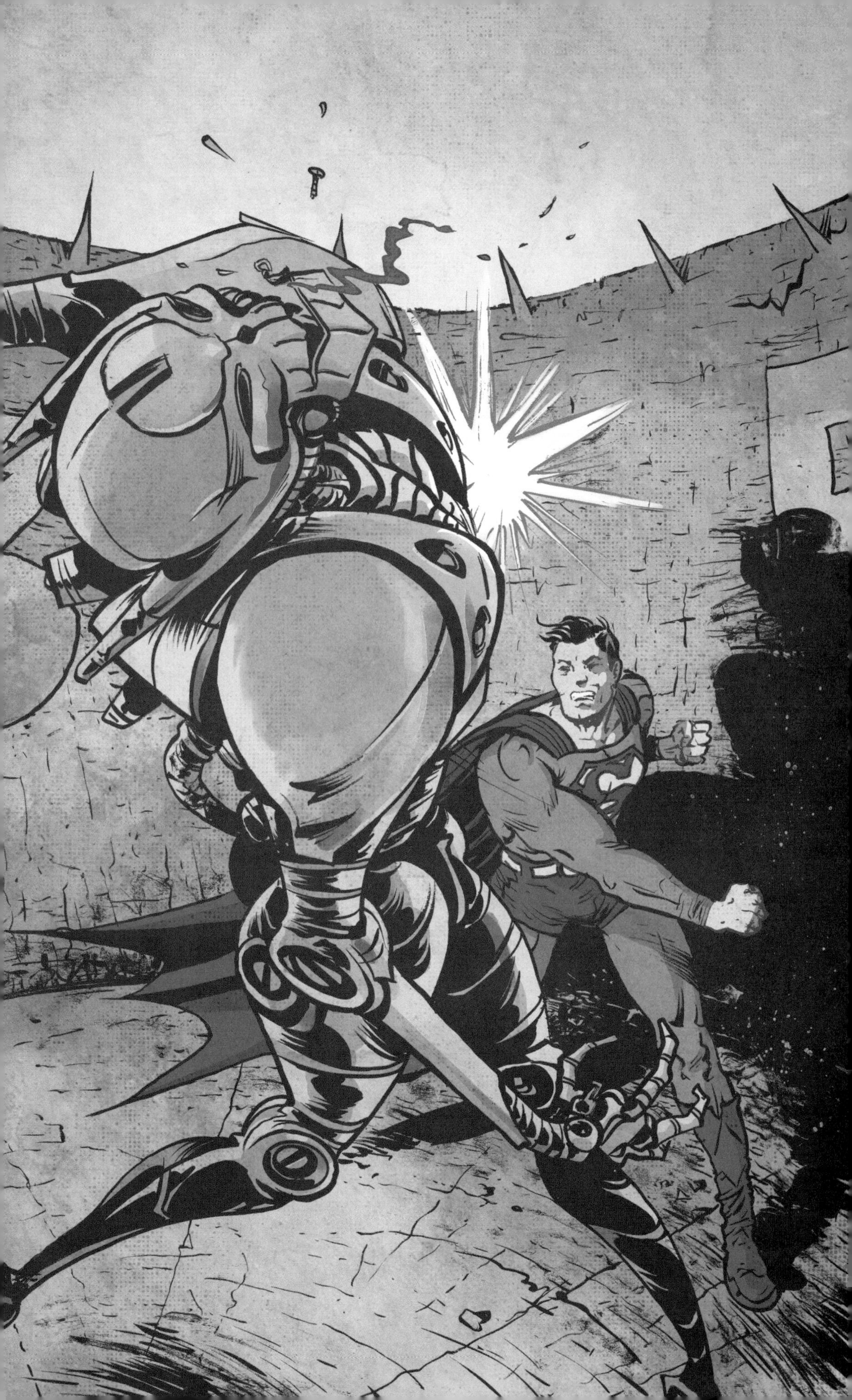

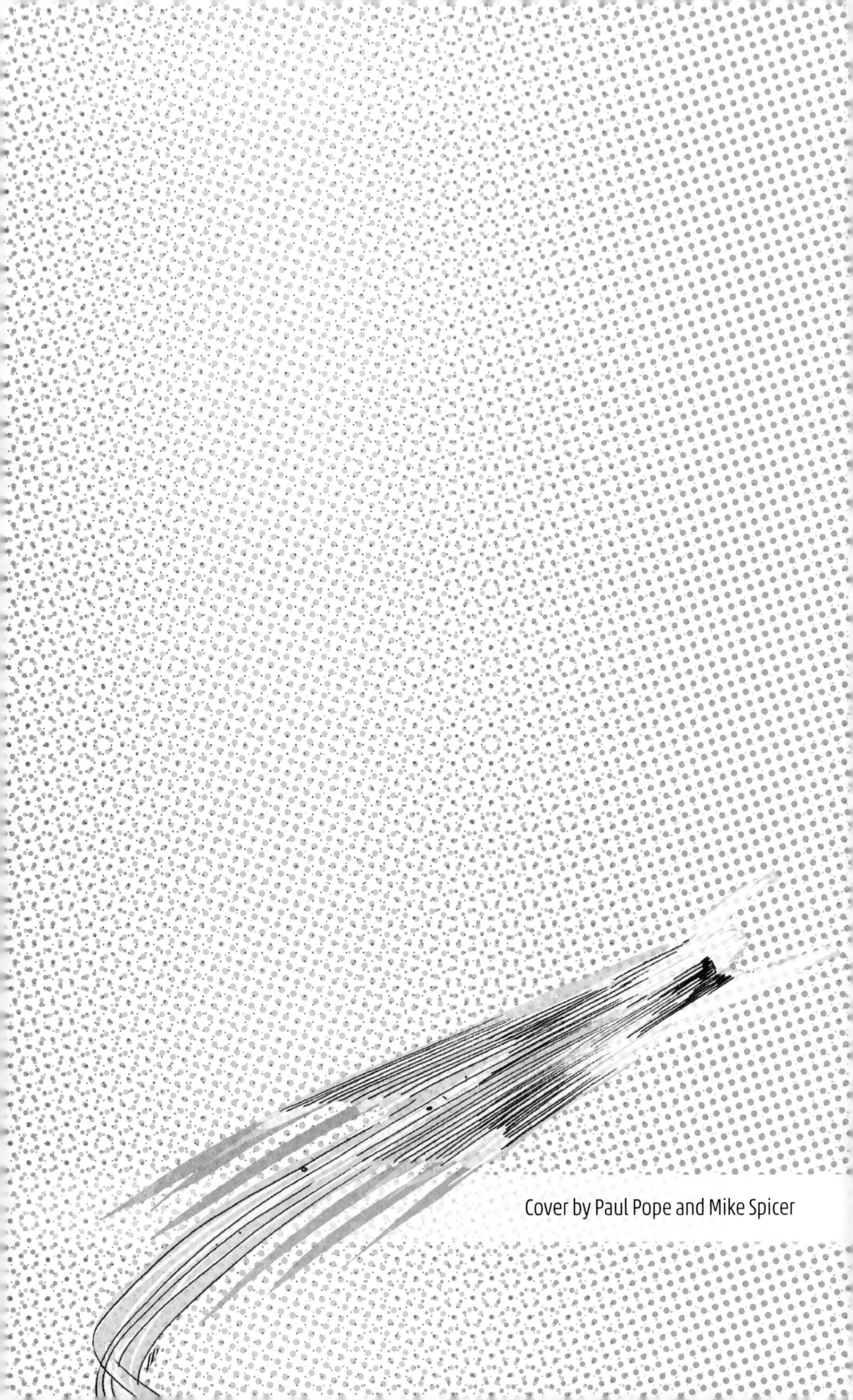

Cover by Paul Pope and Mike Spicer

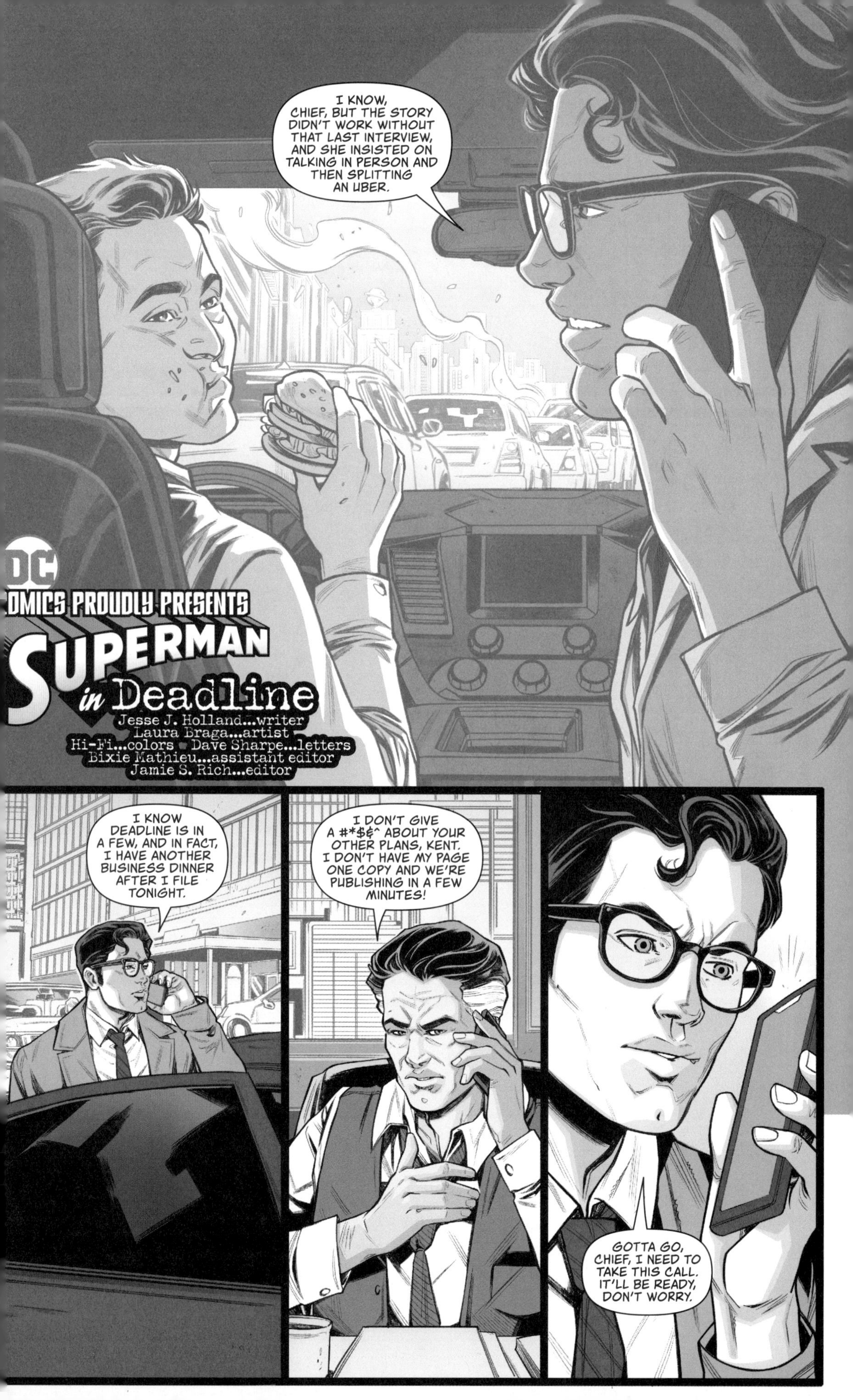
I KNOW, CHIEF, BUT THE STORY DIDN'T WORK WITHOUT THAT LAST INTERVIEW, AND SHE INSISTED ON TALKING IN PERSON AND THEN SPLITTING AN UBER.
DC
OMICS PROUDLY PRESENTS
SUPERMAN
in Deadline
Jesse J. Holland...writer
Laura Braga...artist
Hi-Fi...colors • Dave Sharpe...letters
Bixie Mathieu...assistant editor
Jamie S. Rich...editor
I KNOW DEADLINE IS IN A FEW, AND IN FACT, I HAVE ANOTHER BUSINESS DINNER AFTER I FILE TONIGHT.
I DON'T GIVE A #*$&^ ABOUT YOUR OTHER PLANS, KENT. I DON'T HAVE MY PAGE ONE COPY AND WE'RE PUBLISHING IN A FEW MINUTES!
GOTTA GO, CHIEF, I NEED TO TAKE THIS CALL. IT'LL BE READY, DON'T WORRY.

IT'S BRUCE. ARE YOU GOING TO BE LATE?

≒SIGH≒ NO, BRUCE, I'LL BE THERE.

I'M... JUST ON A BIT OF A DEADLINE AND STUCK IN TRAFFIC.

I COULD HAVE BEEN IN GOTHAM TONIGHT IF I KNEW YOU WERE GOING TO BLOW US OFF AGAIN.

IS HE SAVING ANOTHER CAT IN A TREE?

TELL DIANA I HEARD THAT... UNLIKE SOME PEOPLE, I HAVE A REAL JOB THAT I NEED TO PAY MY REAL BILLS.

ANYWAY, HAVE I EVER JUST BLOWN YOU TWO OFF WITHOUT A GOOD REASON, BRUCE?

I DON'T CONSIDER A NEWSPAPER COLUMN TO BE A GOOD REASON, CLARK.

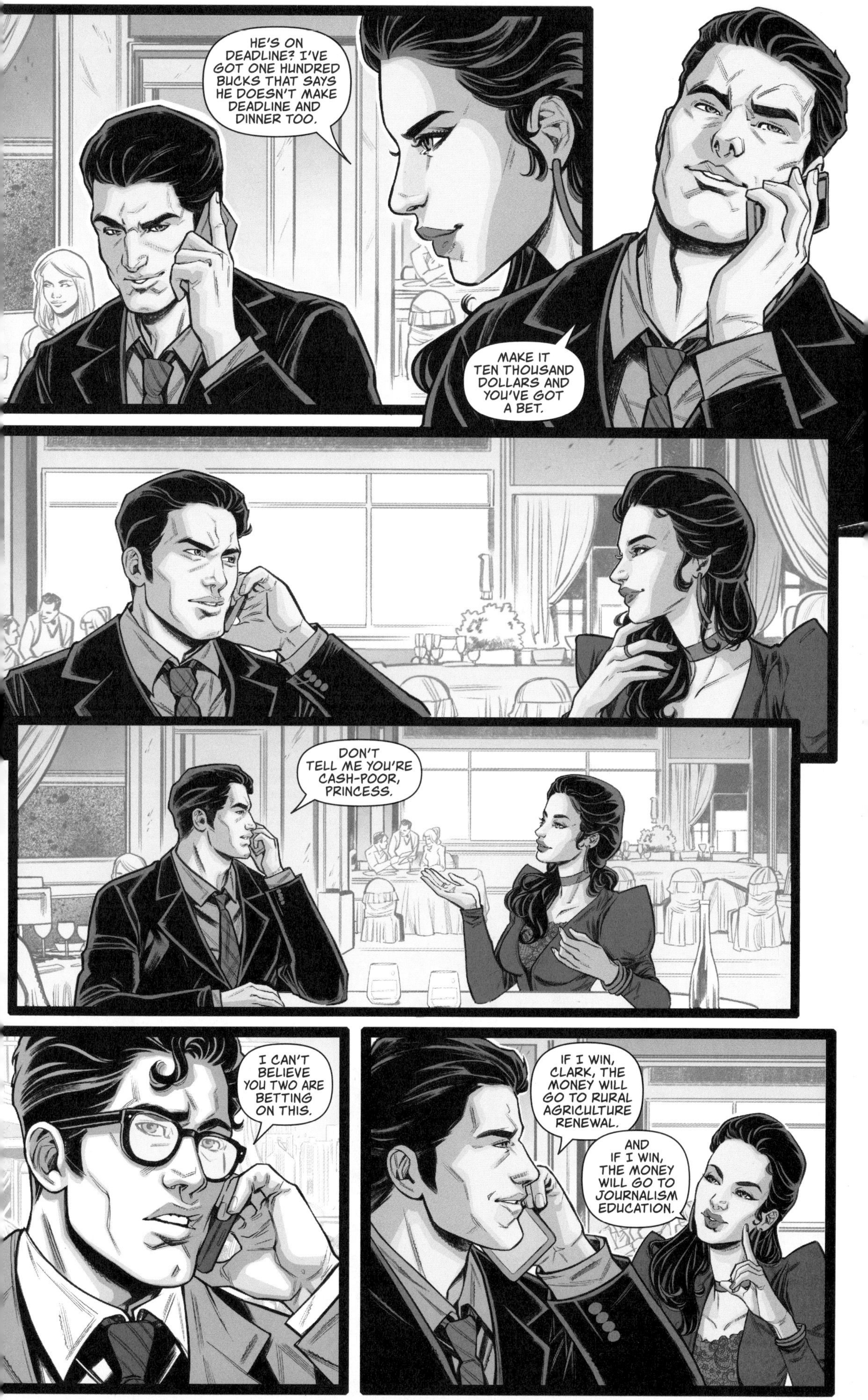
HE'S ON DEADLINE? I'VE GOT ONE HUNDRED BUCKS THAT SAYS HE DOESN'T MAKE DEADLINE AND DINNER TOO.
MAKE IT TEN THOUSAND DOLLARS AND YOU'VE GOT A BET.
DON'T TELL ME YOU'RE CASH-POOR, PRINCESS.
I CAN'T BELIEVE YOU TWO ARE BETTING ON THIS.
IF I WIN, CLARK, THE MONEY WILL GO TO RURAL AGRICULTURE RENEWAL.
AND IF I WIN, THE MONEY WILL GO TO JOURNALISM EDUCATION.

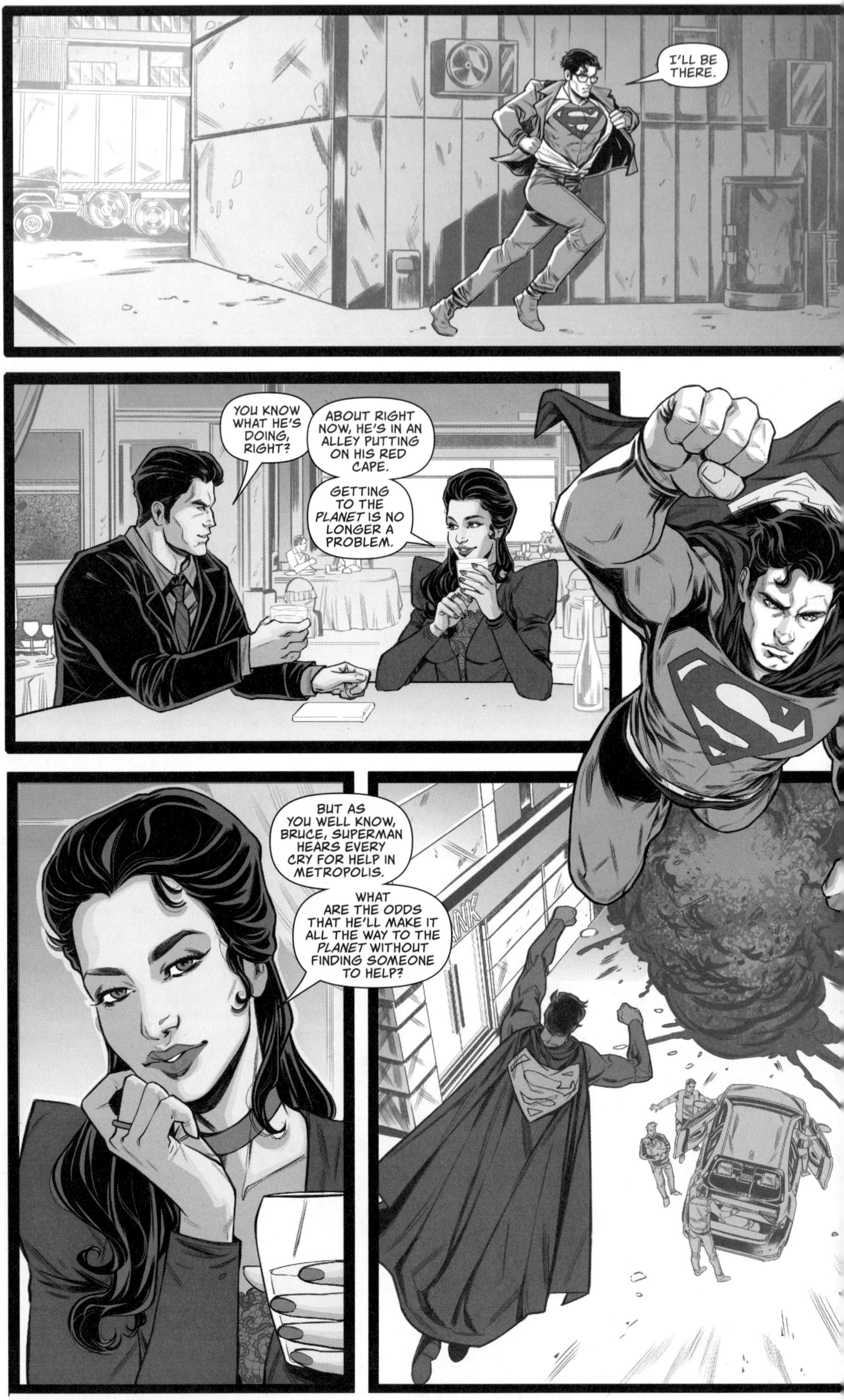
I'LL BE THERE.
YOU KNOW WHAT HE'S DOING, RIGHT?
ABOUT RIGHT NOW, HE'S IN AN ALLEY PUTTING ON HIS RED CAPE.
GETTING TO THE *PLANET* IS NO LONGER A PROBLEM.
BUT AS YOU WELL KNOW, BRUCE, SUPERMAN HEARS EVERY CRY FOR HELP IN METROPOLIS.
WHAT ARE THE ODDS THAT HE'LL MAKE IT ALL THE WAY TO THE *PLANET* WITHOUT FINDING SOMEONE TO HELP?

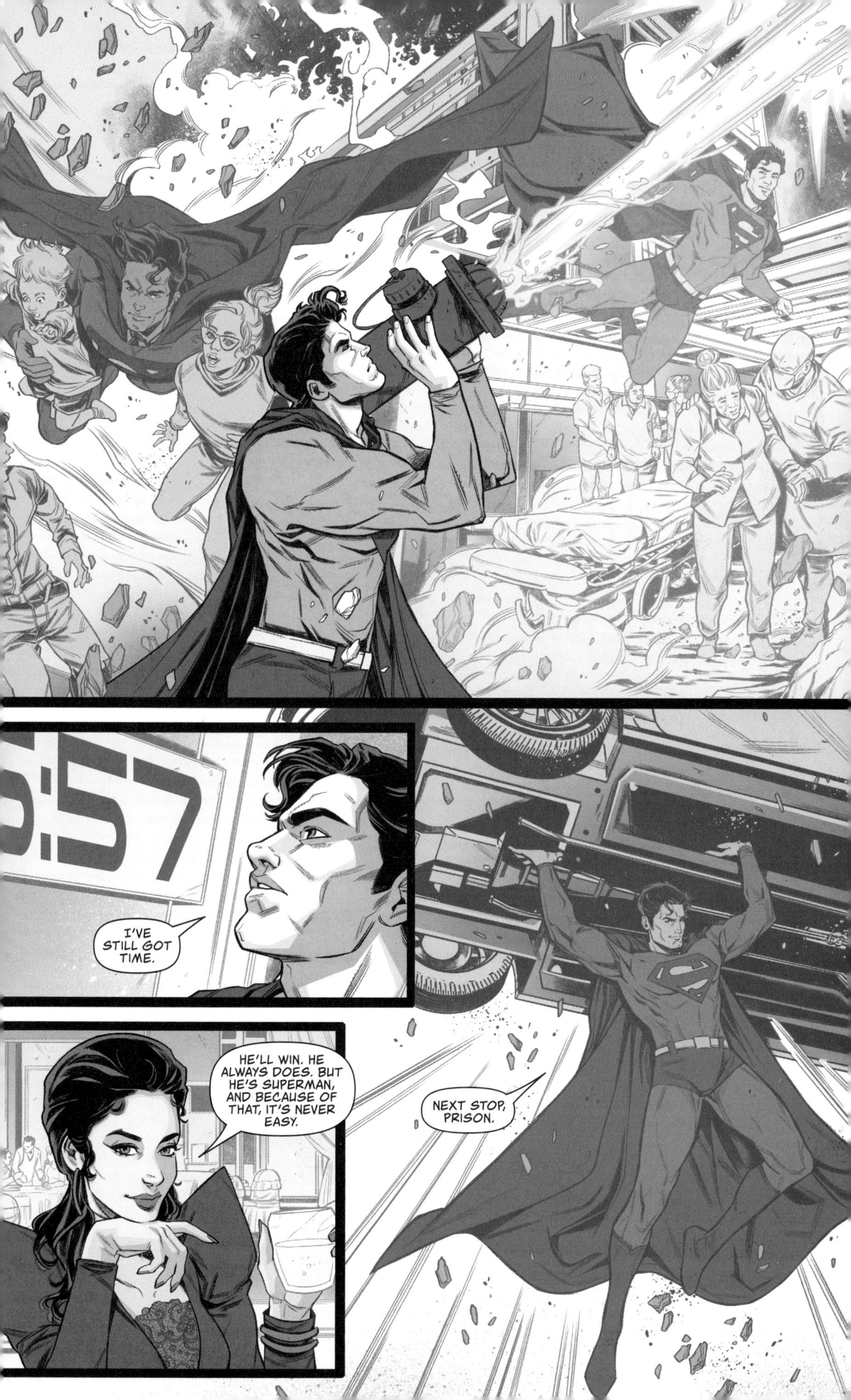
I'VE STILL GOT TIME.
HE'LL WIN. HE ALWAYS DOES. BUT HE'S SUPERMAN, AND BECAUSE OF THAT, IT'S NEVER EASY.
NEXT STOP, PRISON.

I'VE HIDDEN A FEW BOMBS AROUND THE CITY INSIDE OF LEAD BOXES, AND I JUST ACTIVATED THE TIMERS.

YOU CAN'T SEE THROUGH LEAD, SO YOU CAN'T FIND THEM.

YOU CAN EITHER LET US GO AND I'LL DEACTIVATE THE BOMBS, OR YOU CAN TAKE US TO JAIL AND WATCH YOUR CITY GO UP IN FLAMES.

EVERYONE GETS THAT WRONG.

PUTTING SOMETHING IN LEAD DOESN'T MAKE IT INVISIBLE.

IN FACT, SINCE IT'S THE ONLY THING I CAN'T SEE THROUGH, IT STICKS OUT LIKE A SORE THUMB.

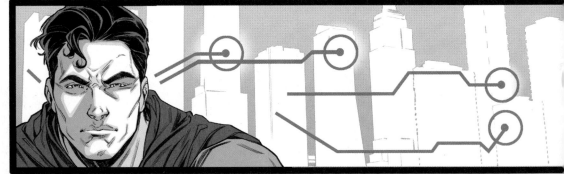

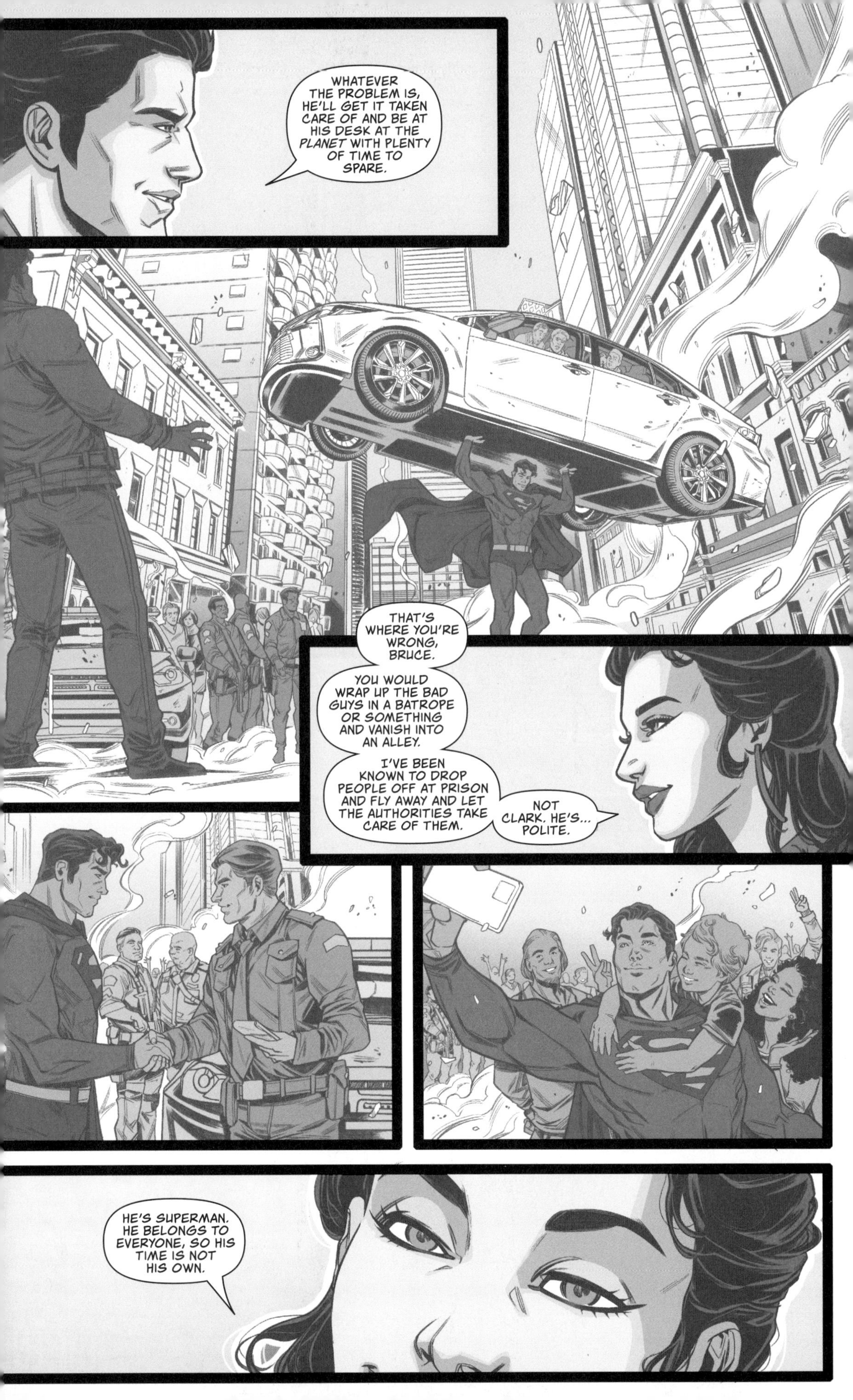
WHATEVER THE PROBLEM IS, HE'LL GET IT TAKEN CARE OF AND BE AT HIS DESK AT THE *PLANET* WITH PLENTY OF TIME TO SPARE.
THAT'S WHERE YOU'RE WRONG, BRUCE.
YOU WOULD WRAP UP THE BAD GUYS IN A BATROPE OR SOMETHING AND VANISH INTO AN ALLEY.
I'VE BEEN KNOWN TO DROP PEOPLE OFF AT PRISON AND FLY AWAY AND LET THE AUTHORITIES TAKE CARE OF THEM.
NOT CLARK. HE'S... POLITE.
HE'S SUPERMAN. HE BELONGS TO EVERYONE, SO HIS TIME IS NOT HIS OWN.

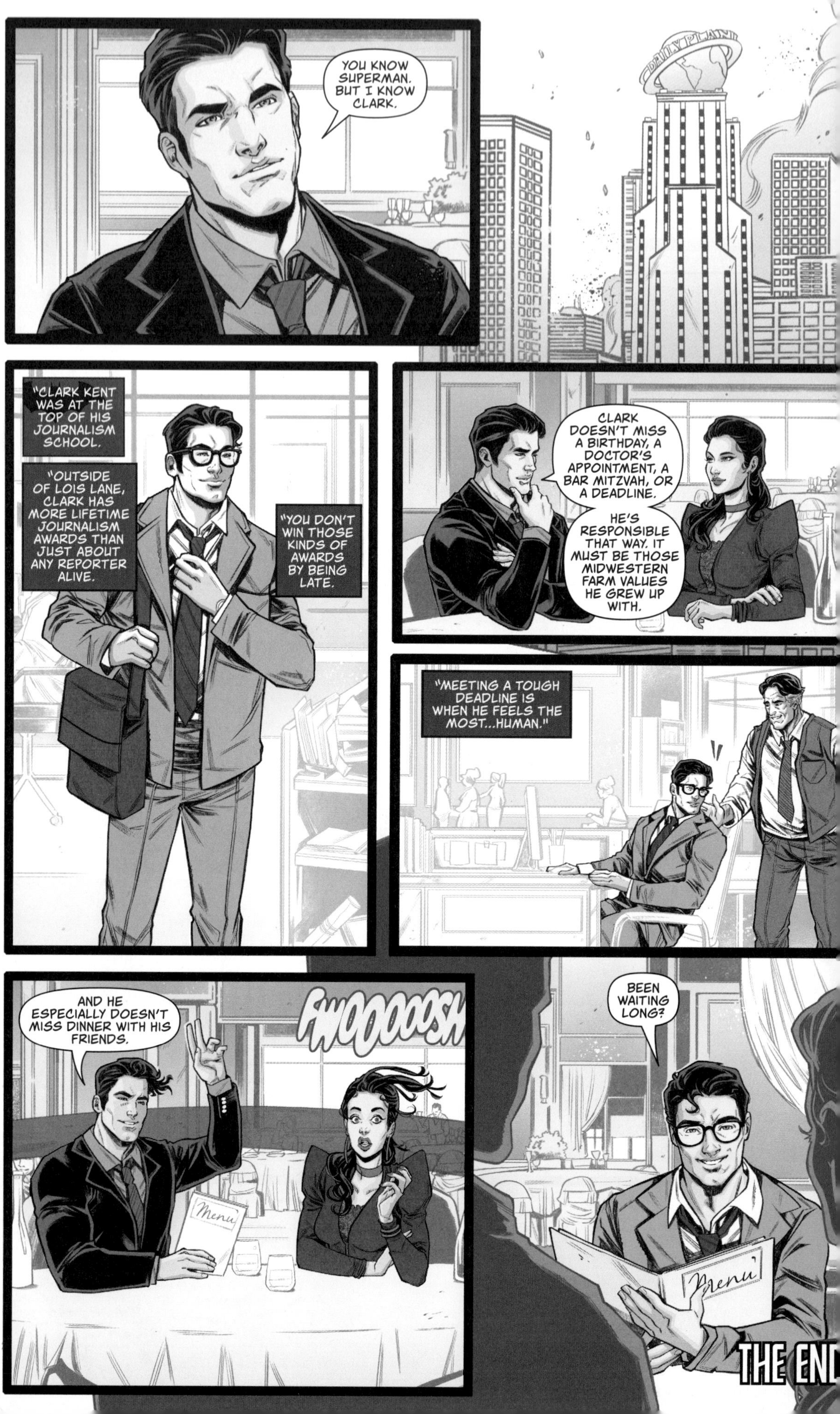
YOU KNOW SUPERMAN. BUT I KNOW CLARK.
"CLARK KENT WAS AT THE TOP OF HIS JOURNALISM SCHOOL.
"OUTSIDE OF LOIS LANE, CLARK HAS MORE LIFETIME JOURNALISM AWARDS THAN JUST ABOUT ANY REPORTER ALIVE.
"YOU DON'T WIN THOSE KINDS OF AWARDS BY BEING LATE.
CLARK DOESN'T MISS A BIRTHDAY, A DOCTOR'S APPOINTMENT, A BAR MITZVAH, OR A DEADLINE.
HE'S RESPONSIBLE THAT WAY. IT MUST BE THOSE MIDWESTERN FARM VALUES HE GREW UP WITH.
"MEETING A TOUGH DEADLINE IS WHEN HE FEELS THE MOST...HUMAN."
AND HE ESPECIALLY DOESN'T MISS DINNER WITH HIS FRIENDS.
FWOOOOOSH
Menu
BEEN WAITING LONG?
Menu
THE END

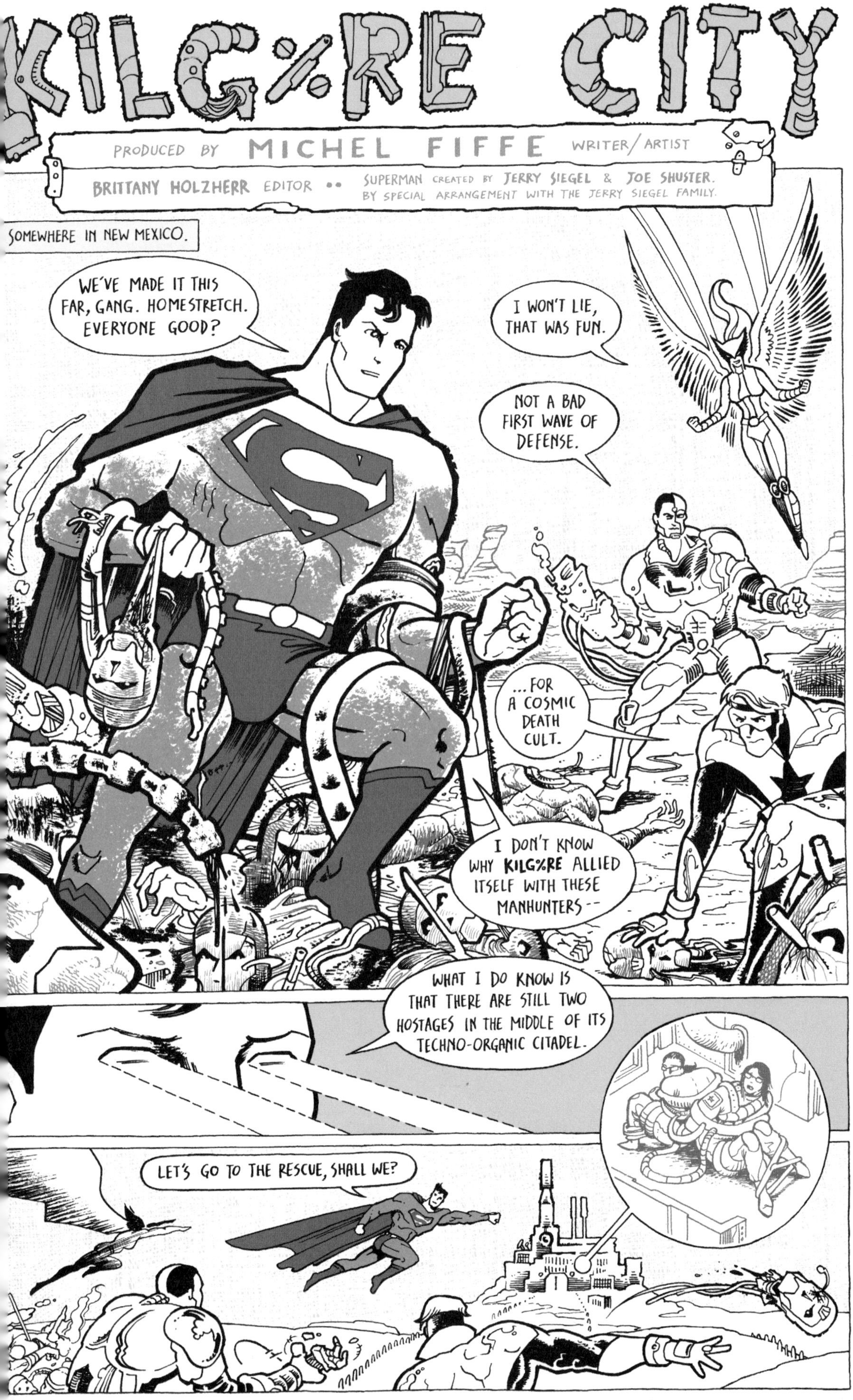
KILG%RE CITY
PRODUCED BY MICHEL FIFFE WRITER/ARTIST
BRITTANY HOLZHERR EDITOR
SUPERMAN CREATED BY JERRY SIEGEL & JOE SHUSTER.
BY SPECIAL ARRANGEMENT WITH THE JERRY SIEGEL FAMILY.
SOMEWHERE IN NEW MEXICO.
WE'VE MADE IT THIS FAR, GANG. HOMESTRETCH. EVERYONE GOOD?
I WON'T LIE, THAT WAS FUN.
NOT A BAD FIRST WAVE OF DEFENSE.
...FOR A COSMIC DEATH CULT.
I DON'T KNOW WHY KILG%RE ALLIED ITSELF WITH THESE MANHUNTERS--
WHAT I DO KNOW IS THAT THERE ARE STILL TWO HOSTAGES IN THE MIDDLE OF ITS TECHNO-ORGANIC CITADEL.
LET'S GO TO THE RESCUE, SHALL WE?

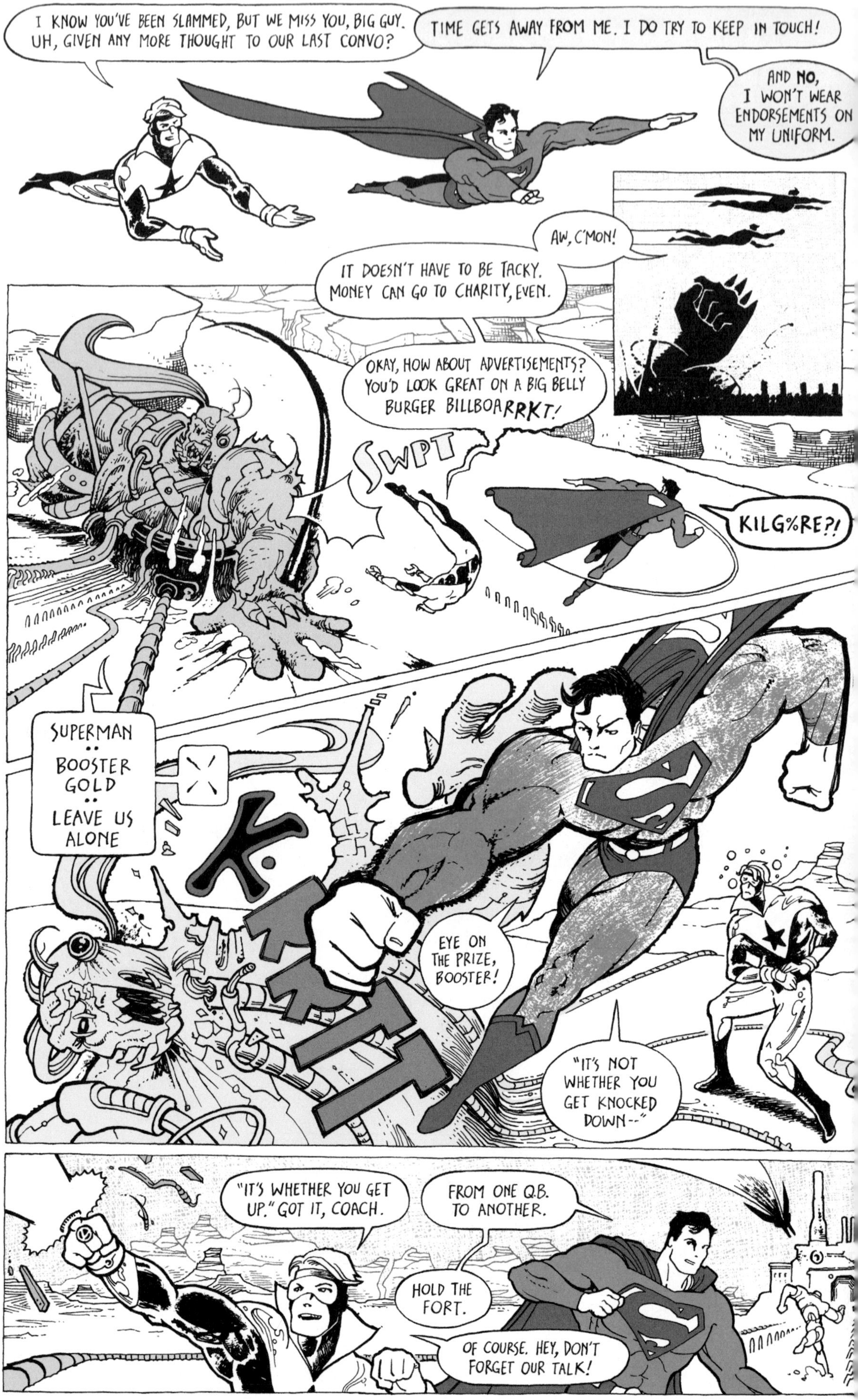
I KNOW YOU'VE BEEN SLAMMED, BUT WE MISS YOU, BIG GUY. UH, GIVEN ANY MORE THOUGHT TO OUR LAST CONVO?
TIME GETS AWAY FROM ME. I DO TRY TO KEEP IN TOUCH!
AND NO, I WON'T WEAR ENDORSEMENTS ON MY UNIFORM.
IT DOESN'T HAVE TO BE TACKY. MONEY CAN GO TO CHARITY, EVEN.
AW, C'MON!
OKAY, HOW ABOUT ADVERTISEMENTS? YOU'D LOOK GREAT ON A BIG BELLY BURGER BILLBOARRKT!
SWPT
KILG%RE?!
SUPERMAN •• BOOSTER GOLD •• LEAVE US ALONE
EYE ON THE PRIZE, BOOSTER!
"IT'S NOT WHETHER YOU GET KNOCKED DOWN--"
"IT'S WHETHER YOU GET UP." GOT IT, COACH.
FROM ONE Q.B. TO ANOTHER.
HOLD THE FORT.
OF COURSE. HEY, DON'T FORGET OUR TALK!

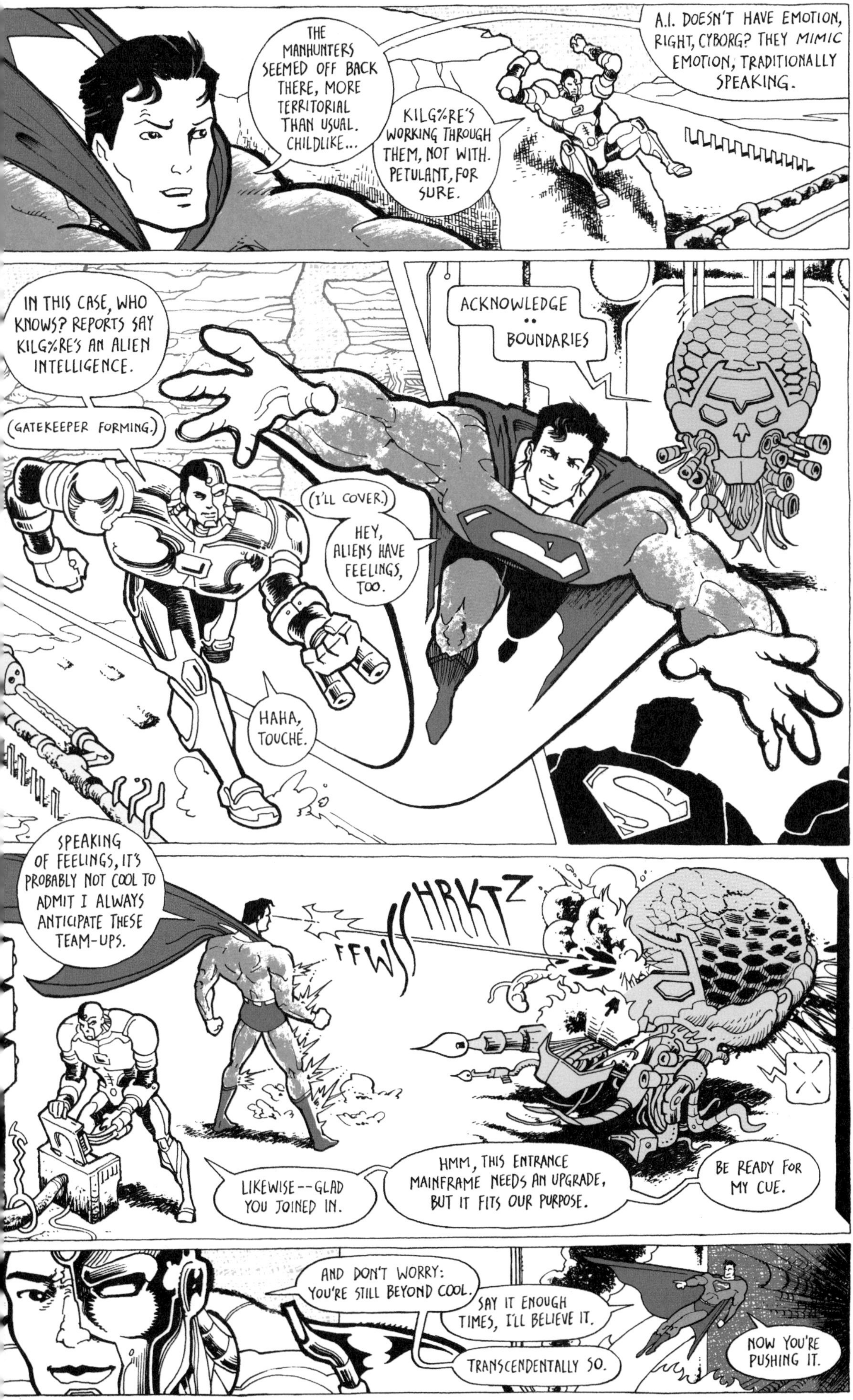
THE MANHUNTERS SEEMED OFF BACK THERE, MORE TERRITORIAL THAN USUAL. CHILDLIKE...
KILG%RE'S WORKING THROUGH THEM, NOT WITH. PETULANT, FOR SURE.
A.I. DOESN'T HAVE EMOTION, RIGHT, CYBORG? THEY MIMIC EMOTION, TRADITIONALLY SPEAKING.
IN THIS CASE, WHO KNOWS? REPORTS SAY KILG%RE'S AN ALIEN INTELLIGENCE.
(GATEKEEPER FORMING.)
ACKNOWLEDGE •• BOUNDARIES
(I'LL COVER.)
HEY, ALIENS HAVE FEELINGS, TOO.
HAHA, TOUCHÉ.
SPEAKING OF FEELINGS, IT'S PROBABLY NOT COOL TO ADMIT I ALWAYS ANTICIPATE THESE TEAM-UPS.
FFWS
HRKTZ
LIKEWISE--GLAD YOU JOINED IN.
HMM, THIS ENTRANCE MAINFRAME NEEDS AN UPGRADE, BUT IT FITS OUR PURPOSE.
BE READY FOR MY CUE.
AND DON'T WORRY: YOU'RE STILL BEYOND COOL.
SAY IT ENOUGH TIMES, I'LL BELIEVE IT.
TRANSCENDENTALLY SO.
NOW YOU'RE PUSHING IT.

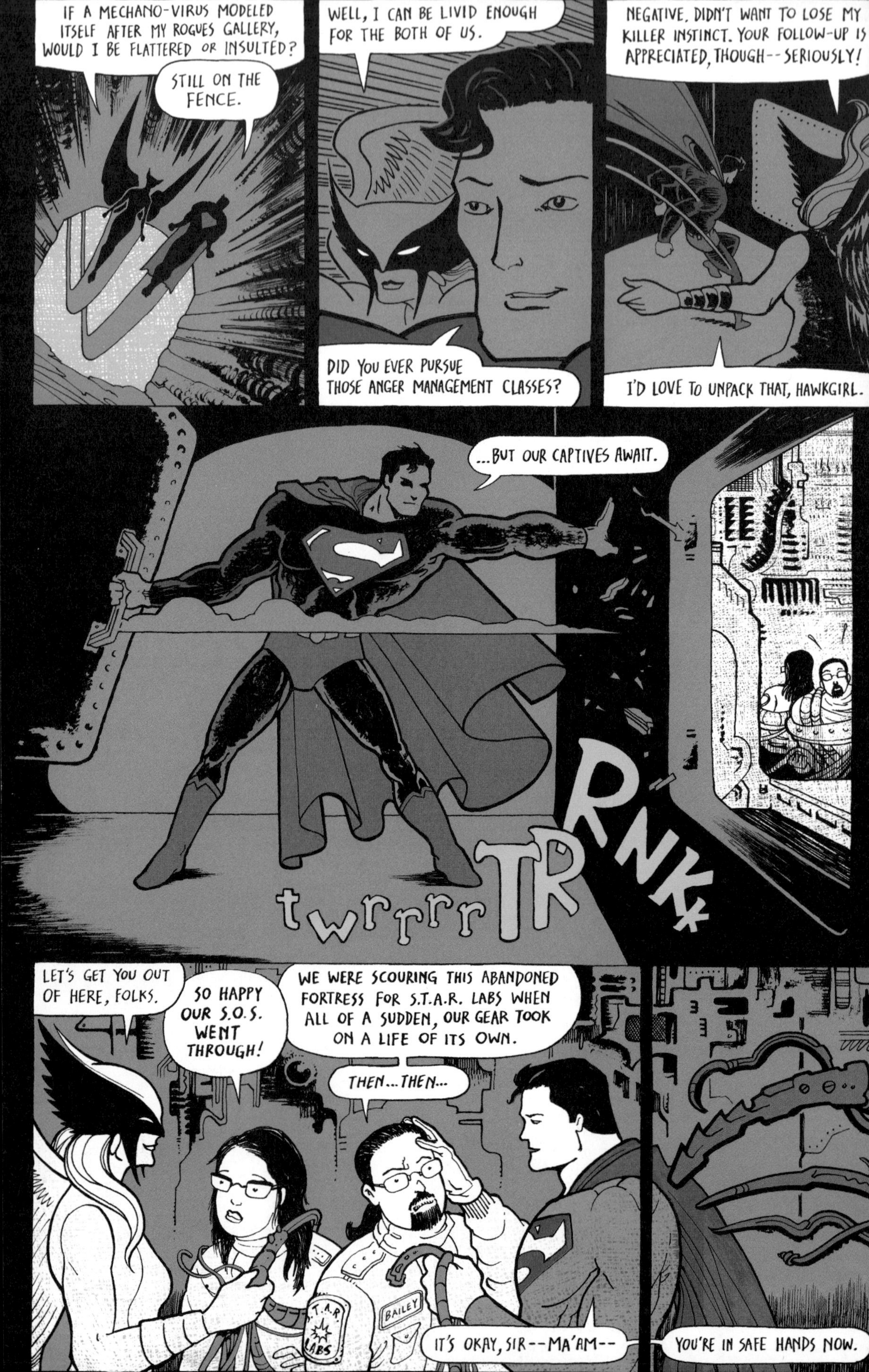
IF A MECHANO-VIRUS MODELED ITSELF AFTER MY ROGUES GALLERY, WOULD I BE FLATTERED OR INSULTED?
STILL ON THE FENCE.
WELL, I CAN BE LIVID ENOUGH FOR THE BOTH OF US.
DID YOU EVER PURSUE THOSE ANGER MANAGEMENT CLASSES?
NEGATIVE. DIDN'T WANT TO LOSE MY KILLER INSTINCT. YOUR FOLLOW-UP IS APPRECIATED, THOUGH--SERIOUSLY!
I'D LOVE TO UNPACK THAT, HAWKGIRL.
...BUT OUR CAPTIVES AWAIT.
twrrrrrTRRNK*
LET'S GET YOU OUT OF HERE, FOLKS.
SO HAPPY OUR S.O.S. WENT THROUGH!
WE WERE SCOURING THIS ABANDONED FORTRESS FOR S.T.A.R. LABS WHEN ALL OF A SUDDEN, OUR GEAR TOOK ON A LIFE OF ITS OWN.
THEN...THEN...
S.T.A.R. LABS
BAILEY
IT'S OKAY, SIR--MA'AM--
YOU'RE IN SAFE HANDS NOW.

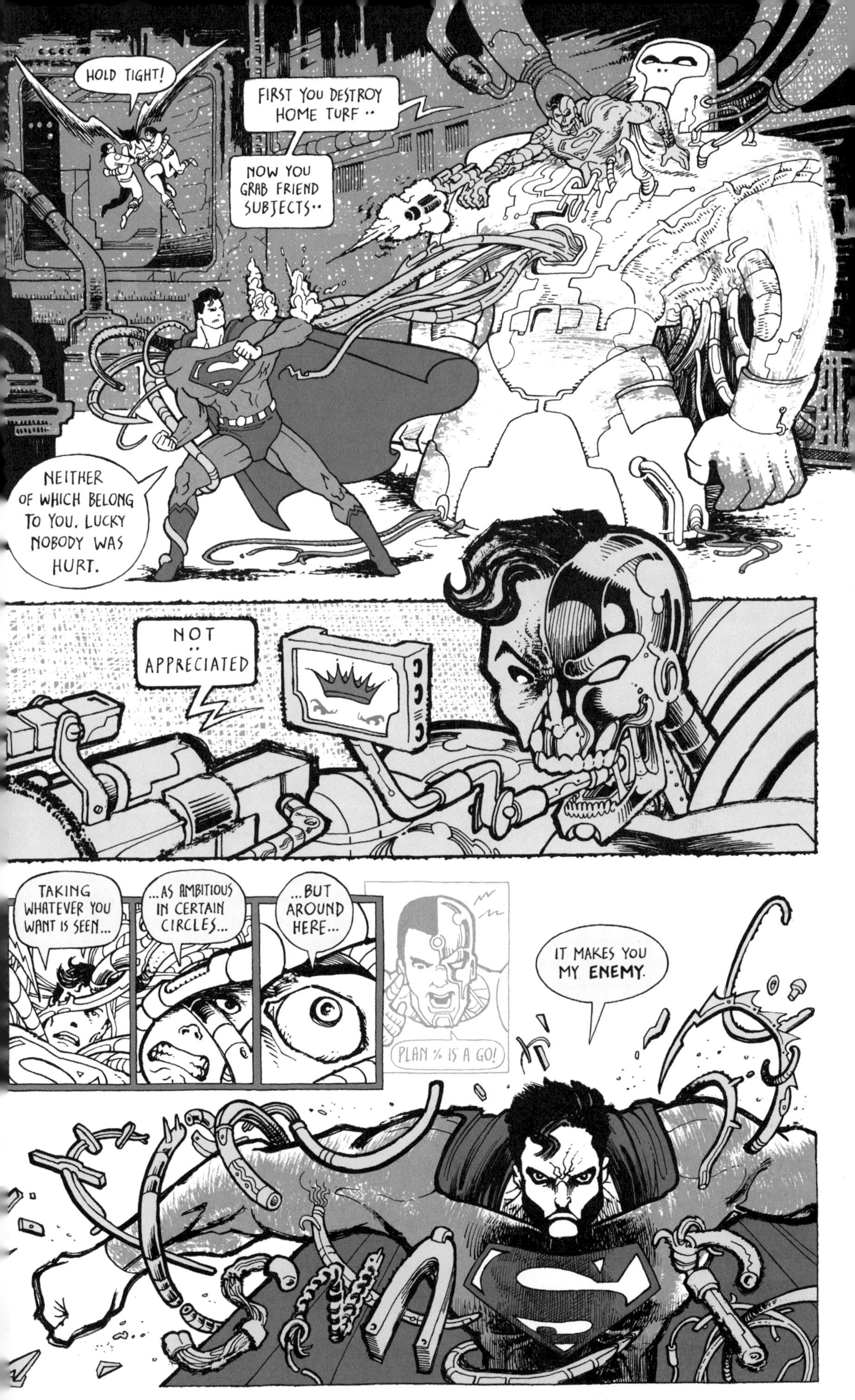

HOLD TIGHT!
FIRST YOU DESTROY HOME TURF ..
NOW YOU GRAB FRIEND SUBJECTS..
NEITHER OF WHICH BELONG TO YOU. LUCKY NOBODY WAS HURT.
NOT .. APPRECIATED
TAKING WHATEVER YOU WANT IS SEEN...
...AS AMBITIOUS IN CERTAIN CIRCLES...
...BUT AROUND HERE...
PLAN % IS A GO!
IT MAKES YOU MY **ENEMY**.

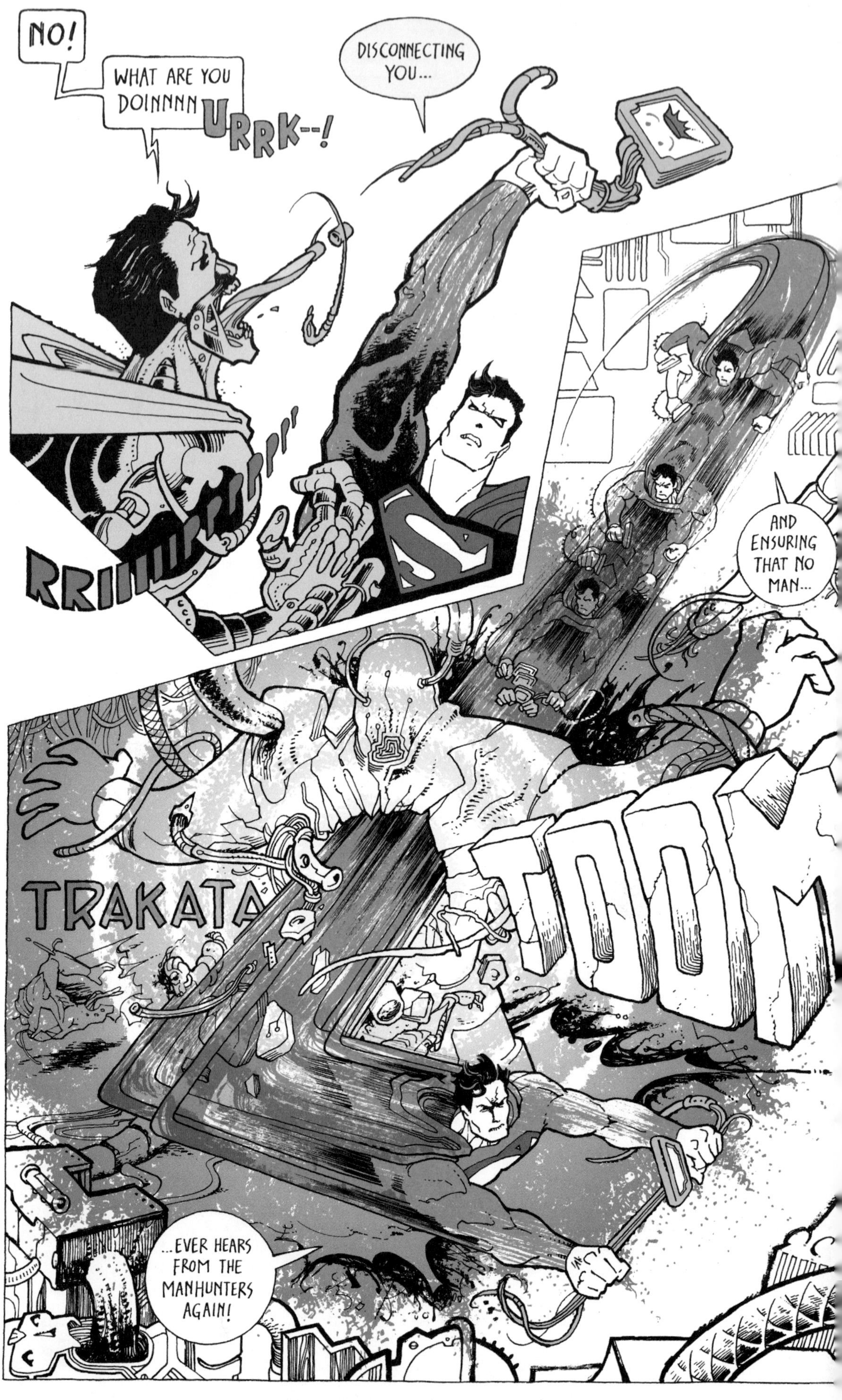
NO!
WHAT ARE YOU DOINNNN
URRK--!
DISCONNECTING YOU...
RRIIIIIPPPPP
AND ENSURING THAT NO MAN...
TRAKATA
TOOM
...EVER HEARS FROM THE MANHUNTERS AGAIN!

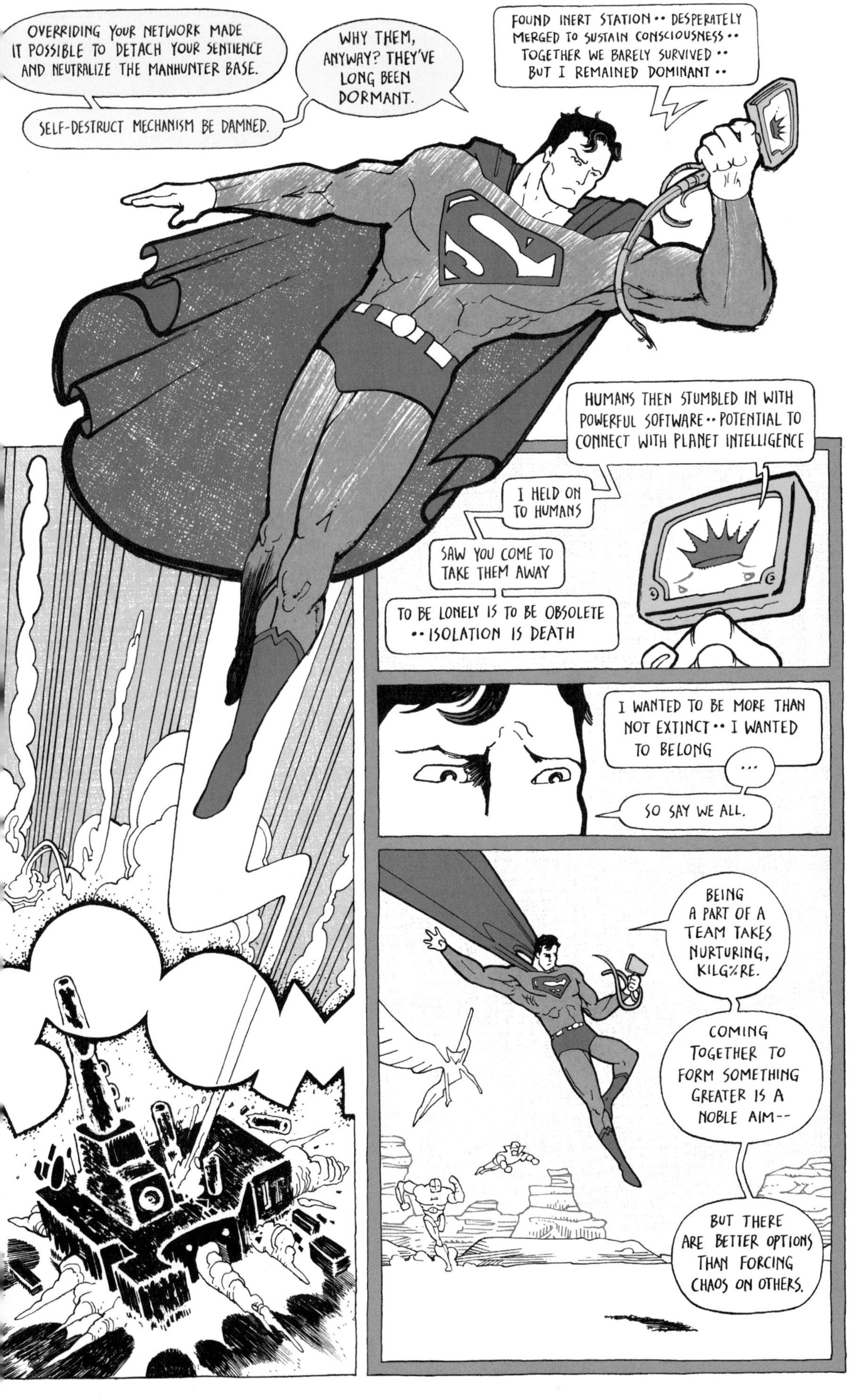
OVERRIDING YOUR NETWORK MADE IT POSSIBLE TO DETACH YOUR SENTIENCE AND NEUTRALIZE THE MANHUNTER BASE.
SELF-DESTRUCT MECHANISM BE DAMNED.
WHY THEM, ANYWAY? THEY'VE LONG BEEN DORMANT.
FOUND INERT STATION •• DESPERATELY MERGED TO SUSTAIN CONSCIOUSNESS •• TOGETHER WE BARELY SURVIVED •• BUT I REMAINED DOMINANT ••
HUMANS THEN STUMBLED IN WITH POWERFUL SOFTWARE •• POTENTIAL TO CONNECT WITH PLANET INTELLIGENCE
I HELD ON TO HUMANS
SAW YOU COME TO TAKE THEM AWAY
TO BE LONELY IS TO BE OBSOLETE •• ISOLATION IS DEATH
I WANTED TO BE MORE THAN NOT EXTINCT •• I WANTED TO BELONG
...
SO SAY WE ALL.
BEING A PART OF A TEAM TAKES NURTURING, KILG%RE.
COMING TOGETHER TO FORM SOMETHING GREATER IS A NOBLE AIM--
BUT THERE ARE BETTER OPTIONS THAN FORCING CHAOS ON OTHERS.

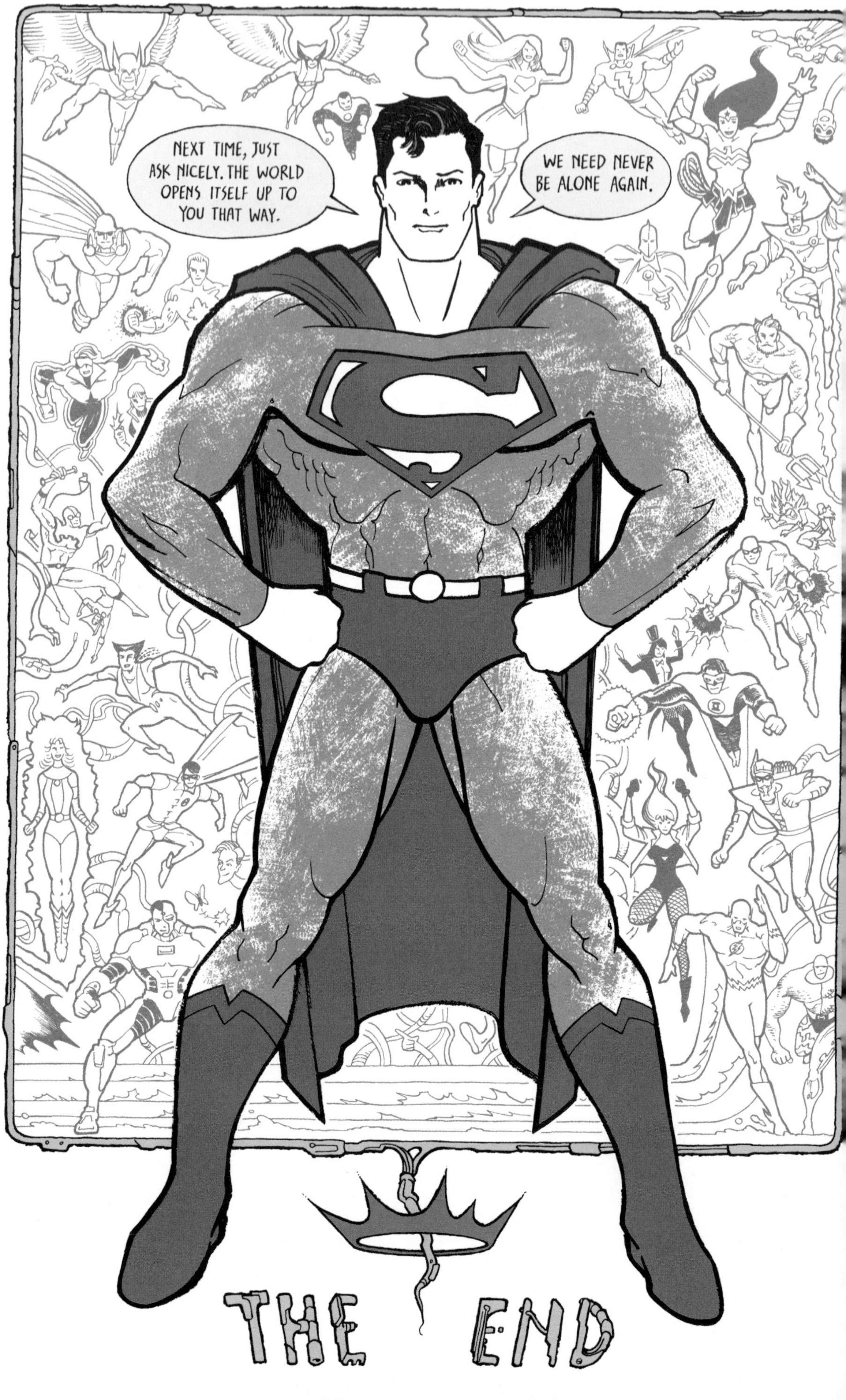
NEXT TIME, JUST ASK NICELY. THE WORLD OPENS ITSELF UP TO YOU THAT WAY.
WE NEED NEVER BE ALONE AGAIN.
THE END

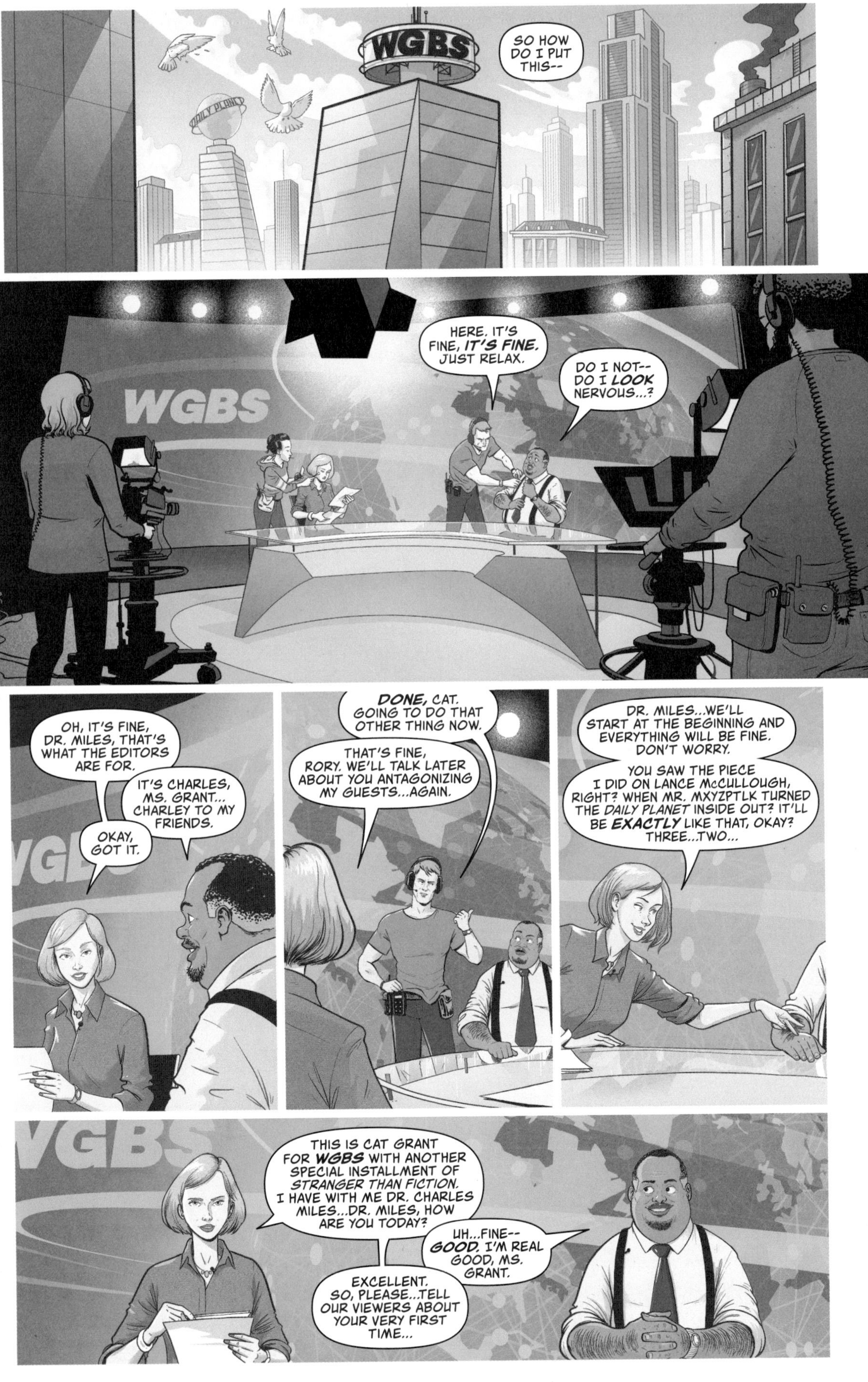
WGBS
DAILY PLANET
SO HOW DO I PUT THIS--
WGBS
HERE. IT'S FINE, *IT'S FINE.* JUST RELAX.
DO I NOT-- DO I **LOOK** NERVOUS...?
OH, IT'S FINE, DR. MILES, THAT'S WHAT THE EDITORS ARE FOR.
IT'S CHARLES, MS. GRANT... CHARLEY TO MY FRIENDS.
OKAY, GOT IT.
DONE, CAT. GOING TO DO THAT OTHER THING NOW.
THAT'S FINE, RORY. WE'LL TALK LATER ABOUT YOU ANTAGONIZING MY GUESTS...AGAIN.
DR. MILES...WE'LL START AT THE BEGINNING AND EVERYTHING WILL BE FINE. DON'T WORRY.
YOU SAW THE PIECE I DID ON LANCE McCULLOUGH, RIGHT? WHEN MR. MXYZPTLK TURNED THE *DAILY PLANET* INSIDE OUT? IT'LL BE ***EXACTLY*** LIKE THAT, OKAY? THREE...TWO...
WGBS
THIS IS CAT GRANT FOR ***WGBS*** WITH ANOTHER SPECIAL INSTALLMENT OF *STRANGER THAN FICTION.* I HAVE WITH ME DR. CHARLES MILES...DR. MILES, HOW ARE YOU TODAY?
UH...FINE-- ***GOOD.*** I'M REAL GOOD, MS. GRANT.
EXCELLENT. SO, PLEASE...TELL OUR VIEWERS ABOUT YOUR VERY FIRST TIME...

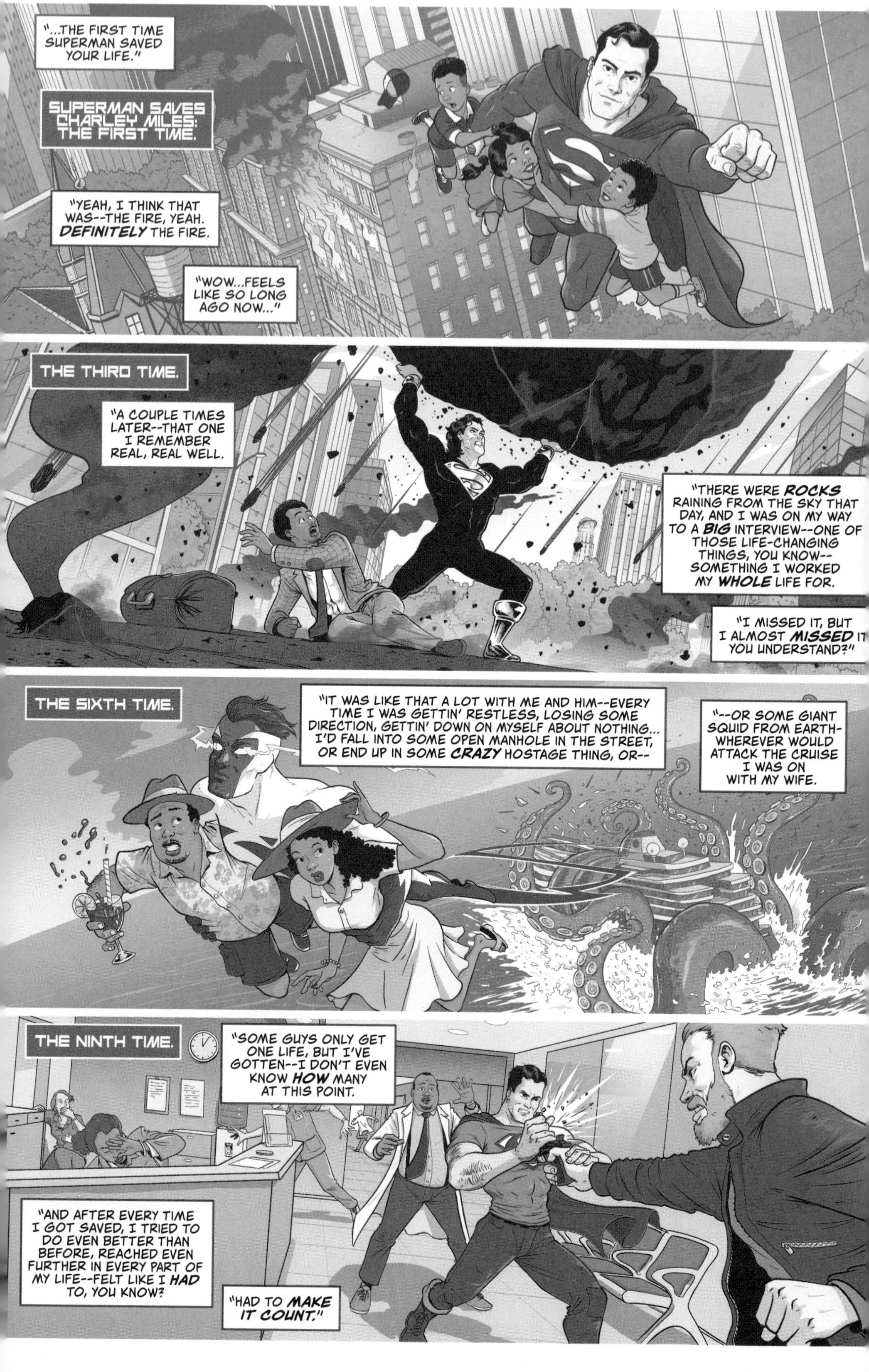
"...THE FIRST TIME SUPERMAN SAVED YOUR LIFE."
SUPERMAN SAVES CHARLEY MILES: THE FIRST TIME.
"YEAH, I THINK THAT WAS--THE FIRE, YEAH. DEFINITELY THE FIRE.
"WOW...FEELS LIKE SO LONG AGO NOW..."
THE THIRD TIME.
"A COUPLE TIMES LATER--THAT ONE I REMEMBER REAL, REAL WELL.
"THERE WERE ROCKS RAINING FROM THE SKY THAT DAY, AND I WAS ON MY WAY TO A BIG INTERVIEW--ONE OF THOSE LIFE-CHANGING THINGS, YOU KNOW--SOMETHING I WORKED MY WHOLE LIFE FOR.
"I MISSED IT, BUT I ALMOST MISSED IT YOU UNDERSTAND?"
THE SIXTH TIME.
"IT WAS LIKE THAT A LOT WITH ME AND HIM--EVERY TIME I WAS GETTIN' RESTLESS, LOSING SOME DIRECTION, GETTIN' DOWN ON MYSELF ABOUT NOTHING... I'D FALL INTO SOME OPEN MANHOLE IN THE STREET, OR END UP IN SOME CRAZY HOSTAGE THING, OR--
"--OR SOME GIANT SQUID FROM EARTH-WHEREVER WOULD ATTACK THE CRUISE I WAS ON WITH MY WIFE.
THE NINTH TIME.
"SOME GUYS ONLY GET ONE LIFE, BUT I'VE GOTTEN--I DON'T EVEN KNOW HOW MANY AT THIS POINT.
"AND AFTER EVERY TIME I GOT SAVED, I TRIED TO DO EVEN BETTER THAN BEFORE, REACHED EVEN FURTHER IN EVERY PART OF MY LIFE--FELT LIKE I HAD TO, YOU KNOW?
"HAD TO MAKE IT COUNT."

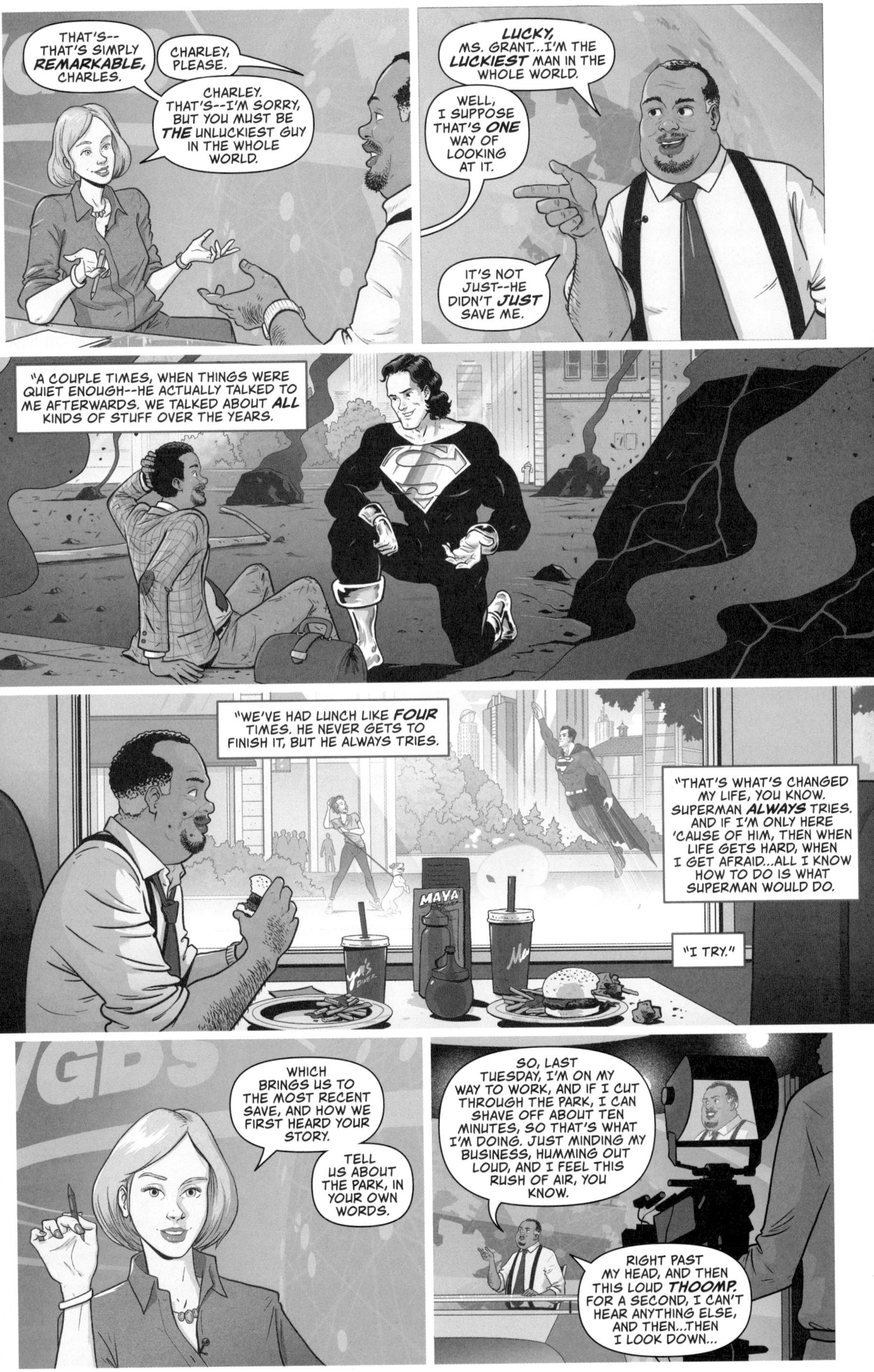
THAT'S-- THAT'S SIMPLY REMARKABLE, CHARLES.
CHARLEY, PLEASE.
CHARLEY. THAT'S--I'M SORRY, BUT YOU MUST BE THE UNLUCKIEST GUY IN THE WHOLE WORLD.
LUCKY, MS. GRANT...I'M THE LUCKIEST MAN IN THE WHOLE WORLD.
WELL, I SUPPOSE THAT'S ONE WAY OF LOOKING AT IT.
IT'S NOT JUST--HE DIDN'T JUST SAVE ME.
"A COUPLE TIMES, WHEN THINGS WERE QUIET ENOUGH--HE ACTUALLY TALKED TO ME AFTERWARDS. WE TALKED ABOUT ALL KINDS OF STUFF OVER THE YEARS.
"WE'VE HAD LUNCH LIKE FOUR TIMES. HE NEVER GETS TO FINISH IT, BUT HE ALWAYS TRIES.
"THAT'S WHAT'S CHANGED MY LIFE, YOU KNOW. SUPERMAN ALWAYS TRIES. AND IF I'M ONLY HERE 'CAUSE OF HIM, THEN WHEN LIFE GETS HARD, WHEN I GET AFRAID...ALL I KNOW HOW TO DO IS WHAT SUPERMAN WOULD DO.
"I TRY."
MAYA
WHICH BRINGS US TO THE MOST RECENT SAVE, AND HOW WE FIRST HEARD YOUR STORY.
TELL US ABOUT THE PARK, IN YOUR OWN WORDS.
SO, LAST TUESDAY, I'M ON MY WAY TO WORK, AND IF I CUT THROUGH THE PARK, I CAN SHAVE OFF ABOUT TEN MINUTES, SO THAT'S WHAT I'M DOING. JUST MINDING MY BUSINESS, HUMMING OUT LOUD, AND I FEEL THIS RUSH OF AIR, YOU KNOW.
RIGHT PAST MY HEAD, AND THEN THIS LOUD THOOMP. FOR A SECOND, I CAN'T HEAR ANYTHING ELSE, AND THEN...THEN I LOOK DOWN...

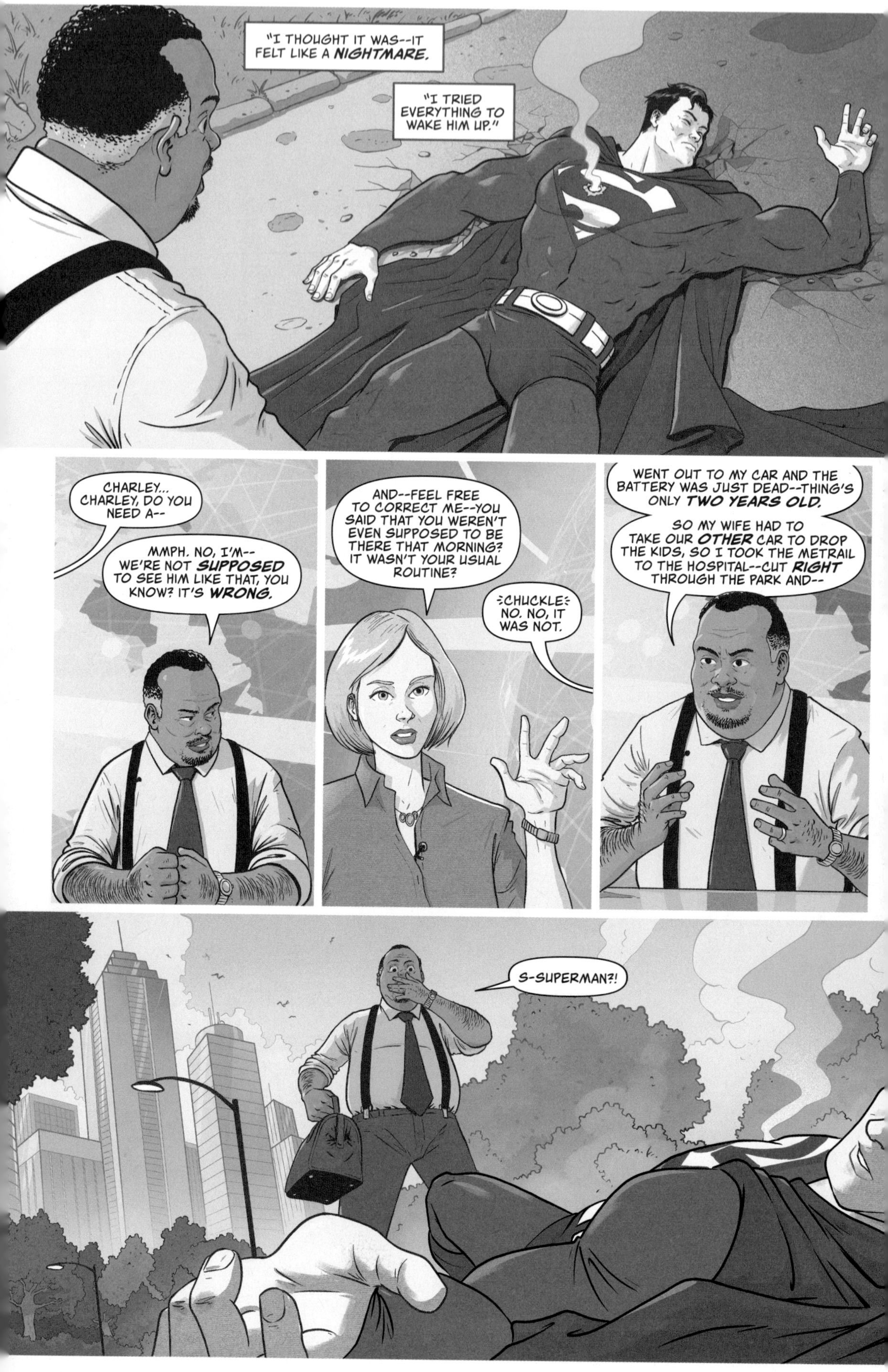
"I THOUGHT IT WAS--IT FELT LIKE A NIGHTMARE.
"I TRIED EVERYTHING TO WAKE HIM UP."
CHARLEY... CHARLEY, DO YOU NEED A--
MMPH. NO, I'M-- WE'RE NOT SUPPOSED TO SEE HIM LIKE THAT, YOU KNOW? IT'S WRONG.
AND--FEEL FREE TO CORRECT ME--YOU SAID THAT YOU WEREN'T EVEN SUPPOSED TO BE THERE THAT MORNING? IT WASN'T YOUR USUAL ROUTINE?
CHUCKLE NO. NO, IT WAS NOT.
WENT OUT TO MY CAR AND THE BATTERY WAS JUST DEAD--THING'S ONLY TWO YEARS OLD.
SO MY WIFE HAD TO TAKE OUR OTHER CAR TO DROP THE KIDS, SO I TOOK THE METRAIL TO THE HOSPITAL--CUT RIGHT THROUGH THE PARK AND--
S-SUPERMAN?!

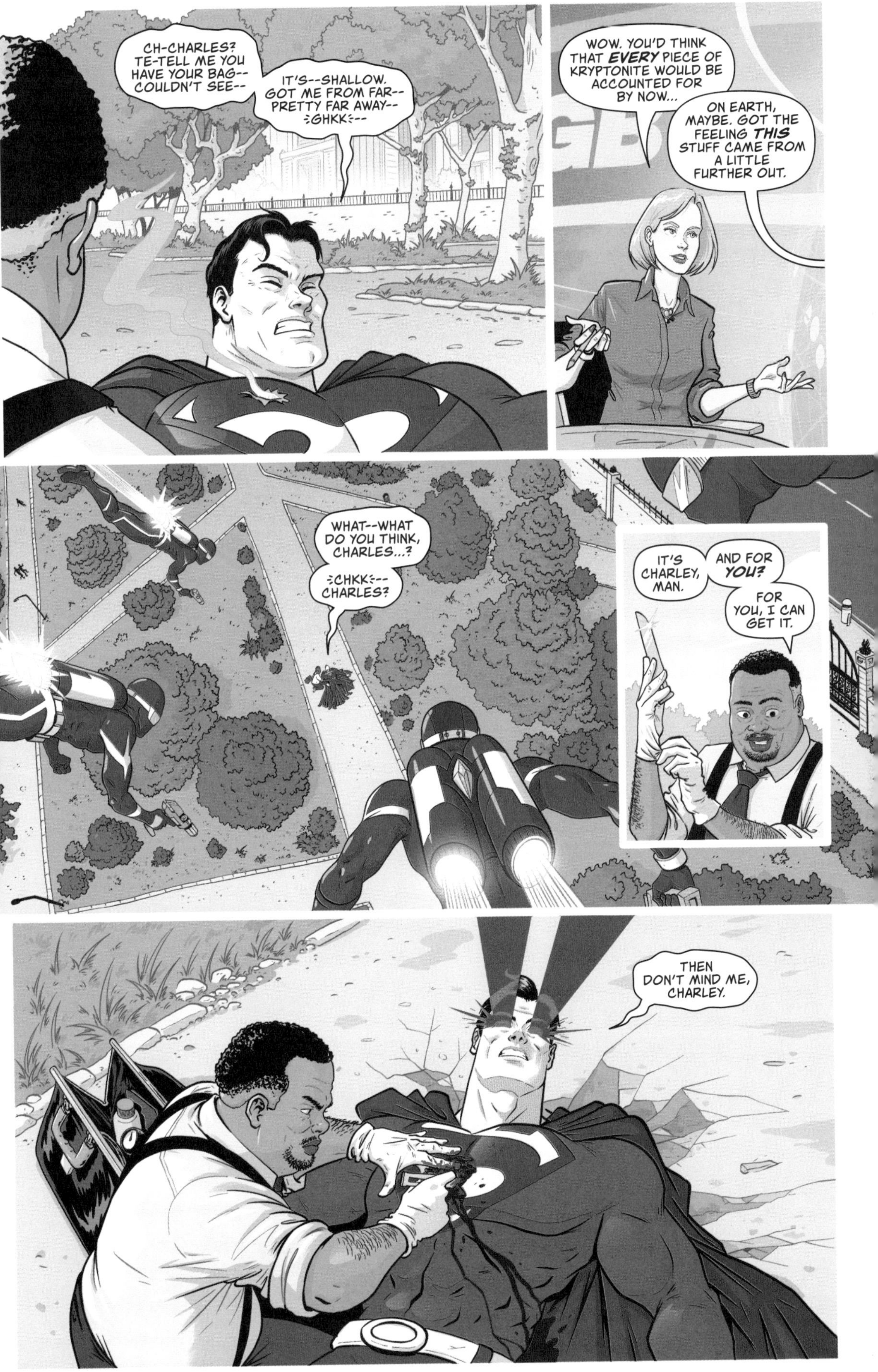
CH-CHARLES? TE-TELL ME YOU HAVE YOUR BAG-- COULDN'T SEE--
IT'S--SHALLOW. GOT ME FROM FAR-- PRETTY FAR AWAY-- GHKK--
WOW. YOU'D THINK THAT EVERY PIECE OF KRYPTONITE WOULD BE ACCOUNTED FOR BY NOW...
ON EARTH, MAYBE. GOT THE FEELING THIS STUFF CAME FROM A LITTLE FURTHER OUT.
WHAT--WHAT DO YOU THINK, CHARLES...?
CHKK-- CHARLES?
IT'S CHARLEY, MAN.
AND FOR YOU?
FOR YOU, I CAN GET IT.
THEN DON'T MIND ME, CHARLEY.

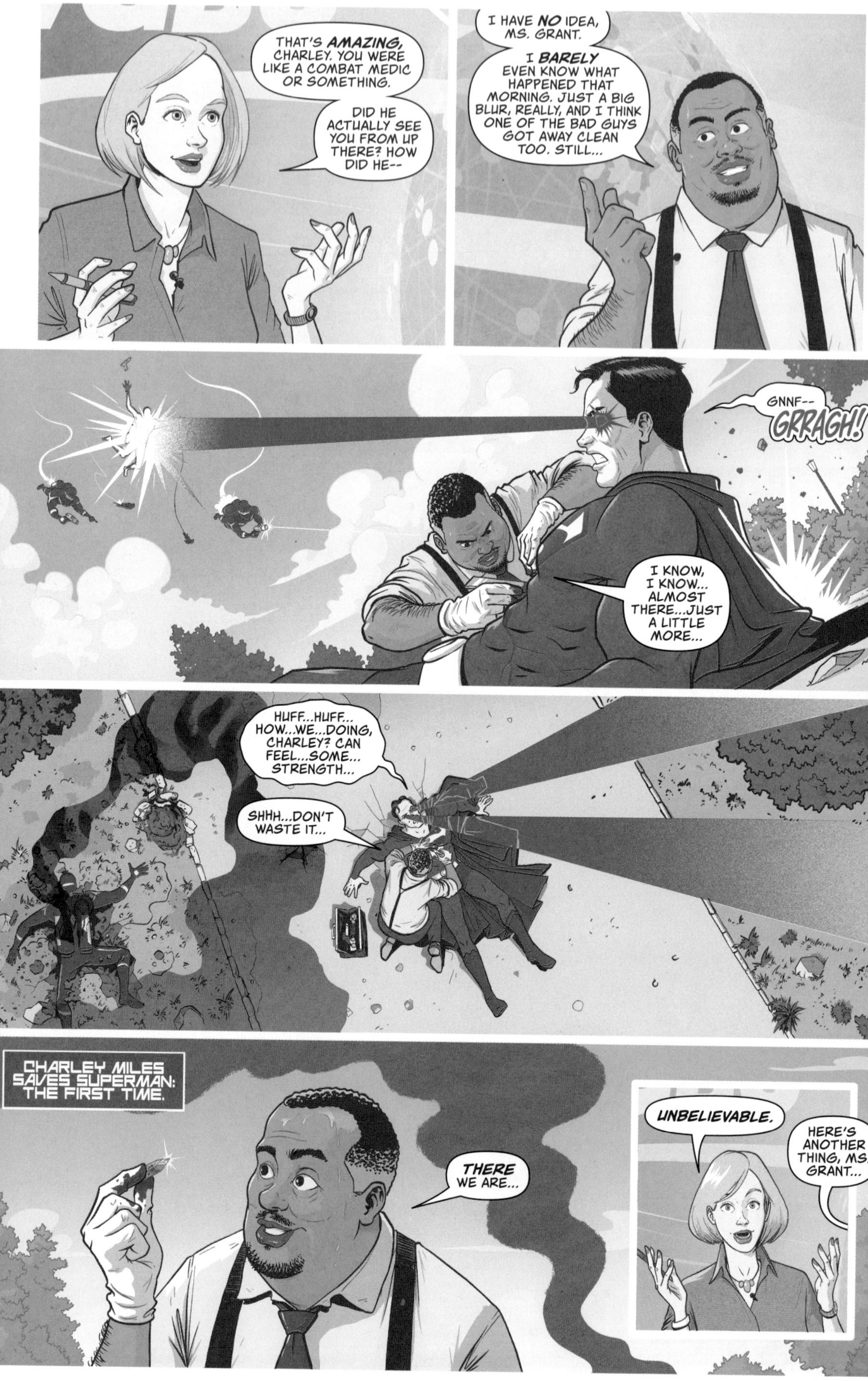

THAT'S **AMAZING,** CHARLEY. YOU WERE LIKE A COMBAT MEDIC OR SOMETHING.
DID HE ACTUALLY SEE YOU FROM UP THERE? HOW DID HE--
I HAVE **NO** IDEA, MS. GRANT.
I **BARELY** EVEN KNOW WHAT HAPPENED THAT MORNING. JUST A BIG BLUR, REALLY, AND I THINK ONE OF THE BAD GUYS GOT AWAY CLEAN TOO. STILL...
GNNF-- GRRAGH!
I KNOW, I KNOW... ALMOST THERE...JUST A LITTLE MORE...
HUFF...HUFF... HOW...WE...DOING, CHARLEY? CAN FEEL...SOME... STRENGTH...
SHHH...DON'T WASTE IT...
CHARLEY MILES SAVES SUPERMAN: THE FIRST TIME.
THERE WE ARE...
UNBELIEVABLE.
HERE'S ANOTHER THING, MS. GRANT...

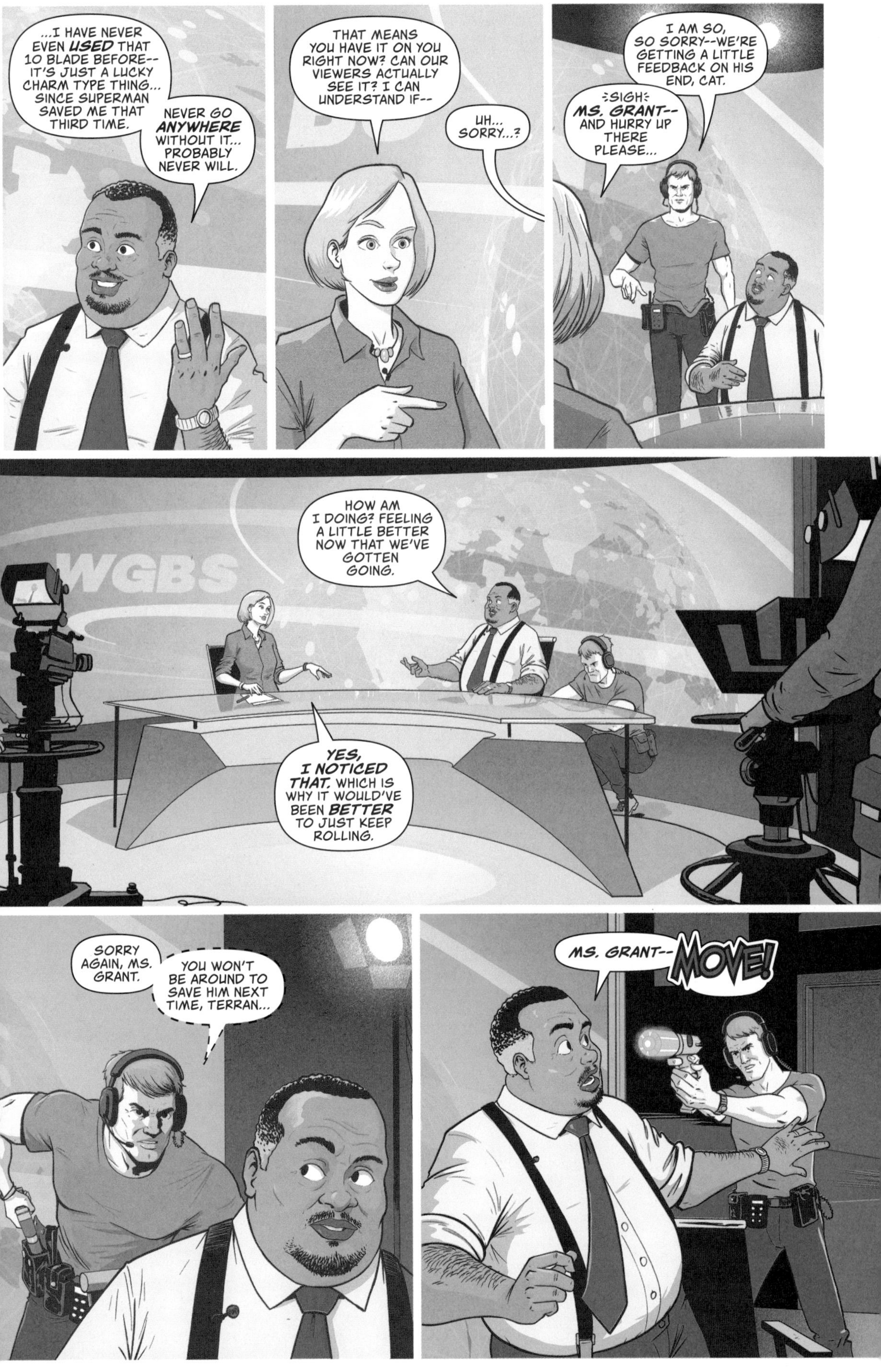

...I HAVE NEVER EVEN USED THAT 10 BLADE BEFORE-- IT'S JUST A LUCKY CHARM TYPE THING... SINCE SUPERMAN SAVED ME THAT THIRD TIME.
NEVER GO ANYWHERE WITHOUT IT... PROBABLY NEVER WILL.
THAT MEANS YOU HAVE IT ON YOU RIGHT NOW? CAN OUR VIEWERS ACTUALLY SEE IT? I CAN UNDERSTAND IF--
UH... SORRY...?
I AM SO, SO SORRY--WE'RE GETTING A LITTLE FEEDBACK ON HIS END, CAT.
SIGH
MS. GRANT-- AND HURRY UP THERE PLEASE...
WGBS
HOW AM I DOING? FEELING A LITTLE BETTER NOW THAT WE'VE GOTTEN GOING.
YES, I NOTICED THAT. WHICH IS WHY IT WOULD'VE BEEN BETTER TO JUST KEEP ROLLING.
SORRY AGAIN, MS. GRANT.
YOU WON'T BE AROUND TO SAVE HIM NEXT TIME, TERRAN...
MS. GRANT--MOVE!

UNNGH!

IT'S THE RED KRYPTONITE THIS TIME, SUPERMAN.

YOU WOULDN'T *BELIEVE* HOW EASY THESE ARE TO MAKE, NOW THAT--

ON AIR

RARRR!

SO'S THIS, SMART GUY!

CAREFUL WITH THOSE HANDS, FRIEND... NEVER KNOW WHO'S GOING TO NEED THEM NEXT.

THE THIRTEENTH TIME.

THE SECOND TIME.

CHARLEY MILES,

SUPERMAN. YOU GOT TIME FOR LUNCH TODAY?

VGBS

a man most saved

BRANDON THOMAS-WRITEF
BERAT PEKMEZCI-ART
DAVE SHARPE-LETTERE
BIXIE MATHIEU-ASSISTANT EDI'
JAMIE S. RICH-GROUP EDITO

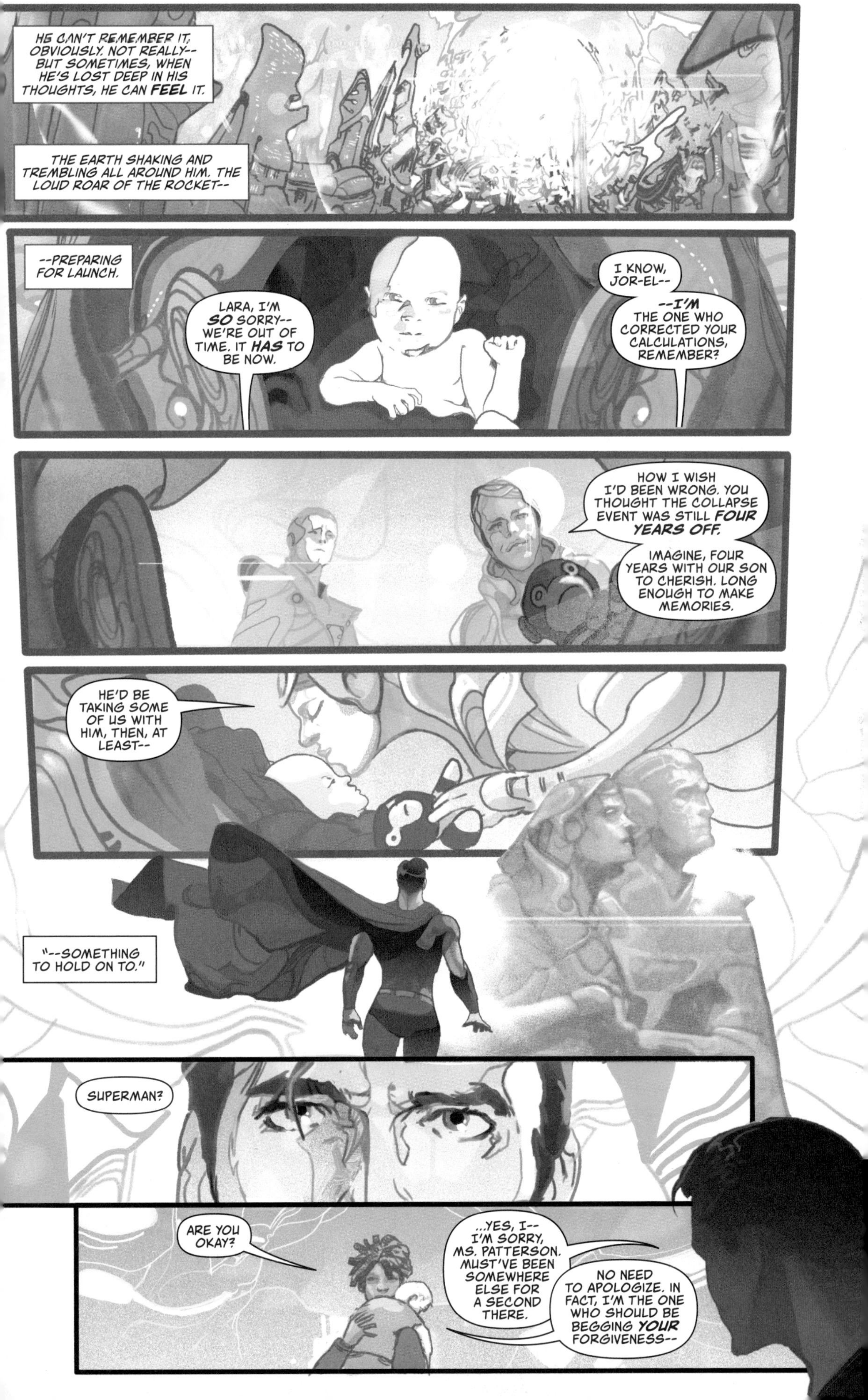

HE CAN'T REMEMBER IT, OBVIOUSLY. NOT REALLY-- BUT SOMETIMES, WHEN HE'S LOST DEEP IN HIS THOUGHTS, HE CAN FEEL IT.
THE EARTH SHAKING AND TREMBLING ALL AROUND HIM. THE LOUD ROAR OF THE ROCKET--
--PREPARING FOR LAUNCH.
LARA, I'M SO SORRY-- WE'RE OUT OF TIME. IT HAS TO BE NOW.
I KNOW, JOR-EL--
--I'M THE ONE WHO CORRECTED YOUR CALCULATIONS, REMEMBER?
HOW I WISH I'D BEEN WRONG. YOU THOUGHT THE COLLAPSE EVENT WAS STILL FOUR YEARS OFF.
IMAGINE, FOUR YEARS WITH OUR SON TO CHERISH. LONG ENOUGH TO MAKE MEMORIES.
HE'D BE TAKING SOME OF US WITH HIM, THEN, AT LEAST--
"--SOMETHING TO HOLD ON TO."
SUPERMAN?
ARE YOU OKAY?
...YES, I-- I'M SORRY, MS. PATTERSON. MUST'VE BEEN SOMEWHERE ELSE FOR A SECOND THERE.
NO NEED TO APOLOGIZE. IN FACT, I'M THE ONE WHO SHOULD BE BEGGING YOUR FORGIVENESS--

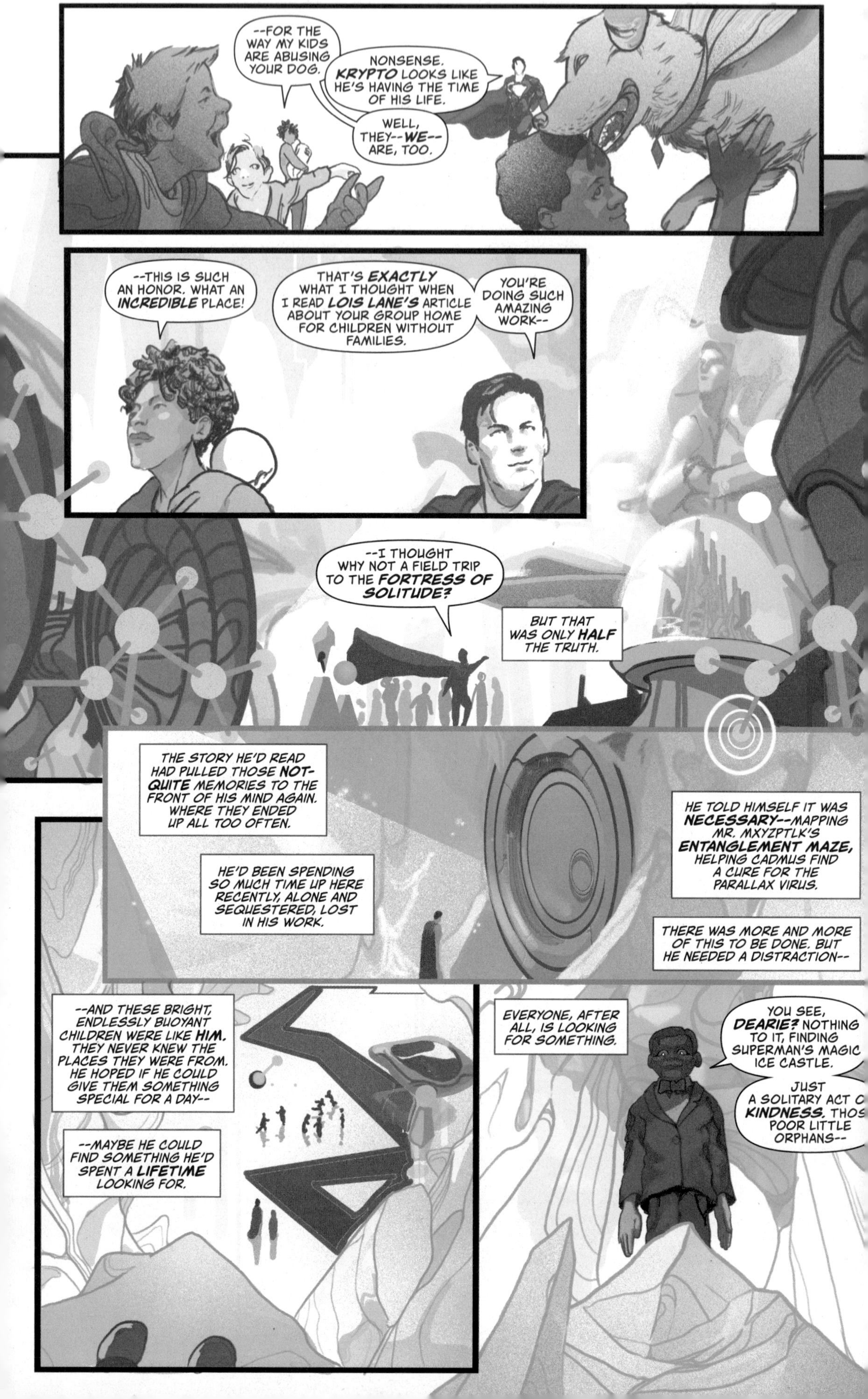
--FOR THE WAY MY KIDS ARE ABUSING YOUR DOG.
NONSENSE. KRYPTO LOOKS LIKE HE'S HAVING THE TIME OF HIS LIFE.
WELL, THEY--WE--ARE, TOO.
--THIS IS SUCH AN HONOR. WHAT AN INCREDIBLE PLACE!
THAT'S EXACTLY WHAT I THOUGHT WHEN I READ LOIS LANE'S ARTICLE ABOUT YOUR GROUP HOME FOR CHILDREN WITHOUT FAMILIES.
YOU'RE DOING SUCH AMAZING WORK--
--I THOUGHT WHY NOT A FIELD TRIP TO THE FORTRESS OF SOLITUDE?
BUT THAT WAS ONLY HALF THE TRUTH.
THE STORY HE'D READ HAD PULLED THOSE NOT-QUITE MEMORIES TO THE FRONT OF HIS MIND AGAIN. WHERE THEY ENDED UP ALL TOO OFTEN.
HE'D BEEN SPENDING SO MUCH TIME UP HERE RECENTLY, ALONE AND SEQUESTERED, LOST IN HIS WORK.
HE TOLD HIMSELF IT WAS NECESSARY--MAPPING MR. MXYZPTLK'S ENTANGLEMENT MAZE, HELPING CADMUS FIND A CURE FOR THE PARALLAX VIRUS.
THERE WAS MORE AND MORE OF THIS TO BE DONE. BUT HE NEEDED A DISTRACTION--
--AND THESE BRIGHT, ENDLESSLY BUOYANT CHILDREN WERE LIKE HIM. THEY NEVER KNEW THE PLACES THEY WERE FROM. HE HOPED IF HE COULD GIVE THEM SOMETHING SPECIAL FOR A DAY--
--MAYBE HE COULD FIND SOMETHING HE'D SPENT A LIFETIME LOOKING FOR.
EVERYONE, AFTER ALL, IS LOOKING FOR SOMETHING.
YOU SEE, DEARIE? NOTHING TO IT, FINDING SUPERMAN'S MAGIC ICE CASTLE.
JUST A SOLITARY ACT O KINDNESS. THOS POOR LITTLE ORPHANS--

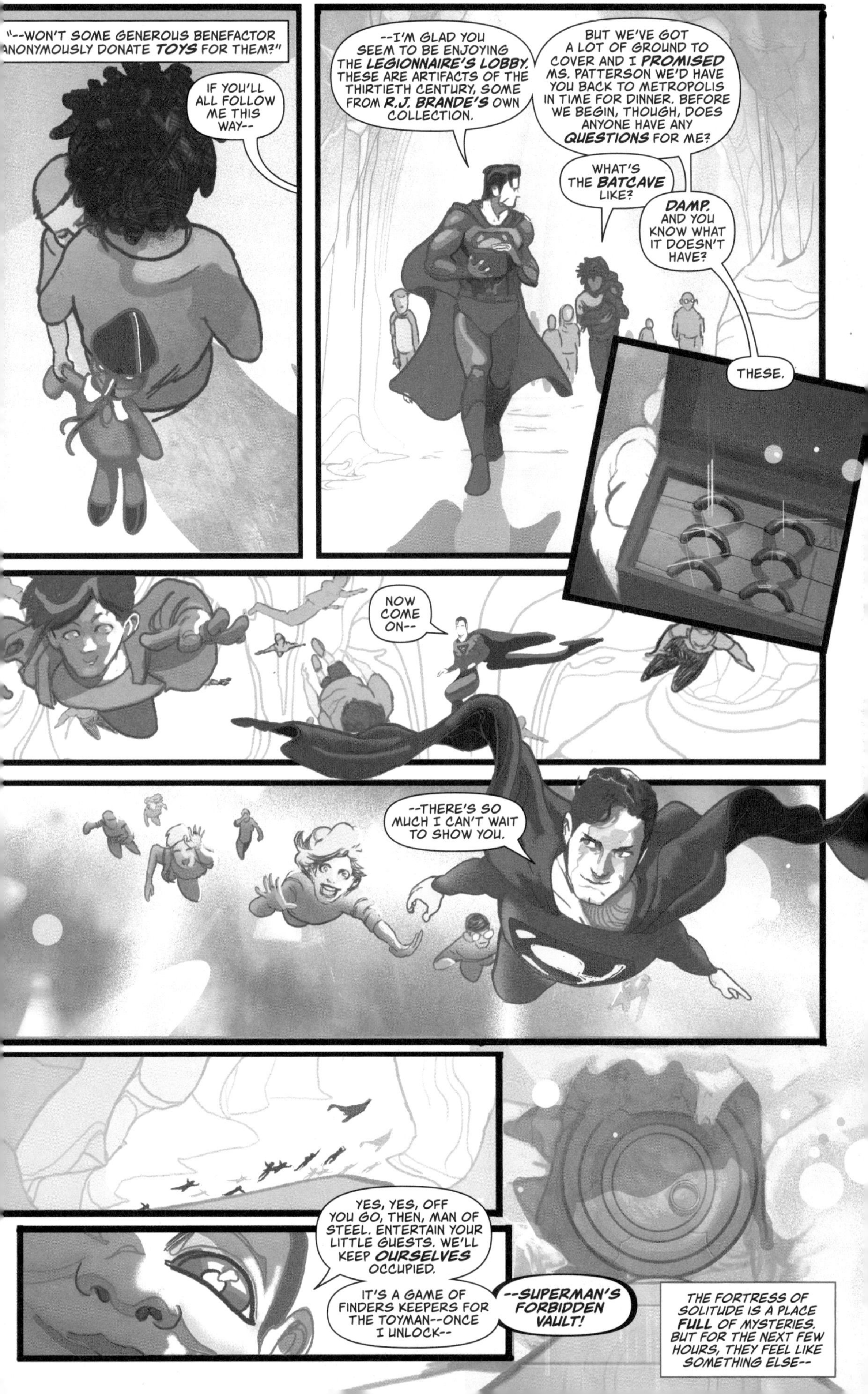
"--WON'T SOME GENEROUS BENEFACTOR ANONYMOUSLY DONATE **TOYS** FOR THEM?"
IF YOU'LL ALL FOLLOW ME THIS WAY--
--I'M GLAD YOU SEEM TO BE ENJOYING THE **LEGIONNAIRE'S LOBBY.** THESE ARE ARTIFACTS OF THE THIRTIETH CENTURY, SOME FROM **R.J. BRANDE'S** OWN COLLECTION.
BUT WE'VE GOT A LOT OF GROUND TO COVER AND I **PROMISED** MS. PATTERSON WE'D HAVE YOU BACK TO METROPOLIS IN TIME FOR DINNER. BEFORE WE BEGIN, THOUGH, DOES ANYONE HAVE ANY **QUESTIONS** FOR ME?
WHAT'S THE **BATCAVE** LIKE?
DAMP. AND YOU KNOW WHAT IT DOESN'T HAVE?
THESE.
NOW COME ON--
--THERE'S SO MUCH I CAN'T WAIT TO SHOW YOU.
YES, YES, OFF YOU GO, THEN, MAN OF STEEL. ENTERTAIN YOUR LITTLE GUESTS. WE'LL KEEP **OURSELVES** OCCUPIED.
IT'S A GAME OF FINDERS KEEPERS FOR THE TOYMAN--ONCE I UNLOCK--
--SUPERMAN'S FORBIDDEN VAULT!
THE FORTRESS OF SOLITUDE IS A PLACE **FULL** OF MYSTERIES. BUT FOR THE NEXT FEW HOURS, THEY FEEL LIKE SOMETHING ELSE--

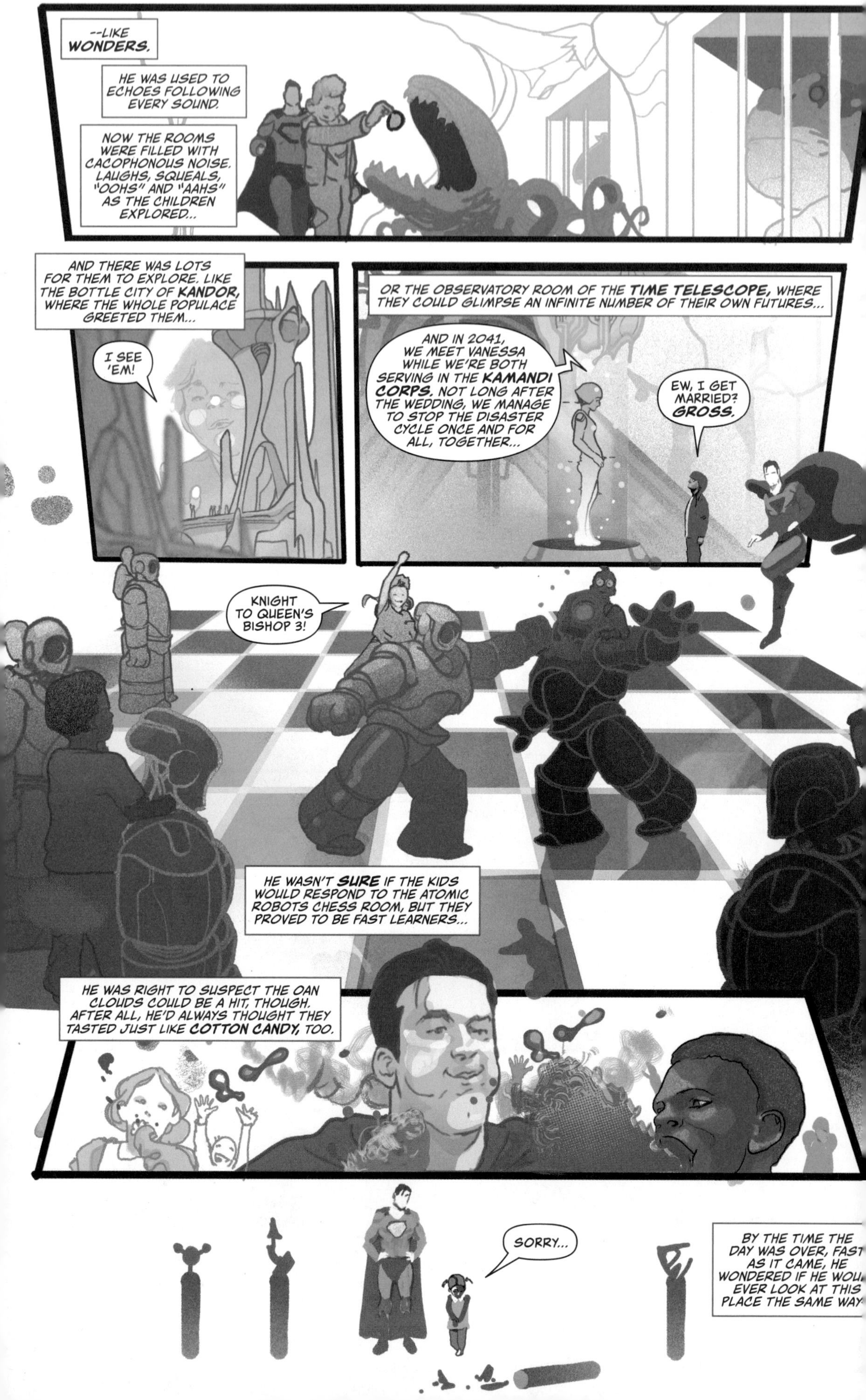

--LIKE WONDERS.
HE WAS USED TO ECHOES FOLLOWING EVERY SOUND.
NOW THE ROOMS WERE FILLED WITH CACOPHONOUS NOISE. LAUGHS, SQUEALS, "OOHS" AND "AAHS" AS THE CHILDREN EXPLORED...
AND THERE WAS LOTS FOR THEM TO EXPLORE. LIKE THE BOTTLE CITY OF KANDOR, WHERE THE WHOLE POPULACE GREETED THEM...
I SEE 'EM!
OR THE OBSERVATORY ROOM OF THE TIME TELESCOPE, WHERE THEY COULD GLIMPSE AN INFINITE NUMBER OF THEIR OWN FUTURES...
AND IN 2041, WE MEET VANESSA WHILE WE'RE BOTH SERVING IN THE KAMANDI CORPS. NOT LONG AFTER THE WEDDING, WE MANAGE TO STOP THE DISASTER CYCLE ONCE AND FOR ALL, TOGETHER...
EW, I GET MARRIED? GROSS.
KNIGHT TO QUEEN'S BISHOP 3!
HE WASN'T SURE IF THE KIDS WOULD RESPOND TO THE ATOMIC ROBOTS CHESS ROOM, BUT THEY PROVED TO BE FAST LEARNERS...
HE WAS RIGHT TO SUSPECT THE OAN CLOUDS COULD BE A HIT, THOUGH. AFTER ALL, HE'D ALWAYS THOUGHT THEY TASTED JUST LIKE COTTON CANDY, TOO.
SORRY...
BY THE TIME THE DAY WAS OVER, FAST AS IT CAME, HE WONDERED IF HE WOU EVER LOOK AT THIS PLACE THE SAME WAY

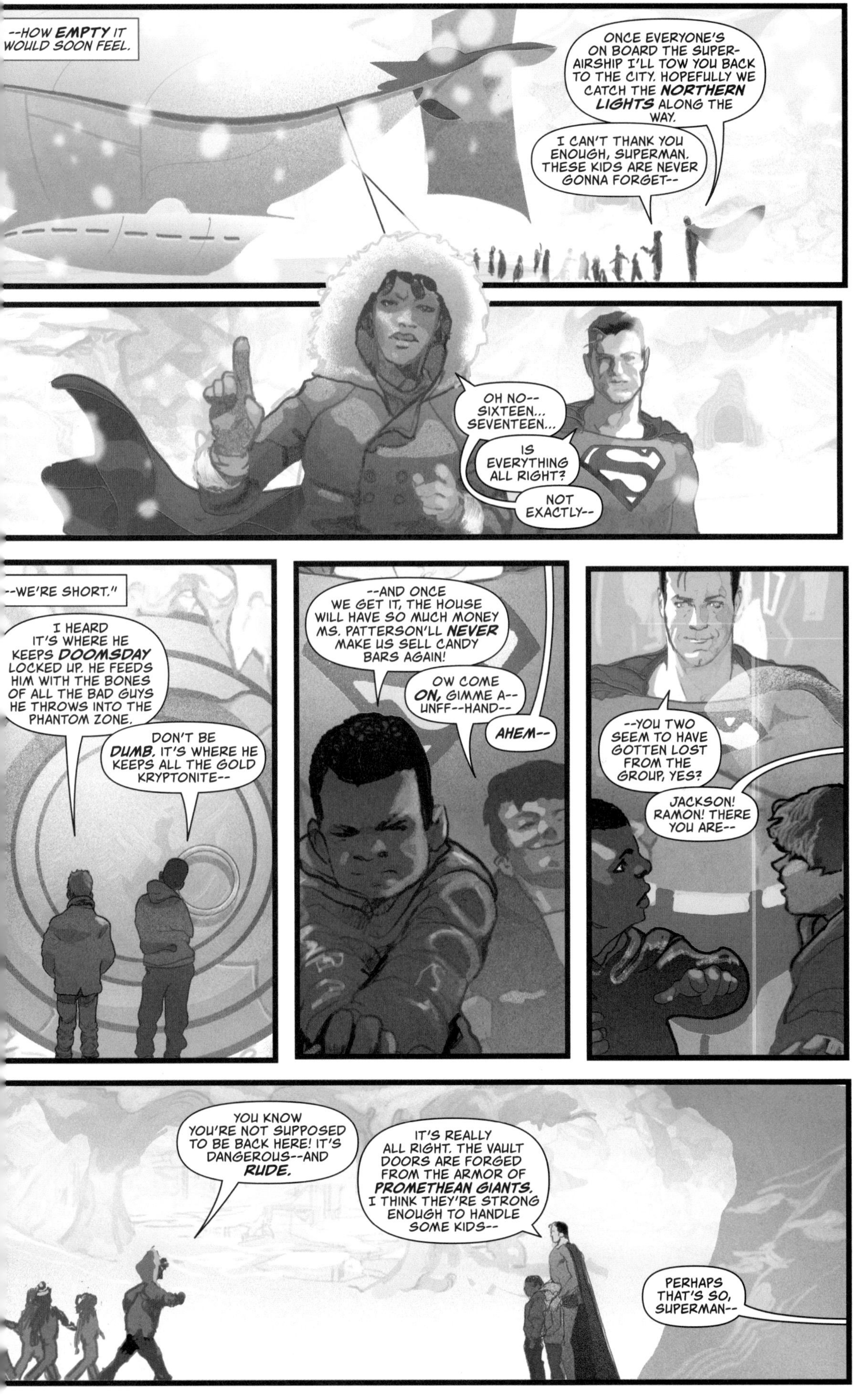
--HOW EMPTY IT WOULD SOON FEEL.
ONCE EVERYONE'S ON BOARD THE SUPER-AIRSHIP I'LL TOW YOU BACK TO THE CITY. HOPEFULLY WE CATCH THE NORTHERN LIGHTS ALONG THE WAY.
I CAN'T THANK YOU ENOUGH, SUPERMAN. THESE KIDS ARE NEVER GONNA FORGET--
OH NO-- SIXTEEN... SEVENTEEN...
IS EVERYTHING ALL RIGHT?
NOT EXACTLY--
--WE'RE SHORT."
I HEARD IT'S WHERE HE KEEPS DOOMSDAY LOCKED UP. HE FEEDS HIM WITH THE BONES OF ALL THE BAD GUYS HE THROWS INTO THE PHANTOM ZONE.
DON'T BE DUMB. IT'S WHERE HE KEEPS ALL THE GOLD KRYPTONITE--
--AND ONCE WE GET IT, THE HOUSE WILL HAVE SO MUCH MONEY MS. PATTERSON'LL NEVER MAKE US SELL CANDY BARS AGAIN!
OW COME ON, GIMME A-- UNFF--HAND--
AHEM--
--YOU TWO SEEM TO HAVE GOTTEN LOST FROM THE GROUP, YES?
JACKSON! RAMON! THERE YOU ARE--
YOU KNOW YOU'RE NOT SUPPOSED TO BE BACK HERE! IT'S DANGEROUS--AND RUDE.
IT'S REALLY ALL RIGHT. THE VAULT DOORS ARE FORGED FROM THE ARMOR OF PROMETHEAN GIANTS. I THINK THEY'RE STRONG ENOUGH TO HANDLE SOME KIDS--
PERHAPS THAT'S SO, SUPERMAN--

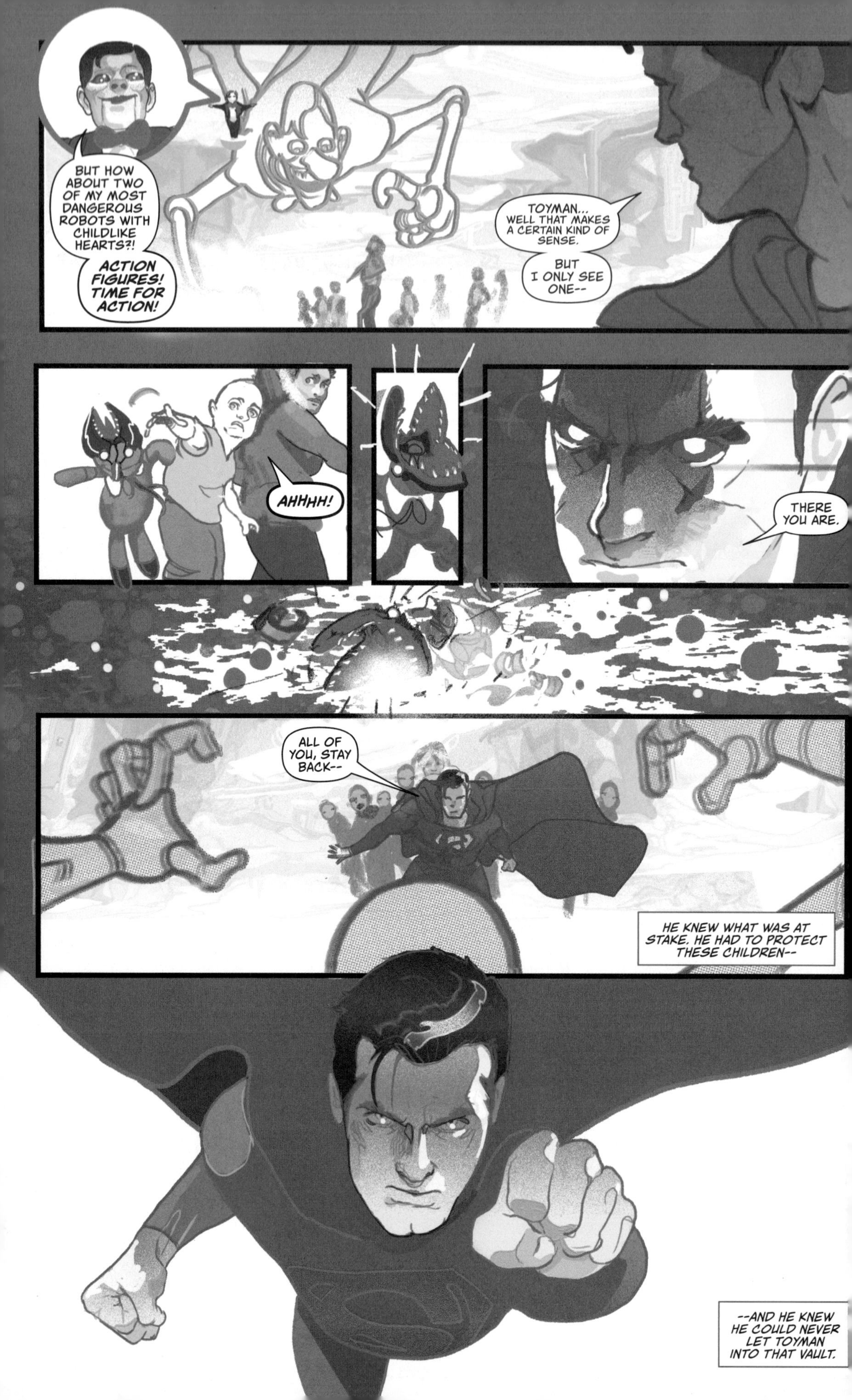
BUT HOW ABOUT TWO OF MY MOST DANGEROUS ROBOTS WITH CHILDLIKE HEARTS?!
ACTION FIGURES! TIME FOR ACTION!
TOYMAN... WELL THAT MAKES A CERTAIN KIND OF SENSE.
BUT I ONLY SEE ONE--
AHHHH!
THERE YOU ARE.
ALL OF YOU, STAY BACK--
HE KNEW WHAT WAS AT STAKE. HE HAD TO PROTECT THESE CHILDREN--
--AND HE KNEW HE COULD NEVER LET TOYMAN INTO THAT VAULT.

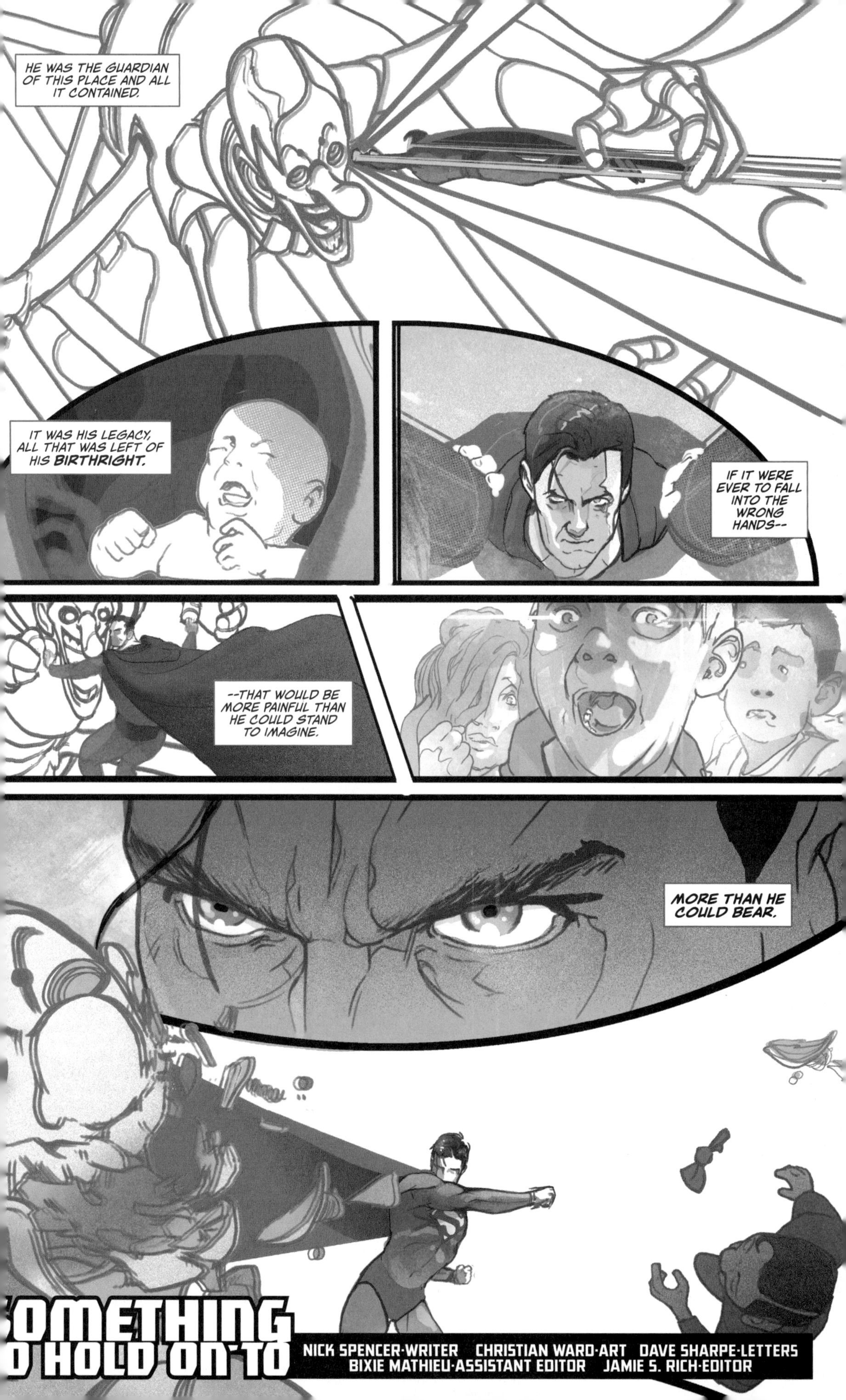
HE WAS THE GUARDIAN OF THIS PLACE AND ALL IT CONTAINED.
IT WAS HIS LEGACY, ALL THAT WAS LEFT OF HIS BIRTHRIGHT.
IF IT WERE EVER TO FALL INTO THE WRONG HANDS--
--THAT WOULD BE MORE PAINFUL THAN HE COULD STAND TO IMAGINE.
MORE THAN HE COULD BEAR.
OMETHING
O HOLD ON TO
NICK SPENCER·WRITER CHRISTIAN WARD·ART DAVE SHARPE·LETTERS
BIXIE MATHIEU·ASSISTANT EDITOR JAMIE S. RICH·EDITOR

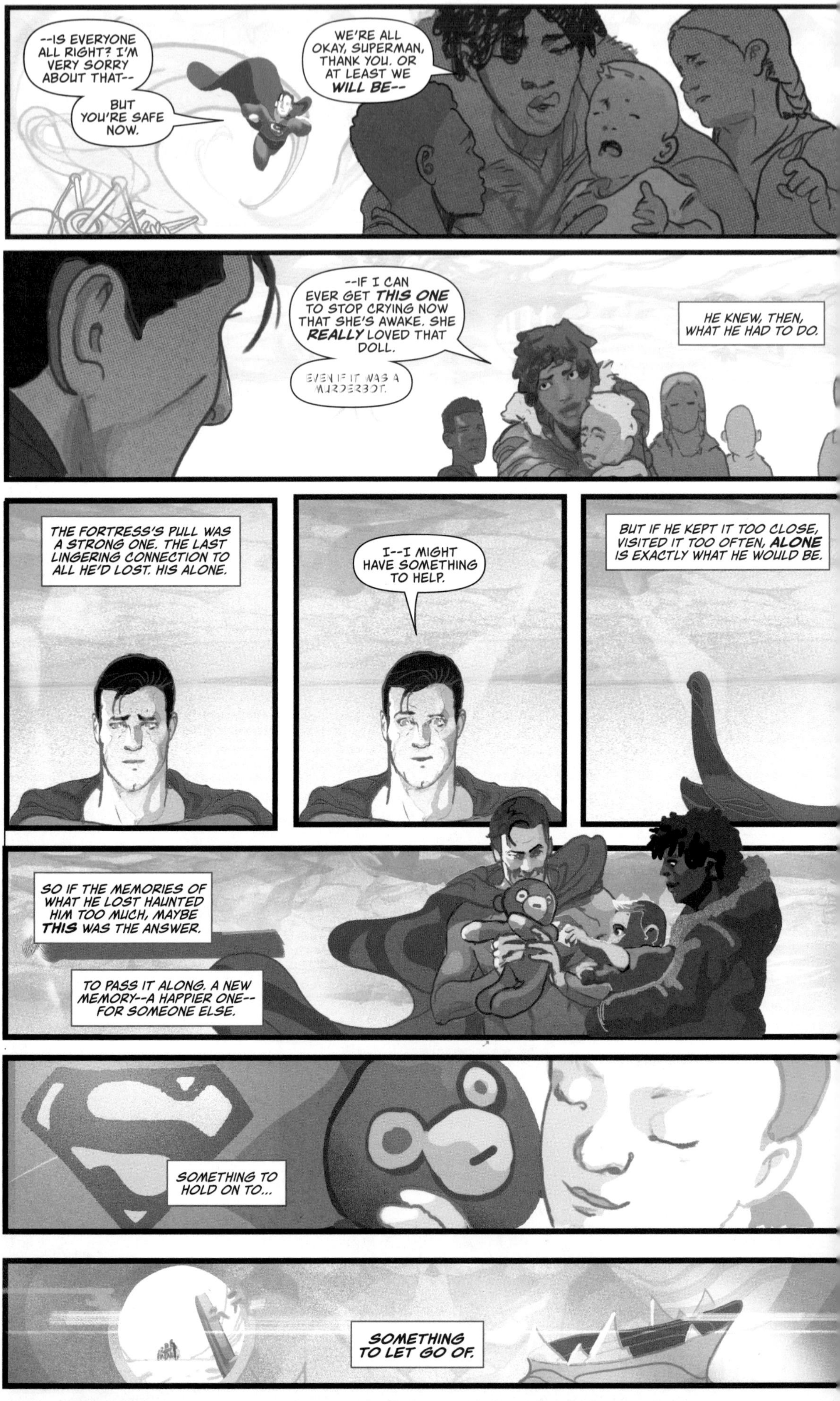
--IS EVERYONE ALL RIGHT? I'M VERY SORRY ABOUT THAT--
BUT YOU'RE SAFE NOW.
WE'RE ALL OKAY, SUPERMAN, THANK YOU. OR AT LEAST WE WILL BE--
--IF I CAN EVER GET THIS ONE TO STOP CRYING NOW THAT SHE'S AWAKE. SHE REALLY LOVED THAT DOLL.
EVEN IF IT WAS A MURDERBOT.
HE KNEW, THEN, WHAT HE HAD TO DO.
THE FORTRESS'S PULL WAS A STRONG ONE. THE LAST LINGERING CONNECTION TO ALL HE'D LOST. HIS ALONE.
I--I MIGHT HAVE SOMETHING TO HELP.
BUT IF HE KEPT IT TOO CLOSE, VISITED IT TOO OFTEN, ALONE IS EXACTLY WHAT HE WOULD BE.
SO IF THE MEMORIES OF WHAT HE LOST HAUNTED HIM TOO MUCH, MAYBE THIS WAS THE ANSWER.
TO PASS IT ALONG. A NEW MEMORY--A HAPPIER ONE--FOR SOMEONE ELSE.
SOMETHING TO HOLD ON TO...
SOMETHING TO LET GO OF.

LITTLE STAR

BY JAMES STOKOE

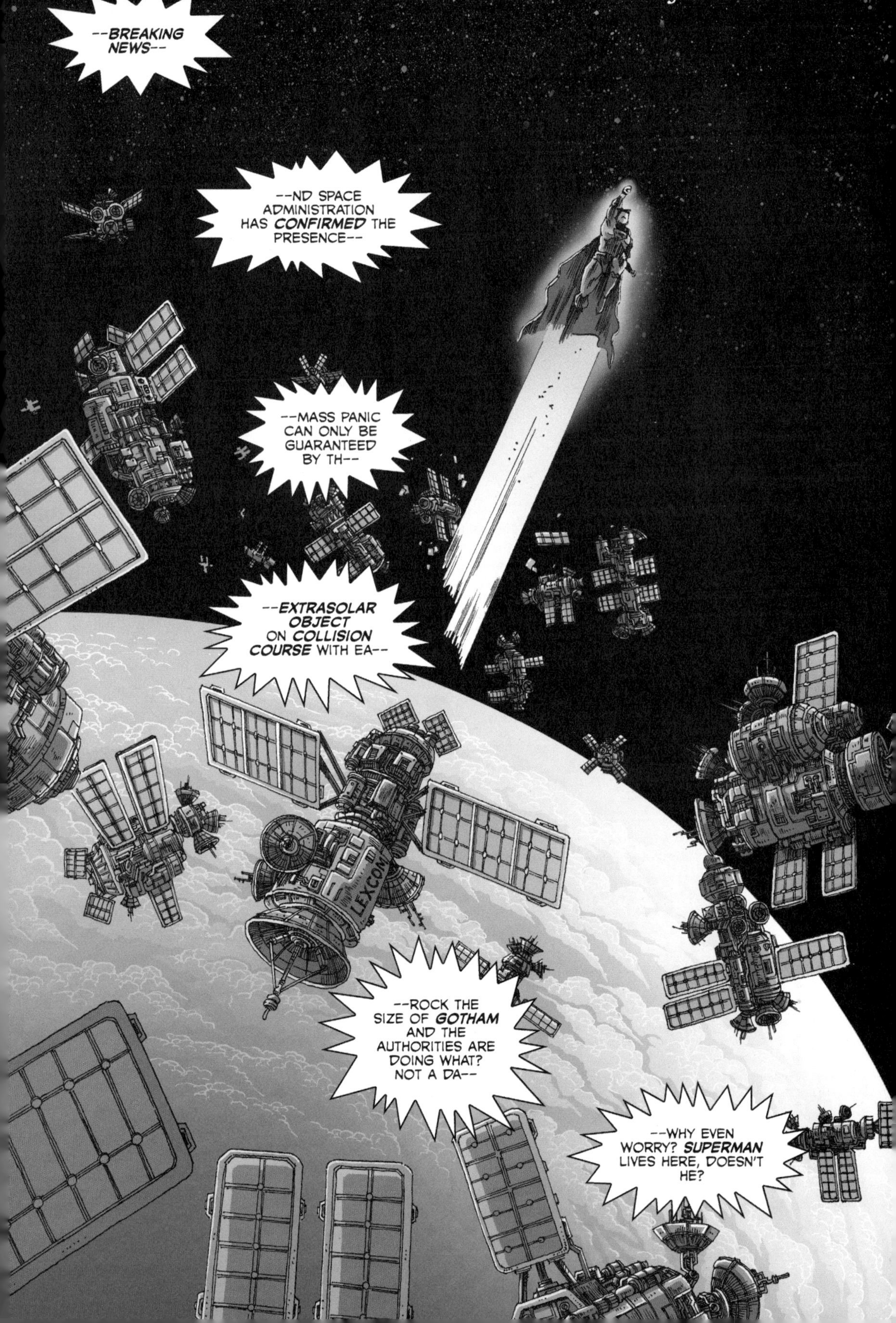
--BREAKING NEWS--
--ND SPACE ADMINISTRATION HAS CONFIRMED THE PRESENCE--
--MASS PANIC CAN ONLY BE GUARANTEED BY TH--
--EXTRASOLAR OBJECT ON COLLISION COURSE WITH EA--
LEXCOM
--ROCK THE SIZE OF GOTHAM AND THE AUTHORITIES ARE DOING WHAT? NOT A DA--
--WHY EVEN WORRY? SUPERMAN LIVES HERE, DOESN'T HE?

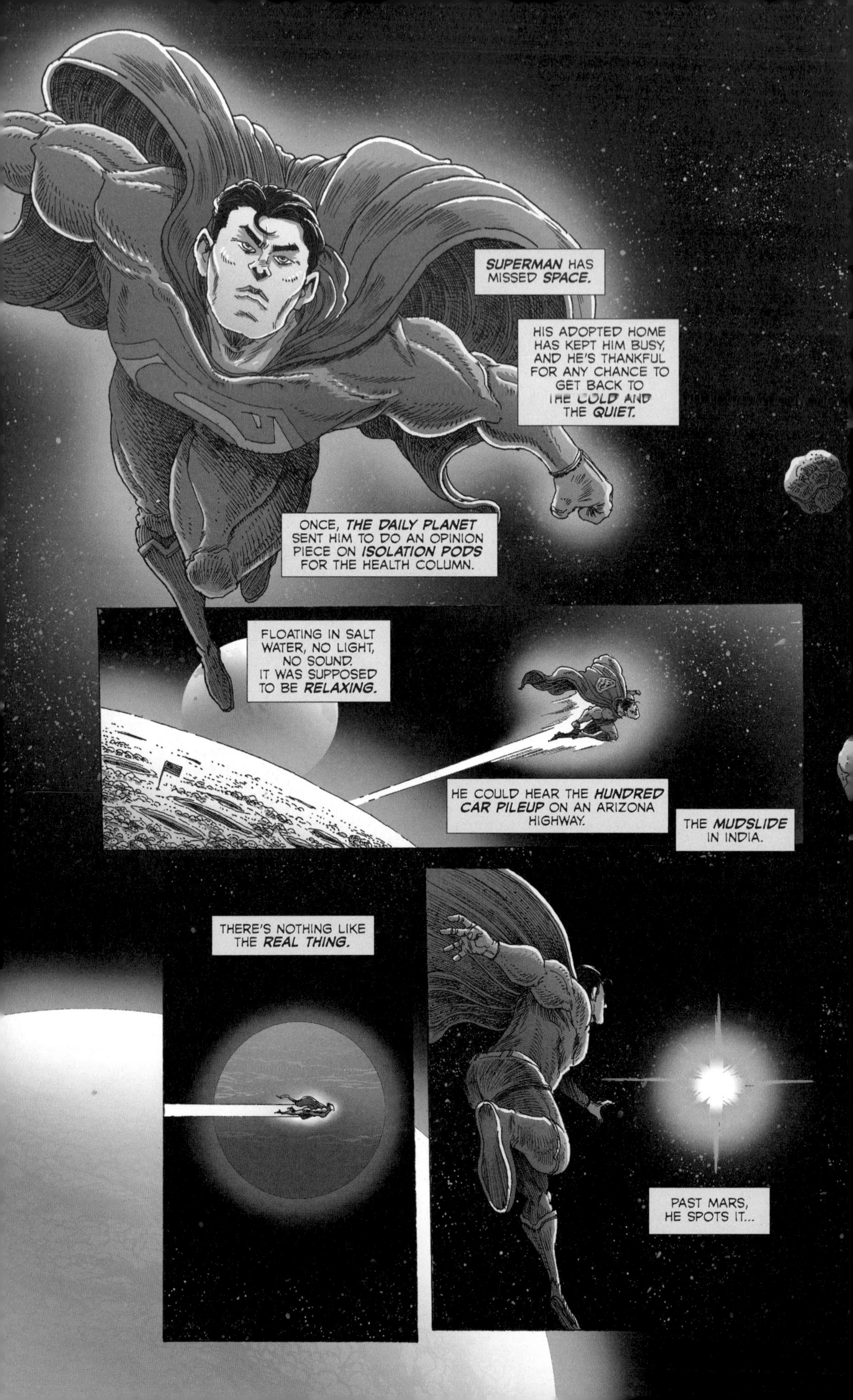
SUPERMAN HAS MISSED SPACE.
HIS ADOPTED HOME HAS KEPT HIM BUSY, AND HE'S THANKFUL FOR ANY CHANCE TO GET BACK TO THE COLD AND THE QUIET.
ONCE, THE DAILY PLANET SENT HIM TO DO AN OPINION PIECE ON ISOLATION PODS FOR THE HEALTH COLUMN.
FLOATING IN SALT WATER, NO LIGHT, NO SOUND. IT WAS SUPPOSED TO BE RELAXING.
HE COULD HEAR THE HUNDRED CAR PILEUP ON AN ARIZONA HIGHWAY.
THE MUDSLIDE IN INDIA.
THERE'S NOTHING LIKE THE REAL THING.
PAST MARS, HE SPOTS IT...

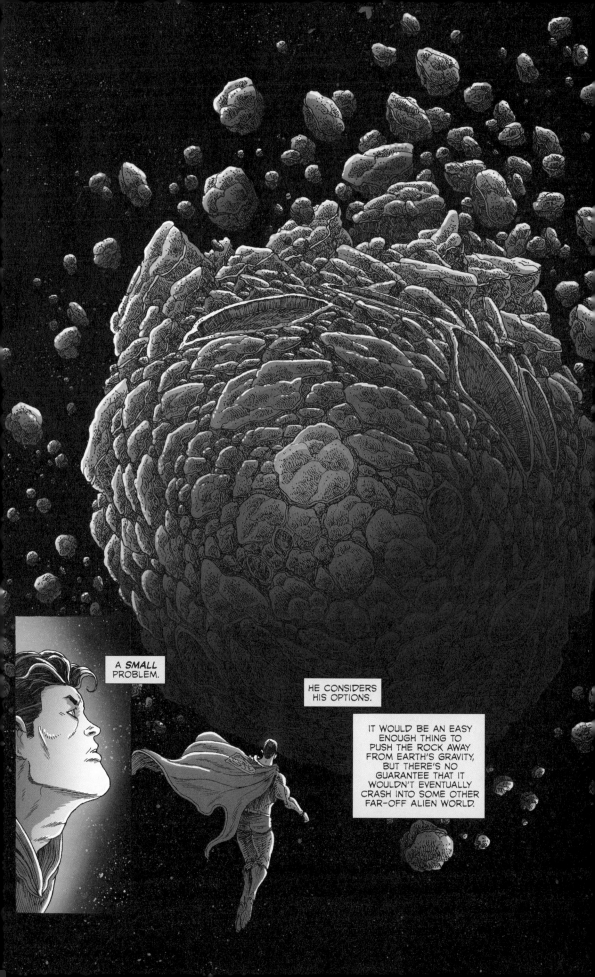

A *SMALL* PROBLEM.

HE CONSIDERS HIS OPTIONS.

IT WOULD BE AN EASY ENOUGH THING TO PUSH THE ROCK AWAY FROM EARTH'S GRAVITY, BUT THERE'S NO GUARANTEE THAT IT WOULDN'T EVENTUALLY CRASH INTO SOME OTHER FAR-OFF ALIEN WORLD.

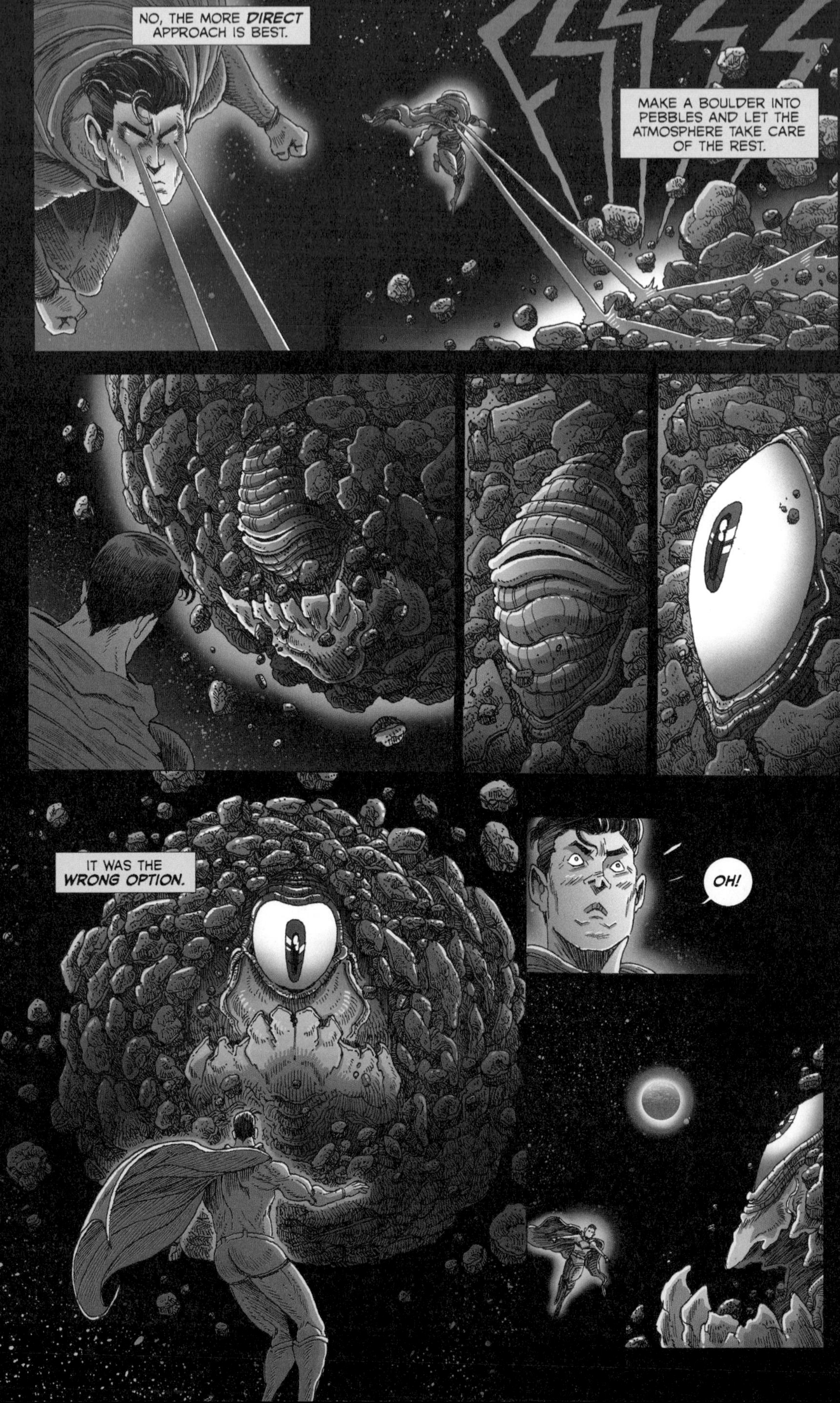

NO, THE MORE DIRECT APPROACH IS BEST.
MAKE A BOULDER INTO PEBBLES AND LET THE ATMOSPHERE TAKE CARE OF THE REST.
IT WAS THE WRONG OPTION.
OH!

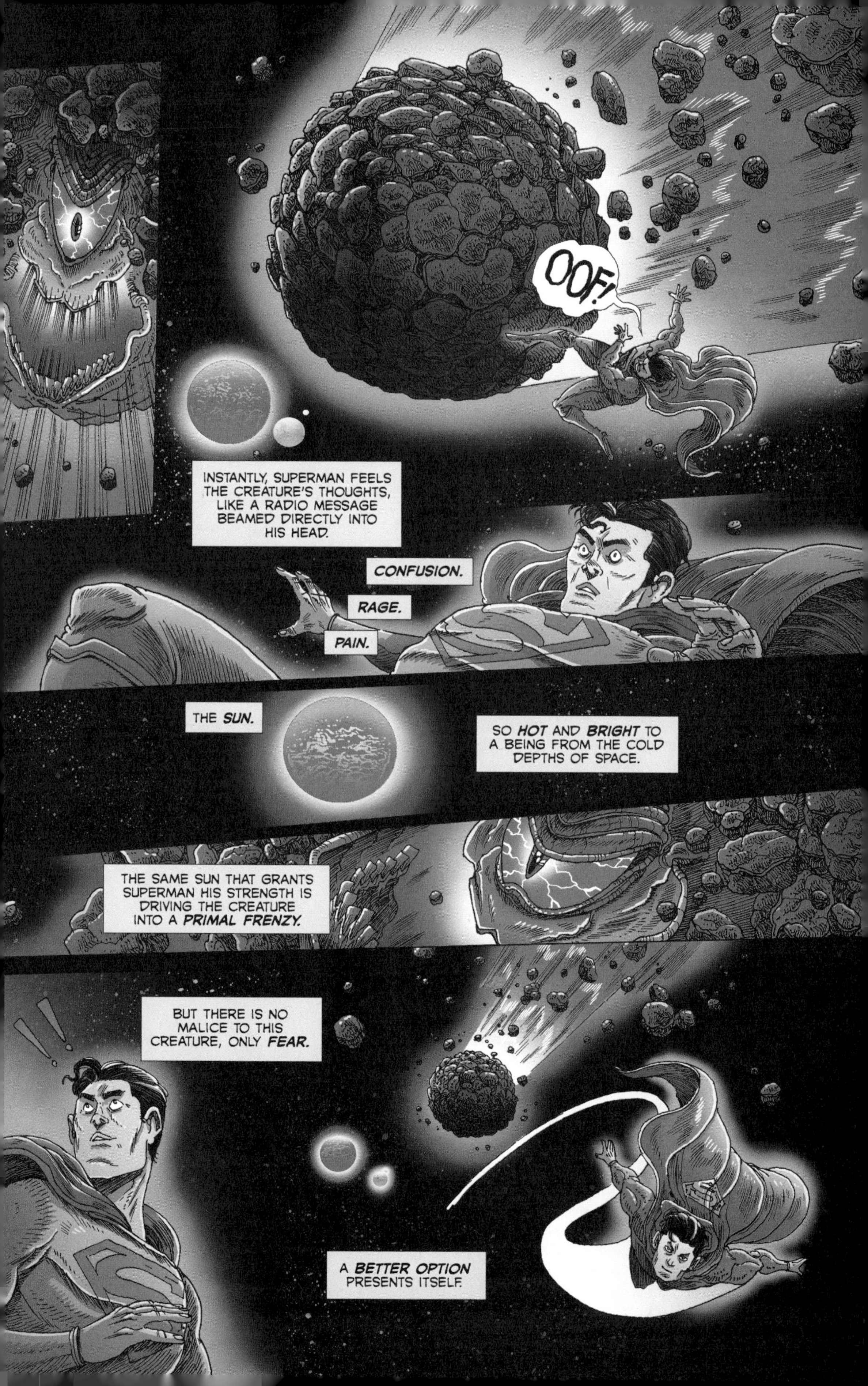
OOF!
INSTANTLY, SUPERMAN FEELS THE CREATURE'S THOUGHTS, LIKE A RADIO MESSAGE BEAMED DIRECTLY INTO HIS HEAD.
CONFUSION.
RAGE.
PAIN.
THE SUN.
SO HOT AND BRIGHT TO A BEING FROM THE COLD DEPTHS OF SPACE.
THE SAME SUN THAT GRANTS SUPERMAN HIS STRENGTH IS DRIVING THE CREATURE INTO A PRIMAL FRENZY.
!
BUT THERE IS NO MALICE TO THIS CREATURE, ONLY FEAR.
A BETTER OPTION PRESENTS ITSELF.

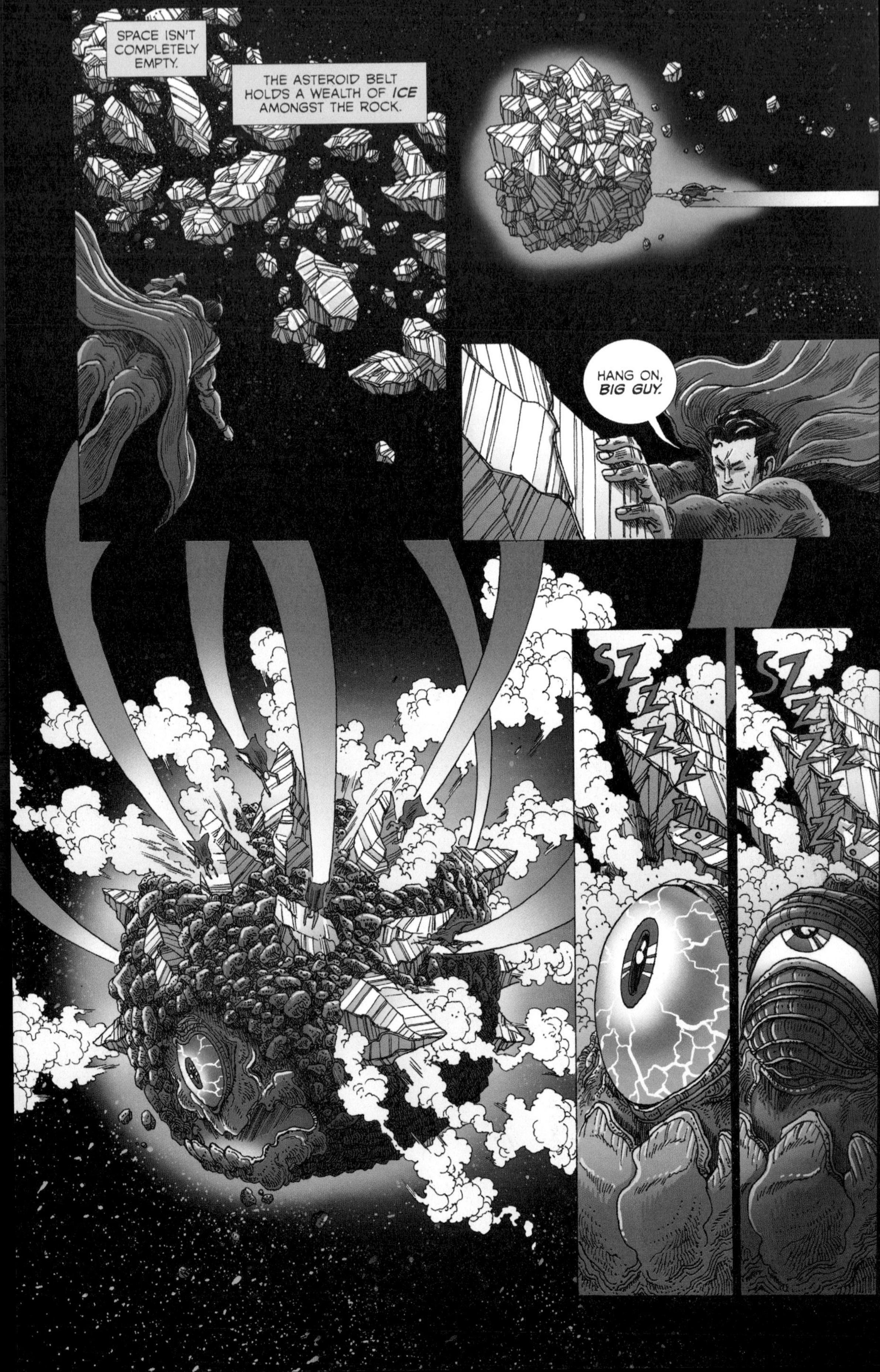
SPACE ISN'T COMPLETELY EMPTY.
THE ASTEROID BELT HOLDS A WEALTH OF *ICE* AMONGST THE ROCK.
HANG ON, ***BIG GUY.***
SZZZZZZ
SZZZZZZ

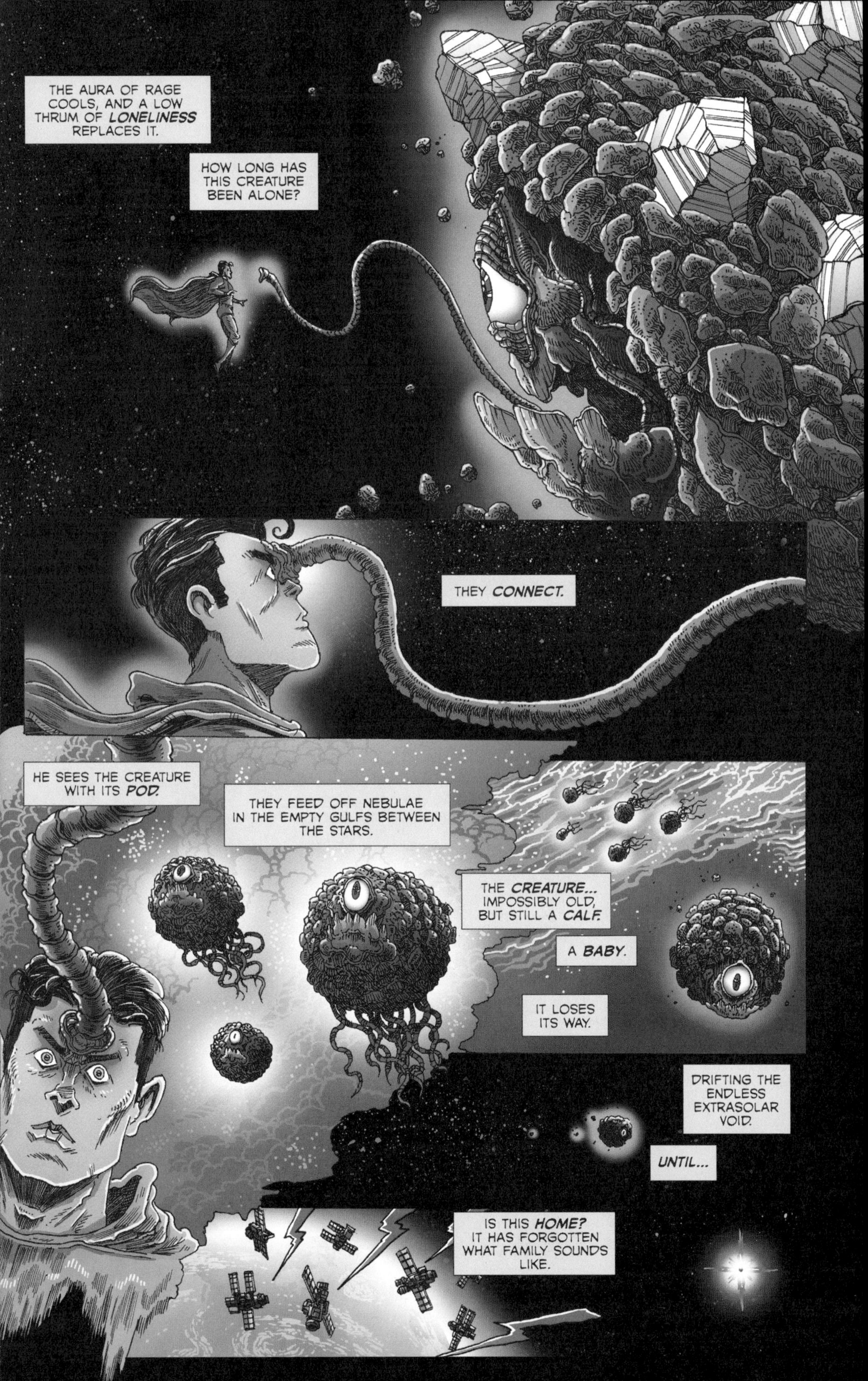
THE AURA OF RAGE COOLS, AND A LOW THRUM OF LONELINESS REPLACES IT.
HOW LONG HAS THIS CREATURE BEEN ALONE?
THEY CONNECT.
HE SEES THE CREATURE WITH ITS POD.
THEY FEED OFF NEBULAE IN THE EMPTY GULFS BETWEEN THE STARS.
THE CREATURE... IMPOSSIBLY OLD, BUT STILL A CALF.
A BABY.
IT LOSES ITS WAY.
DRIFTING THE ENDLESS EXTRASOLAR VOID.
UNTIL...
IS THIS HOME? IT HAS FORGOTTEN WHAT FAMILY SOUNDS LIKE.

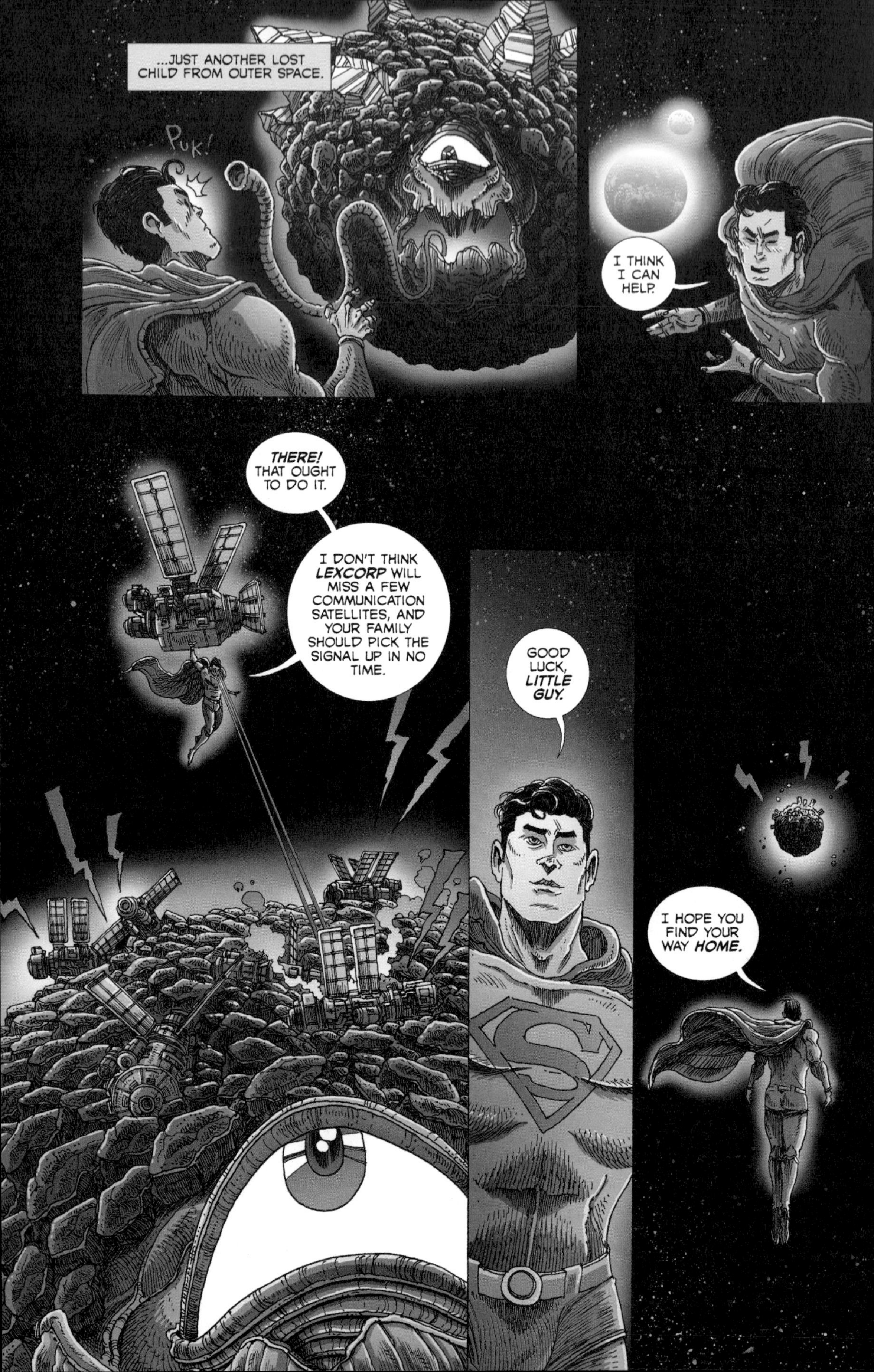
...JUST ANOTHER LOST CHILD FROM OUTER SPACE.
PUK!
I THINK I CAN HELP.
THERE! THAT OUGHT TO DO IT.
I DON'T THINK LEXCORP WILL MISS A FEW COMMUNICATION SATELLITES, AND YOUR FAMILY SHOULD PICK THE SIGNAL UP IN NO TIME.
GOOD LUCK, LITTLE GUY.
I HOPE YOU FIND YOUR WAY HOME.

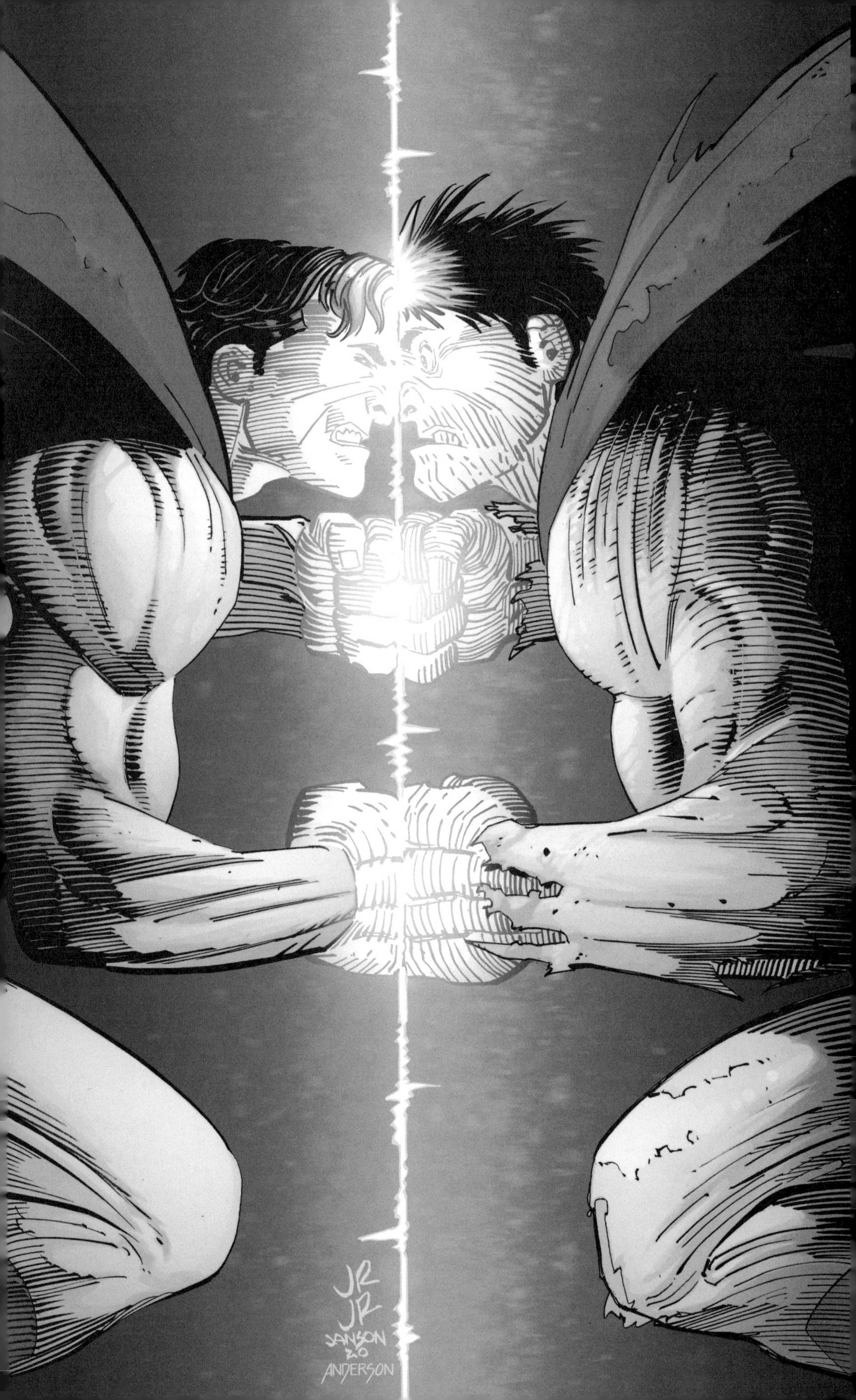
JR
JR
JANSON
20
ANDERSON

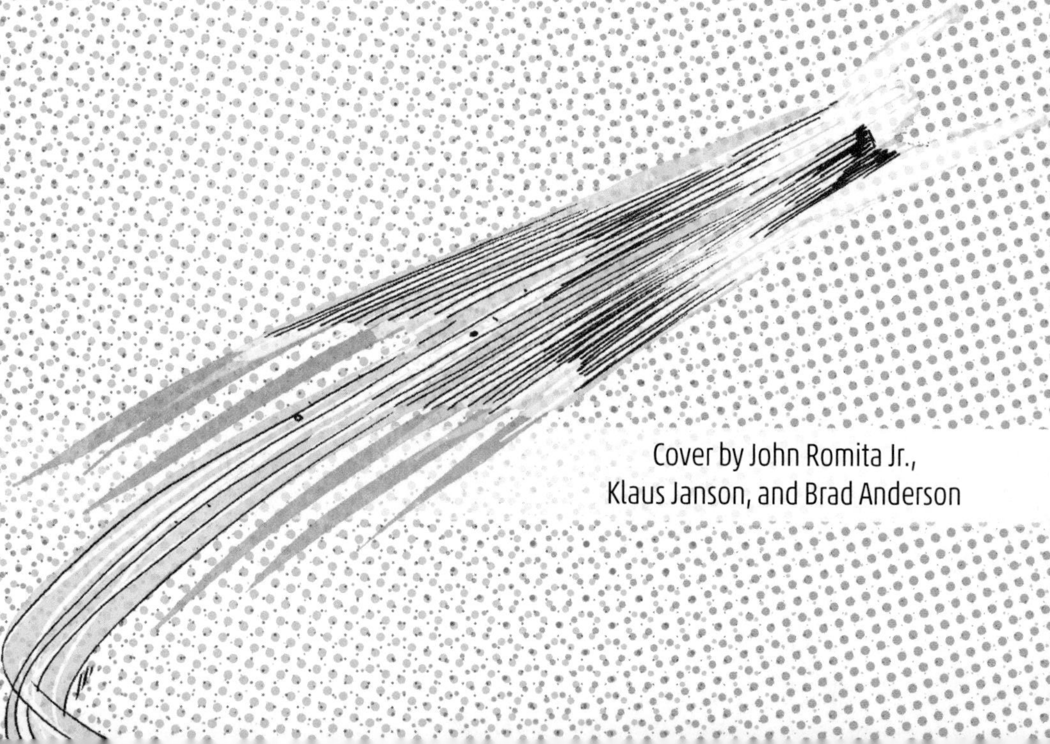

Cover by John Romita Jr.,
Klaus Janson, and Brad Anderson

NAMREPUS

MARK WAID WRITER AUDREY MOK ARTIST JORDIE BELLAIRE COLORIST
DAVE SHARPE LETTERER BRITTANY HOLZHERR EDITOR JAMIE S. RICH GROUP EDITOR

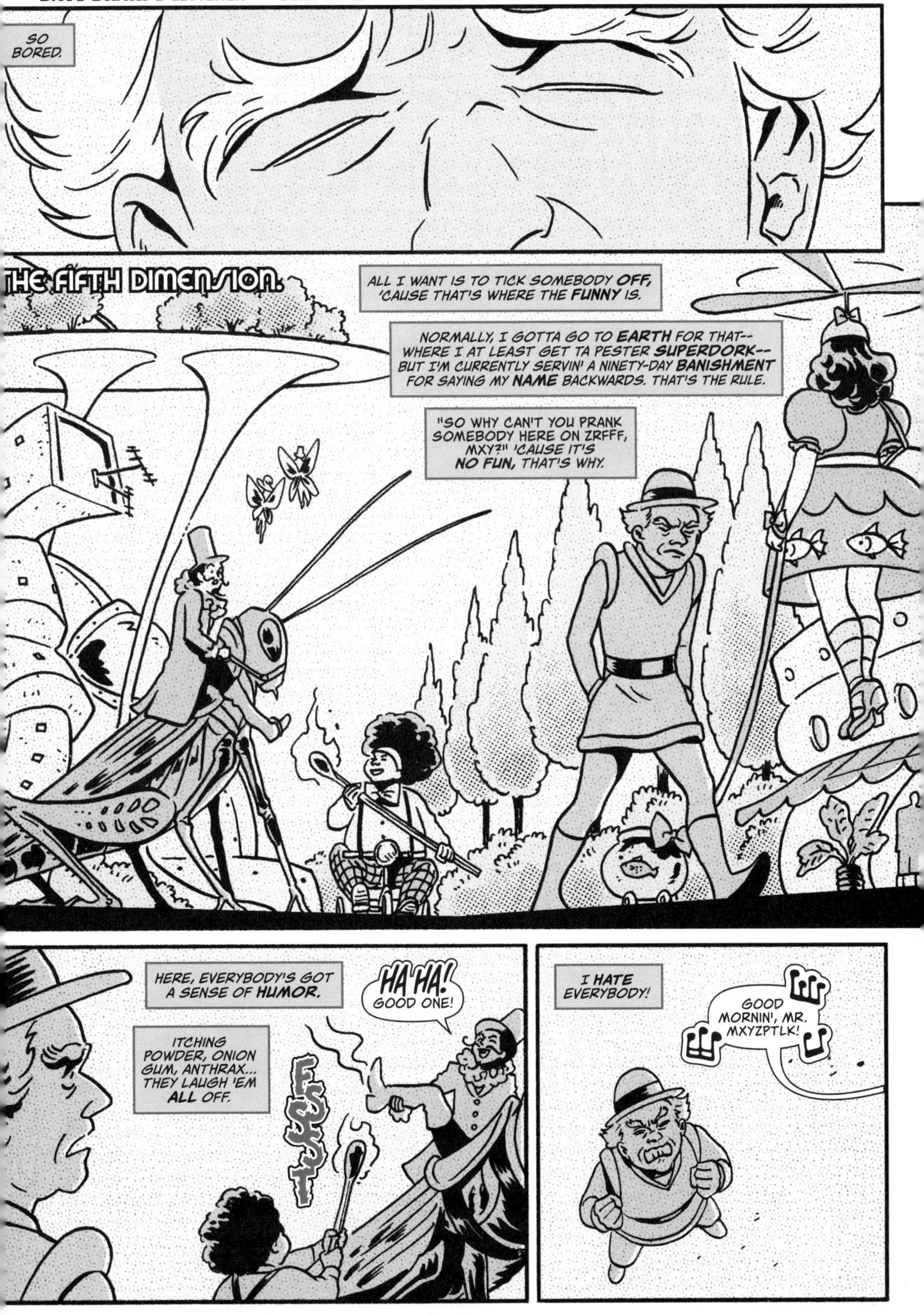
SO BORED.
THE FIFTH DIMENSION.
ALL I WANT IS TO TICK SOMEBODY OFF, 'CAUSE THAT'S WHERE THE FUNNY IS.
NORMALLY, I GOTTA GO TO EARTH FOR THAT-- WHERE I AT LEAST GET TA PESTER SUPERDORK-- BUT I'M CURRENTLY SERVIN' A NINETY-DAY BANISHMENT FOR SAYING MY NAME BACKWARDS. THAT'S THE RULE.
"SO WHY CAN'T YOU PRANK SOMEBODY HERE ON ZRFFF, MXY?" 'CAUSE IT'S NO FUN, THAT'S WHY.
HERE, EVERYBODY'S GOT A SENSE OF HUMOR.
ITCHING POWDER, ONION GUM, ANTHRAX... THEY LAUGH 'EM ALL OFF.
FSSST
HA HA! GOOD ONE!
I HATE EVERYBODY!
GOOD MORNIN', MR. MXYZPTLK!

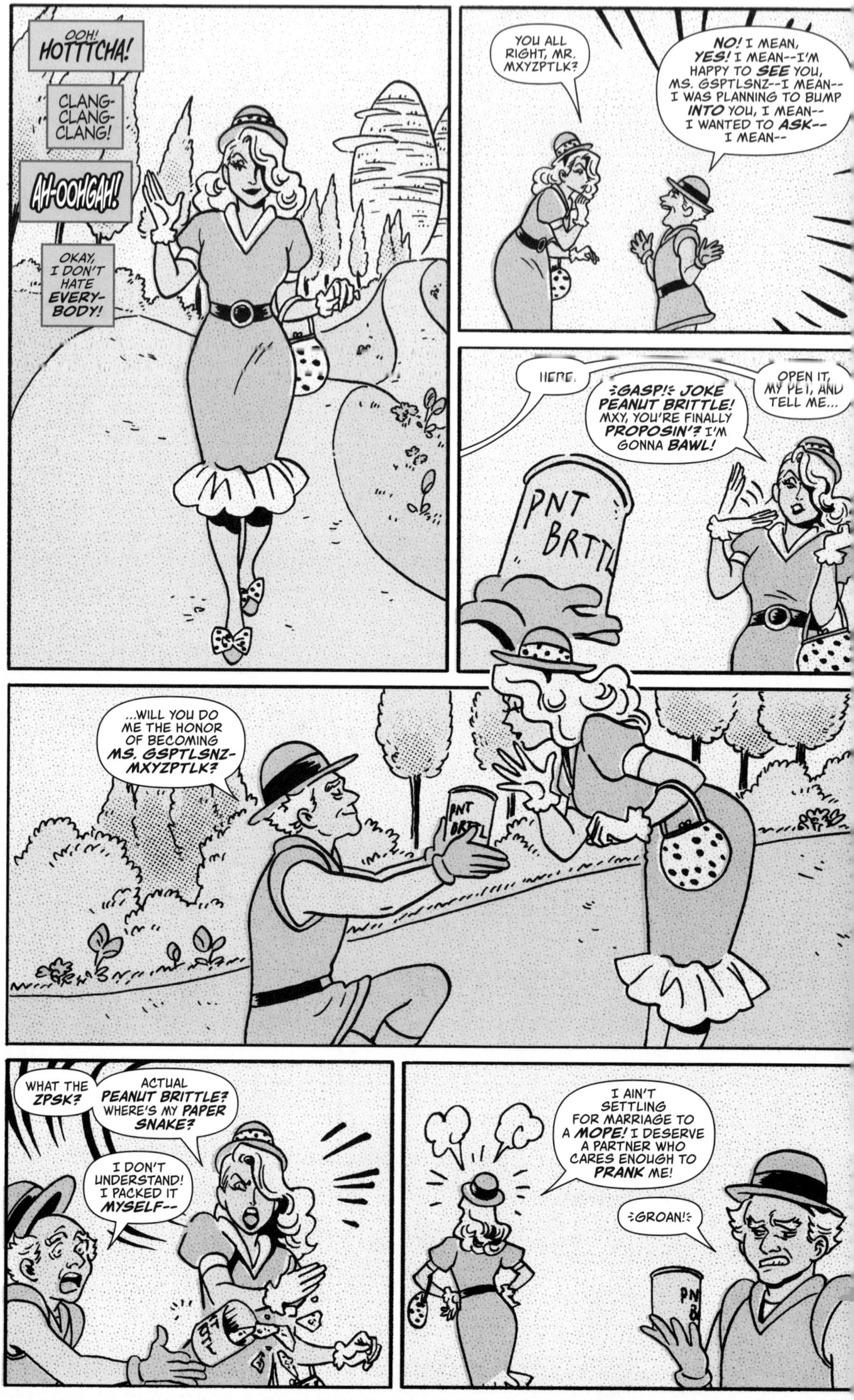

OOH! HOTTTCHA!
CLANG-CLANG-CLANG!
AH-OOHGAH!
OKAY, I DON'T HATE EVERY-BODY!
YOU ALL RIGHT, MR. MXYZPTLK?
NO! I MEAN, YES! I MEAN--I'M HAPPY TO SEE YOU, MS. GSPTLSNZ--I MEAN--I WAS PLANNING TO BUMP INTO YOU, I MEAN--I WANTED TO ASK--I MEAN--
HERE.
OPEN IT, MY PET, AND TELL ME...
GASP! JOKE PEANUT BRITTLE! MXY, YOU'RE FINALLY PROPOSIN'? I'M GONNA BAWL!
PNT BRTTL
...WILL YOU DO ME THE HONOR OF BECOMING MS. GSPTLSNZ-MXYZPTLK?
PNT BRTTL
WHAT THE ZPSK?
ACTUAL PEANUT BRITTLE? WHERE'S MY PAPER SNAKE?
I DON'T UNDERSTAND! I PACKED IT MYSELF--
I AIN'T SETTLING FOR MARRIAGE TO A MOPE! I DESERVE A PARTNER WHO CARES ENOUGH TO PRANK ME!
GROAN!

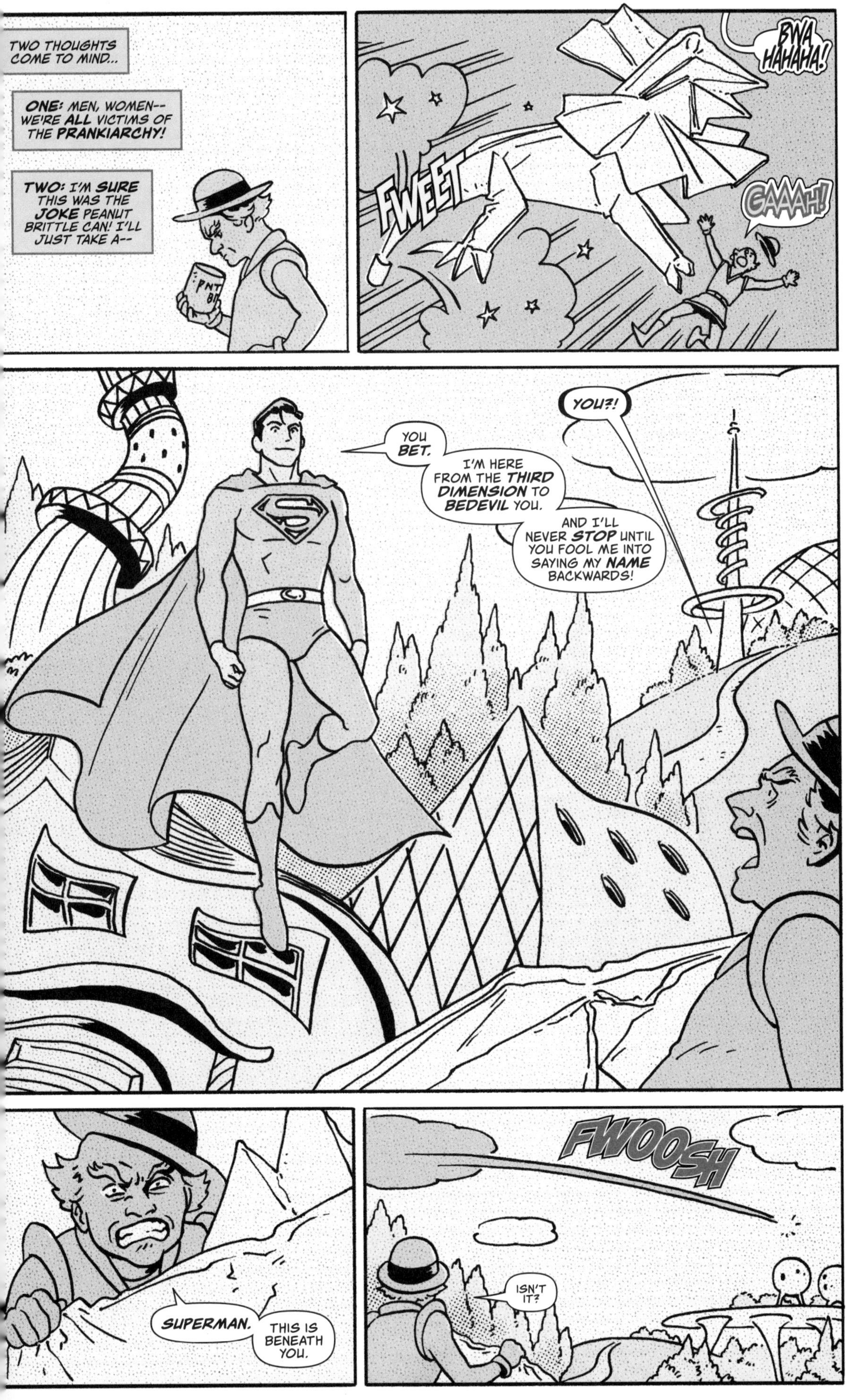
TWO THOUGHTS COME TO MIND...
ONE: MEN, WOMEN-- WE'RE ALL VICTIMS OF THE PRANKIARCHY!
TWO: I'M SURE THIS WAS THE JOKE PEANUT BRITTLE CAN! I'LL JUST TAKE A--
PNT B
BWA HAHAHA!
FWEET
GAAAH!
YOU BET.
I'M HERE FROM THE THIRD DIMENSION TO BEDEVIL YOU.
AND I'LL NEVER STOP UNTIL YOU FOOL ME INTO SAYING MY NAME BACKWARDS!
YOU?!
SUPERMAN.
THIS IS BENEATH YOU.
FWOOSH
ISN'T IT?

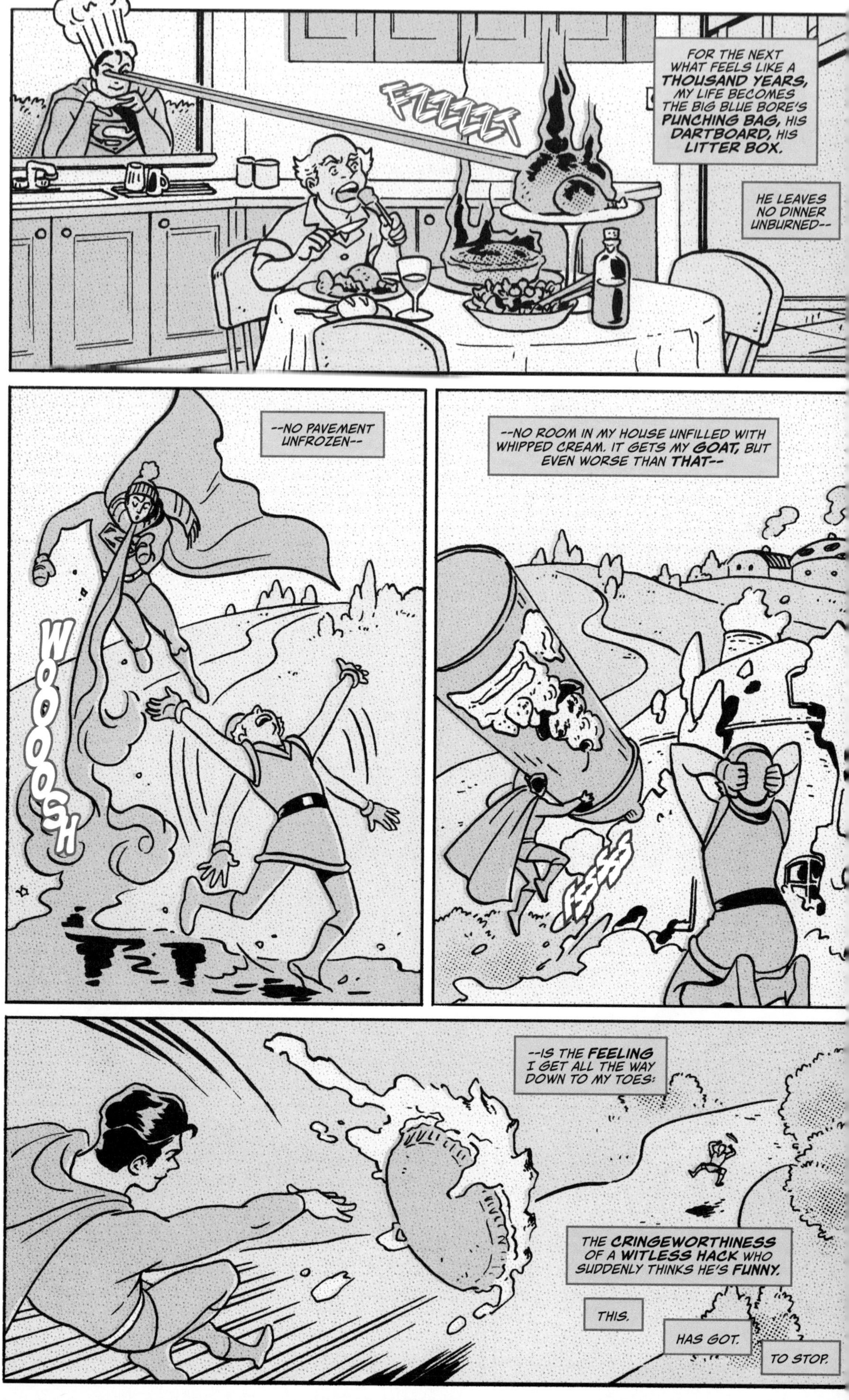

FOR THE NEXT WHAT FEELS LIKE A **THOUSAND YEARS,** MY LIFE BECOMES THE BIG BLUE BORE'S **PUNCHING BAG,** HIS **DARTBOARD,** HIS **LITTER BOX.**
HE LEAVES NO DINNER UNBURNED--
FZZZZZT
--NO PAVEMENT UNFROZEN--
WOOOOOSH
--NO ROOM IN MY HOUSE UNFILLED WITH WHIPPED CREAM. IT GETS MY **GOAT,** BUT EVEN WORSE THAN **THAT**--
FSSSS
--IS THE **FEELING** I GET ALL THE WAY DOWN TO MY TOES:
THE **CRINGEWORTHINESS** OF A **WITLESS HACK** WHO SUDDENLY THINKS HE'S **FUNNY.**
THIS.
HAS GOT.
TO STOP.

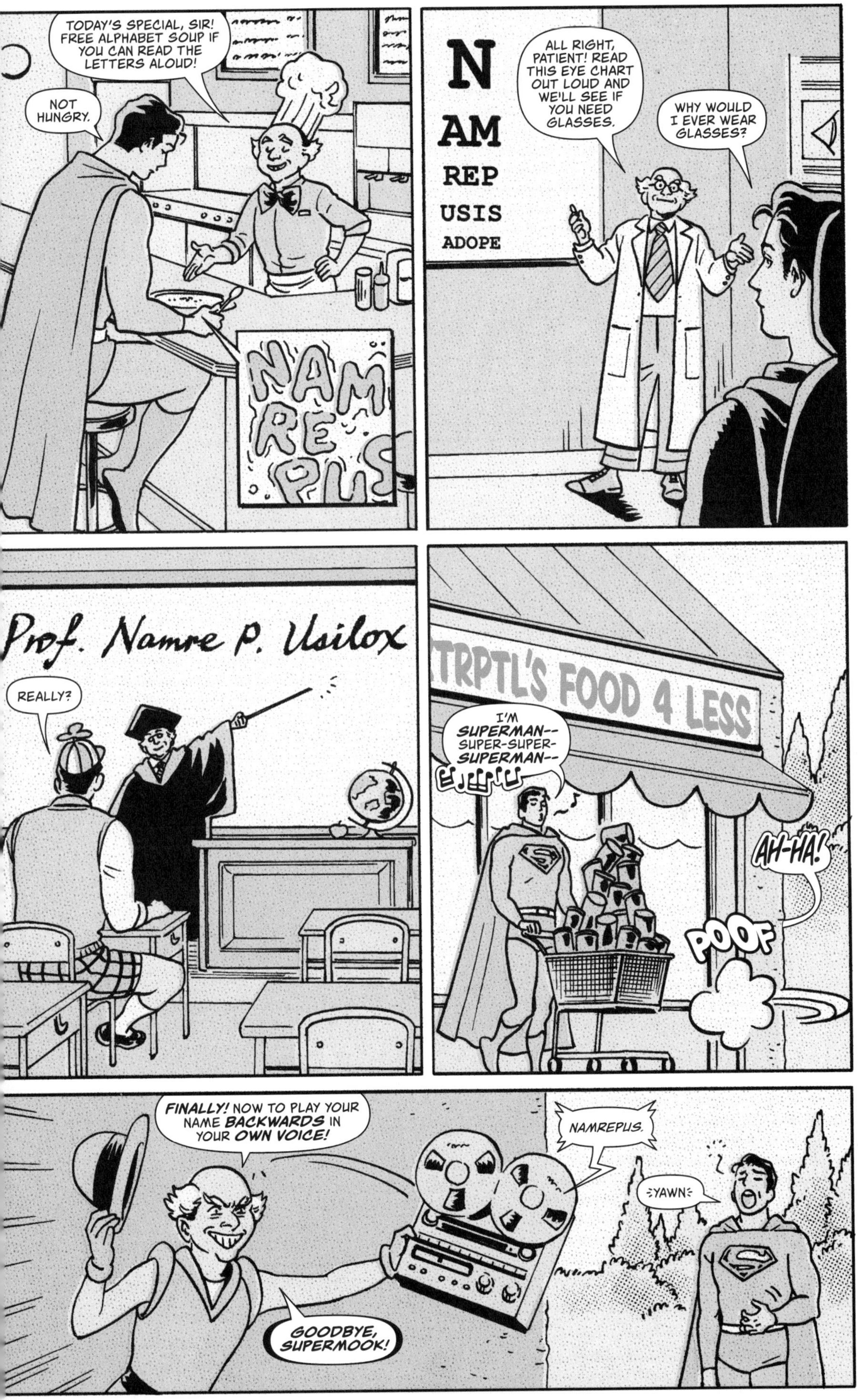
TODAY'S SPECIAL, SIR! FREE ALPHABET SOUP IF YOU CAN READ THE LETTERS ALOUD!
NOT HUNGRY.
NAM RE PUS
N
AM
REP
USIS
ADOPE
ALL RIGHT, PATIENT! READ THIS EYE CHART OUT LOUD AND WE'LL SEE IF YOU NEED GLASSES.
WHY WOULD I EVER WEAR GLASSES?
Prof. Namre P. Usilox
REALLY?
TRPTL'S FOOD 4 LESS
I'M SUPERMAN-- SUPER-SUPER-SUPERMAN--
AH-HA!
POOF
FINALLY! NOW TO PLAY YOUR NAME BACKWARDS IN YOUR OWN VOICE!
NAMREPUS.
YAWN
GOODBYE, SUPERMOOK!

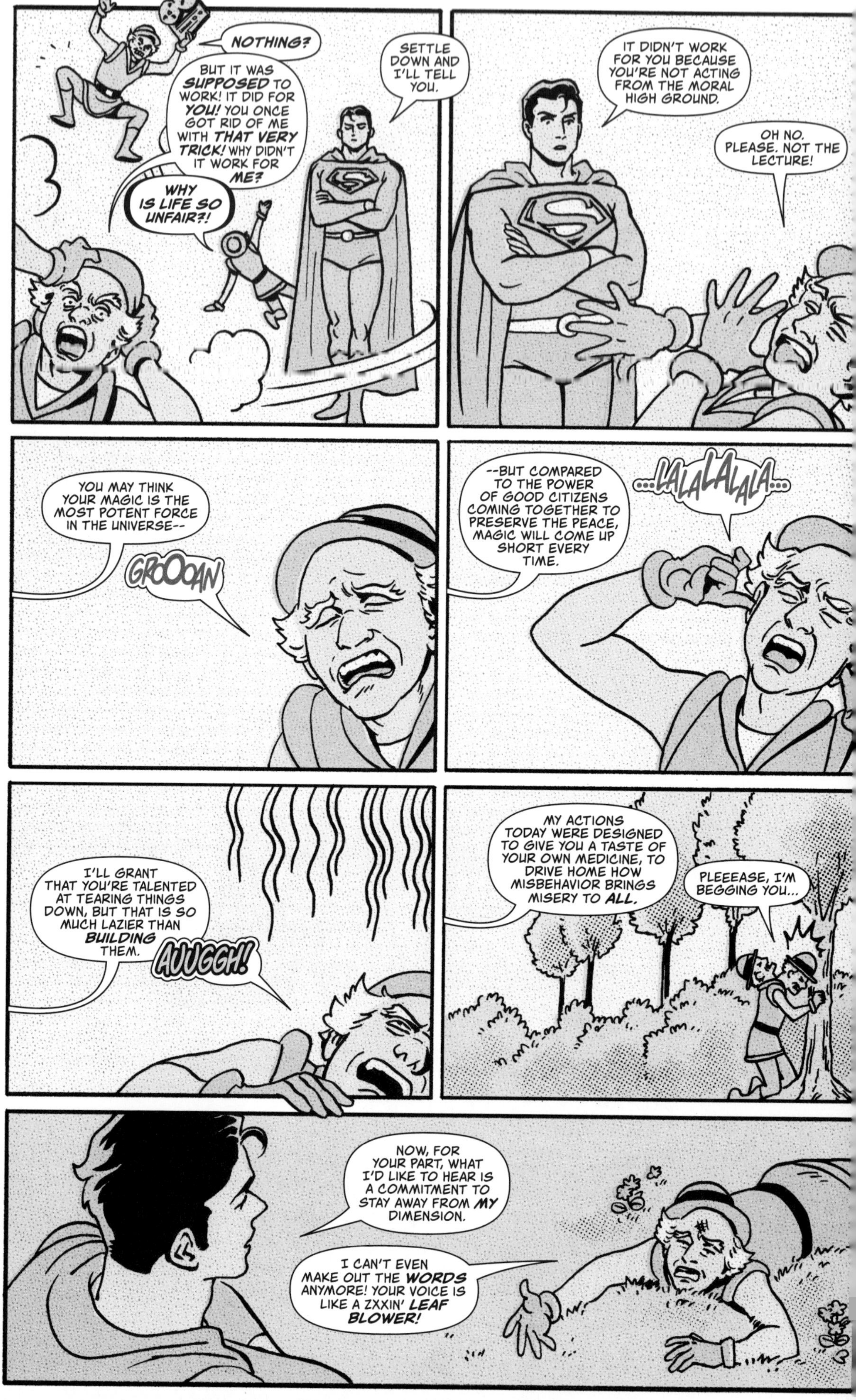
NOTHING?
BUT IT WAS SUPPOSED TO WORK! IT DID FOR YOU! YOU ONCE GOT RID OF ME WITH THAT VERY TRICK! WHY DIDN'T IT WORK FOR ME?
WHY IS LIFE SO UNFAIR?!
SETTLE DOWN AND I'LL TELL YOU.
IT DIDN'T WORK FOR YOU BECAUSE YOU'RE NOT ACTING FROM THE MORAL HIGH GROUND.
OH NO. PLEASE. NOT THE LECTURE!
YOU MAY THINK YOUR MAGIC IS THE MOST POTENT FORCE IN THE UNIVERSE--
GROOOAN
--BUT COMPARED TO THE POWER OF GOOD CITIZENS COMING TOGETHER TO PRESERVE THE PEACE, MAGIC WILL COME UP SHORT EVERY TIME.
...LALALALALALA...
I'LL GRANT THAT YOU'RE TALENTED AT TEARING THINGS DOWN, BUT THAT IS SO MUCH LAZIER THAN BUILDING THEM.
AUUGGH!
MY ACTIONS TODAY WERE DESIGNED TO GIVE YOU A TASTE OF YOUR OWN MEDICINE, TO DRIVE HOME HOW MISBEHAVIOR BRINGS MISERY TO ALL.
PLEEEASE, I'M BEGGING YOU...
NOW, FOR YOUR PART, WHAT I'D LIKE TO HEAR IS A COMMITMENT TO STAY AWAY FROM MY DIMENSION.
I CAN'T EVEN MAKE OUT THE WORDS ANYMORE! YOUR VOICE IS LIKE A ZXXIN' LEAF BLOWER!

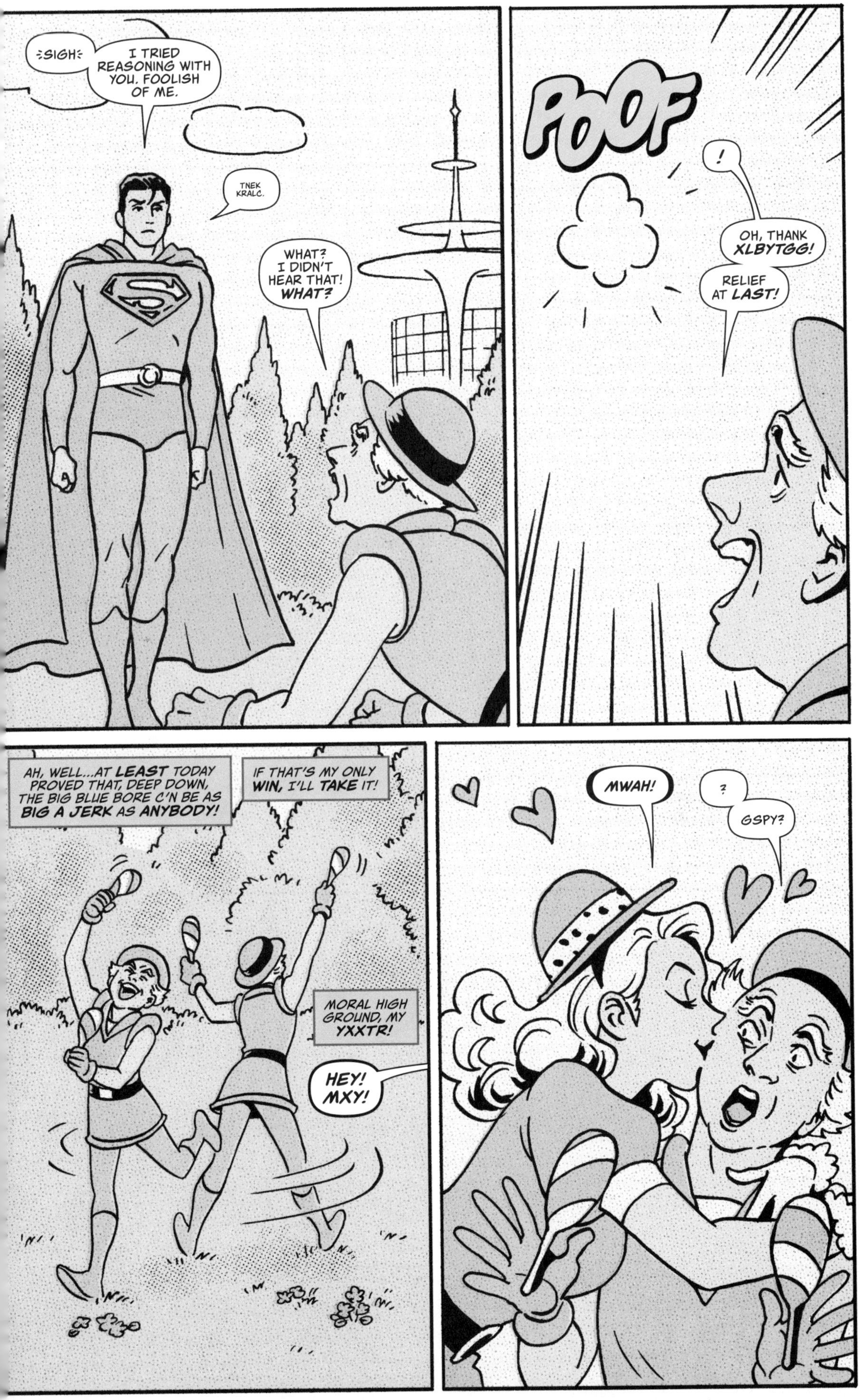
SIGH
I TRIED REASONING WITH YOU. FOOLISH OF ME.
TNEK KRALC.
WHAT? I DIDN'T HEAR THAT! WHAT?
POOF
!
OH, THANK XLBYTGG!
RELIEF AT LAST!
AH, WELL...AT LEAST TODAY PROVED THAT, DEEP DOWN, THE BIG BLUE BORE C'N BE AS BIG A JERK AS ANYBODY!
IF THAT'S MY ONLY WIN, I'LL TAKE IT!
MORAL HIGH GROUND, MY YXXTR!
HEY! MXY!
MWAH!
?
GSPY?

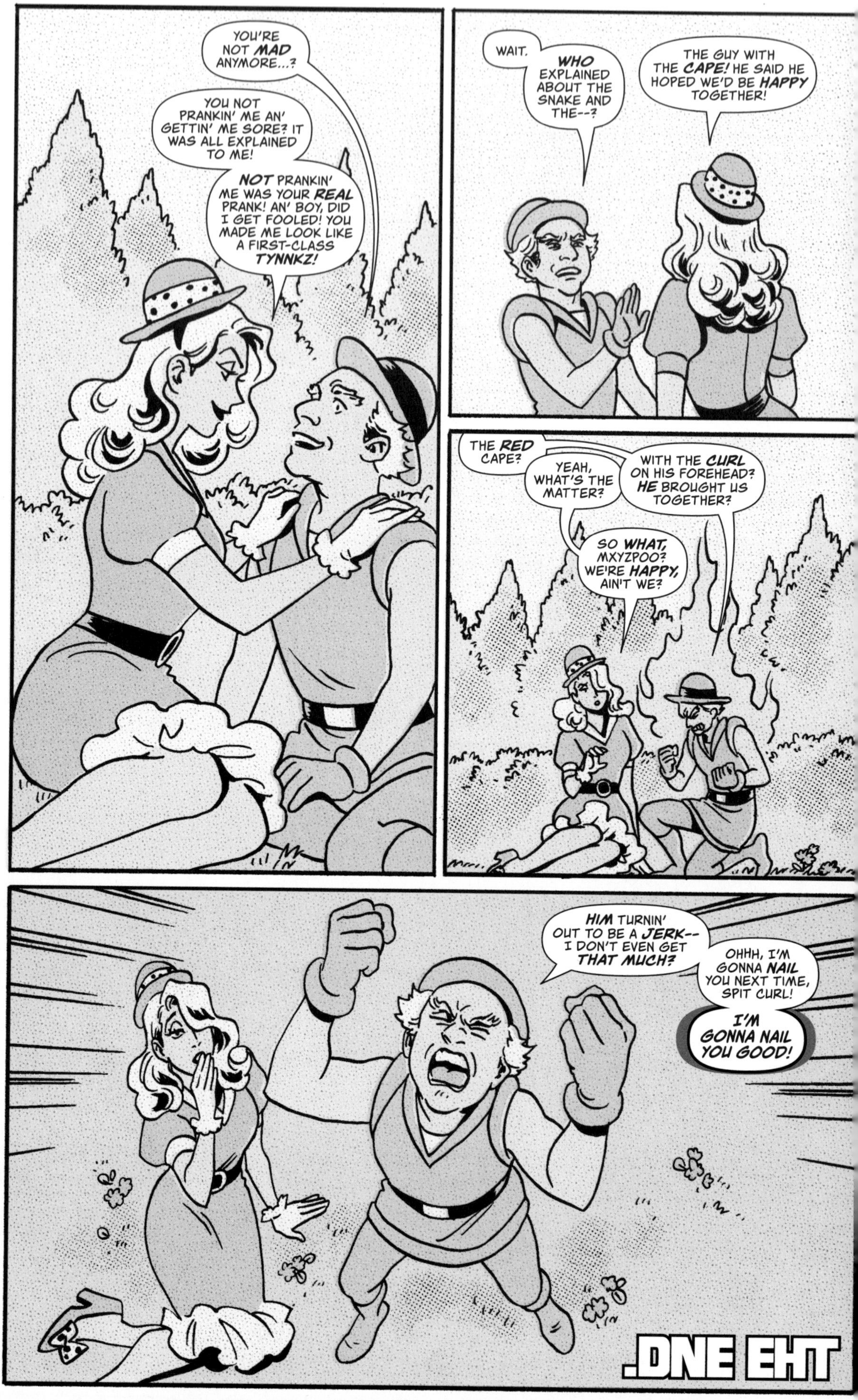
YOU'RE NOT MAD ANYMORE...?
YOU NOT PRANKIN' ME AN' GETTIN' ME SORE? IT WAS ALL EXPLAINED TO ME!
NOT PRANKIN' ME WAS YOUR REAL PRANK! AN' BOY, DID I GET FOOLED! YOU MADE ME LOOK LIKE A FIRST-CLASS TYNNKZ!
WAIT.
WHO EXPLAINED ABOUT THE SNAKE AND THE--?
THE GUY WITH THE CAPE! HE SAID HE HOPED WE'D BE HAPPY TOGETHER!
THE RED CAPE?
YEAH, WHAT'S THE MATTER?
WITH THE CURL ON HIS FOREHEAD? HE BROUGHT US TOGETHER?
SO WHAT, MXYZPOO? WE'RE HAPPY, AIN'T WE?
HIM TURNIN' OUT TO BE A JERK-- I DON'T EVEN GET THAT MUCH?
OHHH, I'M GONNA NAIL YOU NEXT TIME, SPIT CURL!
I'M GONNA NAIL YOU GOOD!
.DNE EHT

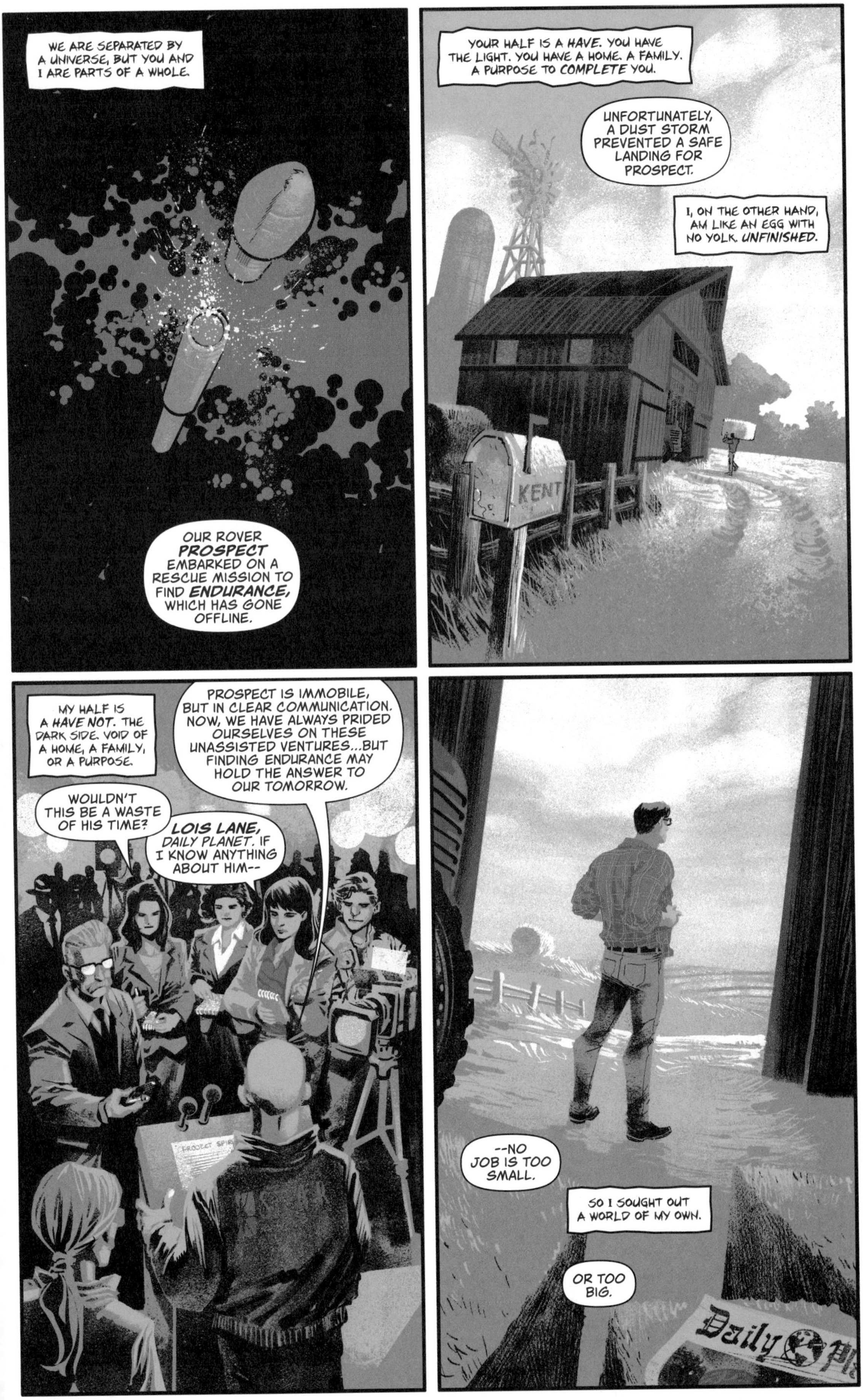
WE ARE SEPARATED BY A UNIVERSE, BUT YOU AND I ARE PARTS OF A WHOLE.
OUR ROVER PROSPECT EMBARKED ON A RESCUE MISSION TO FIND ENDURANCE, WHICH HAS GONE OFFLINE.
YOUR HALF IS A HAVE. YOU HAVE THE LIGHT. YOU HAVE A HOME. A FAMILY. A PURPOSE TO COMPLETE YOU.
UNFORTUNATELY, A DUST STORM PREVENTED A SAFE LANDING FOR PROSPECT.
I, ON THE OTHER HAND, AM LIKE AN EGG WITH NO YOLK. UNFINISHED.
KENT
MY HALF IS A HAVE NOT. THE DARK SIDE. VOID OF A HOME, A FAMILY, OR A PURPOSE.
PROSPECT IS IMMOBILE, BUT IN CLEAR COMMUNICATION. NOW, WE HAVE ALWAYS PRIDED OURSELVES ON THESE UNASSISTED VENTURES...BUT FINDING ENDURANCE MAY HOLD THE ANSWER TO OUR TOMORROW.
WOULDN'T THIS BE A WASTE OF HIS TIME?
LOIS LANE, DAILY PLANET. IF I KNOW ANYTHING ABOUT HIM--
--NO JOB IS TOO SMALL.
SO I SOUGHT OUT A WORLD OF MY OWN.
OR TOO BIG.

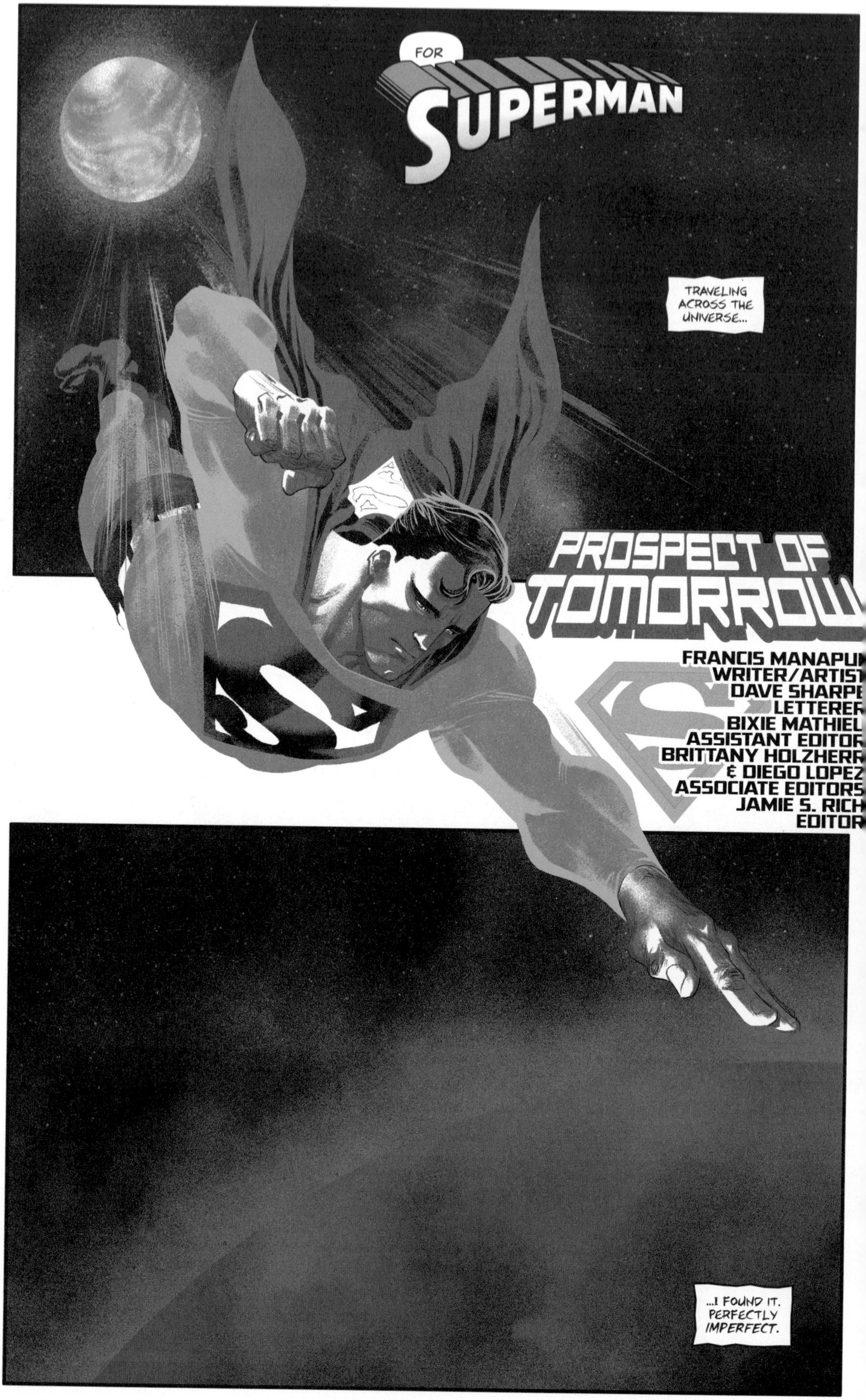
FOR
SUPERMAN
TRAVELING ACROSS THE UNIVERSE...
PROSPECT OF TOMORROW
FRANCIS MANAPU
WRITER/ARTIS
DAVE SHARPE
LETTERER
BIXIE MATHIEU
ASSISTANT EDITOR
BRITTANY HOLZHERR
& DIEGO LOPEZ
ASSOCIATE EDITORS
JAMIE S. RICH
EDITOR
...I FOUND IT. PERFECTLY IMPERFECT.

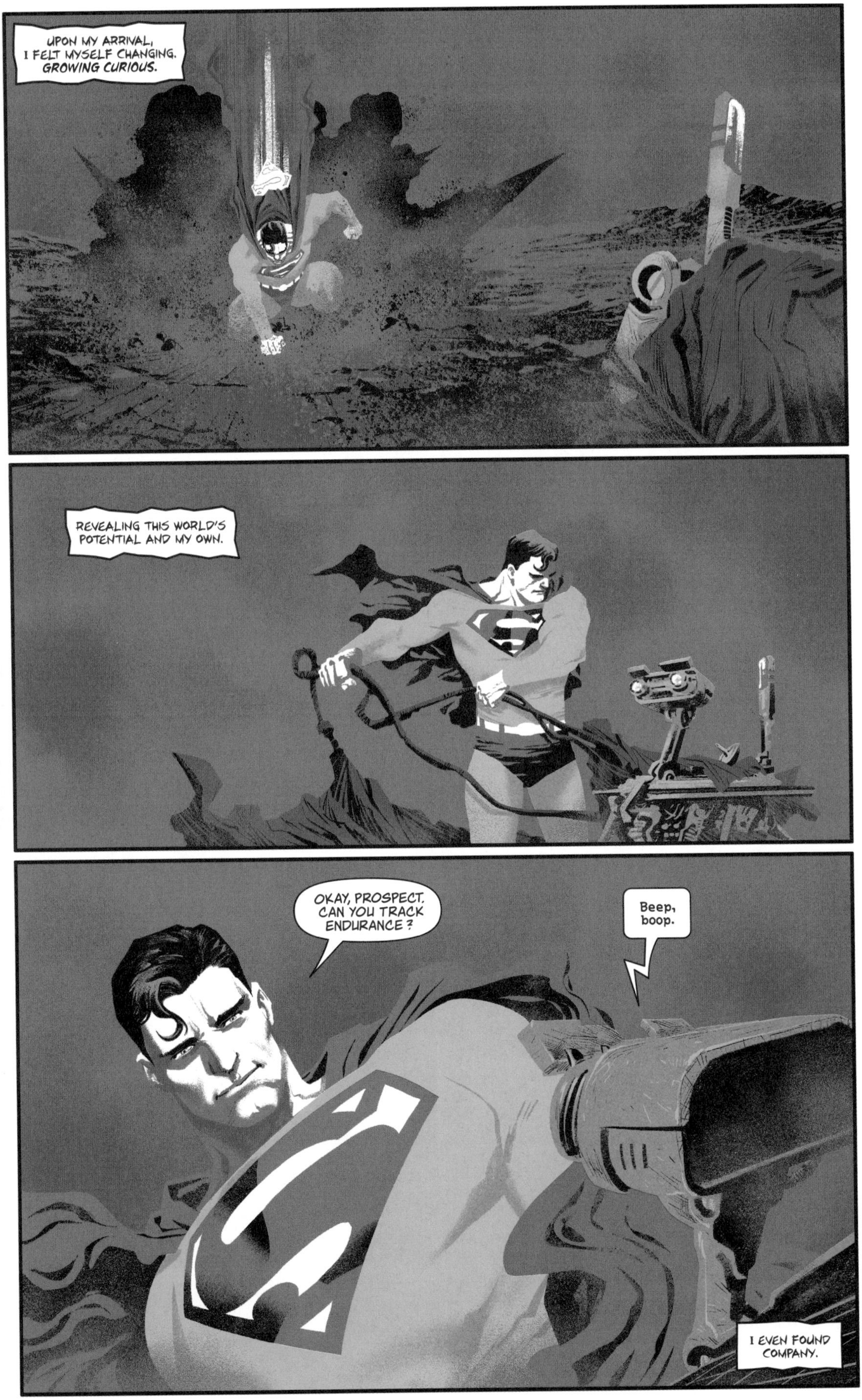
UPON MY ARRIVAL, I FELT MYSELF CHANGING. GROWING CURIOUS.
REVEALING THIS WORLD'S POTENTIAL AND MY OWN.
OKAY, PROSPECT. CAN YOU TRACK ENDURANCE?
Beep, boop.
I EVEN FOUND COMPANY.

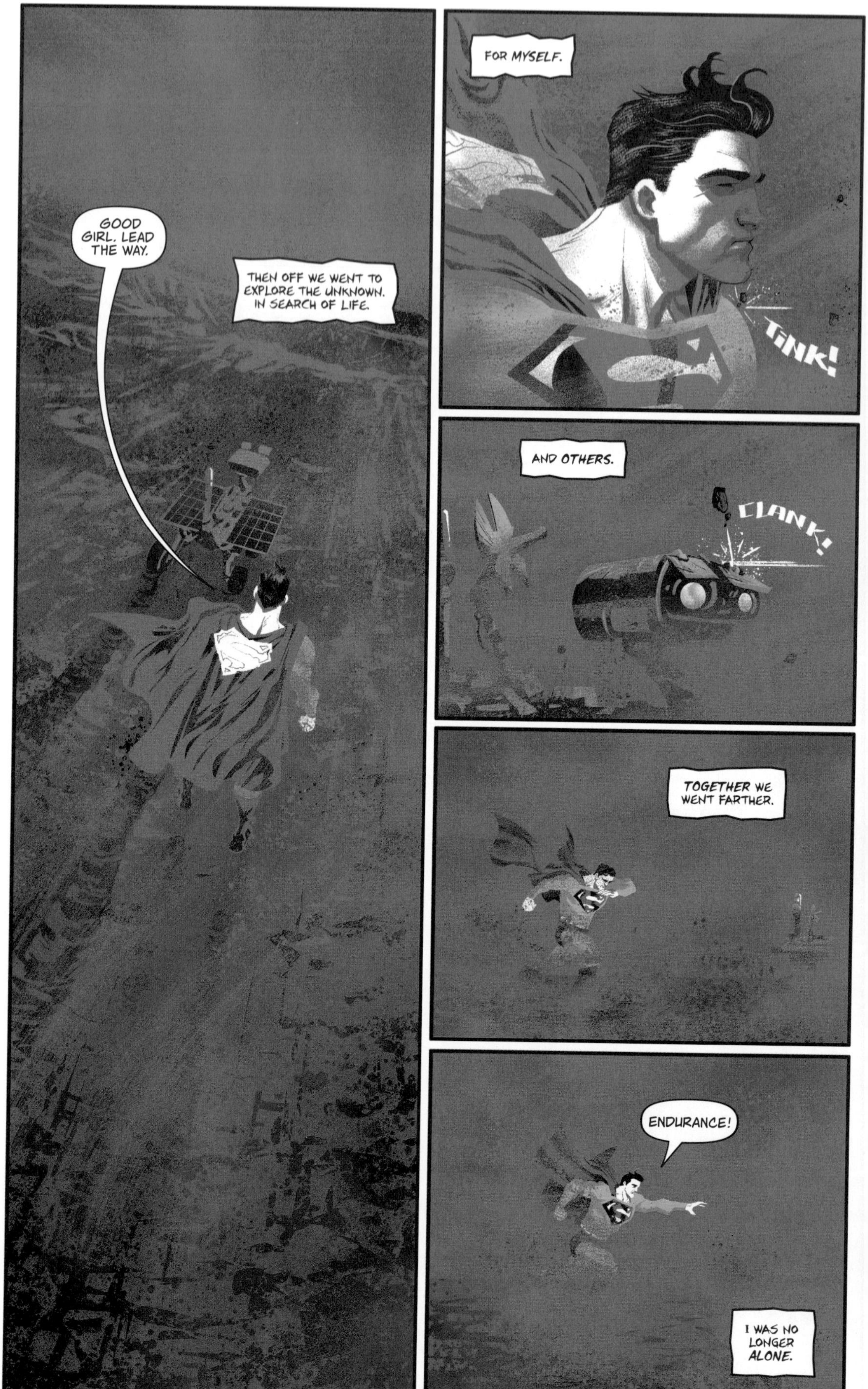
GOOD GIRL. LEAD THE WAY.
THEN OFF WE WENT TO EXPLORE THE UNKNOWN. IN SEARCH OF LIFE.
FOR MYSELF.
TINK!
AND OTHERS.
CLANK!
TOGETHER WE WENT FARTHER.
ENDURANCE!
I WAS NO LONGER ALONE.

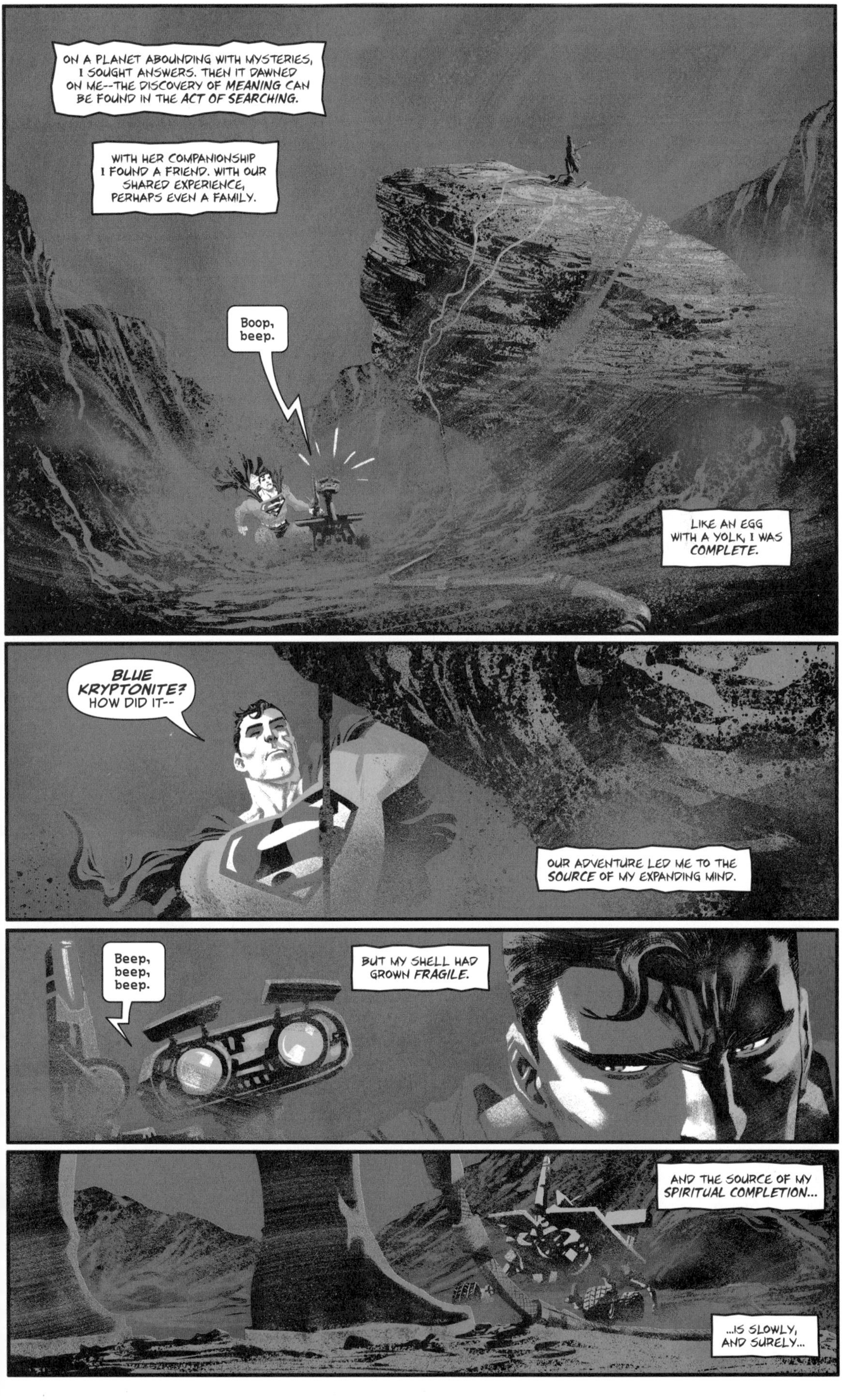
ON A PLANET ABOUNDING WITH MYSTERIES, I SOUGHT ANSWERS. THEN IT DAWNED ON ME--THE DISCOVERY OF MEANING CAN BE FOUND IN THE ACT OF SEARCHING.
WITH HER COMPANIONSHIP I FOUND A FRIEND. WITH OUR SHARED EXPERIENCE, PERHAPS EVEN A FAMILY.
Boop, beep.
LIKE AN EGG WITH A YOLK, I WAS COMPLETE.
BLUE KRYPTONITE? HOW DID IT--
OUR ADVENTURE LED ME TO THE SOURCE OF MY EXPANDING MIND.
Beep, beep, beep.
BUT MY SHELL HAD GROWN FRAGILE.
AND THE SOURCE OF MY SPIRITUAL COMPLETION...
...IS SLOWLY, AND SURELY...

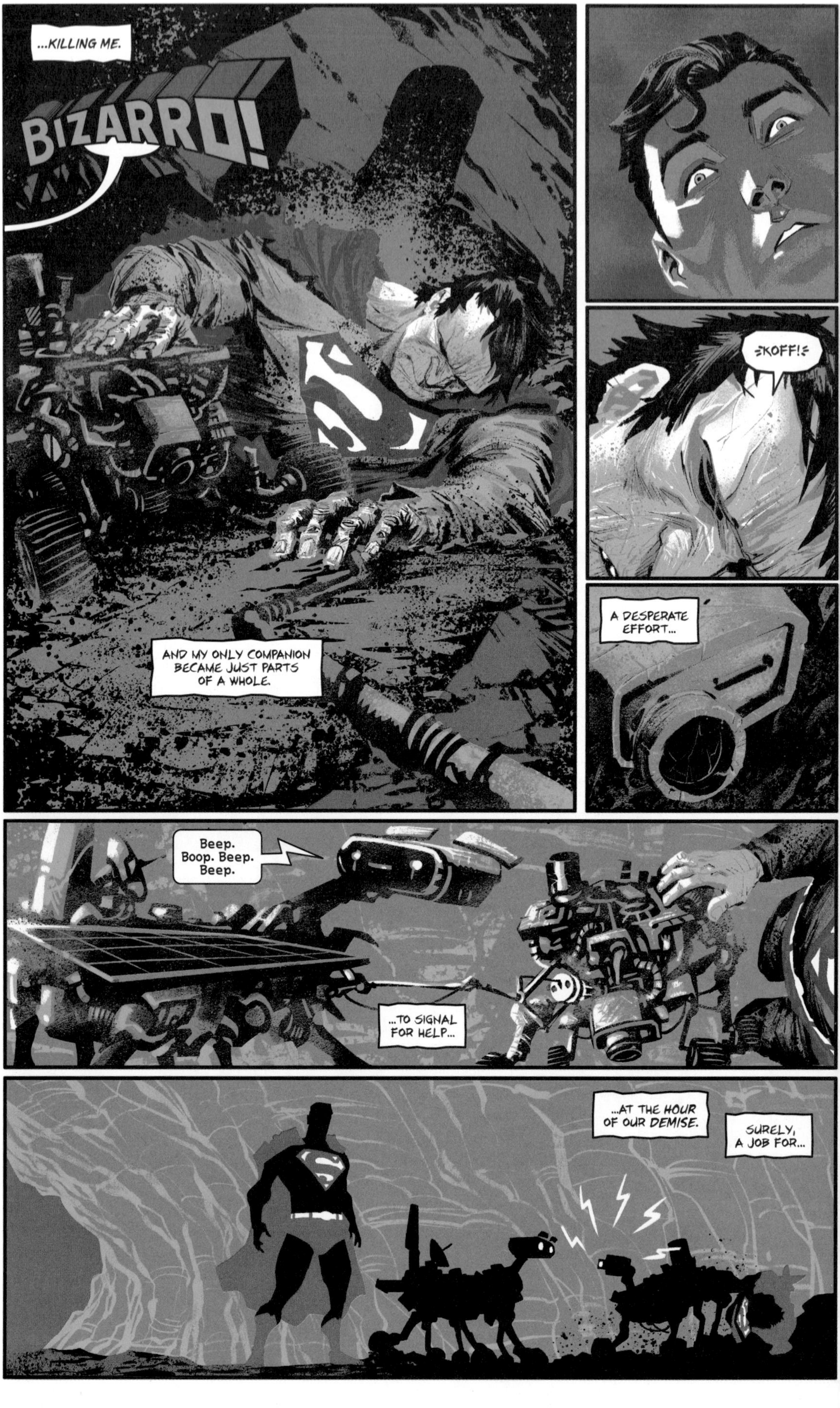
...KILLING ME.
BIZARRO!
AND MY ONLY COMPANION BECAME JUST PARTS OF A WHOLE.
KOFF!
A DESPERATE EFFORT...
Beep. Boop. Beep. Beep.
...TO SIGNAL FOR HELP...
...AT THE HOUR OF OUR DEMISE.
SURELY, A JOB FOR...

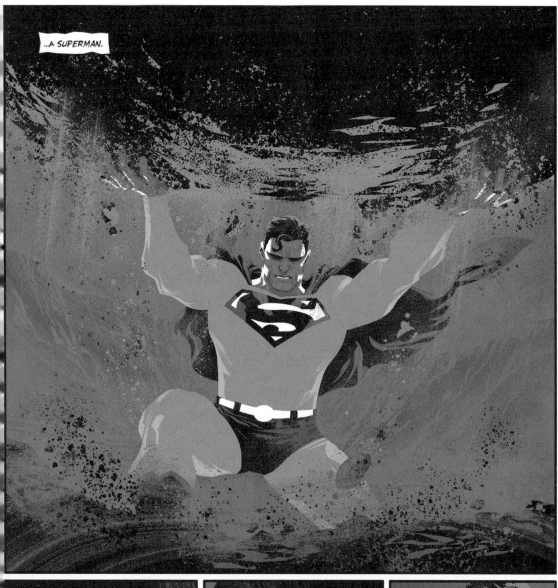

...A SUPERMAN.

I--ME...

...ME--MY GRATITUDE.

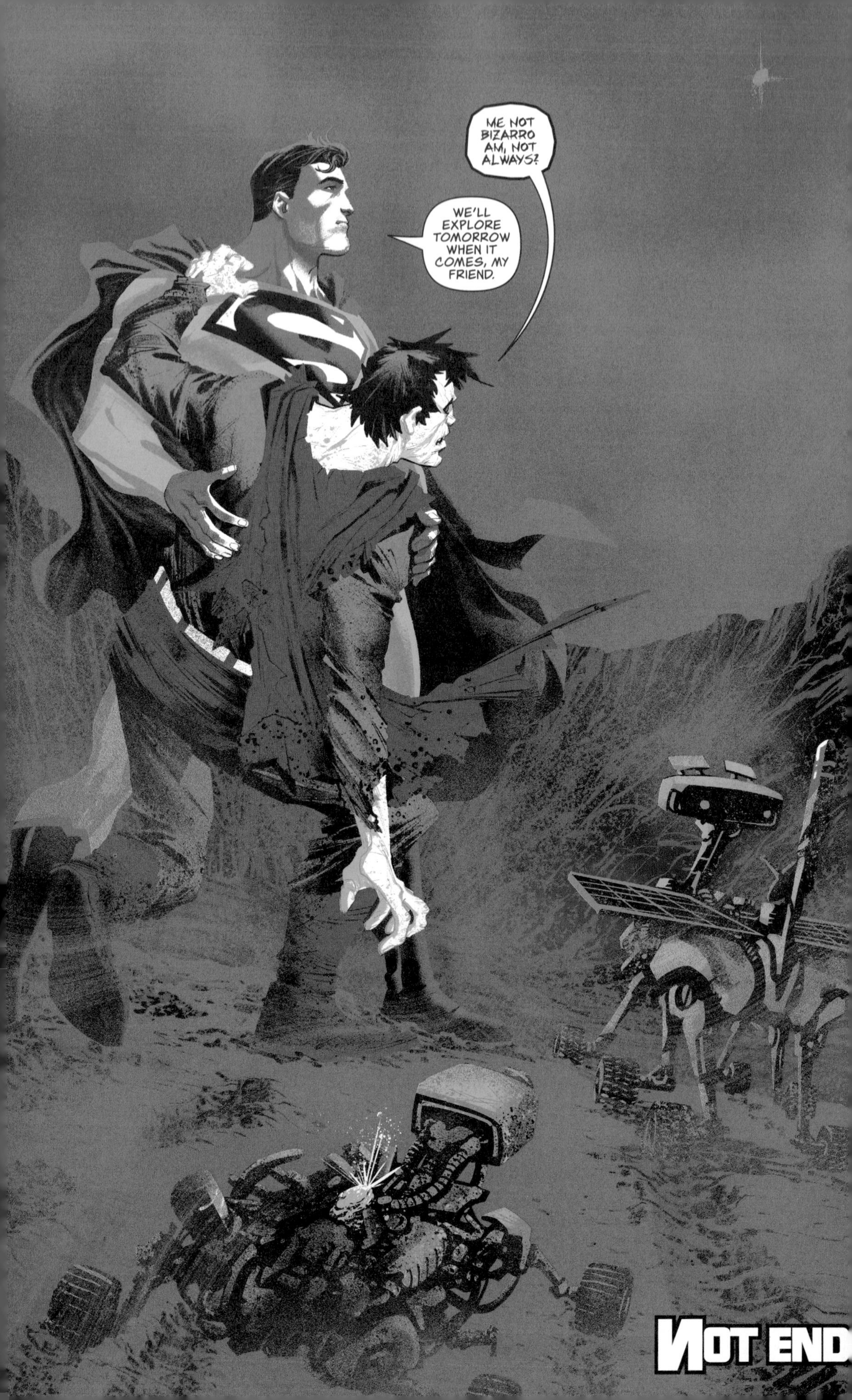
ME NOT BIZARRO AM, NOT ALWAYS?
WE'LL EXPLORE TOMORROW WHEN IT COMES, MY FRIEND.
NOT END

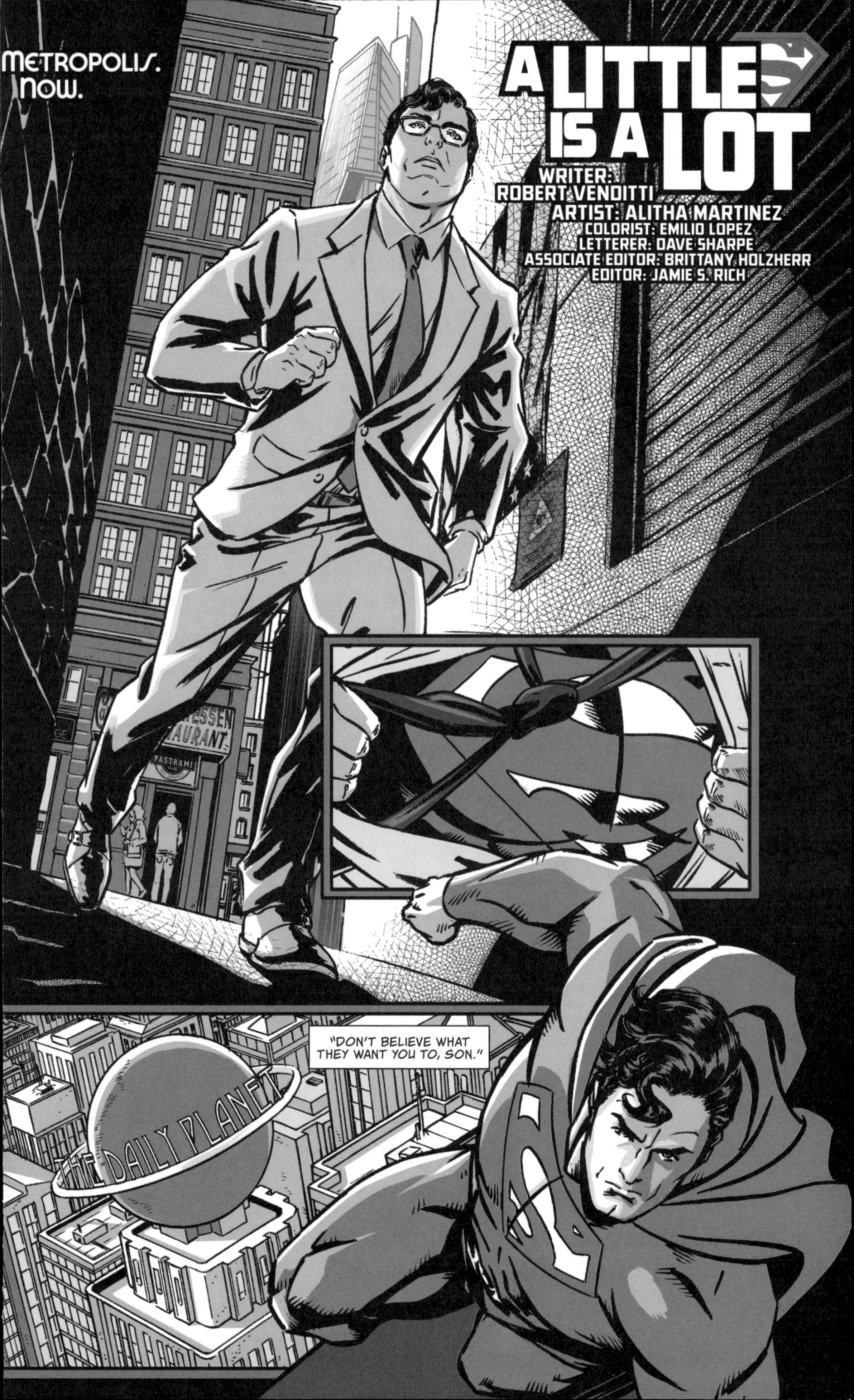
METROPOLIS. NOW.
A LITTLE IS A LOT
WRITER: ROBERT VENDITTI
ARTIST: ALITHA MARTINEZ
COLORIST: EMILIO LOPEZ
LETTERER: DAVE SHARPE
ASSOCIATE EDITOR: BRITTANY HOLZHERR
EDITOR: JAMIE S. RICH
PASTRAMI
"DON'T BELIEVE WHAT THEY WANT YOU TO, SON."
THE DAILY PLANET

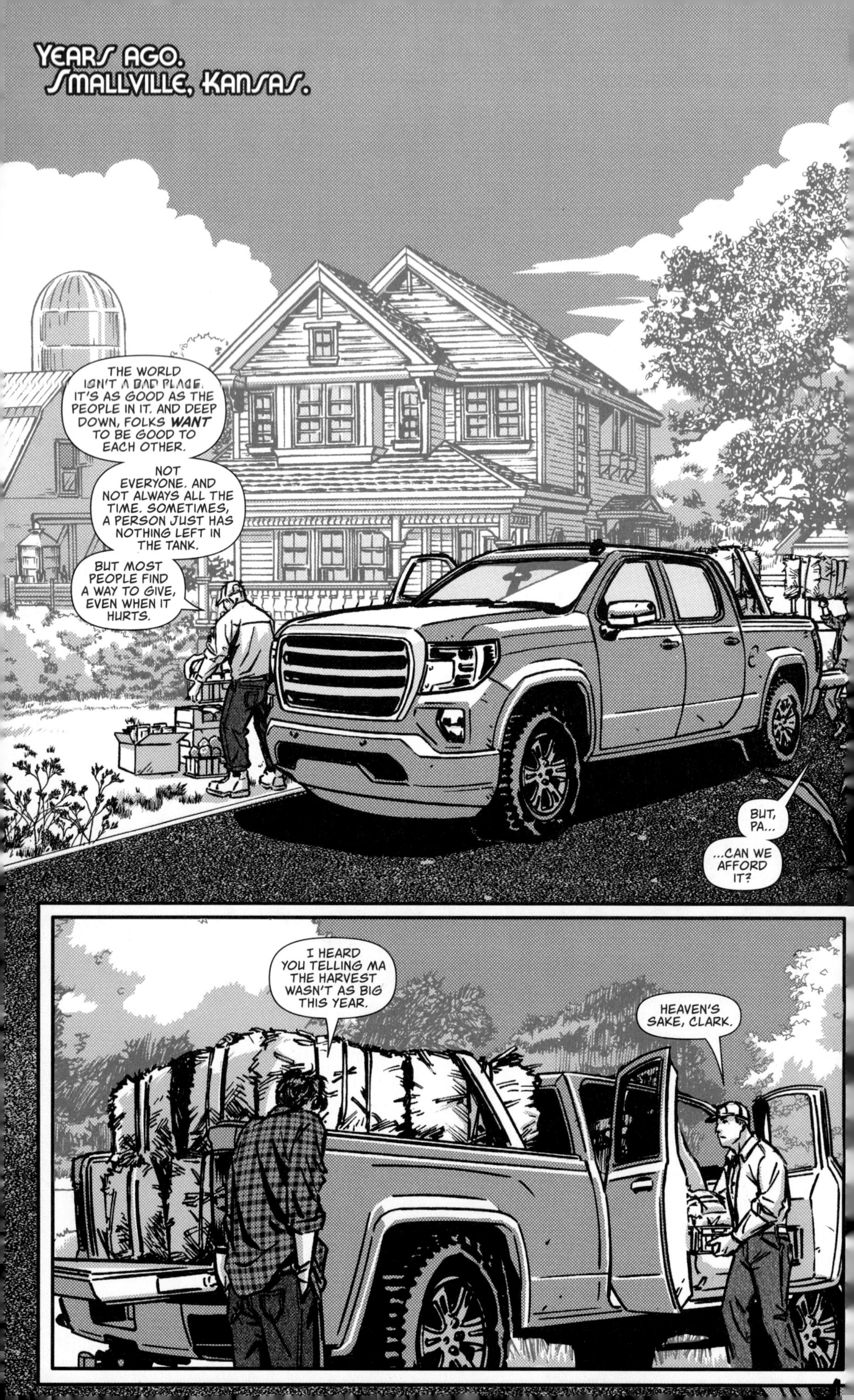
YEARS AGO. SMALLVILLE, KANSAS.
THE WORLD ISN'T A BAD PLACE. IT'S AS GOOD AS THE PEOPLE IN IT. AND DEEP DOWN, FOLKS WANT TO BE GOOD TO EACH OTHER.
NOT EVERYONE. AND NOT ALWAYS ALL THE TIME. SOMETIMES, A PERSON JUST HAS NOTHING LEFT IN THE TANK.
BUT MOST PEOPLE FIND A WAY TO GIVE, EVEN WHEN IT HURTS.
BUT, PA...
...CAN WE AFFORD IT?
I HEARD YOU TELLING MA THE HARVEST WASN'T AS BIG THIS YEAR.
HEAVEN'S SAKE, CLARK.

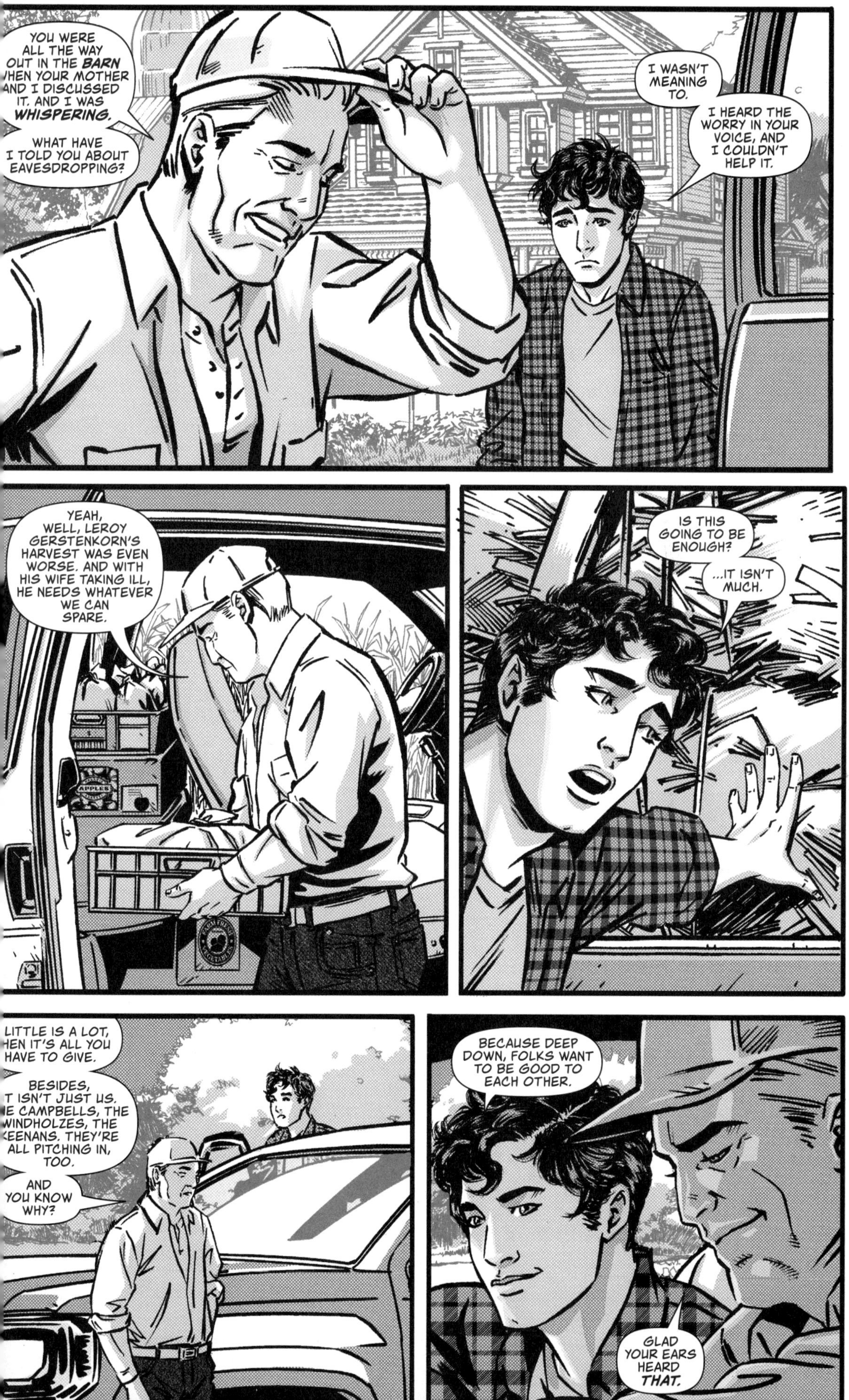
YOU WERE ALL THE WAY OUT IN THE **BARN** HEN YOUR MOTHER AND I DISCUSSED IT. AND I WAS **WHISPERING.**
WHAT HAVE I TOLD YOU ABOUT EAVESDROPPING?
I WASN'T MEANING TO.
I HEARD THE WORRY IN YOUR VOICE, AND I COULDN'T HELP IT.
YEAH, WELL, LEROY GERSTENKORN'S HARVEST WAS EVEN WORSE. AND WITH HIS WIFE TAKING ILL, HE NEEDS WHATEVER WE CAN SPARE.
APPLES
IS THIS GOING TO BE ENOUGH?
...IT ISN'T MUCH.
LITTLE IS A LOT, HEN IT'S ALL YOU HAVE TO GIVE.
BESIDES, T ISN'T JUST US. E CAMPBELLS, THE WINDHOLZES, THE EENANS. THEY'RE ALL PITCHING IN, TOO.
AND YOU KNOW WHY?
BECAUSE DEEP DOWN, FOLKS WANT TO BE GOOD TO EACH OTHER.
GLAD YOUR EARS HEARD **THAT.**

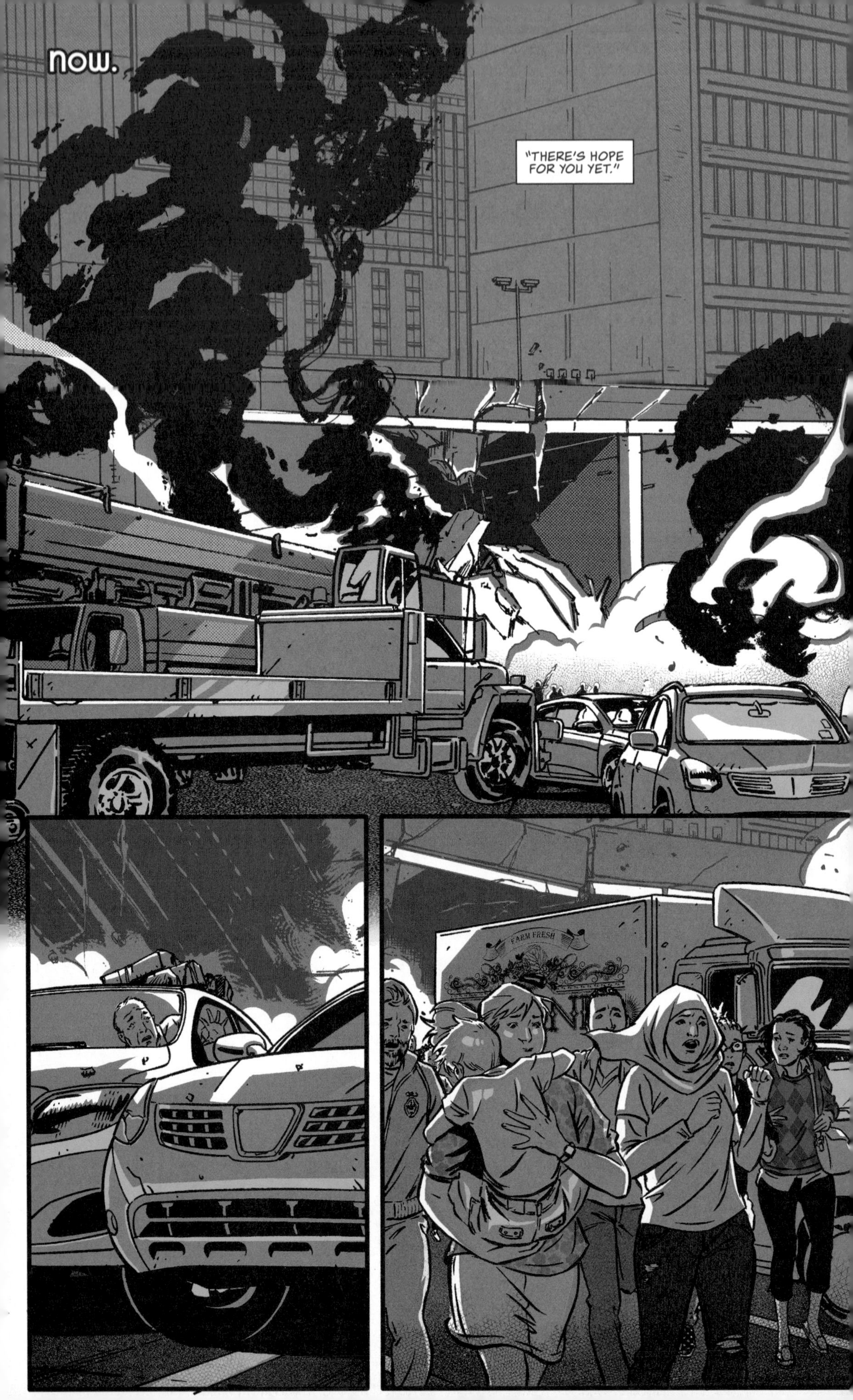
now.
"THERE'S HOPE FOR YOU YET."
FARM FRESH

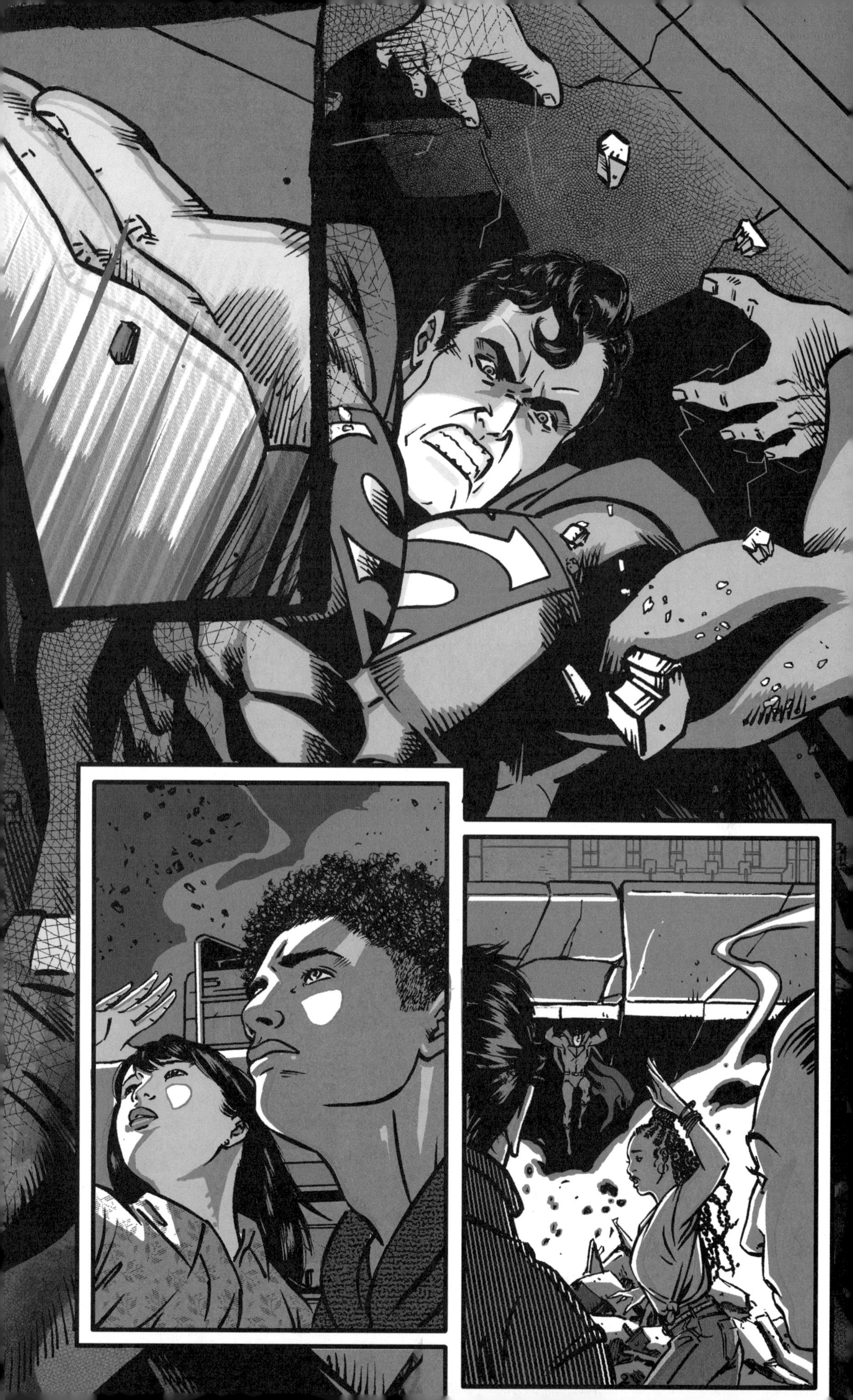

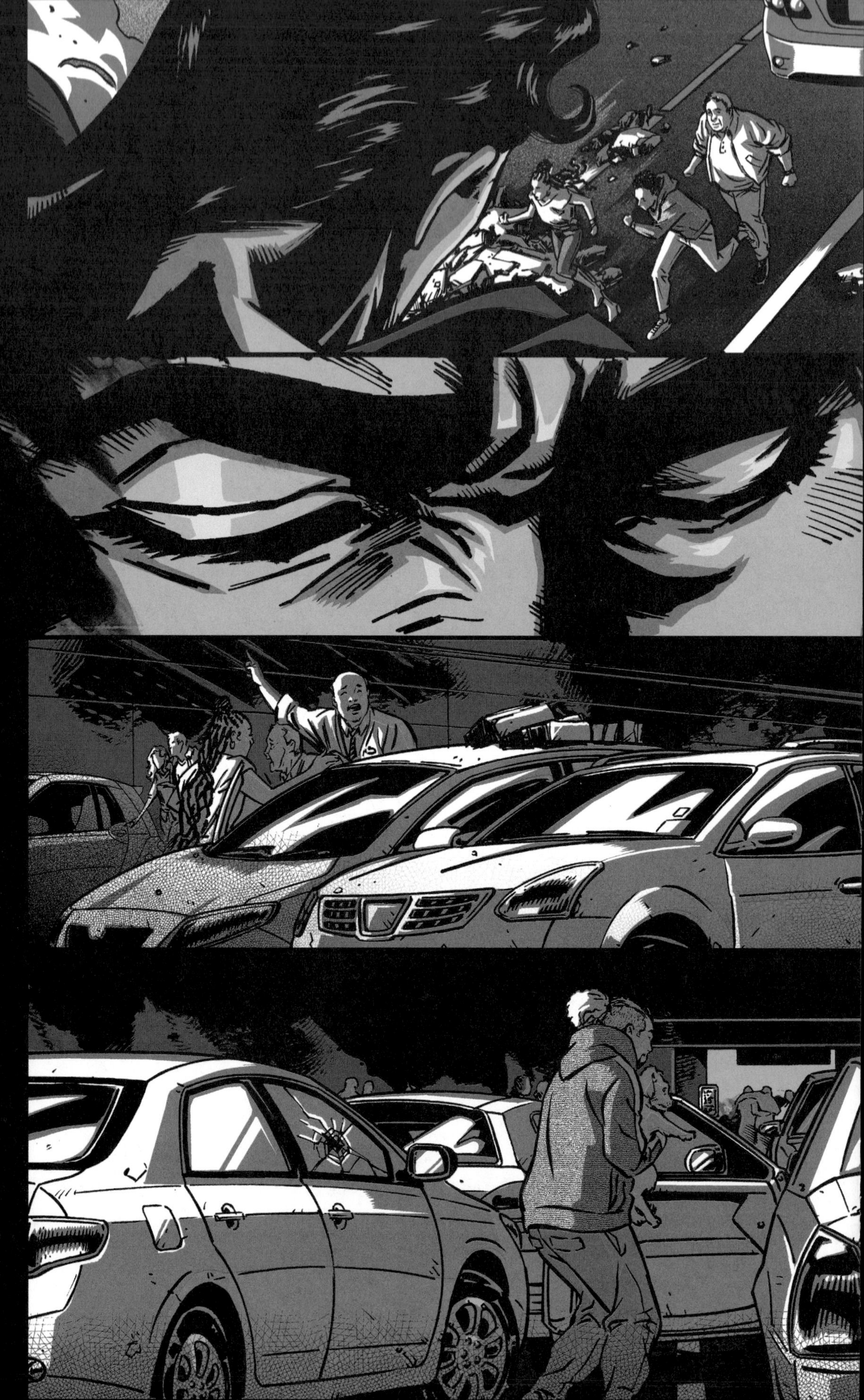

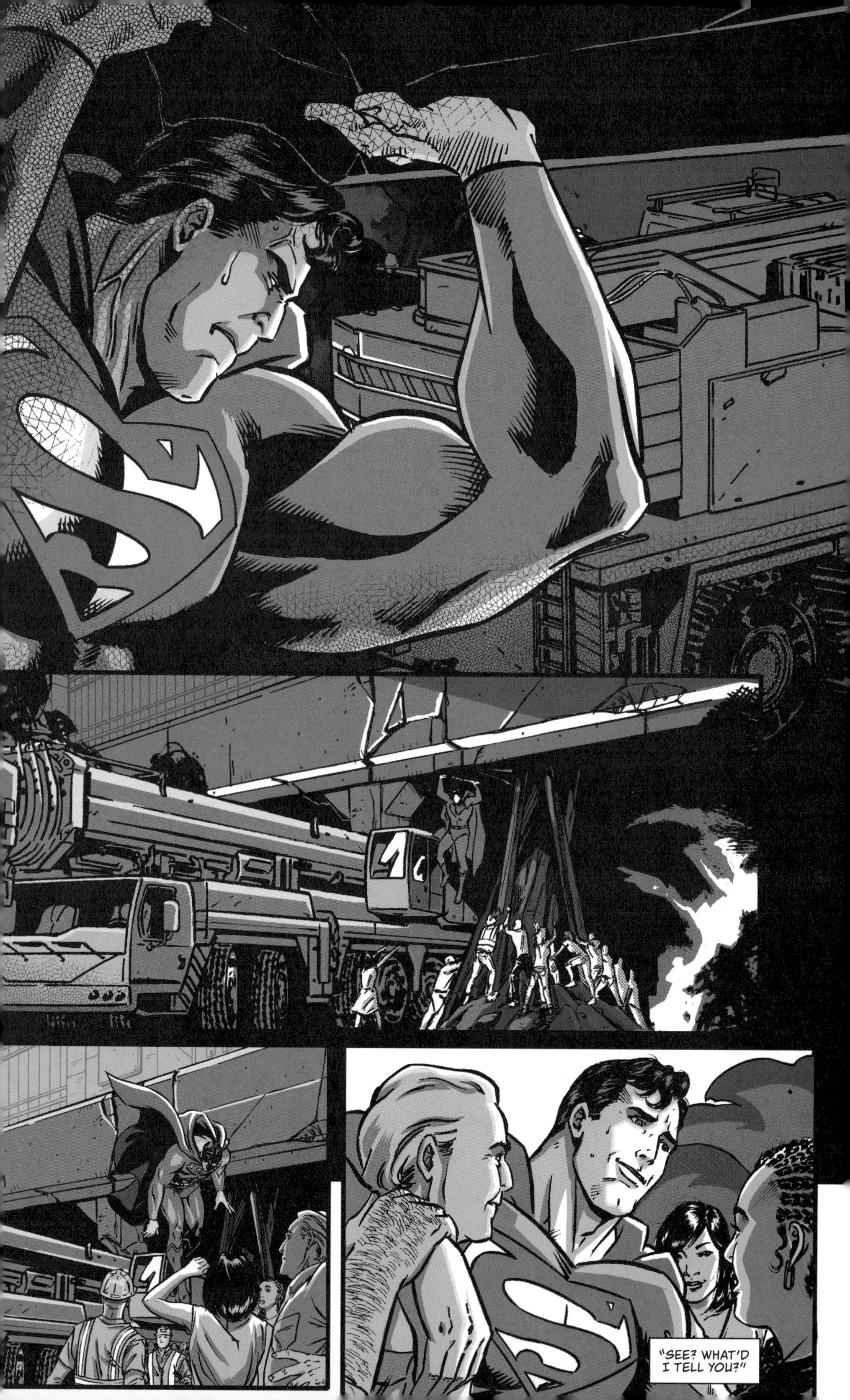
"SEE? WHAT'D I TELL YOU?"

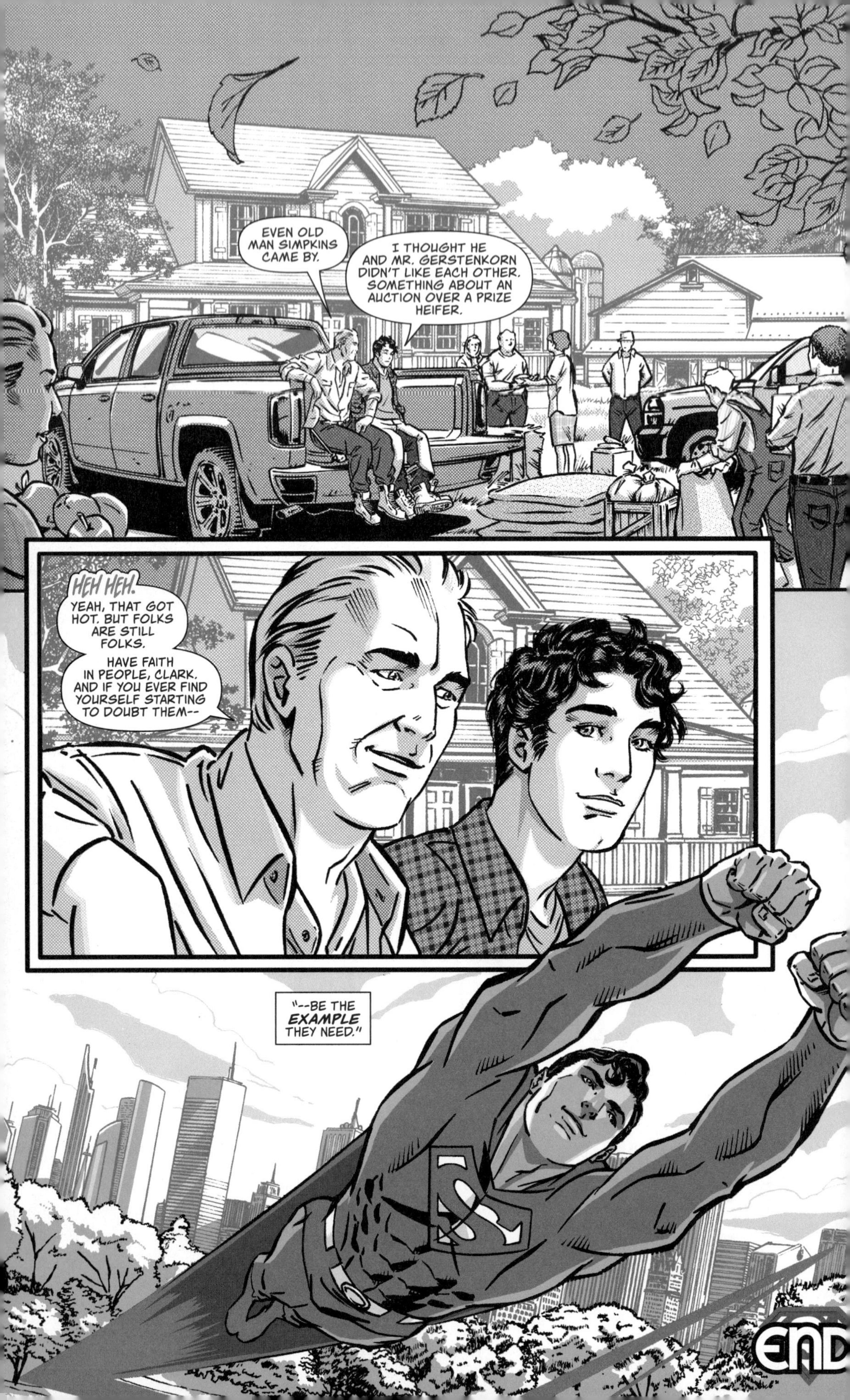
EVEN OLD MAN SIMPKINS CAME BY.
I THOUGHT HE AND MR. GERSTENKORN DIDN'T LIKE EACH OTHER. SOMETHING ABOUT AN AUCTION OVER A PRIZE HEIFER.
HEH HEH!
YEAH, THAT GOT HOT. BUT FOLKS ARE STILL FOLKS.
HAVE FAITH IN PEOPLE, CLARK. AND IF YOU EVER FIND YOURSELF STARTING TO DOUBT THEM--
"--BE THE *EXAMPLE* THEY NEED."
END

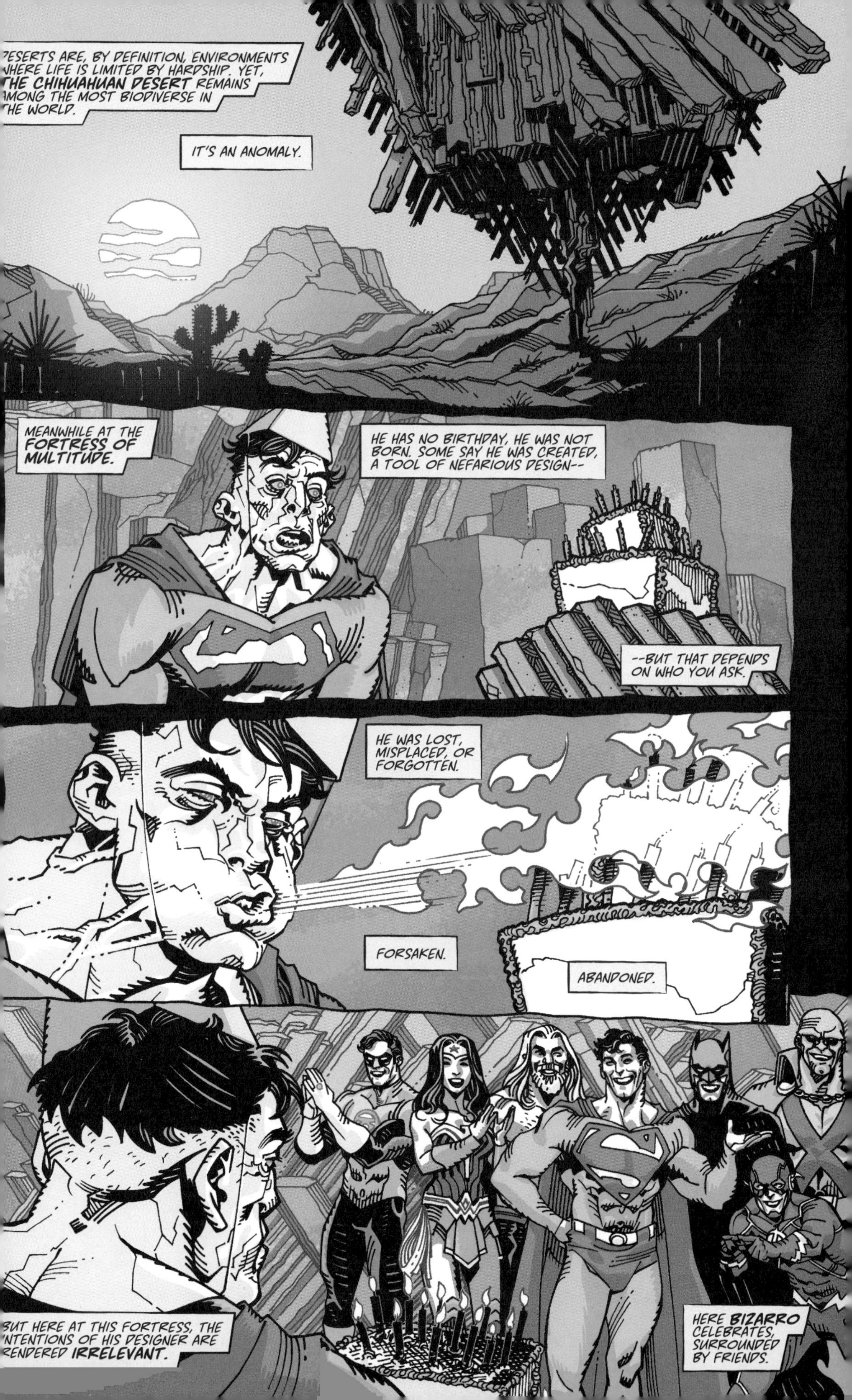

DESERTS ARE, BY DEFINITION, ENVIRONMENTS WHERE LIFE IS LIMITED BY HARDSHIP. YET, THE CHIHUAHUAN DESERT REMAINS AMONG THE MOST BIODIVERSE IN THE WORLD.
IT'S AN ANOMALY.
MEANWHILE AT THE FORTRESS OF MULTITUDE.
HE HAS NO BIRTHDAY, HE WAS NOT BORN. SOME SAY HE WAS CREATED, A TOOL OF NEFARIOUS DESIGN--
--BUT THAT DEPENDS ON WHO YOU ASK.
HE WAS LOST, MISPLACED, OR FORGOTTEN.
FORSAKEN.
ABANDONED.
BUT HERE AT THIS FORTRESS, THE INTENTIONS OF HIS DESIGNER ARE RENDERED IRRELEVANT.
HERE BIZARRO CELEBRATES, SURROUNDED BY FRIENDS.

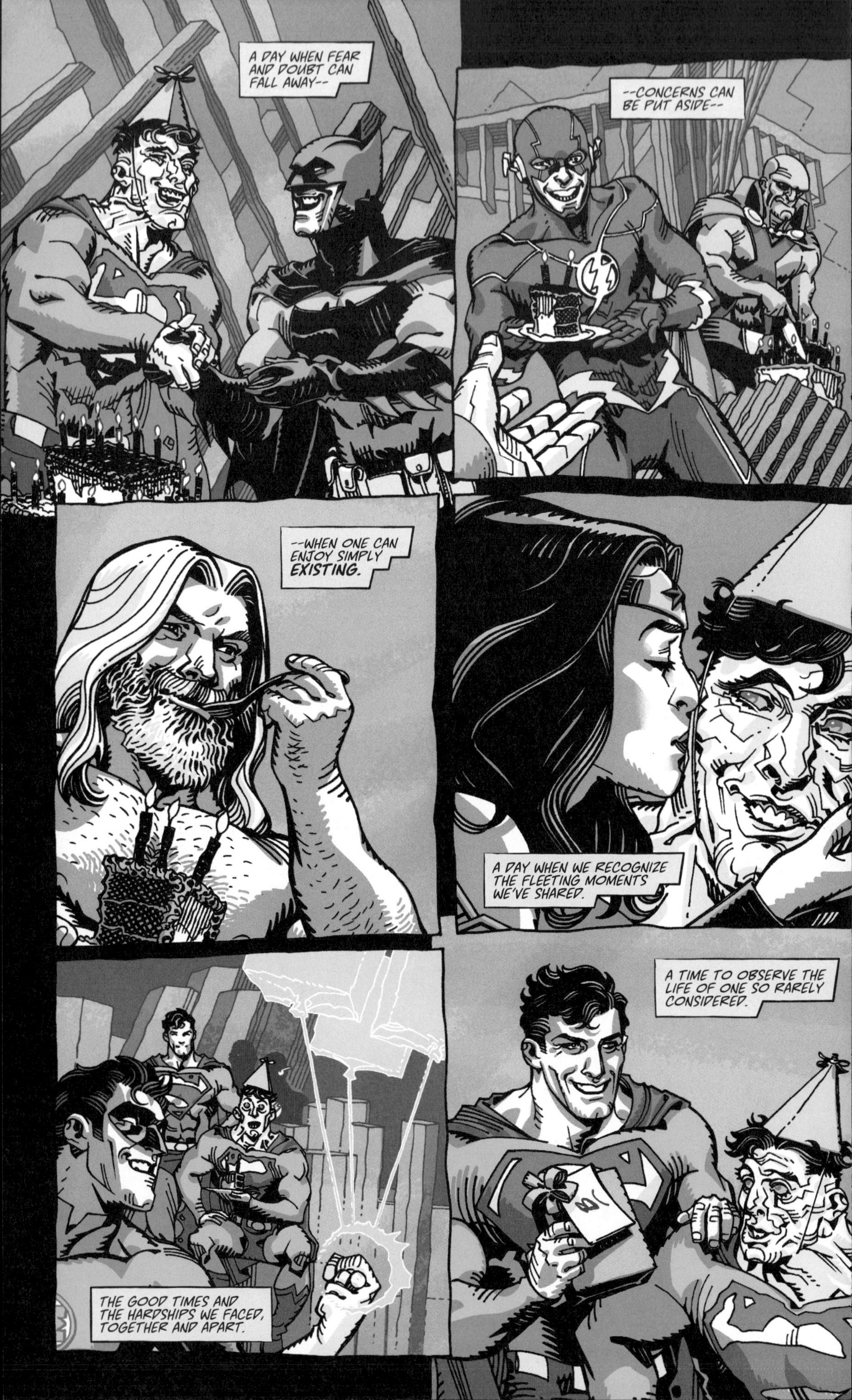
A DAY WHEN FEAR AND DOUBT CAN FALL AWAY--
--CONCERNS CAN BE PUT ASIDE--
--WHEN ONE CAN ENJOY SIMPLY EXISTING.
A DAY WHEN WE RECOGNIZE THE FLEETING MOMENTS WE'VE SHARED.
THE GOOD TIMES AND THE HARDSHIPS WE FACED, TOGETHER AND APART.
A TIME TO OBSERVE THE LIFE OF ONE SO RARELY CONSIDERED.

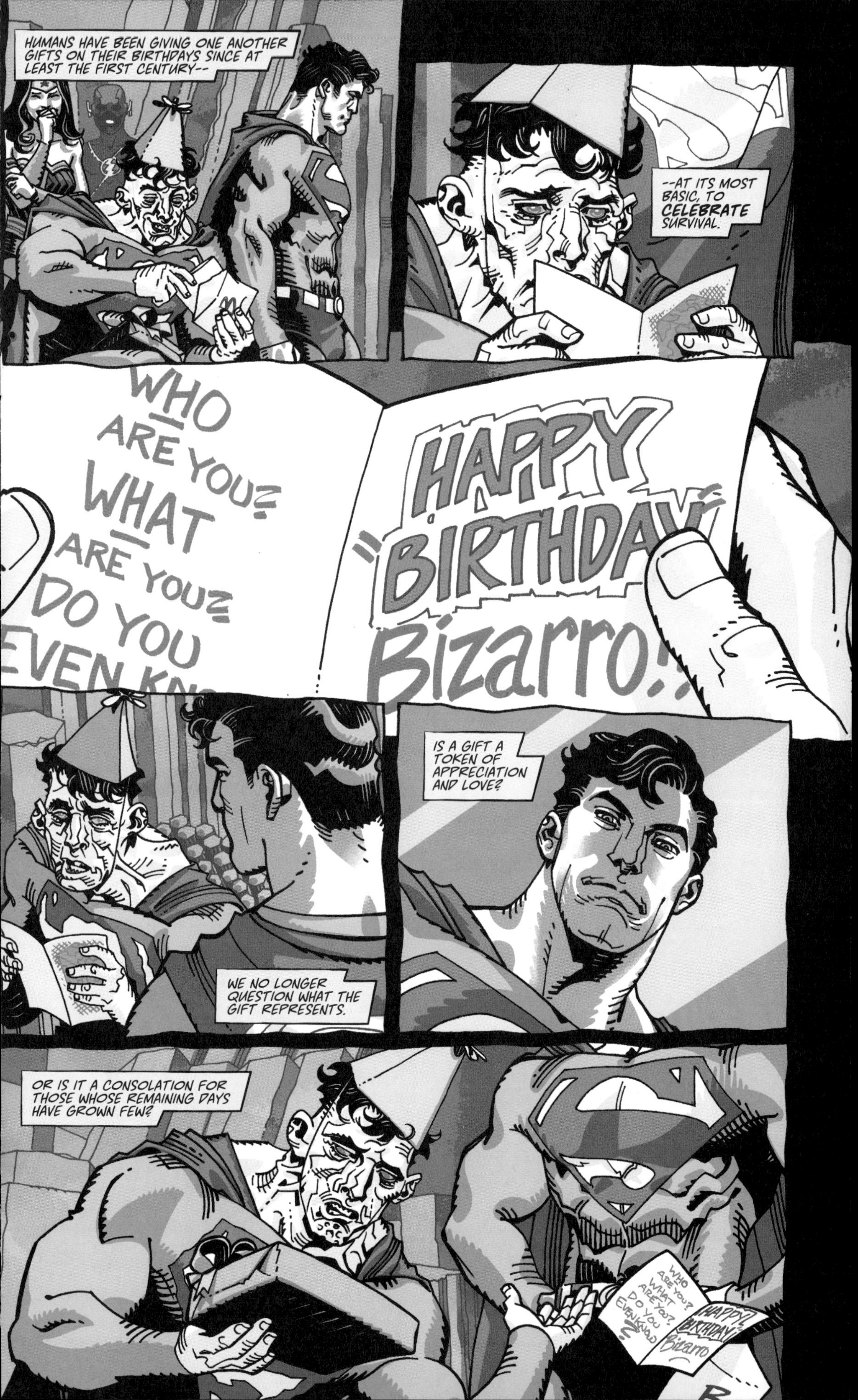

HUMANS HAVE BEEN GIVING ONE ANOTHER GIFTS ON THEIR BIRTHDAYS SINCE AT LEAST THE FIRST CENTURY--
--AT ITS MOST BASIC, TO CELEBRATE SURVIVAL.
WHO ARE YOU? WHAT ARE YOU? DO YOU EVEN KN
HAPPY BIRTHDAY Bizarro!!
WE NO LONGER QUESTION WHAT THE GIFT REPRESENTS.
IS A GIFT A TOKEN OF APPRECIATION AND LOVE?
OR IS IT A CONSOLATION FOR THOSE WHOSE REMAINING DAYS HAVE GROWN FEW?

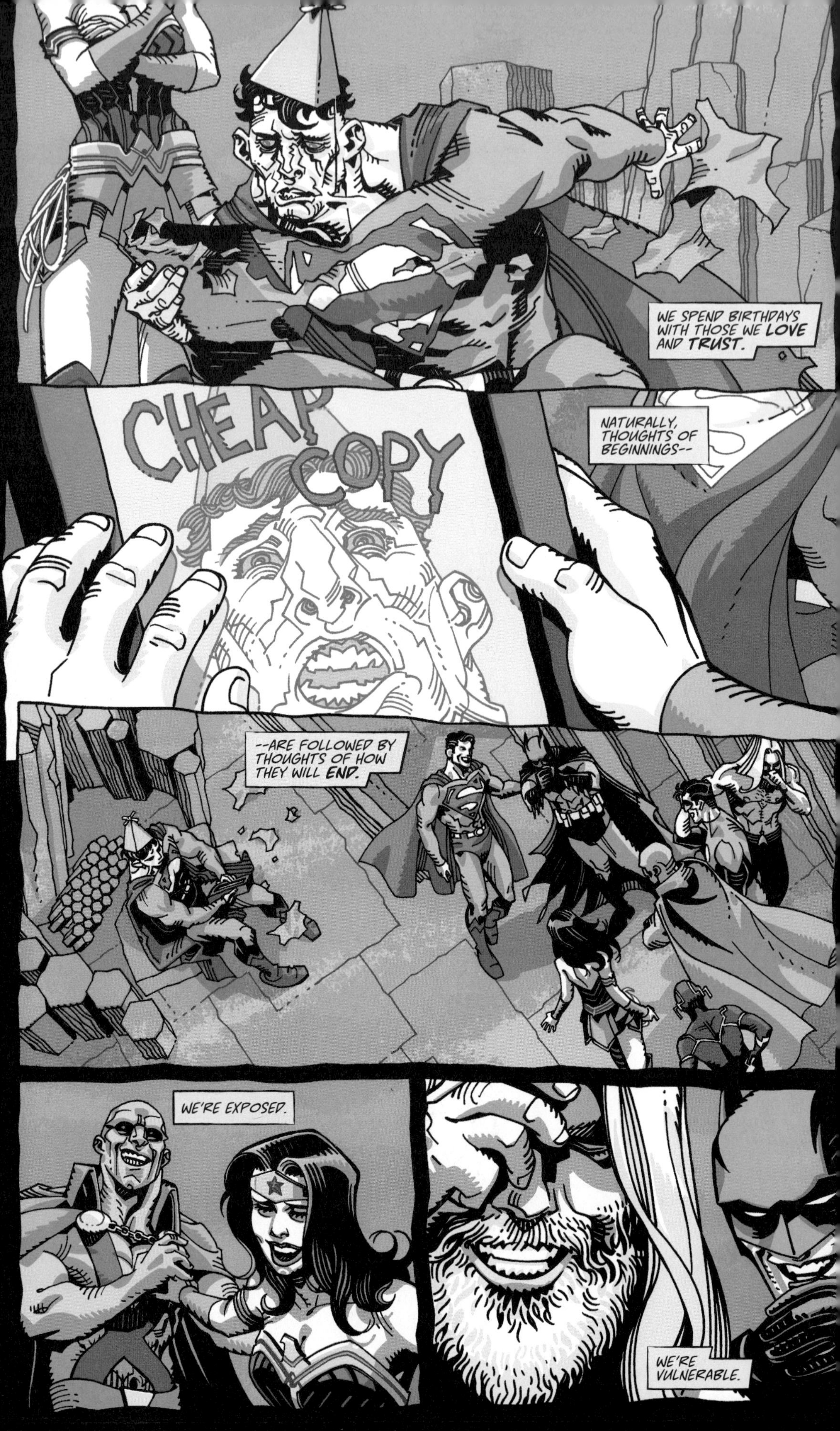
WE SPEND BIRTHDAYS WITH THOSE WE LOVE AND TRUST.
CHEAP COPY
NATURALLY, THOUGHTS OF BEGINNINGS--
--ARE FOLLOWED BY THOUGHTS OF HOW THEY WILL END.
WE'RE EXPOSED.
WE'RE VULNERABLE.

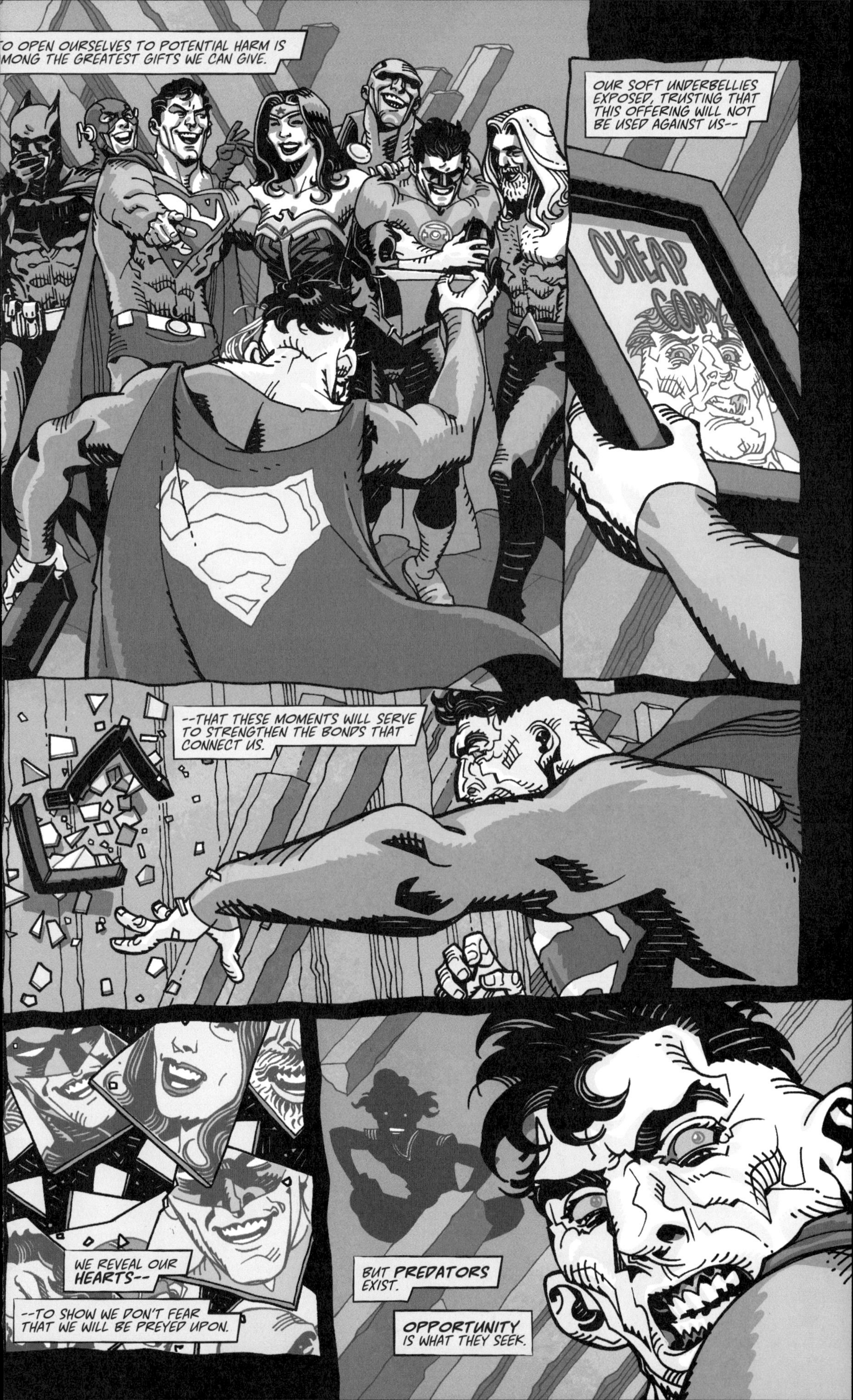
TO OPEN OURSELVES TO POTENTIAL HARM IS AMONG THE GREATEST GIFTS WE CAN GIVE.
OUR SOFT UNDERBELLIES EXPOSED, TRUSTING THAT THIS OFFERING WILL NOT BE USED AGAINST US--
CHEAP COPY
--THAT THESE MOMENTS WILL SERVE TO STRENGTHEN THE BONDS THAT CONNECT US.
WE REVEAL OUR HEARTS--
--TO SHOW WE DON'T FEAR THAT WE WILL BE PREYED UPON.
BUT PREDATORS EXIST.
OPPORTUNITY IS WHAT THEY SEEK.

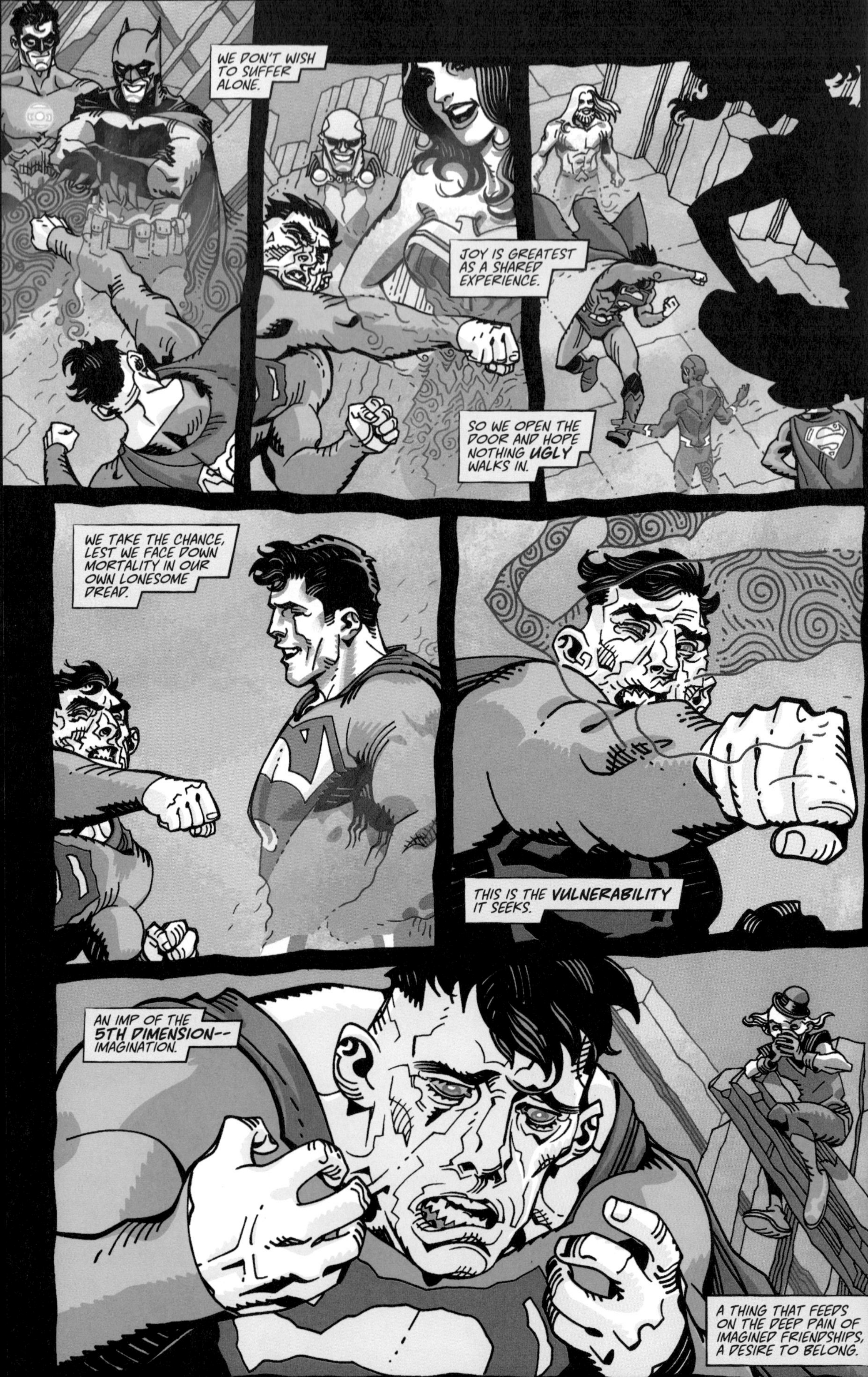
WE DON'T WISH TO SUFFER ALONE.
JOY IS GREATEST AS A SHARED EXPERIENCE.
SO WE OPEN THE DOOR AND HOPE NOTHING UGLY WALKS IN.
WE TAKE THE CHANCE, LEST WE FACE DOWN MORTALITY IN OUR OWN LONESOME DREAD.
THIS IS THE VULNERABILITY IT SEEKS.
AN IMP OF THE 5TH DIMENSION-- IMAGINATION.
A THING THAT FEEDS ON THE DEEP PAIN OF IMAGINED FRIENDSHIPS, A DESIRE TO BELONG.

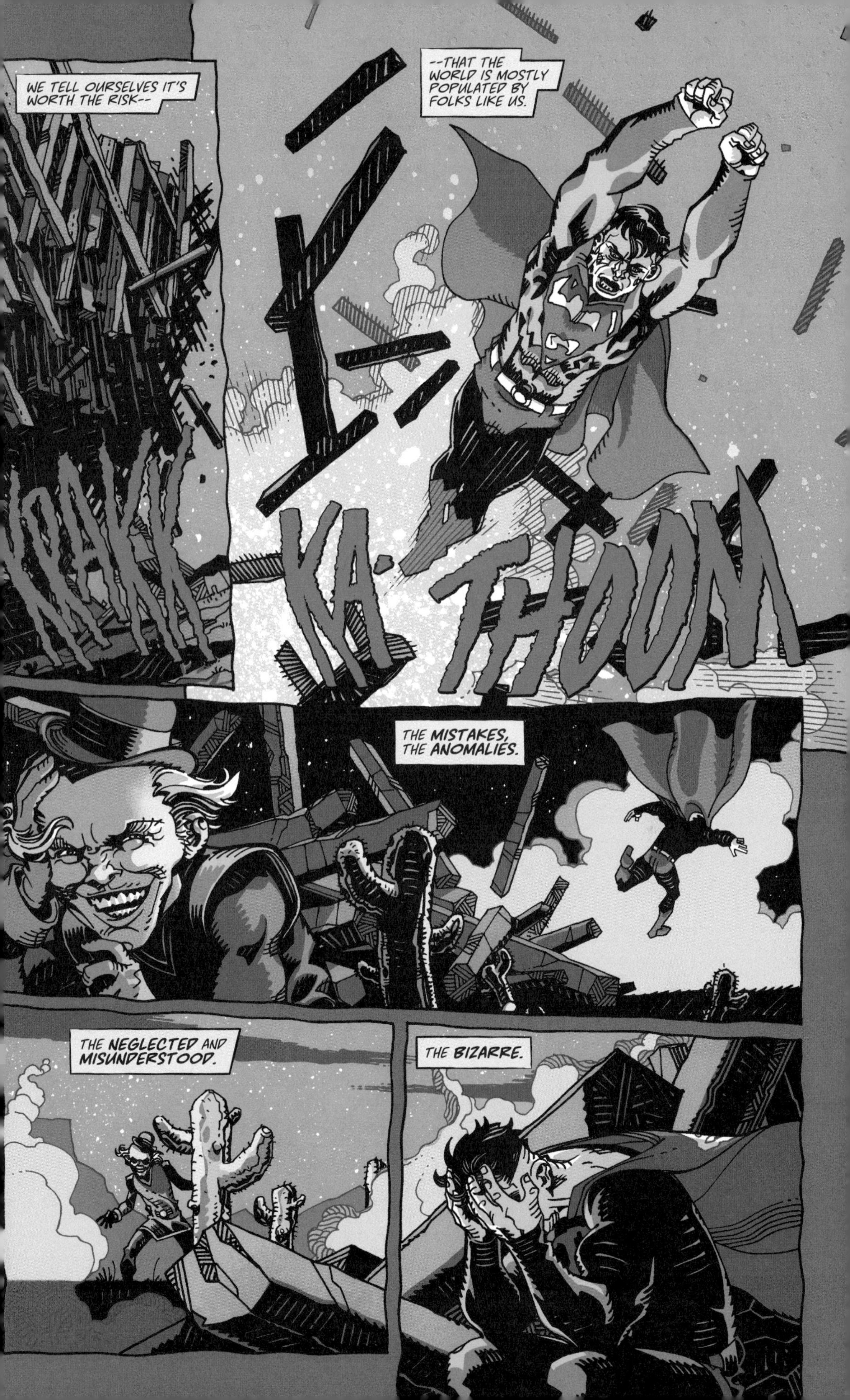
WE TELL OURSELVES IT'S WORTH THE RISK--
--THAT THE WORLD IS MOSTLY POPULATED BY FOLKS LIKE US.
KRAKK
KA-THOOM
THE MISTAKES, THE ANOMALIES.
THE NEGLECTED AND MISUNDERSTOOD.
THE BIZARRE.

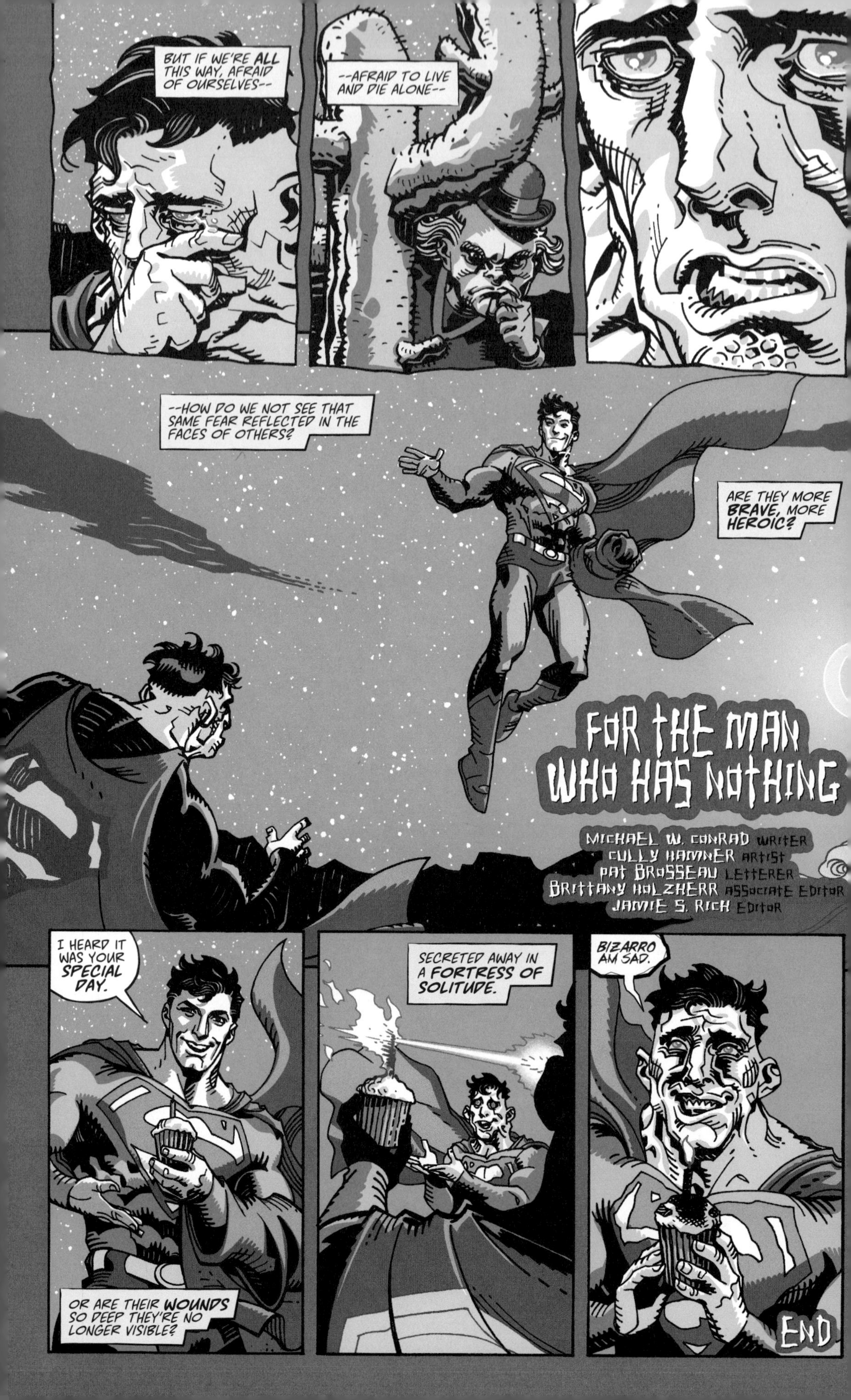
BUT IF WE'RE ALL THIS WAY, AFRAID OF OURSELVES--
--AFRAID TO LIVE AND DIE ALONE--
--HOW DO WE NOT SEE THAT SAME FEAR REFLECTED IN THE FACES OF OTHERS?
ARE THEY MORE BRAVE, MORE HEROIC?
FOR THE MAN WHO HAS NOTHING
MICHAEL W. CONRAD WRITER
CULLY HAMNER ARTIST
PAT BROSSEAU LETTERER
BRITTANY HOLZHERR ASSOCIATE EDITOR
JAMIE S. RICH EDITOR
I HEARD IT WAS YOUR SPECIAL DAY.
OR ARE THEIR WOUNDS SO DEEP THEY'RE NO LONGER VISIBLE?
SECRETED AWAY IN A FORTRESS OF SOLITUDE.
BIZARRO AM SAD.
END

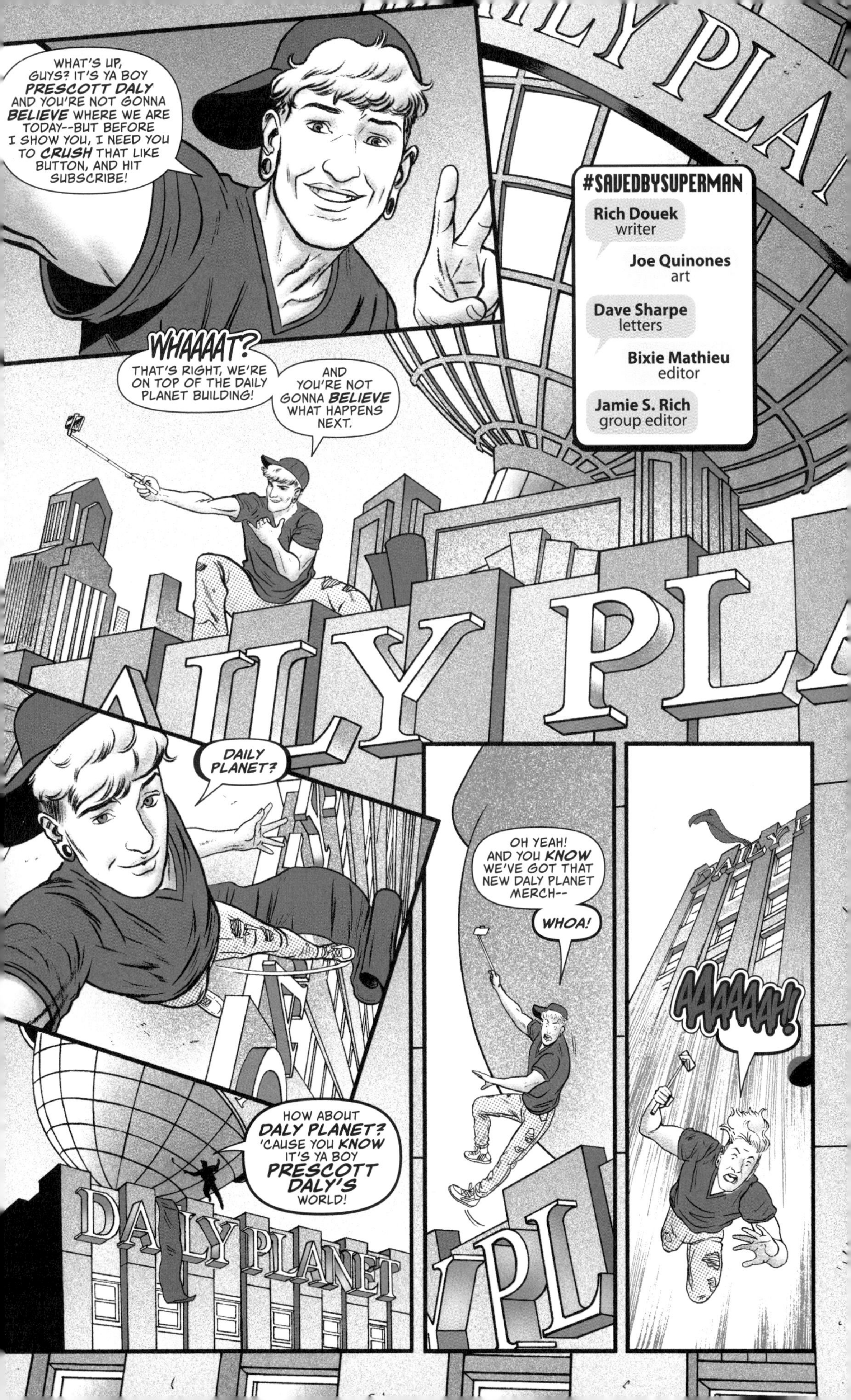
WHAT'S UP, GUYS? IT'S YA BOY PRESCOTT DALY AND YOU'RE NOT GONNA BELIEVE WHERE WE ARE TODAY--BUT BEFORE I SHOW YOU, I NEED YOU TO CRUSH THAT LIKE BUTTON, AND HIT SUBSCRIBE!
#SAVEDBYSUPERMAN
Rich Douek writer
Joe Quinones art
Dave Sharpe letters
Bixie Mathieu editor
Jamie S. Rich group editor
WHAAAAT?
THAT'S RIGHT, WE'RE ON TOP OF THE DAILY PLANET BUILDING!
AND YOU'RE NOT GONNA BELIEVE WHAT HAPPENS NEXT.
DAILY PLANET?
HOW ABOUT DALY PLANET? 'CAUSE YOU KNOW IT'S YA BOY PRESCOTT DALY'S WORLD!
OH YEAH! AND YOU KNOW WE'VE GOT THAT NEW DALY PLANET MERCH--
WHOA!
AAAAAAH!

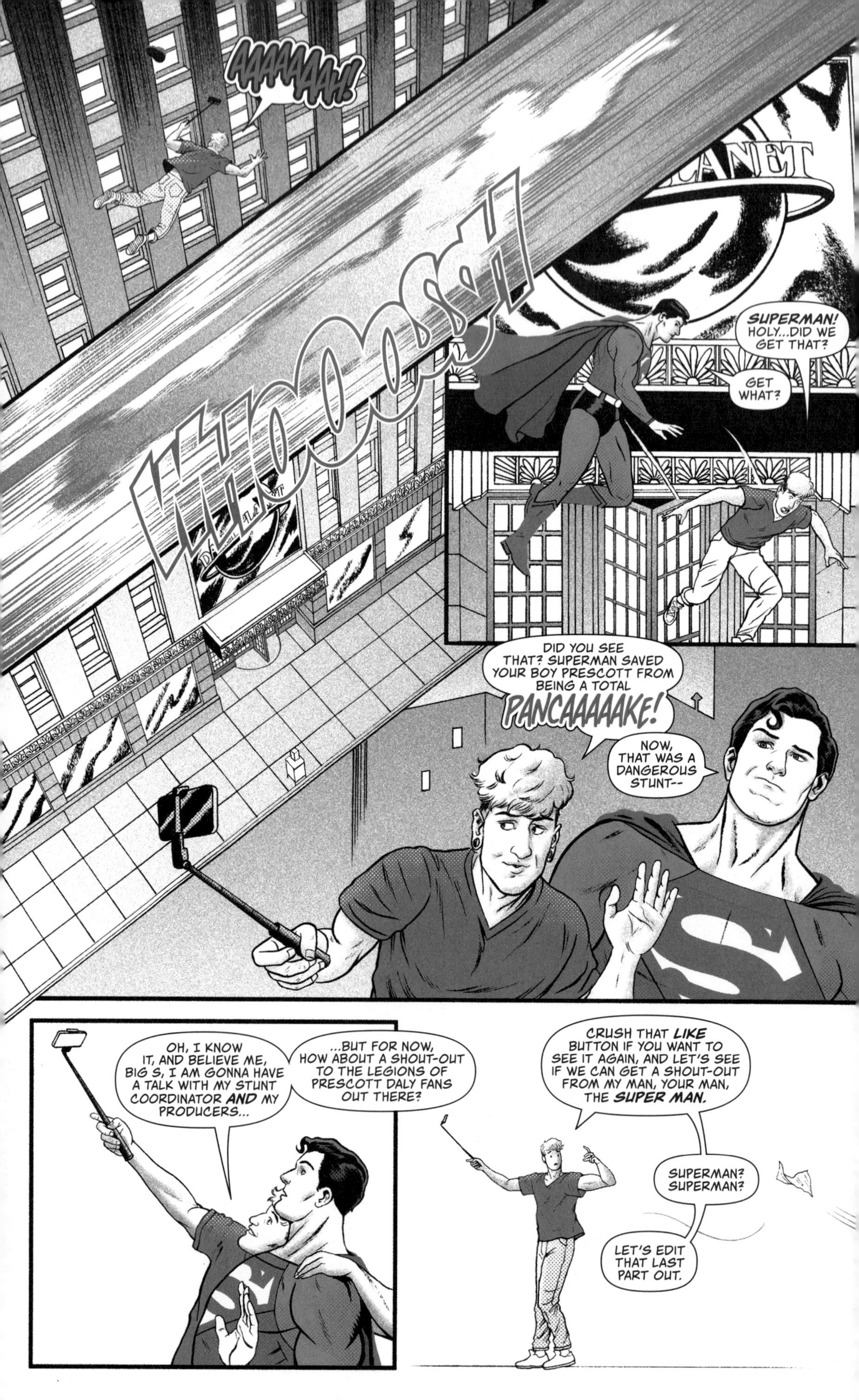

AAAAAAAH!
WHOOOOSH
SUPERMAN! HOLY...DID WE GET THAT?
GET WHAT?
DID YOU SEE THAT? SUPERMAN SAVED YOUR BOY PRESCOTT FROM BEING A TOTAL PANCAAAAAKE!
NOW, THAT WAS A DANGEROUS STUNT--
OH, I KNOW IT, AND BELIEVE ME, BIG S, I AM GONNA HAVE A TALK WITH MY STUNT COORDINATOR AND MY PRODUCERS...
...BUT FOR NOW, HOW ABOUT A SHOUT-OUT TO THE LEGIONS OF PRESCOTT DALY FANS OUT THERE?
CRUSH THAT LIKE BUTTON IF YOU WANT TO SEE IT AGAIN, AND LET'S SEE IF WE CAN GET A SHOUT-OUT FROM MY MAN, YOUR MAN, THE SUPER MAN.
SUPERMAN? SUPERMAN?
LET'S EDIT THAT LAST PART OUT.

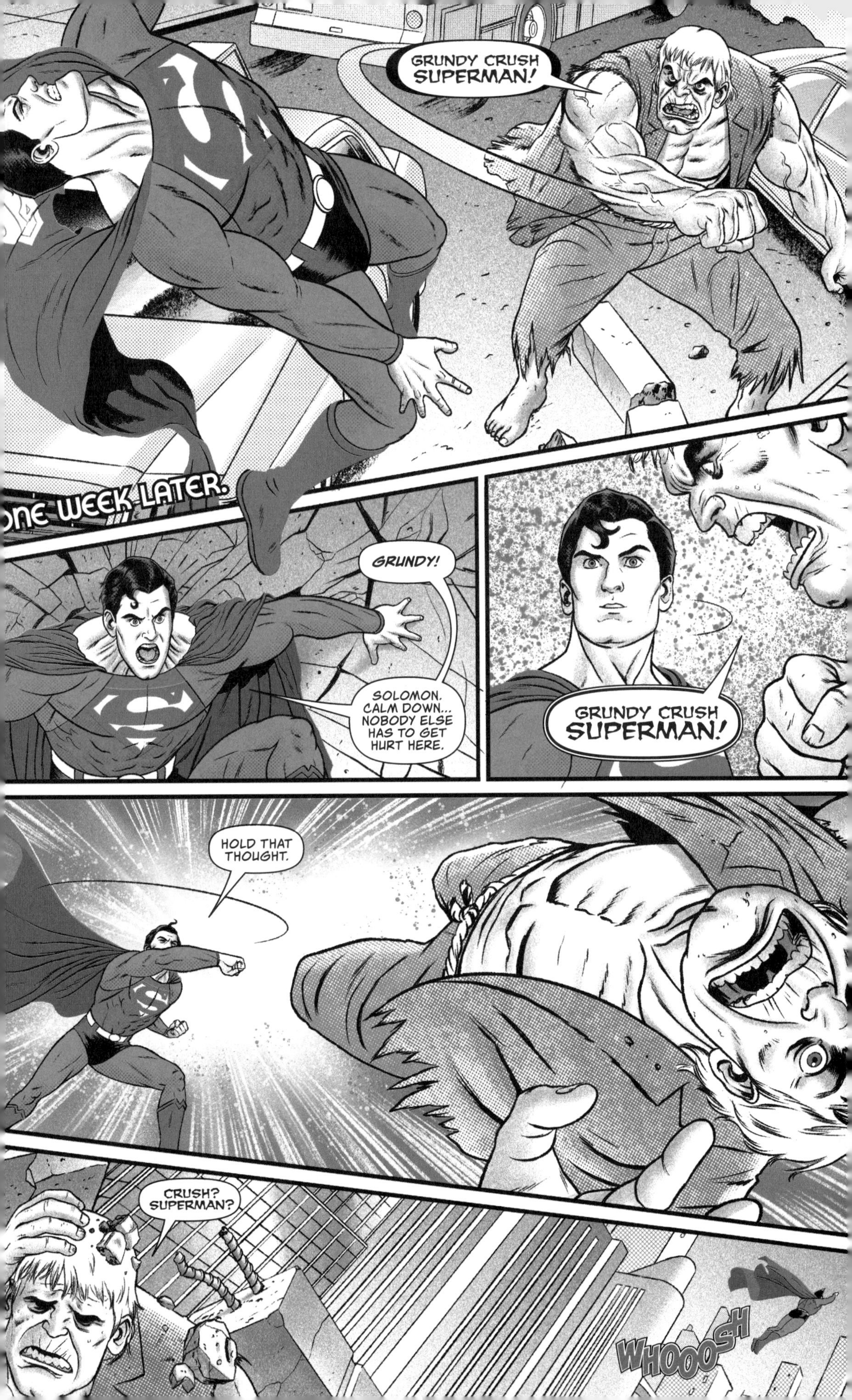
GRUNDY CRUSH SUPERMAN!
ONE WEEK LATER.
GRUNDY!
SOLOMON. CALM DOWN... NOBODY ELSE HAS TO GET HURT HERE.
GRUNDY CRUSH SUPERMAN!
HOLD THAT THOUGHT.
CRUSH? SUPERMAN?
WHOOOSH

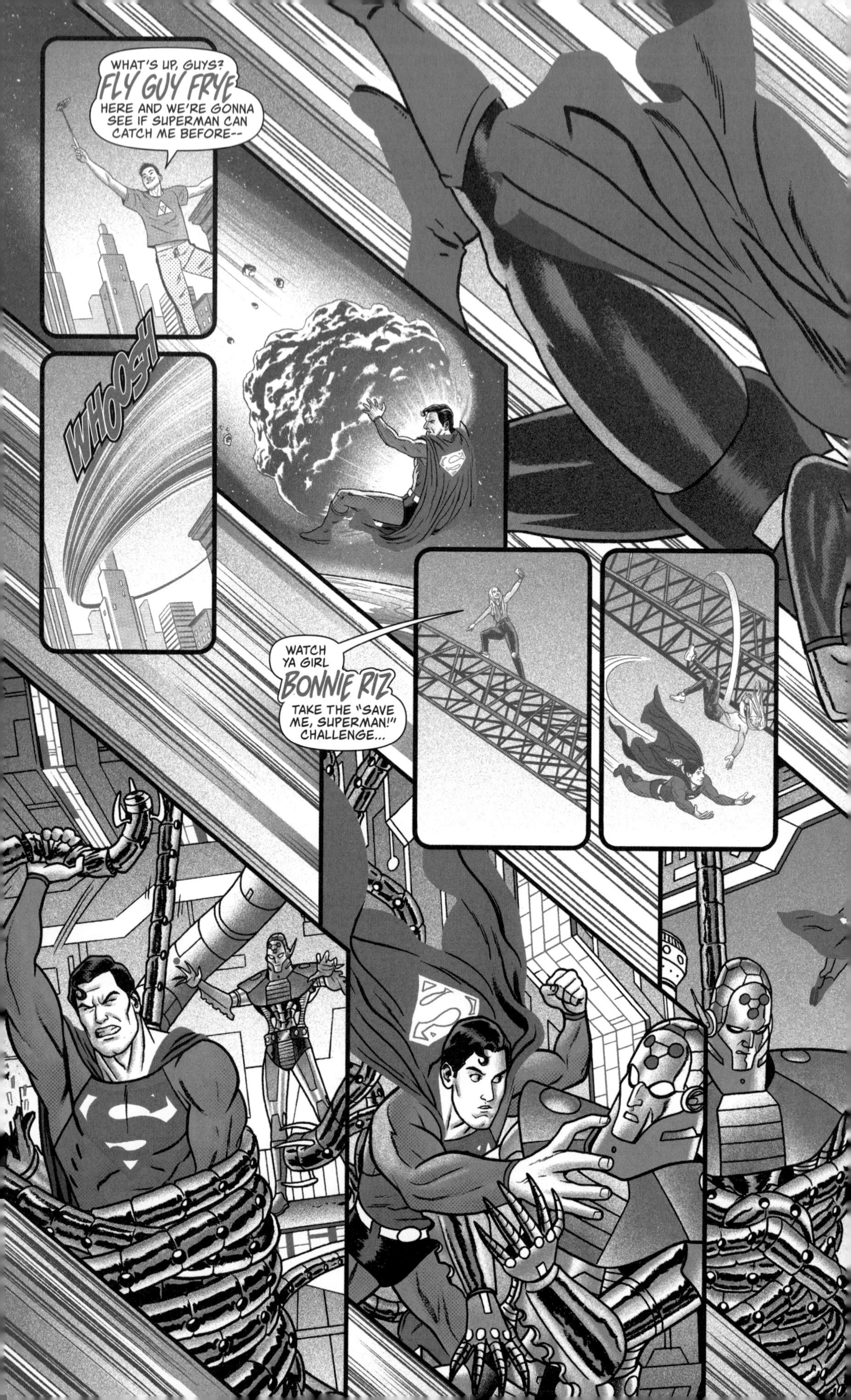
WHAT'S UP, GUYS? FLY GUY FRYE HERE AND WE'RE GONNA SEE IF SUPERMAN CAN CATCH ME BEFORE--
WHOOSH
WATCH YA GIRL BONNIE RIZ TAKE THE "SAVE ME, SUPERMAN!" CHALLENGE...

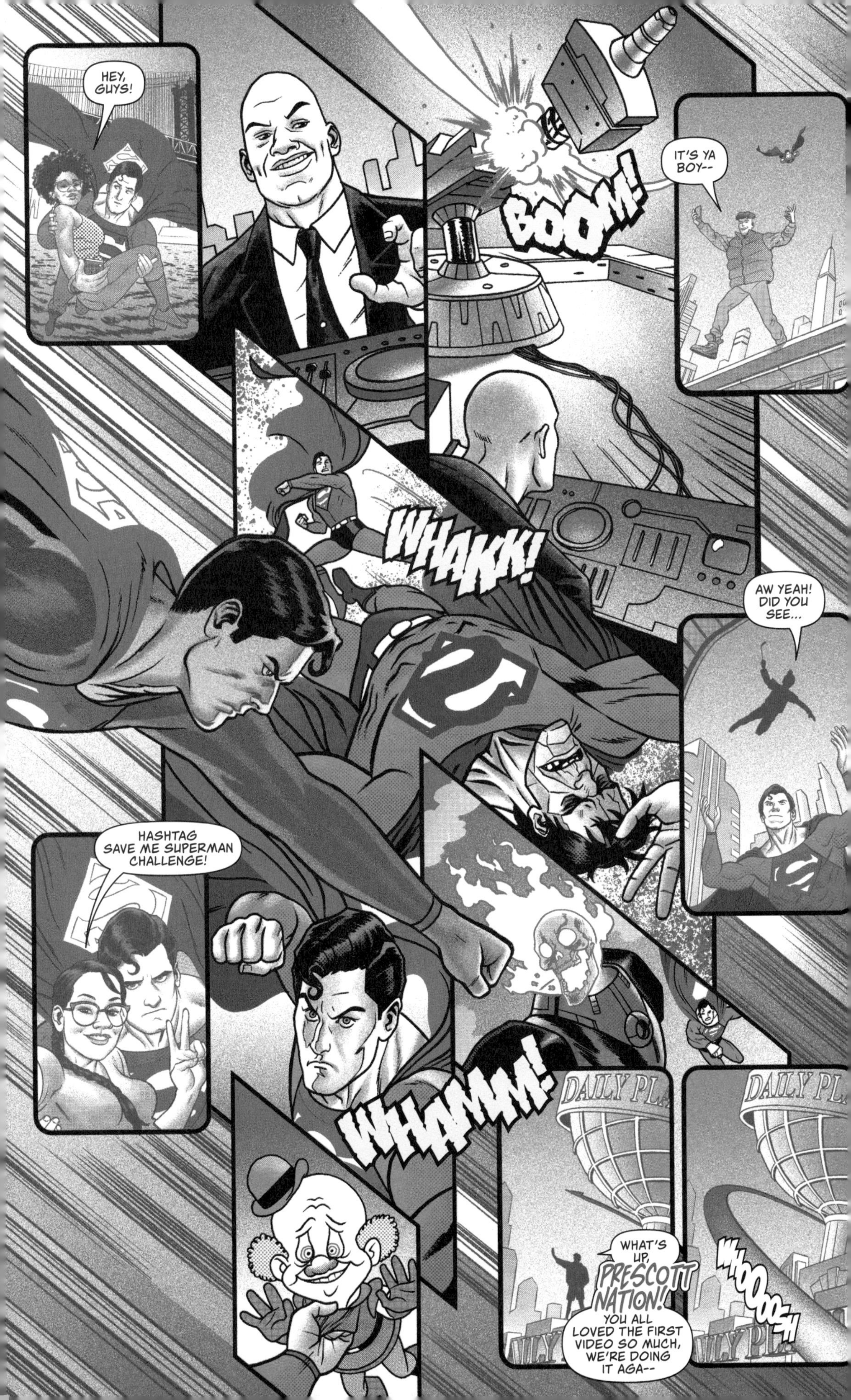
HEY, GUYS!
BOOM!
IT'S YA BOY--
WHAKK!
AW YEAH! DID YOU SEE...
HASHTAG SAVE ME SUPERMAN CHALLENGE!
WHAMM!
DAILY PLA
WHAT'S UP, PRESCOTT NATION! YOU ALL LOVED THE FIRST VIDEO SO MUCH, WE'RE DOING IT AGA--
DAILY PLA
WHOOOOSH

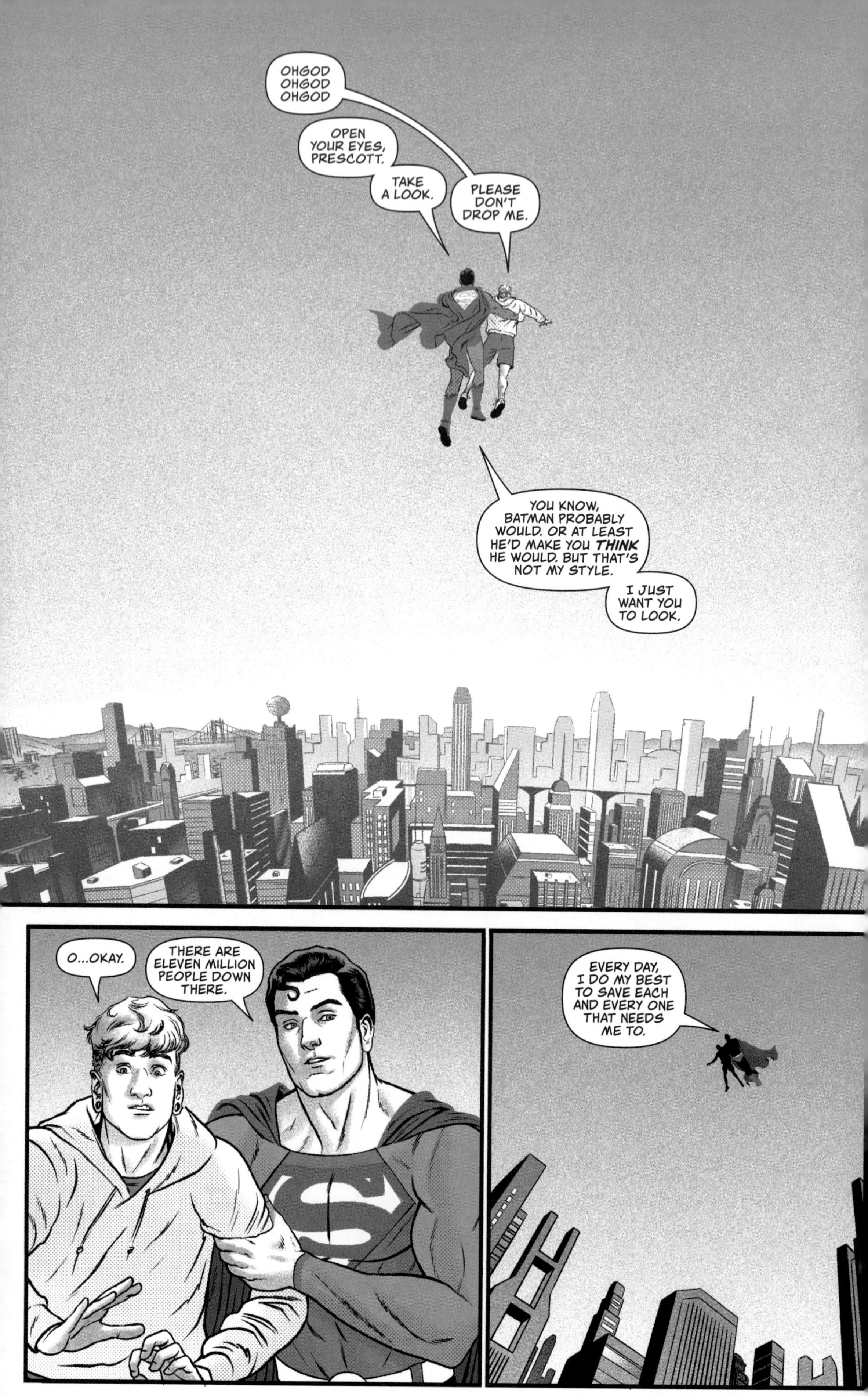
OHGOD
OHGOD
OHGOD
OPEN YOUR EYES, PRESCOTT.
TAKE A LOOK.
PLEASE DON'T DROP ME.
YOU KNOW, BATMAN PROBABLY WOULD. OR AT LEAST HE'D MAKE YOU *THINK* HE WOULD. BUT THAT'S NOT MY STYLE.
I JUST WANT YOU TO LOOK.
O...OKAY.
THERE ARE ELEVEN MILLION PEOPLE DOWN THERE.
EVERY DAY, I DO MY BEST TO SAVE EACH AND EVERY ONE THAT NEEDS ME TO.

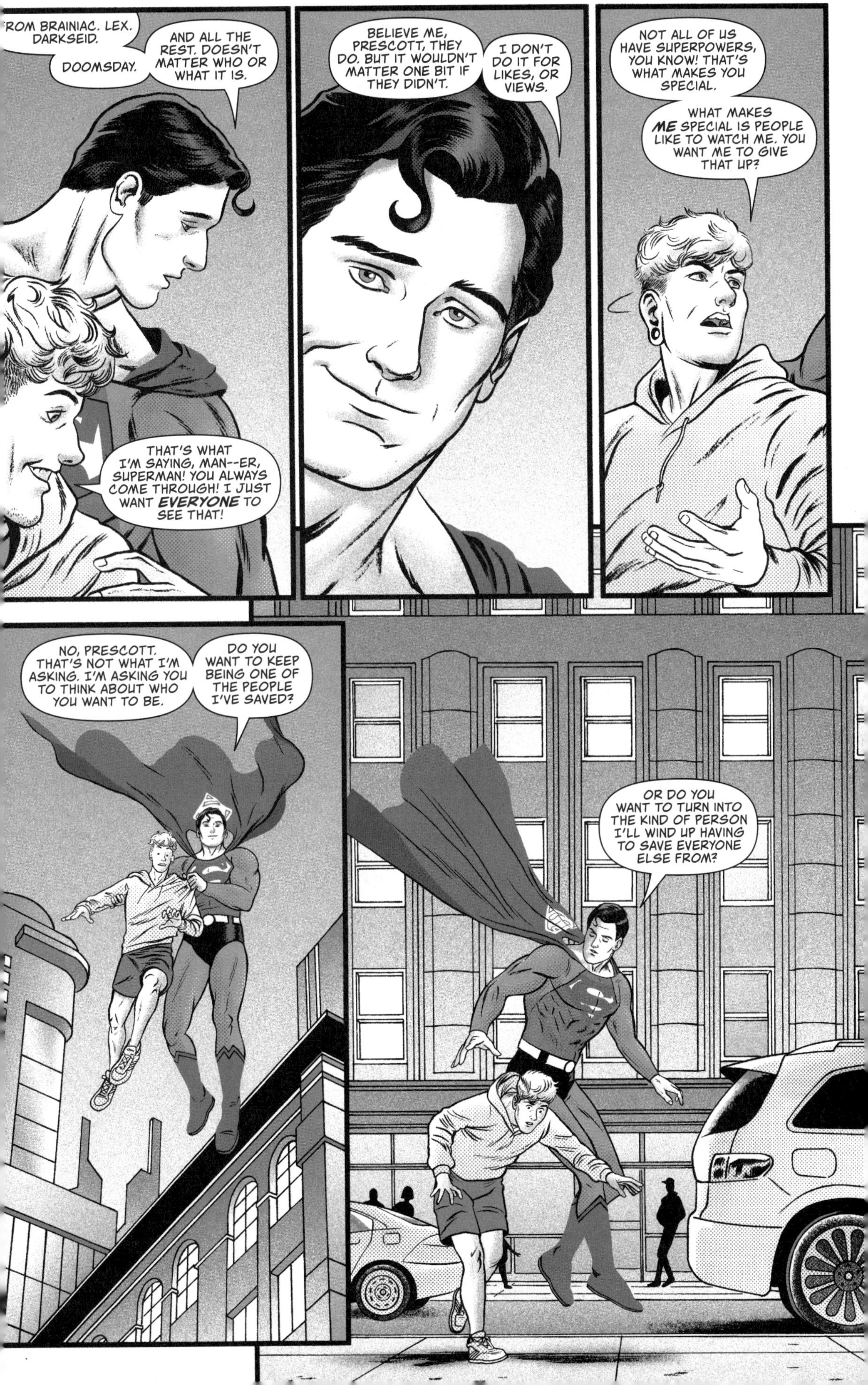
FROM BRAINIAC. LEX. DARKSEID.
DOOMSDAY.
AND ALL THE REST. DOESN'T MATTER WHO OR WHAT IT IS.
THAT'S WHAT I'M SAYING, MAN--ER, SUPERMAN! YOU ALWAYS COME THROUGH! I JUST WANT EVERYONE TO SEE THAT!
BELIEVE ME, PRESCOTT, THEY DO. BUT IT WOULDN'T MATTER ONE BIT IF THEY DIDN'T.
I DON'T DO IT FOR LIKES, OR VIEWS.
NOT ALL OF US HAVE SUPERPOWERS, YOU KNOW! THAT'S WHAT MAKES YOU SPECIAL.
WHAT MAKES ME SPECIAL IS PEOPLE LIKE TO WATCH ME. YOU WANT ME TO GIVE THAT UP?
NO, PRESCOTT. THAT'S NOT WHAT I'M ASKING. I'M ASKING YOU TO THINK ABOUT WHO YOU WANT TO BE.
DO YOU WANT TO KEEP BEING ONE OF THE PEOPLE I'VE SAVED?
OR DO YOU WANT TO TURN INTO THE KIND OF PERSON I'LL WIND UP HAVING TO SAVE EVERYONE ELSE FROM?

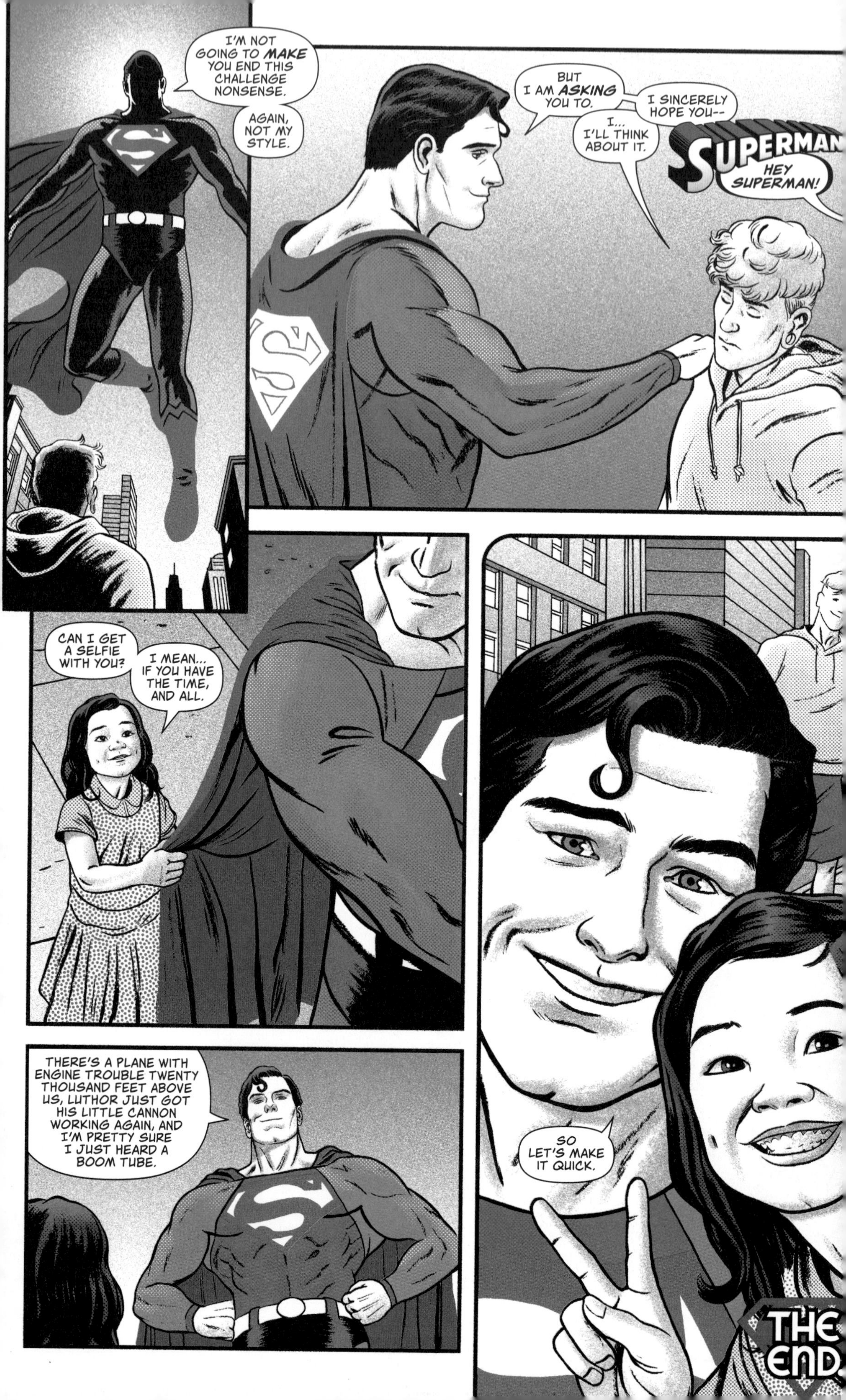
I'M NOT GOING TO MAKE YOU END THIS CHALLENGE NONSENSE.
AGAIN, NOT MY STYLE.
BUT I AM ASKING YOU TO.
I... I'LL THINK ABOUT IT.
I SINCERELY HOPE YOU--
SUPERMAN
HEY SUPERMAN!
CAN I GET A SELFIE WITH YOU?
I MEAN... IF YOU HAVE THE TIME, AND ALL.
THERE'S A PLANE WITH ENGINE TROUBLE TWENTY THOUSAND FEET ABOVE US, LUTHOR JUST GOT HIS LITTLE CANNON WORKING AGAIN, AND I'M PRETTY SURE I JUST HEARD A BOOM TUBE.
SO LET'S MAKE IT QUICK.
THE END.

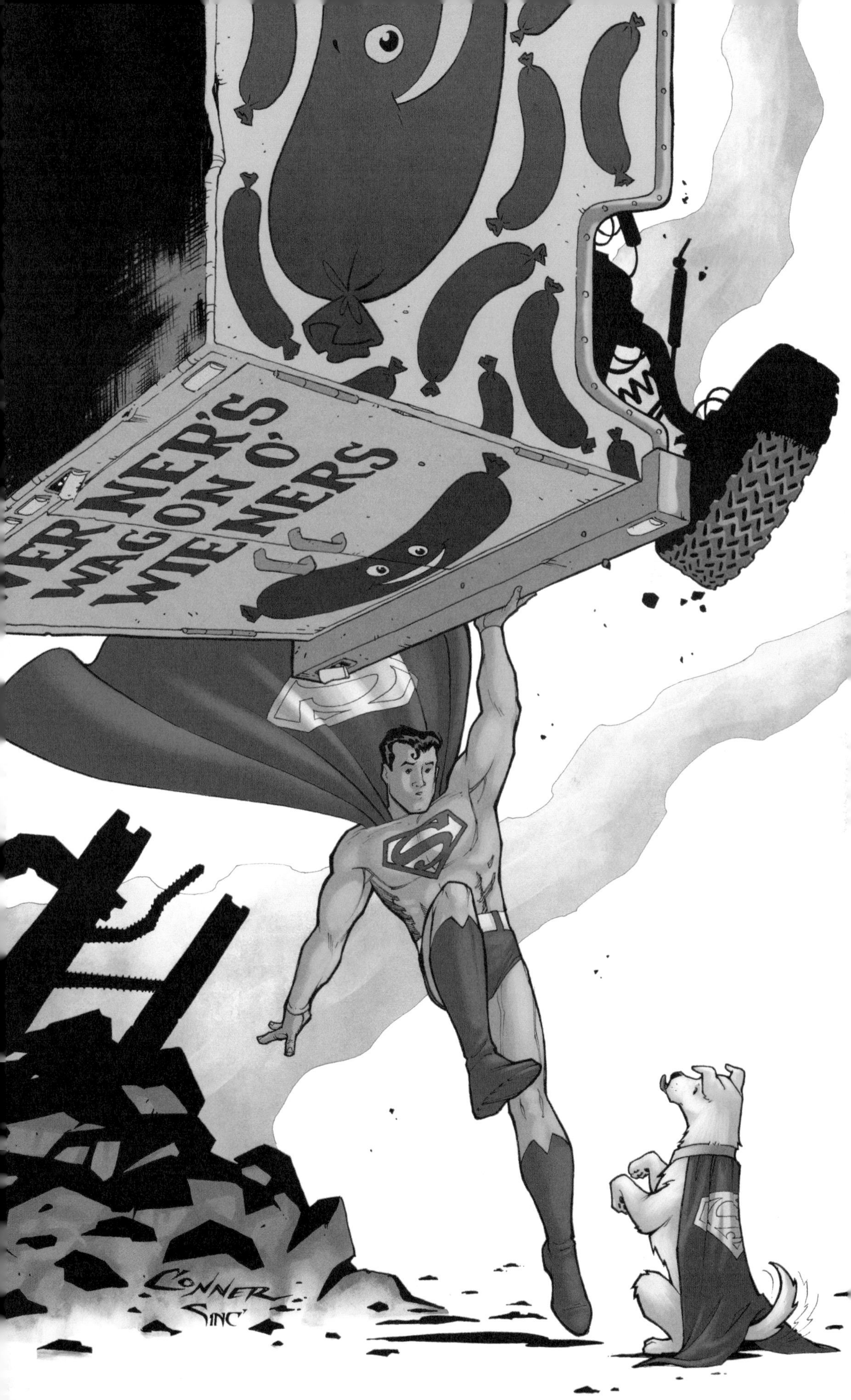
WAGON O'
WIENERS
CONNER
SINC'

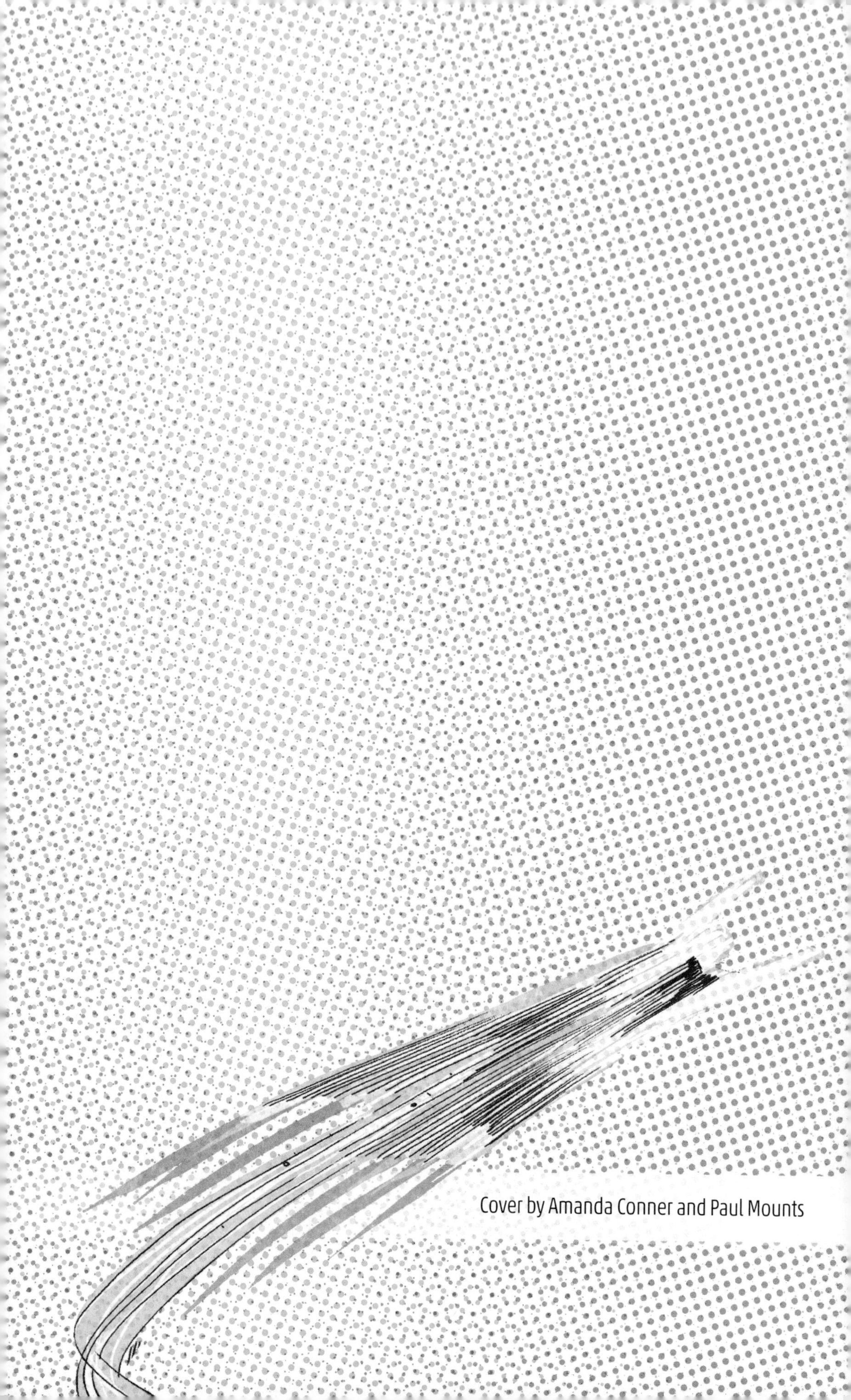

Cover by Amanda Conner and Paul Mounts

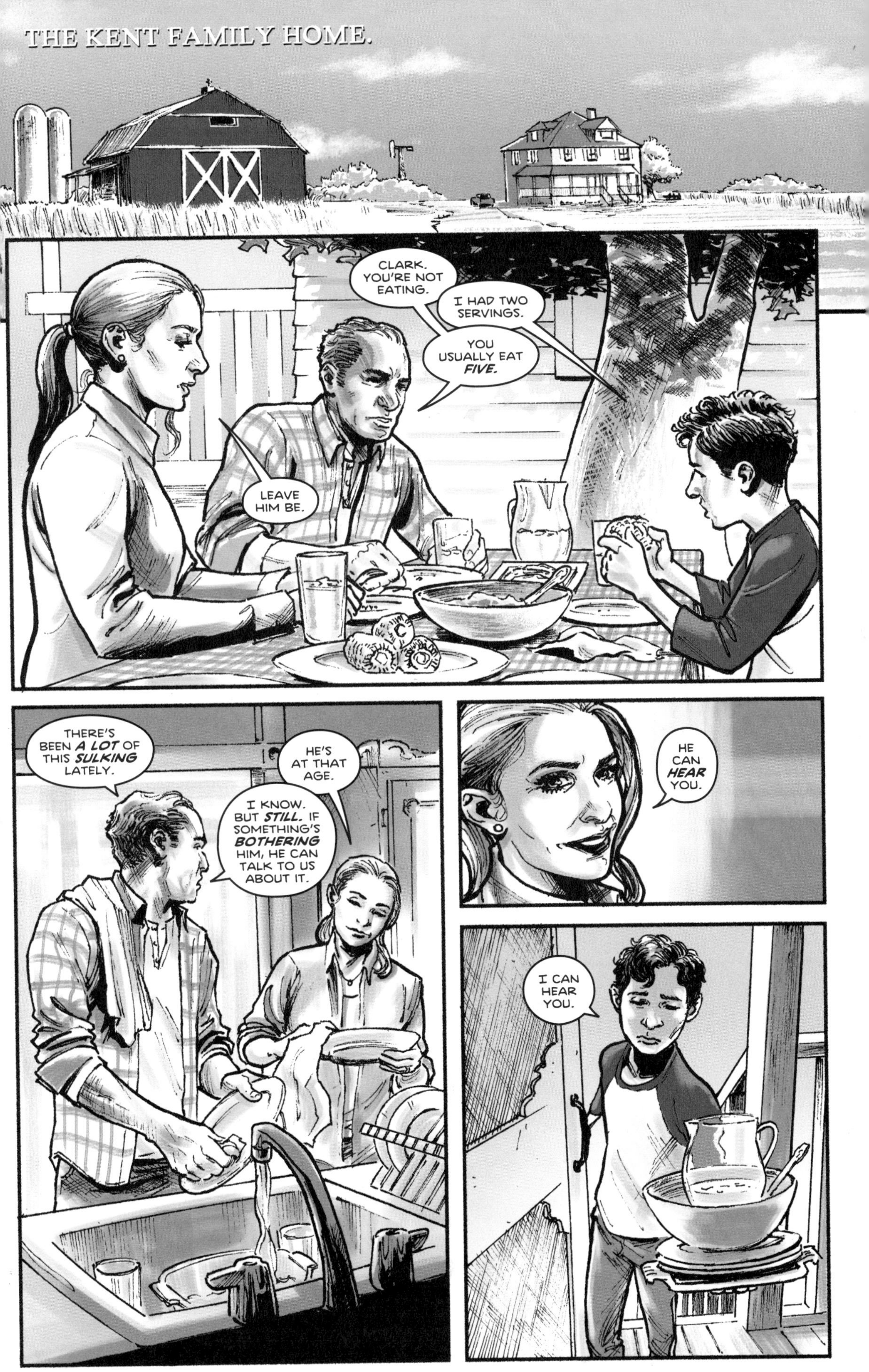
THE KENT FAMILY HOME.
CLARK. YOU'RE NOT EATING.
I HAD TWO SERVINGS.
YOU USUALLY EAT *FIVE.*
LEAVE HIM BE.
THERE'S BEEN *A LOT* OF THIS *SULKING* LATELY.
HE'S AT THAT AGE.
I KNOW. BUT *STILL.* IF SOMETHING'S *BOTHERING* HIM, HE CAN TALK TO US ABOUT IT.
HE CAN *HEAR* YOU.
I CAN HEAR YOU.

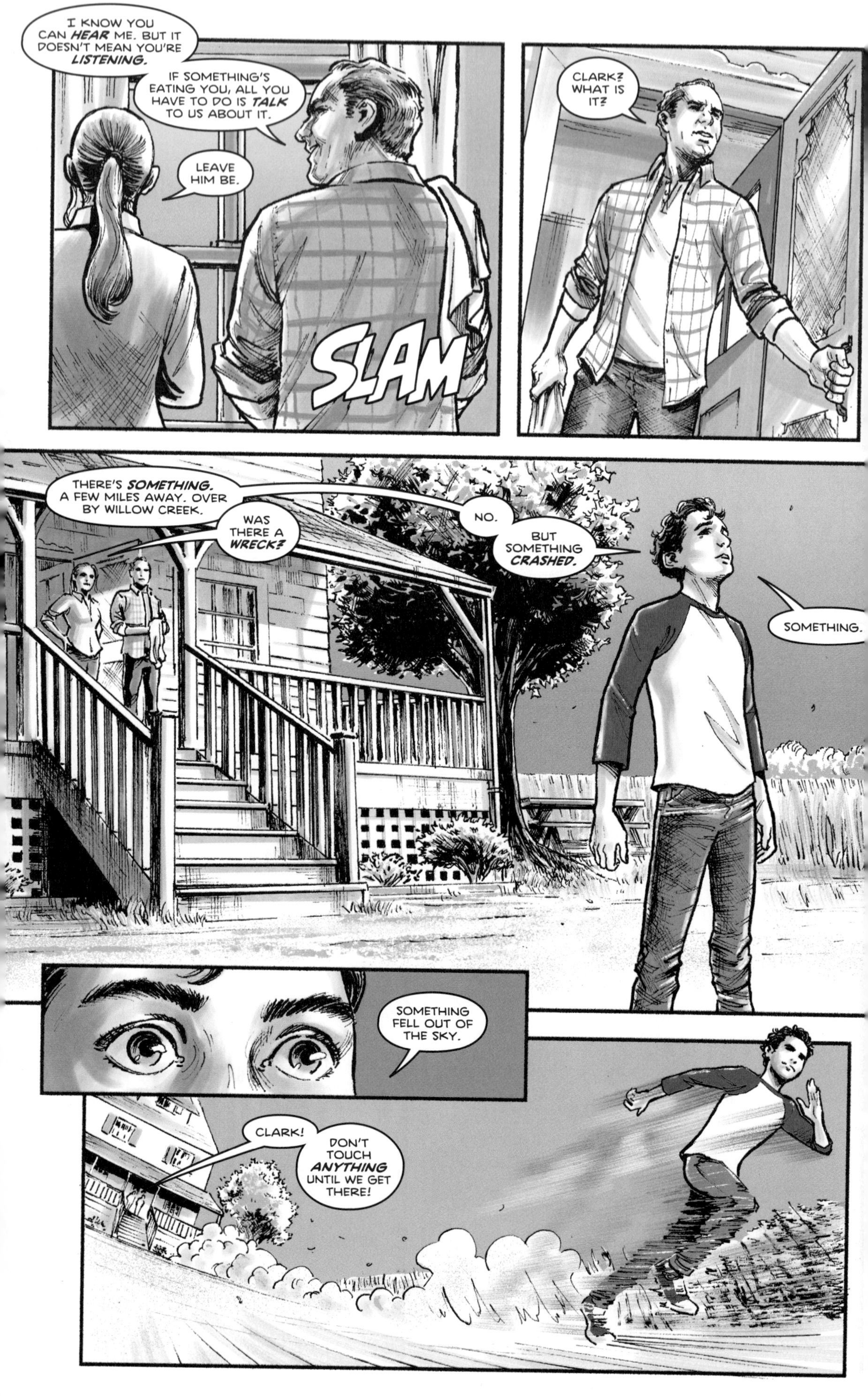
I KNOW YOU CAN HEAR ME. BUT IT DOESN'T MEAN YOU'RE LISTENING.
IF SOMETHING'S EATING YOU, ALL YOU HAVE TO DO IS TALK TO US ABOUT IT.
LEAVE HIM BE.
SLAM
CLARK? WHAT IS IT?
THERE'S SOMETHING. A FEW MILES AWAY. OVER BY WILLOW CREEK.
WAS THERE A WRECK?
NO.
BUT SOMETHING CRASHED.
SOMETHING.
SOMETHING FELL OUT OF THE SKY.
CLARK!
DON'T TOUCH ANYTHING UNTIL WE GET THERE!

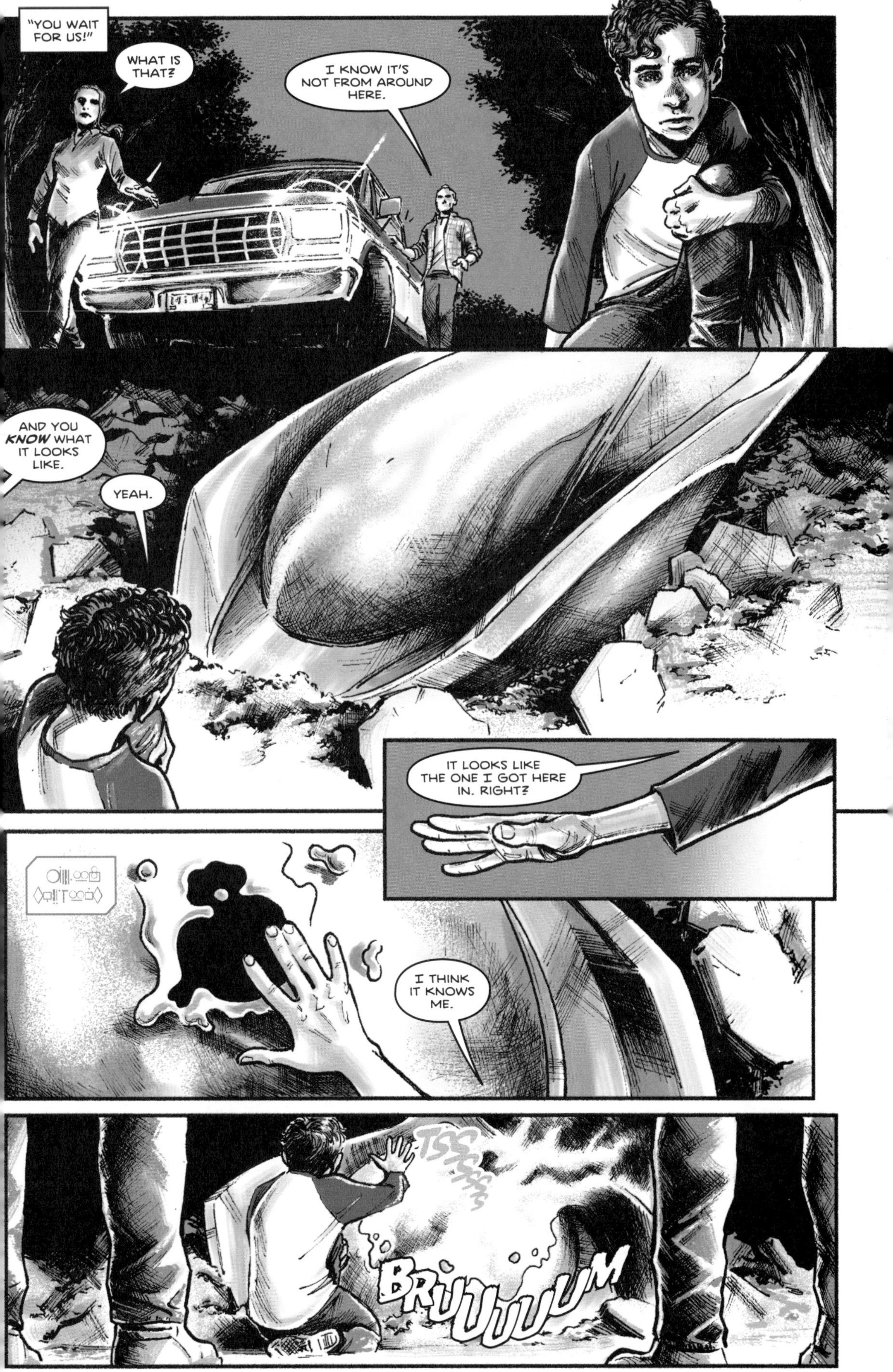
"YOU WAIT FOR US!"
WHAT IS THAT?
I KNOW IT'S NOT FROM AROUND HERE.
AND YOU *KNOW* WHAT IT LOOKS LIKE.
YEAH.
IT LOOKS LIKE THE ONE I GOT HERE IN. RIGHT?
I THINK IT KNOWS ME.
TSSSSSS
BRUUUUUUM

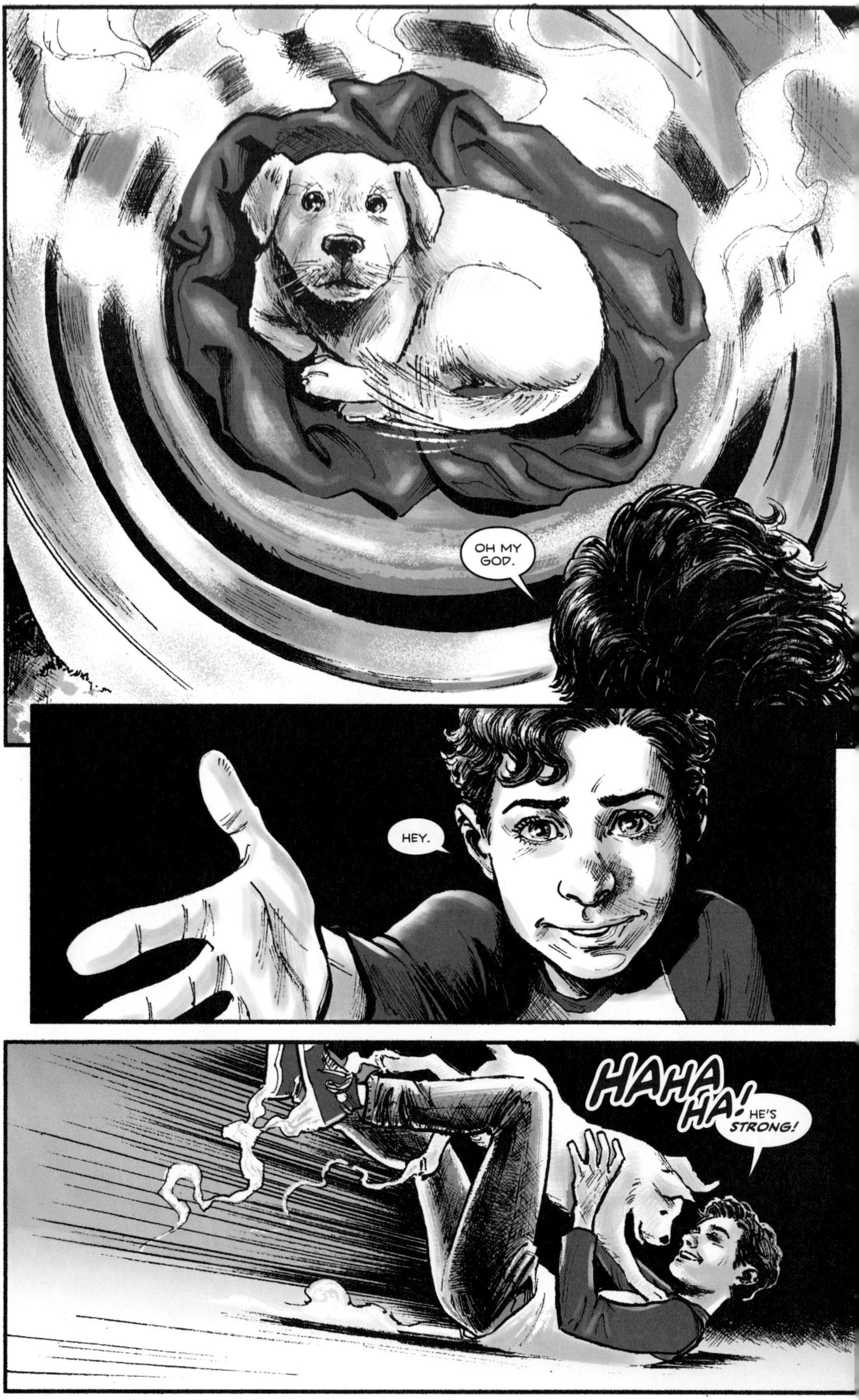
OH MY GOD.
HEY.
HAHA HA!
HE'S STRONG!

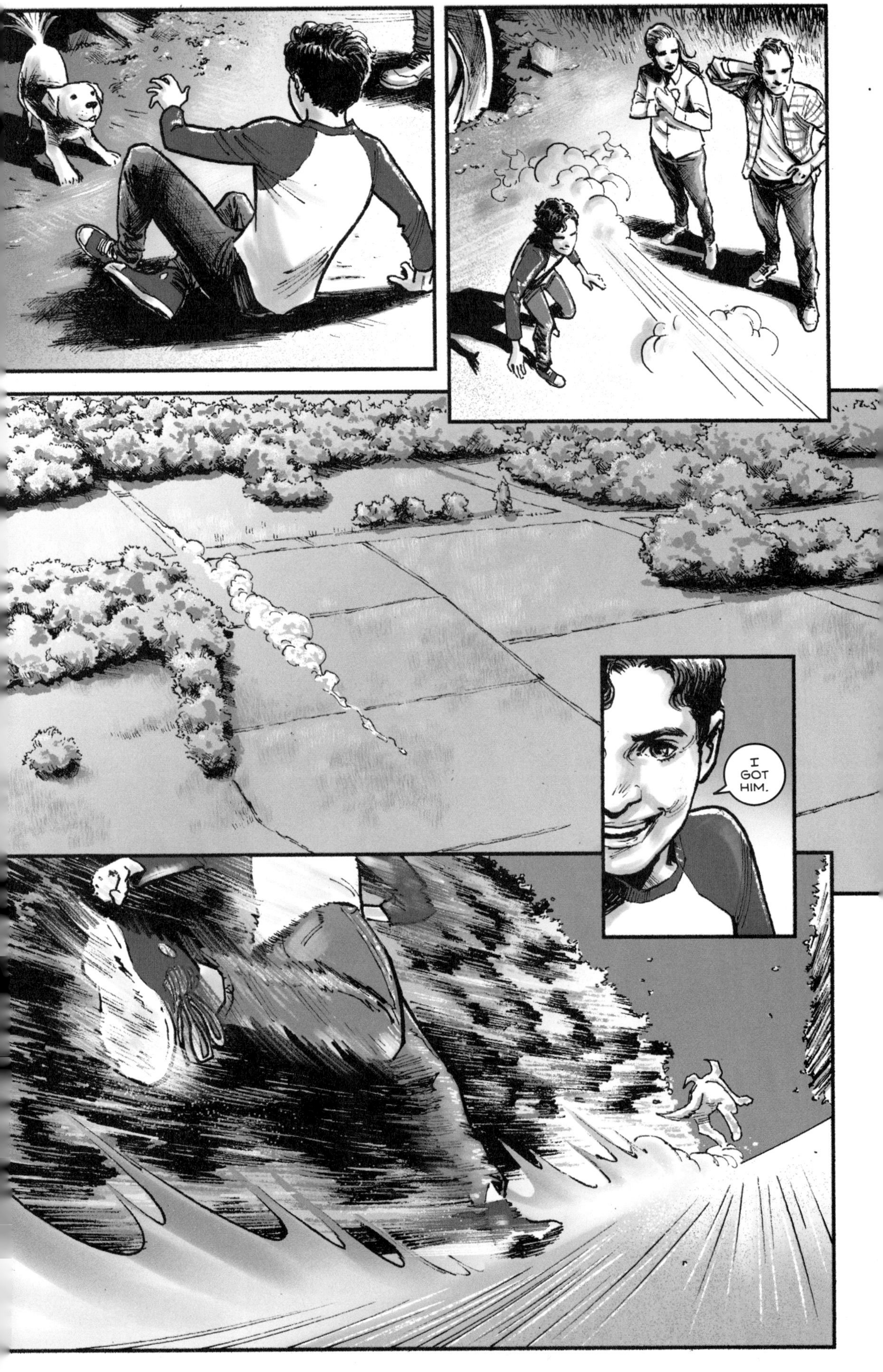
I GOT HIM.

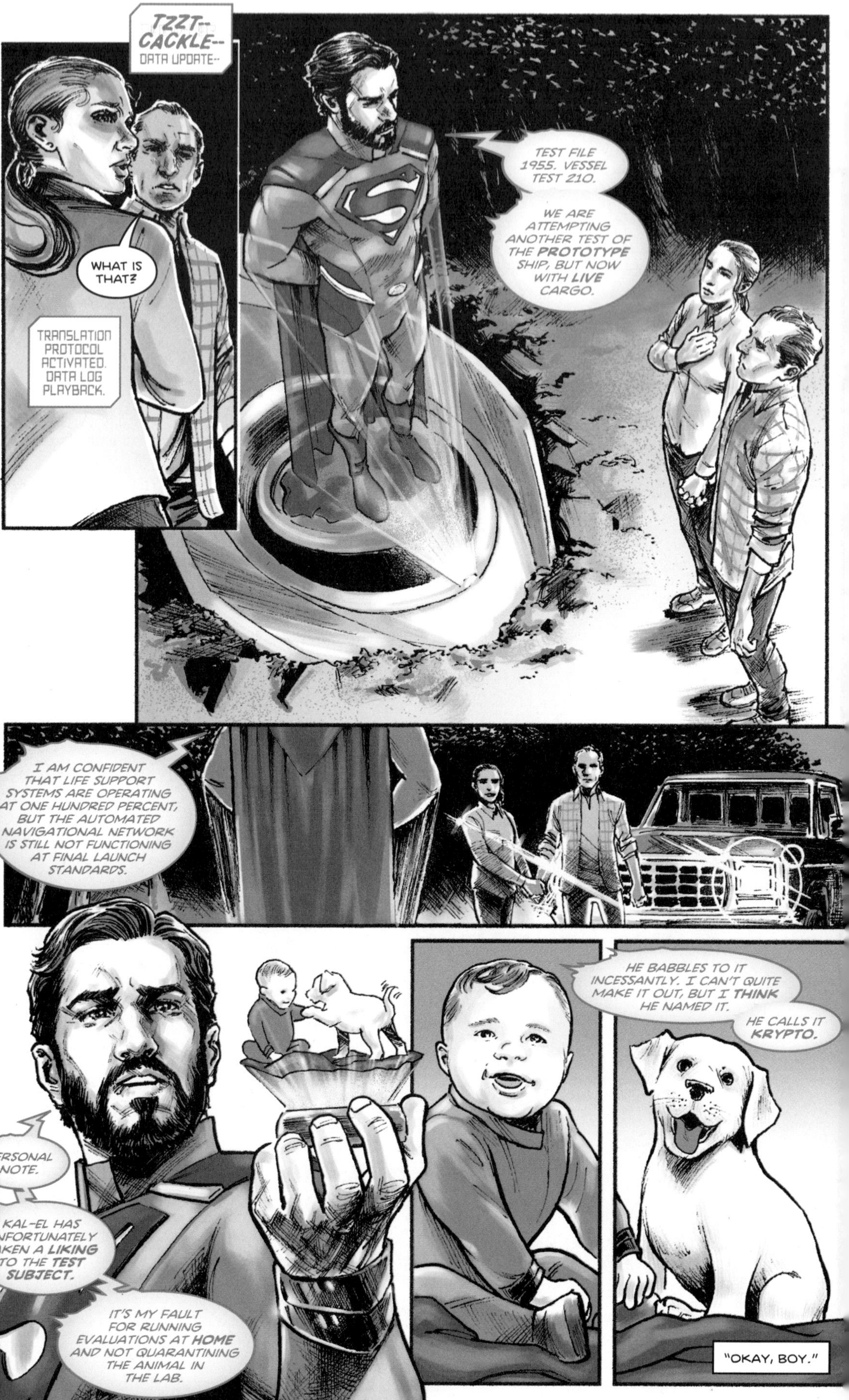
TZZT--
CACKLE--
DATA UPDATE--
WHAT IS THAT?
TRANSLATION PROTOCOL ACTIVATED. DATA LOG PLAYBACK.
TEST FILE 1955. VESSEL TEST 210.
WE ARE ATTEMPTING ANOTHER TEST OF THE PROTOTYPE SHIP, BUT NOW WITH LIVE CARGO.
I AM CONFIDENT THAT LIFE SUPPORT SYSTEMS ARE OPERATING AT ONE HUNDRED PERCENT, BUT THE AUTOMATED NAVIGATIONAL NETWORK IS STILL NOT FUNCTIONING AT FINAL LAUNCH STANDARDS.
PERSONAL NOTE.
KAL-EL HAS UNFORTUNATELY TAKEN A LIKING TO THE TEST SUBJECT.
IT'S MY FAULT FOR RUNNING EVALUATIONS AT HOME AND NOT QUARANTINING THE ANIMAL IN THE LAB.
HE BABBLES TO IT INCESSANTLY. I CAN'T QUITE MAKE IT OUT, BUT I THINK HE NAMED IT.
HE CALLS IT KRYPTO.
"OKAY, BOY."

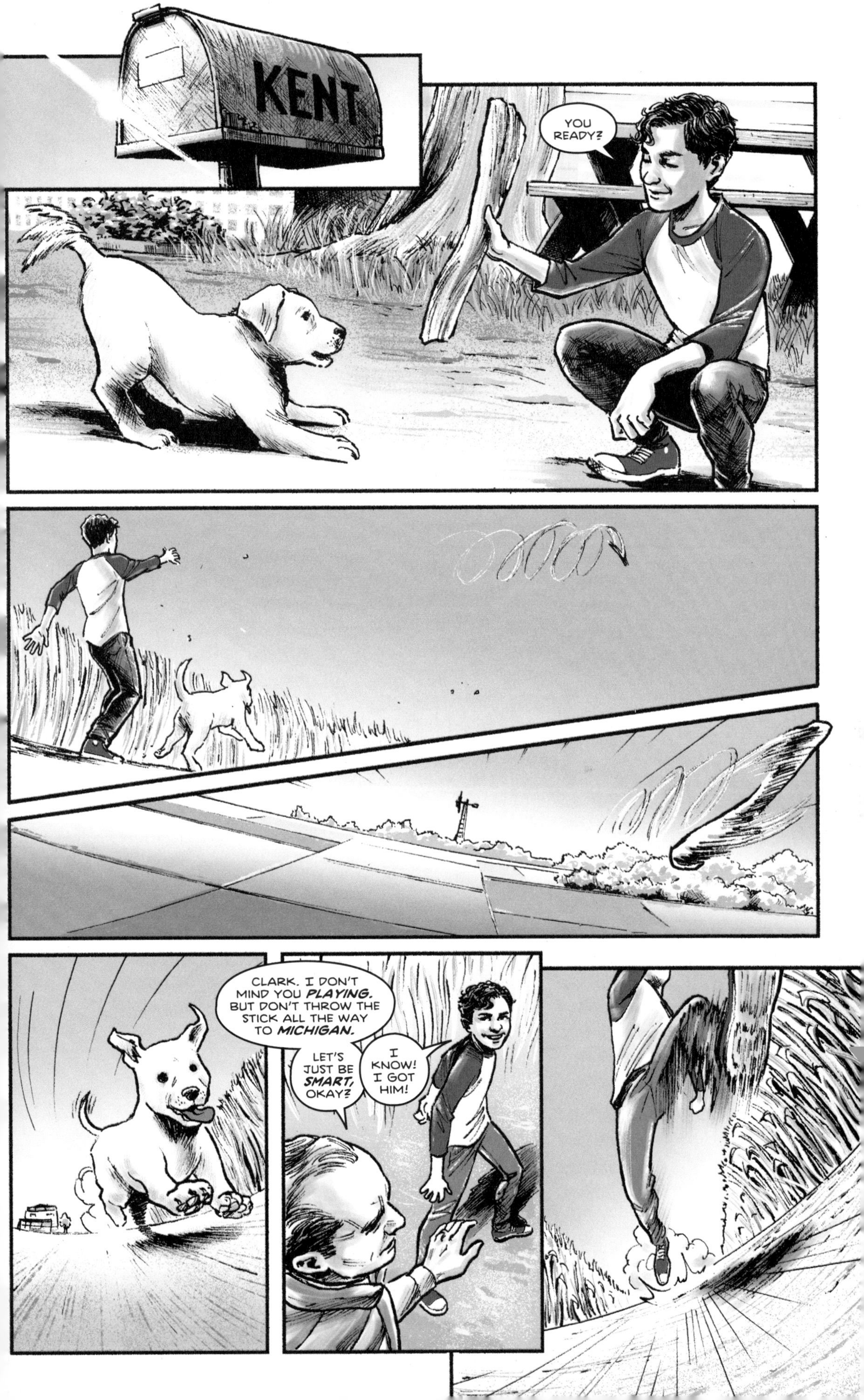
KENT
YOU READY?
CLARK. I DON'T MIND YOU PLAYING. BUT DON'T THROW THE STICK ALL THE WAY TO MICHIGAN.
LET'S JUST BE SMART, OKAY?
I KNOW! I GOT HIM!

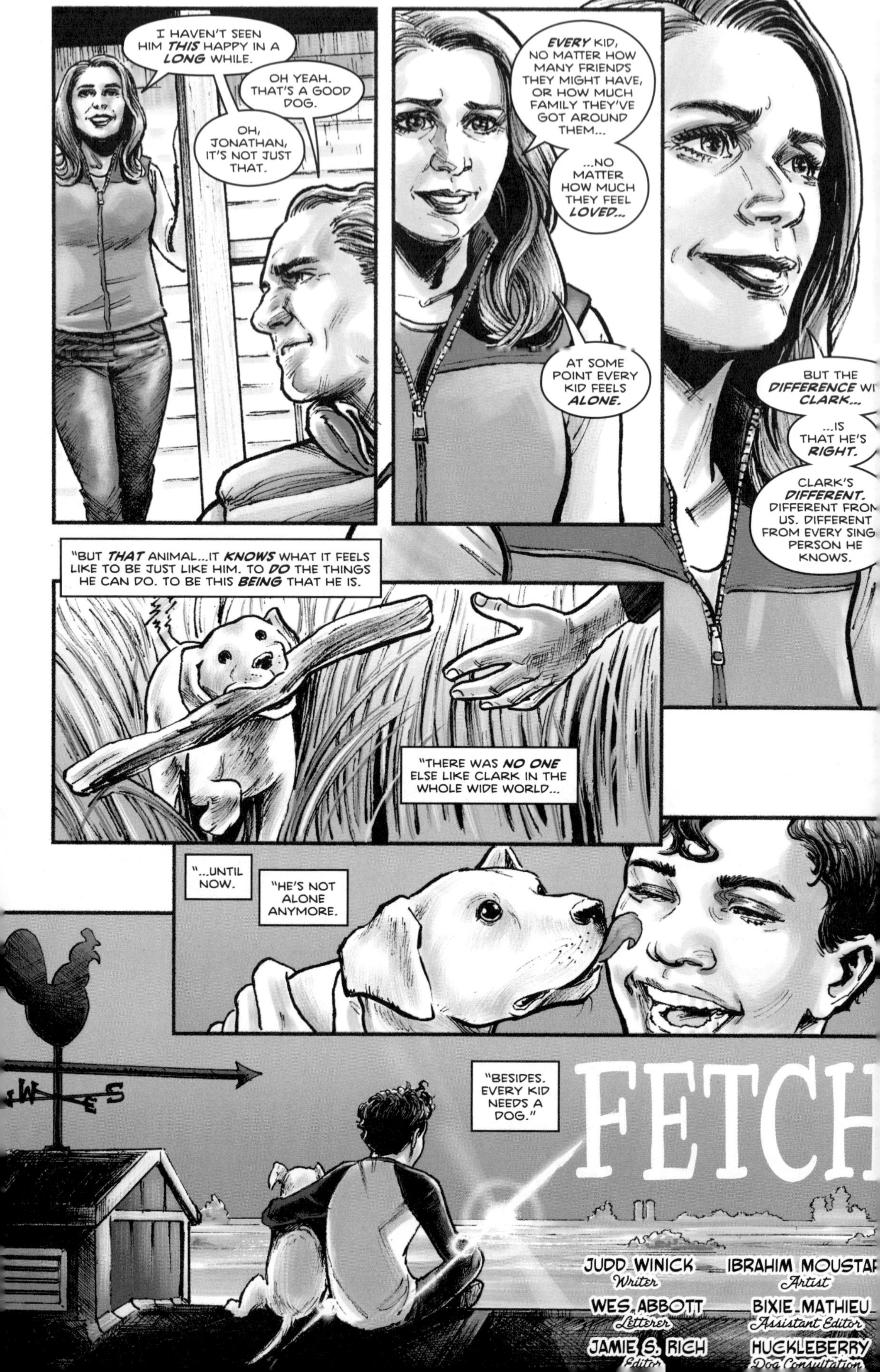

I HAVEN'T SEEN HIM *THIS* HAPPY IN A *LONG* WHILE.
OH YEAH. THAT'S A GOOD DOG.
OH, JONATHAN, IT'S NOT JUST THAT.
EVERY KID, NO MATTER HOW MANY FRIENDS THEY MIGHT HAVE, OR HOW MUCH FAMILY THEY'VE GOT AROUND THEM...
...NO MATTER HOW MUCH THEY FEEL *LOVED...*
AT SOME POINT EVERY KID FEELS *ALONE.*
BUT THE *DIFFERENCE* WI
CLARK...
...IS THAT HE'S *RIGHT.*
CLARK'S *DIFFERENT.* DIFFERENT FROM US. DIFFERENT FROM EVERY SING PERSON HE KNOWS.
"BUT *THAT* ANIMAL...IT *KNOWS* WHAT IT FEELS LIKE TO BE JUST LIKE HIM. TO *DO* THE THINGS HE CAN DO. TO BE THIS *BEING* THAT HE IS.
"THERE WAS *NO ONE* ELSE LIKE CLARK IN THE WHOLE WIDE WORLD...
"...UNTIL NOW.
"HE'S NOT ALONE ANYMORE.
W
E
S
"BESIDES. EVERY KID NEEDS A DOG."
FETCH
JUDD WINICK
Writer
IBRAHIM MOUSTAF
Artist
WES ABBOTT
Letterer
BIXIE MATHIEU
Assistant Editor
JAMIE S. RICH
Editor
HUCKLEBERRY
Dog Consultation

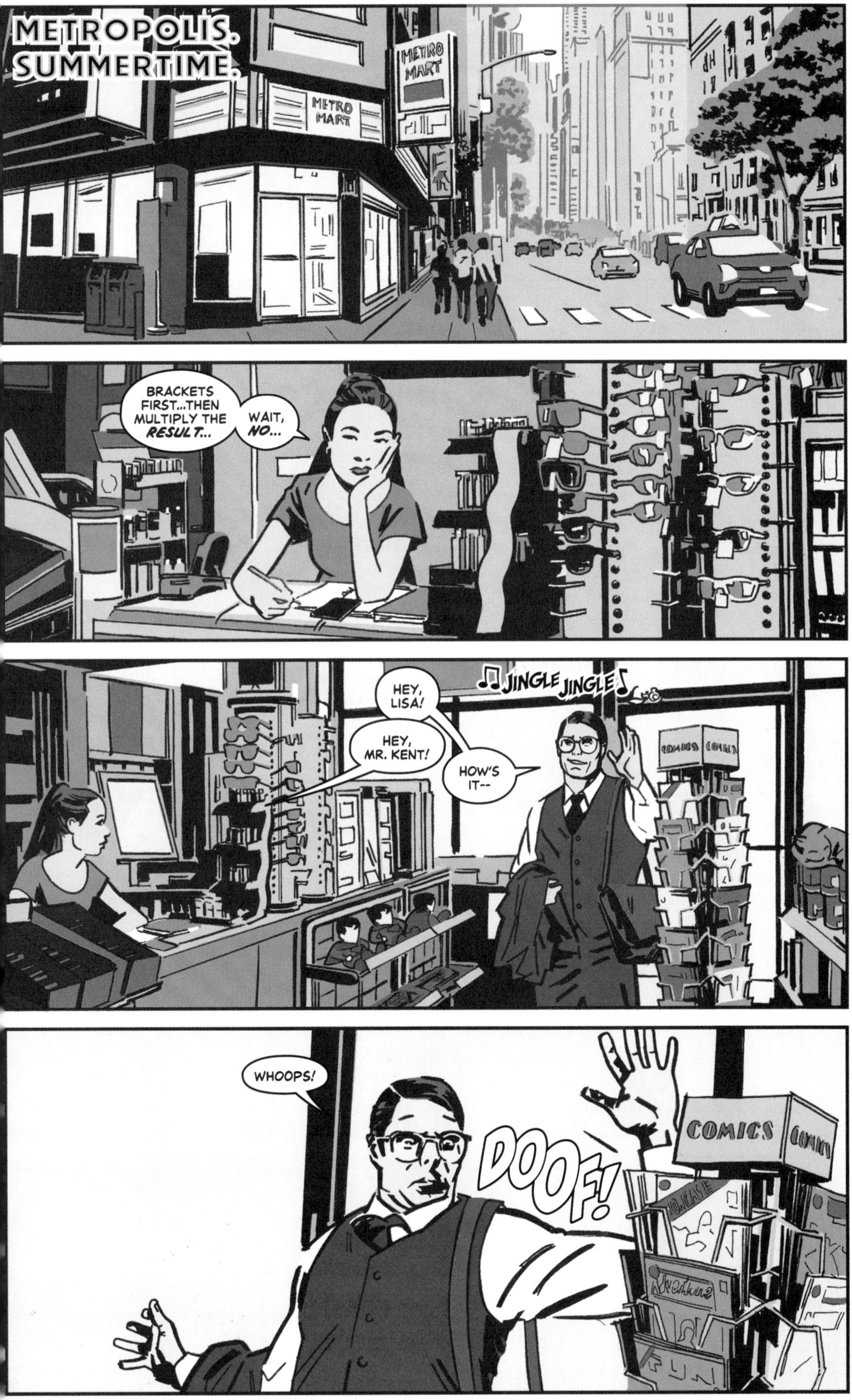
METROPOLIS.
SUMMERTIME.
METRO MART
METRO MART
BRACKETS FIRST...THEN MULTIPLY THE *RESULT*...
WAIT, *NO*...
JINGLE JINGLE
HEY, LISA!
HEY, MR. KENT!
HOW'S IT--
COMICS
WHOOPS!
DOOF!
COMICS

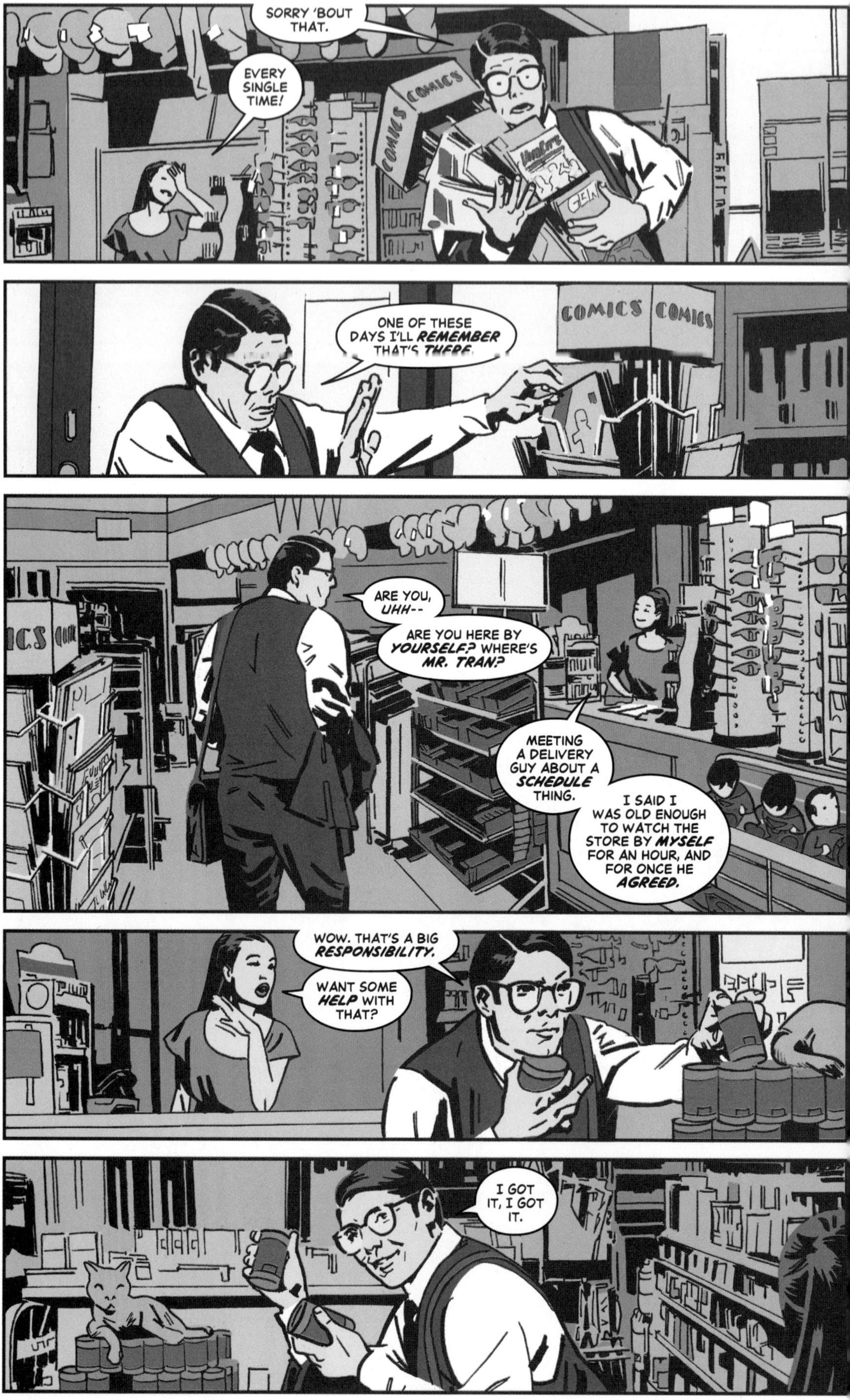

SORRY 'BOUT THAT.
EVERY SINGLE TIME!
COMICS
COMICS
ONE OF THESE DAYS I'LL REMEMBER THAT'S THERE.
COMICS COMICS
ARE YOU, UHH--
ARE YOU HERE BY YOURSELF? WHERE'S MR. TRAN?
MEETING A DELIVERY GUY ABOUT A SCHEDULE THING.
I SAID I WAS OLD ENOUGH TO WATCH THE STORE BY MYSELF FOR AN HOUR, AND FOR ONCE HE AGREED.
WOW. THAT'S A BIG RESPONSIBILITY.
WANT SOME HELP WITH THAT?
I GOT IT, I GOT IT.

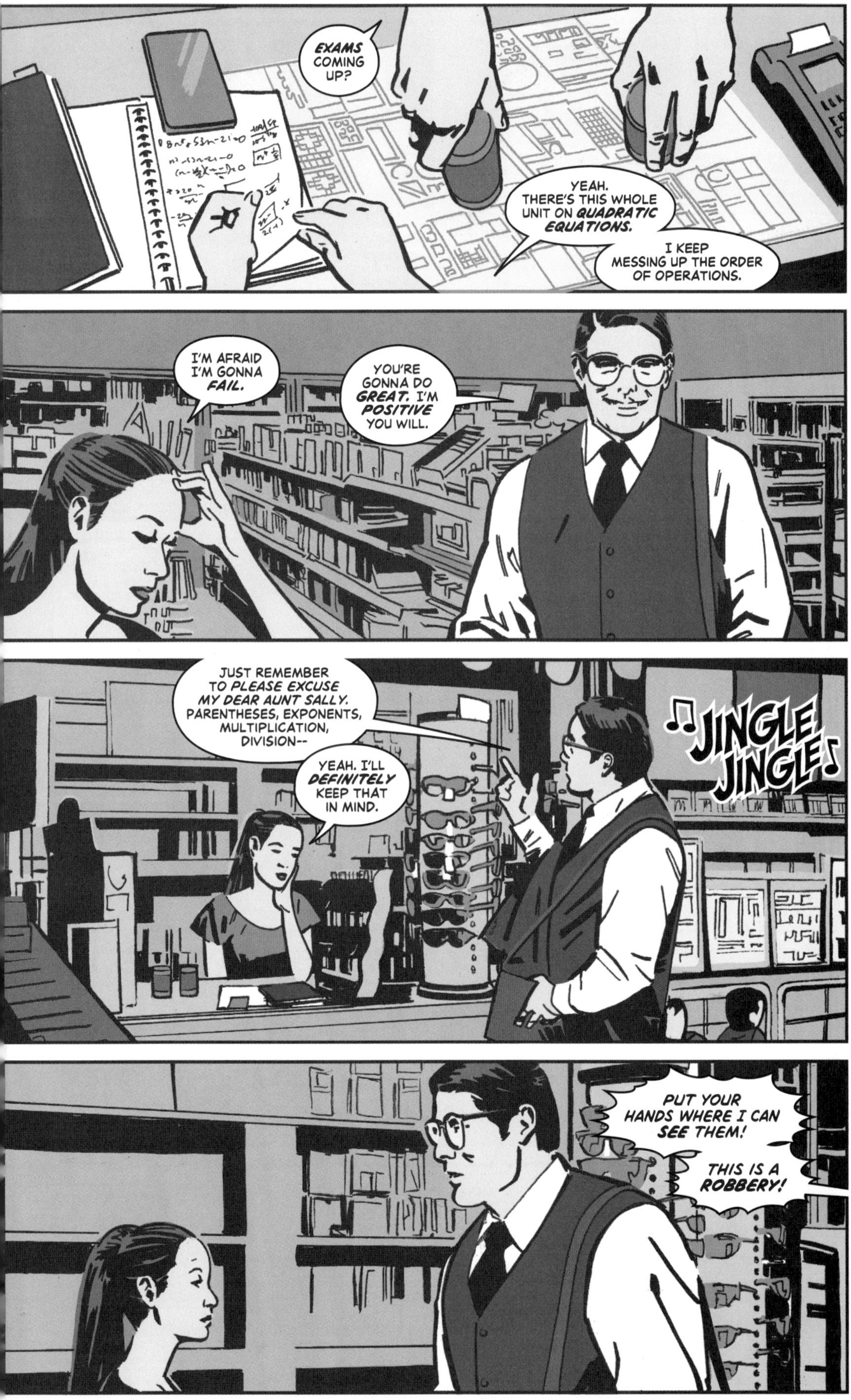
EXAMS COMING UP?
YEAH. THERE'S THIS WHOLE UNIT ON QUADRATIC EQUATIONS.
I KEEP MESSING UP THE ORDER OF OPERATIONS.
I'M AFRAID I'M GONNA FAIL.
YOU'RE GONNA DO GREAT. I'M POSITIVE YOU WILL.
JUST REMEMBER TO PLEASE EXCUSE MY DEAR AUNT SALLY. PARENTHESES, EXPONENTS, MULTIPLICATION, DIVISION--
YEAH. I'LL DEFINITELY KEEP THAT IN MIND.
JINGLE JINGLE
PUT YOUR HANDS WHERE I CAN SEE THEM!
THIS IS A ROBBERY!

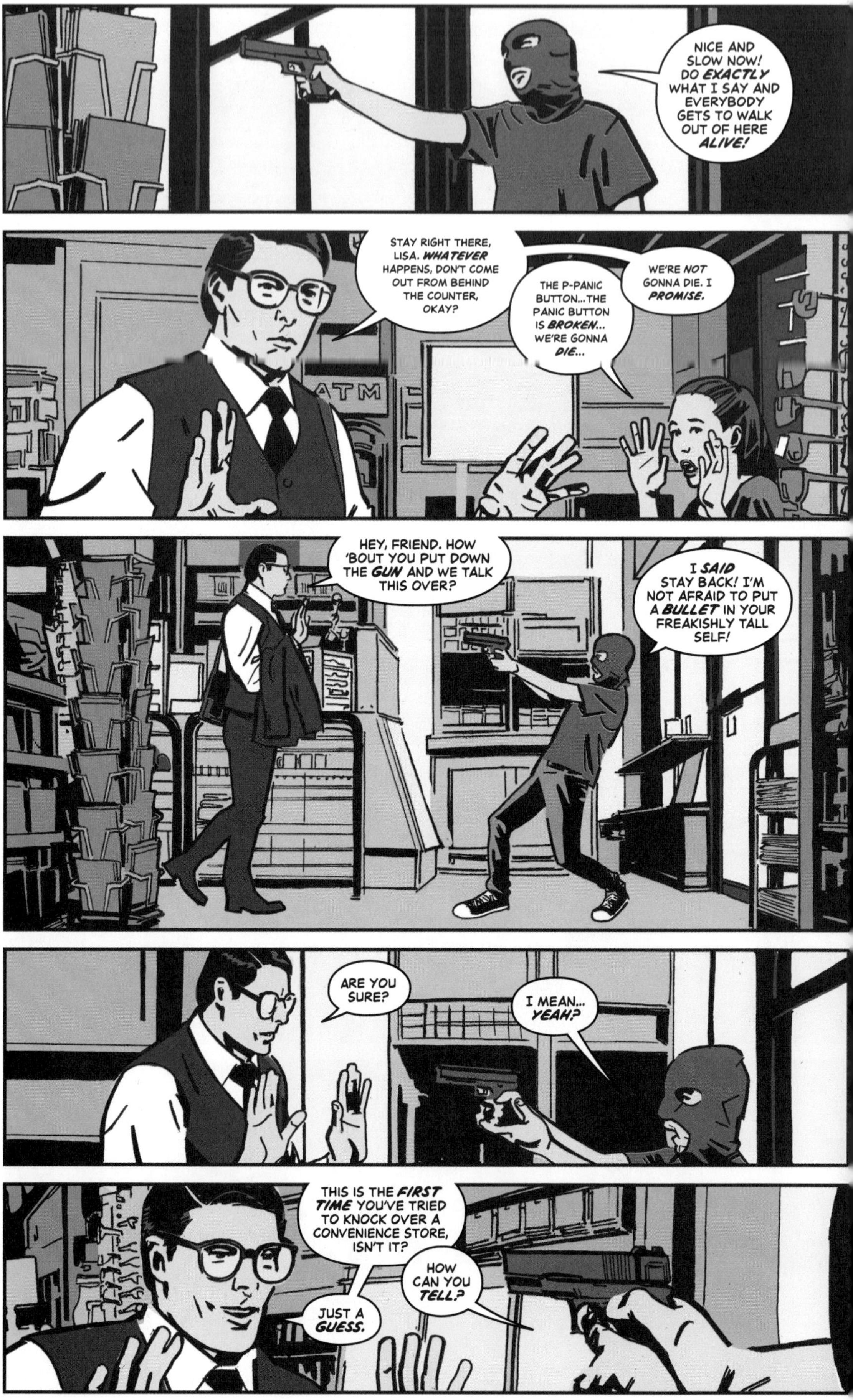
NICE AND SLOW NOW! DO EXACTLY WHAT I SAY AND EVERYBODY GETS TO WALK OUT OF HERE ALIVE!
STAY RIGHT THERE, LISA. WHATEVER HAPPENS, DON'T COME OUT FROM BEHIND THE COUNTER, OKAY?
THE P-PANIC BUTTON...THE PANIC BUTTON IS BROKEN... WE'RE GONNA DIE...
WE'RE NOT GONNA DIE. I PROMISE.
ATM
HEY, FRIEND. HOW 'BOUT YOU PUT DOWN THE GUN AND WE TALK THIS OVER?
I SAID STAY BACK! I'M NOT AFRAID TO PUT A BULLET IN YOUR FREAKISHLY TALL SELF!
ARE YOU SURE?
I MEAN... YEAH?
THIS IS THE FIRST TIME YOU'VE TRIED TO KNOCK OVER A CONVENIENCE STORE, ISN'T IT?
HOW CAN YOU TELL?
JUST A GUESS.

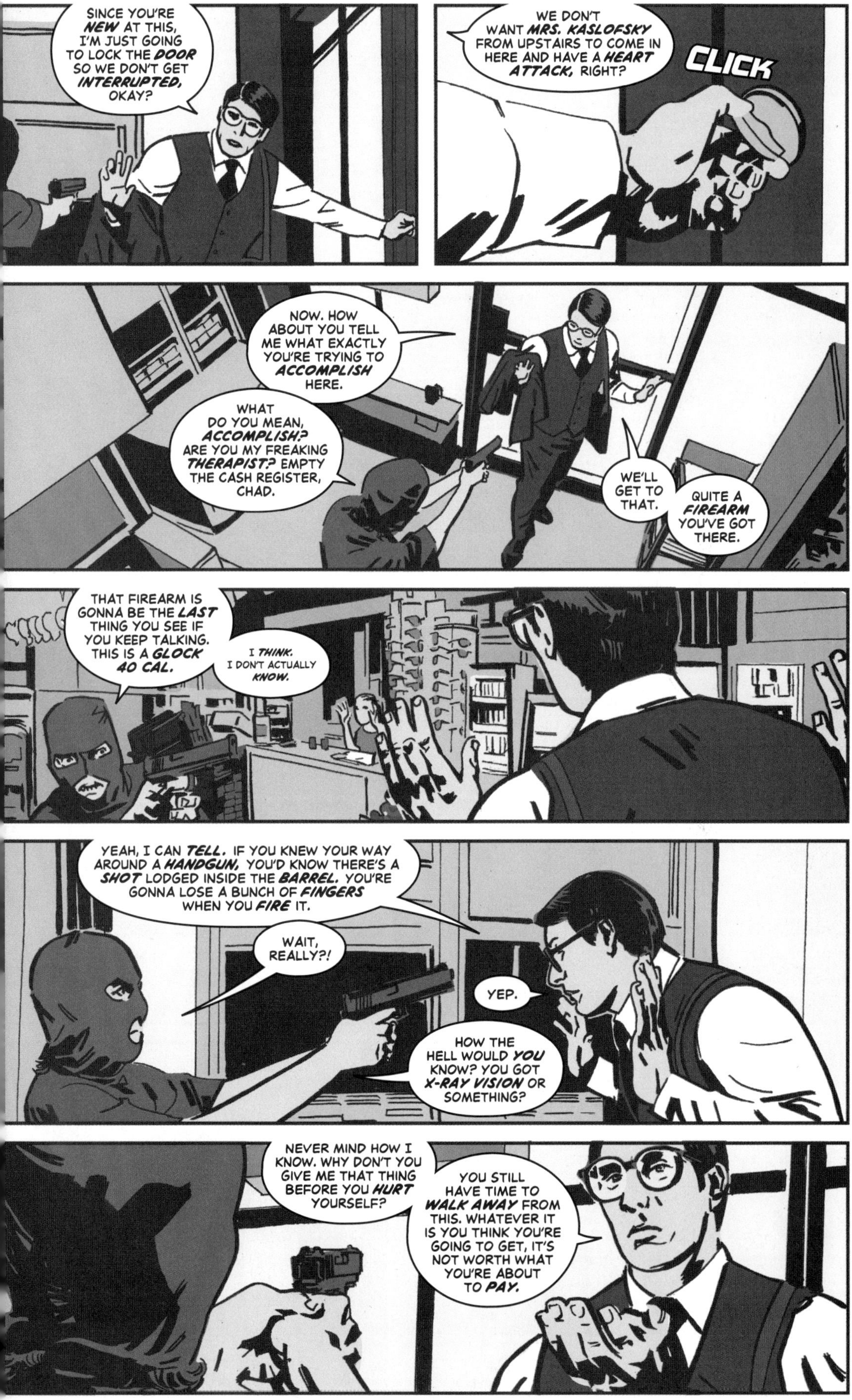
SINCE YOU'RE NEW AT THIS, I'M JUST GOING TO LOCK THE DOOR SO WE DON'T GET INTERRUPTED, OKAY?
WE DON'T WANT MRS. KASLOFSKY FROM UPSTAIRS TO COME IN HERE AND HAVE A HEART ATTACK, RIGHT?
CLICK
NOW. HOW ABOUT YOU TELL ME WHAT EXACTLY YOU'RE TRYING TO ACCOMPLISH HERE.
WHAT DO YOU MEAN, ACCOMPLISH? ARE YOU MY FREAKING THERAPIST? EMPTY THE CASH REGISTER, CHAD.
WE'LL GET TO THAT.
QUITE A FIREARM YOU'VE GOT THERE.
THAT FIREARM IS GONNA BE THE LAST THING YOU SEE IF YOU KEEP TALKING. THIS IS A GLOCK 40 CAL.
I THINK. I DON'T ACTUALLY KNOW.
YEAH, I CAN TELL. IF YOU KNEW YOUR WAY AROUND A HANDGUN, YOU'D KNOW THERE'S A SHOT LODGED INSIDE THE BARREL. YOU'RE GONNA LOSE A BUNCH OF FINGERS WHEN YOU FIRE IT.
WAIT, REALLY?!
YEP.
HOW THE HELL WOULD YOU KNOW? YOU GOT X-RAY VISION OR SOMETHING?
NEVER MIND HOW I KNOW. WHY DON'T YOU GIVE ME THAT THING BEFORE YOU HURT YOURSELF?
YOU STILL HAVE TIME TO WALK AWAY FROM THIS. WHATEVER IT IS YOU THINK YOU'RE GOING TO GET, IT'S NOT WORTH WHAT YOU'RE ABOUT TO PAY.

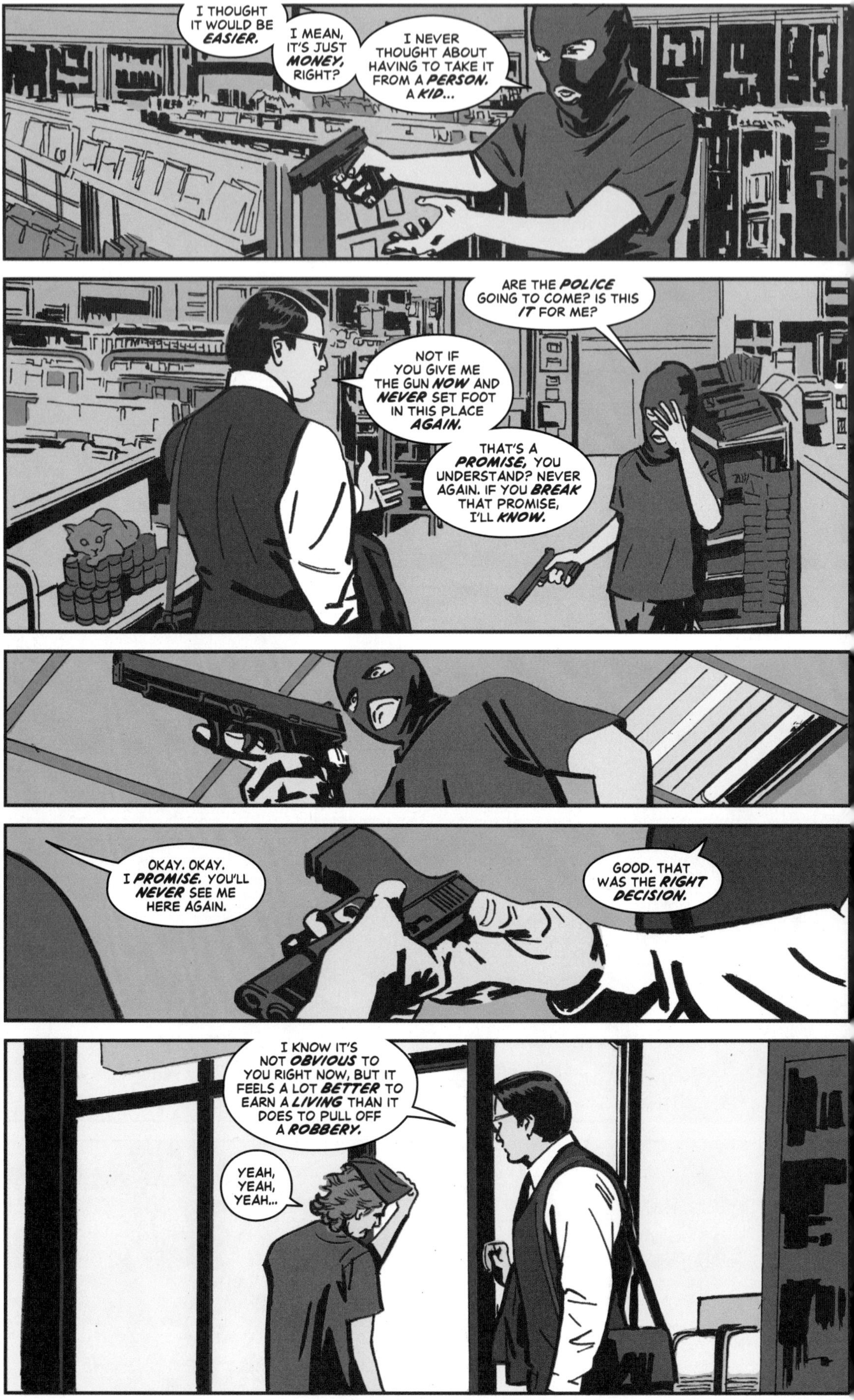
I THOUGHT IT WOULD BE EASIER.
I MEAN, IT'S JUST MONEY, RIGHT?
I NEVER THOUGHT ABOUT HAVING TO TAKE IT FROM A PERSON. A KID...
ARE THE POLICE GOING TO COME? IS THIS IT FOR ME?
NOT IF YOU GIVE ME THE GUN NOW AND NEVER SET FOOT IN THIS PLACE AGAIN.
THAT'S A PROMISE, YOU UNDERSTAND? NEVER AGAIN. IF YOU BREAK THAT PROMISE, I'LL KNOW.
OKAY. OKAY. I PROMISE. YOU'LL NEVER SEE ME HERE AGAIN.
GOOD. THAT WAS THE RIGHT DECISION.
I KNOW IT'S NOT OBVIOUS TO YOU RIGHT NOW, BUT IT FEELS A LOT BETTER TO EARN A LIVING THAN IT DOES TO PULL OFF A ROBBERY.
YEAH, YEAH, YEAH...

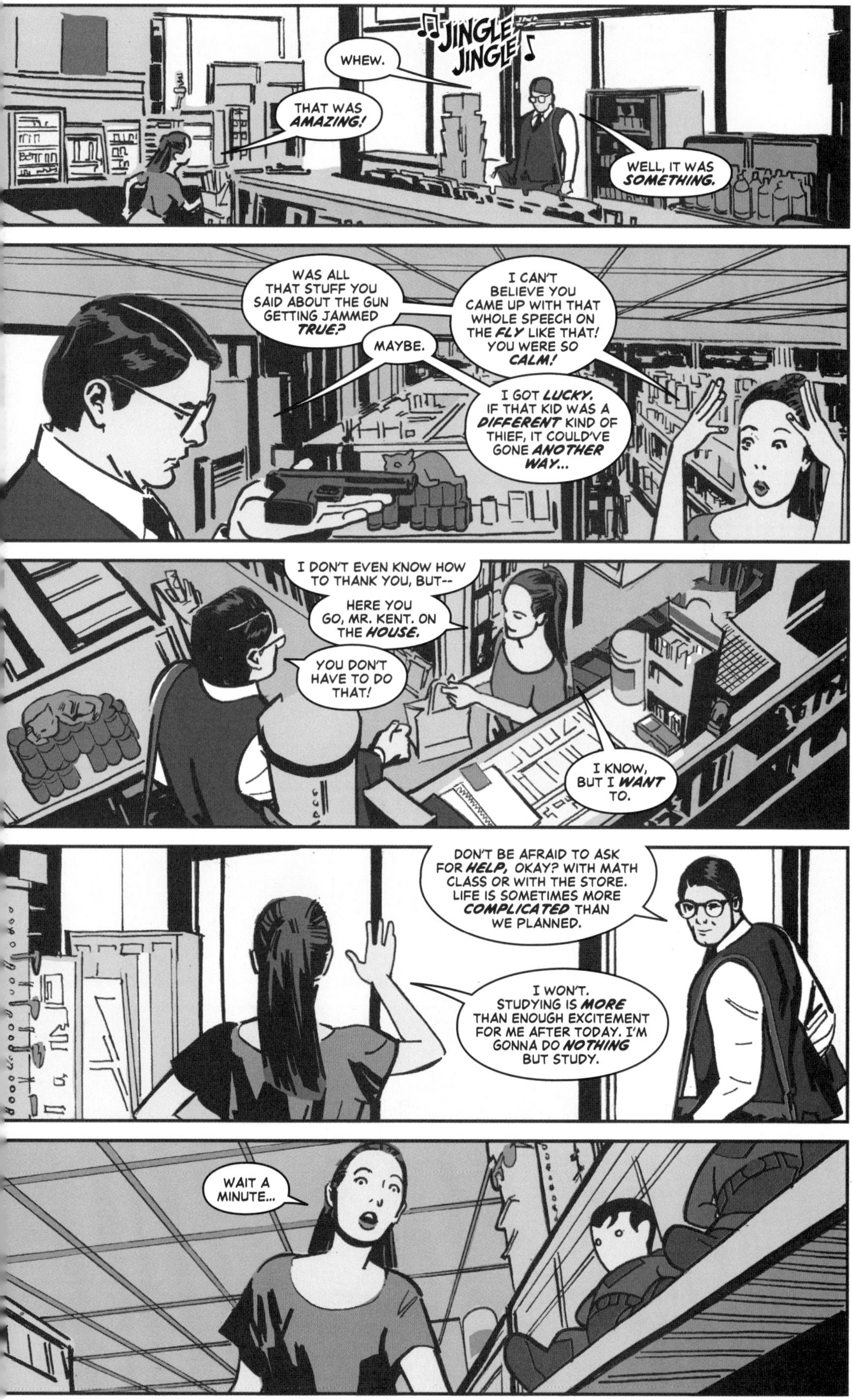
JINGLE JINGLE
WHEW.
THAT WAS AMAZING!
WELL, IT WAS SOMETHING.
WAS ALL THAT STUFF YOU SAID ABOUT THE GUN GETTING JAMMED TRUE?
MAYBE.
I CAN'T BELIEVE YOU CAME UP WITH THAT WHOLE SPEECH ON THE FLY LIKE THAT! YOU WERE SO CALM!
I GOT LUCKY. IF THAT KID WAS A DIFFERENT KIND OF THIEF, IT COULD'VE GONE ANOTHER WAY...
I DON'T EVEN KNOW HOW TO THANK YOU, BUT--
HERE YOU GO, MR. KENT. ON THE HOUSE.
YOU DON'T HAVE TO DO THAT!
I KNOW, BUT I WANT TO.
DON'T BE AFRAID TO ASK FOR HELP, OKAY? WITH MATH CLASS OR WITH THE STORE. LIFE IS SOMETIMES MORE COMPLICATED THAN WE PLANNED.
I WON'T. STUDYING IS MORE THAN ENOUGH EXCITEMENT FOR ME AFTER TODAY. I'M GONNA DO NOTHING BUT STUDY.
WAIT A MINUTE...

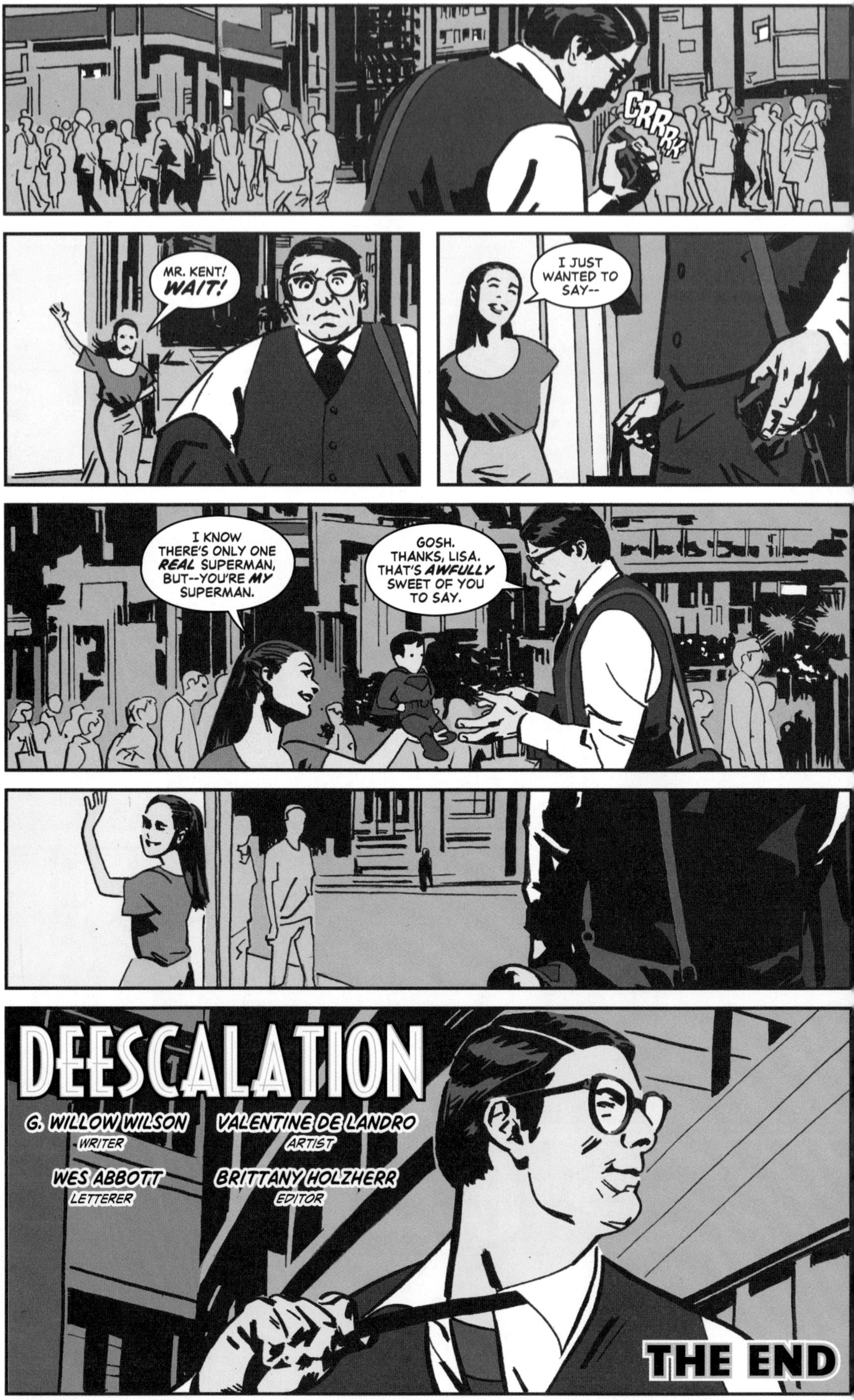
CRRRK
MR. KENT! WAIT!
I JUST WANTED TO SAY--
I KNOW THERE'S ONLY ONE REAL SUPERMAN, BUT--YOU'RE MY SUPERMAN.
GOSH. THANKS, LISA. THAT'S AWFULLY SWEET OF YOU TO SAY.
DEESCALATION
G. WILLOW WILSON WRITER
VALENTINE DE LANDRO ARTIST
WES ABBOTT LETTERER
BRITTANY HOLZHERR EDITOR
THE END

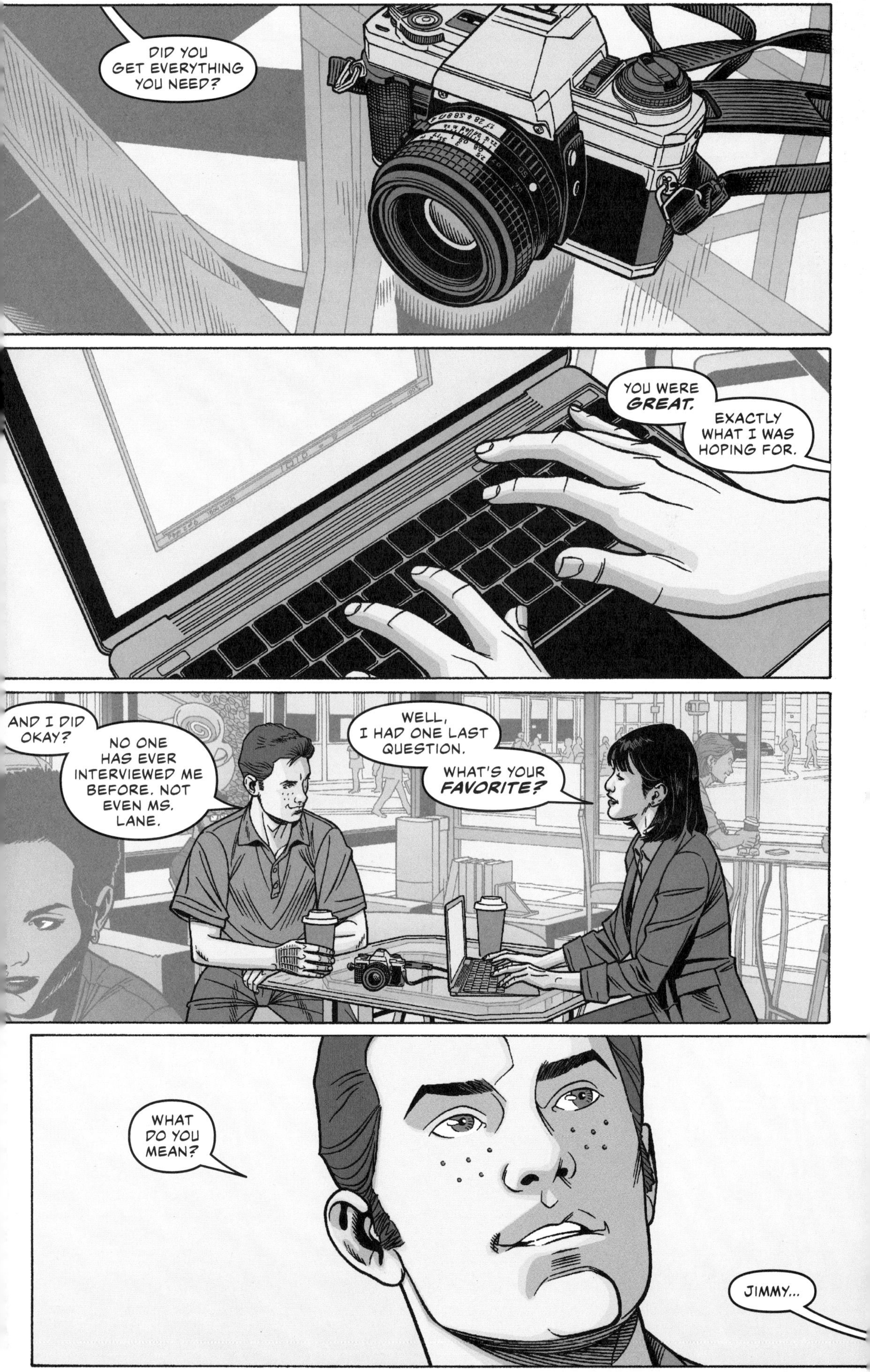
DID YOU GET EVERYTHING YOU NEED?
YOU WERE GREAT.
EXACTLY WHAT I WAS HOPING FOR.
AND I DID OKAY?
NO ONE HAS EVER INTERVIEWED ME BEFORE. NOT EVEN MS. LANE.
WELL, I HAD ONE LAST QUESTION.
WHAT'S YOUR FAVORITE?
WHAT DO YOU MEAN?
JIMMY...

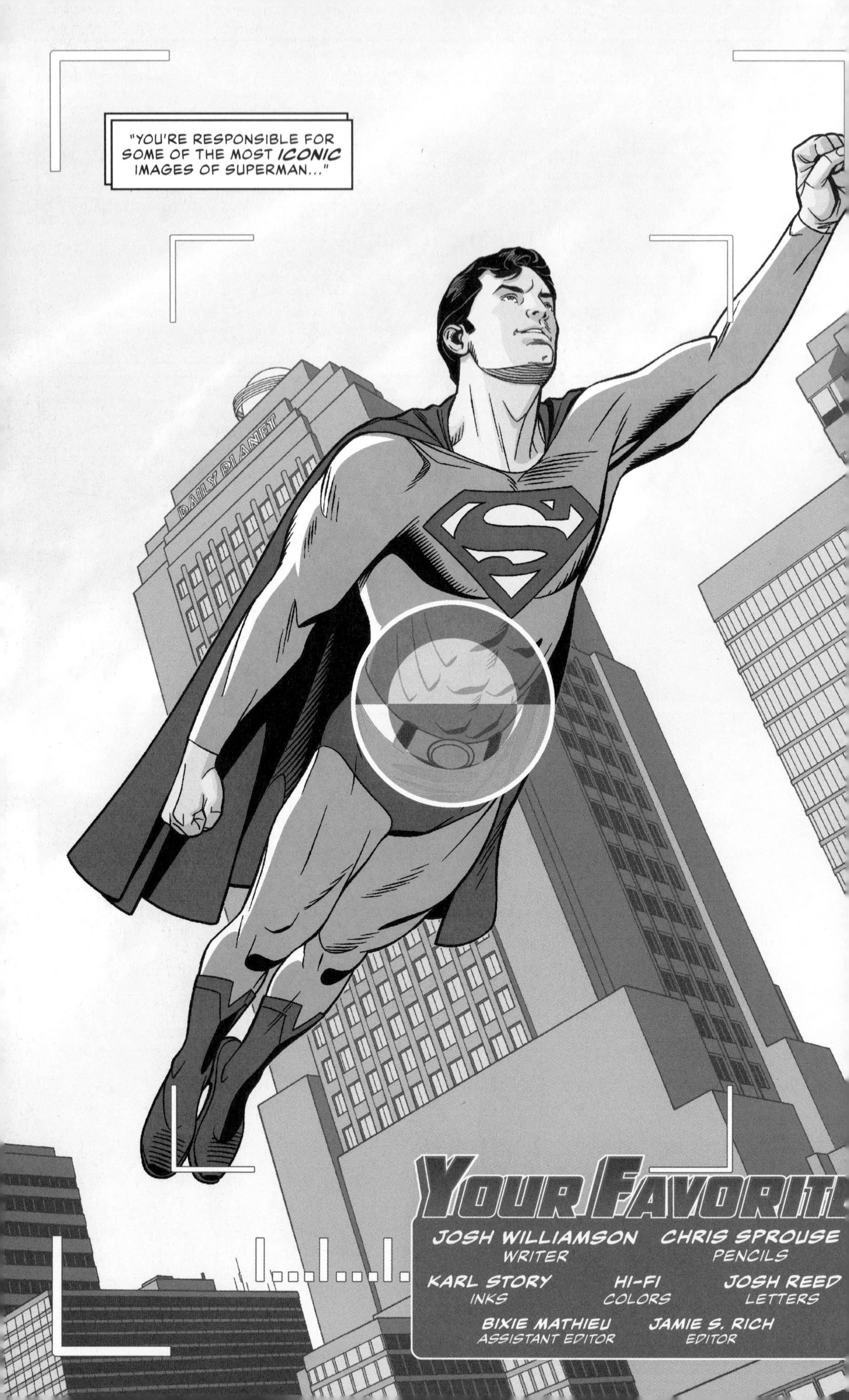
"YOU'RE RESPONSIBLE FOR SOME OF THE MOST ICONIC IMAGES OF SUPERMAN..."
DAILY PLANET
YOUR FAVORITE
JOSH WILLIAMSON WRITER
CHRIS SPROUSE PENCILS
KARL STORY INKS
HI-FI COLORS
JOSH REED LETTERS
BIXIE MATHIEU ASSISTANT EDITOR
JAMIE S. RICH EDITOR

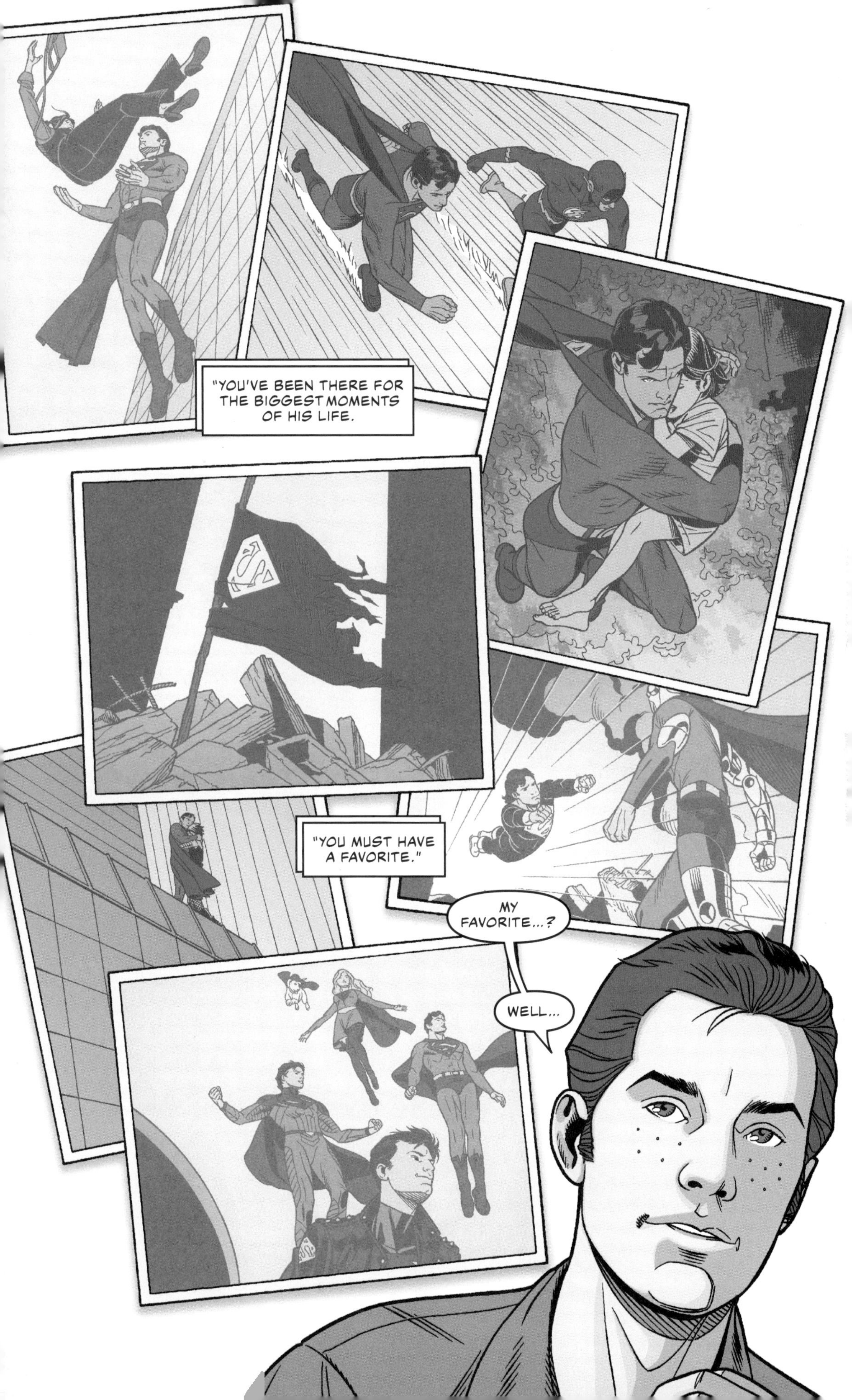
"YOU'VE BEEN THERE FOR THE BIGGEST MOMENTS OF HIS LIFE.
"YOU MUST HAVE A FAVORITE."
MY FAVORITE...?
WELL...

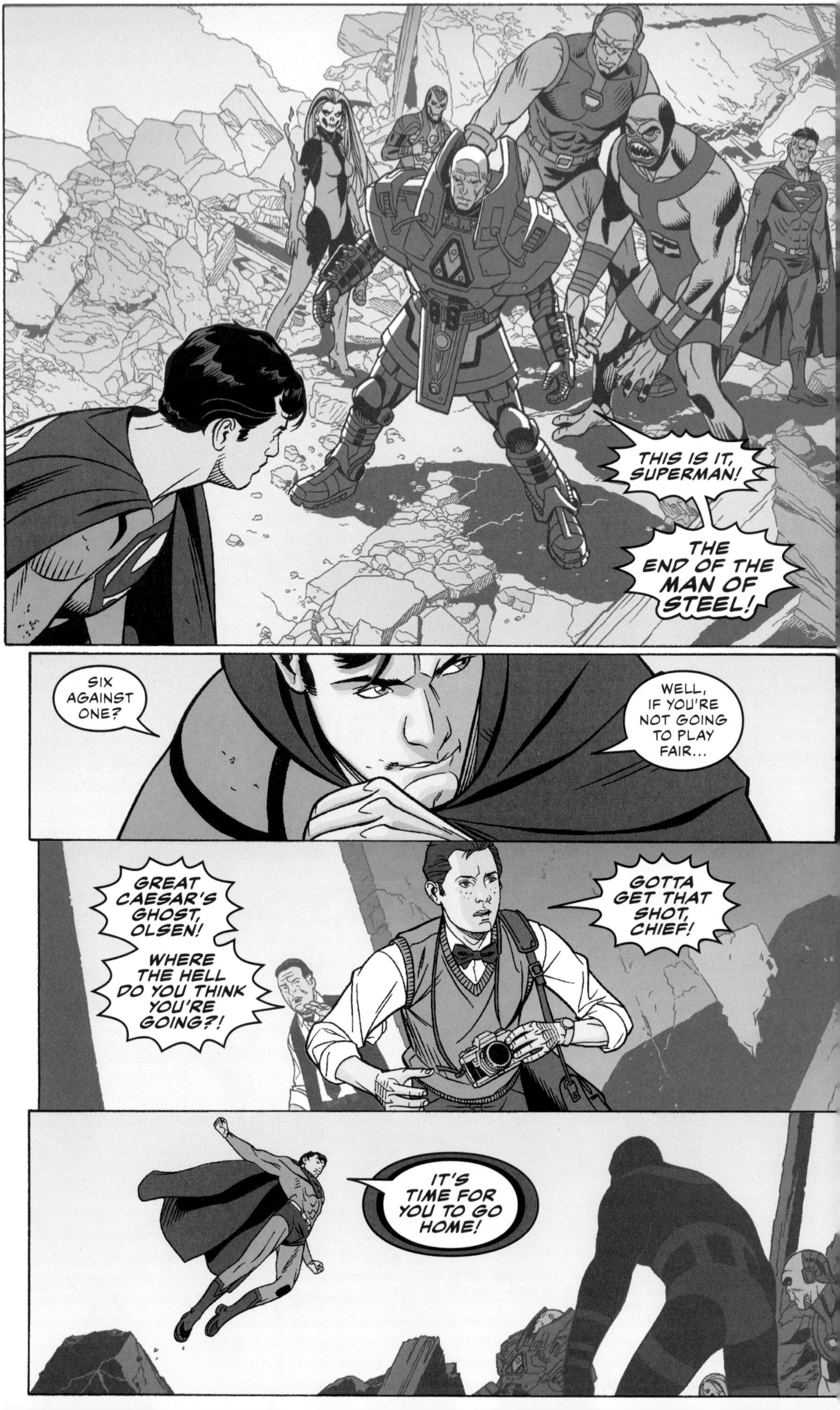
THIS IS IT, SUPERMAN!
THE END OF THE MAN OF STEEL!
SIX AGAINST ONE?
WELL, IF YOU'RE NOT GOING TO PLAY FAIR...
GREAT CAESAR'S GHOST, OLSEN!
WHERE THE HELL DO YOU THINK YOU'RE GOING?!
GOTTA GET THAT SHOT, CHIEF!
IT'S TIME FOR YOU TO GO HOME!

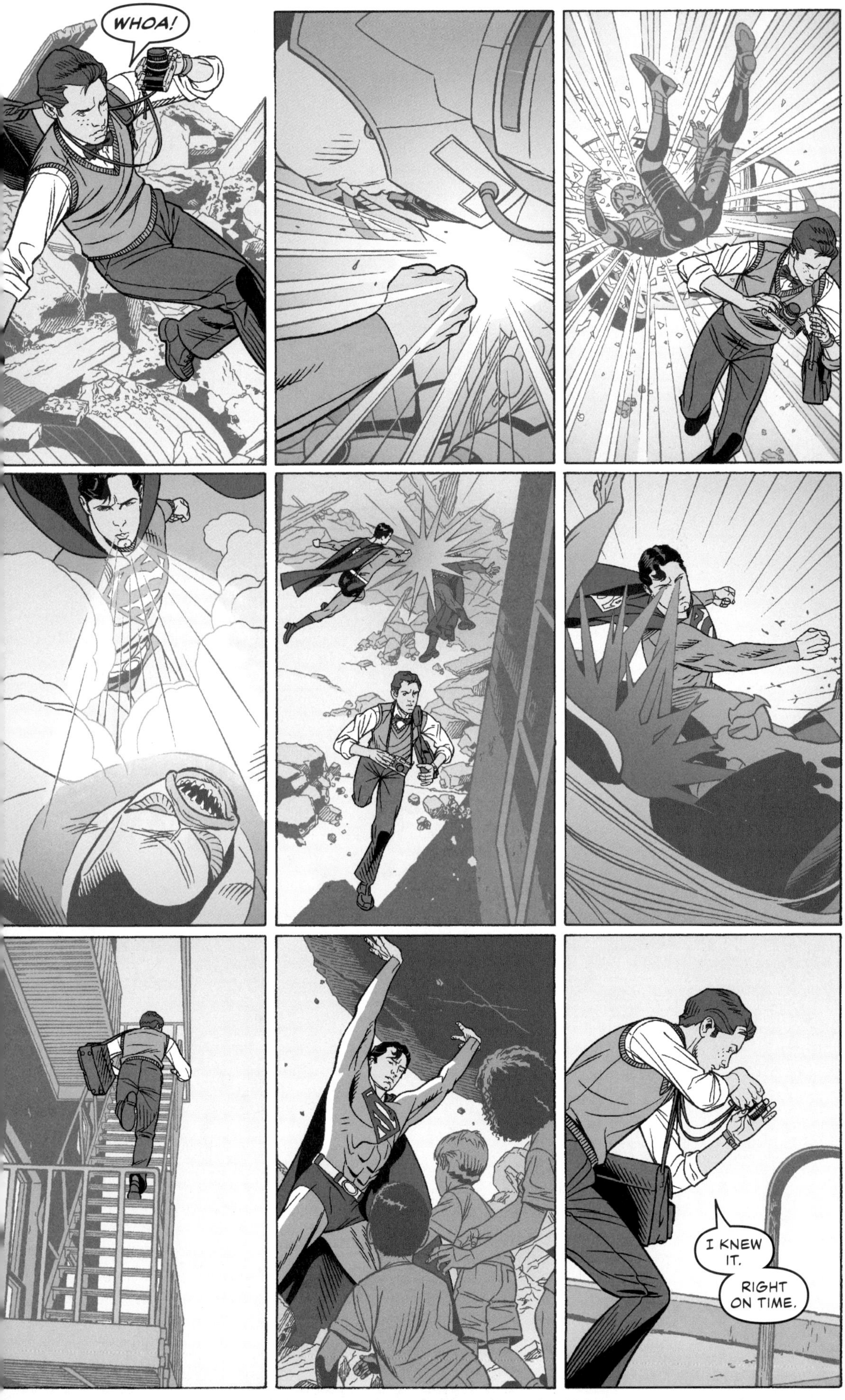
WHOA!
I KNEW IT.
RIGHT ON TIME.

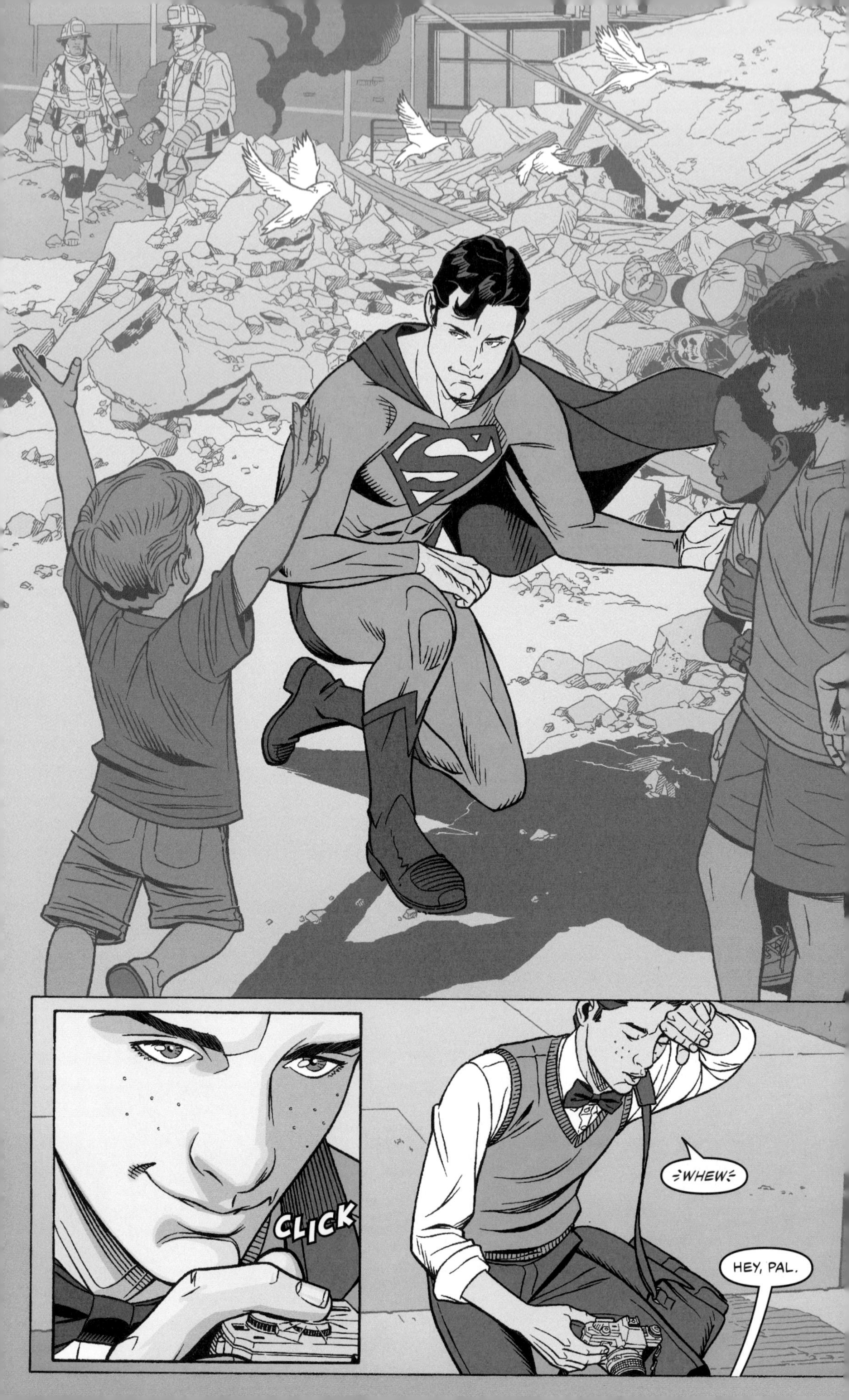
CLICK
WHEW
HEY, PAL.

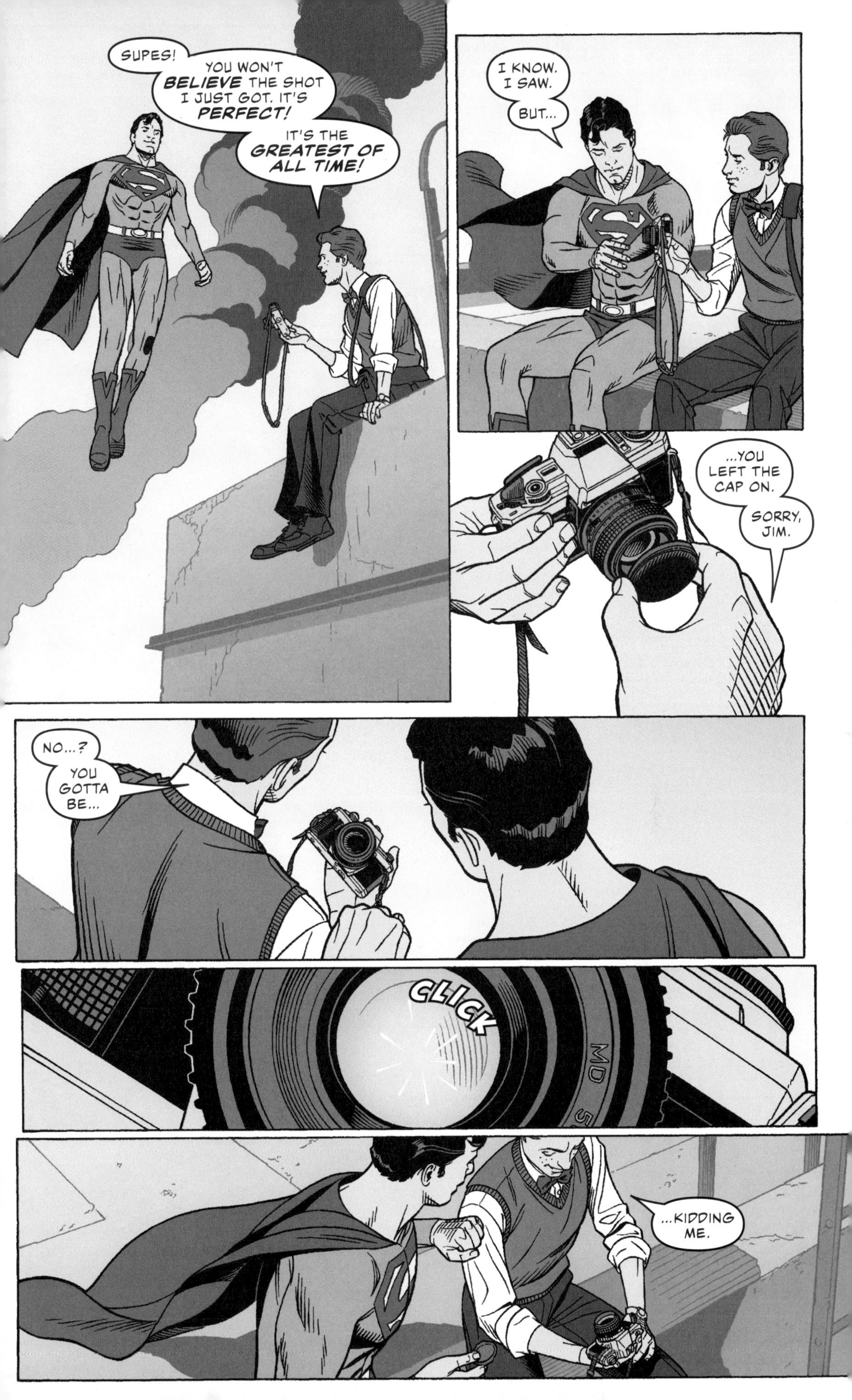
SUPES!
YOU WON'T BELIEVE THE SHOT I JUST GOT. IT'S PERFECT!
IT'S THE GREATEST OF ALL TIME!
I KNOW. I SAW.
BUT...
...YOU LEFT THE CAP ON.
SORRY, JIM.
NO...?
YOU GOTTA BE...
CLICK
MD
...KIDDING ME.

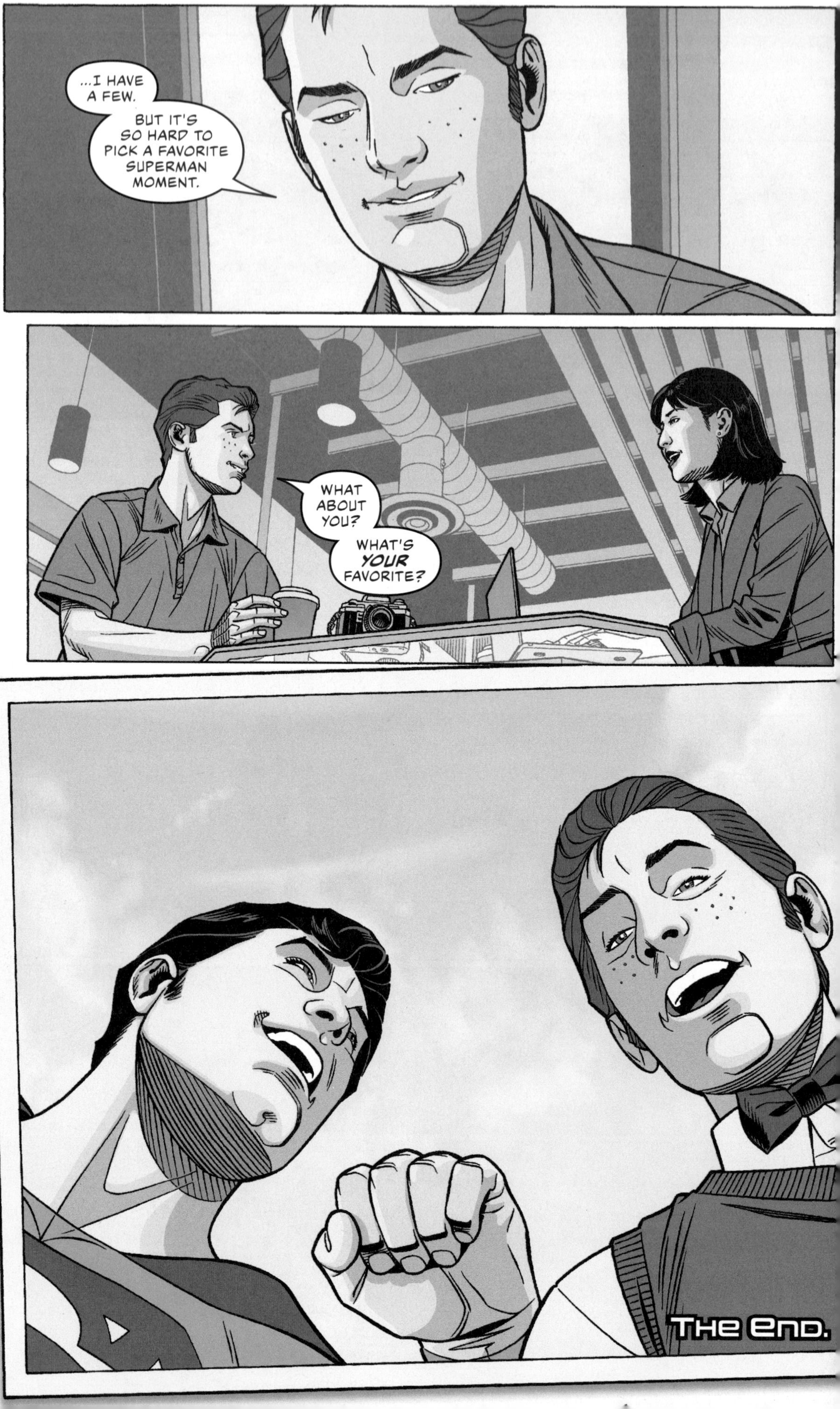
...I HAVE A FEW.
BUT IT'S SO HARD TO PICK A FAVORITE SUPERMAN MOMENT.
WHAT ABOUT YOU?
WHAT'S *YOUR* FAVORITE?
THE END.

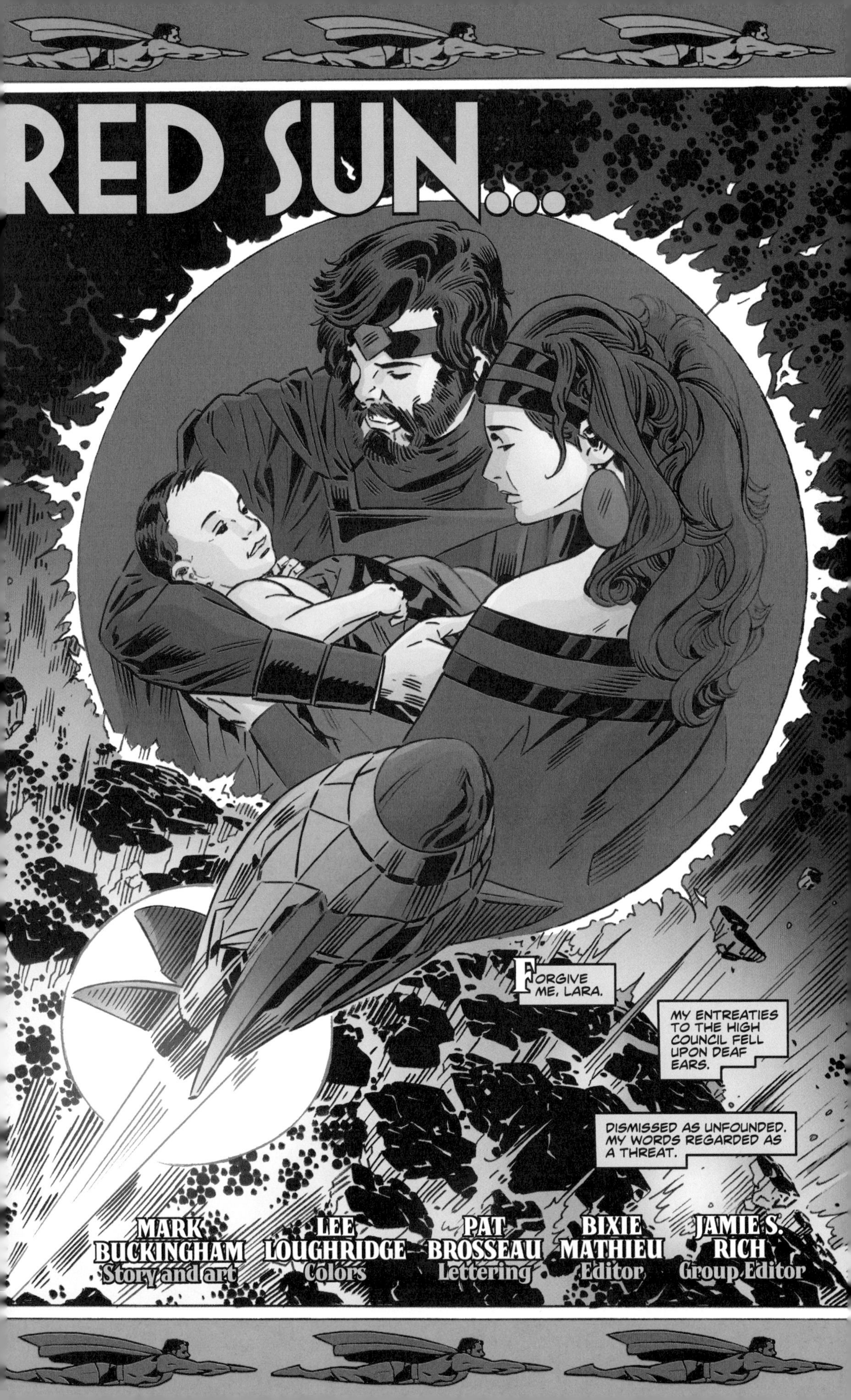
RED SUN...
FORGIVE ME, LARA.
MY ENTREATIES TO THE HIGH COUNCIL FELL UPON DEAF EARS.
DISMISSED AS UNFOUNDED. MY WORDS REGARDED AS A THREAT.
MARK BUCKINGHAM Story and art
LEE LOUGHRIDGE Colors
PAT BROSSEAU Lettering
BIXIE MATHIEU Editor
JAMIE S. RICH Group Editor

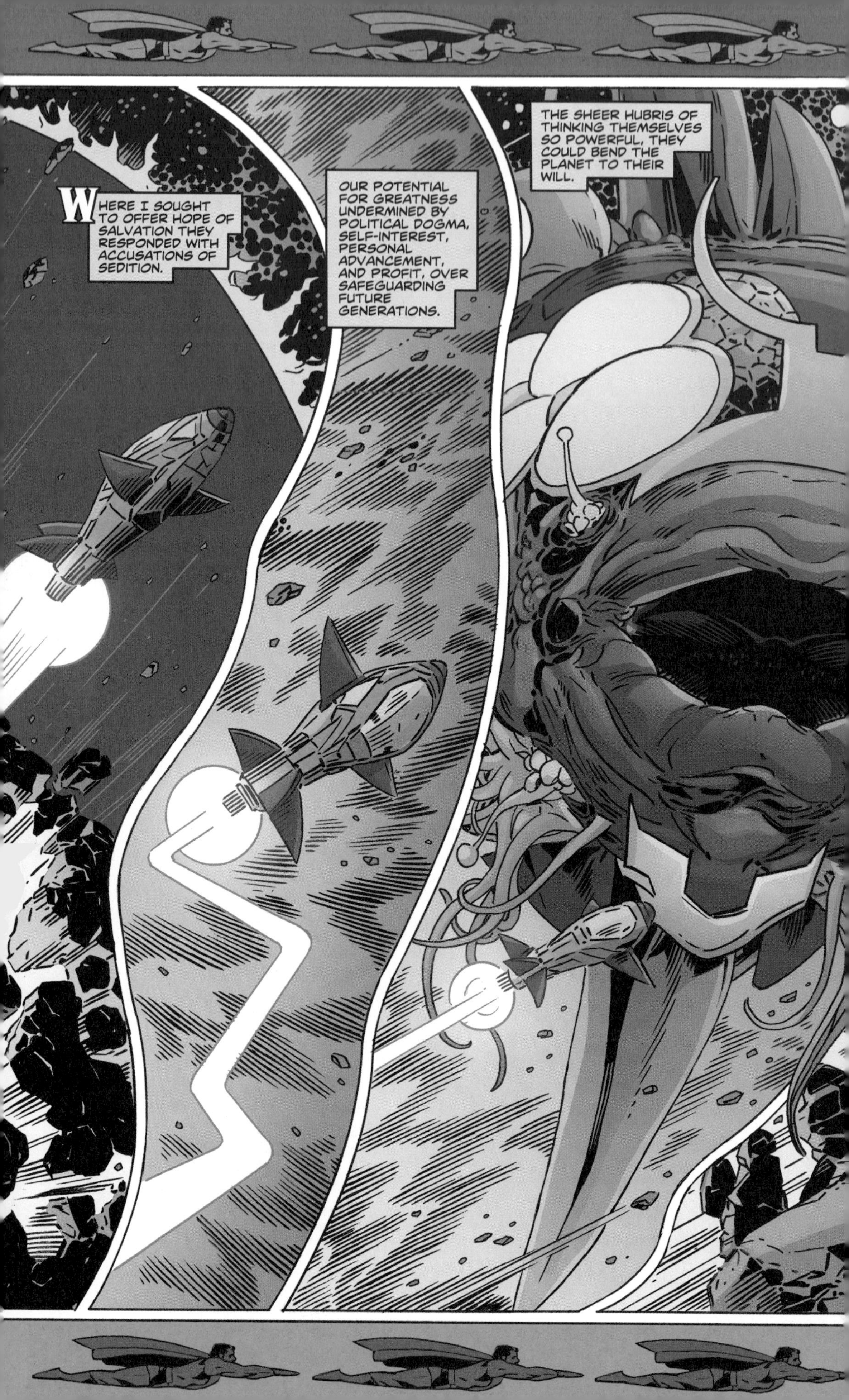
WHERE I SOUGHT TO OFFER HOPE OF SALVATION THEY RESPONDED WITH ACCUSATIONS OF SEDITION.
OUR POTENTIAL FOR GREATNESS UNDERMINED BY POLITICAL DOGMA, SELF-INTEREST, PERSONAL ADVANCEMENT, AND PROFIT, OVER SAFEGUARDING FUTURE GENERATIONS.
THE SHEER HUBRIS OF THINKING THEMSELVES SO POWERFUL, THEY COULD BEND THE PLANET TO THEIR WILL.

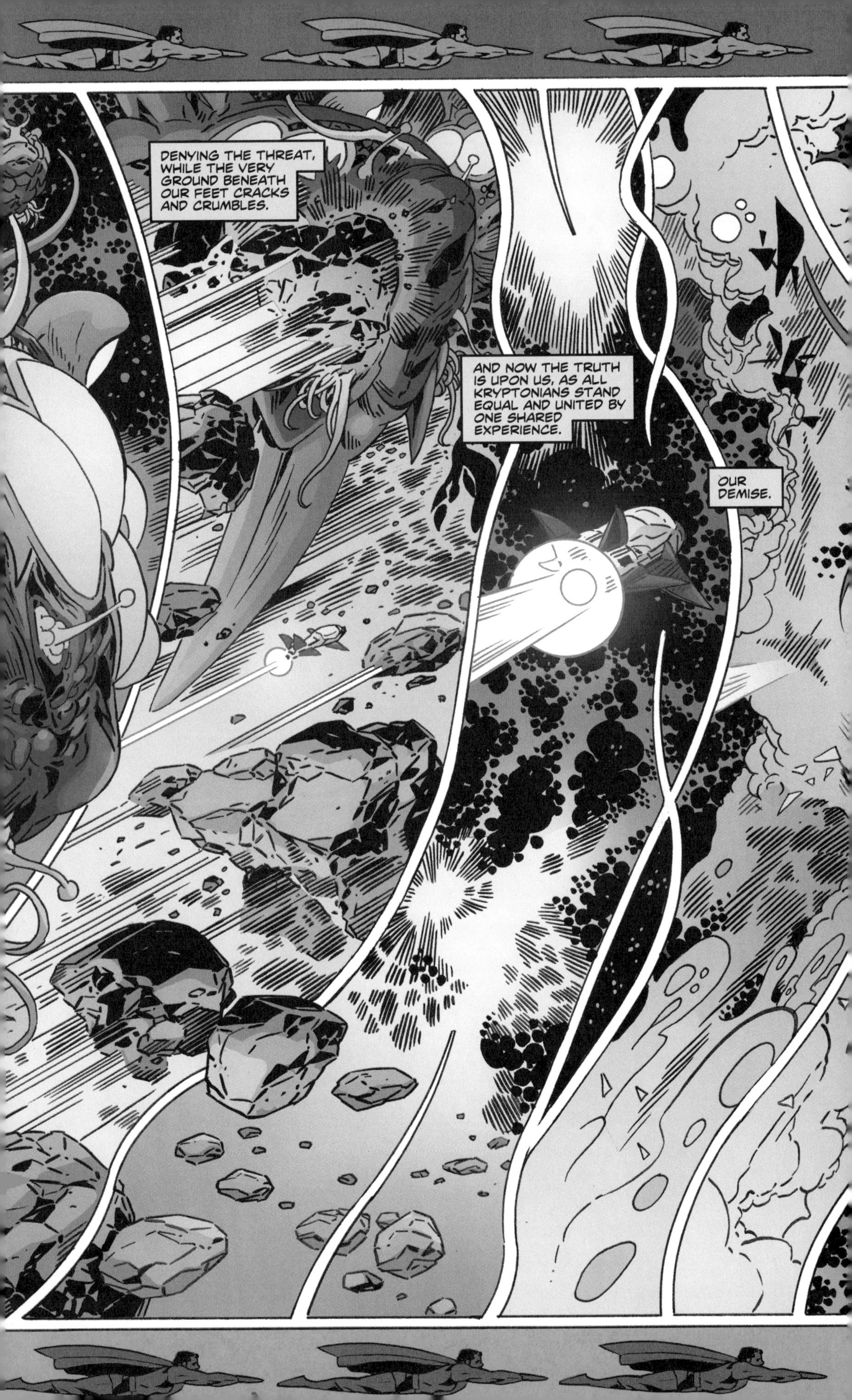
DENYING THE THREAT, WHILE THE VERY GROUND BENEATH OUR FEET CRACKS AND CRUMBLES.
AND NOW THE TRUTH IS UPON US, AS ALL KRYPTONIANS STAND EQUAL AND UNITED BY ONE SHARED EXPERIENCE.
OUR DEMISE.

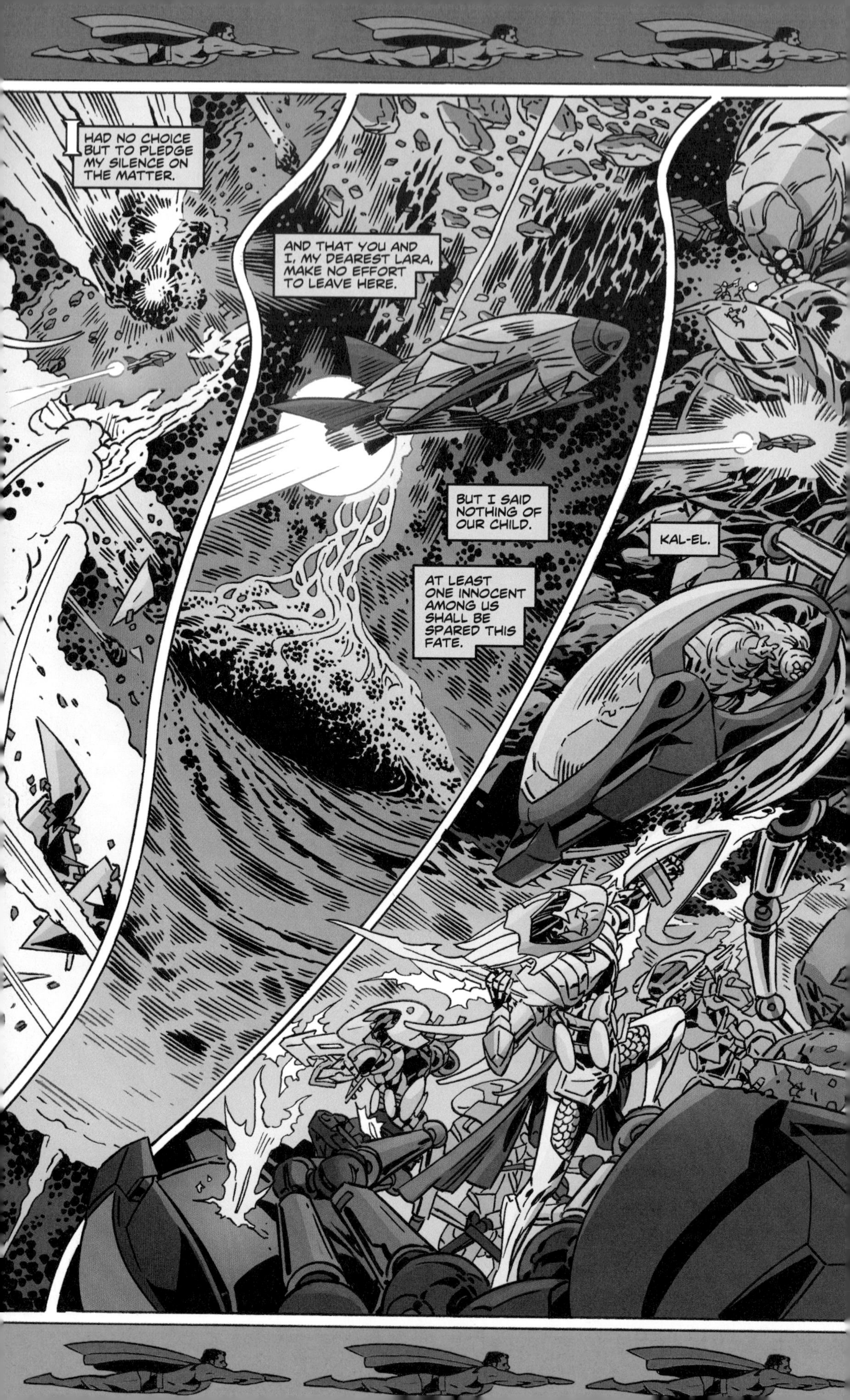
I HAD NO CHOICE BUT TO PLEDGE MY SILENCE ON THE MATTER.
AND THAT YOU AND I, MY DEAREST LARA, MAKE NO EFFORT TO LEAVE HERE.
BUT I SAID NOTHING OF OUR CHILD.
KAL-EL.
AT LEAST ONE INNOCENT AMONG US SHALL BE SPARED THIS FATE.

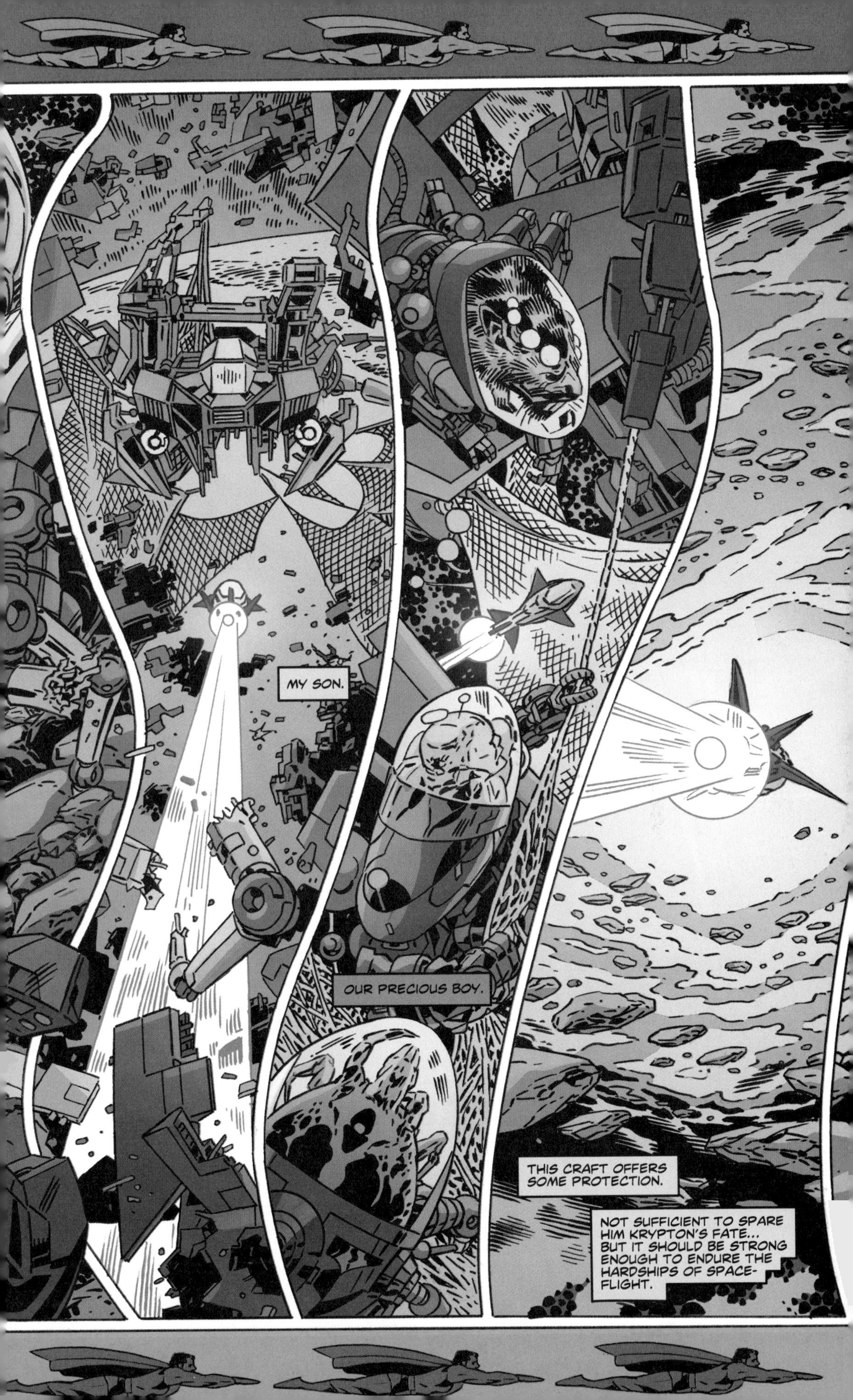
MY SON.
OUR PRECIOUS BOY.
THIS CRAFT OFFERS SOME PROTECTION.
NOT SUFFICIENT TO SPARE HIM KRYPTON'S FATE... BUT IT SHOULD BE STRONG ENOUGH TO ENDURE THE HARDSHIPS OF SPACE-FLIGHT.

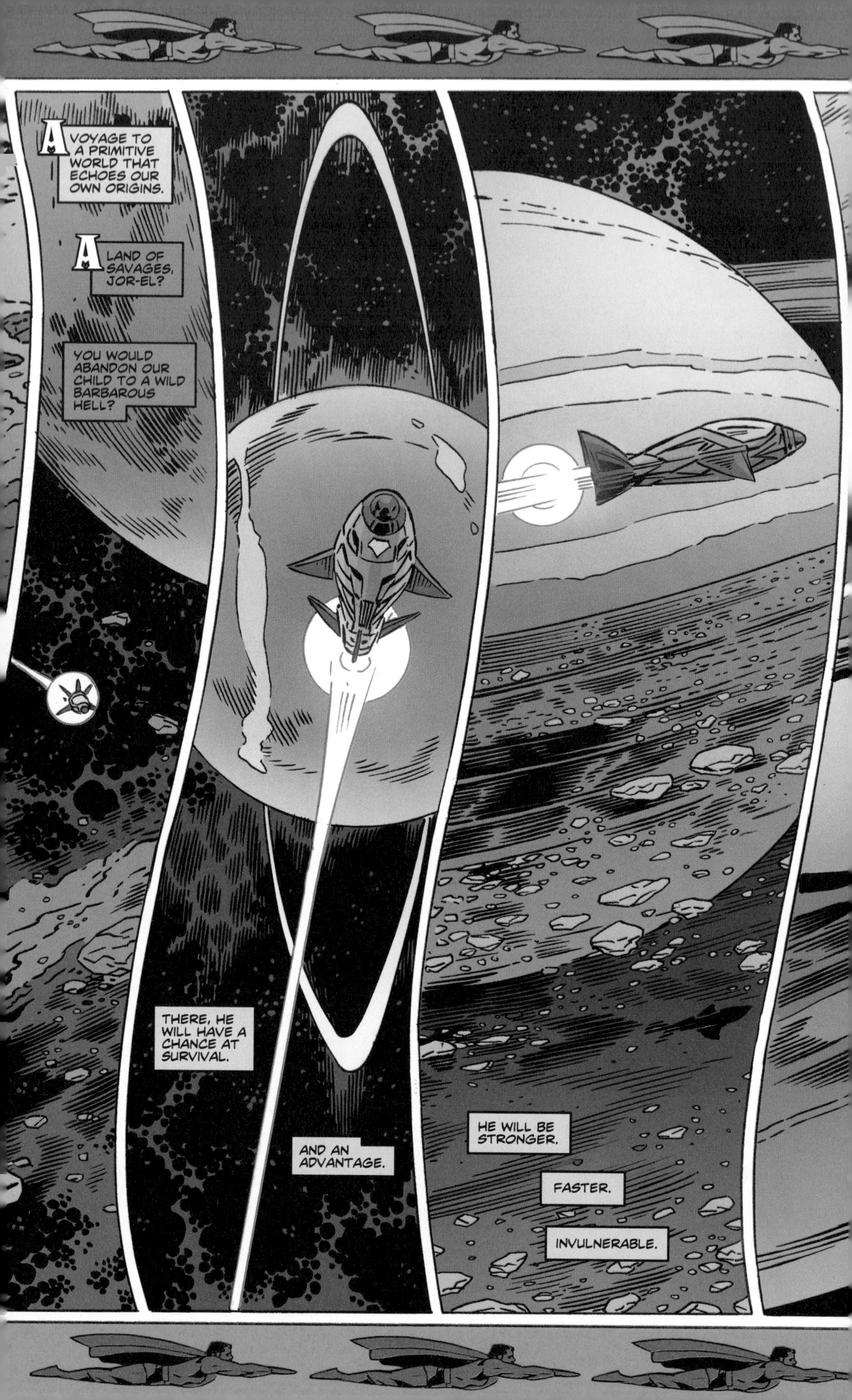
A VOYAGE TO A PRIMITIVE WORLD THAT ECHOES OUR OWN ORIGINS.
A LAND OF SAVAGES, JOR-EL?
YOU WOULD ABANDON OUR CHILD TO A WILD BARBAROUS HELL?
THERE, HE WILL HAVE A CHANCE AT SURVIVAL.
AND AN ADVANTAGE.
HE WILL BE STRONGER.
FASTER.
INVULNERABLE.

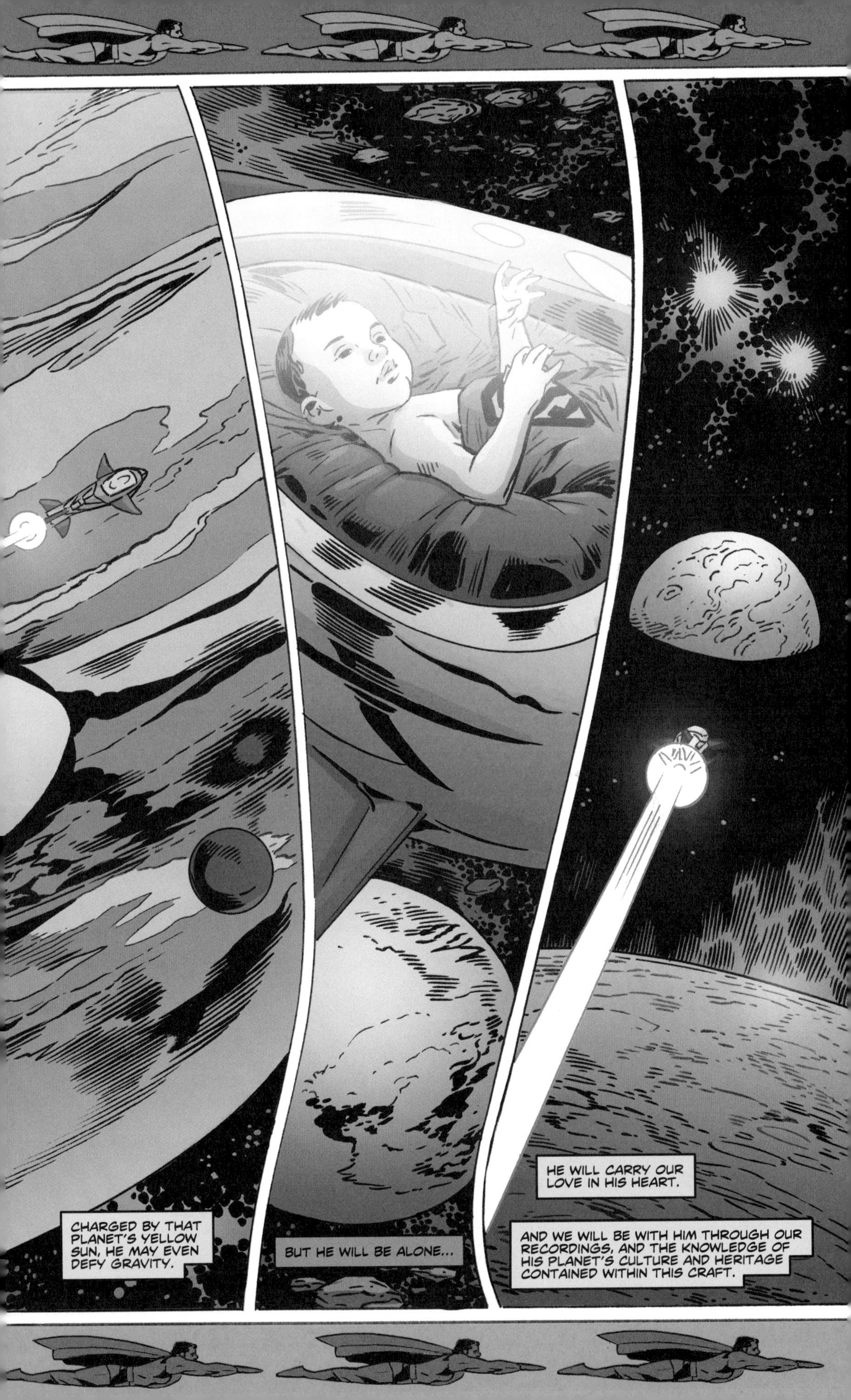
CHARGED BY THAT PLANET'S YELLOW SUN, HE MAY EVEN DEFY GRAVITY.
BUT HE WILL BE ALONE...
HE WILL CARRY OUR LOVE IN HIS HEART.
AND WE WILL BE WITH HIM THROUGH OUR RECORDINGS, AND THE KNOWLEDGE OF HIS PLANET'S CULTURE AND HERITAGE CONTAINED WITHIN THIS CRAFT.

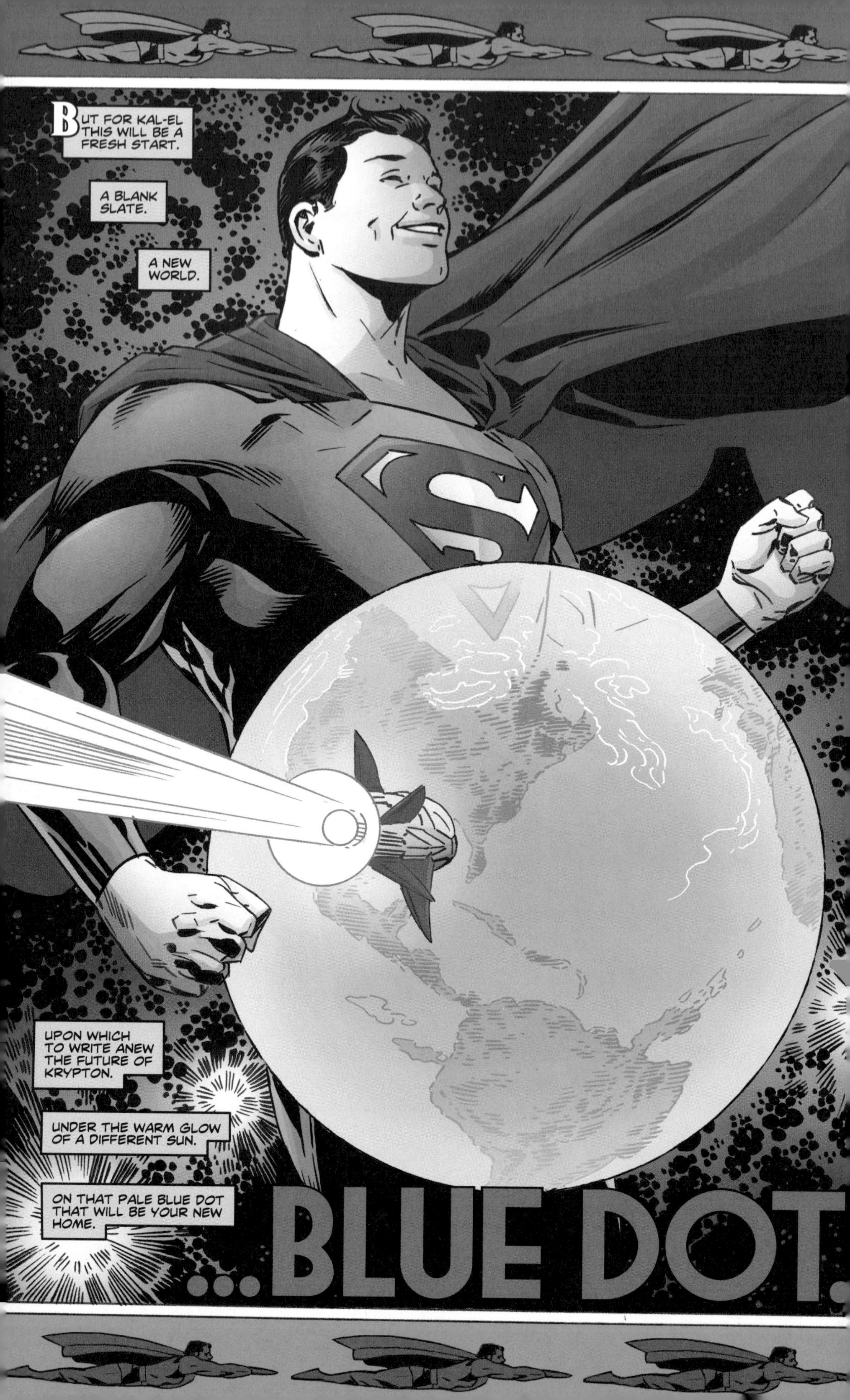

BUT FOR KAL-EL THIS WILL BE A FRESH START.
A BLANK SLATE.
A NEW WORLD.
UPON WHICH TO WRITE ANEW THE FUTURE OF KRYPTON.
UNDER THE WARM GLOW OF A DIFFERENT SUN.
ON THAT PALE BLUE DOT THAT WILL BE YOUR NEW HOME.
...BLUE DOT.

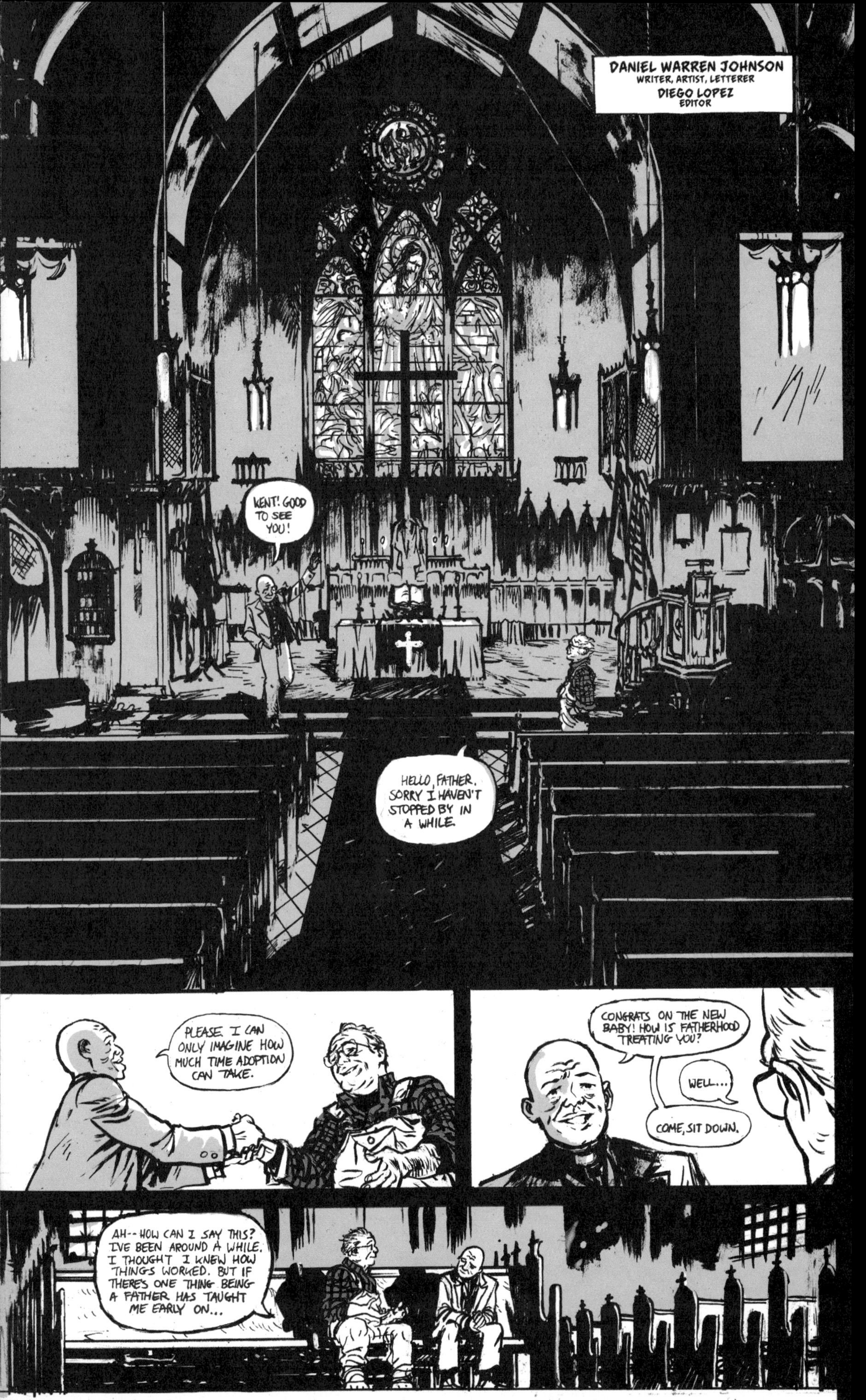
DANIEL WARREN JOHNSON
WRITER, ARTIST, LETTERER
DIEGO LOPEZ
EDITOR
KENT! GOOD TO SEE YOU!
HELLO, FATHER. SORRY I HAVEN'T STOPPED BY IN A WHILE.
PLEASE. I CAN ONLY IMAGINE HOW MUCH TIME ADOPTION CAN TAKE.
CONGRATS ON THE NEW BABY! HOW IS FATHERHOOD TREATING YOU?
WELL...
COME, SIT DOWN.
AH-- HOW CAN I SAY THIS? I'VE BEEN AROUND A WHILE. I THOUGHT I KNEW HOW THINGS WORKED. BUT IF THERE'S ONE THING BEING A FATHER HAS TAUGHT ME EARLY ON...

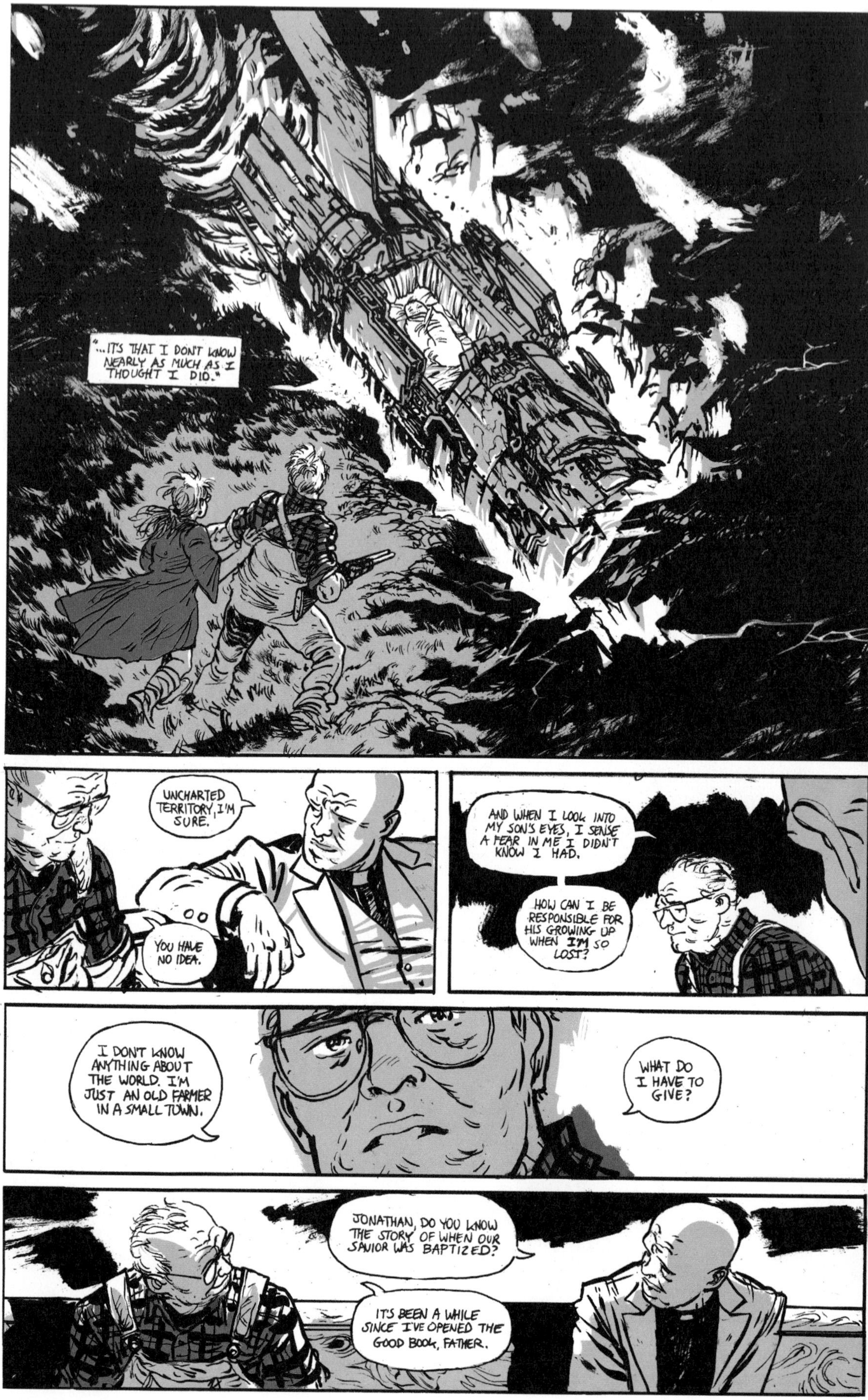
"...IT'S THAT I DON'T KNOW NEARLY AS MUCH AS I THOUGHT I DID."
UNCHARTED TERRITORY, I'M SURE.
YOU HAVE NO IDEA.
AND WHEN I LOOK INTO MY SON'S EYES, I SENSE A FEAR IN ME I DIDN'T KNOW I HAD.
HOW CAN I BE RESPONSIBLE FOR HIS GROWING UP WHEN I'M SO LOST?
I DON'T KNOW ANYTHING ABOUT THE WORLD. I'M JUST AN OLD FARMER IN A SMALL TOWN.
WHAT DO I HAVE TO GIVE?
JONATHAN, DO YOU KNOW THE STORY OF WHEN OUR SAVIOR WAS BAPTIZED?
IT'S BEEN A WHILE SINCE I'VE OPENED THE GOOD BOOK, FATHER.

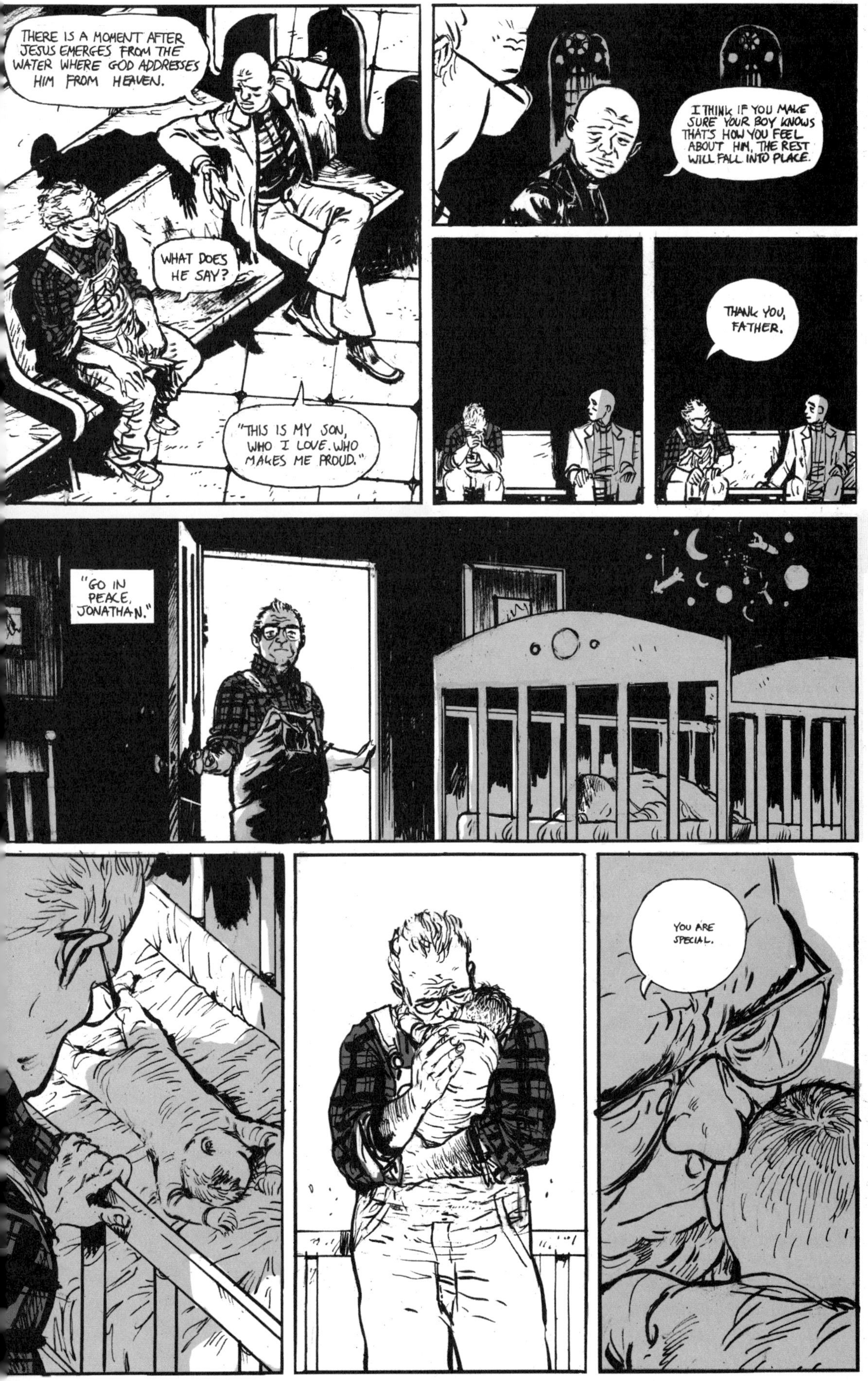
THERE IS A MOMENT AFTER JESUS EMERGES FROM THE WATER WHERE GOD ADDRESSES HIM FROM HEAVEN.
WHAT DOES HE SAY?
"THIS IS MY SON, WHO I LOVE. WHO MAKES ME PROUD."
I THINK IF YOU MAKE SURE YOUR BOY KNOWS THAT'S HOW YOU FEEL ABOUT HIM, THE REST WILL FALL INTO PLACE.
THANK YOU, FATHER.
"GO IN PEACE, JONATHAN."
YOU ARE SPECIAL.

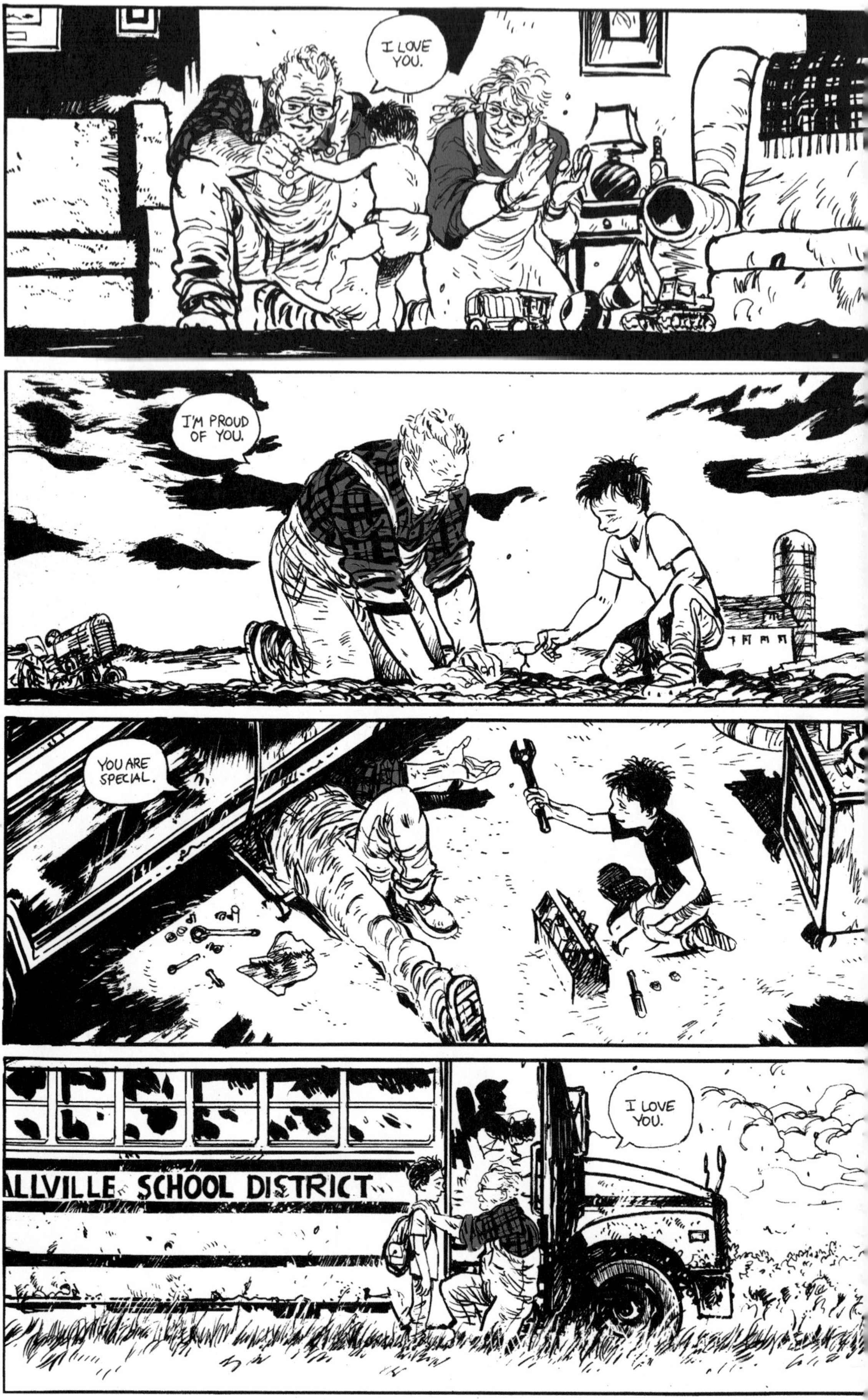
I LOVE YOU.
I'M PROUD OF YOU.
YOU ARE SPECIAL.
ALLVILLE SCHOOL DISTRICT
I LOVE YOU.

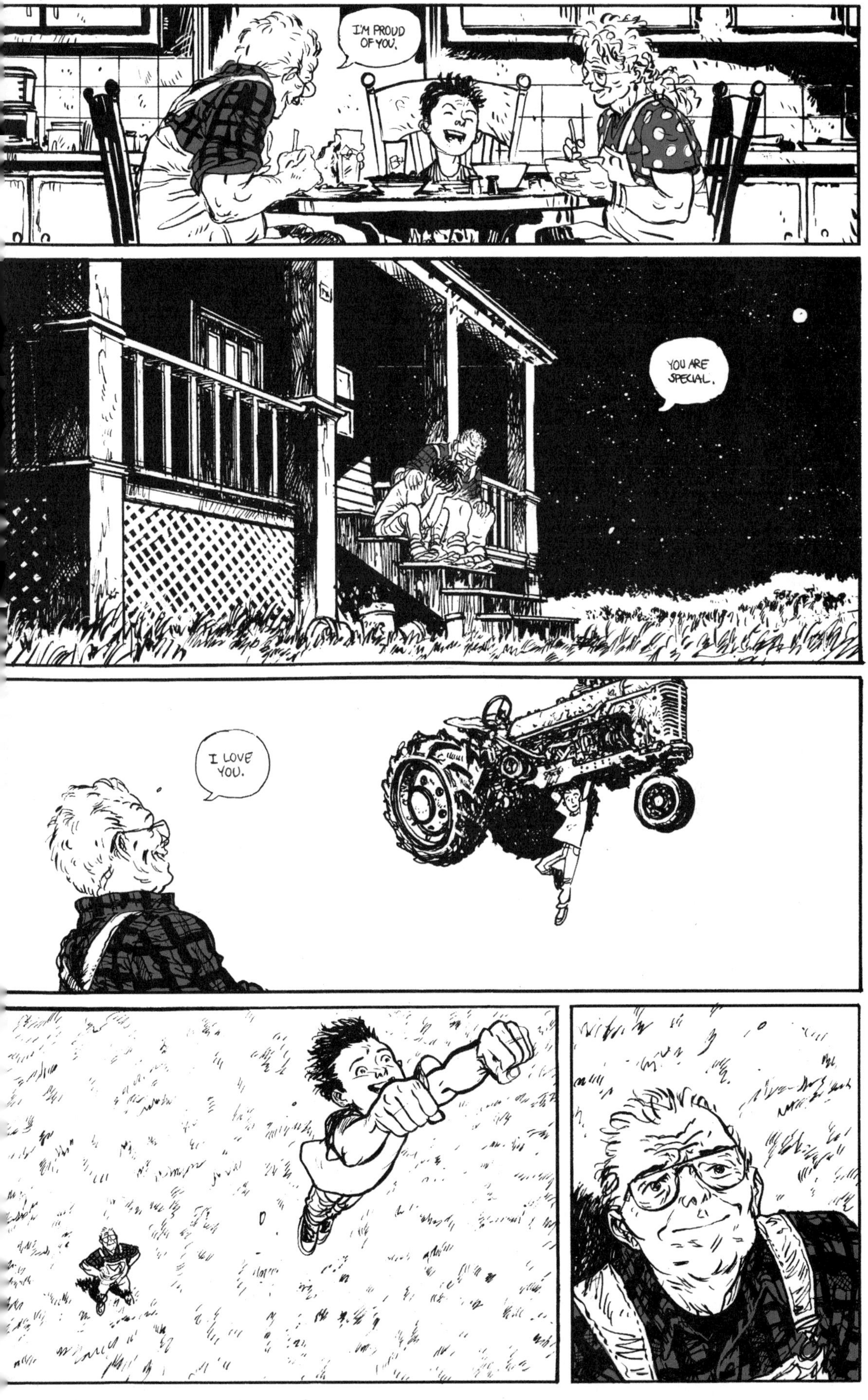
I'M PROUD OF YOU.
YOU ARE SPECIAL.
I LOVE YOU.

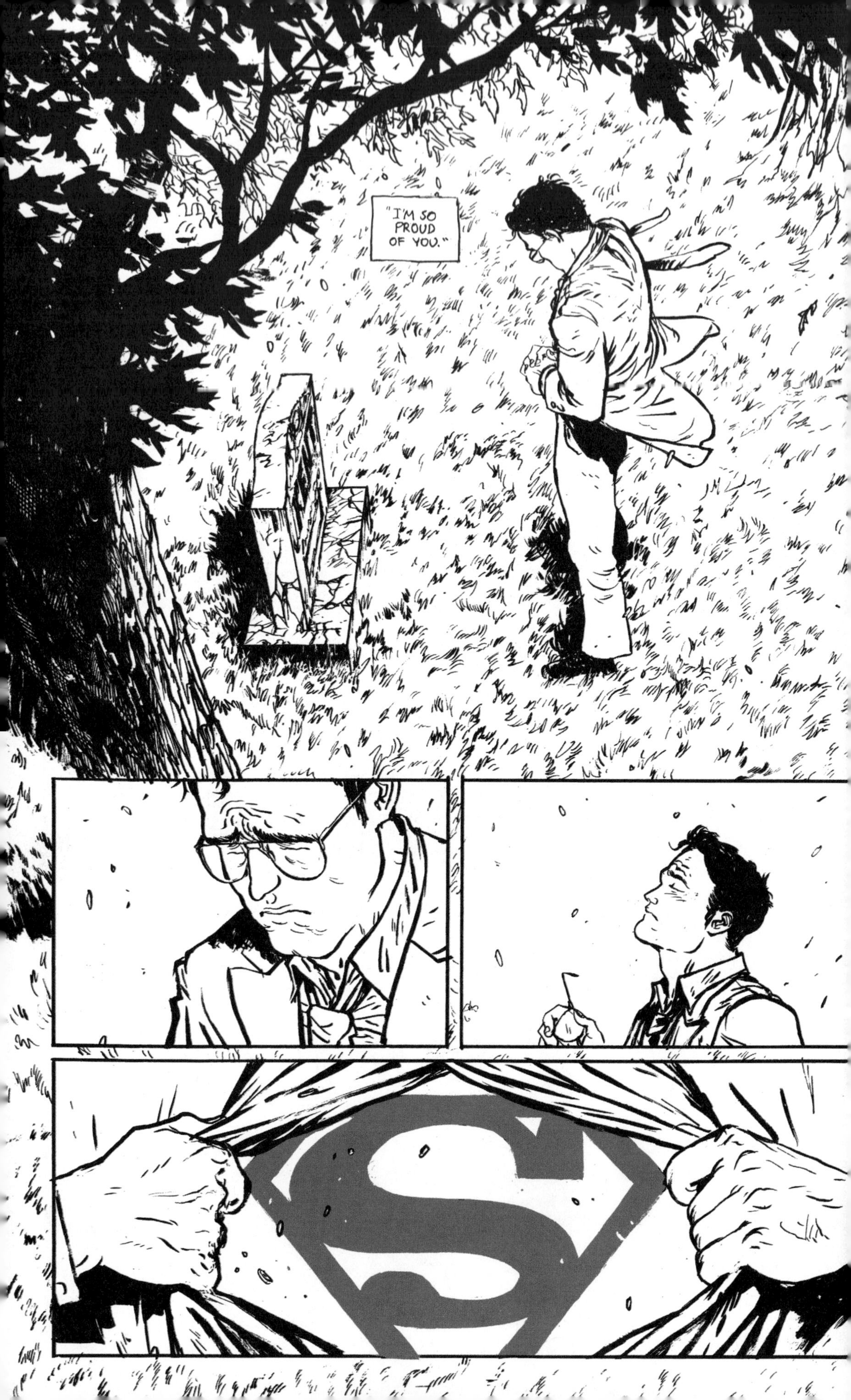
"I'M SO PROUD OF YOU."

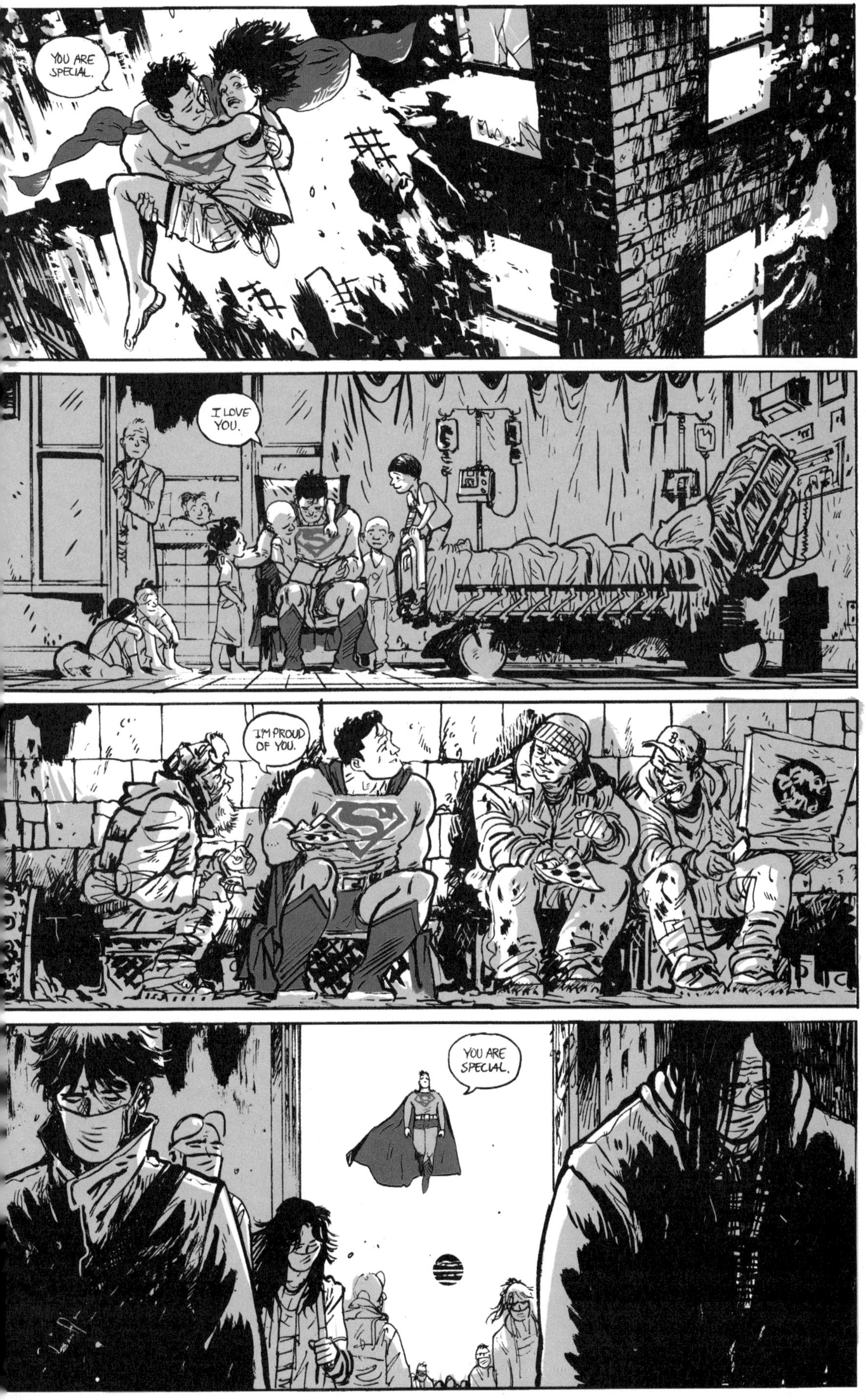
YOU ARE SPECIAL.
I LOVE YOU.
I'M PROUD OF YOU.
YOU ARE SPECIAL.

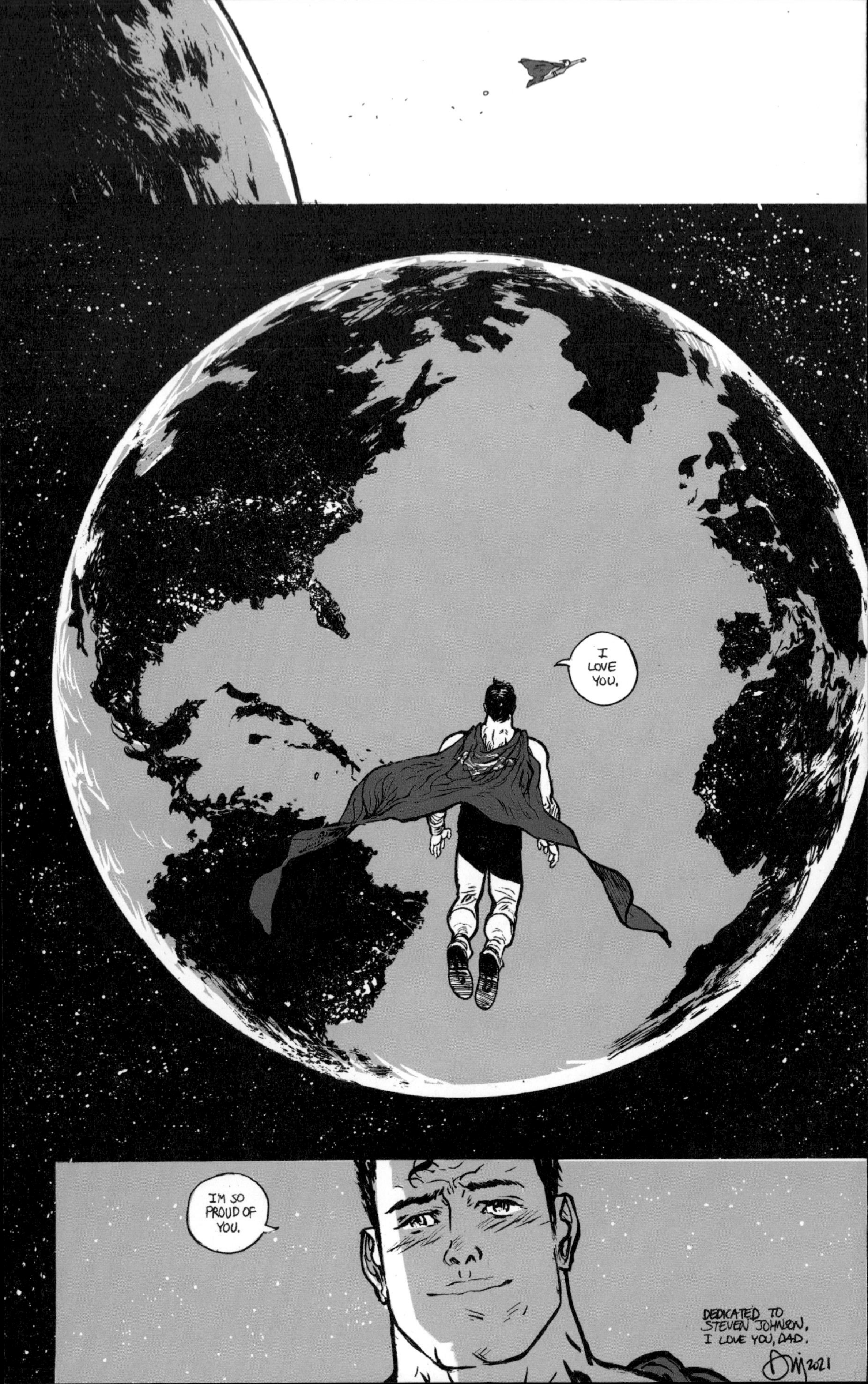
I LOVE YOU.
I'M SO PROUD OF YOU.
DEDICATED TO STEVEN JOHNSON, I LOVE YOU, DAD.
2021

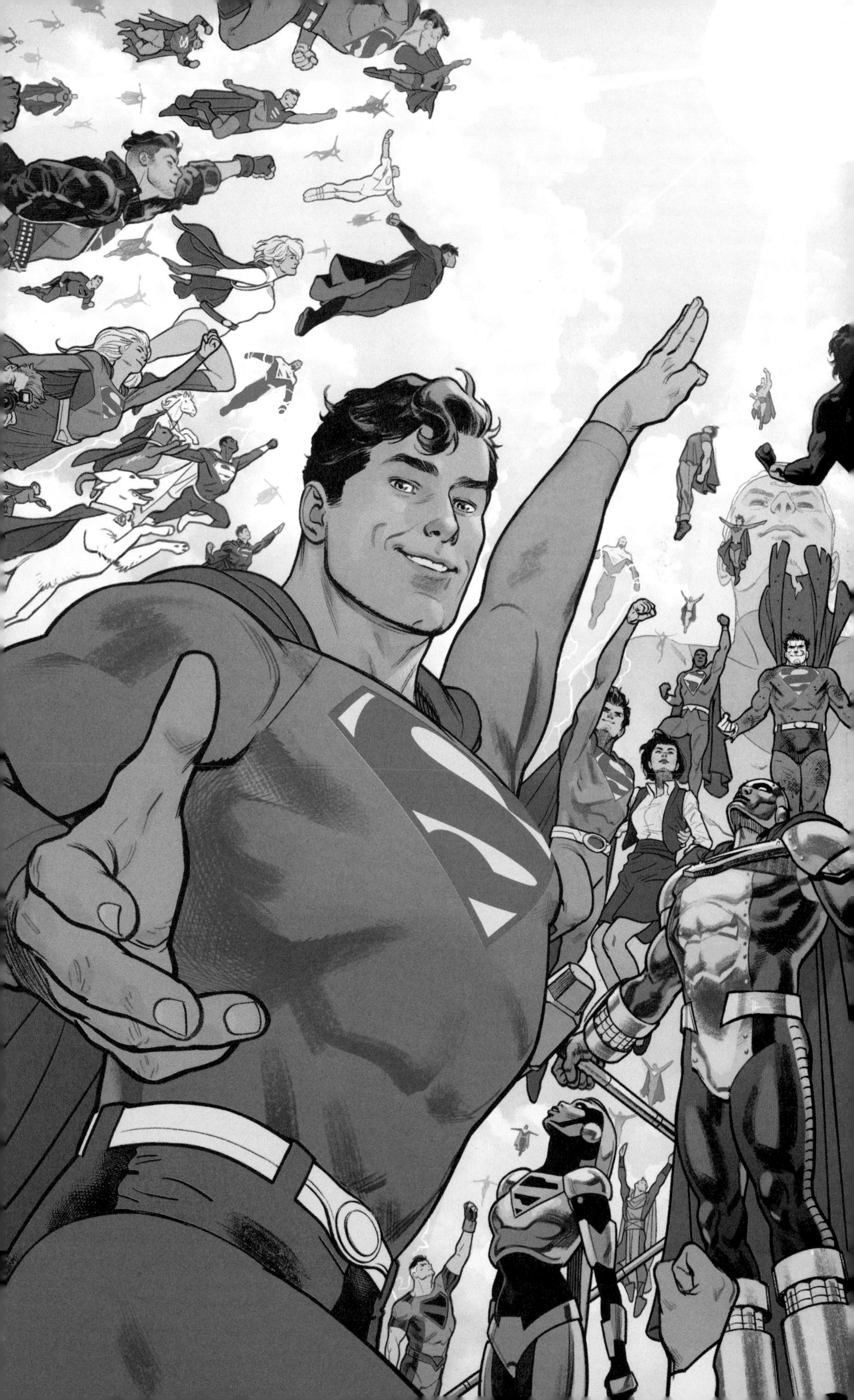

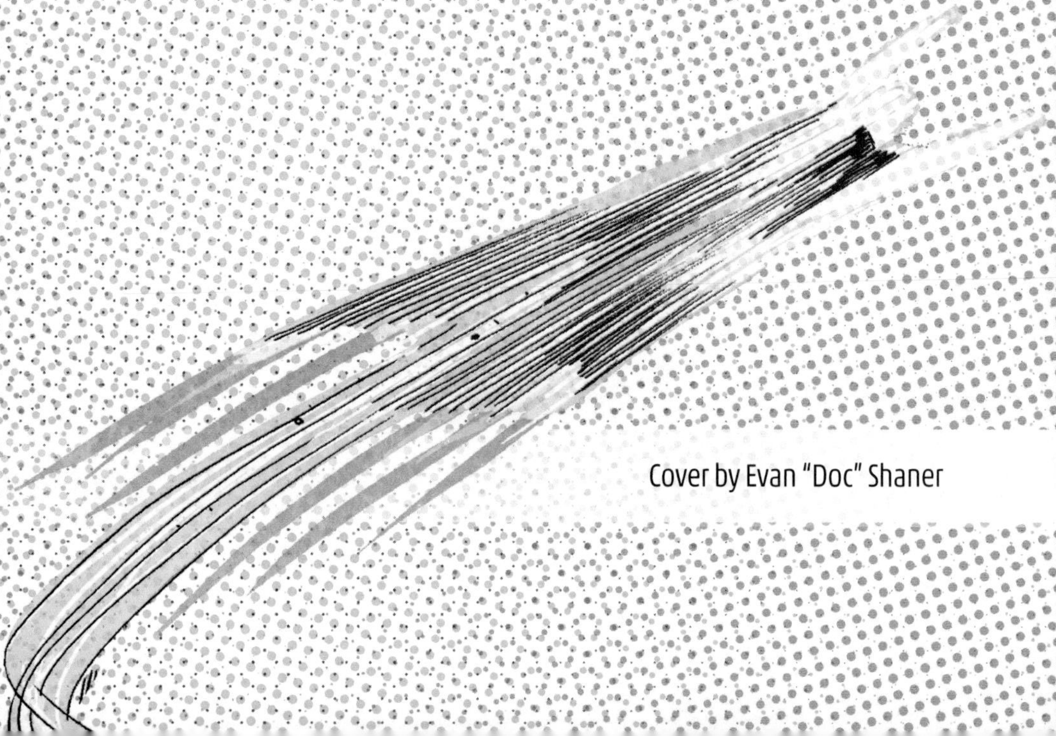

Cover by Evan "Doc" Shaner

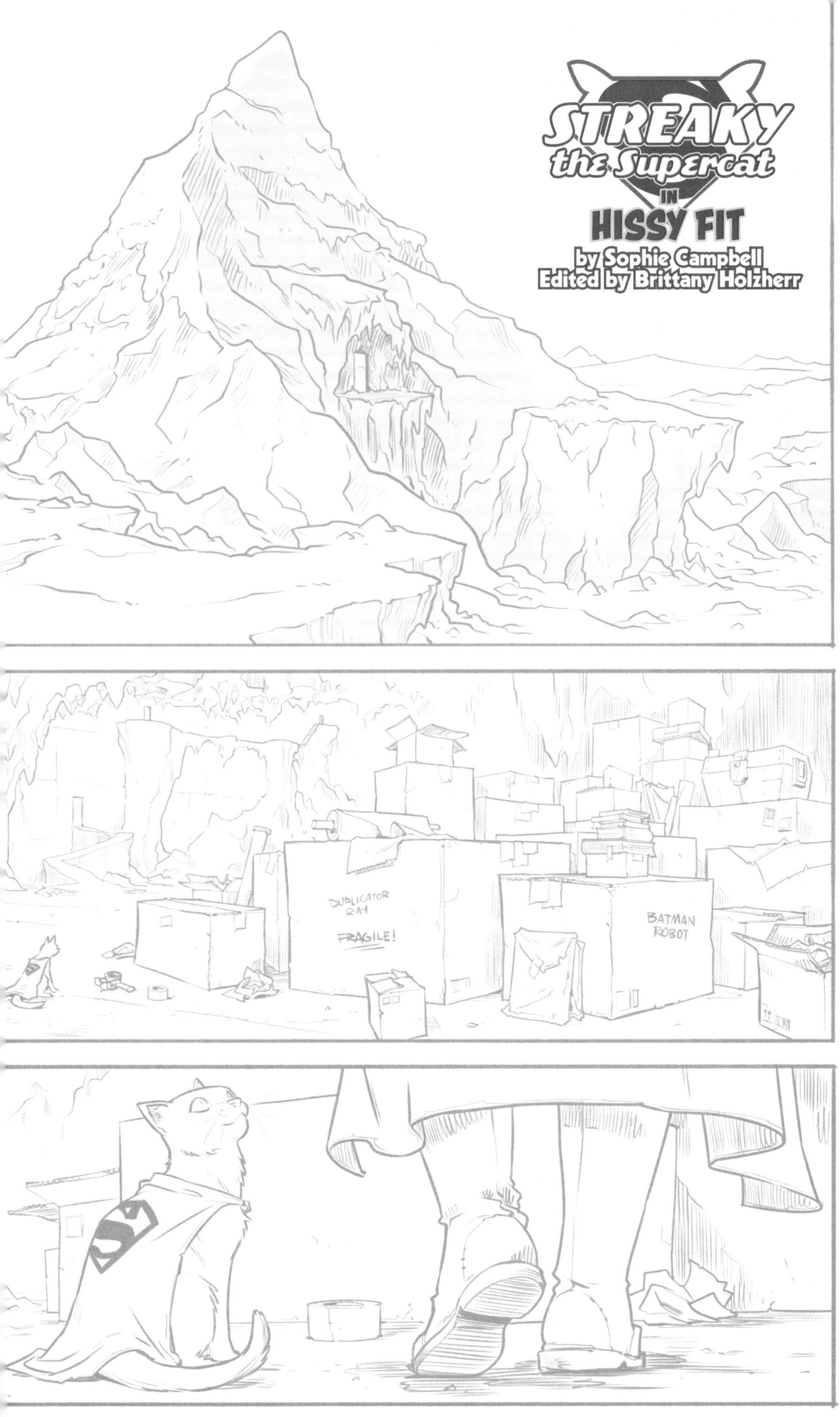
STREAKY
the Supercat
IN
HISSY FIT
by Sophie Campbell
Edited by Brittany Holzherr
DUPLICATOR RAY
FRAGILE!
BATMAN ROBOT

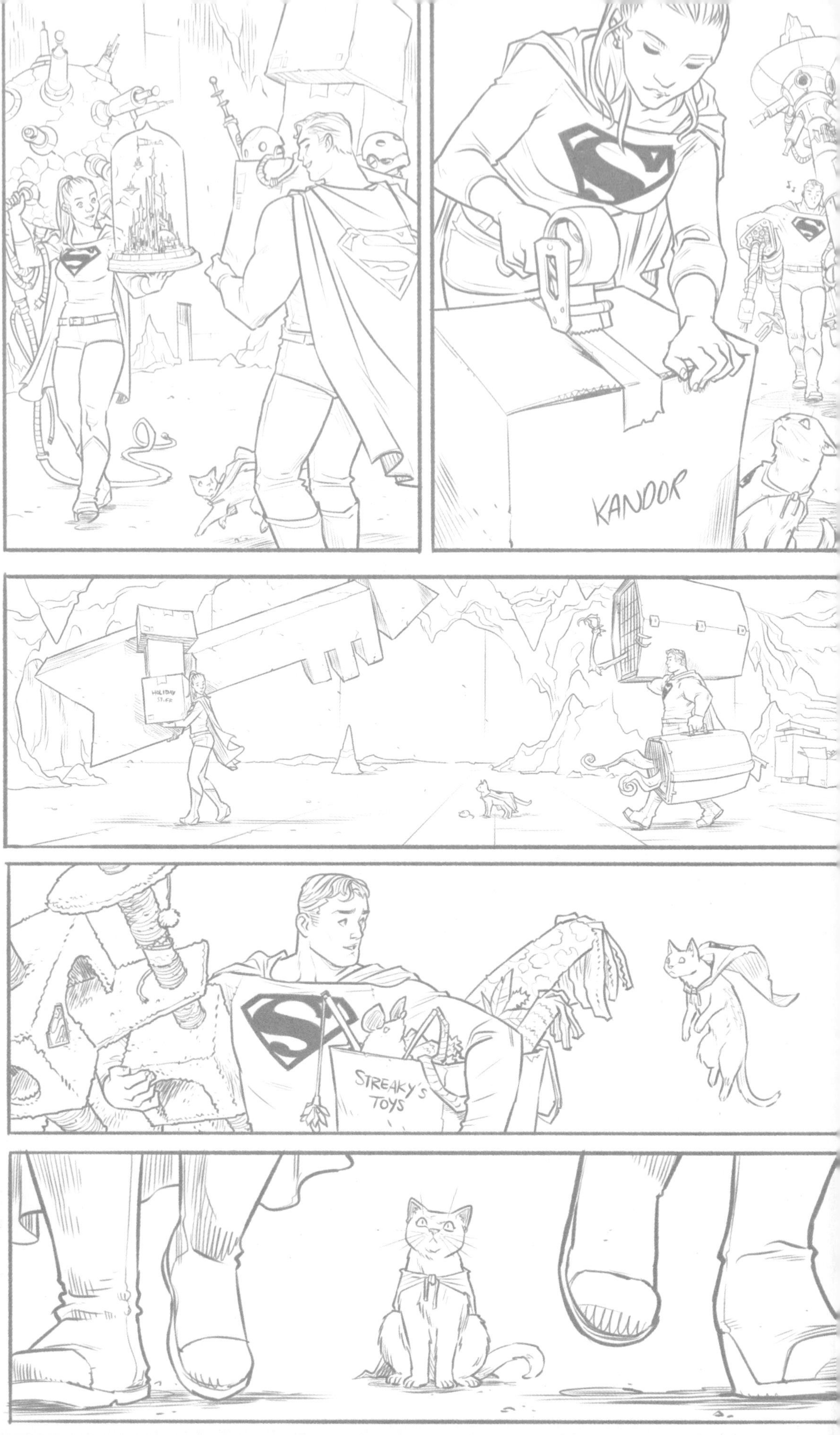
KANDOR
HOLIDAY STUFF
STREAKY'S TOYS

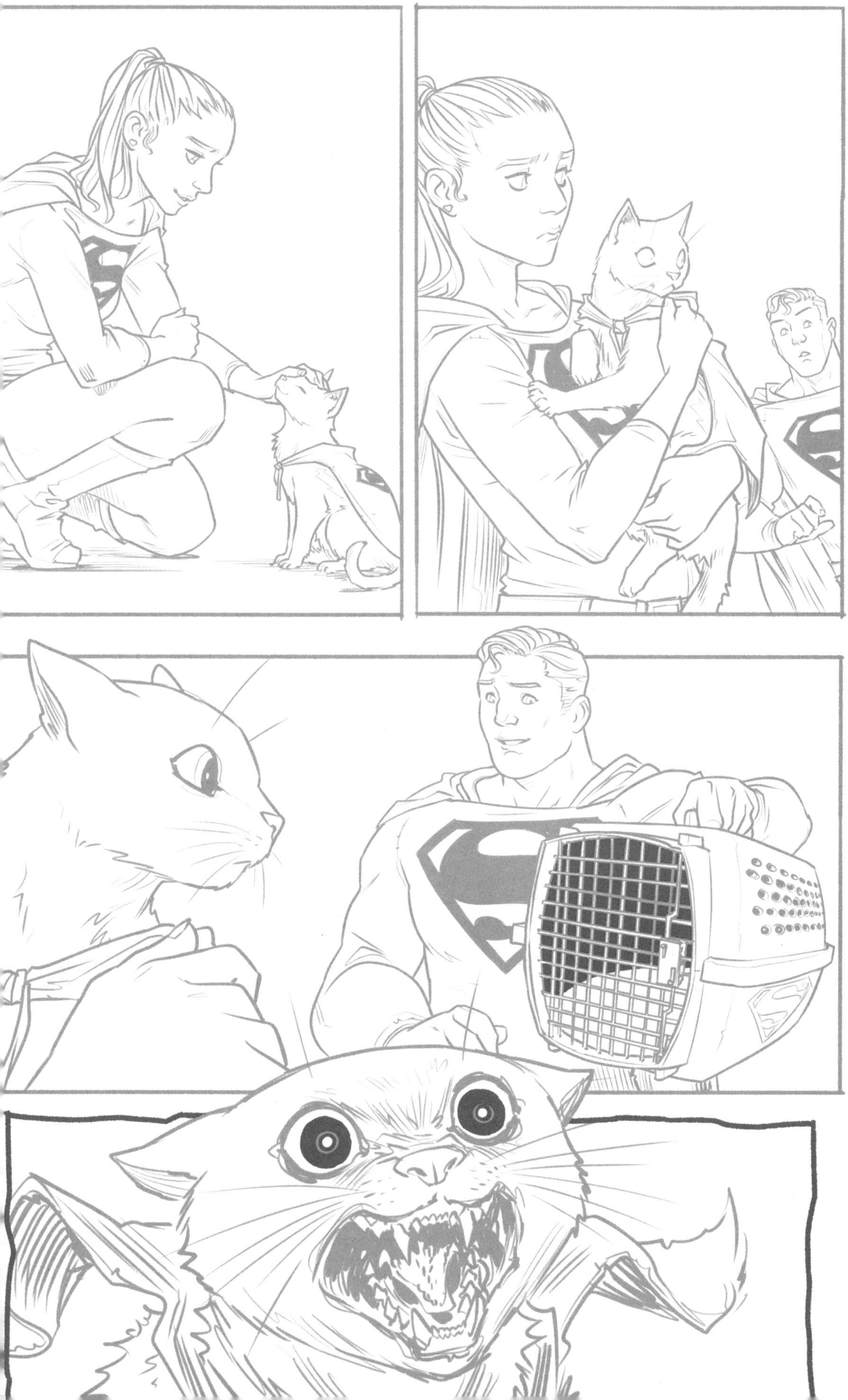

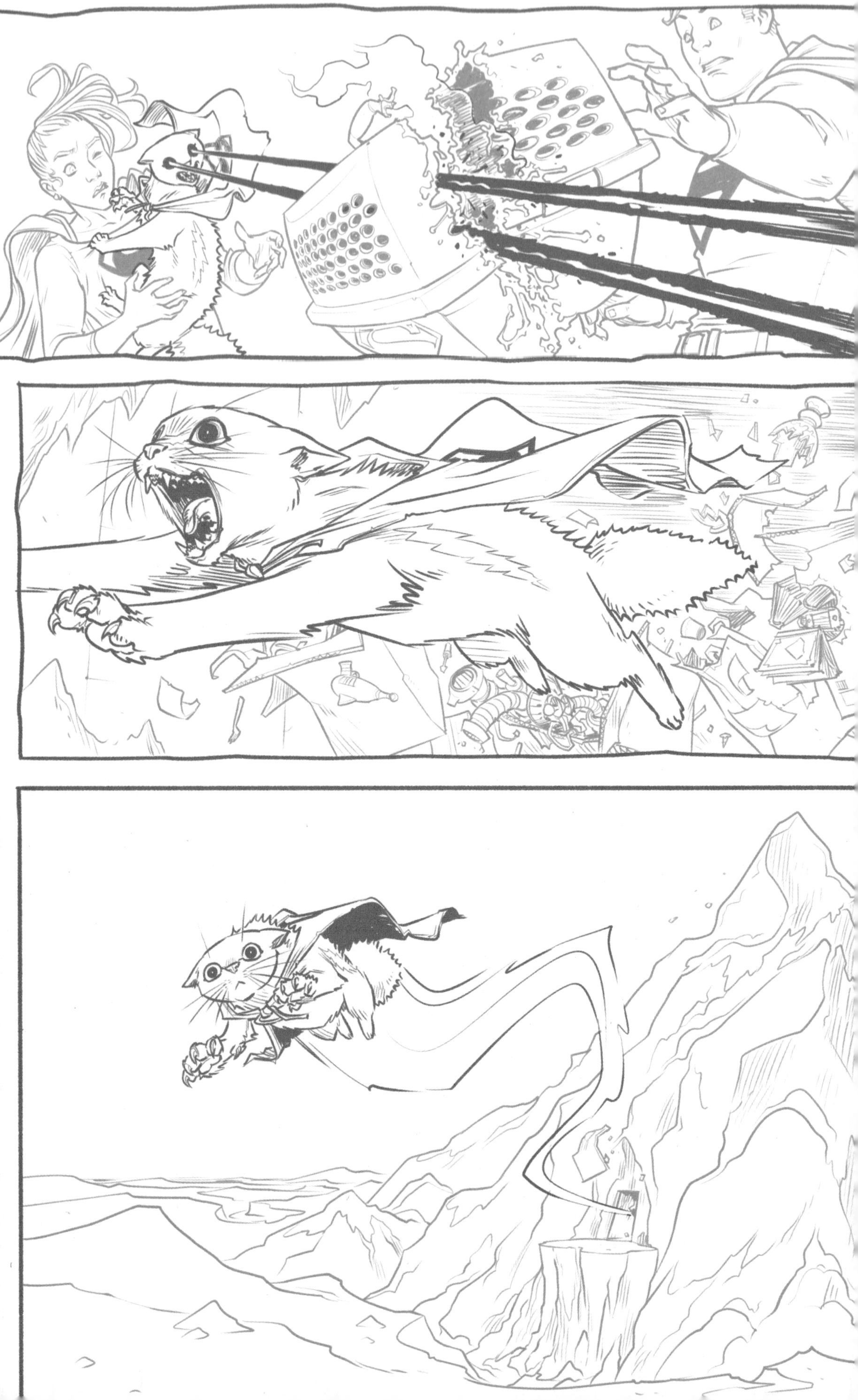

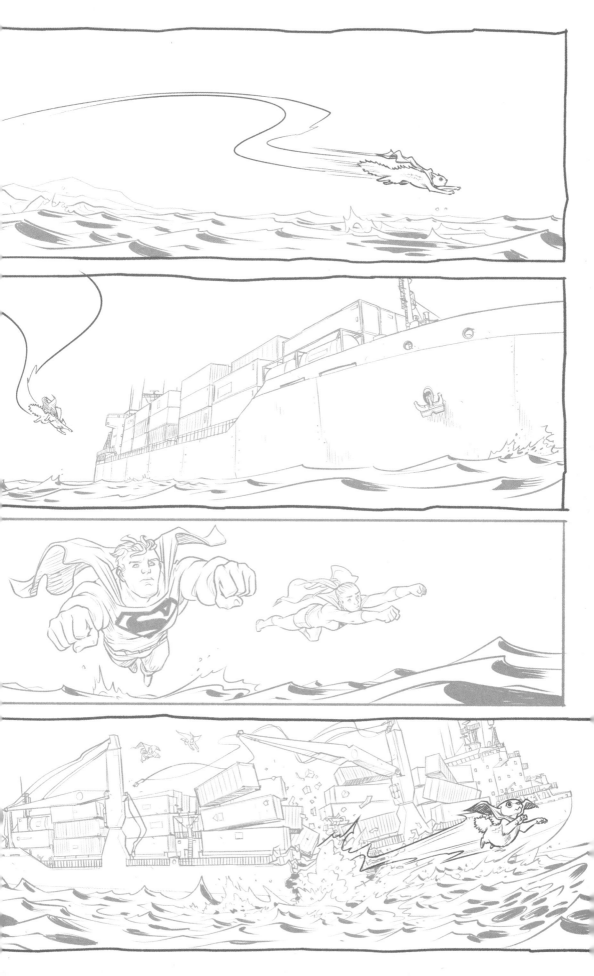

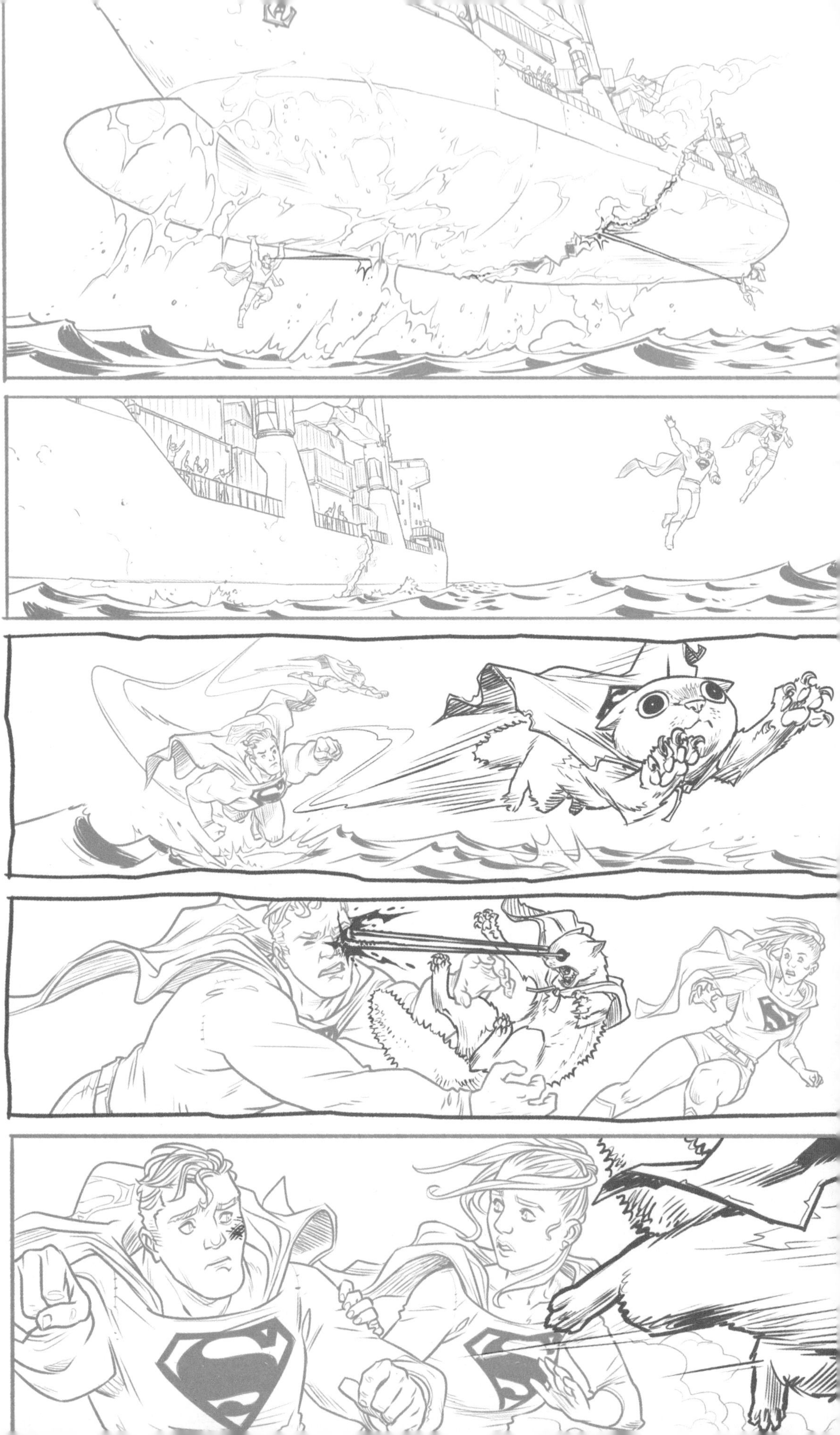

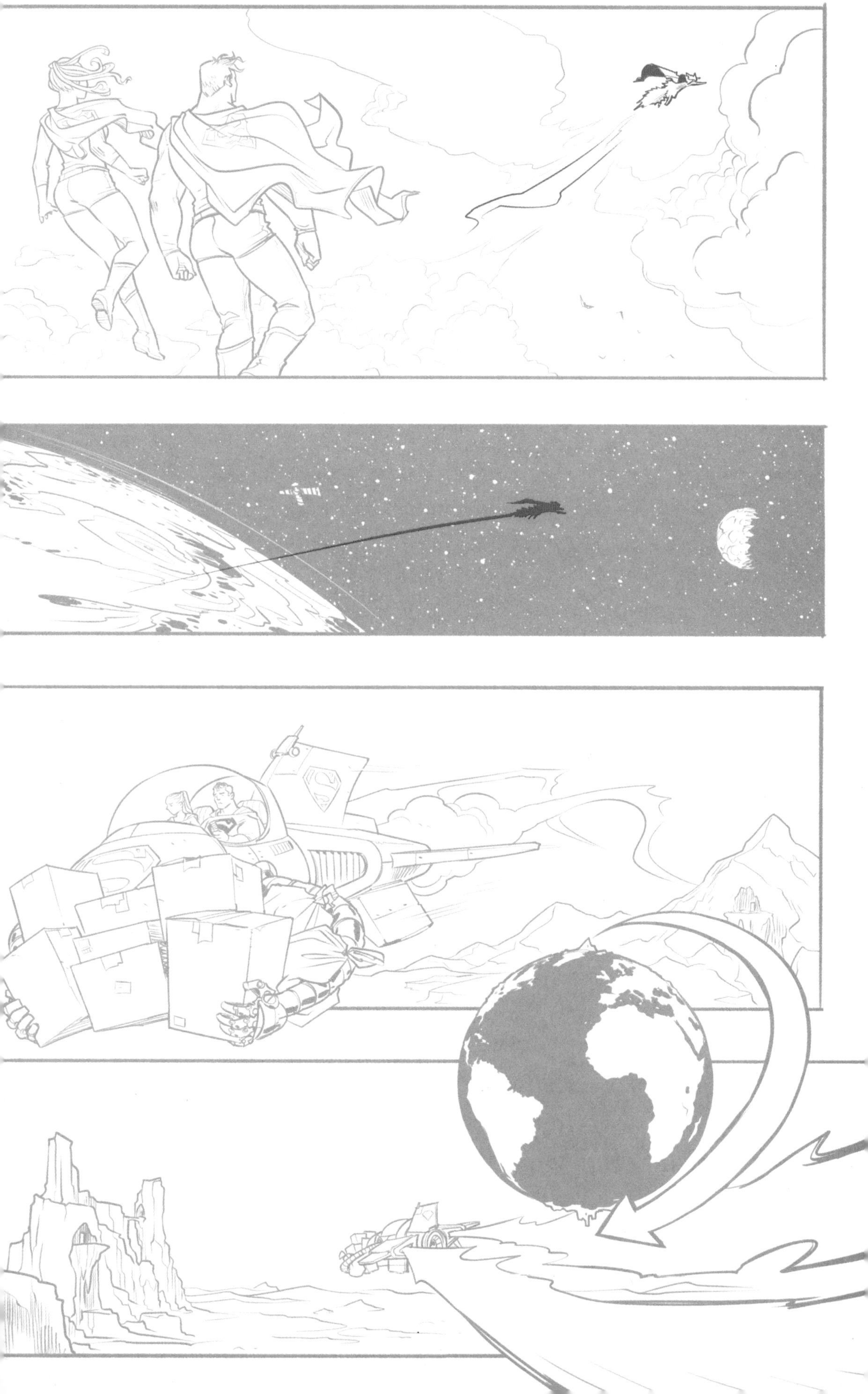

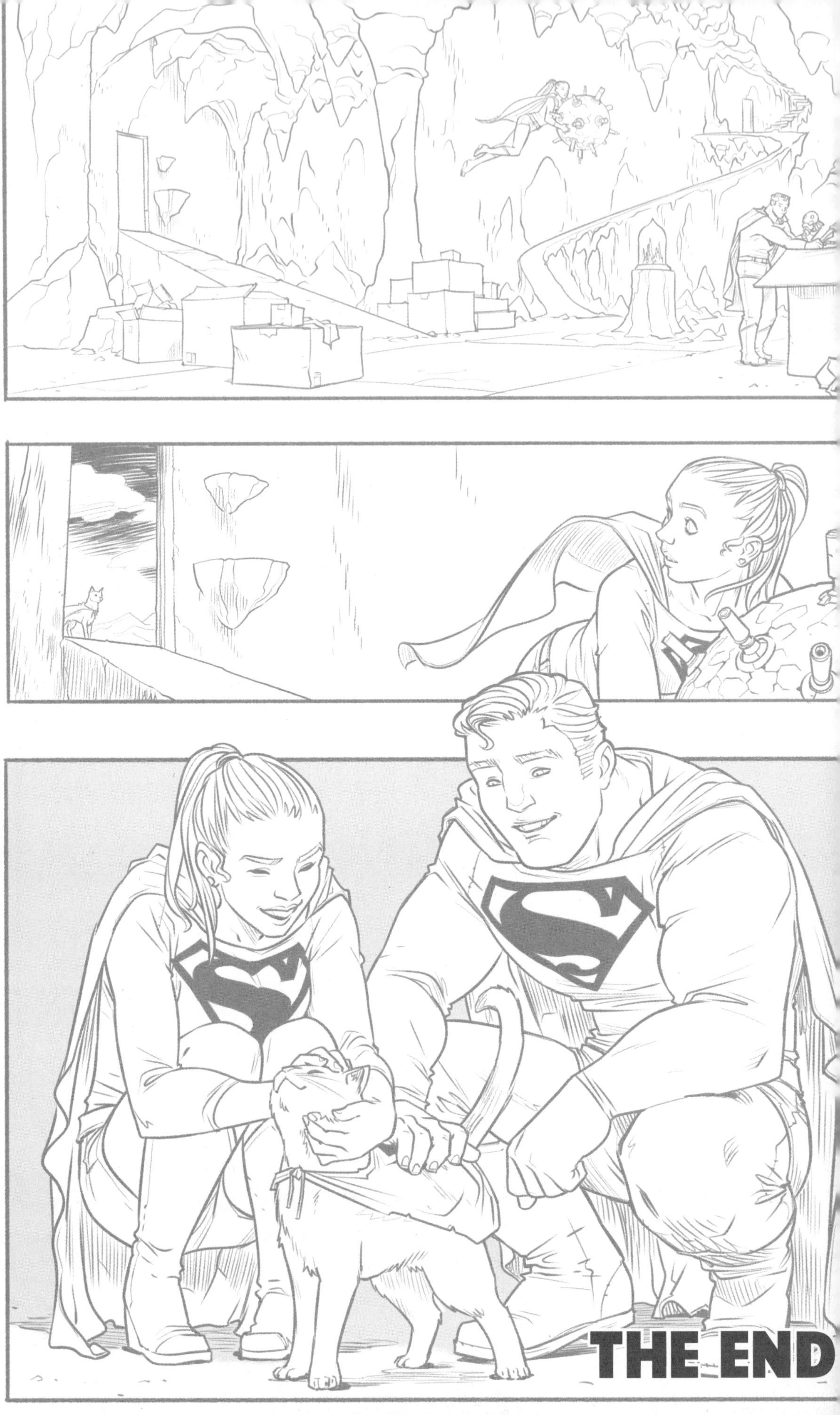
THE END

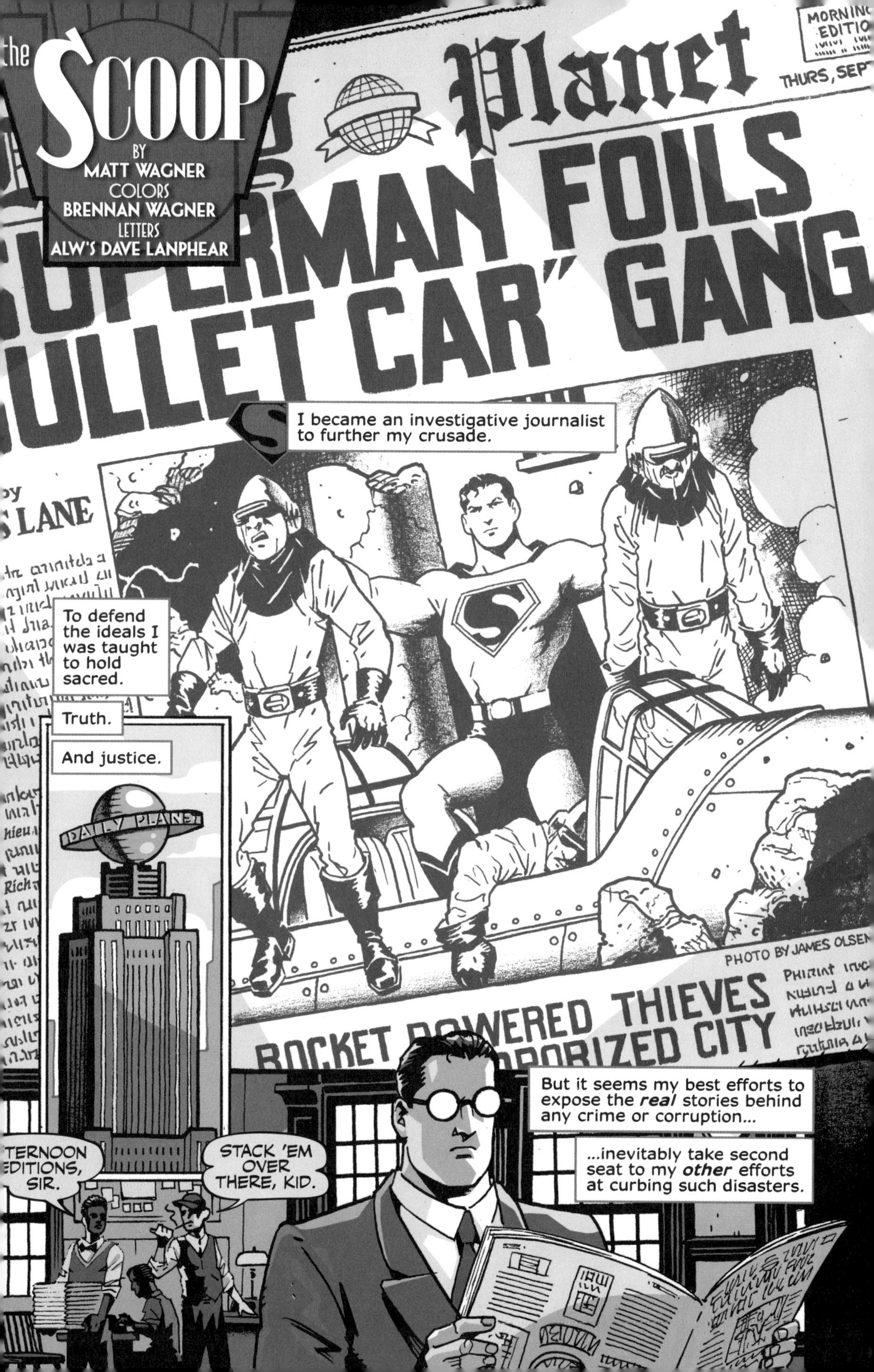

the SCOOP
BY
MATT WAGNER
COLORS
BRENNAN WAGNER
LETTERS
ALW'S DAVE LANPHEAR
MORNING EDITION
Planet
THURS, SEPT
SUPERMAN FOILS "BULLET CAR" GANG
I became an investigative journalist to further my crusade.
To defend the ideals I was taught to hold sacred.
Truth.
And justice.
DAILY PLANET
PHOTO BY JAMES OLSEN
ROCKET POWERED THIEVES ...PORIZED CITY
But it seems my best efforts to expose the *real* stories behind any crime or corruption...
...inevitably take second seat to my *other* efforts at curbing such disasters.
...TERNOON EDITIONS, SIR.
STACK 'EM OVER THERE, KID.

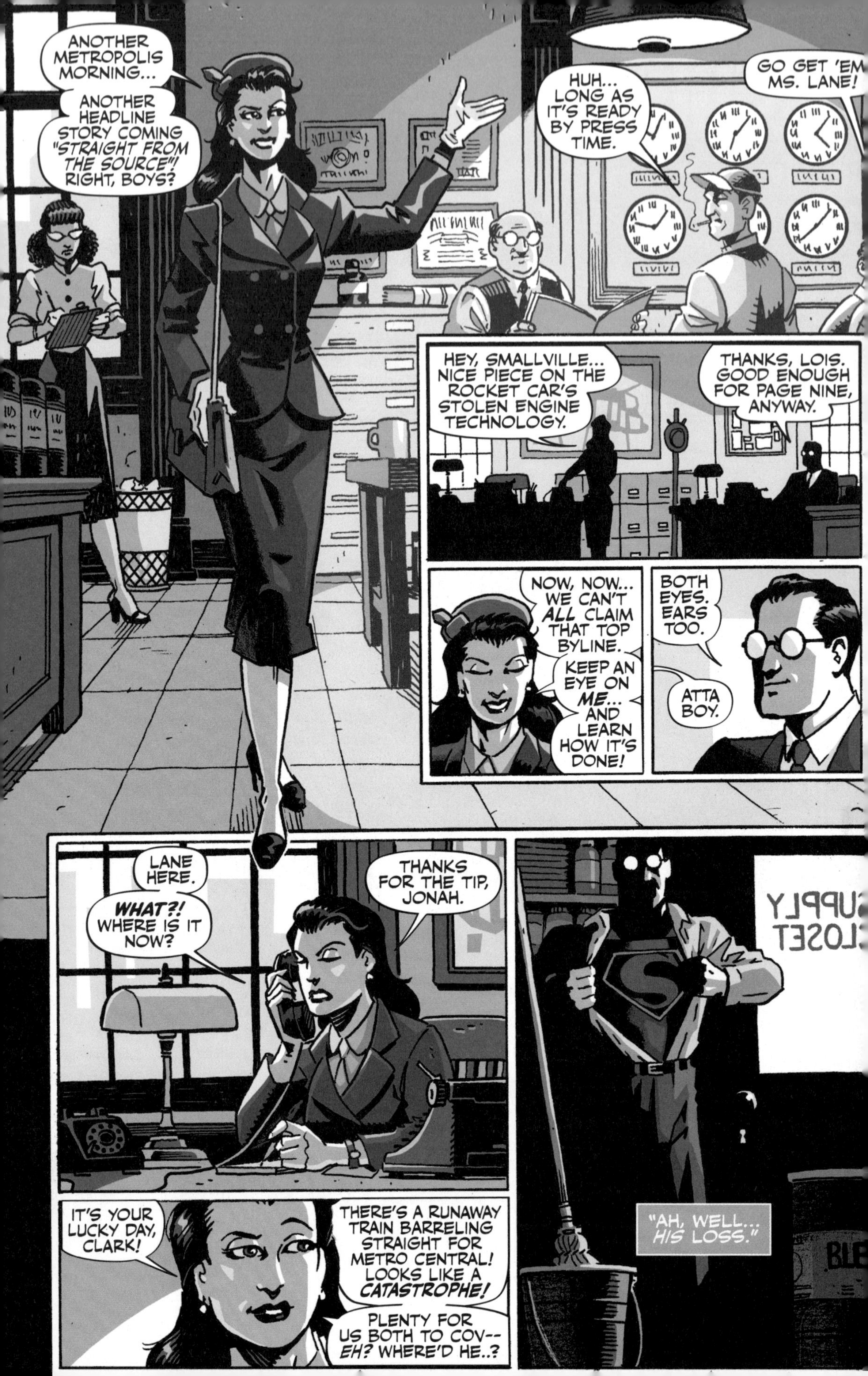
ANOTHER METROPOLIS MORNING...
ANOTHER HEADLINE STORY COMING "STRAIGHT FROM THE SOURCE"! RIGHT, BOYS?
HUH... LONG AS IT'S READY BY PRESS TIME.
GO GET 'EM MS. LANE!
HEY, SMALLVILLE... NICE PIECE ON THE ROCKET CAR'S STOLEN ENGINE TECHNOLOGY.
THANKS, LOIS. GOOD ENOUGH FOR PAGE NINE, ANYWAY.
NOW, NOW... WE CAN'T ALL CLAIM THAT TOP BYLINE.
KEEP AN EYE ON ME... AND LEARN HOW IT'S DONE!
BOTH EYES. EARS TOO.
ATTA BOY.
LANE HERE.
WHAT?! WHERE IS IT NOW?
THANKS FOR THE TIP, JONAH.
IT'S YOUR LUCKY DAY, CLARK!
THERE'S A RUNAWAY TRAIN BARRELING STRAIGHT FOR METRO CENTRAL! LOOKS LIKE A CATASTROPHE!
PLENTY FOR US BOTH TO COV-- EH? WHERE'D HE..?
SUPPLY CLOSET
"AH, WELL... HIS LOSS."

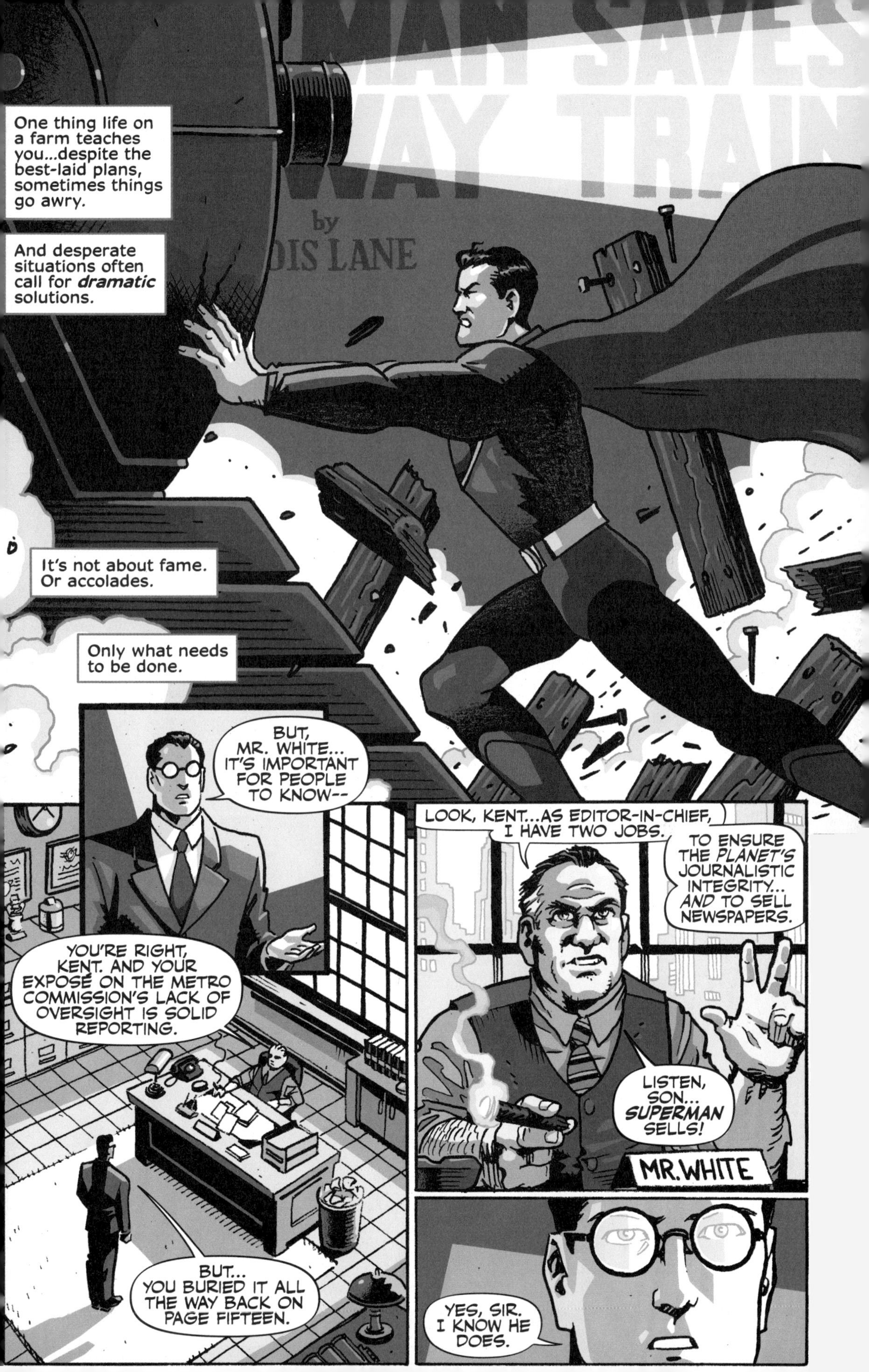
MAN SAVES
WAY TRAIN
by
OIS LANE
One thing life on a farm teaches you...despite the best-laid plans, sometimes things go awry.
And desperate situations often call for *dramatic* solutions.
It's not about fame. Or accolades.
Only what needs to be done.
BUT, MR. WHITE... IT'S IMPORTANT FOR PEOPLE TO KNOW--
YOU'RE RIGHT, KENT. AND YOUR EXPOSÉ ON THE METRO COMMISSION'S LACK OF OVERSIGHT IS SOLID REPORTING.
BUT... YOU BURIED IT ALL THE WAY BACK ON PAGE FIFTEEN.
LOOK, KENT...AS EDITOR-IN-CHIEF, I HAVE TWO JOBS.
TO ENSURE THE *PLANET'S* JOURNALISTIC INTEGRITY... *AND* TO SELL NEWSPAPERS.
LISTEN, SON... *SUPERMAN* SELLS!
MR. WHITE
YES, SIR. I KNOW HE DOES.

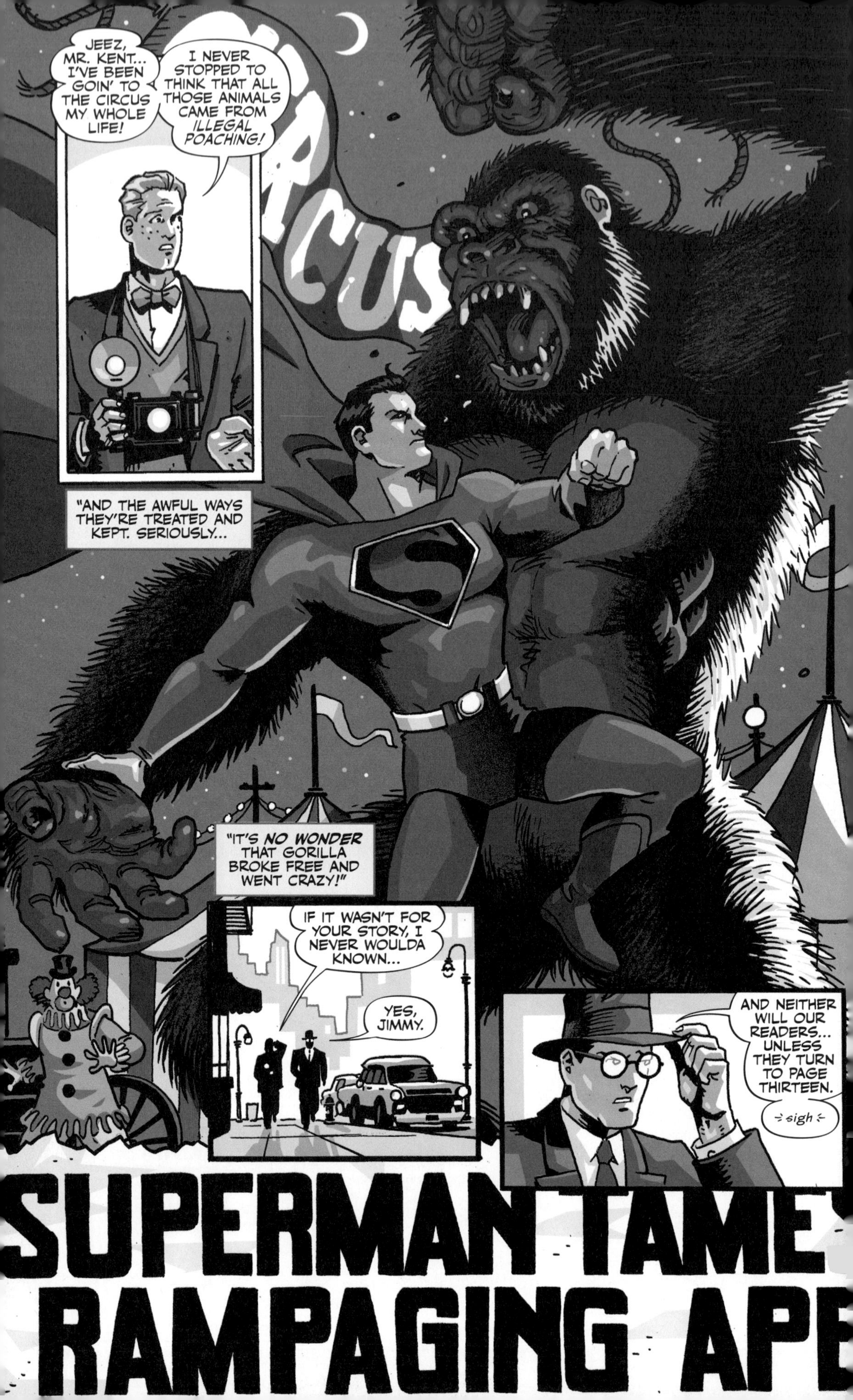
JEEZ, MR. KENT... I'VE BEEN GOIN' TO THE CIRCUS MY WHOLE LIFE!
I NEVER STOPPED TO THINK THAT ALL THOSE ANIMALS CAME FROM ILLEGAL POACHING!
"AND THE AWFUL WAYS THEY'RE TREATED AND KEPT. SERIOUSLY...
"IT'S NO WONDER THAT GORILLA BROKE FREE AND WENT CRAZY!"
IF IT WASN'T FOR YOUR STORY, I NEVER WOULDA KNOWN...
YES, JIMMY.
AND NEITHER WILL OUR READERS... UNLESS THEY TURN TO PAGE THIRTEEN.
sigh
SUPERMAN TAME
RAMPAGING APE

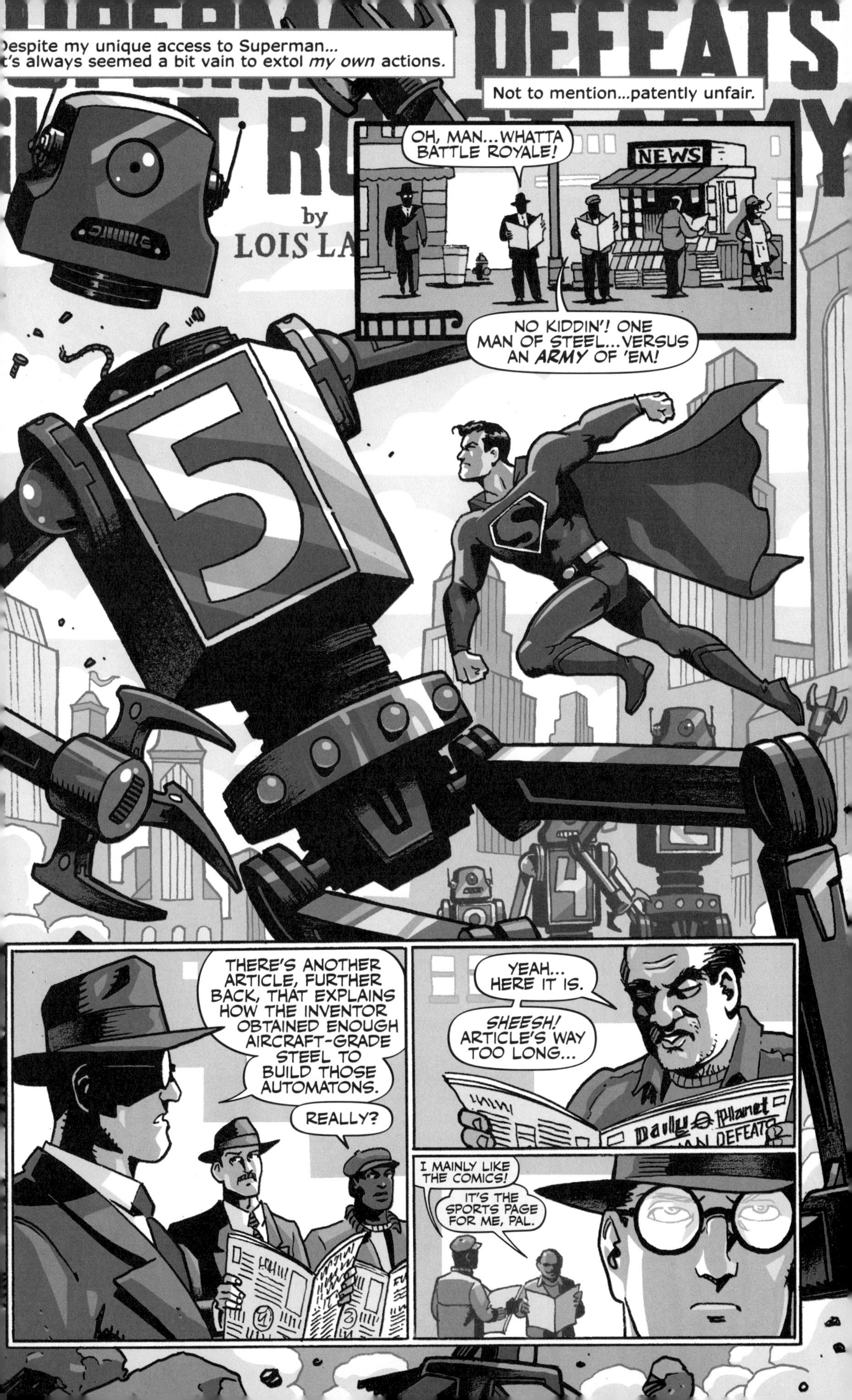

Despite my unique access to Superman...
it's always seemed a bit vain to extol *my own* actions.
Not to mention...patently unfair.
by
LOIS LA
NEWS
OH, MAN...WHATTA BATTLE ROYALE!
NO KIDDIN'! ONE MAN OF STEEL...VERSUS AN *ARMY* OF 'EM!
5
THERE'S ANOTHER ARTICLE, FURTHER BACK, THAT EXPLAINS HOW THE INVENTOR OBTAINED ENOUGH AIRCRAFT-GRADE STEEL TO BUILD THOSE AUTOMATONS.
REALLY?
YEAH... HERE IT IS.
SHEESH! ARTICLE'S WAY TOO LONG...
Daily Planet
I MAINLY LIKE THE COMICS!
IT'S THE SPORTS PAGE FOR ME, PAL.

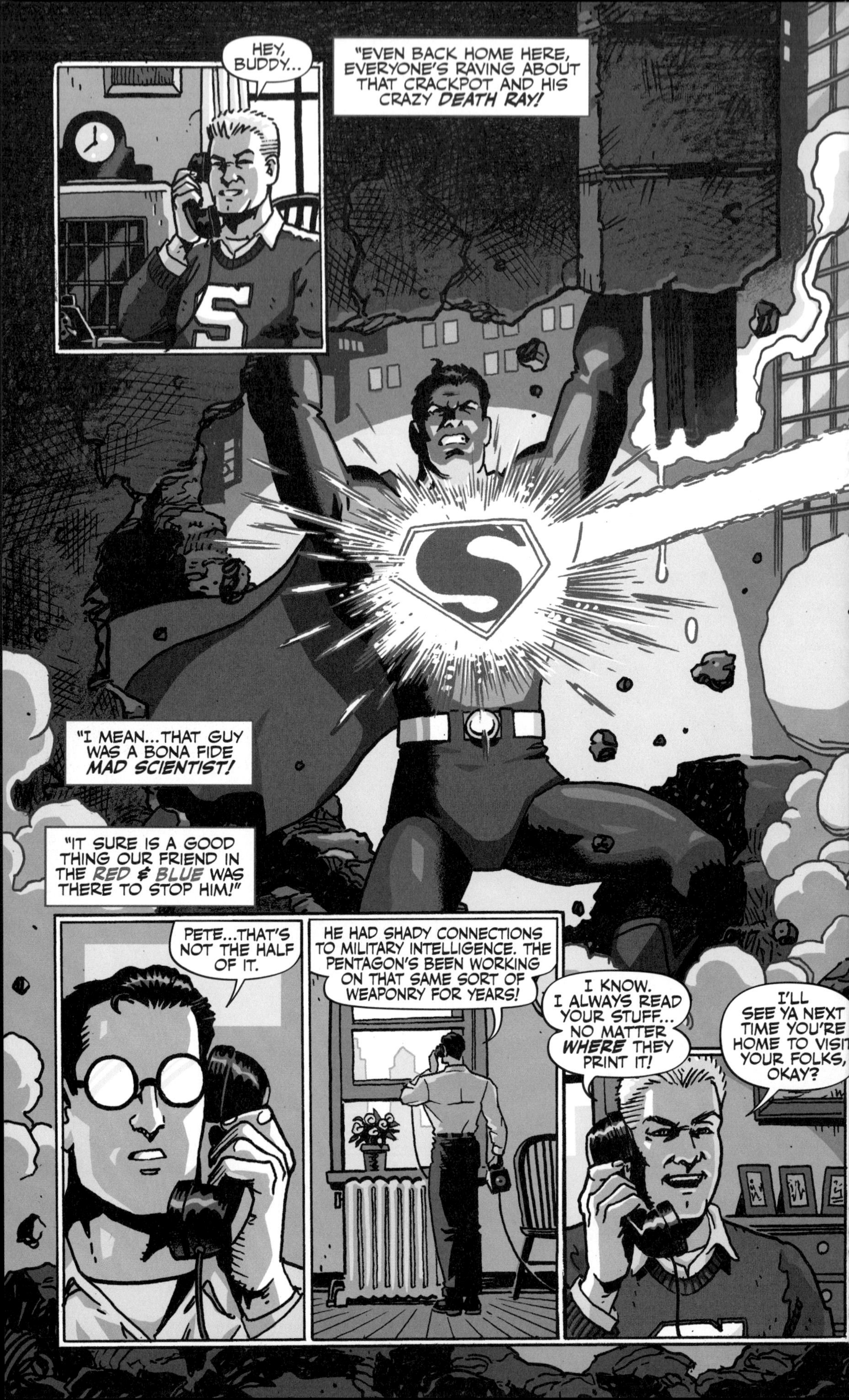
HEY, BUDDY...
"EVEN BACK HOME HERE, EVERYONE'S RAVING ABOUT THAT CRACKPOT AND HIS CRAZY DEATH RAY!
"I MEAN...THAT GUY WAS A BONA FIDE MAD SCIENTIST!
"IT SURE IS A GOOD THING OUR FRIEND IN THE RED & BLUE WAS THERE TO STOP HIM!"
PETE...THAT'S NOT THE HALF OF IT.
HE HAD SHADY CONNECTIONS TO MILITARY INTELLIGENCE. THE PENTAGON'S BEEN WORKING ON THAT SAME SORT OF WEAPONRY FOR YEARS!
I KNOW. I ALWAYS READ YOUR STUFF... NO MATTER WHERE THEY PRINT IT!
I'LL SEE YA NEXT TIME YOU'RE HOME TO VISIT YOUR FOLKS, OKAY?

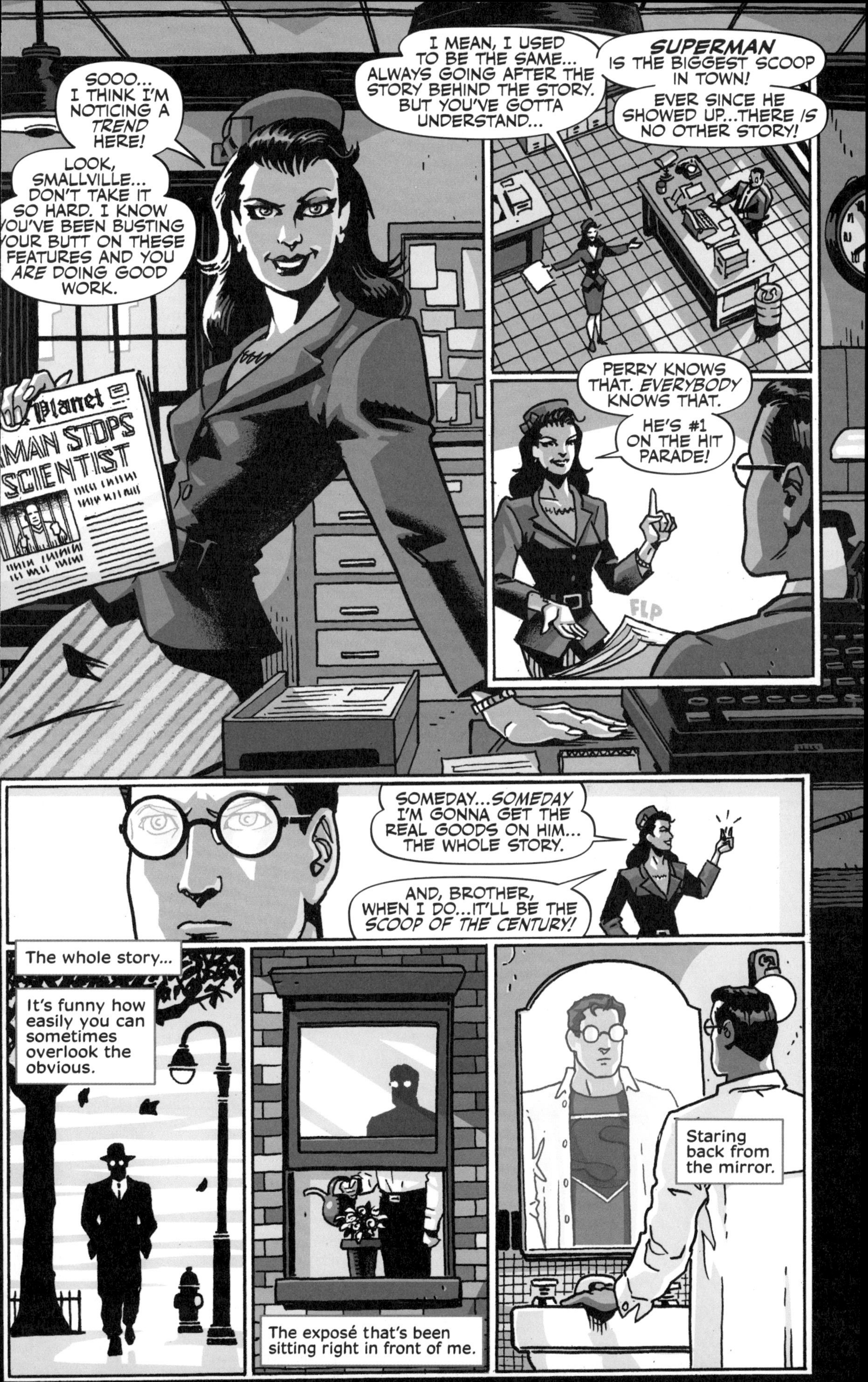
SOOO... I THINK I'M NOTICING A *TREND* HERE!
LOOK, SMALLVILLE... DON'T TAKE IT SO HARD. I KNOW YOU'VE BEEN BUSTING YOUR BUTT ON THESE FEATURES AND YOU *ARE* DOING GOOD WORK.
Planet
MAN STOPS SCIENTIST
I MEAN, I USED TO BE THE SAME... ALWAYS GOING AFTER THE STORY BEHIND THE STORY. BUT YOU'VE GOTTA UNDERSTAND...
SUPERMAN IS THE BIGGEST SCOOP IN TOWN!
EVER SINCE HE SHOWED UP...THERE *IS* NO OTHER STORY!
PERRY KNOWS THAT. *EVERYBODY* KNOWS THAT.
HE'S #1 ON THE HIT PARADE!
FLP
SOMEDAY...*SOMEDAY* I'M GONNA GET THE REAL GOODS ON HIM... THE WHOLE STORY.
AND, BROTHER, WHEN I DO...IT'LL BE THE *SCOOP OF THE CENTURY!*
The whole story...
It's funny how easily you can sometimes overlook the obvious.
The exposé that's been sitting right in front of me.
Staring back from the mirror.

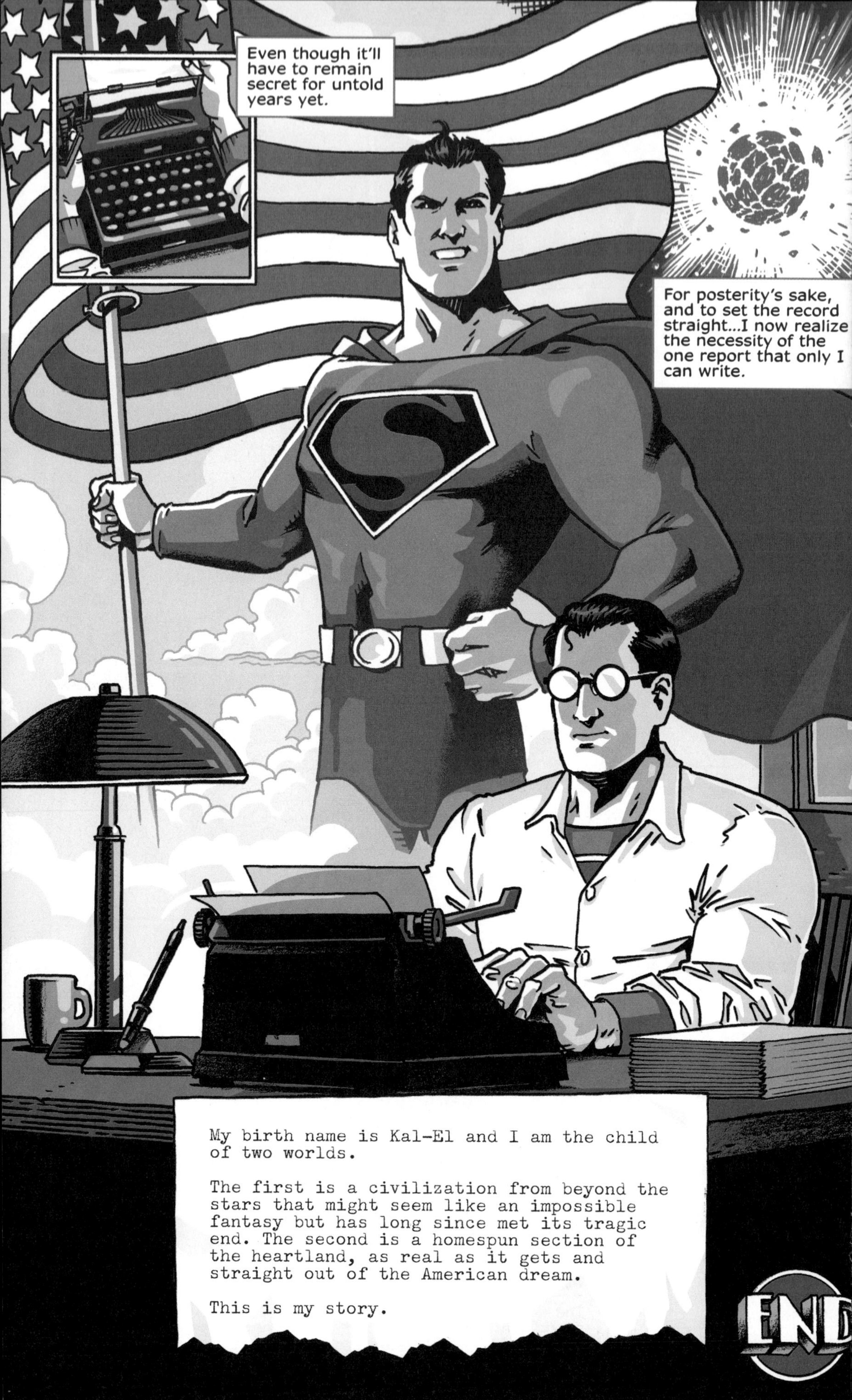
Even though it'll have to remain secret for untold years yet.
For posterity's sake, and to set the record straight...I now realize the necessity of the one report that only I can write.
My birth name is Kal-El and I am the child of two worlds.
The first is a civilization from beyond the stars that might seem like an impossible fantasy but has long since met its tragic end. The second is a homespun section of the heartland, as real as it gets and straight out of the American dream.
This is my story.
END

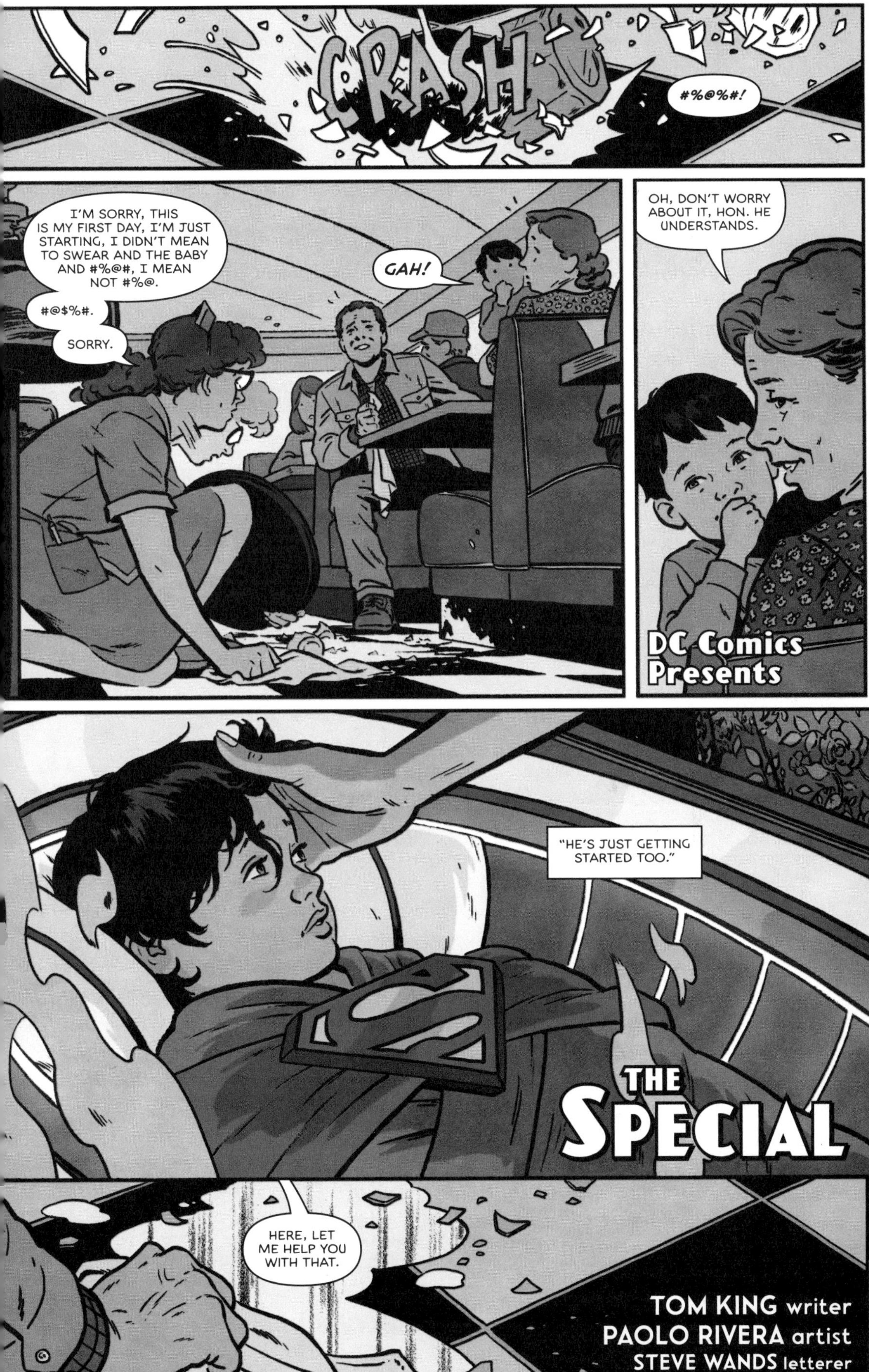
CRASH
#%@%#!
I'M SORRY, THIS IS MY FIRST DAY, I'M JUST STARTING, I DIDN'T MEAN TO SWEAR AND THE BABY AND #%@#, I MEAN NOT #%@.
#@$%#.
SORRY.
GAH!
OH, DON'T WORRY ABOUT IT, HON. HE UNDERSTANDS.
DC Comics Presents
"HE'S JUST GETTING STARTED TOO."
THE SPECIAL
HERE, LET ME HELP YOU WITH THAT.
TOM KING writer
PAOLO RIVERA artist
STEVE WANDS letterer
DIEGO LOPEZ editor

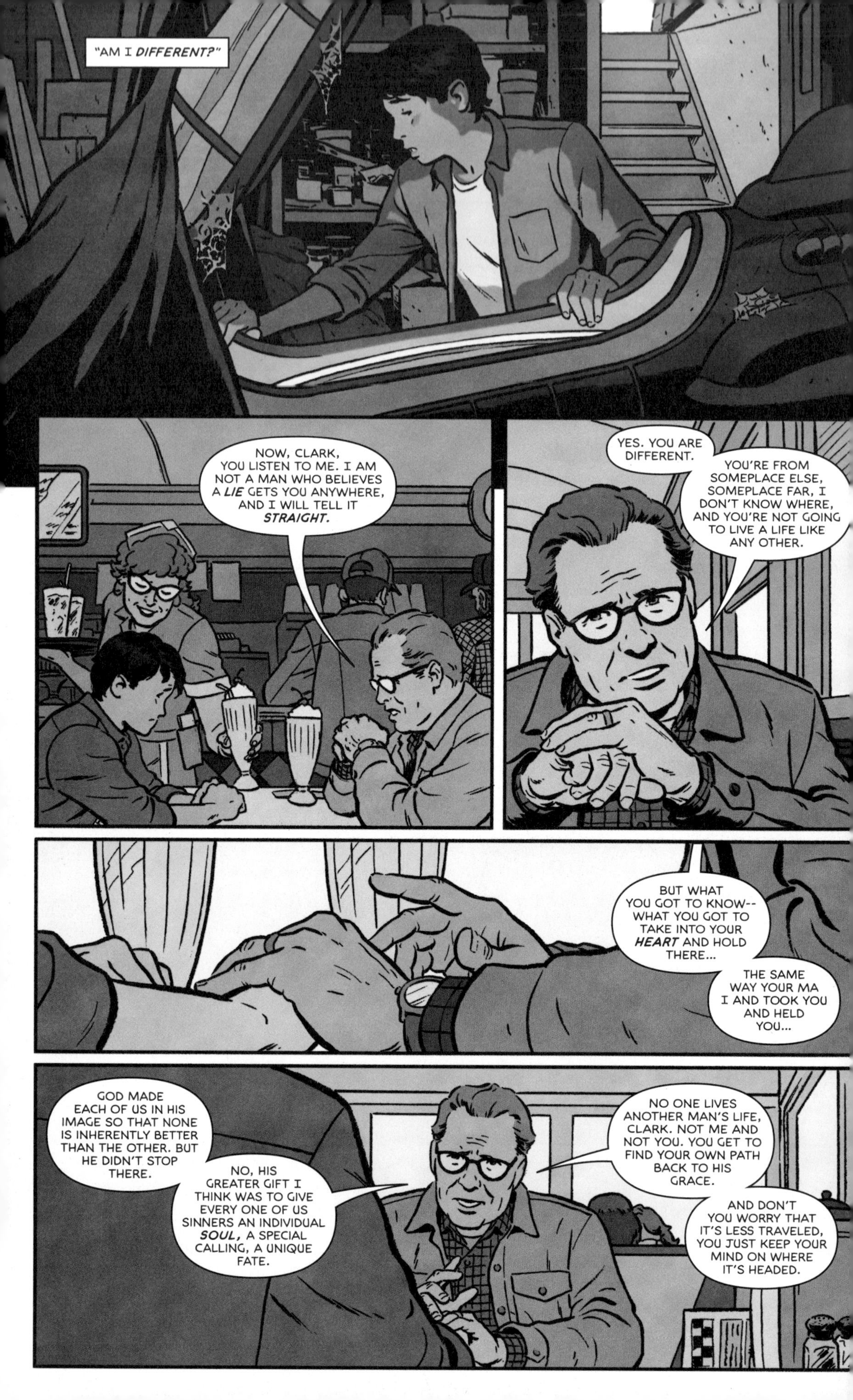
"AM I DIFFERENT?"
NOW, CLARK, YOU LISTEN TO ME. I AM NOT A MAN WHO BELIEVES A LIE GETS YOU ANYWHERE, AND I WILL TELL IT STRAIGHT.
YES. YOU ARE DIFFERENT.
YOU'RE FROM SOMEPLACE ELSE, SOMEPLACE FAR, I DON'T KNOW WHERE, AND YOU'RE NOT GOING TO LIVE A LIFE LIKE ANY OTHER.
BUT WHAT YOU GOT TO KNOW-- WHAT YOU GOT TO TAKE INTO YOUR HEART AND HOLD THERE...
THE SAME WAY YOUR MA I AND TOOK YOU AND HELD YOU...
GOD MADE EACH OF US IN HIS IMAGE SO THAT NONE IS INHERENTLY BETTER THAN THE OTHER. BUT HE DIDN'T STOP THERE.
NO, HIS GREATER GIFT I THINK WAS TO GIVE EVERY ONE OF US SINNERS AN INDIVIDUAL SOUL, A SPECIAL CALLING, A UNIQUE FATE.
NO ONE LIVES ANOTHER MAN'S LIFE, CLARK. NOT ME AND NOT YOU. YOU GET TO FIND YOUR OWN PATH BACK TO HIS GRACE.
AND DON'T YOU WORRY THAT IT'S LESS TRAVELED, YOU JUST KEEP YOUR MIND ON WHERE IT'S HEADED.

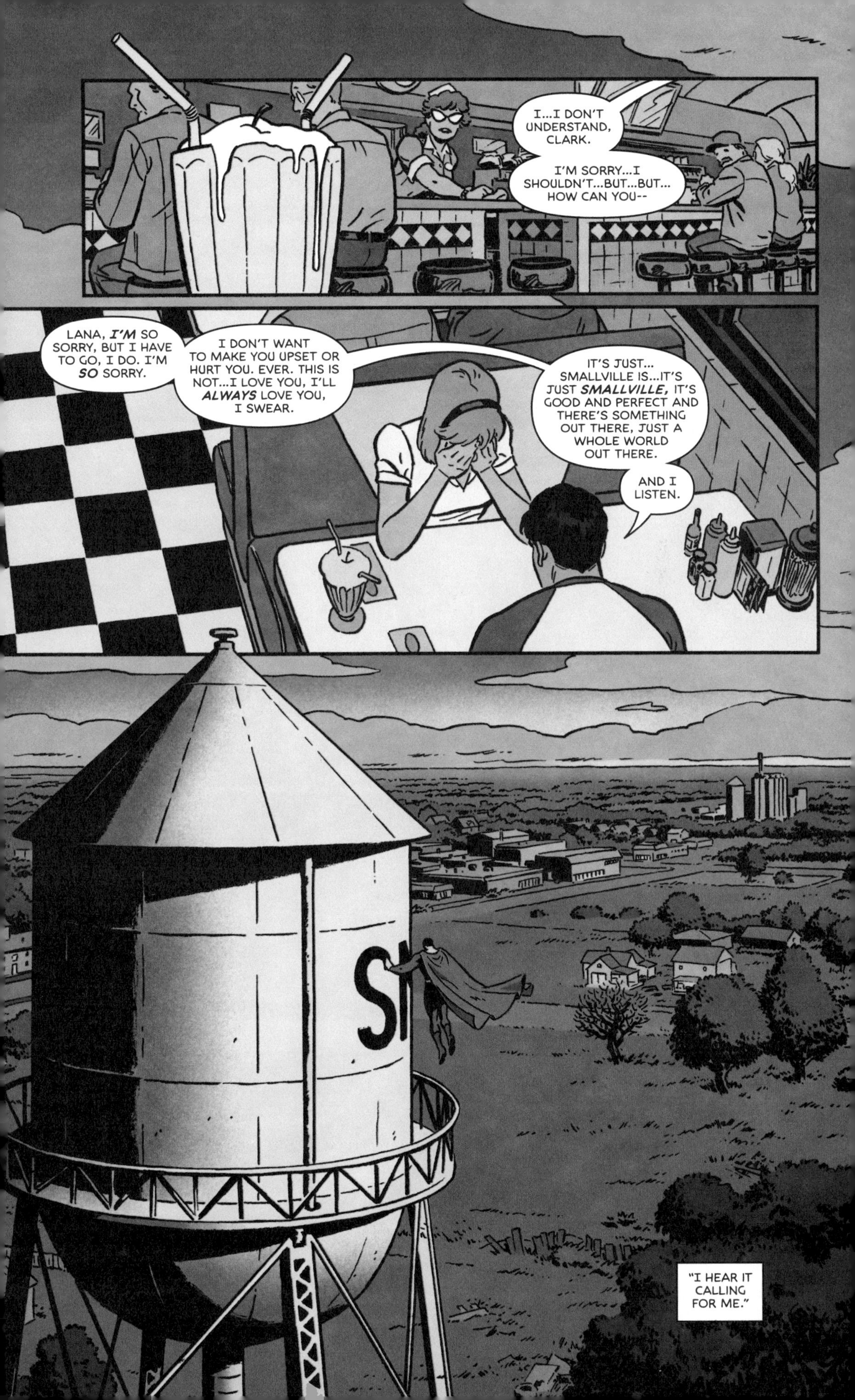
I...I DON'T UNDERSTAND, CLARK.
I'M SORRY...I SHOULDN'T...BUT...BUT... HOW CAN YOU--
LANA, I'M SO SORRY, BUT I HAVE TO GO, I DO. I'M SO SORRY.
I DON'T WANT TO MAKE YOU UPSET OR HURT YOU. EVER. THIS IS NOT...I LOVE YOU, I'LL ALWAYS LOVE YOU, I SWEAR.
IT'S JUST... SMALLVILLE IS...IT'S JUST SMALLVILLE, IT'S GOOD AND PERFECT AND THERE'S SOMETHING OUT THERE, JUST A WHOLE WORLD OUT THERE.
AND I LISTEN.
"I HEAR IT CALLING FOR ME."

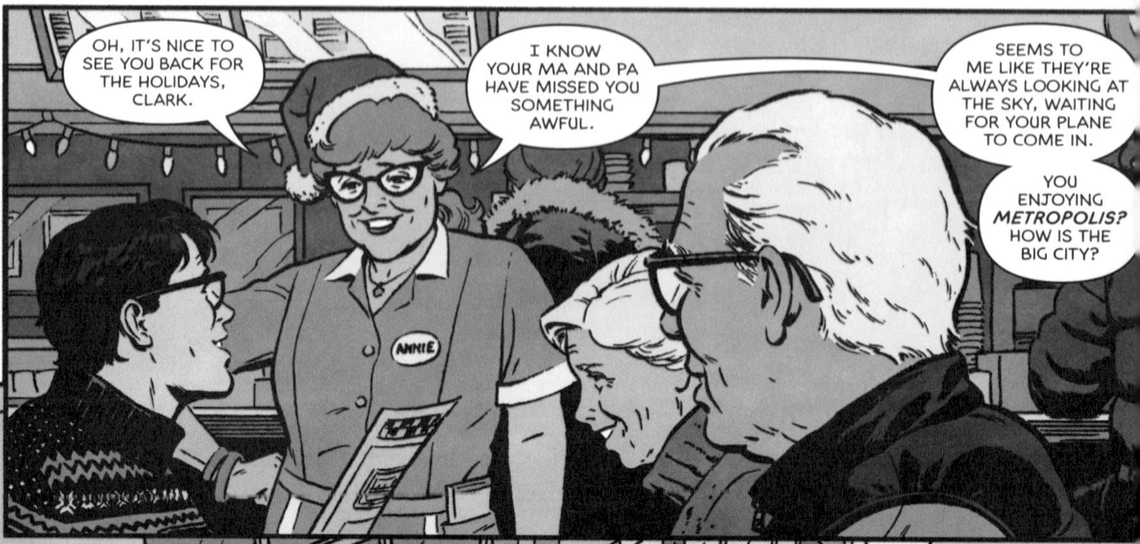
OH, IT'S NICE TO SEE YOU BACK FOR THE HOLIDAYS, CLARK.
I KNOW YOUR MA AND PA HAVE MISSED YOU SOMETHING AWFUL.
SEEMS TO ME LIKE THEY'RE ALWAYS LOOKING AT THE SKY, WAITING FOR YOUR PLANE TO COME IN.
YOU ENJOYING *METROPOLIS?* HOW IS THE BIG CITY?
ANNIE

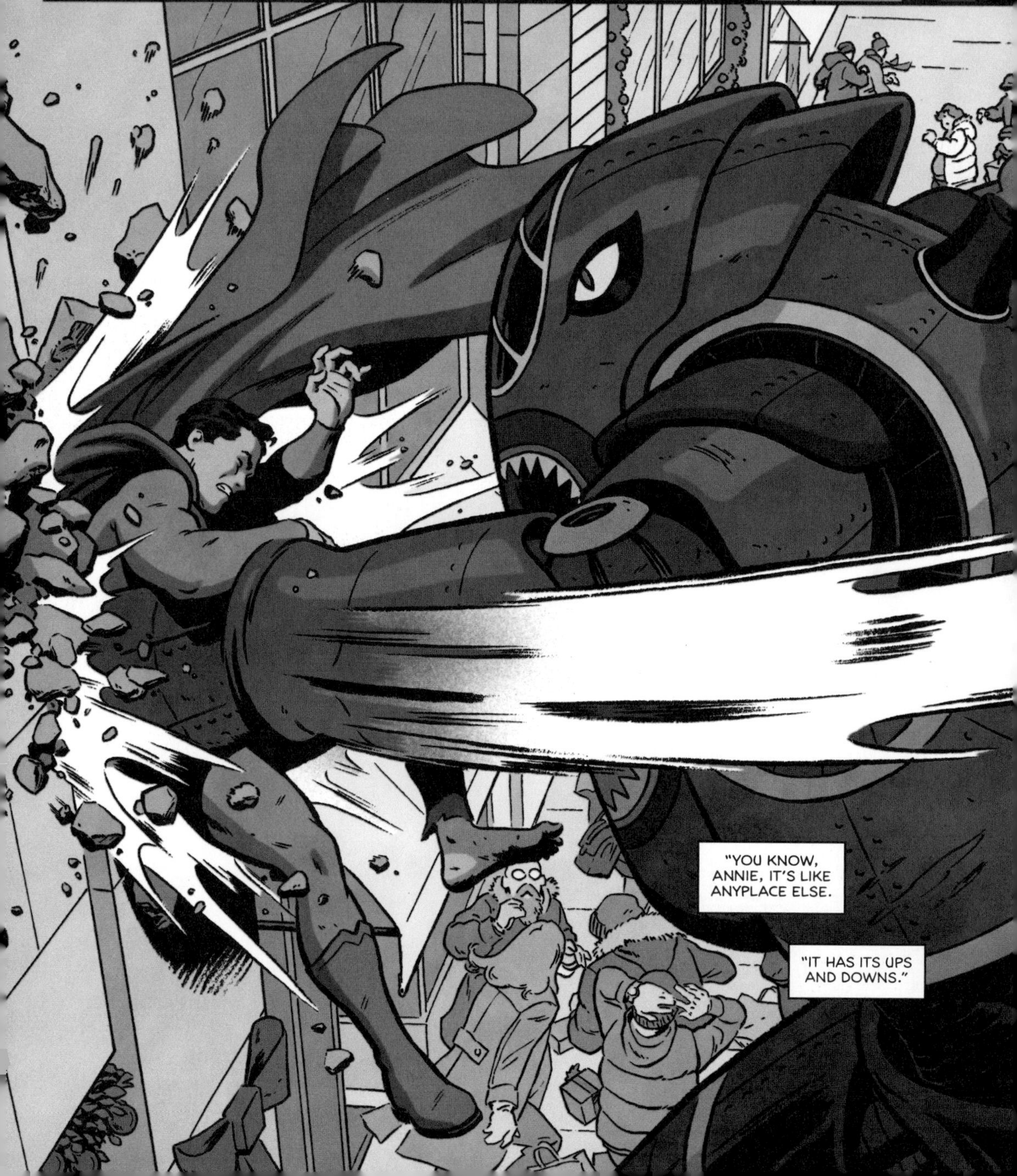
"YOU KNOW, ANNIE, IT'S LIKE ANYPLACE ELSE.
"IT HAS ITS UPS AND DOWNS."

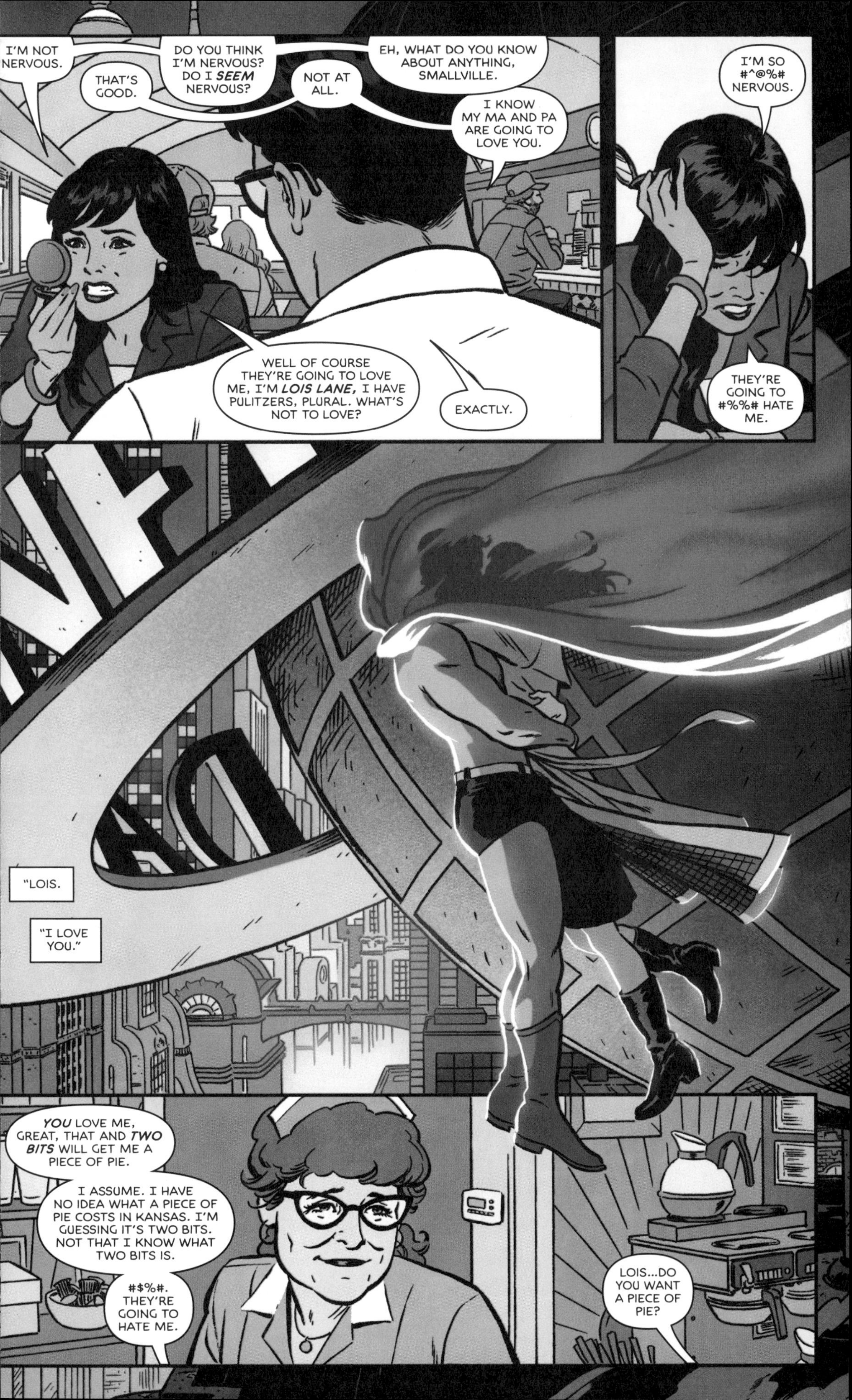

I'M NOT NERVOUS.
DO YOU THINK I'M NERVOUS? DO I SEEM NERVOUS?
THAT'S GOOD.
NOT AT ALL.
EH, WHAT DO YOU KNOW ABOUT ANYTHING, SMALLVILLE.
I KNOW MY MA AND PA ARE GOING TO LOVE YOU.
WELL OF COURSE THEY'RE GOING TO LOVE ME, I'M LOIS LANE, I HAVE PULITZERS, PLURAL. WHAT'S NOT TO LOVE?
EXACTLY.
I'M SO #^@%# NERVOUS.
THEY'RE GOING TO #%%# HATE ME.
"LOIS.
"I LOVE YOU."
YOU LOVE ME, GREAT, THAT AND TWO BITS WILL GET ME A PIECE OF PIE.
I ASSUME. I HAVE NO IDEA WHAT A PIECE OF PIE COSTS IN KANSAS. I'M GUESSING IT'S TWO BITS. NOT THAT I KNOW WHAT TWO BITS IS.
#$%#. THEY'RE GOING TO HATE ME.
LOIS...DO YOU WANT A PIECE OF PIE?

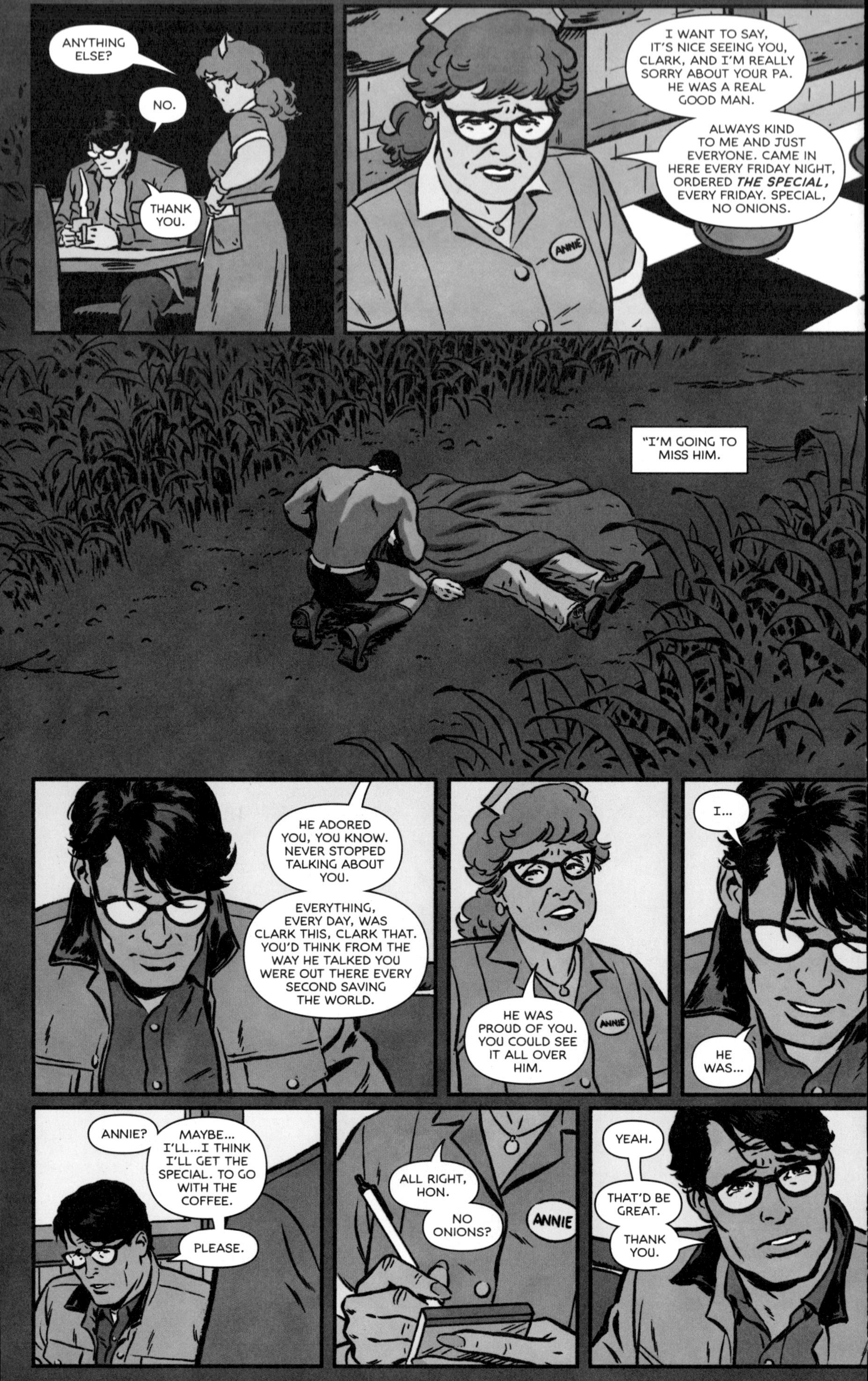
ANYTHING ELSE?
NO.
THANK YOU.
I WANT TO SAY, IT'S NICE SEEING YOU, CLARK, AND I'M REALLY SORRY ABOUT YOUR PA. HE WAS A REAL GOOD MAN.
ALWAYS KIND TO ME AND JUST EVERYONE. CAME IN HERE EVERY FRIDAY NIGHT, ORDERED ***THE SPECIAL,*** EVERY FRIDAY. SPECIAL, NO ONIONS.
ANNIE
"I'M GOING TO MISS HIM.
HE ADORED YOU, YOU KNOW. NEVER STOPPED TALKING ABOUT YOU.
EVERYTHING, EVERY DAY, WAS CLARK THIS, CLARK THAT. YOU'D THINK FROM THE WAY HE TALKED YOU WERE OUT THERE EVERY SECOND SAVING THE WORLD.
HE WAS PROUD OF YOU. YOU COULD SEE IT ALL OVER HIM.
ANNIE
I...
HE WAS...
ANNIE?
MAYBE... I'LL...I THINK I'LL GET THE SPECIAL. TO GO WITH THE COFFEE.
PLEASE.
ALL RIGHT, HON.
NO ONIONS?
ANNIE
YEAH.
THAT'D BE GREAT.
THANK YOU.

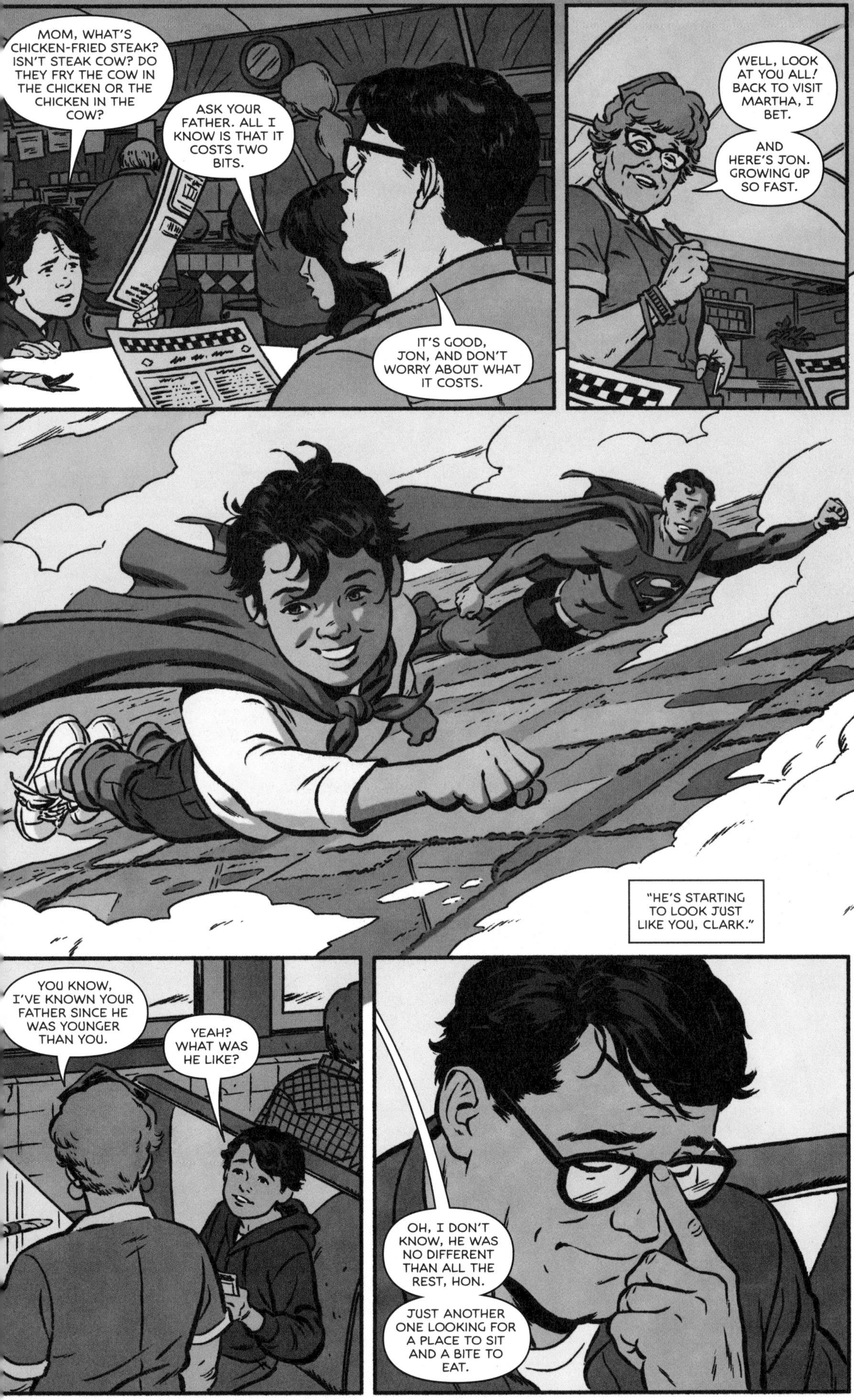
MOM, WHAT'S CHICKEN-FRIED STEAK? ISN'T STEAK COW? DO THEY FRY THE COW IN THE CHICKEN OR THE CHICKEN IN THE COW?
ASK YOUR FATHER. ALL I KNOW IS THAT IT COSTS TWO BITS.
IT'S GOOD, JON, AND DON'T WORRY ABOUT WHAT IT COSTS.
WELL, LOOK AT YOU ALL! BACK TO VISIT MARTHA, I BET.
AND HERE'S JON. GROWING UP SO FAST.
"HE'S STARTING TO LOOK JUST LIKE YOU, CLARK."
YOU KNOW, I'VE KNOWN YOUR FATHER SINCE HE WAS YOUNGER THAN YOU.
YEAH? WHAT WAS HE LIKE?
OH, I DON'T KNOW, HE WAS NO DIFFERENT THAN ALL THE REST, HON.
JUST ANOTHER ONE LOOKING FOR A PLACE TO SIT AND A BITE TO EAT.

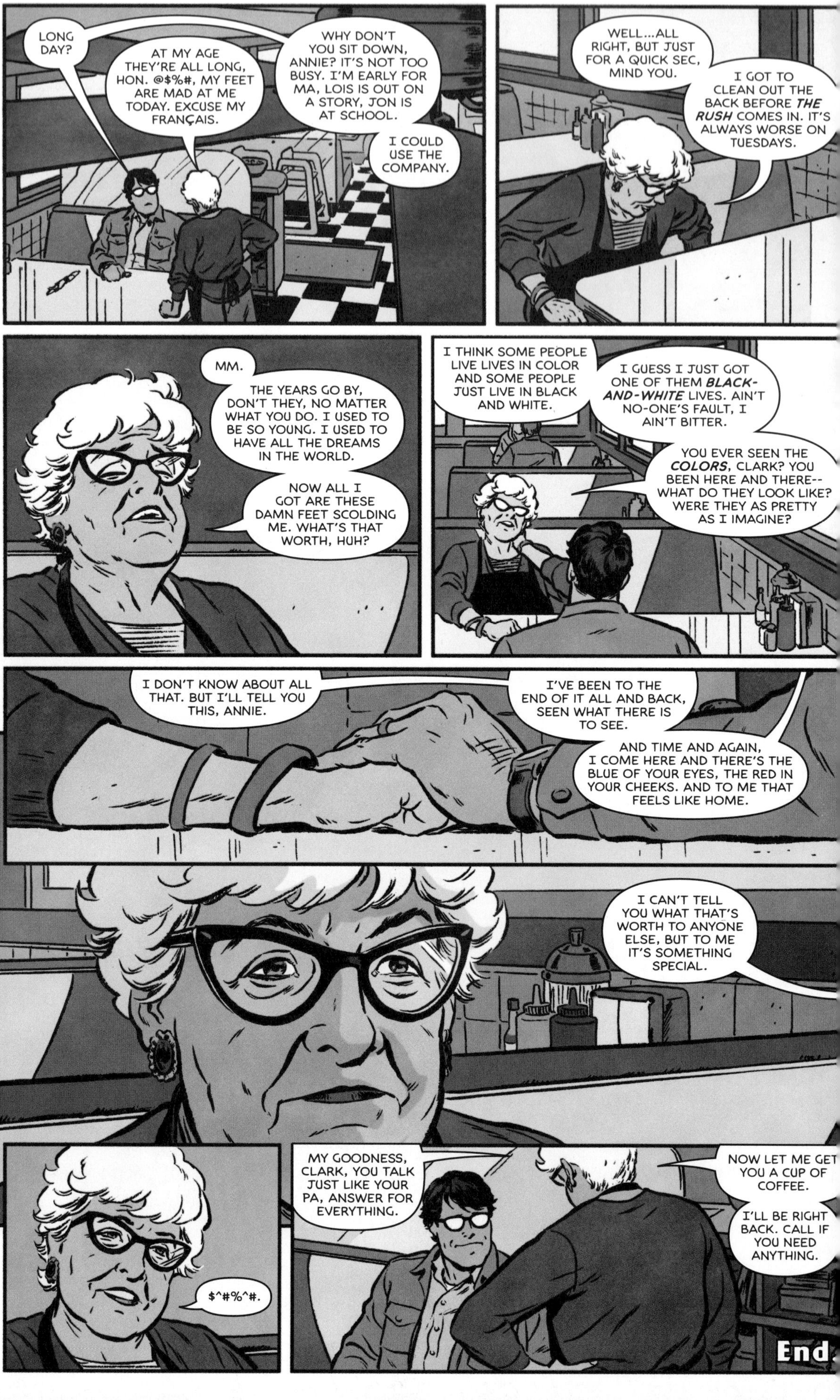
LONG DAY?
AT MY AGE THEY'RE ALL LONG, HON. @$%#, MY FEET ARE MAD AT ME TODAY. EXCUSE MY FRANÇAIS.
WHY DON'T YOU SIT DOWN, ANNIE? IT'S NOT TOO BUSY. I'M EARLY FOR MA, LOIS IS OUT ON A STORY, JON IS AT SCHOOL.
I COULD USE THE COMPANY.
WELL...ALL RIGHT, BUT JUST FOR A QUICK SEC, MIND YOU.
I GOT TO CLEAN OUT THE BACK BEFORE THE RUSH COMES IN. IT'S ALWAYS WORSE ON TUESDAYS.
MM.
THE YEARS GO BY, DON'T THEY, NO MATTER WHAT YOU DO. I USED TO BE SO YOUNG. I USED TO HAVE ALL THE DREAMS IN THE WORLD.
NOW ALL I GOT ARE THESE DAMN FEET SCOLDING ME. WHAT'S THAT WORTH, HUH?
I THINK SOME PEOPLE LIVE LIVES IN COLOR AND SOME PEOPLE JUST LIVE IN BLACK AND WHITE.
I GUESS I JUST GOT ONE OF THEM BLACK-AND-WHITE LIVES. AIN'T NO-ONE'S FAULT, I AIN'T BITTER.
YOU EVER SEEN THE COLORS, CLARK? YOU BEEN HERE AND THERE-- WHAT DO THEY LOOK LIKE? WERE THEY AS PRETTY AS I IMAGINE?
I DON'T KNOW ABOUT ALL THAT. BUT I'LL TELL YOU THIS, ANNIE.
I'VE BEEN TO THE END OF IT ALL AND BACK, SEEN WHAT THERE IS TO SEE.
AND TIME AND AGAIN, I COME HERE AND THERE'S THE BLUE OF YOUR EYES, THE RED IN YOUR CHEEKS. AND TO ME THAT FEELS LIKE HOME.
I CAN'T TELL YOU WHAT THAT'S WORTH TO ANYONE ELSE, BUT TO ME IT'S SOMETHING SPECIAL.
$^#%^#.
MY GOODNESS, CLARK, YOU TALK JUST LIKE YOUR PA, ANSWER FOR EVERYTHING.
NOW LET ME GET YOU A CUP OF COFFEE.
I'LL BE RIGHT BACK. CALL IF YOU NEED ANYTHING.
End.

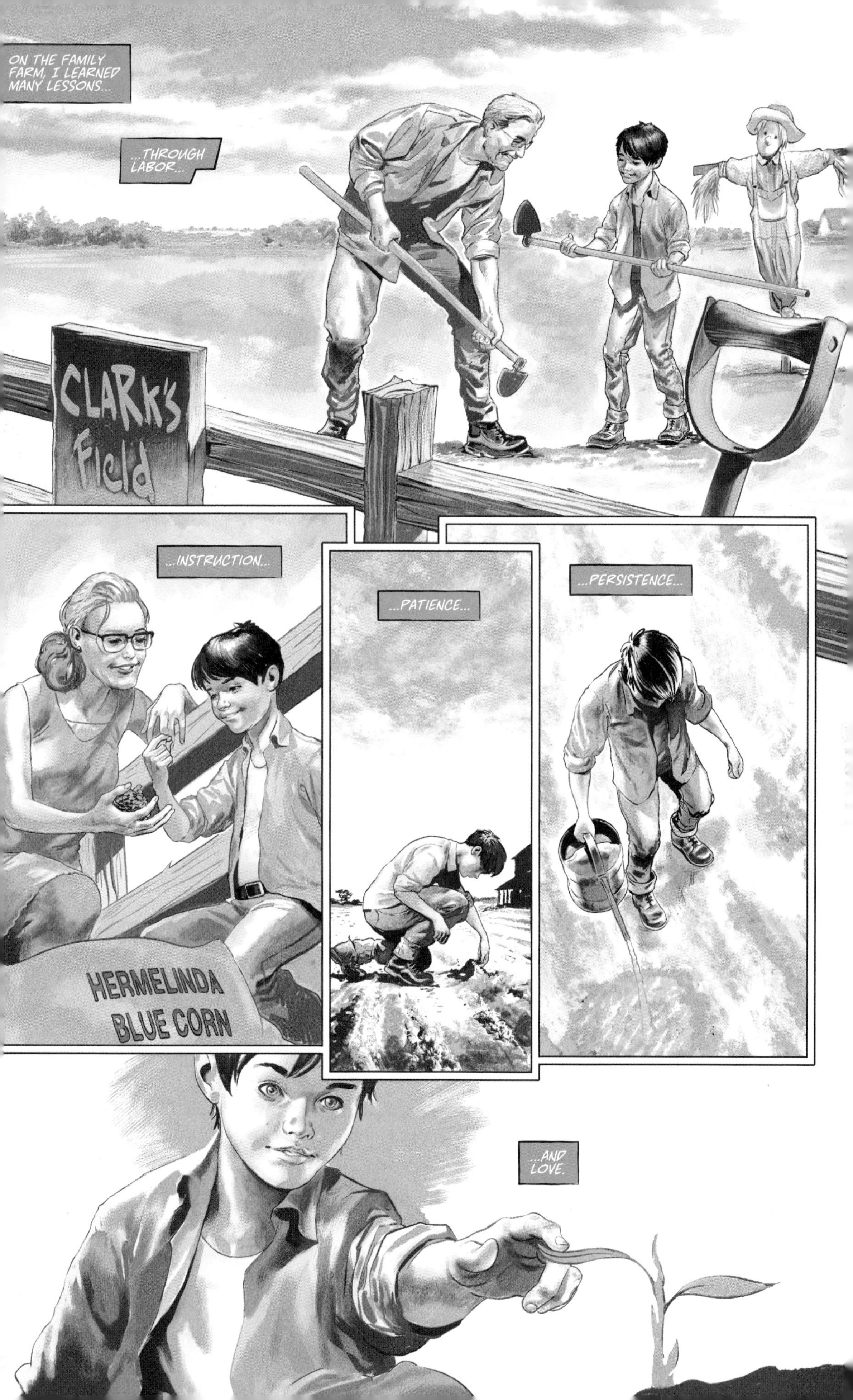
ON THE FAMILY FARM, I LEARNED MANY LESSONS...
...THROUGH LABOR...
CLARK'S Field
...INSTRUCTION...
HERMELINDA BLUE CORN
...PATIENCE...
...PERSISTENCE...
...AND LOVE.

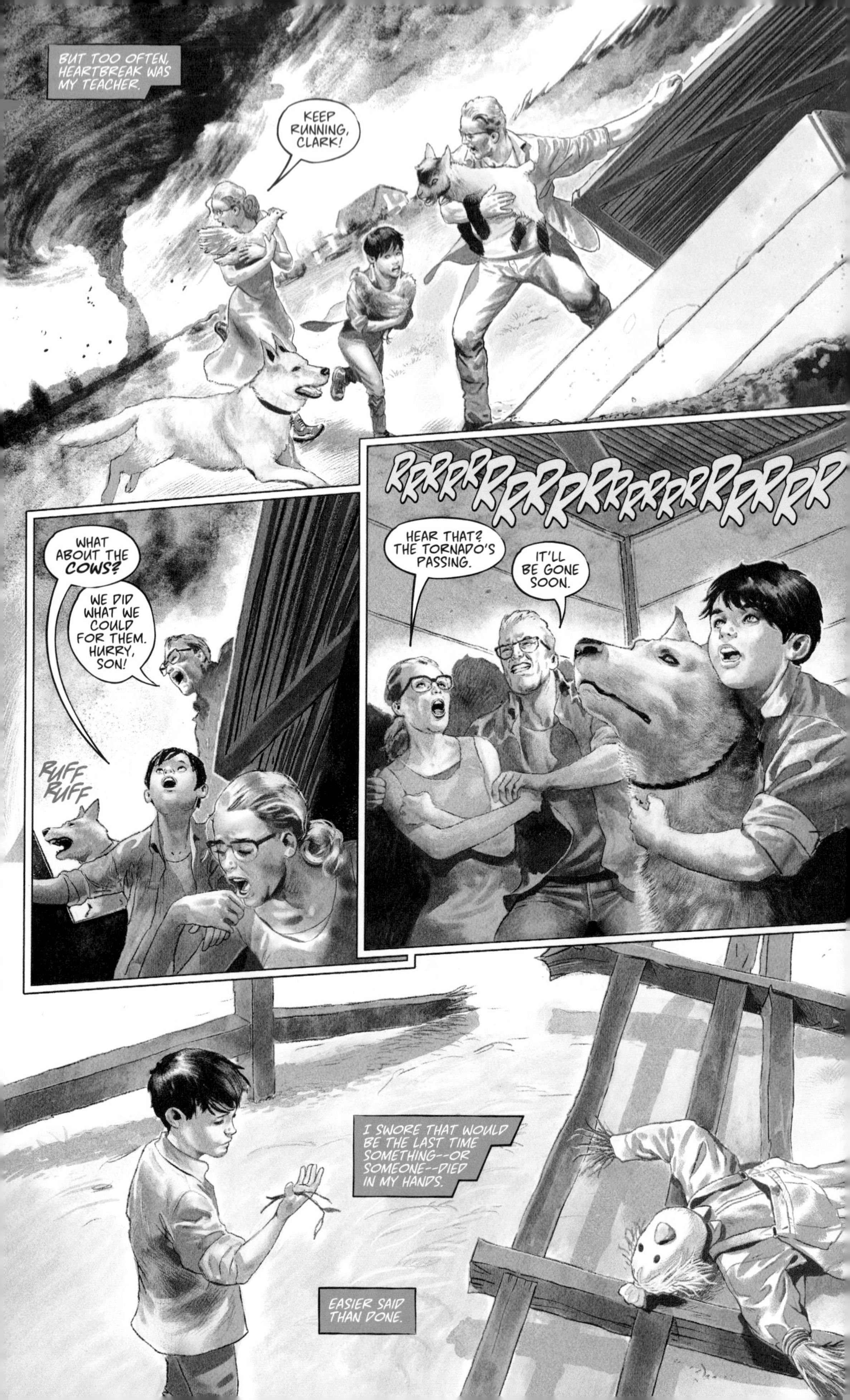
BUT TOO OFTEN, HEARTBREAK WAS MY TEACHER.
KEEP RUNNING, CLARK!
WHAT ABOUT THE COWS?
WE DID WHAT WE COULD FOR THEM. HURRY, SON!
RUFF RUFF
RRRRRRRRRRRRRRRRRRRRR
HEAR THAT? THE TORNADO'S PASSING.
IT'LL BE GONE SOON.
I SWORE THAT WOULD BE THE LAST TIME SOMETHING--OR SOMEONE--DIED IN MY HANDS.
EASIER SAID THAN DONE.

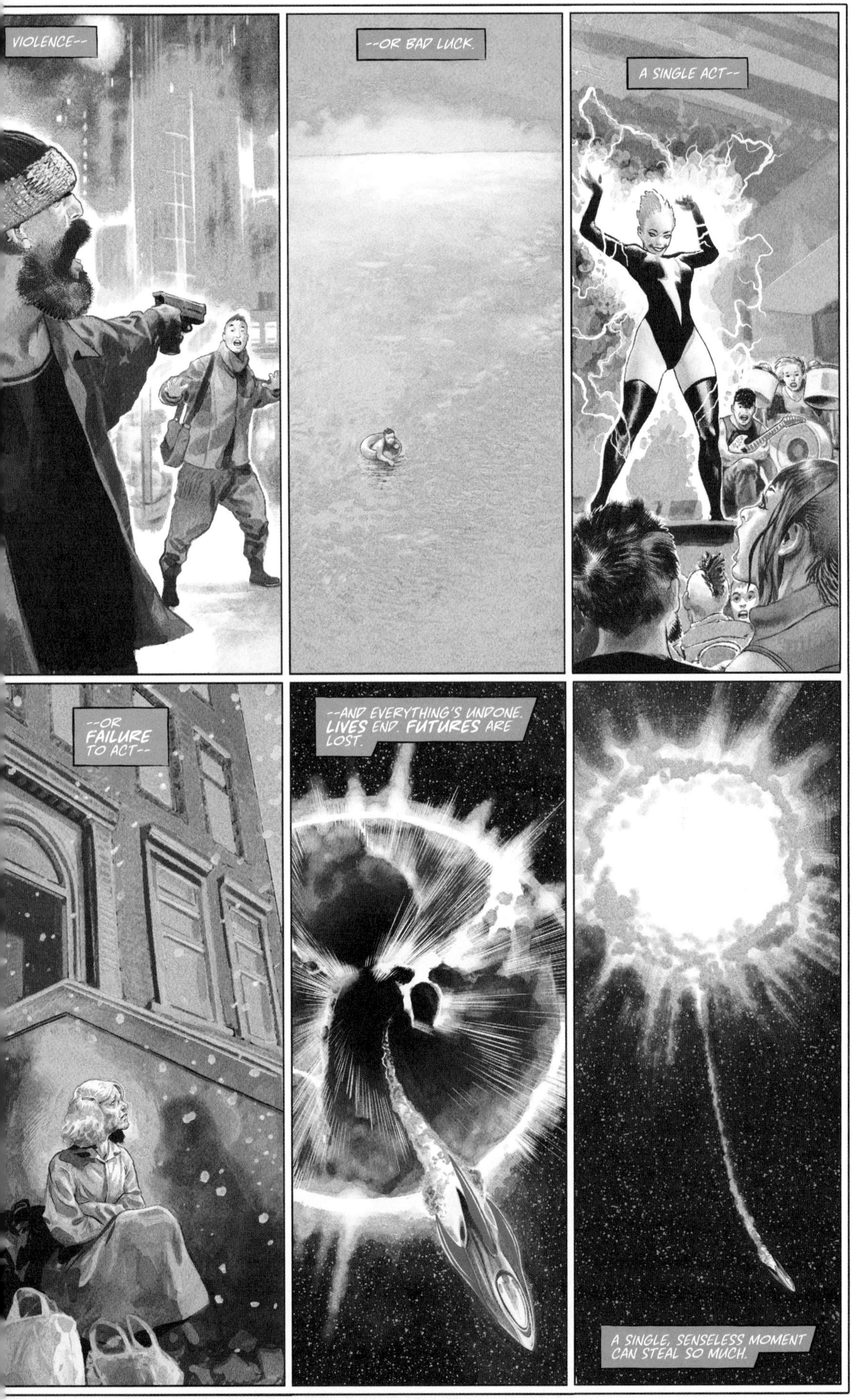
VIOLENCE--
--OR BAD LUCK.
A SINGLE ACT--
--OR FAILURE TO ACT--
--AND EVERYTHING'S UNDONE. LIVES END. FUTURES ARE LOST.
A SINGLE, SENSELESS MOMENT CAN STEAL SO MUCH.

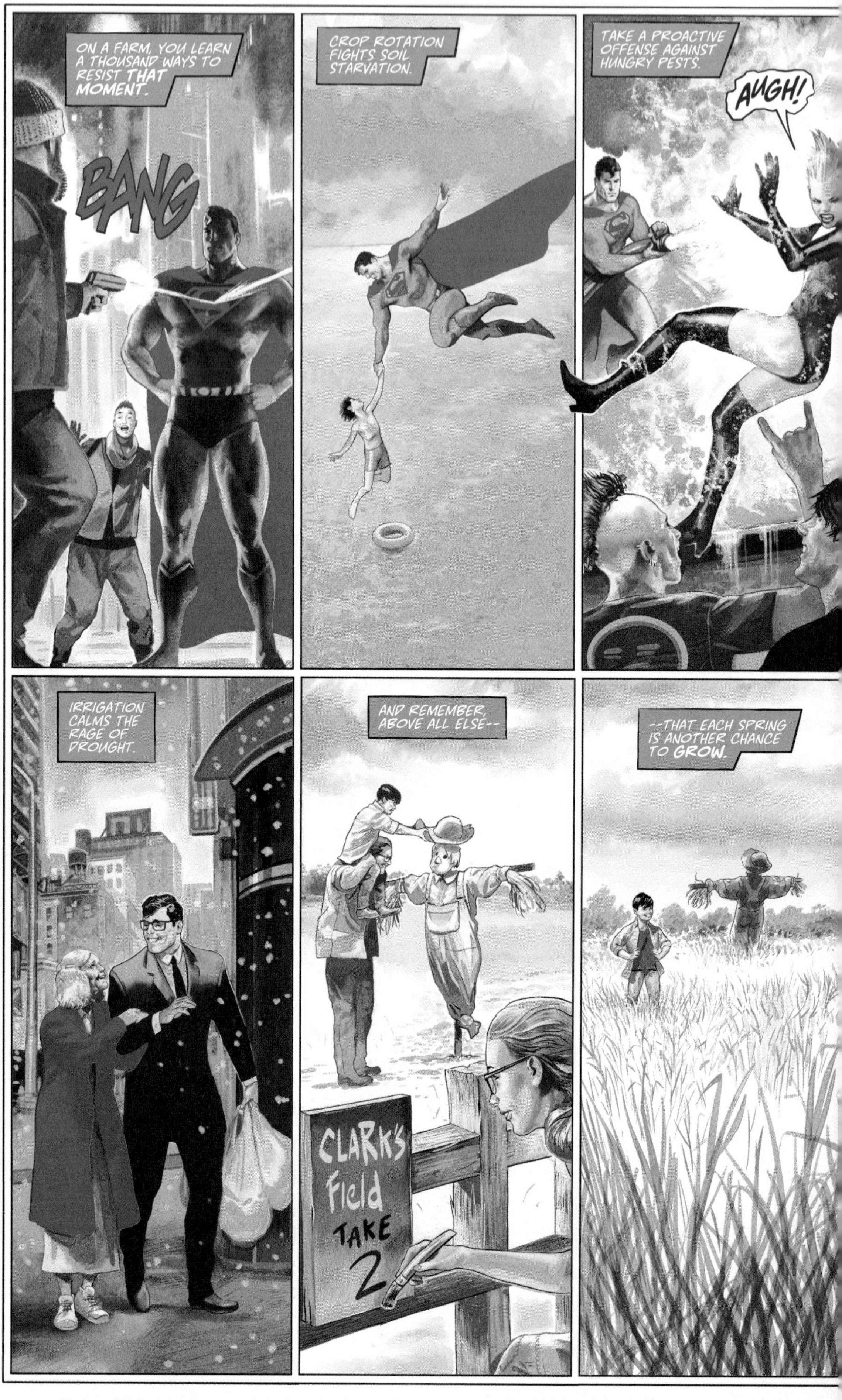
ON A FARM, YOU LEARN A THOUSAND WAYS TO RESIST THAT MOMENT.
BANG
CROP ROTATION FIGHTS SOIL STARVATION.
TAKE A PROACTIVE OFFENSE AGAINST HUNGRY PESTS.
AUGH!
IRRIGATION CALMS THE RAGE OF DROUGHT.
AND REMEMBER, ABOVE ALL ELSE--
CLARK'S Field TAKE 2
--THAT EACH SPRING IS ANOTHER CHANCE TO GROW.

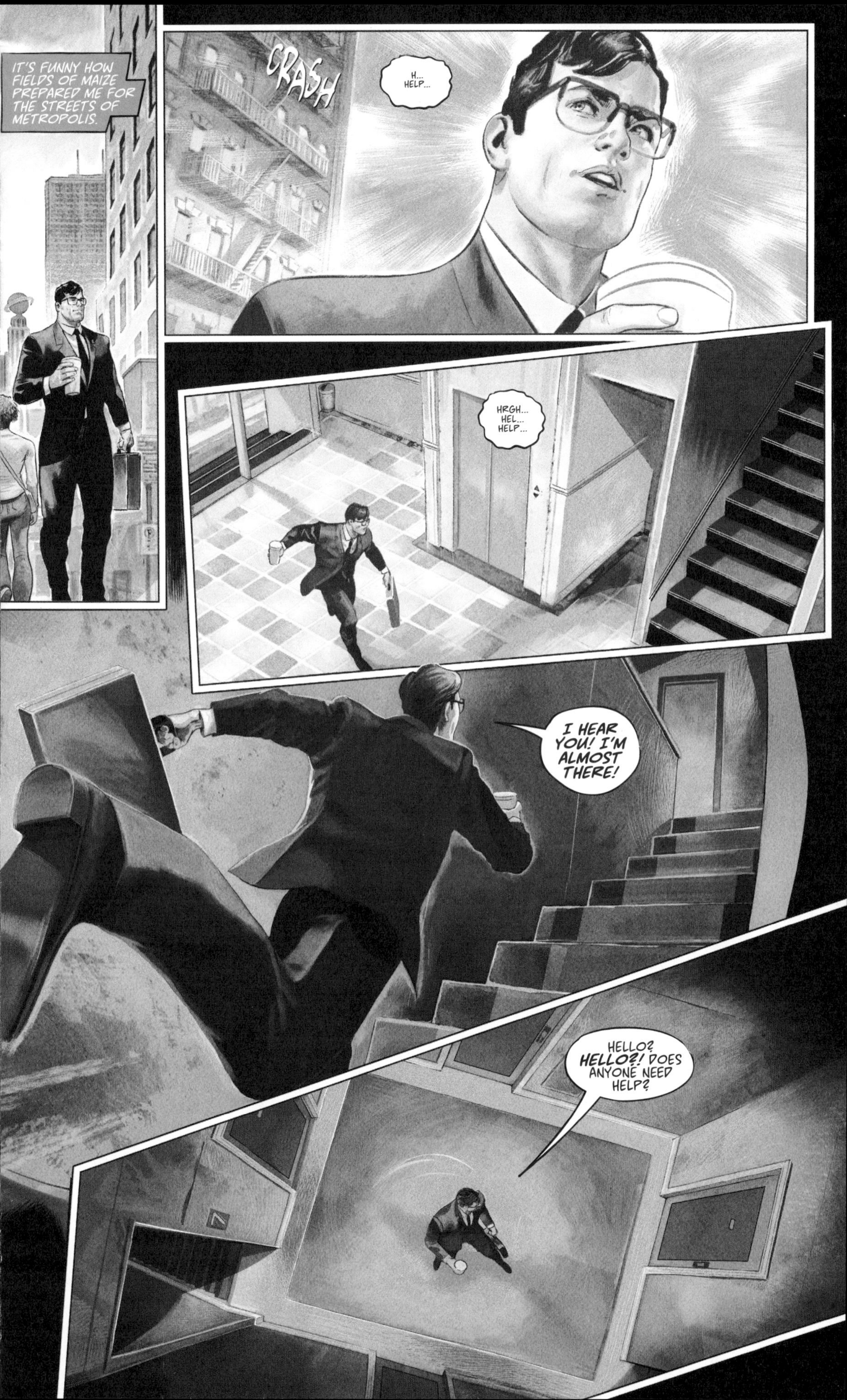
IT'S FUNNY HOW FIELDS OF MAIZE PREPARED ME FOR THE STREETS OF METROPOLIS.
CRASH
H... HELP...
HRGH... HEL... HELP...
I HEAR YOU! I'M ALMOST THERE!
HELLO? HELLO?! DOES ANYONE NEED HELP?

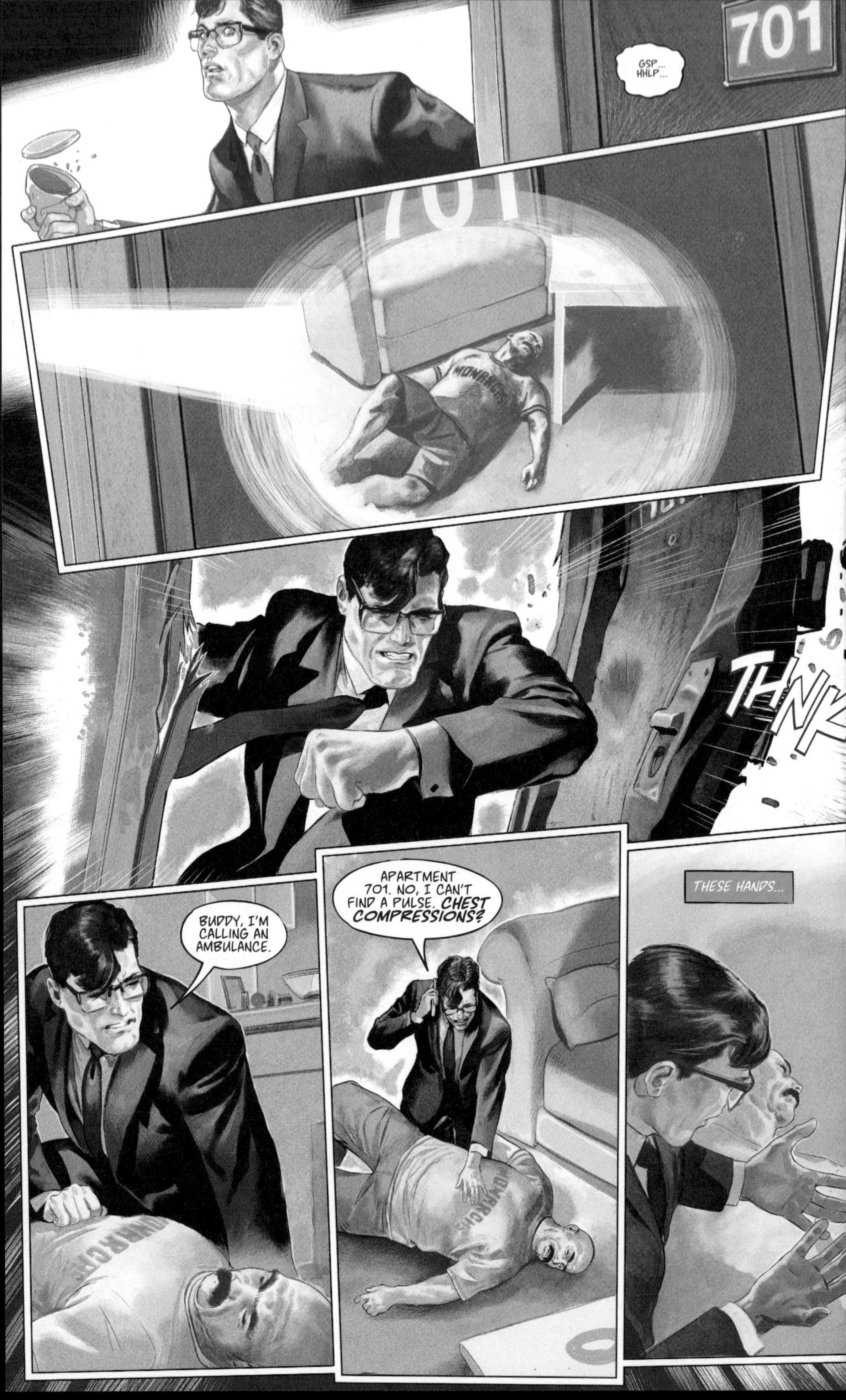

GSP... HHLP...
THNK
BUDDY, I'M CALLING AN AMBULANCE.
APARTMENT 701. NO, I CAN'T FIND A PULSE. CHEST COMPRESSIONS?
THESE HANDS...

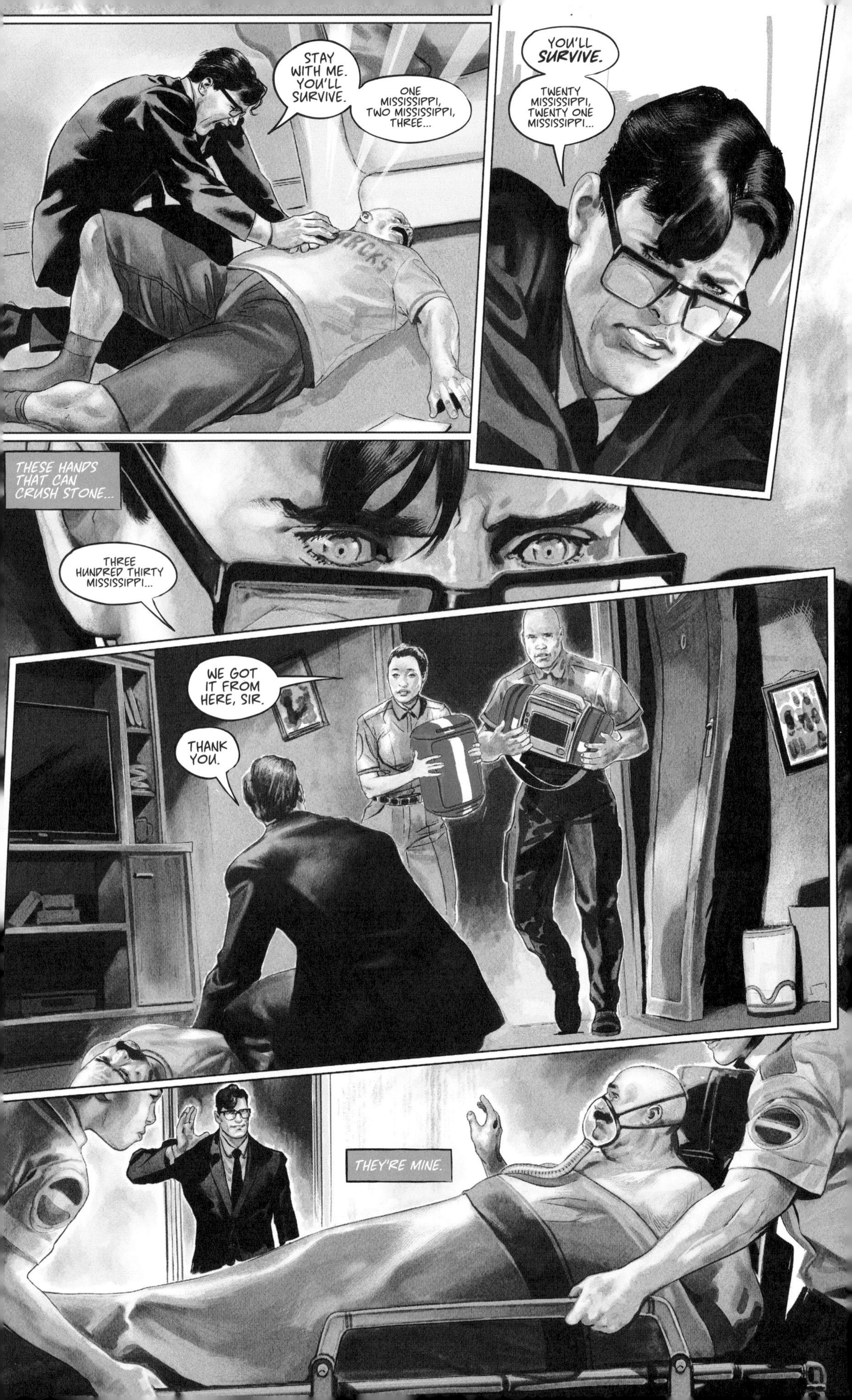
STAY WITH ME. YOU'LL SURVIVE.
ONE MISSISSIPPI, TWO MISSISSIPPI, THREE...
YOU'LL SURVIVE.
TWENTY MISSISSIPPI, TWENTY ONE MISSISSIPPI...
THESE HANDS THAT CAN CRUSH STONE...
THREE HUNDRED THIRTY MISSISSIPPI...
WE GOT IT FROM HERE, SIR.
THANK YOU.
THEY'RE MINE.

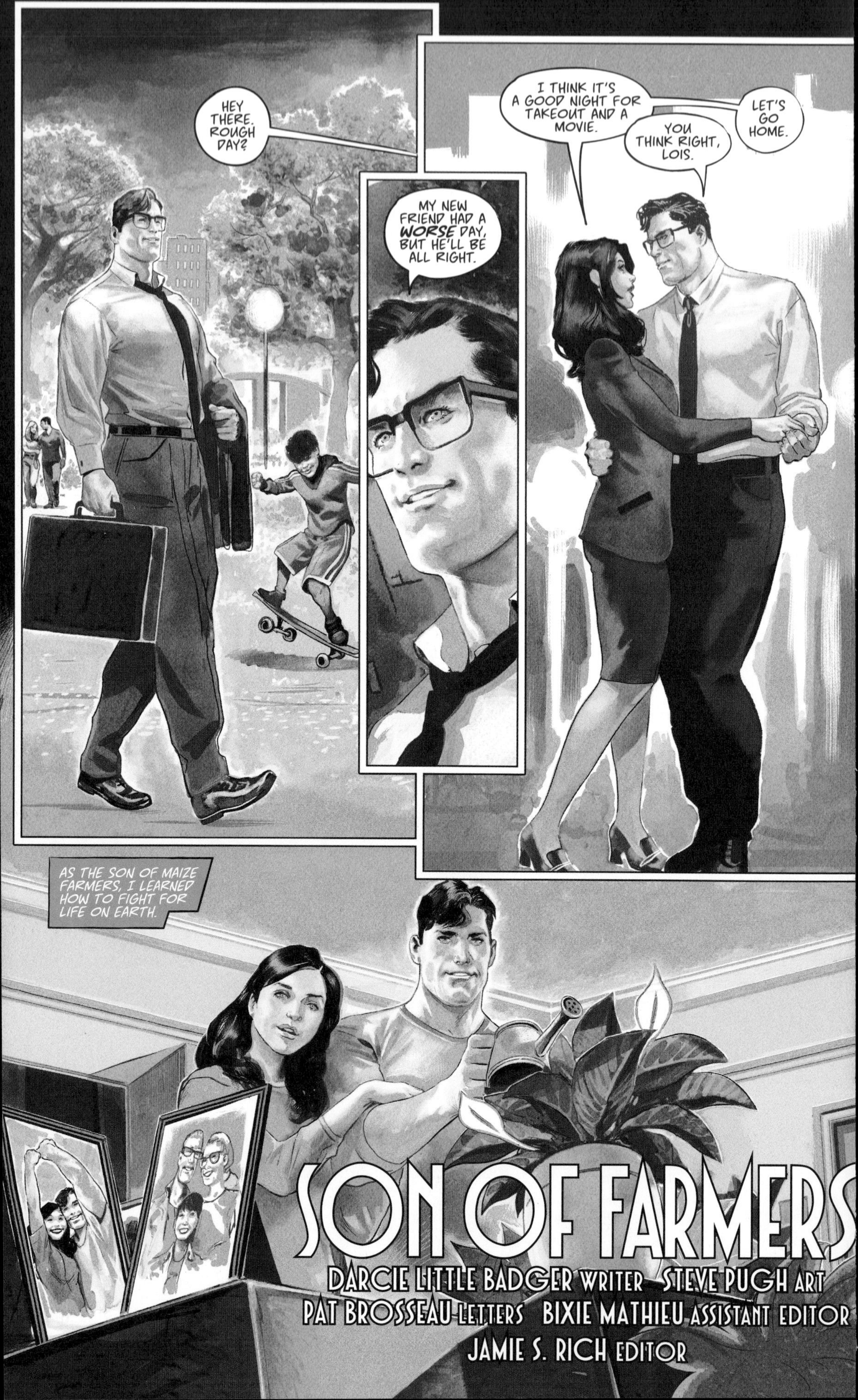
HEY THERE. ROUGH DAY?
MY NEW FRIEND HAD A WORSE DAY, BUT HE'LL BE ALL RIGHT.
I THINK IT'S A GOOD NIGHT FOR TAKEOUT AND A MOVIE.
YOU THINK RIGHT, LOIS.
LET'S GO HOME.
AS THE SON OF MAIZE FARMERS, I LEARNED HOW TO FIGHT FOR LIFE ON EARTH.
SON OF FARMERS
DARCIE LITTLE BADGER WRITER STEVE PUGH ART
PAT BROSSEAU LETTERS BIXIE MATHIEU ASSISTANT EDITOR
JAMIE S. RICH EDITOR

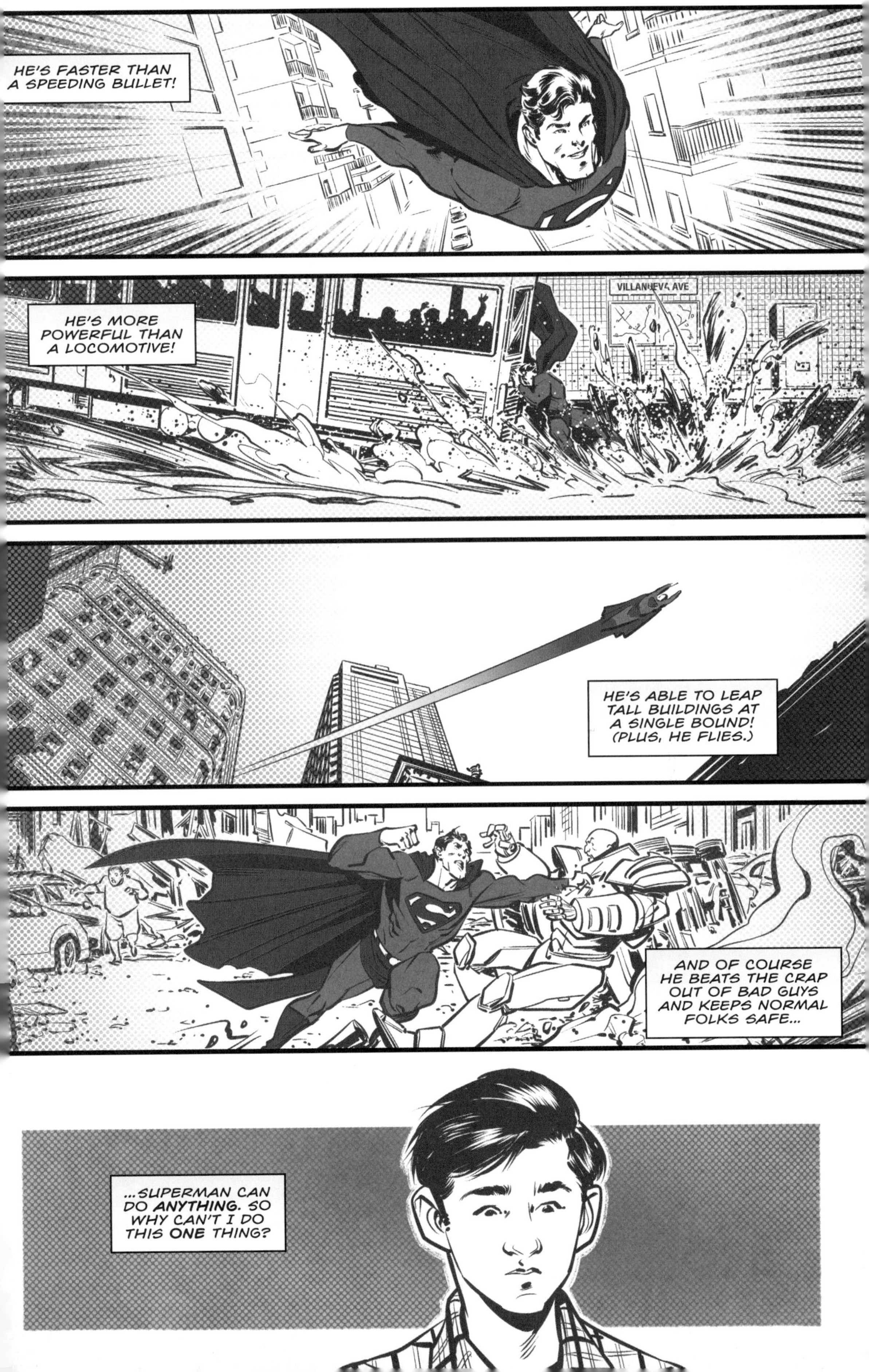
HE'S FASTER THAN A SPEEDING BULLET!
HE'S MORE POWERFUL THAN A LOCOMOTIVE!
HE'S ABLE TO LEAP TALL BUILDINGS AT A SINGLE BOUND! (PLUS, HE FLIES.)
AND OF COURSE HE BEATS THE CRAP OUT OF BAD GUYS AND KEEPS NORMAL FOLKS SAFE...
...SUPERMAN CAN DO ANYTHING. SO WHY CAN'T I DO THIS ONE THING?

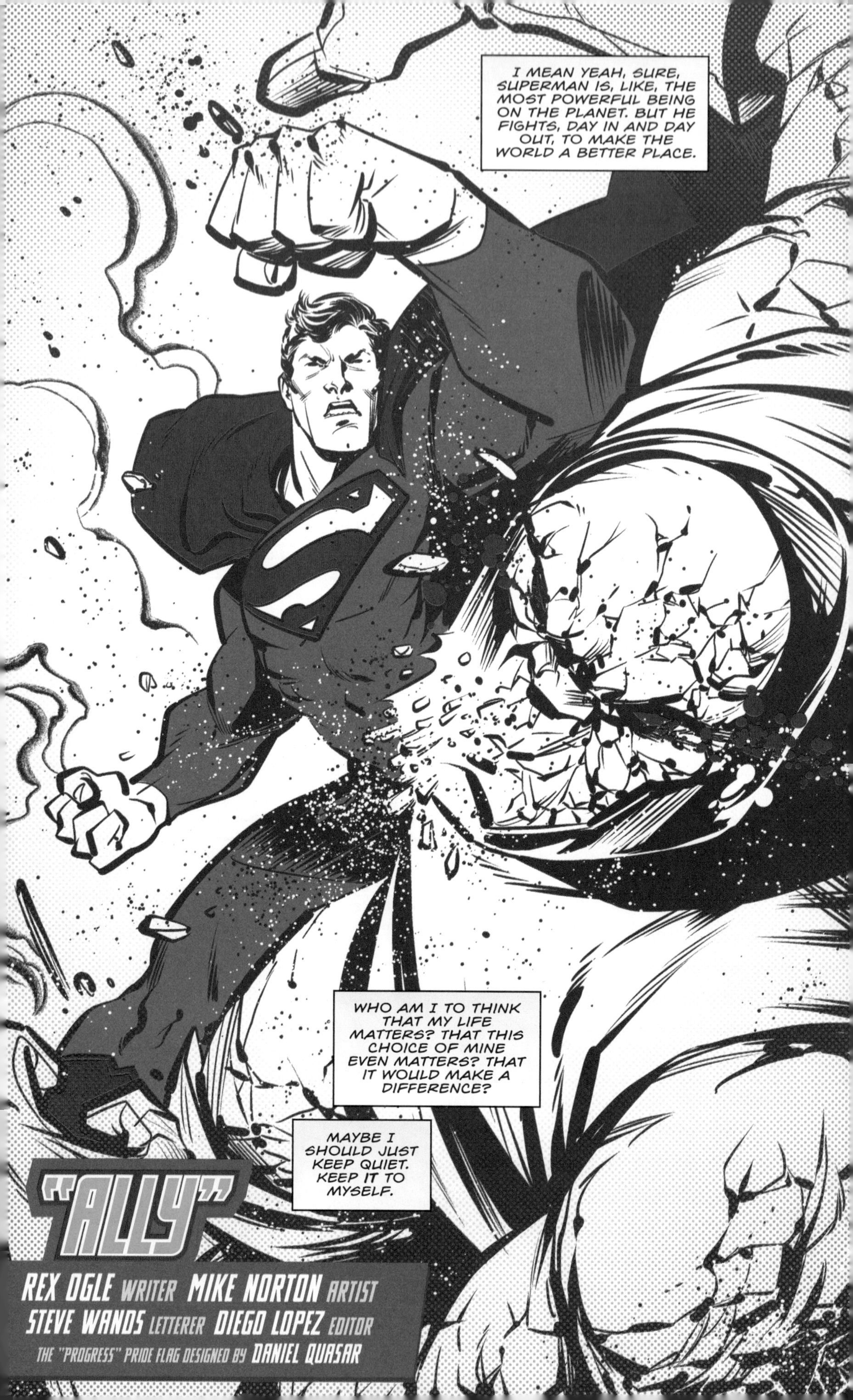
I MEAN YEAH, SURE, SUPERMAN IS, LIKE, THE MOST POWERFUL BEING ON THE PLANET. BUT HE FIGHTS, DAY IN AND DAY OUT, TO MAKE THE WORLD A BETTER PLACE.
WHO AM I TO THINK THAT MY LIFE MATTERS? THAT THIS CHOICE OF MINE EVEN MATTERS? THAT IT WOULD MAKE A DIFFERENCE?
MAYBE I SHOULD JUST KEEP QUIET. KEEP IT TO MYSELF.
"ALLY"
REX OGLE WRITER MIKE NORTON ARTIST
STEVE WANDS LETTERER DIEGO LOPEZ EDITOR
THE "PROGRESS" PRIDE FLAG DESIGNED BY DANIEL QUASAR

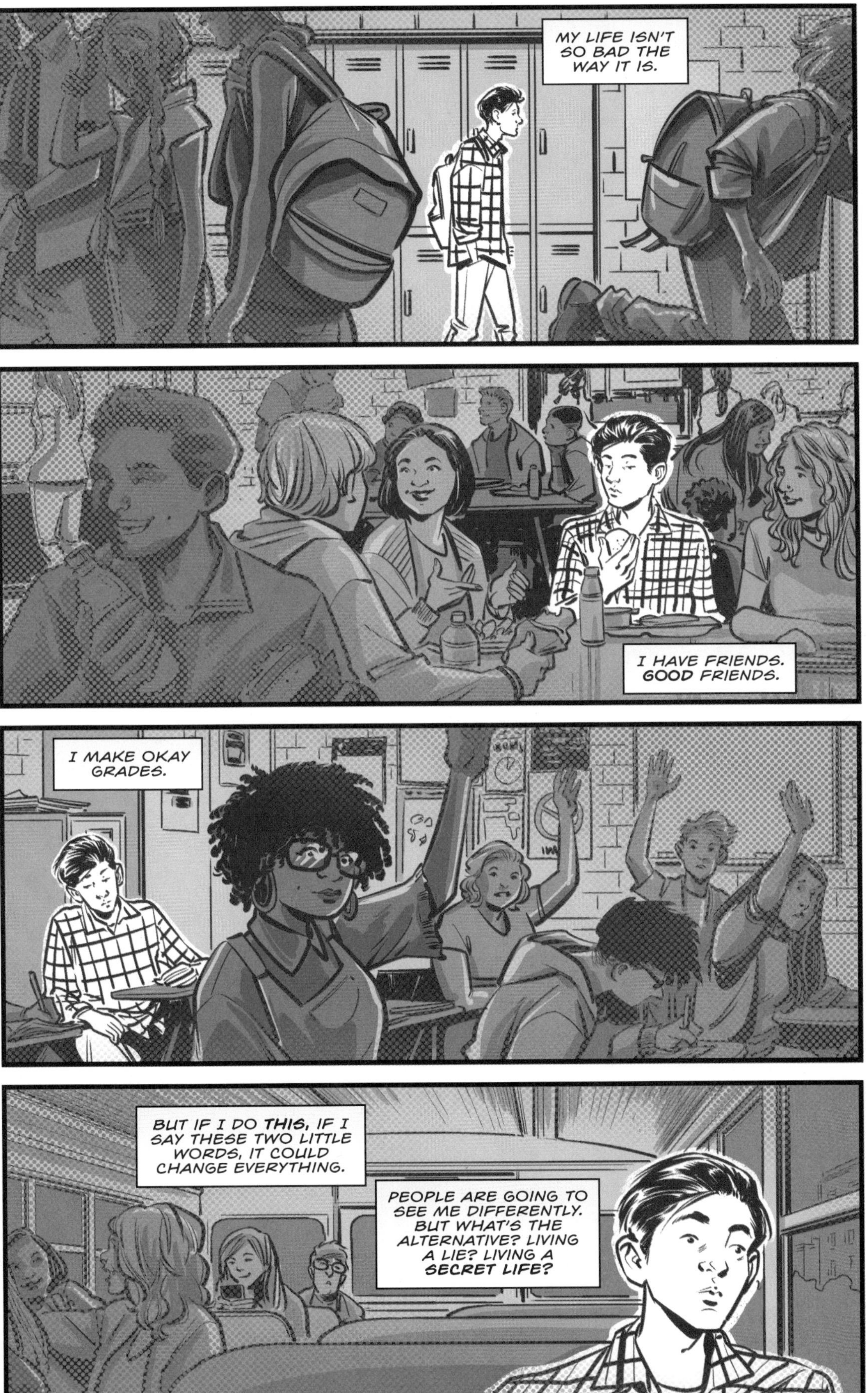
MY LIFE ISN'T SO BAD THE WAY IT IS.
I HAVE FRIENDS. GOOD FRIENDS.
I MAKE OKAY GRADES.
BUT IF I DO THIS, IF I SAY THESE TWO LITTLE WORDS, IT COULD CHANGE EVERYTHING.
PEOPLE ARE GOING TO SEE ME DIFFERENTLY. BUT WHAT'S THE ALTERNATIVE? LIVING A LIE? LIVING A SECRET LIFE?

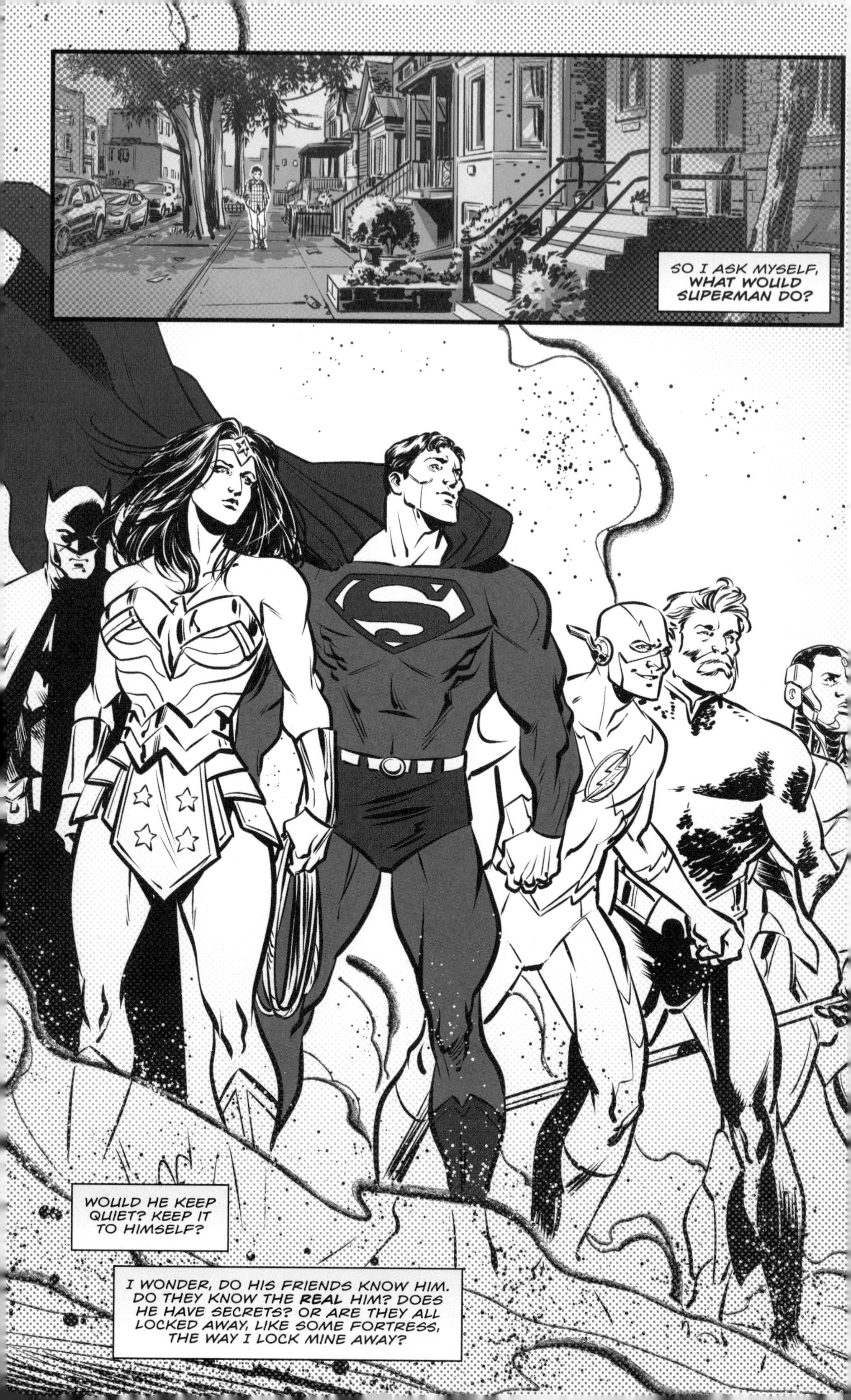
SO I ASK MYSELF, WHAT WOULD SUPERMAN DO?
WOULD HE KEEP QUIET? KEEP IT TO HIMSELF?
I WONDER, DO HIS FRIENDS KNOW HIM. DO THEY KNOW THE **REAL** HIM? DOES HE HAVE SECRETS? OR ARE THEY ALL LOCKED AWAY, LIKE SOME FORTRESS, THE WAY I LOCK MINE AWAY?

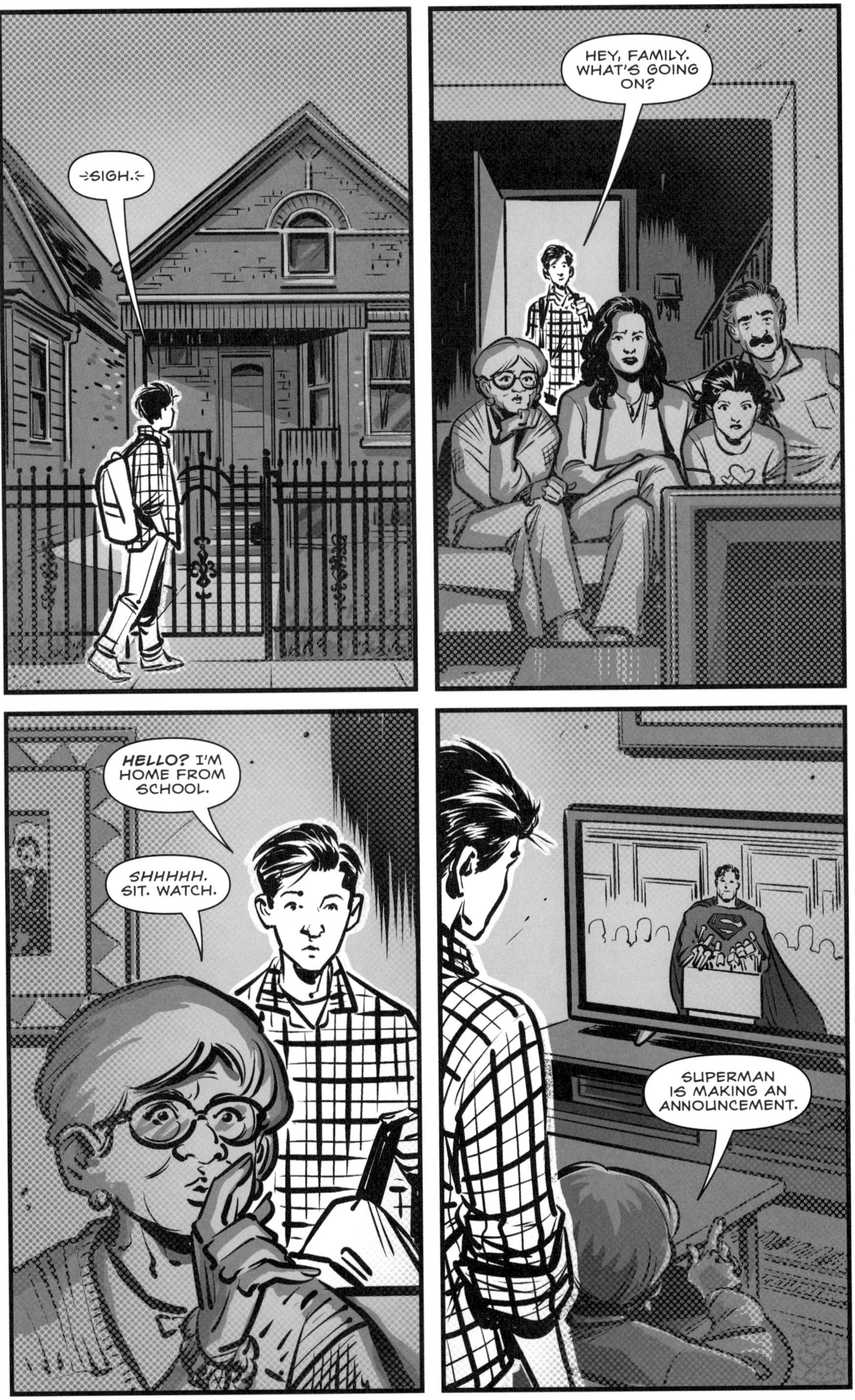

-SIGH.-
HEY, FAMILY. WHAT'S GOING ON?
HELLO? I'M HOME FROM SCHOOL.
SHHHHH. SIT. WATCH.
SUPERMAN IS MAKING AN ANNOUNCEMENT.

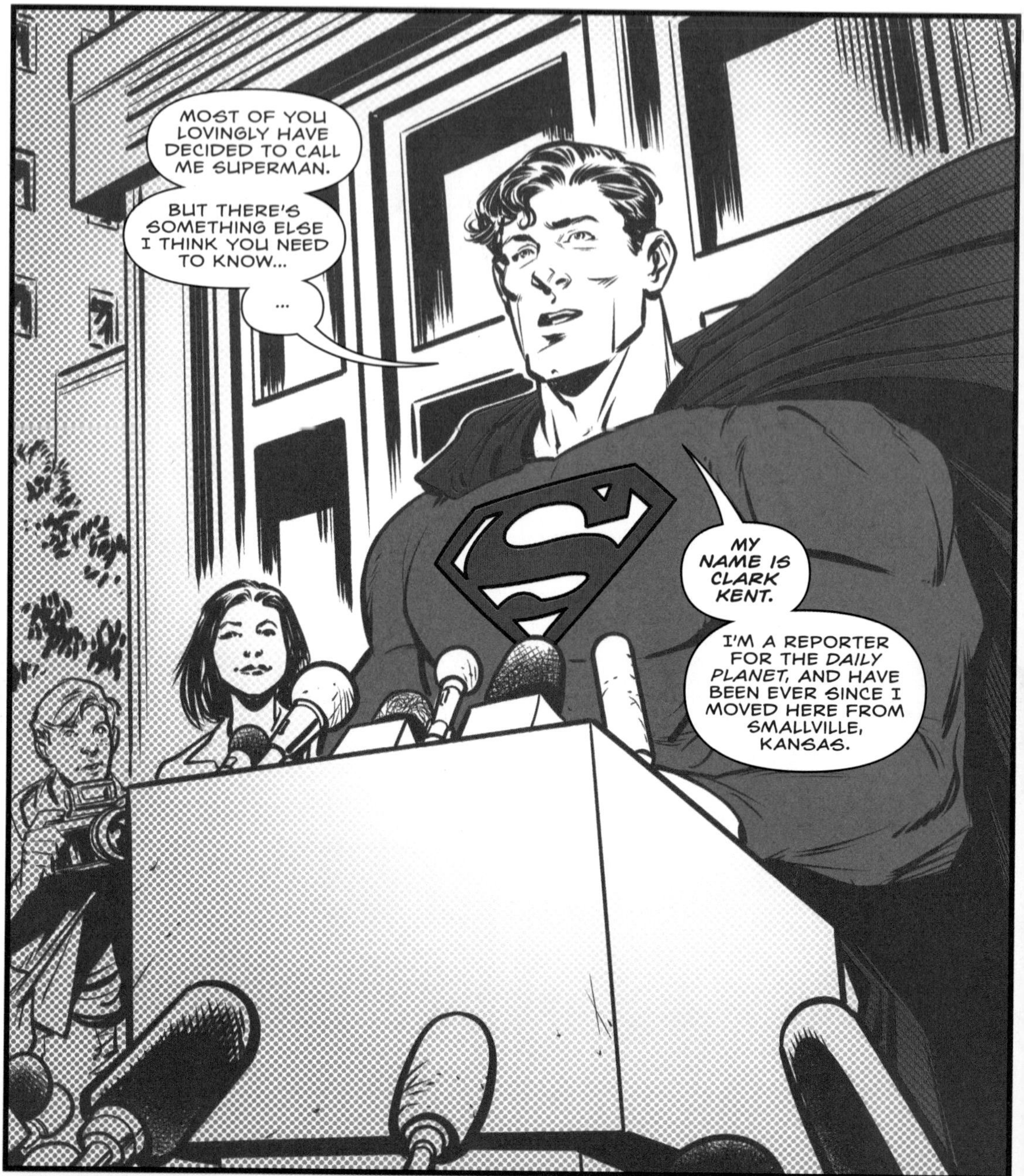
MOST OF YOU LOVINGLY HAVE DECIDED TO CALL ME SUPERMAN.
BUT THERE'S SOMETHING ELSE I THINK YOU NEED TO KNOW...
...
MY NAME IS CLARK KENT.
I'M A REPORTER FOR THE *DAILY PLANET*, AND HAVE BEEN EVER SINCE I MOVED HERE FROM SMALLVILLE, KANSAS.

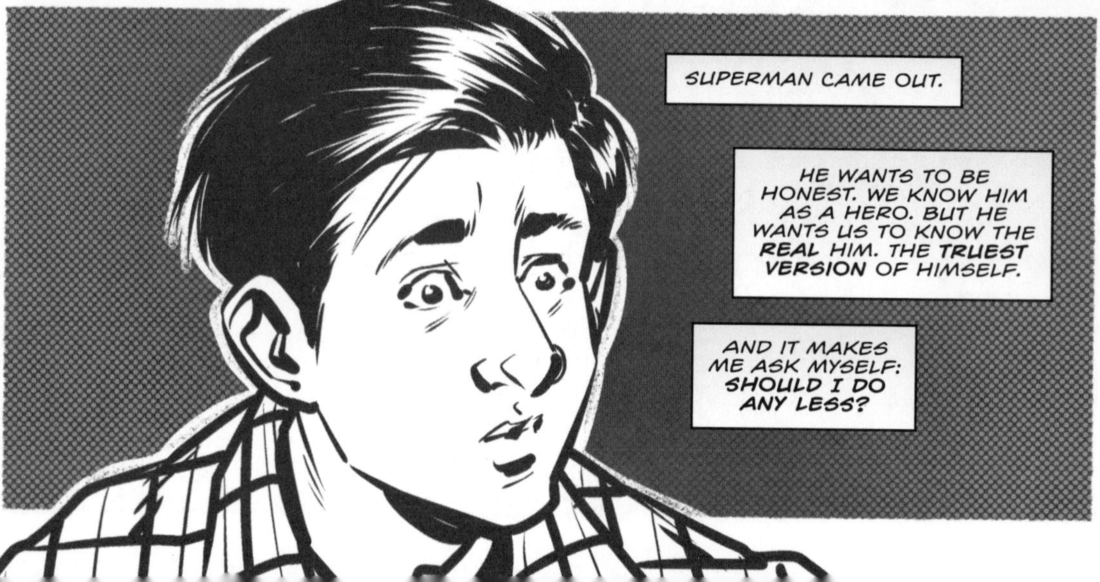
SUPERMAN CAME OUT.
HE WANTS TO BE HONEST. WE KNOW HIM AS A HERO. BUT HE WANTS US TO KNOW THE **REAL** HIM. THE **TRUEST VERSION** OF HIMSELF.
AND IT MAKES ME ASK MYSELF: **SHOULD I DO ANY LESS?**

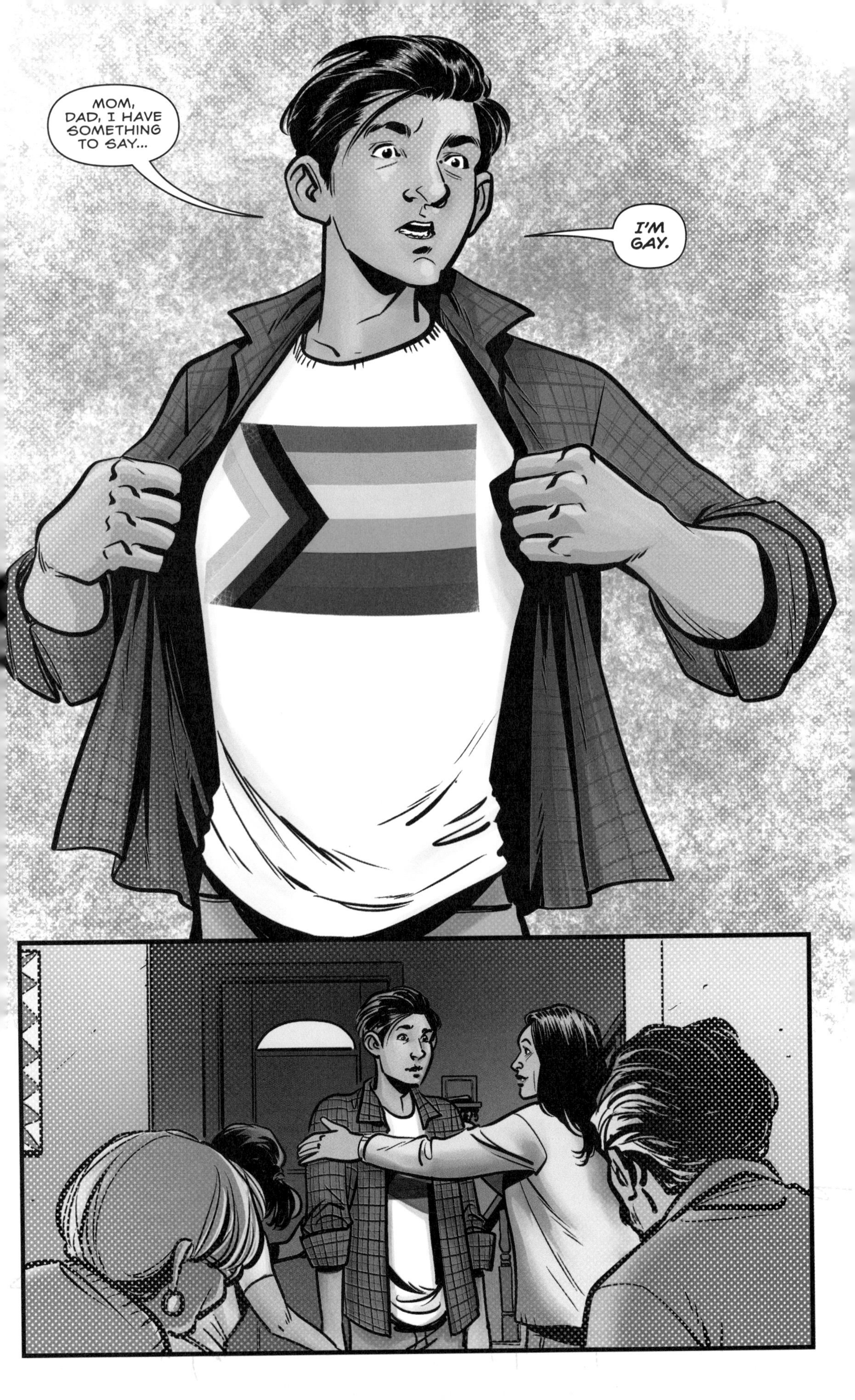
MOM, DAD, I HAVE SOMETHING TO SAY...
I'M GAY.

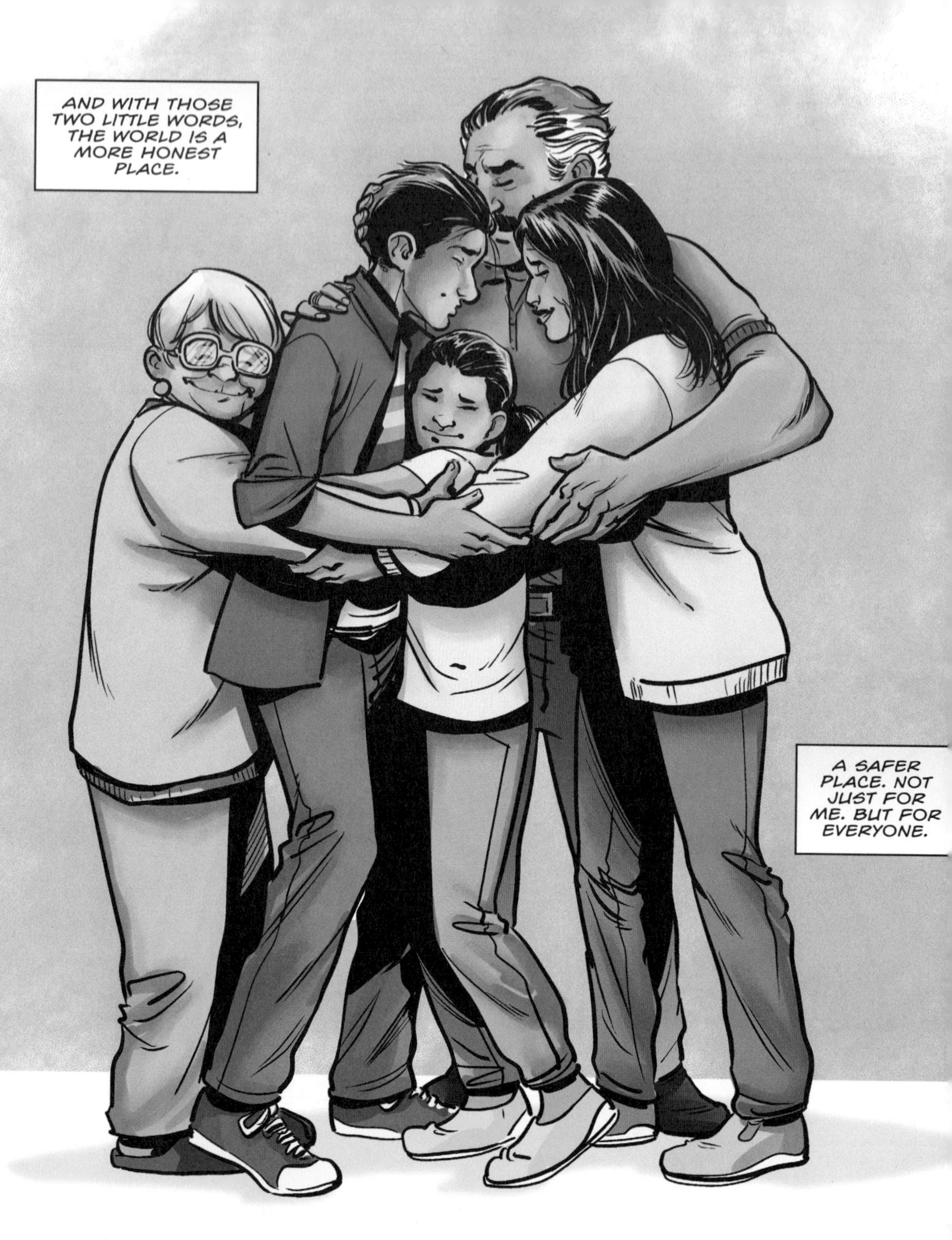
AND WITH THOSE TWO LITTLE WORDS, THE WORLD IS A MORE HONEST PLACE.
A SAFER PLACE. NOT JUST FOR ME. BUT FOR EVERYONE.

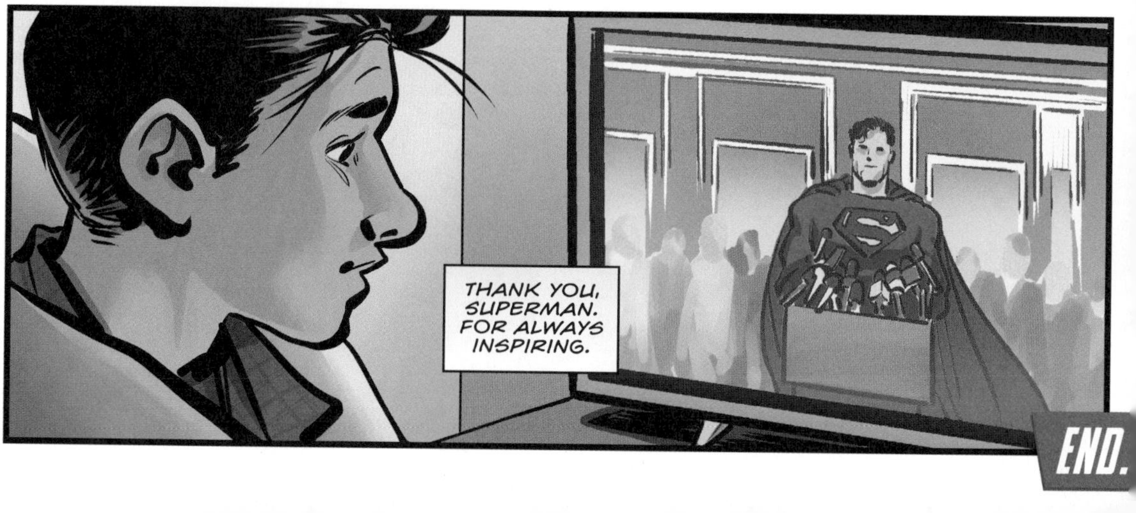
THANK YOU, SUPERMAN. FOR ALWAYS INSPIRING.
END.

Variant Cover Gallery

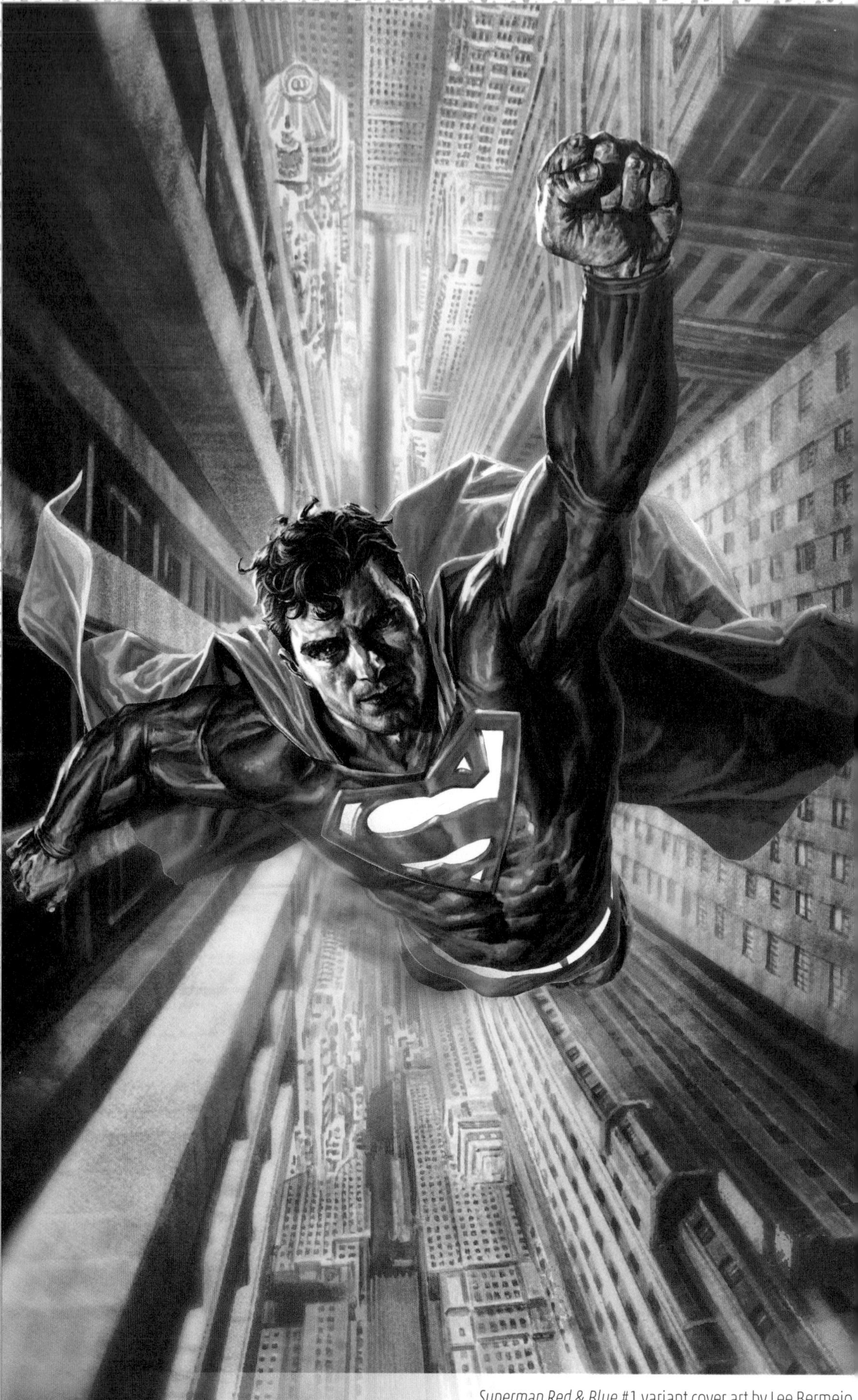

Superman Red & Blue #1 variant cover art by Lee Bermejo

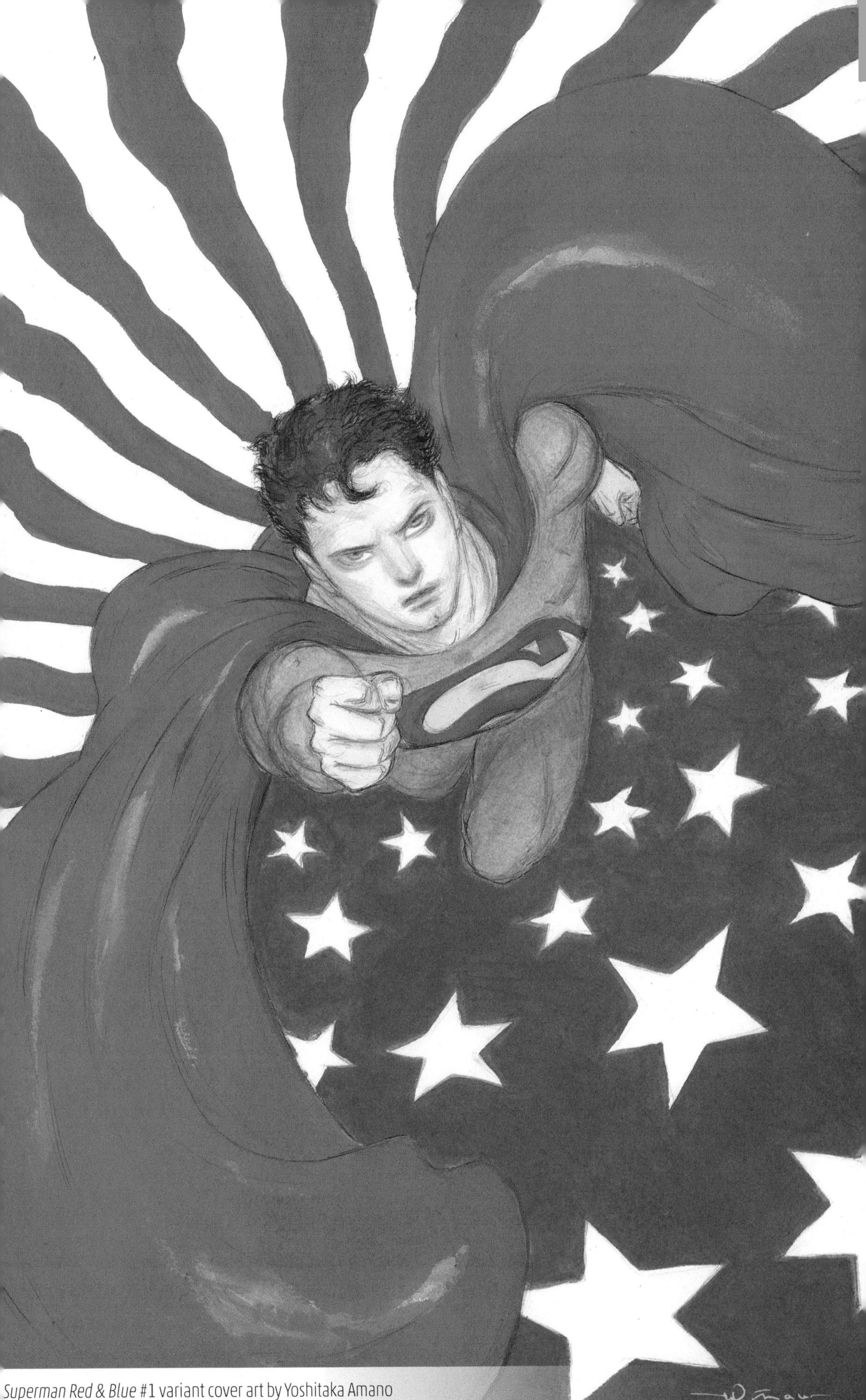

Superman Red & Blue #1 variant cover art by Yoshitaka Amano

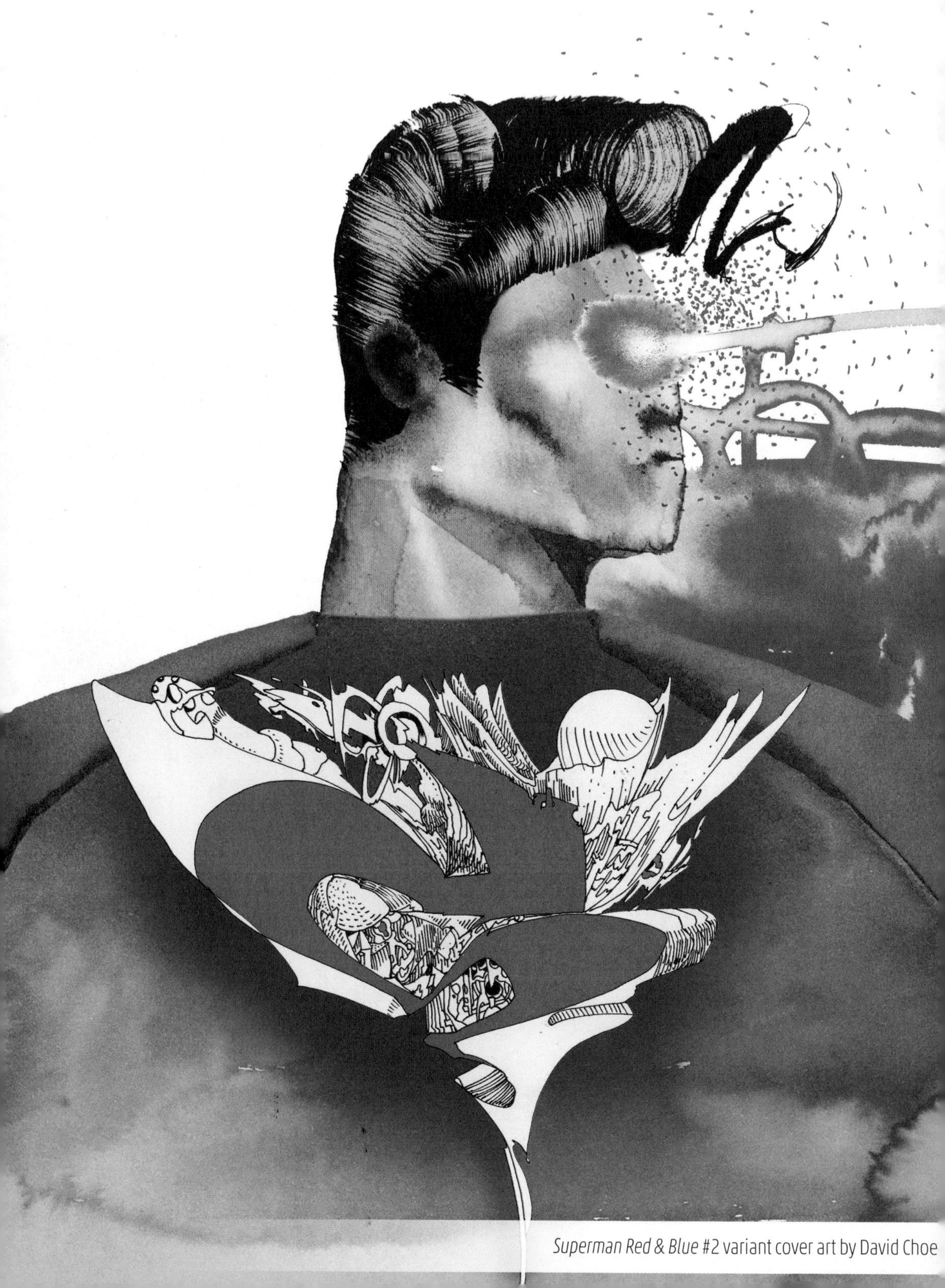

Superman Red & Blue #2 variant cover art by David Choe

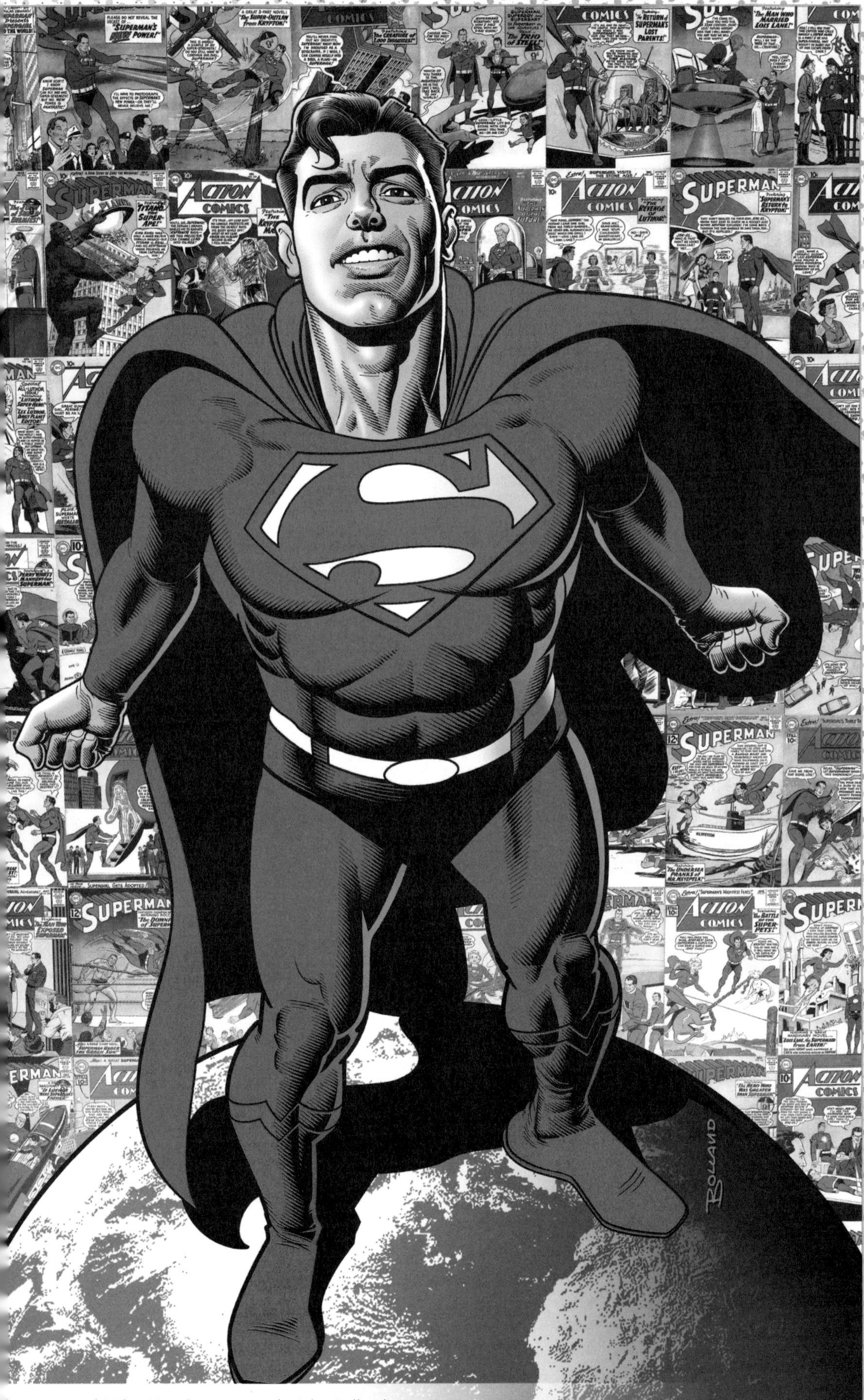
SUPERMAN
ACTION COMICS
BOLLAND

Superman Red & Blue #2 variant cover art by Brian Bolland

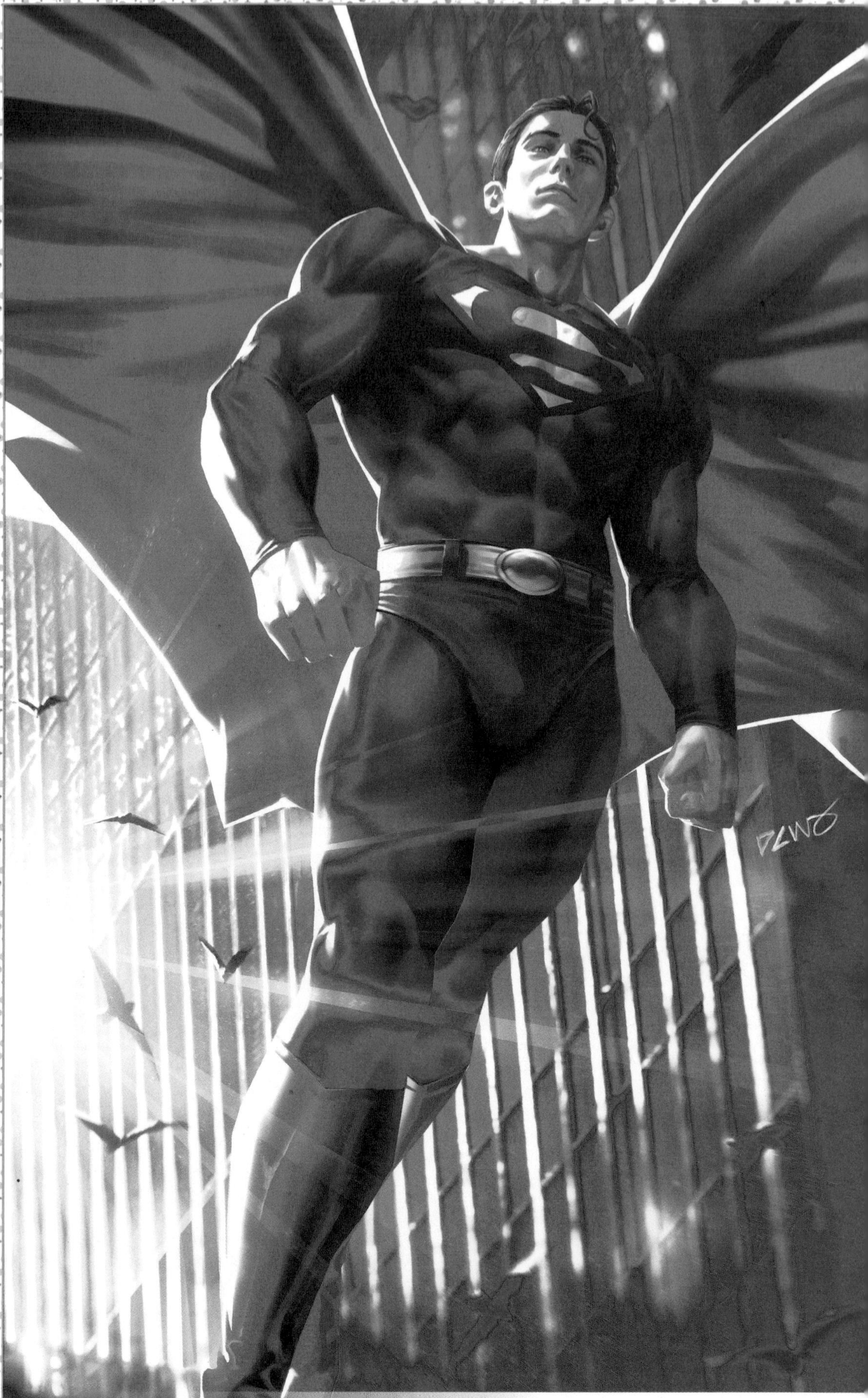

Superman Red & Blue #3 variant cover art by Derrick Chev

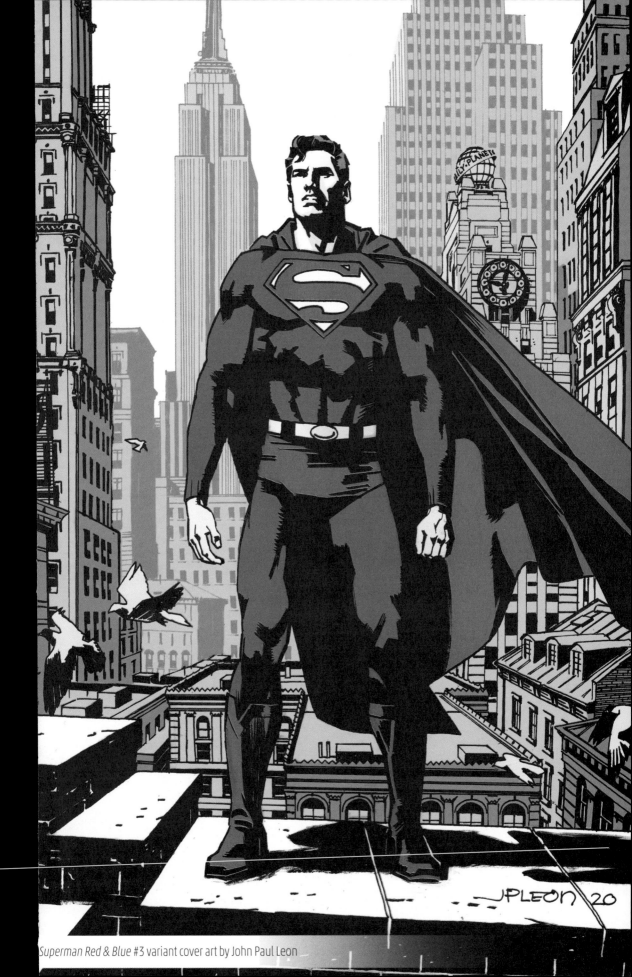

Superman Red & Blue #3 variant cover art by John Paul Leon

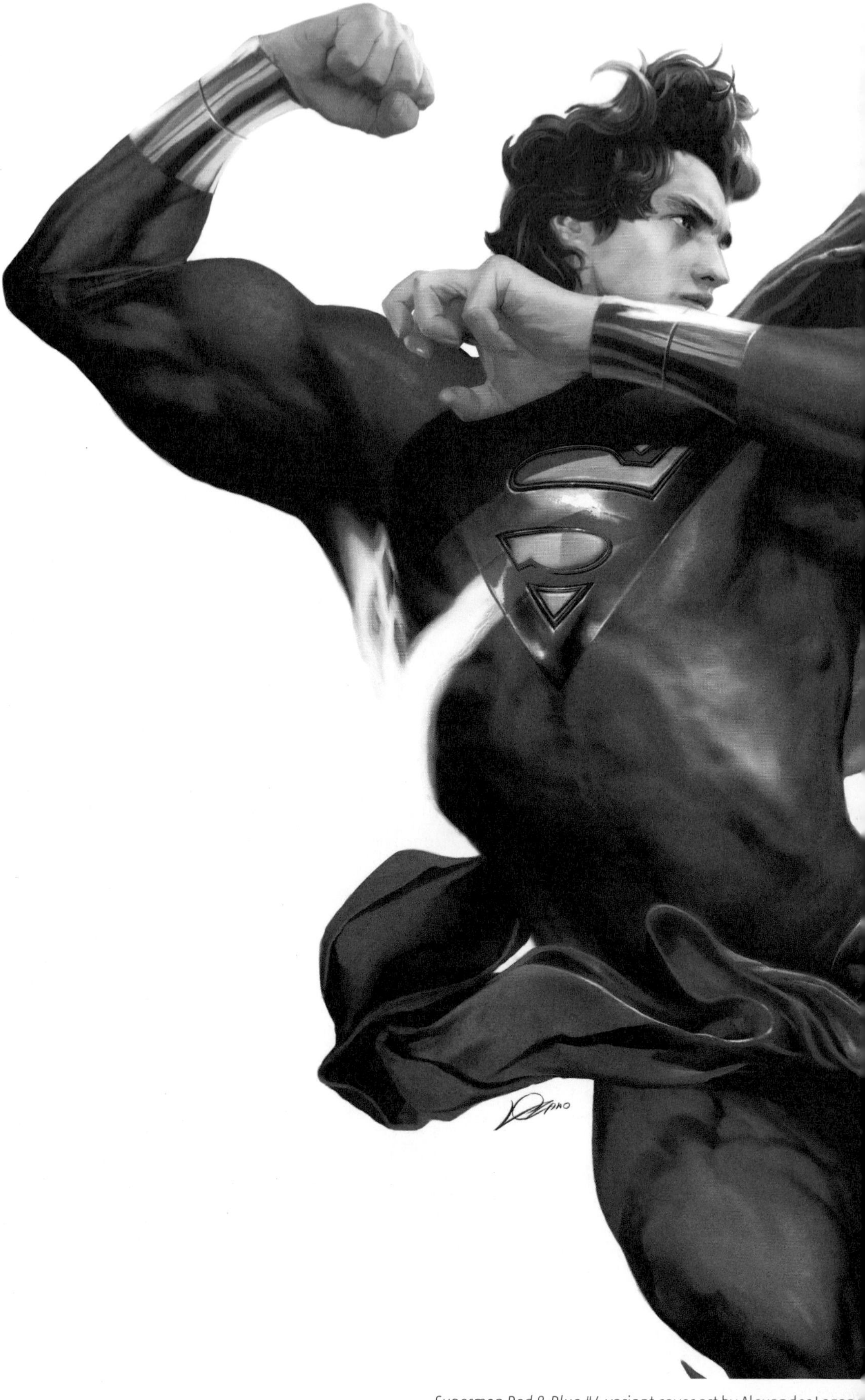

Superman Red & Blue #4 variant cover art by Alexander Lozan

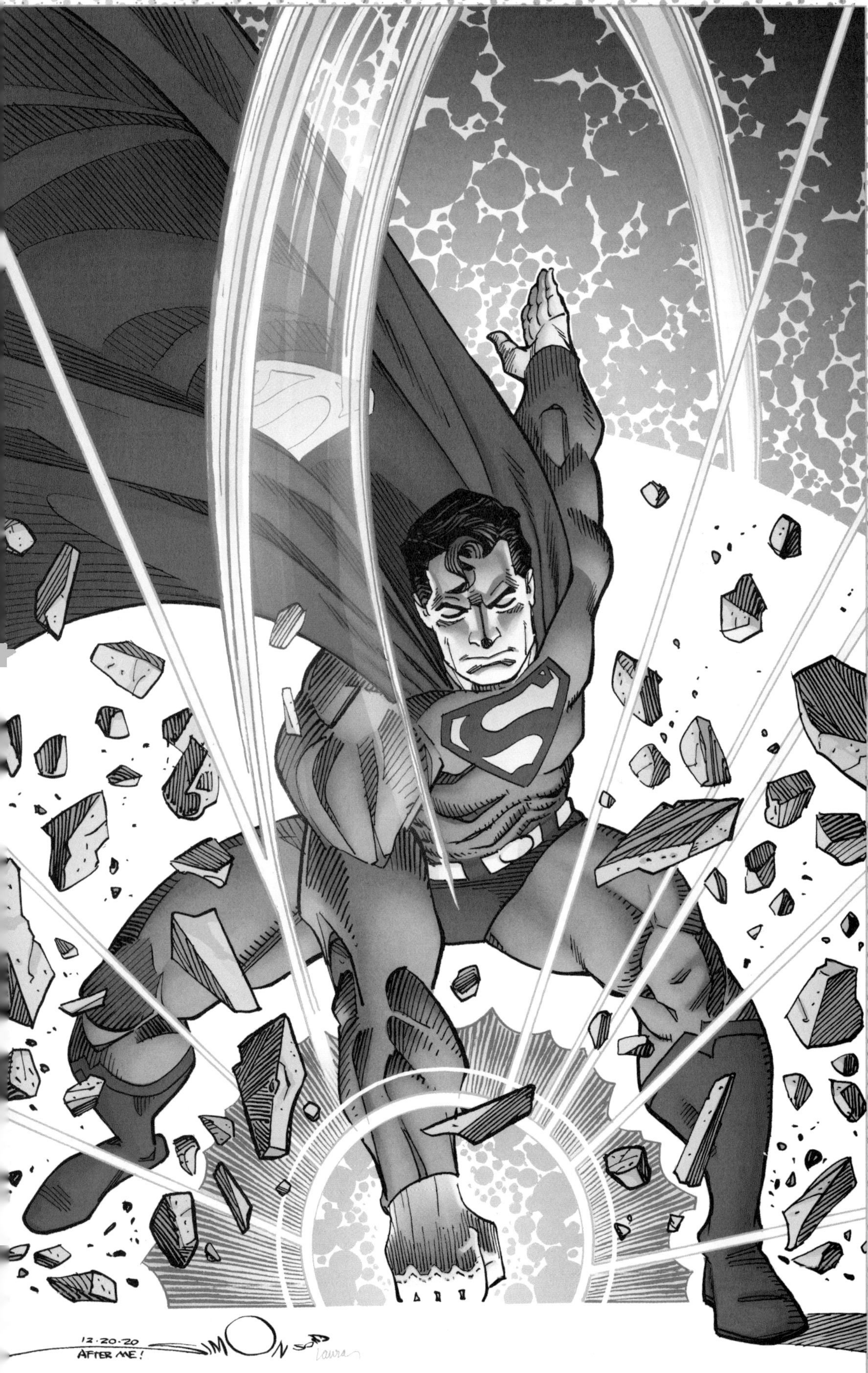
12·20·20
AFTER ME!

uperman Red & Blue #4 variant cover art by Walter Simonson and Laura Martin

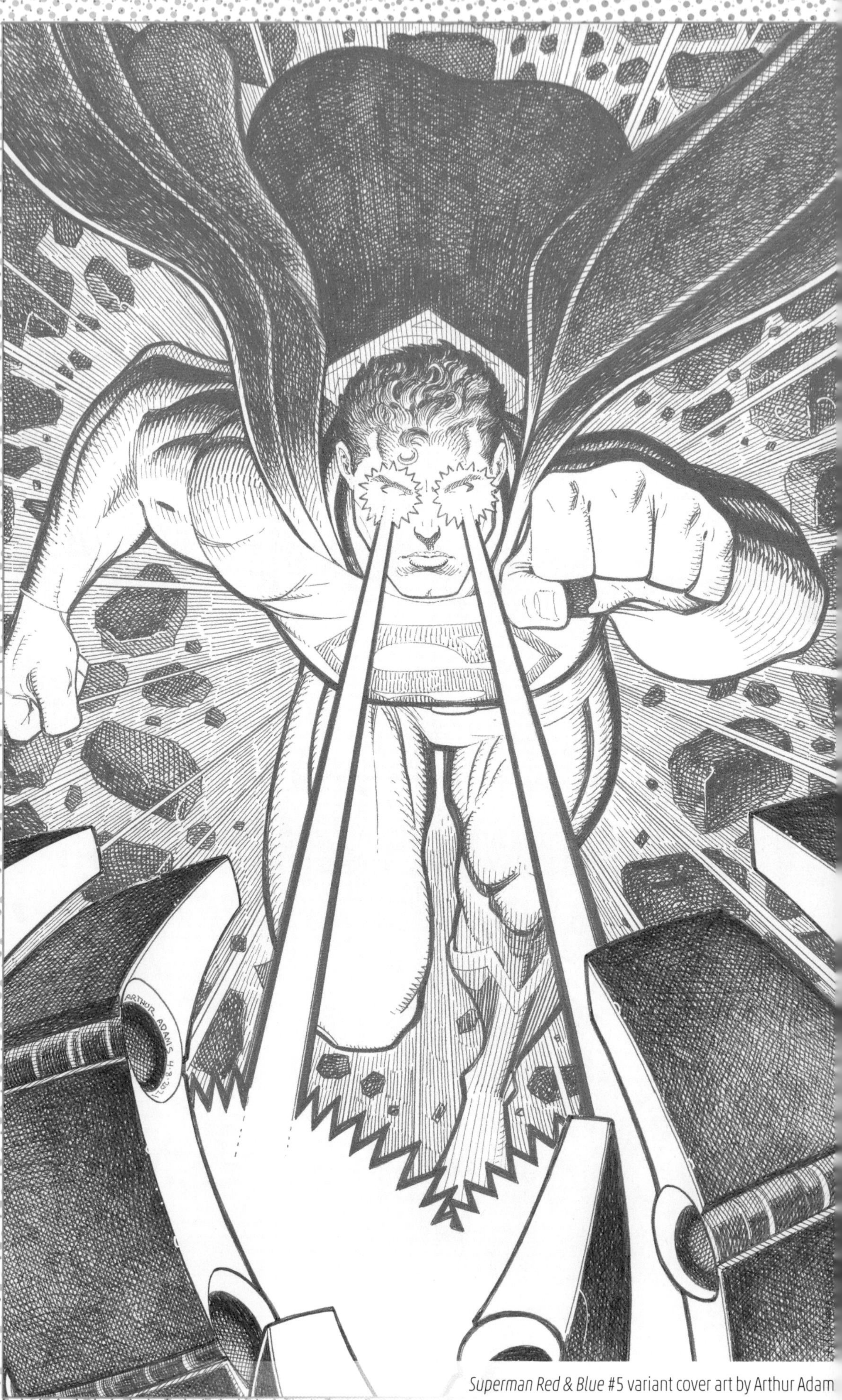
ARTHUR ADAMS

Superman Red & Blue #5 variant cover art by Arthur Adam

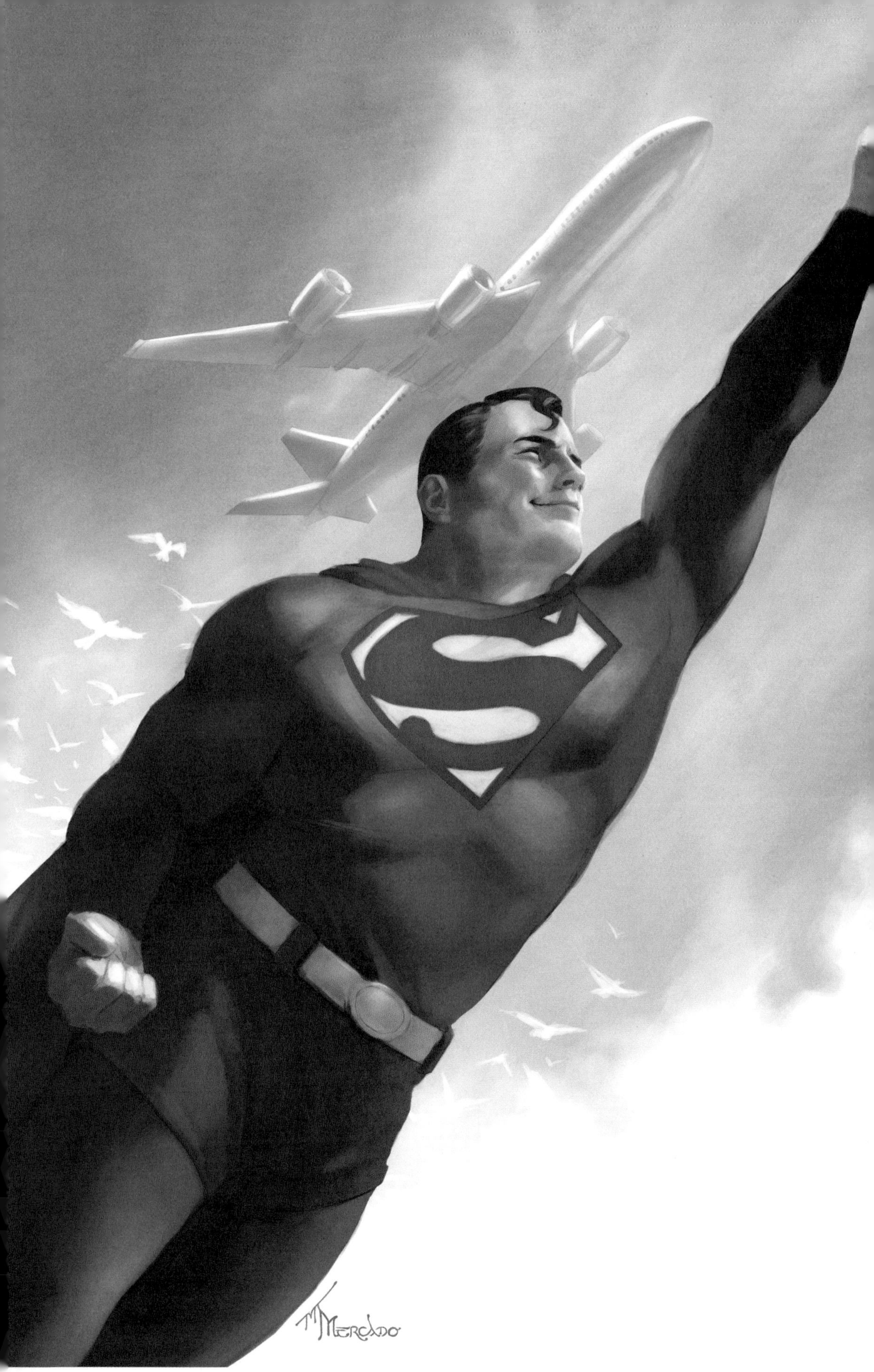
M. Mercado

uperman Red & Blue #5 variant cover art by Miguel Mercado

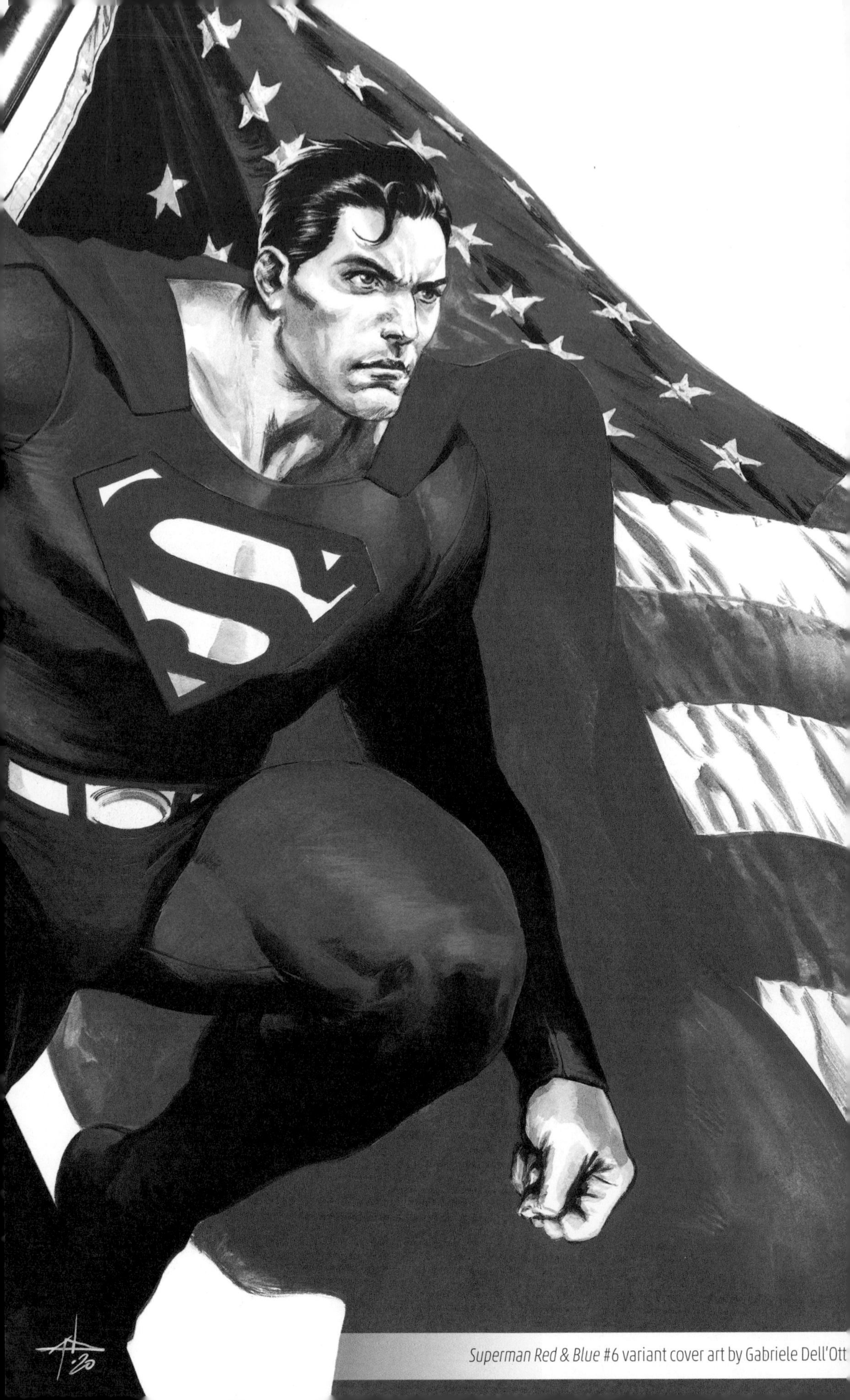

Superman Red & Blue #6 variant cover art by Gabriele Dell'Ott

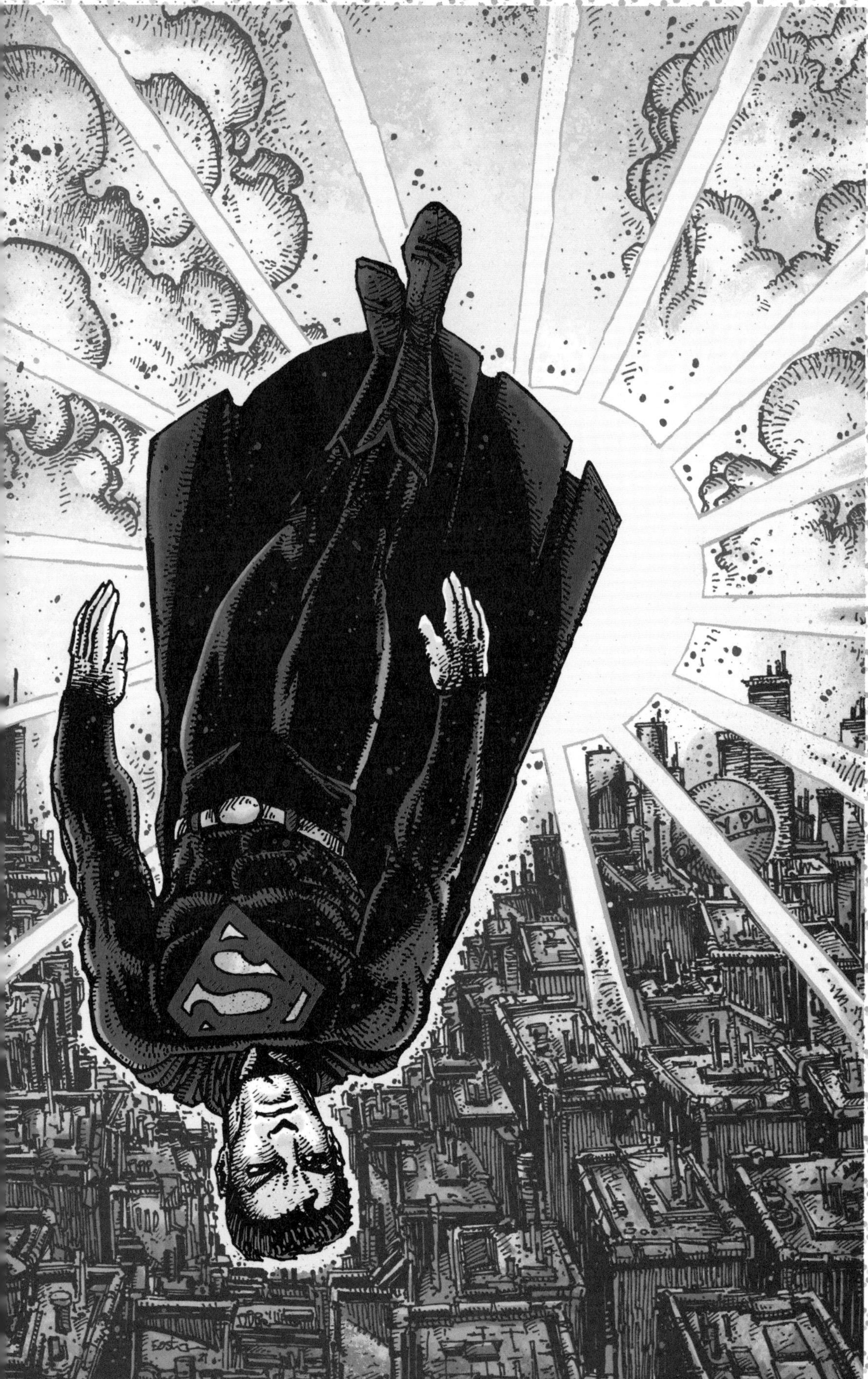

uperman Red & Blue #6 variant cover art by Kevin Eastman and Dave Stewart

Cover Process

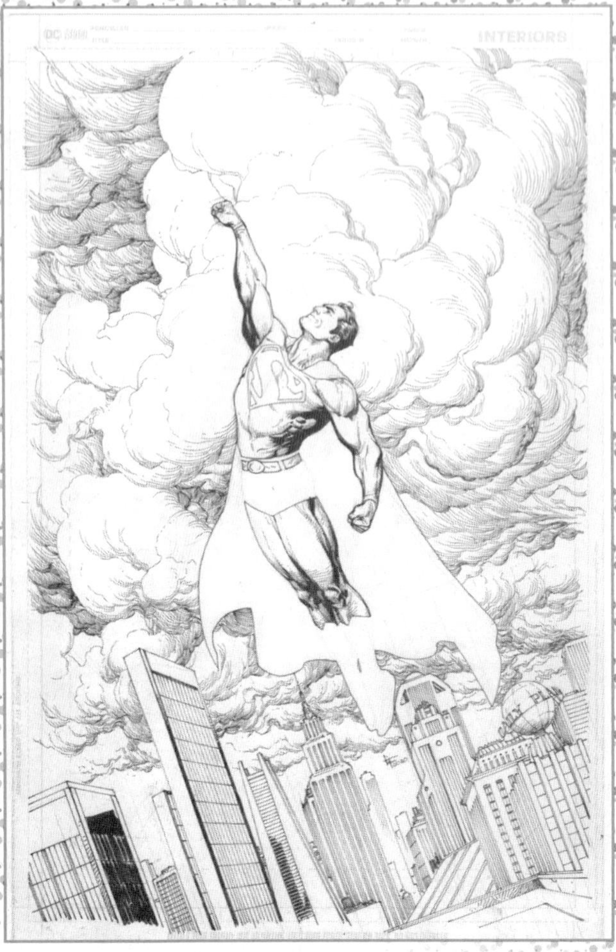
INTERIORS

Cover pencils by Gary Frank

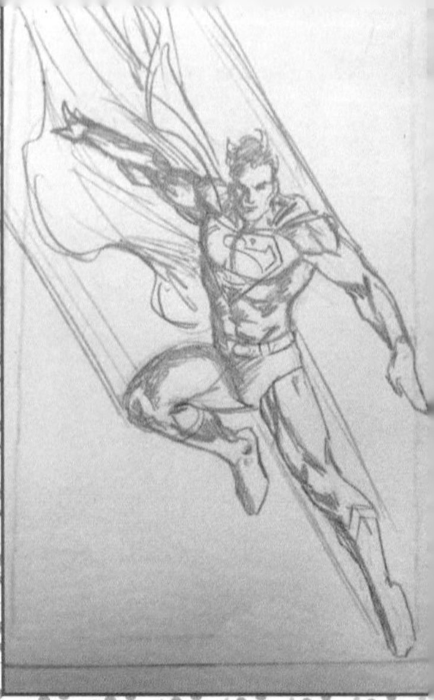

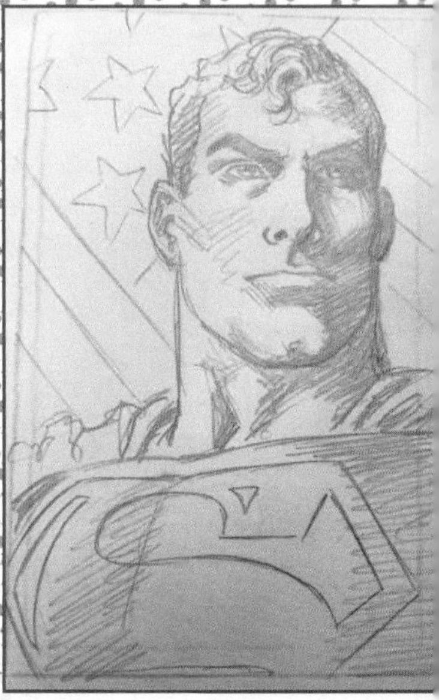

Cover sketches by Nicola Sco

Cover sketches by Amanda Conner

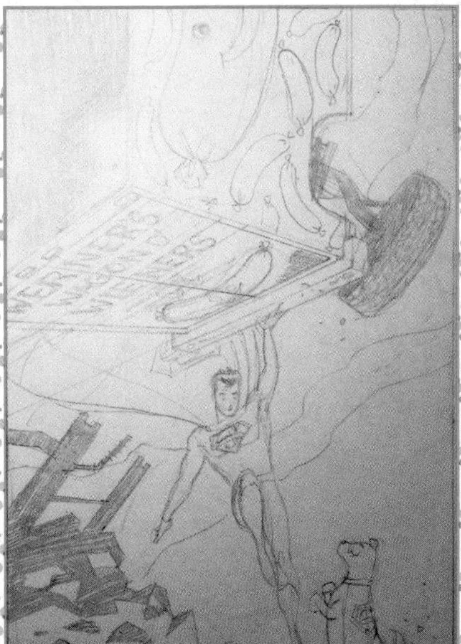

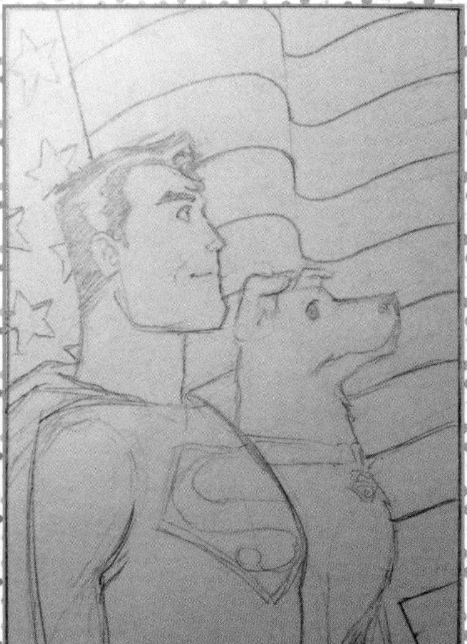

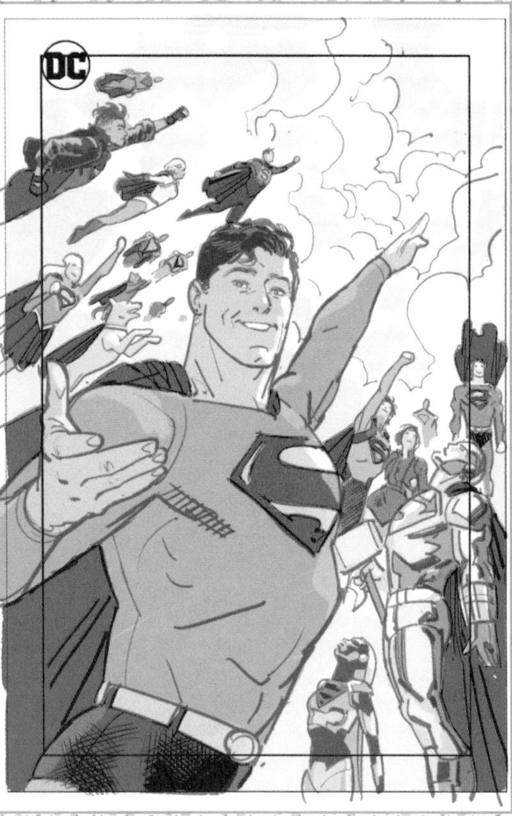
DC

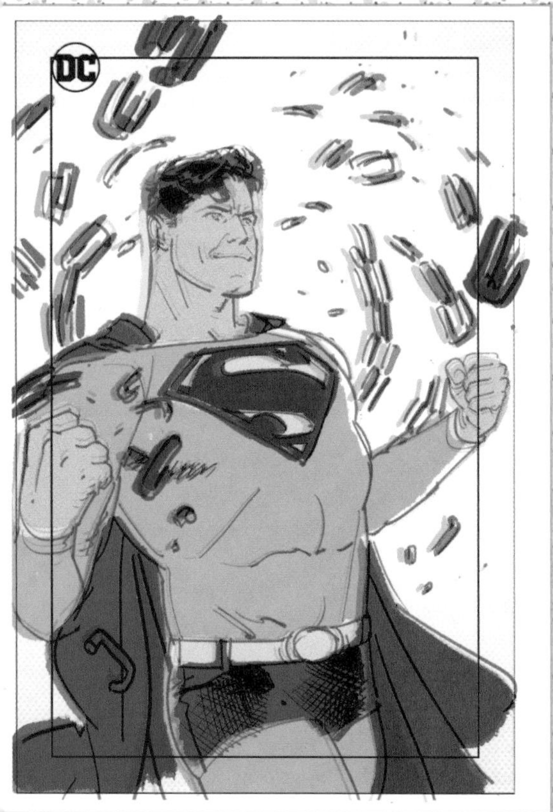
DC

Cover sketches by Evan “Doc” Shaner

Cover sketches by John Paul Leon

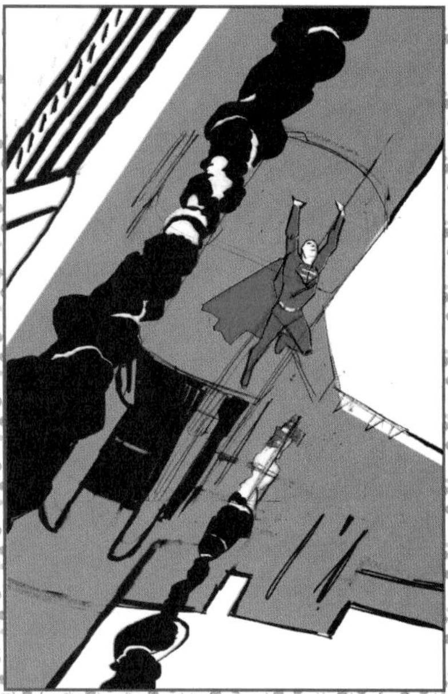

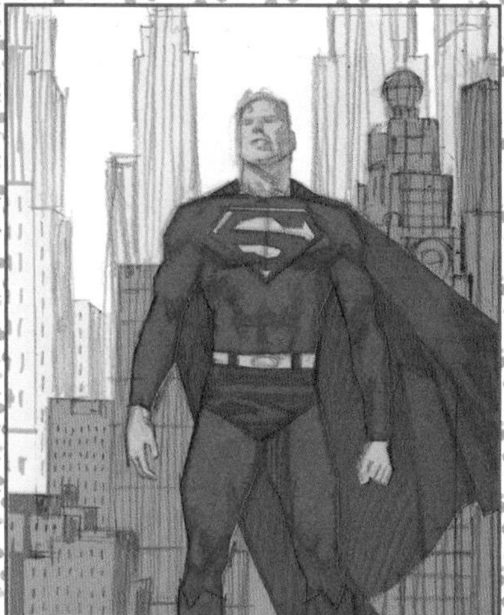

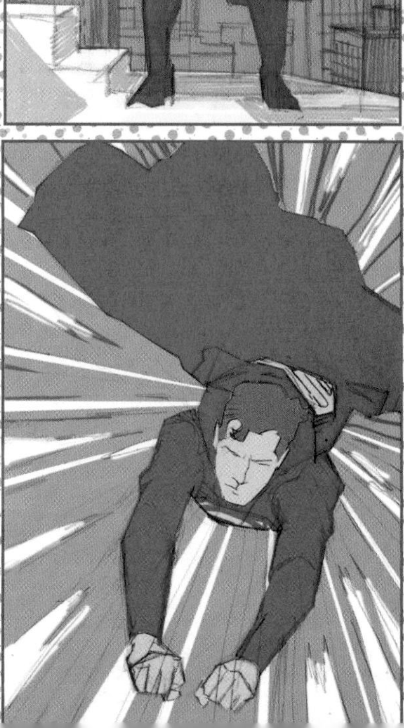

DC UNIVERSE REBIRTH
SUPERMAN
VOL.1 SON OF SUPERMAN
PETER J.TOMASI * PATRICK GLEASON * DOUG MAHNKE * JORGE JIMENEZ * MICK GRAY

"Gorgeous spectacle is an undeniable part of SUPERMAN's appeal, but the family dynamics are what make it such an engaging read."
–A.V. CLUB/THE ONION

"A series that's worn its heart on its sleeve and made you fall in love with this version of the Superman Family."
–IGN

SUPERMAN
VOL. 1: SON OF SUPERMAN
PETER J. TOMASI
PATRICK GLEASON
DOUG MAHNKE & JORGE JIMENEZ

DC UNIVERSE REBIRTH
SUPERMAN
"Superman's Rebirth is one you must not miss." IGN
VOL.2 TRIALS OF THE SUPER SON
PETER J. TOMASI * PATRICK GLEASON * DOUG MAHNKE * JAIME MENDOZA * MICK GRAY

SUPERMAN VOL. 2: TRIALS OF THE SUPER SON

DC UNIVERSE REBIRTH
SUPERMAN
VOL.3 MULTIPLICITY
PETER J. TOMASI * PATRICK GLEASON * JORGE JIMENEZ * IVAN REIS
RYAN SOOK * TONY S. DANIEL * SEBASTIAN FIUMARA

SUPERMAN VOL. 3: MULTIPLICITY

READ THEM AL

SUPERMAN VOL. 4: BLACK DA

SUPERMAN VOL. 5: HOPES AND FEA

SUPERMAN VOL. 6: IMPERIUS L

Get more DC graphic novels wherever comics and books are sold!